THE
PLAY
AND
THE READER

PRENTICE-HALL ENGLISH LITERATURE SERIES

Maynard Mack, Editor

PRENTICE-HALL INTERNATIONAL, INC., *London*
PRENTICE-HALL OF AUSTRALIA, PTY., LTD., *Sydney*
PRENTICE-HALL OF CANADA, LTD., *Toronto*
PRENTICE-HALL OF INDIA (PRIVATE), LTD., *New Delhi*
PRENTICE-HALL OF JAPAN, INC., *Tokyo*

THE
PLAY
AND THE READER

Stanley Johnson
Judah Bierman
James Hart

DEPARTMENT OF ENGLISH
PORTLAND STATE COLLEGE
PORTLAND, OREGON

Prentice-Hall, Inc.
Englewood Cliffs, N.J.

Library of Congress Catalog Card No.: 66-10238

Printed in the United States of America [68227-C]

Current printing (last digit):

10 9 8

The editors wish to acknowledge their indebtedness to the following for permission to reprint the plays included in this book:

Random House, Inc., for *Rosmersholm* by Henrik Ibsen and *The Madwoman of Chaillot* by Jean Giraudoux. *Rosmersholm* © Copyright 1957 by Eva Le Gallienne. Reprinted from *Six Plays by Henrik Ibsen*, translated by Eva Le Gallienne, by permission of Random House, Inc. *The Madwoman of Chaillot*, Copyright 1947 by Maurice Valency, under the title "La Folle de Chaillot" by Jean Giraudoux. English version, Copyright 1949 by Maurice Valency. Reprinted by permission of Random House, Inc.

David McKay Company for *Lysistrata* by Aristophanes, translated into English by Charles T. Murphy. From *Greek Literature in Translation* by C. T. Murphy and W. J. Oates. Reprinted through the courtesy of David McKay Company, Inc.

Dodd, Mead & Company, Inc., for *Caesar and Cleopatra* by Bernard Shaw. Copyright 1900 by Herbert S. Stone & Co. Copyright 1928 by George Bernard Shaw. By arrangement with Dodd, Mead & Company, Inc.

Harcourt, Brace & World, Inc., for *The Oedipus Rex of Sophocles:* An English Version by Dudley Fitts and Robert Fitzgerald. Copyright 1949 by Harcourt, Brace and Company, Inc., and reprinted with their permission.

Penguin Books Inc for *King Lear* by William Shakespeare, text and glossary edited by Alfred Harbage. Reprinted by permission Penguin Books Inc. Copyright © 1958.

E. P. Dutton & Co., Inc., for *Henry IV* by Luigi Pirandello, translated into English by Edward Storer. From the book *Naked Masks: Five Plays* by Luigi Pirandello. Copyright, 1922, by E. P. Dutton & Co., Inc. Renewal, ©, 1950, by Stefano, Fausto, and Lietta Pirandello. Dutton Paperback Series. Reprinted by permission of the publishers.

Grove Press, Inc., for *Mother Courage* by Bertolt Brecht and *The Chairs* by Eugène Ionesco. *Mother Courage and Her Children:* A Chronicle of the Thirty Years' War, by Bertolt Brecht, English version by Eric Bentley, Copyright © 1955, 1959, 1961, 1962, 1963 by Eric Bentley. Published by Grove Press, Inc.; Canadian rights granted by Methuen & Co., Ltd., Publishers, and Suhrkamp. *The Chairs* from *Four Plays* by Eugène Ionesco, translated by Donald M. Allen, Copyright © 1958, by Grove Press, Inc. Published by Grove Press, Inc.

The editors also wish to express their appreciation to the following for permission to reprint the essays included in this book:

Routledge & Kegan Paul Ltd. and The Macmillan Company, for "The Art of Drama." From *The Art of Drama*, Copyright 1957 by Ronald Peacock. Reprinted by permission of Routledge & Kegan Paul Ltd., London, and the Macmillan Company, New York.

Atheneum Publishers, for "Enactment." From *The Life of the Drama* by Eric Bentley. Copyright © 1964 by Eric Bentley. Reprinted by permission of Atheneum Publishers.

The New York Times Company, for "An Encounter with 'King Lear.' " © 1963 by the New York Times Company. Reprinted by permission.

New Directions, for "The Timeless World of a Play." From *The Rose Tattoo* by Tennessee Williams. Copyright 1950, 1951 by Tennessee Williams. All rights reserved. Reprinted by permission of the publishers, New Directions.

Alfred A. Knopf, Inc., for "Some Prefatory Words on Comedy." Copyright 1952 by Louis Kronenberger. Reprinted from *The Thread of Laughter*, by Louis Kronenberger, by permission of Alfred A. Knopf, Inc.

Princeton University Press, for "Comic Fictional Modes." Reprinted from *Anatomy of Criticism*, by Northrup Frye by permission of Princeton University Press. Copyright © 1957 by Princeton University Press.

Duell, Sloan & Pearce, Inc., for "The Meaning of Comedy." From *Aesthetics* by James K. Feibleman, by permission of Duell, Sloan & Pearce, Inc. Copyright 1949 by James K. Feibleman.

New York Post, for "A Fated Family." Reprinted by permission of *New York Post*. Copyright 1964, New York Post Corporation.

New York University Press, for "A Definition of Tragedy." From *A Definition of Tragedy* by Oscar Mandel.

Essays in Criticism, for "The Psychology of Tragic Pleasure." From *Essays in Criticism* VI (1956).

Michigan Quarterly Review, for "The Modern Temper and Tragic Drama." From the *Michigan Alumnus Quarterly*, LXI, No. 18 (May 21, 1955). Also by permission of the author.

The New York Times Company and the Ashley Famous Agency, Inc., for "Tragedy and the Common Man." © 1949 by the New York Times Company. Reprinted by permission.

The Yale Review, for "Comedy and Tragedy Transposed." Copyright Yale University.

George Braziller, Inc., for "Beyond Tragedy." George Braziller, Inc.—"Beyond Tragedy" from *Beyond the Tragic Vision* by Morse Peckham reprinted with the permission of the publisher. Copyright © 1962 by Morse Peckham.

Doubleday & Company, Inc., for "The Absurdity of the Absurd." From *The Theatre of the Absurd* by Martin Esslin. Copyright © 1961 by Martin Esslin. Reprinted by permission of Doubleday & Company, Inc.

Cover photograph: Oregon Shakespearean Festival Association, Ashland, Oregon (Angus L. Bowmer, director; William W. Patton, general manager), for permission to use photographs from their production of King Lear.

CONTENTS

v

Part One

THE NATURE OF

DRAMA

A NOTE TO THE STUDENT

Though critics and students still debate whether a play can fully exist apart from a stage performance of it, *reading* a play is of necessity a different experience from *seeing* a play. Given a choice, one would in general opt for seeing; but given the choice of seeing the play once and being able to read it again and again, then the greater the play the more likely one would choose the printed text and a lifetime of re-reading. For no single performance can exhaust the meaning of a great drama; neither can a single reading. The choice is, however, irrelevant to our immediate purpose; our concern here is to enlarge your capacity to experience the drama through reading.

Let us begin with the obvious: the drama is dramatic. To call a scene or spectacle *dramatic* is to point out that it is rooted in action and conflict, that it arouses emotion and reflection, that it moves and is moving. In the drama we are moved in a unique way. One reason is the play's compactness, its being a concentrate in which the trivial, the routine, and the irrelevant of daily life have no place. (To be sure, good plays have been written about the trivial and the routine, plays in which the irrelevant has a thematic function; but in such plays the trivial assumes significance precisely because it is trivial.) A second reason for the uniqueness of the dramatic experience lies in our being witness to action and conflict, of our being present during the very unfolding of the action. This *presentness* significantly conditions our response in the theater; but it is in fact a property not only of the acted drama, but of drama generally. It becomes a property of the drama as read as soon as the reader has prepared himself to assume responsibilities different from those demanded of him by the novel or the short story.

The drama, like music, is a performing and therefore preeminently a collaborative art, and the responsibilities it imposes are precisely these collaborative responsibilities. Once you have learned to assume them, you can stage the performance in your mind's eye and ear. And this imagined performance, which the reader stages as he reads, is not without compensations for the loss of the visual and aural impact provided by an actual performance in the theater. For the dramatist's collaborators are, after all, limited by their full share of human fallibility. A poorly designed setting,

3

the wooden behavior of a single inept actor, a miscalculated or badly timed gesture—any one of these may call attention to itself, and in so doing prove inimical to the audience's illusion and the author's intention. The *reader* of a play is fortunately not subject to distractions of this kind. While he reads, his imagination produces for him his own performance, and this will be as nearly ideal as his own experience and his increasing sophistication will allow.

The following text offers a selection of plays productive of both emotion and reflection; it aims to foster, through drama and commentary, the sophistication requisite to an ideal imagined performance. The achievement of this initial objective is, in its turn, prerequisite to an understanding of the drama as a genre of literature.

INTRODUCTION : THE DRAMATIC GENRE

The generic differences that distinguish the performed play from the spoken poem and the silently read novel can best be understood by imagining the differing spatial relations among the author, the characters, and the audience. In the epic poem the poet spoke directly to his audience; his characters did not appear at all. In the lyric poem, a solitary voice is heard; whether or not that voice is the poet's, the poet himself remains hidden, while we overhear a disembodied voice. In the novel or short story, the reader actually sees neither the author nor his characters. But what distinguishes the drama from all other literary genres is the acting out of the story by its characters directly before us, and always in the present tense; in a play, the characters are alone with each other, in the presence of a witnessing audience. The dramatist must remain hidden from both.

The dramatist may not permit his own voice to be heard, and he cannot stop the action, as can the novelist, to explicate to the reader the motivations and responses of his characters; nevertheless, he knows that actors (people like those who make up his audience) will play out the life of his story. Though his characters may be citizens of ancient Argos, or medieval Britain, or modern France, they will move across a three-dimensional stage where their words and deeds enlist our minds and emotions as co-participants with the characters in the story. Further, as we sit in a darkened auditorium, we take part in a communal experience that has within it archetypal elements of ritual: in turn, we bring to this communal experience that psychological "set" which Coleridge described as our "willing suspension of disbelief." We are, in fact, so eager to believe, to be enlisted as co-participants, that only the grossest ineptitude can destroy our willing suspension. Indeed, recent dramatic history suggests that even deliberate attempts to destroy that suspension, to remind us that what we are looking at is only a story and is not reality nor even a substitute for it, will fail to overcome our determination to participate. In any case, what *we* bring to the drama combines with what we find there—presentness, human beings, and three-dimensional settings—to produce the magic of the theater. These characteristics also suggest the condition that limits and defines the dramatist's craft: objectivity.

We soon discover that, even in our reading of a play, we never move outside the circumscribing orbit of the characters' world. Our attention never shifts from the characters themselves, who, once they are set in motion, must seem from that moment forth to be moving independently of their creator, to be working out their own destinies without visible assistance from the author. We stand directly in the presence of these created human beings, at the very moment when they move and speak, and if the author is to succeed in sustaining our belief, he must ensure that we remain conscious only of his characters and their world. They must seem to us to be—what in fact they are not—autonomous beings; as soon as they lose their autonomy and become mere puppets subserving the author's ulterior purposes they lose for us, first, their believability and second (in most cases), their interest. The creator of dramatic figures must therefore never allow us to become conscious of *his* manipulating hand; just as soon as, and insofar as, he does so, we cease to credit his invention. The dramatist's ideas and attitudes can be articulated only through the voices of his characters, speaking in their own persons. On stage, the dramatist has no voice of his own.

Since dialogue is the dramatist's primary medium for revealing his characters to us, the credibility of these characters as human beings is necessarily measured chiefly by their speech. The dramatist, knowing that every individual possesses his own distinctive personality, knows also that that personality finds expression in an individualized tone of voice and in idiosyncrasies of vocabulary. Such a generalization holds good even when the author follows the verbal-theatrical conventions of his age; for example, it holds good even when all the characters of a drama speak to us in blank verse: the idiosyncratic speech of Lear, for instance, is distinct from the equally idiosyncratic speech of Oswald or of the First Servant who dispatches Cornwall. That is, in the drama, as in life, tone of voice and vocabulary reflect environmental factors, climate and geography, economic status and education, the psychological and emotional set of the characters, as well as the exigencies of the immediate situation. Hence the dramatist will put into the mouth of each character only such words as may arise readily and naturally from a distinctive personality in a distinctive situation. He therefore finds it necessary to create a variety of voices, each the right one for each character at each moment, but none of them identifiable as his own.

Being thus unable to speak directly to the audience or reader, the dramatist must rely on the dialogue in his script and on what is sometimes called the subscript—the gesture and movement through which performers, like people, also speak. Only the play itself, the whole play, can speak for the dramatist. This enforced objectivity does not imply any desire by the playwright to detach himself from commitment to his materials; it simply stems from the mode of the drama, the given conditions inherent in its very nature. Playwrights have been among the most accurate and sensitive observers of the human scene, but they can translate what their eyes and ears record into comments on the human condition *only* through the dramatic vehicle itself. Direct statement is proscribed; the created world of the play alone must speak for its creator. The stage differs in this respect from the platform and the pulpit. What the dramatist would have us understand, he must have us overhear and oversee.

But though the sensitive reader will properly regard the dialogue of words and gestures as the life blood of a performance, he will also follow the printed stage directions as carefully as he follows the dialogue itself. For while it is true that the dramatist conceives his work in terms of its ultimate staging, he is yet powerless to bring his play to life in the theater unaided. He writes with the full knowledge that a word or phrase can be translated on the stage into the raising of a skeptical eyebrow or into the complex movement of an angry mob. What the novelist provides through a detailed description of the external scene across which his characters move, or through his analysis of human motives that lie too deep for articulation, the dramatist can provide only through his stage directions. By means of such directions he enables the director, designer, and actor to *real*-ize the play, to bring his dramatic world to life. Stage directions obviously extend beyond initial descriptions of setting, important as these are; they appear throughout the play, recording for his professional collaborators the particularities of tone of voice, of gesture, of setting and movement, which, like the architect's blueprint, will hopefully lead to the realization of his vision. If the reader wishes to participate fully in the dramatic experience, he must assume the collective responsibilities of the dramatist's allies in the theater. He must become his own director, designer, and actor; he must collaborate with the playwright in giving life to the printed page.

DRAMA AND MEANING

Whenever one encounters a play, he is immediately aware that something happens, that it happens to someone, and that it happens somewhere. At once, then, we can name three obvious elements of drama: action, character, and setting. All must be present in every work designed for the theater, although the emphasis each one receives will vary with the intention of the dramatist, his skill in making appropriate use of them, and the mode in which he chooses to express himself. But to name the obvious is not to exhaust the possibilities of analysis. In finding out how a play works, why it does what it does, we must eventually go further than the naming of these elements. We must discern the controlling purpose that causes the dramatist to arrange his raw materials in one order rather than another, and we must look for the "meaning" revealed by the pattern his play imposes on its action, characters, and setting. That pattern is its plot.

Drama begins and ends in action, and sheer movement accounts for some of the attractions of a play, as it accounts also for the child's pleasure in the toys that dangle in front of him and for the sports fan's excitement at a track meet or a boxing match. But a moment's reflection will reveal that random action alone, or the repetition of a single movement, will not keep us engrossed for very long. There must be some complicating factor, some outcome for us to be concerned about. It is conflict that provides this concern, that gives the play its shape by particularizing the central issue in specific clashes that pit the characters against each other. Yet we must not let the metaphor of contest mislead us. Dramatic action is always more than a synonym for mere action; dramatic conflict always involves the collision of ideas and forces. The conflict in a play may be seen in physical, intellectual, or spiritual terms; it may be presented as the clash of political, economic, or psychological forces. And though conflict is traditionally thought of as a clash between the hero and his antagonist, the greatest struggles often take place within the mind of the hero, or between the hero and the ethos of his society, or the will of his God. Nor need we think of conflict as limited to "serious" plays. The conflict between Lysistrata's group of determined women and their warrior husbands in Aristophanes' comedy, or between Countess Aurelia and the rulers and exploiters in *The Madwoman of Chaillot*, is not less urgent than that between Oedipus and Creon in Sophocles' tragedy. Problem plays, farce and melodrama, comedy and tragedy, all involve some conflict, and the nature of the struggle and the significance of its outcome state the meaning of the play in dramatic terms.

These are not the only means that convey the play's meaning. In addition to action, character, and setting, there is the element that the play shares with all literary forms: language. The language of plays must in one sense be dramatic language, for characters under stress, characters engaged in conflicts, must be heard to speak in heightened tones, whether whispers or shouts. When we turn from those speaking voices to the words themselves, we begin to treat the play as though it were a poem. That is, we explore the recurrent images and dominant metaphors of its lines, we look in them for the underlying meaning of its actions and the identifying profile of its characters. What the players say will seem at first the most obvious key to what the play means; in the end, especially in the greatest plays, the imagery will reveal the play's meaning in subtler but more comprehensive ways. The literal and symbolic meanings of the dialogue, the actions, characters, and setting of the play, speak to us in patterns of their own. It is by ordering all the elements into a common pattern—what Aristotle called a plot—that the dramatist constructs a play. The pattern of the plot, the ordering of all the elements, holds the key to meaning in the drama.

Discussions of conflict treat the subject of a play as though it were a life action, and in general we value plays to the degree that they embody conflicts that continue to confront us in life. In seeking meaning, therefore, we must always ask, why did the dramatist choose *this* story, these characters, this place and time to embody the human experience he saw as meaningful? But whatever the reason, the conflict he chooses to dramatize determines the structure the playwright builds, and to discuss that structure we must use terms that are partly psychological and partly structural: exposition, complication, crisis, climax, and dénouement.

Concentration on conflict necessarily requires the dramatist to eliminate nonessential actions and to focus on those which, for his purpose, are most engrossing and most meaningful. If acted out in their entireties, most stories would contain too many incidents and cover too long a period of time. Limited by theatrical convention and the audience's capacity, the dramatist must decide where in the total action to begin, and he usually chooses a point well along in the story. He must therefore be prepared, in his *exposition*, to tell his audience quickly, and without intruding too obviously into the ongoing action, all they need to know of the antecedent action, the origins of his characters, and their previous relationships. But once the audience knows enough to become engrossed in the situation, or once the dramatist judges that he has told us enough, his structural problem changes. His concern now shifts to the process of deliberate entanglement known as dramatic *complication;* he becomes engaged in weaving the various strands of his conflict into a rising action. From this moment forward, his story will mount, through a complex interweaving of motives and actions, to the *crisis*, that point in the plot where, because of a decisive step taken by the protagonist or central character, the play's resolution becomes inevitable. At the same time, the interweaving of actions produces a rising tension, until the play comes to its emotional *climax*, the moment of greatest intensity and greatest empathy. Climax may coincide with crisis or come after it; what follows climax is dénouement. Seen structurally, the dénouement, borrowed from the French and translatable as "untying," refers to the disentangling of the strands of the conflict. Seen psychologically, it refers to that closing period of the play, past the climax, in which the audience's tension is relieved so that it can leave the theater and return to reality. Plays need not solve all of life's problems, but they must resolve their own conflicts.

This created world of the play, like all the worlds that man creates, has what our actual world so frequently seems to lack—an organizing principle that gives it meaning. The vitalizing principle that makes the play more than a mere copy of life is the playwright's vision—his ability, as T. S. Eliot once said of the powers of a poet, to see the skull beneath the skin, to go beneath the surfaces of things and see basic relationships and realities. This vision is not something the poet or playwright deliberately seeks or willfully shapes; it grows out of his total experience in his society and his world, and it reflects his total commitment to an attitude toward life. It is both the initiating spirit and the point of view from which he sees the events he records.

Between the playwright's vision, which refers to the world he lives in, and the play, which is the world he creates, stands the theme of the play. In simplest terms, theme is what the play is about. Theme differs from all the other terms used in the analysis of plays because, unlike the action or the characters, theme does not exist in the play alone. To state the theme of a play is to verbalize one's own experience of the world of that play. Thus, though theme is tied to, in fact begins in, action, setting, characters, and the languages they speak, it always involves something more than the plot and its elements. Theme states the implied meaning of those actions and their consequences, and it often involves a judgment on the life they reveal. If we assume that we can equate theme with the intention of the playwright, we see then that like all literature the play attempts to persuade the reader to understand the experiences recorded and to accept the view of life that underlies them. It is the special requirement of the dramatic form that the theme must be ostensibly overshadowed by the specifics of action, setting, and character; but if the dramatist is successful in translating his vision of the world he creates, he will permit the reader to share the same view he has seen, and to grasp the same meaning in the events he records. What he shows will lead inevitably to what he means.

As an art designed ultimately to be a collaborative effort, the drama poses special questions not relevant to other genres. Through the ages, it has elicited comment and study from many viewpoints: from scholars concerned with its theoretical foundations, from historians interested in its reflection of society, and from the professionals who create it and perform it. In the essays that follow, some of the drama's creators and partisans offer their views on this form, and make us aware, from their informed "inside" positions, of various problems and demands inherent in it. These comments may serve as a preface to the reading of the plays themselves.

In the first essay, Ronald Peacock, a scholar of the drama, propounds a theory of the dramatic, and surveys the various forms it takes. Considering the inner structure of the play itself, Professor Peacock comments on and expands the traditional notions of plot, character, and setting, and shows how the nature of its conflict defines a play. Next, one of the contemporary theater's most eminent critics, Eric Bentley, explores the "enactment" of a play by turning an analytic eye on the actor as player. What, he asks, makes an actor tick, what makes him want to exhibit himself before an audience? Is his a pathological urge, or a "normal" one—that is, one we all share? And what is our role as viewers of this exhibitionism? In answering these questions, in suggesting that something of the essence of theatrical enactment can be understood by considering its roots in human play, Mr. Bentley emphasizes elements in the drama often avoided by some who pretend to love it. There is an old argument, often called Puritan, that attacks the theater and drama because its plays and players are immoral. Mr. Bentley takes a closer look at the morality of play and play-acting, a look which requires us to see the creation of the play as involving our own personality needs in ways we might not have suspected.

The remaining two essays offer the views of practitioners within the theater. A famous actor, Morris Carnovsky, explains some of the problems an actor faces in bringing a complex character to life on the stage. His comments about an actor's job illuminate the nature of a parallel task faced by the reader: both must do more than merely read lines of dialogue on a printed page; they are equally responsible for seeing those lines, and the accompanying stage directions, as external manifestations of a real personality, as clues that reveal the soul that exists behind them. Though Mr. Carnovsky's remarks apply specifically to his recent portrayal of King Lear, they have a wider application to the problems of characterization in general. They emphasize the intellectual, physical, and spiritual challenge faced by an actor in attempting to recreate a character "more real than real." Had he been theorizing rather than recounting his own experience, Mr. Carnovsky might have talked about acting not as mere impersonation, not as the imitation of a person like someone he knows, but as the creation of a *persona*, an image that embodies a set of human characteristics so typical that we can all recognize the man they make. But even in their treatment of the special problem of creating Lear, these comments clarify the general function of the actor and point the way toward the reader's assumption of the same task. Finally, Tennessee Williams, author of *The Glass Menagerie*, *A Streetcar Named Desire*, and *The Rose Tattoo*, sums up the role of drama in bestowing significance on the subjects it chooses to treat. He suggests that the power of drama lies in the special kind of time it keeps; he shows the playwright to be a man who rescues the meaningful events of life from their transitory surroundings and "fixes" them permanently in the enduring time of the drama.

THE ART OF DRAMA

Ronald Peacock

Every aspect of art . . . may be illustrated from the form of drama. It is an art; it is imagery for eye and ear and mind; it shows a characteristic intertexture. There are in it elements of representation and of expression. It incorporates the visual images of scene and persons, it uses words in dialogue, which may however include many uses of speech, emotive, analytic, declamatory, exclamatory, rhetorical, descriptive, lyrical, musical, and so on. It may express moods, emotions, subjective conflicts. It springs from experience and reflects it; it is clearly and intensely a re-enactment. And finally, it resembles all other forms in that it exploits many kinds of imagery and expressive tones whilst maintaining its typical character. As a branch of art it is an interpretation of experience by means of images and words in which the representational and the expressive intermingle and in which, indeed, the law of functional assimilation holds in respect of all the kinds of image used.

VARIETY OF DRAMATIC FORMS

The question: what is drama? admits of two answers, one historical and complicated, the other theoretical and by comparison simple, and each complementary to the other. Drama is all drama as we know it in a multitude of historical examples; and it is also a type of art, the concept of which we construct by generalizing from recurrent features.

The first meaning is complicated because so many varieties of the form have existed, each with a different significance and func-

From *The Art of Drama*, Copyright 1957 by Ronald Peacock. Reprinted by permission of Routledge & Kegan Paul, Ltd., London, and The Macmillan Company, New York.

tion in extremely diverse cultures and in more recent times showing increased elements of personal idiosyncrasy as against drama based firmly, like religious plays, on communal cults or beliefs. Greek tragedy and comedy, the mysteries and moralities of the medieval Church, Elizabethan drama, French classical plays, the comedy of manners, the *commedia dell' arte, comédie larmoyante*, Ibsen, Claudel, expressionists, romantic and symbolist plays, to mention only a few types, have each an original way of associating dramatic form with a view of life held by a society or an individual, and from them we learn forcibly that "drama" has been many things to many people. It can be the handmaiden of a creed, a simple but moving story, an analysis of character, a portrayal of manners, a declaration of subjective feeling, a vehicle of the acquisition or loss of faith, a fairy-tale or fantasy, a "proverb," a history, an allegory; every drama is either a common type, that is, one of the predominant historical kinds, or, drawing on several of the features associated with drama, it is a mixture.

The second, theoretical, answer to the question about what drama is appears simple by comparison because it is easy to enumerate a set of characteristics necessary to the form. There must be an action; that is, events and situations must be presented with accompanying tension, sudden changes and a climax. Persons must be portrayed with sympathy and truth. The conception must embrace possibilities for the actor's art. And there must be some central meaning, whether religious, moral, emotional or psychological, which strikes home to the spectator's head and heart. These ingredients, present in the simplest and most intricate, the most ritualistic and the most sophisticated, the most tragic and most comic, drama, arise from the aesthetic conditions of the art. Starting from the fact that a play—life depicted by acting—gives pleasure, it is natural to seek those actions that are best for the purpose; they are the tense and exciting ones that keep the spectator interested. From this initial simple condition everything else flows; the art of subtle dramatic construction, of portraying persons to the life, and of drawing on every means of intensifying the expression. But let us not anticipate a more

detailed treatment; it is only necessary here to indicate in the briefest and most general terms what drama is, reserving more precise analysis for the following sections. It is moreover appropriate, before embarking on theoretic statements about aspects and types of drama, to tabulate the many possible sources of pleasure in plays. We enjoy the story, the character-drawing, taking a sympathetic interest in the fortunes and misfortunes of the persons, their problems and feelings. We enjoy the unfolding of an idea in dramatic situations and the release of feeling that it occasions. We take pleasure in the skill of the dramatist, in his construction, his sense of the theater, the opportunities he gives his actors. Another source of delight derives from the style and language, whether prose or verse, the eloquence, poetry, wit, epigram, rhetoric, the sentiments and ideas expressed *en passant* or as the immediate product of the situations. And finally we enjoy the décor, the production, the acting, and the personalities of actors and actresses which are inseparable from their art. This immensely rich and varied arsenal of delights lures us perennially to the theater and it is a poor play indeed that does not offer one or the other. Some of them constitute a snare, as purists always point out, since the superficial sensuous attractions of décor and acting may degenerate into gratuitous and vulgar spectacle. On the other hand the harmonious use of such varied means of expression can secure effects so intense and moving that they bestow a particular aura on the form. . . .

THE IDEA OF "THE DRAMATIC"

Our notion of the dramatic derives in the first place from exciting things observed in nature and human life, but it has been refined by the art of drama itself, with the result that life and the art form are inextricably intertwined in the idea. The word "dramatic" has a natural meaning in relation to any events of a sudden, surprising, disturbing, and violent kind, or to situations

and sequences of events characterized by tension. Thunderstorms, high seas and floods, animals pursuing and killing their prey, are dramas of nature. Accidents, sudden death, battles, rescues, crimes, quarrels, politics, adventures, failures, triumphs, constitute the natural dramas of human destiny, winning a place in the columns of the daily newspapers. It is usual to denigrate these as sensational but they are a touchstone for what strikes men and arrests their interest, and it was no accident that Ibsen pored daily over his newspaper. It is commonly held that conflict makes drama, but surprise, and particularly tension, are the truer symptoms. They both arise from conflict, of course, but not always, and conflict is only dramatic when they do. A cricket match involves a conflict, yet with most variable tension, as foreign spectators are apt to observe; it is only a dramatic conflict at particular moments when the pace increases and puts the game in the balance. On the other hand what is more dramatic than a train moving at speed towards a broken viaduct? Yet there is only tense expectation here, no conflict.

When the imagery of art incorporates such features we ascribe to it "dramatic" quality, and clearly this process is not confined to drama and theater alone. The baroque style in architecture, the sculptures of Michelangelo, the paintings of Delacroix and Picasso, offer examples of the dramatic in the plastic arts, whilst many features of music—rhythms, change of tonality, tempi, in fact all its "dynamics"—and of ballet, which approaches close to drama, come under the same head. Sonata form is commonly looked upon as a structure of dramatic quality. Masks, although fixed in a single immobile expression, are charged with dramatic effect.

In drama proper the basic formula is that persons make decisions and act on them, which has consequences involving other persons, and complications and crisis follow. Some events and actions have always occurred before the start; the beginning of a play implies that a certain situation exists between a group of people, the play showing the further evolution. In other words a past and a future are always implicit in the opening scenes. And indeed this may be said of any subsequent moment in the course of the play; it constitutes the essential feature of a *plot* in which all hangs together in tense relationship for a short space of time. When we speak of dramatic situations we mean such as spring from cross-related human characters and their circumstances, and in which destiny and fatality inhere. One of the distinctive and most powerful effects of drama, as against the narrative or the film, is to show a *group* of people, present simultaneously on the stage, held together in this way by the embrace of fate. The events and actions and cross-currents of human living are then felt, one might even say "seen," as presences amidst the group.

The Greek drama established very early this general pattern, though according to Aristotle (*Poetics*, III, 1) the name itself appears originally to have meant simply that kind of poetry which "imitated" by representing the characters as real and employed in the action itself. Obviously characters and actions not exciting or tense may be represented in this way, so that if drama had done no more it would never have become "dramatic." Hence the importance of exciting complications and crisis. The form of enactment requires, in order to be successful by nature, and hold the emotions of spectators, a concentration of effects, which is derived from the increased tempo of events, from involved situations, and from the gravity of the issues at stake in the action represented. The nonliterary drama of entertainment (comedy-thriller, for example) cultivates only the external excitements. The literary drama derives its excitements from serious subject matter.

The practice of the great dramatists has followed these natural requirements of the form of representation. They have always cultivated the good "plot." Some, like Sophocles and Racine, have been more skilful·than others; none have denied its importance. And they have learnt from the suggestions of life itself what a good plot is. In other words, they exploit for dramatic art the dramatic imagery generated by life.

Thus it comes about that our notion of "the dramatic" is influenced constantly by the interplay of the two ideas of drama in life and the cultivated dramatic quality of art. And as the word assumes a technical meaning in connection with the drama it suggests the possibility of concentrating various modes of the dramatic. In this way a stylization occurs which involves a *sustained* complication and intensity not in fact usually found in real life. When we judge a play not dramatic enough we mean that it falls short of this stylization.

Many things, functioning sometimes alone and sometimes together, can be dramatic about a play; the action, if complicated or tense or impetuous; the speeches, revealing personal dilemma and confusion and a range of emotions and passions explosive or tempestuous; surprises of every category, such as confrontations, discoveries, confessions, turns of thought and situation; rhythms of various kinds, the modulations of which, apprehended in the language and the developing action, are among the most powerful dramatic elements; the dialectic of ideas, scenes and situations. No play uses all forms of the dramatic all the time but it will use them sufficiently to establish the feeling that the dramatic is predominant. Even so "a drama" is any variation of dramatic form that lies within two limits, the one being the greatest concentration conceivable, the other the point at which the dramatic is altogether negated. Racine and Ibsen are near to the one, Chekhov sometimes near to the other, limit.

None of these features should be taken, however, in an external or superficial sense. In good drama the sensuous appearances are all related to meanings, to thought, beliefs, philosophies, religious feelings, moral judgements. Indeed it must be categorically stated that the intensest dramatic quality will be realized where the most vital meanings are involved. This can be illustrated even from nonliterary drama. Melodrama depends, with all its falsities, on the actuality in the audience's minds of the conflict between "virtue" and "vice" as embodied in the stock hero and villain. It flourished in England particularly in Victorian times when the sense of this conflict was acute. The thriller, playing on the whole gamut of nervous shock, relies by implication on a moral sense of horror at murder. The "fatalistic" drama of the early nineteenth century (in Germany especially), mechanical in its use of theatrical clichés, and devoid of poetic quality, rested

nevertheless on an appeal to the genuine sense of fatality and the supernatural. These examples show sufficiently that the images of drama, all the vivid sensuous experience that is thrust upon the spectators from the illuminated stage or arena, the persuasive illusion of violent and catastrophic action, are impregnated with human thought and judgements. In such cases the latter are stereotyped or conventional, since the writer of a thriller does not reveal anything new about human nature. But they are present, incorporated in the raw material of the story. They may in fact be called agents of the form because they release the dramatic element.

The sense of meaning is important however for action itself, the element so universally invoked as indispensable in drama. In the "action" of a play people are expected to "do things" and thus create a concatenation of actions, situations, and events. We perform daily innumerable actions that are not in the least dramatic since they belong to a peaceful routine. But when actions are fraught with consequences, they become dramatic. "To be fraught with consequences" is a phrase we can only use in relation to the meaning of an action and its possible effects. Into that enter all the beliefs and principles by which we live and all our general interpretations of experience. The peculiar prestige of "action" for the drama is not simply the result of the material sense of something happening, or people creating a commotion, but it derives from the general sense of fate and fatality in actions that have important consequences. "Destiny" has always been a well-worked topic in discussing drama; and no wonder, for they are by nature linked. There is, it is true, an undramatic form of destiny, as when we say of a man that "it was his destiny to live a long and uneventful life in the village of his birth." On the other hand destiny emerges often as an almost tangible presence, with the force of a personality, from the interaction of events and people; and where this interaction appears most striking, where man seems to be the plaything of forces quite beyond his control, the notion of destiny becomes most pregnant. A situation in which a man is subject to reversal of fortune, or unprecedented success, or persecution, and so on, shows destiny in command, generating drama.

Just as actions are dramatic by the fatality in them, so, too, tragedy is highly dramatic because its meanings are complex, profound, and sublime, involving our sense of divine purpose, of order and justice in the universe and in human life, and our beliefs in good and evil. The moments in the course of a play when these meanings are clarified are always of great emotional intensity. For this reason, no doubt, tragedy has by tradition been especially associated with the dramatic form, while tragic elements in another literary form, as for example the novel, almost always induce dramatic quality.

In a similar way the dramatic force of ritual depends entirely on the meanings involved. Rites belong to religion from which they derive all their mystery and significance; they are intense and dramatic because they pertain to gods. Emotions are keyed up in their performance because of this sense of significance, and the formalization of ritual is a fixing of the ceremonial pattern found most adequate to evoke the highest emotional response to the religious meanings invoked. The same principle applies to trials and arraignments which are dramatic in life and have in consequence always been a stock device of the theater; trial scenes always warm up plays. It is not merely that they represent an obvious example of "conflict"; the conflict in any particular instance is heightened and the suspense raised because of all the meanings associated with law, with right and wrong, crime and punishment, because the fate of a person depends on the issue, and because justice is reaffirmed or contaminated by the judgement. One might also mention a situation like a royal abdication. This is dramatic, as Shakespeare knew, because of the institution of kingship and all that it implies in a religious, political, and social sense. When a king abdicates kingship itself is in question and is seen to be.

From these examples it may be concluded that to define drama simply as "action" or "conflict," as so often happens, is to rely too much on a narrow abstraction. Physical incident and conflict provide something dramatic, it is true; but the dramatic quality of any moment or situation in a play is directly commensurate with all the meanings involved. These include of course the "conflict" of ideas or beliefs as represented in the persons of the play, but extend also to all the meanings operative in a given social context. Human situations only stand out in relief against such a background of spiritual and social meanings, as we immediately apprehend in the subjects and plots of Elizabethan plays, or, equally strikingly, in Ibsen's plays, with their later nineteenth-century period atmosphere.

The force of this point about meaning in drama may be gathered from the effect created by overstatement. Meaning very deliberately pointed produces the effect we call theatrical. What constitutes legitimate emphasis, and what impairs the quality of this by exaggeration, provides a nice problem of balance. All the best drama carries with it a sense of the scene being set, which in itself adds an emphasis to the drama that is to come, pointing deliberately to its meaning. Sometimes this is implicit in the exposition, as in the opening scenes of *Hamlet*, or *Macbeth*, or *Antony and Cleopatra*, where secondary characters both help to initiate the action and also, being secondary, are a preliminary audience wondering at events and scanning them for their significance. But sometimes a dramatist sets his scene with still greater deliberation. An eminent example is the opening of Hofmannsthal's *The Great World Theatre*, where God distributes parts to souls about to enter life. Here the image of the "theater of life," embodying the quality of the theatrical, is itself used to lend force to the scene. It sets the tone, grandiose and solemn, warning the spectators that something is to be enacted, and with significance, something full of consequence. A play is beginning, its meaning hidden at first but progressively to be revealed. The sense of the dramatic and theatrical radiates from this image, by means of which the poet determines his aim, and doubles his effect.

Wagner, constantly singled out for praise —sometimes a little ambiguous—by Nietzsche and Thomas Mann as a genius with the deepest theatrical instincts, was a master of the "magic" that emanates from an elaborately pointed scene. One of the best examples is Act III, scene 5, of *The Mastersingers*, which leads from the homage to Sachs to the contest between the singers, the foreseen but demonstrative victory of Walter, and then, at the very crest of the huge and wonderful theatrical build-up, the exaltation of *deutsche Ehre* and *deutsche Kunst*. All the power of music, here incorporated in the theatrical texture, is lavished on the expression of the expectation and *Ergriffenheit* of the crowd, on meaningful ceremony and the triumph of an idea. The great scenes of Wagner's operas are all "staged" in this way; they all have a meaning which is not only shown in an action and in characters, but is exhibited with grandiose stress in the whole apparatus of theatrical and musical imagery. Wagner's *Leitmotive* were a device to help this purpose and they fit aptly into the scheme. They are a set of pointers with which Wagner constantly and solemnly draws attention to the central meanings of his fable or myth. They share in the ambiguity of the theatrical quality in that they are sometimes sounded with beautiful discretion and suggestiveness, and sometimes appear blatant. Thus they strike one now as a wonderful invention, and now as a device so obvious as to be rather childish. But all these features of Wagner make him a superb example for the specific quality of the theatrical, the essence of which is dramatic meaning set in relief, overstated, deliberately exhibited, and washed round with feeling, excitement, awe, and exaltation.

This theatrical quality, in its purest forms, strengthens the fabric of drama, and in its debased forms impairs it. On the one hand it heightens the sense of the dramatic image, stirs the spectators to excited participation, and thus enhances the enactment of a play in its social liaison. The *scène-à-faire*, the "big scene," the "great aria" in opera, Ibsen's framed discussion scenes, as well as the incorporation of trial scenes, arraignments, and ceremonies, "naturally" dramatic scenes with crowd effects, constituting plays within plays, theatre within theatre—all these show the subtle interweaving of dramatic and theatrical, the legitimate conjuring up of the sense of dramatic import in the audience, a positive theatrical enhancement. Brecht's technique of distancing (*Verfremdungseffekt*) derives also from this process of making one conscious of the theatrical *image*, though his method is rather crude. On the other hand this process can be so mismanaged that the mark is overshot. Instead of heightened and more impressive effect we get artificiality, affectation, and exaggeration; there is either too much emphasis of meaning or a large effort at emphasis on a nonexistent meaning. Many works of the baroque style in sculpture and architecture, with their ample and agitated gestures and forms, stand uncertainly on the narrow frontier between the positive dramatic and the negative theatrical. The histrionic, we should note at this point, is the personal form of the phenomenon, the theatrical quality bursting out of the individual. The last degradation is the resort to the cheap tricks that show the hollow shells of the dramatic-theatrical, as when, to take simple and obvious examples, an author makes easy points with actors, or better still actresses, and their histrionic behavior, among his *dramatis personae*, or introduces too often inset scenes of acting and mimicry. This is relying on effects, mere empty forms, on the theatrical not as an overemphasis on meaning but emptied of meaning.

ENACTMENT

Eric Bentley

TO IMPERSONATE, TO WATCH, AND TO BE WATCHED

The theatrical situation, reduced to a minimum, is that A impersonates B while C looks on. Such impersonation is universal among small children, and such playing of a part is not wholly distinct from the other playing that children do. All play creates a world within a world—a territory with laws of its own—and the theater might be regarded as the most durable of the many magic palaces which infantile humanity has built. The distinction between art and life begins there.

Impersonation is only half of this little scheme. The other half is watching—or, from the viewpoint of A, being watched. Even when there is actually no spectator, an impersonator imagines that there is, often by dividing himself into two, the actor and his audience. That very histrionic object, the mirror, enables any actor to watch himself and thereby to become C, the audience. And the mirror on the wall is only one: the mirrors in the mind are many.

What is it to want to be watched? Impossible to ask such a question these days without eliciting the word: exhibitionism. To want to be watched is to be exhibitionistic. Is this merely to say: to want to be watched is to want to be watched? Not quite. "Exhibitionism" is a clinical phenom-enon, and the word carries a connotation of the socially inappropriate as well as the mentally unhealthy. Which, I am afraid, only makes it the more applicable to the theater. Wishing to be watched, sometimes and in a small way, is one thing, but wishing to become an actor is wishing to be watched all the time and in a big way. Such a wish would take a lot of justifying and even more explaining. It is bizarre, and brings to mind Thomas Mann's notion that there is a natural affinity between art and pathology.

Is the Folies-Bergère the quintessence of theater? That depends, I think, on how one takes the Folies-Bergère. Sir Kenneth Clark has distinguished between the naked and the nude. A nude body is one that calls for no clothing; a naked body is a clothed body temporarily stripped of its clothing. Sir Kenneth's interest in the distinction lies in the fact that the arts he is professionally concerned with—painting and sculpture——deal, not with the naked, but with the nude; in fact (so far as Europe is concerned) they invented it. Not so the theater, however. Even in places and at times which had nothing against the body, the method of the theater has been concealment by mask and costume. True, one of the archetypal acts of the theater is to remove this concealment.

17

But one can only take off what is on. Or, in Sir Kenneth's terms, theater can present the naked, but never the nude. When therefore the girls of the Folies-Bergère are made a highbrow tableau of in the likeness of classical nude paintings, in trying to be nude they succeed in being untheatrical. When, on the other hand, they take off their clothes for us, or parade around in *almost* no clothing, they become theatrical through the act or simulation of unmasking. In short, if these girls are nude, they are art; if they are naked, they are theater. Parts of the French audience take them to be nude, or try to. The foreign tourists take them to be naked. That is because the tourists have "dirty minds." But the tourists are right. The nudity is spurious; the nakedness, genuine.

Hence, theater has less in common with the tradition of the nude in painting than with the tradition of the striptease in "vulgar" entertainment. Theater is shamelessly "low"; it cannot look down on the body, because it *is* the body. If you want the soul, why pay to see chorus girls? Why pay to *see* nonchorus girls? To begin to understand and accept theatrical art, we must be willing to say, yes, it's true, *we do* wish to see, and we do wish to be stimulated by seeing bodies—we decline to say "titillated" because the word "titillate" belongs to the puritan enemy of the theater. We must be willing to aver, further, that the bodies we wish to see are not "spiritualized" as Sir Kenneth Clark says nudes are, they are "naked," their spiritual credit is nil, their appeal is "prurient." We are prying into filthy secrets: the police department and the post office can begin to shift uneasily in their shoes.

How indecent the theater is! Yet, for our peace of mind, the indecency is in general placed at a remove: the nakedness is usually of the soul, not the body—and it is Phaedra's nakedness we see, not Gypsy Rose Lee's. For once that we see Salome remove her seven veils in Wilde's play or Strauss's opera, we see the veils removed a thousand times in other operas and plays from the individual spirit, from society, from the universe.

The problem with this is that to show the naked spirit is impossible. Only the spirit's envelope can be shown, and this is the body. And though a philosopher may represent the body as a mere shadow of a more substantial spiritual reality, and a playwright may follow him in this, our crude retort is inevitably that the shadow is itself pretty substantial. "Can spirit set to a leg? No. Or an arm? No." Platonic thoughts can be entertained in the mind, but not lived by from breakfast to lunch. And though the great nakednesses of the theater are spiritual, the immediate reality of theater is aggressively physical, corporeal. . . . Does an actor exhibit *himself?* There has been much discussion on this head. Educators usually tell students of theater that the actor does not exhibit himself: that would be egotistic. He submerges himself in his roles: a noble example of self-discipline, if not self-sacrifice. Louis Jouvet was saying as much when he stated that to embody a role the actor disembodies himself. One knows what he meant. When Sir Laurence Olivier plays Justice Shallow, the noble Olivier face and erect body are gone. Yet the very fact that I put it this way proves that I am not looking at the performance as I would if it were played by an actor who did not have a handsome face and an erect carriage. Does this signify only that I am a gossip, unable to concentrate on the show itself? I think not. The knowledge that an acrobatic trick is difficult is not irrelevant to the experience of watching it. On the contrary. We know it is easy for many creatures to fly up and down at great speed: the interest is *only* in seeing men and women do it, because it is not easy for them to do it. To see Olivier as Shallow is to see comparable difficulties overcome, comparable laws of nature defied by human prowess. Hence we are not enjoying the role alone, but also the actor. And he, on his side, is not exhibiting the role alone, he is exhibiting his prowess, he is exhibiting himself. Nor is the self-exhibition confined to the skill with which he portrays someone we define as "so different from himself." To wear a heavy, senile make-up and hunch the shoulders would not be enough if there were not a Justice Shallow in Olivier, if Shallow were not something he might yet become, or might have become. In such roles the actor is exhibiting the many different possibilities of being that he finds in himself.

No need to say anything about actors who all too evidently exhibit nothing but themselves. I am saying that even the actor who seems to be at the opposite pole from this is still exhibiting himself. Exceptional in Sir Laurence is the talent. Unexceptional is the original, naïve impulse that said: Watch me!

What of the pleasure of watching? In some respects, there is no difference between the theater spectator and the "consumer" of other arts—the listener to music, the reader of novels. It might be imagined that his position is identical with that of the observer of painting, sculpture, and architecture: all are onlookers. But the phenomenon is less straightforward. If theater is a visual art like painting, it is also a temporal art like music. The watcher is also a listener—the voyeur is also an eavesdropper.

Such words as *exhibitionist* and *voyeur*—though some will discount them as jargon—add to the purely descriptive words an implication of guilt.

> I have heard
> That guilty creatures sitting at a play
> Have by the very cunning of the scene
> Been struck so to the soul that presently
> They have proclaimed their malefactions.

Literal-minded persons will find Hamlet's ideas on crime detection somewhat far-fetched, but poetic drama deals in essences, and here Shakespeare, Hamlet, and all audiences of *Hamlet* take it that the essence of theater is to strike guilty creatures to the soul—or, as we would say in prose cliché, to play on the guilt feelings of the audience. Seen in this way, the logic is good.

> The play's the thing
> Wherein I'll catch the conscience of the king.

—because plays *are* things wherein consciences are caught.

This makes it sound as if watching were very unpleasurable indeed—as, for King Claudius, it was. Hamlet plotted to defy the distinction between art and life, to exploit the possibility of a leap from art to life. When that happens we are no longer dealing with drama but with the destruction of its main convention. If we are not King Claudius, and have not literally killed our brother, we are also spared his reaction. Instead of calling for lights and making our exit, we stay on to "enjoy the show." Is our conscience *not* caught, then? Are our withers unwrung? It is. They are. But in art, not life. Such is the paradox of pain in drama: we do and do not suffer. We are suffering; we are also enjoying ourselves. When we watch, though we do not watch in the way we watch actual happenings, neither do we watch in the spirit of "scientific detachment" but always with some degree of emotional involvement. I am suggesting that this involvement is not an innocent one.

It would be impossible to draw the line between drama and gossip, drama and scandal, drama and the front page of the worst newspapers—which, understandably enough, claim to be dramatic. Even what is called pornography is by no means in any separate realm from the realm of the tragic and comic poets. All these things are enjoyed by human beings, and to all some measure of guilt is attached. Perhaps if one took the guilt away, the dirty picture, so called, would lose much of its appeal, and perhaps if one took from theater the element of voyeurism, the occasion would lose much of its appeal.

Certainly that element has been on the increase in modern times. The Greek, Elizabethan, and Spanish theaters were less voyeuristic because the plays were put on in broad daylight. It is the modern age that worked out the idea of a pitch-dark auditorium. Scholars call the modern stage the peepshow stage. The corollary is that this is a theater for Peeping Toms. It is; and the classical criticism of it is that, from the eighteenth century to Tennessee Williams, it has been so too crudely. It has been, all too often, a theatre of domestic triviality.

The pleasure of looking on is in itself an equivocal thing. It includes such delights as feeling one has committed the crime yet is able to escape the penalty because the final curtain descends and one finds "it was all a dream."

SUBSTITUTIONS

Such is the infantile basis of theatre. When he impersonates B, A is an exhibitionist, and when C looks on, he is a voyeur. But of course A does not need B if exhibition is all he desires, for he could exhibit himself, and necessarily that is one thing he does exhibit.

B, the person impersonated, who is he? Originally, he is the little actor's father, the mother, and the siblings. Any other persons are likely to be members of the household interchangeable with a parent or a sibling. The interesting thing is that this continues to be true in adult theater. There the persons impersonated are the work of a playwright. But the classic preoccupation of the playwright has been with the family. Comedy has often shown the family in the making. Both comedy and tragedy have often shown the family in the unmaking, and from the *Agamemnon* to *Ghosts*, from *The Mandrake* to *Candida*, have dealt with marriage and the threats to it.

It was the psychoanalysts who pointed out that the family was often still the subject even when it seemed not to be. Otto Rank, for example, maintained that Julius Caesar is about parricide and that Brutus, Cassius, and Marc Antony are, symbolically speaking, Caesar's sons. Such a thing cannot be directly demonstrated but it comes to seem likely if we follow a certain line of reasoning. It is a matter of those other persons in the household whom, when we are children, we take to be members of the family, the nurse who is a kind of mother, the uncle who is a kind of father, the cousin who is an older or younger brother. The fact is that we continue to enlarge our family in this way as long as we live or, putting it the other way round, we assign all our acquaintances membership in the family which we knew as children. The play of life, as each of us writes it, has a very small cast—though for each role there may be innumerable understudies. If we felt our own father to be tyrannical, the role known as Father may be played by anyone we feel to be tyrannical. If we had the coddling kind of mother, the role known as Mother may be played by anyone, even a male, who coddles us. And so on. In short we have made ourselves a list of very definite types and, far from being tenuous and nebulous as types are reputed to be, they suggest to us strong emotion and clear-cut attitude.

IDENTIFICATIONS

There is a peculiarity about these little systems. One does not include oneself in the cast of characters, and so it is impossible for one to identify a whole class of people with oneself. It is the other way round. Unable to see oneself at all, one gropes in the dark, one guesses, one decides one is like some other person. One does not identify others with oneself but oneself with others. Again, the family is likely to play a guiding role. A little boy is likely to identify himself with his father. In this there is another source of tragic art: oneself as the great god Daddy. Here is the root of the idea of the hero: identification with strength.

The world, I have been saying, consists

of oneself and others. One makes a cast of characters out of the ensemble, and a play out of living. A tragedy can well be made out of oneself and one's identification with Father, a comedy out of one's sense of those few archetypes, "the others." Two psychological processes are involved: *substitution* of all and sundry persons for the few in one's own original background, and *identification* of oneself with someone else. To analyze any "interpersonal" situation, one might well ask: who has been substituted for whom? and: with whom am I identified?

It would be hard to overestimate the influence of the identifications we all make. Though certainly we do not become the people we model ourselves on, what we become depends upon the people we model ourselves on. This is an element in upbringing which the Victorian age understood better than ours. Identifications, at home, and later at school, are everything. Central in the dynamics of living and growing up, they are central in this so intimately human art: the drama. Even Broadway knows as much. Its reviewers know how to account for the failure of a play by its lack of anyone in the cast they can identify themselves with. Precisely in its crudity, Broadway dramaturgy is suited to illustrate an argument I am presenting in broad lines only: a Broadway cast of characters consists of the person one identifies oneself with plus the rest of one's family put there in the form most quickly recognizable, old Uncle Tom Cobley and all.

Broadway producers presuppose in their audience very little spiritual ambition. They don't expect people to identify themselves with anyone of any stature. The old melodramas were more enterprising, because there, for the space of two hours, one could make a Douglas Fairbanks of oneself. At the other pole, there is the kind of protagonist who probably is beyond one's reach —T. S. Eliot's Becket, for example. In *Murder in the Cathedral* Mr. Eliot put in a chorus of women for us to identify ourselves with. They are slightly better than half-witted. In this way the "highbrow" playwright reaches a conclusion not dissimilar to that of the "lowbrows"; and indeed this play achieved a certain popularity.

EMPATHY AND ALIENATION

In challenging the traditional principles of the drama, Bertolt Brecht has in our day questioned the value of identification. The word was *Einfühlung*, translated as empathy. As used early in this century, by Vernon Lee, for example, the word empathy had to do with the mental process by which we say that a mountain rises from the plain. Since then it has come to bear one of the meanings Vernon Lee said it should not bear: more or less the literal meaning of *sich einfühlen*, "to feel oneself into." It is sympathy without the moral implication or the sentimental overtone. It is identification.

Brecht coined another word for what he saw as the theatrical alternative to empathy. This is *Verfremdung*—Alienation or Estrangement. Brecht asks that we not identify ourselves with his characters but that we stand back from them. Object is to be seen as object, with astonishment. Brecht claims to derive this latter clause from science. Most people take for granted that apples fall; Isaac Newton was astonished. In the Brechtian theater, the playwright is to be an Isaac Newton, and make Isaac Newtons of his audience. There was really no need to go outside the drama for such an aim. Corneille would have understood it well; and something of the sort is implied in most comedy.

Brecht is perhaps overconfident in assuming that when we abandon empathy we can see "the object in itself as it really is." He reckons without the process of substitution as I have described it. And failing to notice the inescapability of identifications, he himself makes them only unconsciously. Indeed his unconscious identification with his supposed enemies becomes a source of unintended drama.

THE ADULT AND THE INFANTILE

This comment on Brecht brings to a head my presentation of theater as an infantile system. Brecht's objection is precisely to infantility. His Epic Theater would be a completely adult theater *if such a thing were possible*. As he writes in his Prospectus of the Diderot Society:

> Only in recent decades did a theater develop which placed greater value upon a correct presentation of the world, whereby, to fit this correctness, objective, nonindividual criteria should be allowed. No more did the artist feel himself bound to create "his own world" and, taking the actual world as known and unalterable, feel bound to enrich the catalogue of images which are really images of the image-makers; rather did he feel himself bound to take the world as alterable and unknown and to deliver images which give information more about the world than about him. . . . The "inner eye" needs no microscope or telescope; the outer eye needs both. For the visionary the experiences of other people are dispensable. Experiment is not in the repertoire of the seer. No, the artist who takes up the new task must, when he seeks to communicate images, deny himself the methods of hypnosis and even at need the customary empathy. . . .

In which it is taken for granted that a man "of the age of science" can become independent of the primitive side of his own nature by taking thought.

Everything in Brecht's theory of theater— from the white light to the "presentational" acting—is dedicated to the same end: replacing a magical theater with a scientific one, a childish theater with an adult one. There is obviously a good deal to be said for this. What you cannot say for it, however, is that it is possible. For "growing up," so far as mental growth is concerned, is only a manner of speaking. The most mature person bristles with immaturities; the least neurotic person is still neurotic. The human race cannot reasonably be divided into two groups, the childish and the adult, because the child is not only father of the man, he is the man's Siamese twin.

The only odd thing is that an artist should not know it, since the child lives on more unabashedly in the artist than in any other class, and many artists are rather too happy about the fact. If I went back to infantile psychology in order to introduce the subject of this chapter, I did so in the interests not of simplicity but of relevance. For the theater of grownups is much closer to the little system that children work out than the casual observer would think, the reason being, as Richard Sterba has put it, that "the pleasure of acting and looking on at a theatrical performance is a very narcissistic one, through regression to the early childhood stage of magic world creation." Brecht, who welcomed the blow to the world's narcissism that was administered by Galileo, should not have been above admitting that there are regressive and narcissistic and magical elements in all effective theater, including of course his own. They have their negative side (immaturity is immaturity) but "becoming again like a little child" has its positive side too, and is a requirement not only of higher ethics but of higher theater.

PLAY, PLAY-ACTING, ACTING

The greatest part of our energy is expended in repeating what we and others have done many times before. To all appearances the aim of life is to make sure that tomorrow shall duplicate today. The same round of little duties and meals, followed by the same spell in bed! Our early education had only this kind of thing in mind. Toilet training was at first to repeat what our elders did, and later to repeat what we ourselves had begun to do. To learn language was nothing if not to repeat what the others said. To learn gesture was to repeat what the others did with their arms. So much indeed would seem to be necessary to the life process. But as if this were not enough of repetition, we add more. Repetition is a leading feature of our pleasures too. To learn a little dance is to learn a small figure which is then repeated *ad libitum.* We learn a tune in order to sing it a thousand times, not to mention that in most songs the theme is repeated even within one verse. We attach prestige to repetition. "Solemn occasions" are occasions on which oft-repeated words and music are repeated again. Ritual would not be itself if not constantly repeated. And so, if life is action, it should not seem surprising that acting—going through our actions again—is a universal art.

Of this art it can confidently be said that, if it became extinct, it would be reinvented again by children of two and three. Children of that age, giving up as hopeless the notion of being grownups on the full scale, become little imitation grownups and, as such, actors of the human comedy. This can be regarded, and often has been, as part of the educational process. We learn to grow up by pretending to be grown-up. To which some psychologists add that play-acting in children is also experimental. This means not only that we acquire (for example) a grownup vocabulary by repeating the grown-up vocabulary but that the world of play is a workshop or laboratory for experiment by trial and error. There is no doubt a defensive side to it as well. Not having mastered the "real" world, by play-acting we construct a refuge from it, a haven whose inviolability we jealously guard.

Play, play-acting, acting: it is hard, in observing three-year-old children, to say where play leaves off and play-acting begins.

Pure play would seem to belong more especially to a later age where rules are understood and adhered to. Games are a kind of abstract art, all geometry and numbers. What the three-year-olds mostly do has an element of pretending in it, and so of play-acting: there is a role and there is a drama. But it is not acting because there is no audience: it is not there to be looked at, noted, appreciated, enjoyed. Children, notoriously, are audience-conscious, they wish to be noted, appreciated, enjoyed, but what they at first exhibit to their audience is precisely not their make-believe dramas but their conquests of "reality." If the grownup is to be included in the drama he must be included as a fellow actor, not observing the fantasy, but entering into it. Not until the impulse to play-act can be brought together with the impulse to be watched and appreciated is a child ready to be, even in the most rudimentary sense, an actor.

It would be a naïve psychology indeed that saw acting as a device of childhood to be later discarded. "All the world's a stage, and all the men and women merely players," or, in the words written up at the Globe Theatre: *totus mundus facit histrionem*—"all the world plays the actor." Even everyday talk concedes that grown people are often "just acting," "putting on an act," "doing a song and dance," and the Germans even say: "*Machen Sie keine Oper!*"—"Don't make an opera!" The limitation of this popular understanding of acting in everyday life is that it is marked with disapproval, applies only to hypocritical activity, and presupposes that most action is not acting. More sophisticated opinion allows that acting tends to characterize human behavior in general. Indeed to make this allowance in Anglo-Saxon countries is itself to *be* sophisticated, since our tradition in these matters is puritanic and philistine. It is for an Irishman like Shaw to tell us that the actor is the least hypocritical of men since he alone admits he is acting. It is for Irishmen like Wilde and Yeats to explain to us that our choice is not between mask and face, but between bad masks and good. And it is for the Spaniard Santayana, as provoked by Boston and Harvard, to represent, with hauteur, that the mask is the only alternative to the fig leaf, the fig leaf being "only a more ignominious mask."

> In this world [says Santayana in the *Soliloquies in England*], we must institute conventional forms of expression or else pretend that we have nothing to express.

And again:

> What . . . could be more splendidly sincere than the impulse to play in real life, to rise on the rising wave of very feeling and let it burst, if it will, into the foam of exaggeration? Life is not a means, the mind is not a slave nor a photograph: it has a right to enact a pose, to assume a panache, and to create what prodigious allegories it will for the mere sport and glory of it. . . . To embroider upon experience is not to bear false witness against one's neighbor, but to bear true witness to oneself.

Such a philosophy, which might be traced all the way back to a passage in Plato's *Laws*, makes us see play, play-acting, and acting, not only as natural and childish, but also as a human achievement and an adult goal. If, as phenomena of childhood, they seem to clinicians merely the preparation for unplayful adulthood, the philosopher can question the value of unplayfulness—that Puritanic notion of maturity—and place at the goal of experience a renewed childhood, a second playfulness, a regained innocence. Such an idea has even as good a claim to orthodoxy as the contrary, Puritan notion (latterly adopted more, perhaps, by scientific than religious folk), for what is the traditional conception of heavenly bliss? Its image, in its familiar if vulgar form, is that of angels sitting, harp in hand, on clouds— angels playing, angels performing. Condemned, as we may see ourselves, to eat bread in the sweat of our brow, we do so only in the hope of a celestial songfest or heavenly hootenanny.

AN ENCOUNTER WITH " KING LEAR "

Lewis Funke

When an actor wants to play King Lear, the reason cannot be dissimilar from that given by the late George Leigh Mallary when he was asked why he wanted to climb Mount Everest: "Because it is there."

Lear is a veritable Everest in the realm of the English-speaking theater, a monumental challenge to skill, comprehension and endurance. Many regard the play as one of the most powerful complex dramas ever written, and Shaw once observed that no man ever would write a greater one.

Morris Carnovsky, receiving plaudits for his performance of the title role at the American Shakespeare Festival, remembers his final meeting with director Allen Fletcher before the start of rehearsals.

"We'd had several conferences," Mr. Carnovsky recalls. "I'd vowed that I would not go on until I understood the meaning of every word, every phrase, every motivation. Allen and I had gone over our concepts, all the details, looked for a common ground, for mutual understanding of what we were after. At last, we were finished. I looked at him and I said, 'Of course, you know it's impossible.' Allen nodded. 'Yes,' he said, 'it's impossible. But we're going to try.' 'Good,' I said. 'We go for broke.'"

Mr. Carnovsky's "we go for broke" will not rank with Mallary's classically simple and by now classic "because it is there." But

in its own way it bears its own awareness of reality, its own recognition of the loftiness of the goal. To attempt Lear is to risk health, reputation, self-esteem. Few try. In the 63 years of this century only 11 British actors have dared, including such masters as John Gielgud, Laurence Olivier, and Paul Scofield. Here, there have been ten in the same period, the last on Broadway having been Orson Welles.

What is it that makes Lear so difficult to capture? What are the problems that confront an actor as he wrestles with this monarch whose will and anger lead him to disaster?

Mr. Carnovsky is not a big man, about 5 feet 8 inches tall, though he is broad of shoulder. He has a strong head, a deep forehead, now deeper because his hair has thinned through 65 years. He has a sharp, strong nose and the air and manner of a man who has read a great deal, felt deeply about art and society, and come to definite conclusions about himself in relationship to his world. Sitting on the lawn here the other day, behind the festival's administration building, he sought to give some answers. Even now, after weeks, months and years of contemplating the part, he finds it necessary to pick his way.

"There is something about this role," he began slowly, his gray-blue eyes narrowed in concentrated thought, "there is something about Lear that overpowers the imagination. Unlike Hamlet, which is translatable for an actor in personal terms, Lear is more real than real. He is like those doom-eager Norse heroes I've read about somewhere. Doom-eager, you understand, what I mean? Human beings up against the forces of nature, knowing that they have only their courage to carry them on, knowing that in the end they will fail and yet, at the same time, hoping somehow to outwit the ultimate decree.

LEAR NO FOOL

"Here is Lear, a man over 80 who has enjoyed a lifetime of rule, a despot, but a despot who has been loved. He's had everything. Everyone has given him respect, love, admiration. He has come to a point where he no longer wishes to rule. When by a whim in a moment of wrath, he chooses to distribute his kingdom and cut off Cordelia, he knows that he is wrong. He is no fool. But this is what he has done, what he chose to do and is ready for the consequences. When nature and the forces around him set out to destroy him, he has nothing with which to oppose them except his strength. When nature takes revenge he accepts the challenge and stands there, as it were, crying out, 'Pour it on, I will endure.'

"And it seems to me that this is what Shakespeare was saying. After the years of his experience, he was saying, look at what I have seen in the world. The world is black and evil, full of pretense and fraud. I have seen stupidity and cupidity and men deluded. And yet there is a certain beauty in life, even goodness. And I have beheld the indomitability of man. The mirror is black and yet I affirm. I am part of life and I affirm."

If the play is a major intellectual challenge for an actor, it is no less a physical ordeal. Mr. Carnovsky points out that it is "crowded with climaxes—it's a series of volcanic masses." From the first scene the pitch is set high and it goes higher still until a point is reached "where I have to outshout the gods of thunder. I remember stopping rehearsals one day and saying to Allen, "Enough of this. Let's try to make it a dialogue. Let me say what I have to say and let the heavens answer." I'm not sure that we've got it right yet.

"The role demands almost superhuman strength. It is necessary to discover in the playing how to relax, how to conserve yourself as the play plunges on. There is always the danger that you will give too much of yourself too soon. I try to hold back. I try to look for places where I can relax, like when my fool speaks his long speech. Believe me, I try to relax every muscle in my body. I drop my stomach, my eyes. These moments —they're like a vacation trip to the Virgin Islands."

Mr. Carnovsky, warmed now to his subject, turned to the problem of relating to Lear, of trying to translate the character in terms of personal experience. In creating Shylock, he recalled, he could summon his own experience as a Jew, he could remember the persecution of Jews through their long history of martydom, he could understand repression, insult, and rejection. He could remember artistic examples that fitted Shylock—"Man with a Broken Nose," by Rodin, a mask of Picasso's, Marc Chagall's "The Vitebsk Rabbi," and Ivan Mestrovic's "Moses."

He could recall, as he has, a character from his youth, "a crazy, half-demented fellow. His name was Yussel, and they called him Yussel the Meshuganeh—Yussel the crazy one. He was a terribly pathetic creature. And I remember the kids used to throw stones at him and he had no way of protecting himself. He had a broken nose and a dirty, bedraggled beard and now and then he would turn on them and ask them, 'Why do you do this? What have I done to you?' " And, he says, the pathos was almost unbearable.

"But for Lear—I've had trouble as most men have. But I had no such sources. Yes, I could use a little of Yussel and I suppose

I have. But mostly I've had to rely on my intellect, my sympathies, my imagination, and isolated recollections. They say that Garrick, when he prepared for Lear, would go to a certain street and watch a man standing day after day at a window enduring anguish. The man had dropped his child from that window and had gone completely crazy. They say that Garrick, who was a great mime, reproduced the agony of that man so that it tore your heart out."

FEW SOURCES

"I did, of course, have certain things that helped. You know, in one scene where I cover my eye with the palm of my hand—it's a gesture of horror and despair—I got that from Michelangelo's "Last Judgment." And there is an impression I have carried with me since my college days. I had a professor, a most sensitive and poetic man who, I remember, one day read to us from "King Lear" and came to that passage in which Lear awakens in the presence of Cordelia. He was reading Cordelia's lines, and when he came to 'Mine enemy's dog though he had bit me, should have stood that night against my fire'—he stopped, he got stuck and then he muttered in a deep, hushed whisper, 'dreadful, dreadful, dreadful.' These I have remembered and they helped. But they are impressions and nothing more. No, Lear is not easily translatable for an actor in terms of his own experience."

Mr. Carnovsky rose from his chair, gazed out toward the Housatonic River, around the beautiful festival landscape. It was the time of day he liked best—late afternoon. "Every so often," he said, "a Gauguin-like light settles here, like now. It's magnificent." He was relaxed now. He had gone for broke and if he was not yet completely satisfied that he was Lear's master, at least he felt he was on the right road. "A few more performances," he mused, "then, maybe...."

THE TIMELESS WORLD OF A PLAY

Tennessee Williams

Carson McCullers concludes one of her lyric poems with the line: "Time, the endless idiot, runs screaming 'round the world." It is this continual rush of time, so violent that it appears to be screaming, that deprives our actual lives of so much dignity and meaning, and it is, perhaps more than anything else, the *arrest of time* which has taken place in a completed work of art that gives to certain plays their feeling of depth and significance. In the London notices of *Death of a Salesman* a certain notoriously skeptical critic made the remark that Willy Loman was the sort of man that almost any member of the audience would have kicked out of an office had he applied for a job or detained one for conversation about his troubles. The remark itself possibly holds some truth. But the implication that Willy Loman is consequently a character with whom we have no reason to concern ourselves in drama, reveals a strikingly false conception of what plays are. Contemplation is something that exists outside of time, and so is the tragic sense. Even in the actual world of commerce, there exists in some persons a sensibility to the unfortunate situations of others, a capacity for concern and compassion, surviving from a more tender period of life outside the present whirling wire-cage of business activity. Facing Willy Loman across an office desk, meeting his nervous glance and hearing his querulous voice, we would be very likely to glance at our wrist watch and our schedule of other appointments. We would not kick him out of the office, no, but we would certainly *ease* him out with more expedition than Willy had feebly hoped for. But suppose there had been no wrist watch or office clock and suppose there had *not* been the schedule of pressing appointments, and suppose that we were not actually facing Willy across a desk—and facing a person is *not* the best way to *see* him!—suppose, in other words, that the meeting with Willy Loman had somehow occurred in a world *outside* of time. Then I think we would receive him with concern and kindness and even with respect. If the world of a play did not offer us this occasion to view its characters under that special condition of a *world without time*, then, indeed, the characters and occurrences of drama would become equally pointless, equally trivial, as corresponding meetings and happenings in life.

The classic tragedies of Greece had tremendous nobility. The actors wore great masks, movements were formal, dance-like, and the speeches had an epic quality which doubtless were as removed from the normal conversation of their contemporary society as they seem today. Yet they did not seem false to the Greek audiences: the magnitude of the events and the passions aroused by them did not seem ridiculously out of proportion to common experience. And I wonder if this was not because the Greek audiences knew, instinctively or by training, that the created world of a play is removed from that element which makes people *little* and their emotions fairly inconsequential.

Great scupture often follows the lines of the human body: yet the repose of great sculpture suddenly transmutes those human lines to something that has an absoluteness, a purity, a beauty, which would not be possible in a living mobile form.

A play may be violent, full of motion: yet it has that special kind of repose which allows contemplation and produces the climate in which tragic importance is a possible thing, provided that certain modern conditions are met.

In actual existence the moments of love are succeeded by the moments of satiety and sleep. The sincere remark is followed by a cynical distrust. Truth is fragmentary, at best: we love and betray each other not in quite the same breath but in two breaths that occur in fairly close sequence. But the fact that passion occurred in *passing*, that it then declined into a more familiar sense of indifference, should not be regarded as proof of its inconsequence. And this is the very truth that drama wishes to bring us . . . .

Whether or not we admit it to ourselves, we are all haunted by a truly awful sense of impermanence. I have always had a particularly keen sense of this at New York cocktail parties, and perhaps that is why I drink the martinis almost as fast as I can snatch them from the tray. This sense is the febrile thing that hangs in the air. Horror of insincerity, of *not meaning*, overhangs these affairs like the cloud of cigarette smoke and the hectic chatter. This horror is the only thing, almost, that is left unsaid at such functions. All social functions involving a group of people not intimately known to each other are always under this shadow.

They are almost always (in an unconscious way) like that last dinner of the condemned: where steak or turkey, whatever the doomed man wants, is served in his cell as a mockingly cruel reminder of what the great-big-little-transitory world had to offer.

In a play, time is arrested in the sense of being confined. By a sort of legerdemain, events are made to remain *events*, rather than being reduced so quickly to mere *occurrences*. The audience can sit back in a comforting dusk to watch a world which is flooded with light and in which emotion and action have a dimension and dignity that they would likewise have in real existence, if only the shattering intrusion of time could be locked out.

About their lives people ought to remember that when they are finished, everything in them will be contained in a marvelous state of repose which is the same as that which they unconsciously admired in drama. The rush is temporary. The great and only possible dignity of man lies in his power deliberately to choose certain moral values by which to live as steadfastly as if he, too, like a character in a play, were immured against the corrupting rush of time. Snatching the eternal out of the desperately fleeting is the great magic trick of human existence. As far as we know, as far as there exists any kind of empiric evidence, there is no way to beat the game of *being* against *non-being*, in which non-being is the predestined victor on realistic levels.

Yet plays in the tragic tradition offer us a view of certain moral values in violent juxtaposition. Because we do not participate, except as spectators, we can view them clearly, within the limits of our emotional equipment. These people on the stage do not return our looks. We do not have to answer their questions nor make any sign of being in company with them, nor do we have to compete with their virtues nor resist their offenses. All at once, for this reason, we are able to *see* them! Our hearts are wrung by recognition and pity, so that the dusky shell of the auditorium where we are gathered anonymously together is flooded with an almost liquid warmth of unchecked human sympathies, relieved of self-consciousness, allowed to function . . . .

Men pity and love each other more deeply than they permit themselves to know. The moment after the phone has been hung up, the hand reaches for a scratch pad and scrawls a notation: "Funeral Tuesday at five, Church of the Holy Redeemer, don't forget flowers." And the same hand is only a little shakier than usual as it reaches, some minutes later, for a highball glass that will pour a stupefaction over the kindled nerves. Fear and evasion are the two little beasts that chase each other's tails in the revolving wirecage of our nervous world. They distract us from feeling too much about things. Time rushes toward us with its hospital tray of infinitely varied narcotics, even while it is preparing us for its inevitably fatal operation . . . .

So successfully have we disguised from ourselves the intensity of our own feelings, the sensibility of our own hearts, that plays in the tragic tradition have begun to seem untrue. For a couple of hours we may surrender ourselves to a world of fiercely illuminated values in conflict, but when the stage is covered and the auditorium lighted, almost immediately there is a recoil of disbelief. "Well, well!" we say as we shuffle back up the aisle, while the play dwindles behind us with the sudden perspective of an early

Chirico painting. By the time we have arrived at Sardi's, if not as soon as we pass beneath the marquee, we have convinced ourselves once more that life has as little resemblance to the curiously stirring and meaningful occurrences on the stage as a jingle has to an elegy of Rilke.

This modern condition of his theater audience is something that an author must know in advance. The diminishing influence of life's destroyer, time, must be somehow worked into the context of his play. Perhaps it is a certain foolery, a certain distortion toward the grotesque, which will solve the problem for him. Perhaps it is only restraint, putting a mute on the strings that would like to break all bounds. But almost surely, unless he contrives in some way to relate the dimensions of his tragedy to the dimensions of a world in which time is *included*—he will be left among his magnificent debris on a dark stage, muttering to himself: "Those fools . . . ."

And if they could hear him above the clatter of tongues, glasses, chinaware and silver, they would give him this answer: "But you have shown us a world not ravaged by time. We admire your innocence. But we have seen our photographs, past and present. Yesterday evening we passed our first wife on the street. We smiled as we spoke but we didn't really see her! It's too bad, but we know what is true and not true, and at 3 A.M. your disgrace will be in print!"

A play by the Norwegian dramatist Henrik Ibsen is uniquely useful as an illustration both of the story-telling methods of the stage and of the use of plot to further a dramatist's purpose; for Ibsen, though a skillful artisan, was also an insistent moralist who believed that drama should have a crusading purpose or function. As an example of the combination and balance of the various elements of drama, as an illustration of the manner in which a drama may blend action, character, and setting in such a way as to point toward an over-all "meaning," Ibsen's *Rosmersholm* will serve us well as a starting point in the study of the range of drama.

Rosmersholm is typical not only of the work of its author, but of the "problem play" or "drama of ideas" that rose to a dominant position in the theater late in the nineteenth century and influenced much of twentieth-century drama. Its author was thus an innovator in his own day, his drama a precursor of things to come. Ibsen found the sentimental and romantic drama of the nineteenth century sickly and tiresome, devoid of purpose; in the new kind of play he came to write, he insisted that the dramatist should not merely "entertain" his audiences, he should also "engage" them by requiring them to take sides on significant social, political, and ethical issues.

Though sometimes described condescendingly as only a lecturer in the theater, Ibsen nevertheless, by means of this emphasis, imbued drama with a new vitality and seriousness of purpose. Thus in one early play, *Brand* (1866), he exposed the self-gratifying sanctimoniousness that often passes as piety; in another, *Pillars of Society* (1877), he attacked the craftiness and opportunism of those who lead society. In perhaps his most famous play, *A Doll's House* (1879), he encouraged the feminist movement by dramatizing for the first time the demand for a single standard of conduct for men and women alike. In these and other plays, Ibsen showed that the dramatist could extract significant themes from the issues that confront and perplex ordinary people.

In some of Ibsen's earlier plays, the events are arbitrarily manipulated in order to make the plot come out right, and some of the characters are flat or stock figures who seem to exist primarily to speak the author's views. But in *Rosmersholm*, written in 1886, many of these weaknesses are overcome; it dates from a period in Ibsen's life when increased skill in plot construction was combined with greater insight into human nature to produce a dramatically mature work that makes adept use of action and character as vehicles for ideas.

Basically, *Rosmersholm* is a play about an intelligent and skeptical man caught in a conflict between the contradictory demands of a traditional, conservative past and a liberal, progressive future. Its central character, Johannes Rosmer, a former clergyman, has left his post because his inquiring mind has led him to a radical skepticism toward the institutions of his society. As the play opens, his rejection of political and religious absolutes has left him in so ambivalent a state that he cannot make a brave leap in any direction. His inner conflict is exemplified by the two women who overshadow his life: his dead first wife, who links him to the past, and the calculating and efficient Rebekka West, the prototype of the "new woman," so emancipated that she can pretend to be unburdened by love and the ordinary human emotions. Ibsen projects the sources of conflict through Rebekka and Ulrik Brendel on the one hand, representing the forces of social upheaval, and Professor Kroll and the dead wife Beata on the other, representing the status quo in society and the burden of the past in Rosmer's mind.

At the action level, mysterious hints about the death of the first wife, about the origins of Rebekka West, and about past relationships of the other characters, provide the exposition and prepare the reader for the revelations that come in the last two acts. At the same time, the frequent references to the ghostly White Horses, symbolic of the dead weight of the past which threatens to crush the present, foreshadow the violence of the dénouement. As the personal and the broader social implications of the plot merge, there emerges, too, not a pat "moral" arbitrarily grafted onto the story, but a generalization inherent in the very action of the play itself. Ibsen forces the reader to confront the problem of balancing his debt to the past against the claims of the future: he offers no ready-made solution.

Thus *Rosmersholm* prefaces our study of types and modes of drama because it stands as an example of a well-constructed play that knits all its elements together into one entity; because it uses these elements, despite their individual natures and the inherent interest they possess, for an ultimate thematic purpose; and because its characters prefigure the concern of so much twentieth-century drama with the common man, seeing as much dramatic import in his failures and pettinesses as in his triumphs. All these traits combine to illustrate "meaning" in drama for the modern reader.

ROSMERSHOLM

Henrik Ibsen

Translated by
Eva Le Gallienne

JOHANNES ROSMER, *owner of Rosmersholm; a former clergyman*
REBEKKA WEST, *a member of the household*
PROFESSOR KROLL, *Rosmer's brother-in-law*
ULRIK BRENDEL

PEDER MORTENSGAARD*
MRS. HELSETH, *housekeeper at Rosmersholm*
The action takes place at Rosmersholm, an old estate in the neighborhood of a small town on a fjord on the west coast of Norway.

ACT I

SCENE: *Sitting-room at Rosmersholm; spacious, old-fashioned, and comfortable. In front, on the right, a stove decked with fresh birch branches and wild flowers. Farther back, on the same side, a door. In the back wall, folding doors opening into the hall. To the left, a window, and before it a stand with flowers and plants. Beside the stove a table with a sofa and easy chairs. On the walls, old and more recent portraits of clergymen, officers and government officials in uniform. The window is open; so are the door into the hall and the house door beyond. Outside can be seen an avenue of fine old trees, leading* up to the house. It is a summer evening, after sunset. REBEKKA WEST *is sitting in an easy chair by the window, and crocheting a large white woolen shawl, which is nearly finished. She now and then looks out expectantly through the leaves of the plants.* MRS. HELSETH *presently enters.*

MRS. HELSETH: I suppose I had better start laying the table for supper, Miss?

REBEKKA: Yes, do. Mr. Rosmer should be back in a few minutes.

MRS. HELSETH: Aren't you sitting in a draught there, Miss?

REBEKKA: Yes, there is a little draught. You might just close the window.

---

* For stage purposes, often PETER.

33

(MRS. HELSETH *shuts the door into the hall, and then comes to the window.*)

MRS. HELSETH (*About to shut the window, looks out*): Isn't that Mr. Rosmer out there now?

REBEKKA (*Hastily*): Where? (*Rises*) Yes, so it is. (*Stands behind the curtain*) Stand back a little. Don't let him see us.

MRS. HELSETH (*Draws back from window*): You see, Miss?—He's beginning to use the path by the mill again.

REBEKKA: He used it the day before yesterday too. (*Peeps out between the curtains and the windowframe*) But I wonder whether—

MRS. HELSETH: Will he bring himself to cross the foot-bridge, do you think?

REBEKKA: That's just what I want to see. (*After a pause*) No, he's turning back. Today, again! He's going by the upper road. (*Leaves the window*) A long way round.

MRS. HELSETH: Well—Good Lord!—you can't blame him for not wanting to cross that bridge, Miss. When you think of what happened there—

REBEKKA (*Folding up her work*): They certainly cling to their dead at Rosmersholm.

MRS. HELSETH: Do you know what *I* think, Miss? I think it's the dead that cling to Rosmersholm.

REBEKKA (*Looks at her*): How do you mean —the dead?

MRS. HELSETH: It's as if they kept trying to come back; as if they couldn't quite free themselves from those they've left behind.

REBEKKA: What an idea! What put that into your head?

MRS. HELSETH: That would account for the White Horse, you see.

REBEKKA: What is all this about a White Horse, Mrs. Helseth?

MRS. HELSETH: It's no use talking to you about it, Miss; you don't believe such things.

REBEKKA: Do *you* believe them?

MRS. HELSETH (*Goes and shuts the window*): You'd only make fun of me, Miss. (*Looks out*) Look! Isn't that Mr. Rosmer on the path again—?

REBEKKA (*Looks out*): Let me see. (*Goes to the window*) No. Why—it's Professor Kroll!

MRS. HELSETH: Yes, so it is.

REBEKKA: What a funny thing! He seems to be coming here.

MRS. HELSETH: He makes no bones about going over the footbridge—even if she was his own sister! Well, I suppose I'd better lay the table, Miss.

(*She goes out.* REBEKKA *stands at the window for a short time; then smiles and nods to someone outside. It begins to grow dark.*)

REBEKKA (*Goes to the door*): Oh, Mrs. Helseth! You'd better prepare a little something extra; something the Professor's specially fond of.

MRS. HELSETH (*Outside*): Very well, Miss; I'll see to it.

REBEKKA (*Opens the door to the hall*): Well— what a surprise! Welcome, my dear Professor!

KROLL (*In the hall, laying down his stick*): Many thanks. I hope I'm not disturbing you?

REBEKKA: You! How can you say such things!

KROLL (*Comes in*): Charming as ever! (*Looks around*) Is Rosmer up in his room?

REBEKKA: No, he's out for a walk. He's been gone a bit longer than usual; but he's sure to be here any minute. (*Indicating the sofa*) Won't you sit down till he comes?

KROLL (*Laying down his hat*): Many thanks. (*Sits down and looks about him*) What nice things you've done to the old place! It's all so cheerful—flowers everywhere!

REBEKKA: Mr. Rosmer's very fond of flowers.

KROLL: And you are too, I suppose.

REBEKKA: Yes, I am; I find them very soothing. We had to do without them though—until quite recently.

KROLL (*Nods sadly*): I know; on account of poor Beata. Their scent seemed to overpower her.

REBEKKA: Their colors, too. They upset her terribly.

KROLL: Yes, I remember. (*In a lighter tone*) Well—how are things going out here?

REBEKKA: Oh, quietly and peacefully as usual; the days slip by—one day just like the last. But what about you? I hope Mrs. Kroll is well?

KROLL: Oh, my dear Miss West, I'd rather

not talk about my affairs. In family life one has to expect complications—especially in times like there.

REBEKKA (*Sits in an armchair by the sofa*): You haven't been to see us once, all during the holidays. Why haven't you? Tell me.

KROLL: I didn't want to make a nuisance of myself.

REBEKKA: I can't tell you how we've missed you—

KROLL: Besides—I've been away—

REBEKKA: But only for a couple of weeks. I hear you've been attending a lot of meetings—You've been going in for politics—?

KROLL (*Nods*): Yes, what do you say to that? Who would ever have thought I'd become a political firebrand in my old age?

REBEKKA (*Smiling*): Well, you have always been a bit of a firebrand, Professor Kroll.

KROLL: In private life, perhaps—for my own amusement. But this is a serious matter. Do you ever read any of these radical newspapers, by any chance?

REBEKKA: I must admit, my dear Professor, that I—

KROLL: As far as you're concerned, my dear Miss West, there's no reason why you shouldn't—

REBEKKA: No, that's what I feel. I like to know what's going on—to keep up with the times—

KROLL: Certainly. And one naturally doesn't expect a woman to take an active part in this controversy—one might almost call it a civil war—that is raging all about us. Then you're no doubt familiar with the disgraceful way these gentlemen of "the people" have seen fit to treat me? The infamous abuse they've dared to heap upon me?

REBEKKA: I must say you gave as good as you got!

KROLL: I did indeed. And I'm proud of it. Now that I've tasted blood they'll soon find out I'm not the man to turn the other cheek—(*Breaks off*) But why should we discuss this painful subject?

REBEKKA: No, dear Professor, don't let us talk about it.

KROLL: I'd rather talk about you; how are you getting on at Rosmersholm, now that our poor Beata—?

REBEKKA: Thank you, well enough. It seems so empty here without her; one can't help feeling very sad—we miss her in so many ways. But, apart from that—

KROLL: Do you plan to go on staying here? —permanently, I mean?

REBEKKA: I really haven't given it much thought. I've grown so accustomed to this place— It's almost as if I, too, belonged here.

KROLL: But you *do!* You *do* belong here!

REBEKKA: And as long as Mr. Rosmer needs me—as long as I can be of any help or comfort to him—I feel I should remain.

KROLL (*Looks at her much moved*): It's a very wonderful thing, Miss West, for a woman to give up the best years of her life to others, as you have.

REBEKKA: What else had I to live for?

KROLL: Your devotion to your foster-father was admirable. It must have been very hard for you; half-paralyzed and unreasonable as he was—

REBEKKA: You mustn't think Dr. West was always so unreasonable—at least, not during the first years in Finmark. It was those terrible sea voyages that undermined his health. It wasn't until afterwards, when we moved down here—those last two years before his death—that things became so difficult.

KROLL: And presumably the years that followed were more difficult still—

REBEKKA: How can you say that! I was devoted to Beata—Poor darling! She had such need of tenderness and care.

KROLL: How kind you are to speak of her with so much understanding.

REBEKKA (*Moves a little nearer*): Dear Professor, you reassure me! You couldn't say that with such sincerity if you had any resentment in your heart towards me.

KROLL: Resentment! Why should you think that?

REBEKKA: Well, mightn't it be natural that you should resent a stranger presiding over things at Rosmersholm?

KROLL: What on earth—!

REBEKKA: But you have no such feeling, have you? (*Takes his hand*) Thank you, my dear Professor; many, many thanks!

KROLL: What on earth put that into your head?

REBEKKA: You've been to see us so seldom lately—I began to be a little frightened.

KROLL: Then you were totally mistaken, my dear Miss West. And, after all, things haven't really changed; you were in full charge here long before poor Beata died.

REBEKKA: Yes—but that was only a kind of stewardship on her behalf—

KROLL: All the same—For my part, Miss West—I should be only too happy to see you— But perhaps I shouldn't mention such a thing.

REBEKKA: What do you mean?

KROLL: I'd be only too happy to see you take poor Beata's place.

REBEKKA: I have the only place I want, Professor.

KROLL: For all practical purposes, yes; but not as far as—

REBEKKA (*Interrupting gravely*): Shame on you, Professor Kroll. You shouldn't joke about such things!

KROLL: I dare say our good Rosmer feels he's had more than enough of married life. But still—

REBEKKA: Don't be so absurd, Professor!

KROLL: But still—Tell me —how old are you now, Miss West?—if you'll forgive the question!

REBEKKA: I'm ashamed to admit, Professor, I'm past twenty-nine—I'm in my thirtieth year.

KROLL: And Rosmer—how old is he? Let me see: he is five years younger than I am, so that would make him forty-three. That seems to me most suitable.

REBEKKA (*Rises*): No doubt—yes; very suitable indeed! You'll stay for supper, won't you?

KROLL: Yes, thank you; I'd like to very much. There's a matter I must discuss with Rosmer. And from now on, Miss West, I shall resume my former practice of coming out more often; we can't have you getting your head full of foolish notions!

REBEKKA: Yes—*do* that! I wish you would! (*Shakes both his hands*) Again—many thanks! How kind and good you are!

KROLL (*Gruffly*): Am I? That's not what I hear at home!

(JOHANNES ROSMER *enters by the door on the right.*)

REBEKKA: Mr. Rosmer! Just look who's here!

ROSMER: Mrs. Helseth told me. (PROFESSOR KROLL *has risen;* ROSMER *takes his hand; with quiet emotion*) Welcome back to this house, my dear Kroll. (*Lays his hands on* KROLL's *shoulders and looks into his eyes*) My dear, dear friend! I was certain things would straighten out between us.

KROLL: My dear fellow—don't tell me you've been imagining things too?

REBEKKA (*To* ROSMER): Isn't it wonderful, Rosmer? It was all imagination!

ROSMER: Is that really true? Then what made you stay away from me?

KROLL (*Gravely, in a low voice*): I didn't want to be a constant reminder of those unhappy years—and of poor Beata's tragic death.

ROSMER: How good of you! But then—you always were considerate. Still—it wasn't necessary to stay away on that account— Let's sit here on the sofa. (*They sit down*) No, I assure you, the thought of Beata isn't painful to me. She seems so close to us. We speak of her every day.

KROLL: Do you really?

REBEKKA (*Lighting the lamp*): Yes, indeed we do.

ROSMER: It's natural enough. We were both so devoted to her. And Rebek—Miss West and I did everything in our power to help her— We're confident of that; there's no room for self-reproach. That's why we can think of her with a sense of peace—a quiet tenderness.

KROLL: What splendid people you are! That settles it—I shall come out and see you every single day!

REBEKKA (*Seats herself in an arm-chair*): Be sure and keep your word!

ROSMER (*With some hesitation*): You know— I regret even this short interruption in our friendship. Ever since we've known each other you've been my chief adviser—since my student days, in fact.

KROLL: Yes—I've always been proud of it. But is there anything in particular—?

ROSMER: There are a number of things I'm most anxious to discuss with you. I'd like to talk to you quite frankly—heart to heart.

REBEKKA: It would do you good, wouldn't it, Mr. Rosmer? It must be such a comfort —between old friends—

KROLL: And I've a great deal to discuss with you. You know, of course, I've begun to take an active part in politics?

ROSMER: I know. How did that come about?

KROLL: I was forced into it—I had no choice. It's no longer possible to stand by idly looking on. Now that the radical party has, so unfortunately, come into power, it is high time that something was done about it. I have persuaded some of our friends in town to band together—to take some constructive action. I tell you it is high time!

REBEKKA (*With a faint smile*): Perhaps it might even be a little late?

KROLL: Oh, unquestionably, we should have stemmed the tide long ago—that would have been far better! But who could possibly foresee what was to happen? Not I, certainly! (*Rises and walks up and down*) But I can tell you my eyes are open now. You'd never believe it—but this seditious element has actually gained a foothold in the school!

ROSMER: The school? You surely don't mean *your* school?

KROLL: Yes, I tell you! What do you say to that? And it has come to my knowledge that for the past six months the senior boys—a considerable number of them at any rate—have been members of a secret society and subscribe to Mortensgaard's paper.

REBEKKA: What! *The Beacon?*

KROLL: Yes; nice mental sustenance for fur-ture government officials, is it not? But the most distressing thing is, that it's the most gifted students who have taken part in this conspiracy against me. The only ones who seem to have kept away from

it are the dunces—at the bottom of the class.

REBEKKA: Does this really affect you so very deeply, Professor Kroll?

KROLL: Does it affect me? To see the work of a lifetime thwarted and undermined? (*Lower*) Still—all this might be endurable, perhaps. There's something worse, how-ever. (*Looks around*) You're sure no one can hear us?

REBEKKA: No, no; of course not.

KROLL: Then, listen to this: the spirit of revolt has actually crept into my own house—into my own quiet home; the harmony of my family life has been ut-terly destroyed.

ROSMER (*Rises*): What do you mean? Into your home—!

REBEKKA (*Goes over to the Professor*): What can have happened, dear Professor?

KROLL: You wouldn't believe it, would you, that my own children—? In short—I find that Lauritz is the ringleader of this con-spiracy; and my daughter Hilda has em-broidered a red portfolio to keep *The Beacon* in.

ROSMER:—Your own home? It seems impos-sible!

KROLL: Yes—doesn't it? The very home of duty and obedience—where, at my insist-ence, order and decency have always reigned supreme—

REBEKKA: How does your wife take all this?

KROLL: That's the most astonishing thing about it. My wife, who has always shared my opinion on all subjects—has undevia-tingly upheld my principles—seems in-clined to take the children's point of view in this affair. She tells me I'm to blame— that I'm too harsh with them. Yet, surely there are times when discipline— Well, you see how my house is divided against itself. I naturally say as little about it as possible. Such things are best kept quiet. (*Wanders about the room*) Ah, well, well, well. (*Stands at window with hands behind his back and looks out.*)

REBEKKA (*Comes up close to* ROSMER, *and says rapidly and in a low voice so that the Professor does not hear her*): Tell him!

ROSMER (*Also in a low voice*): Not this evening.

REBEKKA (*As before*): Yes! Tell him *now*! (*Goes to the table and busies herself with the lamp.*)

KROLL (*Comes forward*): Well, my dear Rosmer, now you know how the spirit of the times has cast its shadow over me —over my domestic as well as my official life. I could hardly be expected not to resist this dangerous and destructive force —this anarchy. I shall fight it with every weapon I can lay my hands on. I shall fight it by word and deed.

ROSMER: What do you expect to gain by that?

KROLL: I shall at least have done my duty as a citizen. And I hold it the duty of every right-thinking man with an atom of patriotism to do likewise. This was my main reason for wanting to talk to you this evening.

ROSMER: But, my dear Kroll, how do you mean—? How could I possibly—?

KROLL: You must stand by your old friends. You must join our ranks—march with us to battle!

REBEKKA: Professor Kroll, you know how Mr. Rosmer dislikes that sort of thing.

KROLL: Then he must get over his dislike. You've let yourself get out of touch with things, Rosmer. You bury yourself away out here, delving into the past, absorbed in your genealogical research—oh, far be it from me to scoff at such things—but this is no time to indulge in these pursuits. You have no conception of what is happening throughout the country. There is scarcely an established principle that hasn't been attacked; the whole order of Society is threatened! It will be a colossal task to set things right again.

ROSMER: Yes—I quite agree. But that sort of work isn't at all in my line.

REBEKKA: Besides, I think Mr. Rosmer has gradually acquired a wider view on life.

KROLL (*With surprise*): A wider view?

REBEKKA: Well—freer, if you like; less prejudiced.

KROLL: What does this mean? Rosmer, you are surely not so weak as to be taken in by any temporary advantage these anarchists have won?

ROSMER: As you know, I've very little understanding of politics, dear Kroll. But it does seem clear that in the past few years, men have at last begun to think for themselves —as individuals.

KROLL: And you immediately assume this to be to their advantage? You are mistaken, I assure you. I don't think you quite realize what these ideas are, that the radicals are spreading among the people —not only in the city, but out here in the country too. You should make some inquiries! You'd find them based on the brand of wisdom proclaimed in the pages of *The Beacon*.

REBEKKA: Yes; Mortensgaard certainly has great influence.

KROLL: It's inconceivable! A man with such a record—who was dismissed from his position as schoolteacher on moral grounds—to set himself up as a leader of the people! And he succeeds too! He actually succeeds! He is about to enlarge his paper, I understand. He's on the lookout for a capable assistant.

REBEKKA: I'm surprised you and your friends don't start a paper of your own.

KROLL: That is precisely what we intend to do. Only today we purchased the *County News*. Financial backing is no problem to us, of course, but—(*Turns to* ROSMER)— and now I come to the real purpose of my visit— Where are we to find an editor? That is the vital question. Tell me, Rosmer —don't you feel it your duty, for the good of the cause, to undertake this task?

ROSMER (*Almost in consternation*): I!

REBEKKA: You can't be serious!

KROLL: I can well understand your dislike of public meetings, and all that they imply. But this position would enable you to keep in the background—or rather—

ROSMER: No, no!—Please don't ask me to do this.

KROLL: I'd have no objection to trying my own hand at it. But that's out of the question—I'm burdened with too many duties as it is; while you have ample leisure—there's nothing to prevent you from undertaking it. We'd naturally give you all the help we could.

ROSMER: I can't do it, Kroll. I'm not suited to it.

KROLL: That's what you said when your father procured you the ministry here—

ROSMER: And I was right. That's why I resigned it.

KROLL: If you're as good an editor as you were a clergyman, we shan't complain!

ROSMER: Once and for all, my dear Kroll, I cannot do it.

KROLL: Well—but you'll lend us your name, at any rate?

ROSMER: My name?

KROLL: Yes, the mere name, Johannes Rosmer, will be a great help to the paper. We are all of us looked upon as hopeless reactionaries. I believe I myself am supposed to be a desperate fanatic! This will make it difficult for us to reach the people —poor misguided wretches that they are! You, on the other hand, have always kept aloof. Everyone knows and appreciates your integrity, your humanity, your fine mind and unimpeachable honor. Then, too, you are esteemed and respected as a former clergyman. And think of what the name "Rosmer" stands for in this part of the country!

ROSMER: No doubt—

KROLL (*Pointing to the portraits on the walls*): Rosmers of Rosmersholm—clergymen and soldiers, high-ranking officials; worthy, honorable gentlemen all!—A family that for nearly two centuries has held its place as the first in the district. (*Lays his hand on* ROSMER's *shoulder*) You owe it to yourself, Rosmer, to all the traditions of your race, to defend those things that have always been held most precious in our society. (*Turns round*) Don't you agree with me, Miss West?

REBEKKA (*Laughing softly, as if to herself*): I'm afraid it all strikes me as utterly ludicrous—

KROLL: Ludicrous?

REBEKKA: Yes, ludicrous. I think I'd better tell you—

ROSMER (*Quickly*): No, no—don't! Not just now!

KROLL (*Looks from one to the other*): But, my dear friends, what does this mean—? (*interrupting himself*) H'm!

(MRS. HELSETH *appears in doorway.*)

MRS. HELSETH: There's a man at the kitchen-door; he says he wants to see you, Sir.

ROSMER (*Relieved*): Well—show him in.

MRS. HELSETH: In *here*, Sir?

ROSMER: Yes, of course.

MRS. HELSETH: But he doesn't look like the sort you'd bring into the drawing room.

REBEKKA: What *does* he look like, Mrs. Helseth?

MRS. HELSETH: He's not much to look at, Miss, and that's a fact.

ROSMER: Did he give his name?

MRS. HELSETH: I think he said he was called Hekman—or something of the sort.

ROSMER: I know no one of that name.

MRS. HELSETH: And then he said something about Uldrik, too.

ROSMER (*In surprise*): Ulrik Hetman! Was that it?

MRS. HELSETH: That's it—Hetman.

KROLL: I seem to have heard that name—

REBEKKA: It's the name that strange man used to write under—

ROSMER (*To* KROLL): It's Ulrik Brendel's pen name.

KROLL: Quite right! That scoundrel Brendel!

REBEKKA: He's still alive, then.

ROSMER: I heard he had joined a troupe of actors.

KROLL: When I last heard of him, he was in the workhouse.

ROSMER: Ask him to come in, Mrs. Helseth.

MRS. HELSETH: Very well. (*She goes out.*)

KROLL: You're not going to let a man like that into your house?

ROSMER: He was once my tutor.

KROLL: I know. And I know too that he filled your head with a lot of revolutionary notions and that your father showed him the door—with a horsewhip.

ROSMER (*With a touch of bitterness*): Yes. Father was a martinet at home as well as in his regiment.

KROLL: You should be forever grateful to him for that, my dear Rosmer—Well! (MRS. HELSETH *opens the door on the right for* ULRIK BRENDEL, *and then withdraws, shutting the door behind him. He is a handsome man, with gray hair and beard; somewhat gaunt but active and well set up. He is dressed like a common tramp: threadbare frock-coat; worn-out shoes; no shirt visible. He wears an old pair of black gloves, and carries a soft, greasy felt hat under his arm, and a walking-stick in his hand.*)

BRENDEL (*Hesitates at first, then goes quickly up to* KROLL, *and holds out his hand*): Good evening, Johannes!

KROLL: I beg your pardon—

BRENDEL: I'll be bound you never expected to see me again! And within these hated walls, too?

KROLL: I beg your pardon—(*Pointing*) Over there—

BRENDEL (*Turns*): Oh, of course! There you are! Johannes—my own beloved boy—!

ROSMER (*Takes his hand*): My dear old teacher.

BRENDEL: I couldn't pass by Rosmersholm without paying you a flying visit—in spite of certain painful memories!

ROSMER: You are heartily welcome here now —I assure you.

BRENDEL: And who is this charming lady—? (*Bows*) Mrs. Rosmer, no doubt.

ROSMER: Miss West.

BRENDEL: A near relation, I expect. And yonder stranger—? A brother of the cloth, I see.

ROSMER: Professor Kroll.

BRENDEL: Kroll? Kroll? Wait a bit— Weren't you a student of philology in your young days?

KROLL: Of course I was.

BRENDEL: Why, *Donnerwetter*—then I must have known you!

KROLL: I beg your pardon.

BRENDEL: Of course! You were—

KROLL: I beg your pardon—

BRENDEL: Yes! You were one of those para-gons of virtue that got me kicked out of the Debating Club!

KROLL: It's very possible. But I acknowledge no closer acquaintance.

BRENDEL: Well, well! *Nach Belieben, Herr Doktor.* It's all one to me. Ulrik Brendel remains Ulrik Brendel just the same!

REBEKKA: I suppose you're on your way to town, Mr. Brendel?

BRENDEL: You have hit it, most charming lady. At certain intervals, I am constrained to strike a blow for existence. It goes against the grain; but—*enfin*—imperious necessity—

ROSMER: Oh, but my dear Mr. Brendel, mayn't I be allowed to help you. In one way or another, I am sure—

BRENDEL: To propose such a thing to me! You surely wouldn't wish to desecrate our friendship? Never, my dear Johannes; never!

ROSMER: But what do you plan to do in town? I'm afraid you won't find it easy to—

BRENDEL: Leave that to me, my boy. The die is cast. You see before you a man about to embark on a great campaign—greater and more intensive than all my previous excursions put together. (*To* KROLL) May I be so bold as to ask the *Herr Professor*— *unter uns*—have you such a thing as a reasonably clean, respectable and commodious Assembly Hall in your esteemed city?

KROLL: There is the Workers Union Hall— that is the largest.

BRENDEL: And has the *Herr Professor* any official influence in this, no doubt worthy, organization?

KROLL: I have nothing whatever to do with it.

REBEKKA (*To* BRENDEL): You should apply to Peder Mortensgaard.

BRENDEL: Pardon, Madame—what sort of an idiot is he?

ROSMER: What makes you suppose that he's an idiot?

BRENDEL: The name has such a distinctly plebian sound.

KROLL: I never expected *that* answer.

BRENDEL: However I will conquer my reluctance; there's no alternative. When a man finds himself at a turning point in his career, as I do—So be it. I will get in touch with this person—open direct negotiations with him—

ROSMER: Are you really at a turning point in your career—in all seriousness?

BRENDEL: Doesn't my own boy know that wherever I am and whatever I do, it's always in all seriousness? I'm about to put on a new man—to discard this modest reserve I have hitherto maintained.

ROSMER: How so?

BRENDEL: I intend to take hold of life with a strong hand—Go forward. Mount upward. We live in a tempestuous, an equinoctial age—I am about to lay my mite on the altar of Emancipation.

KROLL: So, you too—?

BRENDEL (*To them all*): Is the public in these parts at all familiar with my infrequent writings?

KROLL: No; I must honestly admit that—

REBEKKA: I've read some of them. My foster-father had them in his library.

BRENDEL: Then you wasted your time, fair lady. They're all so much trash, let me tell you.

REBEKKA: Indeed?

BRENDEL: Those that you've read, yes. My really significant works no man or woman knows. No one—except myself.

REBEKKA: Why is that?

BRENDEL: For the simple reason that I have never written them.

ROSMER: But my dear Mr. Brendel—

BRENDEL: You know I've always been a bit of a sybarite, my dear Johannes; a *Feinschmecker*. I like to enjoy things in solitude; then I enjoy them doubly—tenfold. Glorious dreams come to me—intoxicating thoughts—bold, lofty, unique ideas, that carry me aloft on powerful pinions; these I transform into poems, visions, pictures —all in the abstract, you understand.

ROSMER: Yes, yes.

BRENDEL: The joys, the ecstasy I have reveled in, Johannes! The mysterious bliss of creation—in the abstract, as I said before. I have been showered with applause, gratitude and fame; I have been crowned with laurel-wreaths; all these tributes I have garnered with joyous, tremulous hands. In my secret imaginings I have been satiated with delight—with a rapture so intense, so intoxicating—

KROLL: H'm.

ROSMER: But you've never written down any of these things?

BRENDEL: Not a word. The vulgar business of writing has always nauseated me—filled me with disgust. Besides, why should I profane my own ideals, when I can enjoy them by myself in all their purity? But now they must be offered up. I assure you I feel as a mother must when she delivers her young daughters into their bridegrooms' arms. Nevertheless—they must be offered up—offered upon the altar of Freedom. I will start with a series of carefully planned lectures—all over the country—

REBEKKA (*With animation*): How splendid of you, Mr. Brendel! You'll be giving the most precious thing you have.

ROSMER: The only thing.

REBEKKA (*Looking significantly at* ROSMER): There aren't many people who'd do that —who'd have the courage to do that!

ROSMER (*Returning the look*): Who knows?

BRENDEL: I see my audience is touched. That puts new heart into me—strengthens my will. So now I will proceed to action. Just one thing more. (*To the Professor*) Tell me, *Herr Preceptor*—is there a Temperance Society in town? A Total Abstinence Society? But of course there must be!

KROLL: I am the president, at your service.

BRENDEL: Of course! One only has to look at you! Then—be prepared! I may come and join up for a week or so.

KROLL: I beg your pardon—we do not accept members by the week.

BRENDEL: *A la bonne heure, Herr Pedagogue.* Ulrik Brendel has never been one to force his way into such Societies. (Turns) But I dare not prolong my stay in this house, so rich in memories. I must get to town and select a suitable lodging. There is a decent hotel in the place, I hope.

REBEKKA: You'll have a hot drink before you go?

BRENDEL: What sort of a hot drink, gracious lady?

REBEKKA: A cup of tea, or—

BRENDEL: I thank my bountiful hostess—but I dislike taking advantage of private hospitality. (*Waves his hand*) Farewell, gentlefolk all! (*Goes toward door but turns again*) Oh, I almost forgot, Johannes—Pastor Rosmer—would you do your former teacher a favor, for old time's sake?

ROSMER: I should be delighted.

BRENDEL: Then, could you lend me a dress shirt—just for a day or two?

ROSMER: Is that all?

BRENDEL: You see, I happen to be traveling on foot—just for the time being. They're sending my trunk after me.

ROSMER: I see. But are you sure there's nothing else?

BRENDEL: Yes—come to think of it—if you could spare me a light overcoat—

ROSMER: Of course I can.

BRENDEL: And perhaps a respectable pair of shoes as well—?

ROSMER: I'll see to it. As soon as we know your address, we'll send them off to you.

BRENDEL: I wouldn't dream of putting you to so much trouble! Give me the bagatelles now—I'll take them with me.

ROSMER: Very well. Just come upstairs with me.

REBEKKA: No, let me go. Mrs. Helseth and I will see to it.

BRENDEL: I could never allow this distinguished lady—!

REBEKKA: Oh, nonsense, Mr. Brendel! Come along. (*She goes out.*)

ROSMER (*Detaining him*): There must be something else I can do for you?

BRENDEL: No; I can't think of a thing. But, of course—damnation take it! It just occurred to me; I wonder if you happen to have eight crowns on you, Johannes?

ROSMER: Let me see. (*Opens his purse*) Here are two tencrown notes.

BRENDEL: Never mind—they'll do. I can always get change in town. Meanwhile —many thanks. Don't forget—that was two tens you lent me. Good night, my own

dear boy. Good night, honored Sir! (*Goes out right.*)

(ROSMER *takes leave of him, and shuts the door behind him.*)

KROLL: Merciful Heaven!—so this is that Ulrik Brendel people once expected such great things of.

ROSMER (*Quietly*): At least he's had the courage to live life in his own way. It seems to me that's something to his credit.

KROLL: What do you mean? A life like his! Don't tell me he still has the power to influence you?

ROSMER: Far from it. My mind is quite clear now, on all points.

KROLL: I wish I could believe that, Rosmer. You're easily swayed, you know.

ROSMER: Sit down. I've got to talk to you.

KROLL: Very well. (*They seat themselves on the sofa.*)

ROSMER (*After a slight pause*): Our life here must strike you as very comfortable and pleasant.

KROLL: Yes, indeed; it's comfortable and pleasant now—and peaceful, too. You have found a home, Rosmer—and I have lost one.

ROSMER: My dear friend, don't say that. The wound will heal in time.

KROLL: Never. The sting can never be removed. Things can never be the same.

ROSMER: Now listen to me, Kroll. We have been close friends for a great many years. Does it seem to you conceivable that anything could ever break our friendship?

KROLL: I can think of nothing that could ever come between us. What makes you ask that question?

ROSMER: I ask it because I know how intolerant you are of any opposition to your way of seeing things.

KROLL: That may be; but you and I have always agreed—at least on essentials.

ROSMER (*In a low voice*): I'm afraid that's no longer true.

KROLL (*Tries to jump up*): What's that you say?

ROSMER (*Holds him back*): No, please sit still!

KROLL: What does this mean? I don't understand you. Explain yourself.

ROSMER: It's as though my spirit had grown young again. I see things now with different eyes—with *youthful* eyes, Kroll; that's why I no longer agree with you, but with—

KROLL: With whom? Tell me!

ROSMER: With your children.

KROLL: With my children?

ROSMER: With Lauritz and Hilda—yes.

KROLL (*Bows his head*): A traitor! Johannes Rosmer a traitor!

ROSMER: I should have been happy—completely happy—in being what you call a traitor! But the thought of you saddened me. I knew it would be a great grief to you.

KROLL: I shall never get over it, Rosmer. (*Looks gloomily at him*) That you should be willing to share in this work of destruction—bring ruin on our unhappy country!

ROSMER: I intend to work for Freedom.

KROLL: Oh, yes—I know! That's what these false prophets call it—that's what their wretched followers call it too. But what sort of freedom can come from Anarchy, I ask you? From this spirit of evil that is spreading poison throughout our entire society?

ROSMER: I'm not wedded to this spirit of evil, as you call it, and I belong to neither party. I want to bring men together regardless of which side they may be on. I want them to unite for the common good. I intend to devote my whole life and all my strength to this one end: the creation of a true democracy.

KROLL: Haven't we democracy enough already! It's my opinion that we are all of us rapidly being dragged down into the mud where, hitherto, only the common people have seemed to prosper.

ROSMER: For that very reason I have faith in the true purpose of Democracy.

KROLL: What purpose?

ROSMER: That of giving all men a sense of their own nobility.

KROLL: All men—!

ROSMER: As many as possible, at any rate.

KROLL: By what means, may I ask?

ROSMER: By freeing their thoughts and purifying their aims.

KROLL: You're a dreamer, Rosmer. And you think *you* can do this?

ROSMER: No, my dear friend; but I can at least open their eyes. They must do it for themselves.

KROLL: And you think they can?

ROSMER: Yes.

KROLL: By their own strength?

ROSMER: It must be by their own strength. There is no other.

KROLL (*Rises*): A strange way for a clergyman to talk!

ROSMER: I am no longer a clergyman.

KROLL: But what about your faith? The faith you were brought up in?

ROSMER: I no longer believe in it.

KROLL: You no longer—!

ROSMER: I've given it up. I *had* to give it up, Kroll.

KROLL: I see. I suppose one thing leads to another. So this was why you resigned your position in the church?

ROSMER: Yes. When it finally dawned on me that this was no temporary aberration—but, rather, a deep conviction that I neither could nor would shake off—then I left the church.

KROLL: To think that all this time, we, your friends, had no suspicion of what was going on inside you. Rosmer, Rosmer, how could you bring yourself to hide the truth from us!

ROSMER: I felt it concerned no one but myself. And I didn't want to cause you and my other friends unnecessary grief. I intended to go on living here just as before, quietly, serenely, happily. Reading, studying; steeping myself in all the books that had hitherto been closed to me. I wanted to become thoroughly familiar with this great world of truth and freedom that was suddenly revealed to me.

KROLL: Every word proves what you are—a traitor! But why did you change your mind? What made you decide to admit your guilt? And why just now?

ROSMER: You yourself forced me to it, Kroll.

KROLL: *I* did?

ROSMER: I was shocked to hear of your violence on the platform; to read your bitter speeches; the scurrilous attacks, the cruel, contemptuous scorn you heaped on your opponents. How could *you* be like that, Kroll? Then I realized I had an imperative duty to perform. Men are becoming evil in this struggle. We must get back to peace, and joy and mutual understanding. That's why I've made up my mind to declare my beliefs openly—to try my strength. Couldn't you—on your side —join in this work, and help me?

KROLL: Never! I shall never make peace with the destroyers of society.

ROSMER: Then if we must fight, let us, at least, use honorable weapons.

KROLL: Any man who goes against my fundamental principles I shall refuse to recognize; nor do I owe him any consideration.

ROSMER: Does that include me, as well?

KROLL: It is you who have broken with me, Rosmer; our friendship is at an end.

ROSMER: You *can't* mean that?

KROLL: Not *mean* it! This is an end to all your former friendships; now you must take the consequences.

(REBEKKA WEST *enters, and opens the door wide.*)

REBEKKA: He's gone. He is on his way to his great sacrifice! And now we can go to supper. Come, Professor.

KROLL (*Takes up his hat*): Good night, Miss West. I have nothing more to do here.

REBEKKA (*Eagerly*): What does he mean? (*Shuts the door and comes forward*) Did you tell him?

ROSMER: Yes. He knows now.

KROLL: We shan't let you go, Rosmer. You'll come back to us again.

ROSMER: I shall never go back to your opinions.

KROLL: Time will tell. You are not a man to stand alone.

ROSMER: But I shan't be alone; there are two of us to share the loneliness.

KROLL: You mean—? (*A suspicion crosses his face*) I see! Just What Beata said—!

ROSMER: Beata—?

KROLL (*Shaking off the thought*): No, no, forgive me; that was vile.

ROSMER: Why? What do you mean?

KROLL: Never mind! Forgive me! Good-bye. (*Goes toward door.*)

ROSMER (*Follows him*): Kroll! Our friendship can't end like this. I'll come and see you tomorrow.

KROLL (*In the hall turns*): You shall never set foot in my house again. (*Takes up his stick and goes out.*)

(ROSMER *stands for a moment in the doorway; then shuts the door and walks up to the table.*)

ROSMER: It can't be helped, Rebekka. We'll face it together—like the loyal friends we are.

REBEKKA: What do you suppose he meant by "that was vile"?

ROSMER: Don't give it a thought, my dear. He himself didn't believe what he was saying. I'll go and talk to him tomorrow. Good night.

REBEKKA: Are you going up already, just as usual? I thought perhaps—after what had happened—

ROSMER: No—I'll go up, as usual. I can't tell you how relieved I feel now that it's over. You see—I'm quite calm about it all, Rebekka, dear. And you must take it calmly too. Good night.

REBEKKA: Good night, dear Rosmer; sleep well!

(ROSMER *goes out by the hall door, and his steps are heard ascending the staircase;* REBEKKA *goes and pulls a bell-rope. Shortly after,* MRS. HELSETH *enters.*)

REBEKKA: You might as well clear the table, Mrs. Helseth. Mr. Rosmer doesn't care for anything, and Professor Kroll's gone home.

MRS. HELSETH: Gone home? Is anything the matter with him?

REBEKKA (*Takes up work*): He said he felt a storm coming on—

MRS. HELSETH: That's queer. There's not a cloud in the sky this evening.

REBEKKA: I hope he won't run into that White Horse. I've a feeling the ghosts may be quite busy for a while.

MRS. HELSETH: Good gracious, Miss! Don't say such dreadful things.

REBEKKA: Well, well—who knows?

MRS. HELSETH (*Softly*): You mean you think

someone's going to be taken from us, Miss?

REBEKKA: Of course not! Why should I think that? But there are all sorts of white horses in this world, Mrs. Helseth—Well, good night. I'm going to my room.

MRS. HELSETH: Good night, Miss.

(REBEKKA *goes out with her work.*)

MRS. HELSETH (*Turns the lamp down, shaking her head and muttering to herself*): Lord, Lord! That Miss West! What queer things she does say!

CURTAIN

ACT II

SCENE: JOHANNES ROSMER'S *study. Entrance door on the left. At the back, a doorway with a curtain drawn aside, leading into* ROSMER'S *bedroom. On the right a window, and in front of it a writing table covered with books and papers. Bookshelves and bookcases round the room. The furniture is simple. On the left, an old-fashioned sofa, with a table in front of it.*

JOHANNES ROSMER, *in a smoking-jacket, is sitting in a highbacked chair at the writing table. He is cutting and turning over the leaves of a pamphlet, and reading a little here and there. There is a knock at the door.*

ROSMER (*Without moving*): Come in.

REBEKKA (*Enters; she is wearing a dressing-gown*): Good morning.

ROSMER (*Turning the leaves of the pamphlet*): Good morning, dear. Is there anything you want?

REBEKKA: I just wanted to know if you had slept well.

ROSMER: Yes, I had a good restful night—no dreams; what about you?

REBEKKA: I slept well; at least toward morning—

ROSMER: I don't know when I've ever felt so light-hearted! It was good to get that off my chest at last.

REBEKKA: You should have done it long ago.

ROSMER: I can't imagine why I was such a coward.

REBEKKA: Well, it wasn't exactly cowardice—

ROSMER: Oh yes, it was; it was partly cowardice, at any rate—I realize that now.

REBEKKA: That makes it all the braver. (*Sits on a chair at writing table, close to him*) Rosmer, I want to tell you something I did last night—I hope you won't object—

ROSMER: Object? You know I never—

REBEKKA: You may think it was unwise of me—

ROSMER: Well—tell me.

REBEKKA: I gave Ulrik Brendel a note to Mortensgaard, before he left.

ROSMER (*A little doubtful*): Did you, Rebekka? What did you say?

REBEKKA: I told him he'd be doing you a favor if he were to keep an eye on Brendel; help him in any way he could.

ROSMER: Oh, you shouldn't have done that, dear. I'm afraid it will do more harm than good. And Mortensgaard is not the sort of man I choose to have dealings with. You know all about that former unpleasantness between us.

REBEKKA: But wouldn't it be as well to be on good terms with him again?

ROSMER: I? With Mortensgaard? What for?

REBEKKA: I thought it might be to your advantage—now that your old friends have turned against you.

ROSMER (*Looks at her and shakes his head*): You surely don't believe that Kroll or any of the others would try to take revenge on me? That they'd ever think of—?

REBEKKA: You never know what people will do in the first heat of anger. After the way the Professor took it—it seemed to me—

ROSMER: You should know him better than that. Kroll is a thoroughly honorable man. I'll go in and see him after lunch. I'd like to talk to all of them. You'll see—things will come out all right.

(MRS. HELSETH *appears at door.*)

REBEKKA (*Rises*): What is it, Mrs. Helseth?

MRS. HELSETH: Professor Kroll is downstairs in the hall.

ROSMER (*Rises hastily*): Kroll!

REBEKKA: The Professor! Fancy!

MRS. HELSETH: He wants to know if he may come up and talk to Mr. Rosmer.

ROSMER (*To* REBEKKA): What did I tell you? —of course he may. (*Goes to door and calls downstairs*) Come up, dear friend! I am delighted to see you.

(ROSMER *holds the door open for him;* MRS. HELSETH *exits.* REBEKKA *closes the curtain to the alcove and tidies up here and there. Enter* KROLL, *hat in hand.*)

ROSMER (*With quiet emotion*): I was sure we hadn't said good-bye for good.

KROLL: I see things in quite a different light today.

ROSMER: I was sure you would, Kroll; now that you've had time to think things over—

KROLL: You misunderstand me. (*Lays his hat on table beside sofa*) It is of the utmost importance that I speak to you, alone.

ROSMER: But, why shouldn't Miss West—?

REBEKKA: No, no, Mr. Rosmer. I'll go.

KROLL (*Looks at her from head to foot*): I must ask Miss West's pardon for coming at such an early hour—for taking her unawares, before she has had time to—

REBEKKA (*Surprised*): How do you mean? Do you see anything wrong in my wearing a dressing gown about the house?

KROLL: Heaven forbid! Who am I to know what may now be customary at Rosmersholm?

ROSMER: Why, Kroll—you are not yourself today!

REBEKKA: My respects, Professor Kroll! (*Goes out.*)

KROLL: With your permission—(*Sits.*)

ROSMER: Yes, do sit down, let's talk things over amicably. (*Sits opposite the Professor.*)

KROLL: I haven't closed my eyes since yesterday. All night long I lay there turning things over in my mind.

ROSMER: And what have you to say today?

KROLL: It will be a long story, Rosmer. As a kind of preliminary—let me give you news of Ulrik Brendel.

ROSMER: Has he called on you?

KROLL: No. He took up quarters in a disreputable tavern, in the lowest possible company. There he started drinking and playing host to the others till his money ran out. In the end he turned on them; abused

them as a pack of thieves and blackguards —in which he was undoubtedly quite right —whereupon they beat him up and pitched him into the gutter.

ROSMER: So he's incorrigible, after all.

KROLL: He had pawned the overcoat, but I hear that has been redeemed for him. Can you guess by whom?

ROSMER: By you, perhaps?

KROLL: No. By the noble Mr. Mortensgaard.

ROSMER: Indeed!

KROLL: Yes. It seems Mr. Brendel's first visit was to the "plebian idiot."

ROSMER: That was a lucky thing for him.

KROLL: To be sure it was. (*Leans across the table towards* ROSMER) This brings me to a matter I feel it my duty to warn you about, for our old—or rather for our former—friendship's sake.

ROSMER: What matter, my dear Kroll?

KROLL: I warn you: there are things going on behind your back in this house.

ROSMER: What makes you think that? Is it Reb—is it Miss West you're referring to?

KROLL: Precisely. Oh, it's not surprising. All this time she's been given such a free hand here. But still—

ROSMER: You're quite mistaken in this, Kroll. She and I are completely honest with each other—on all subjects.

KROLL: Then has she informed you that she has started a correspondence with the editor of *The Beacon?*

ROSMER: You mean those few words she gave to Ulrik Brendel?

KROLL: Oh, so you know about it. And you mean to say that you approve of her associating with this cheap journalist— this scandalmonger who never ceases to hold me up to ridicule?

ROSMER: My dear Kroll, I don't suppose it occurred to her to look at it from that angle. And, besides, she's a free agent— just as I am.

KROLL: I see. It's all part of this new line of conduct, I presume. Miss West undoubtedly shares your present point of view?

ROSMER: Yes, she does. We've worked towards it together—in loyal friendship.

KROLL (*Looks at him and slowly shakes his*

head): You're a blind, deluded man, Rosmer!

ROSMER: I? Why should you call me that?

KROLL: Because I dare not—*will* not think the worst. No, no! Let me finish! You really do value my friendship, don't you, Rosmer? And my respect?

ROSMER: Surely that question should require no answer.

KROLL: Very well. But there are other questions that do require an answer—a full explanation on your part. Are you willing to submit to a sort of cross-examination—?

ROSMER: Cross-examination?

KROLL: Yes. Will you allow me to inquire frankly into various matters that it may pain you to be reminded of? You see— this apostasy of yours—this emancipation, as you prefer to call it—is bound up with many other things, that for your own sake you must explain to me.

ROSMER: Ask me anything you like, my dear Kroll. I have nothing to hide.

KROLL: Then tell me—what do you think was the real—the basic—reason for Beata's suicide?

ROSMER: Have you doubts on that score? You can hardly expect to find a reasonable explanation for the actions of a poor demented invalid.

KROLL: But are you quite certain Beata was completely irresponsible? Remember, the doctors were by no means convinced of that.

ROSMER: If the doctors had ever seen her as I so often saw her—day after day, night after night—they would have had no doubts.

KROLL: I had no doubts either, then.

ROSMER: No, unfortunately there wasn't the slightest room for doubt. Those paroxysms of morbid passion she was seized with! How could I respond to them—they appalled me; I told you all about it at the time. And then the constant reproaches she heaped upon herself in those last years; without basis—without reason.

KROLL: After she found out she could never have children; yes—I know.

ROSMER: She suffered untold agonies of mind —tormented herself incessantly—over

something entirely out of her control. No normal human being would behave like that.

KROLL: Tell me—do you remember having any books in the house at that time, dealing with marital relations? From the so-called modern point of view, I mean?

ROSMER: Yes—I believe Miss West once lent me such a book; she inherited Doctor West's library, you know. But, my dear Kroll, you don't suppose for a moment we were careless enough to let it fall into poor Beata's hands? I give you my solemn word, we were both entirely blameless in this matter. It was her own sick brain that drove Beata to the verge of madness.

KROLL: I can tell you one thing, at any rate: Beata—poor, tormented creature that she was—put an end to her own life in order to bring happiness to yours; to set you free to live—after your own heart.

ROSMER (*Starts half up from chair*): What do you mean by that?

KROLL: Listen to me quietly, Rosmer! I must speak about it now. Not long before she died she came to see me twice and poured out all her sorrow and despair.

ROSMER: On this same subject?

KROLL: No. The first time she kept insisting you were about to break with the Faith— to leave the church.

ROSMER (*Eagerly*): That's quite impossible— utterly impossible! You're mistaken, I assure you!

KROLL: What makes you think that?

ROSMER: Because as long as Beata lived I'd come to no decision. I was in a turmoil —that is true—wrestling with doubts; but I never said a word to anyone; I fought it out alone and in the utmost secrecy. I don't think even Rebekka—

KROLL: Rebekka?

ROSMER: Well—Miss West then; I call her Rebekka for convenience' sake.

KROLL: So I have noticed.

ROSMER: It's quite inconceivable that Beata could ever have suspected such a thing. And if she had, why didn't she mention it to me? She never did—she never said a single word.

KROLL: Poor thing—she begged and implored me to talk to you.

ROSMER: Why didn't you, then?

KROLL: Because I thought she was unbalanced! I took that for granted at the time. To accuse a man like you of such a thing! The second time she came—it was about a month later—she seemed much calmer. But just as she was leaving, she turned to me and said: "It won't be long now before the White Horse appears at Rosmersholm."

ROSMER: The White Horse, yes—she often spoke of that.

KROLL: I tried to steer her away from such sad thoughts—but she continued: "I haven't long to live. Rosmer must marry Rebekka at once."

ROSMER (*Almost speechless*): What are you saying? I marry—?

KROLL: That was a Thursday afternoon— The following Saturday evening she threw herself from the bridge into the mill-race.

ROSMER: And you never warned us—!

KROLL: You know she was always saying she hadn't long to live.

ROSMER: I know; but still—you should have warned us!

KROLL: I thought of it, but by then it was too late.

ROSMER: But after it happened—why didn't you? Why haven't you told me this before?

KROLL: I didn't want to add to your grief— what good would it have done? In any case, at the time I took everything she said for the hysterical ravings of an unsound mind. Until yesterday evening I believed that firmly—

ROSMER: And now?

KROLL: Didn't Beata see quite clearly when she declared you were about to desert the faith you were brought up in?

ROSMER (*Looks fixedly straight before him*): That I *cannot* understand! It's quite incomprehensible—

KROLL: Incomprehensible· or not—there it is. And now—what about her other accusation, Rosmer? How much truth is there in that?

ROSMER: Was that an accusation?

KROLL: Perhaps you did not notice the way she worded it. She had to go, she said— why?—Well? Answer me!

ROSMER: So that I might marry Rebekka—

KROLL: That is not exactly the way she put it. Beata expressed it differently. She said: "I haven't long to live; Johannes must marry Rebekka at once."

ROSMER (*Looks at him for a moment; then rises*): Now I understand you, Kroll!

KROLL: Well? And what is your answer?

ROSMER (*Still quiet and self-restrained*): To something so unheard of—? The only right answer would be to show you the door.

KROLL (*Rises*): Well and good.

ROSMER (*Stands in front of him*): Wait a minute, Kroll! For well over a year—ever since Beata left us—Rebekka West and I have lived here alone at Rosmersholm. All that time you have been aware of Beata's accusation against us. Yet I've never noticed the slightest sign of disapproval on your part.

KROLL: Until yesterday evening I had no idea you were an atheist; and that the woman sharing your home was a freethinker.

ROSMER: I see. You don't believe there can be purity of mind among free-thinkers? You don't believe there's such a thing as an instinctive sense of morality?

KROLL: I have no great faith in any morality that is not founded on the teachings of the church.

ROSMER: And does this apply to Rebekka and me as well? To our relationship?

KROLL: Consideration for you cannot alter my opinion that there is very little separation between free-thought and—

ROSMER: And?

KROLL: Free love—since you force me to put it into words.

ROSMER (*In a low voice*): Aren't you ashamed to say such a thing to me! You, who have known me since I was a boy?

KROLL: All the more reason for me to say it. I know how easily you are influenced by those around you. And this Rebekka of yours—well, this Miss West then—what do we really know about her? Next to nothing! In short, Rosmer—I refuse to give you up. I urge you to try and save yourself while there's still time.

ROSMER: In what way—Save myself?

(MRS. HELSETH *peeps in at the door.*)

ROSMER: What do you want?

MRS. HELSETH: I'm to ask Miss West to come downstairs.

ROSMER: Miss West is not up here.

MRS. HELSETH: Isn't she? (*Looks around room*) That's strange. (*Goes.*)

ROSMER: You were saying—

KROLL: Listen to me. What went on here in secret while Beata was alive—what may be going on here now, I shall inquire into no further. Your marriage was a most unhappy one; that may serve to excuse you, to some extent—

ROSMER: How little you really know me—!

KROLL: Don't interrupt me. What I mean is this: if your relationship with Miss West is to continue, at least keep your new opinions, your tragic fall from faith—for which she is undoubtedly to blame—keep these things to yourself! No! Let me speak! Let me speak! If the worst comes to the worst then for heaven's sake, think and believe and do whatever you like, but be discreet about it. It's a purely personal matter! It's not necessary to shout it from the house-tops.

ROSMER: Perhaps not. But it is necessary for me to free myself from a false and ambiguous position.

KROLL: It's your duty to uphold the traditions of your race, Rosmer! Remember that! For countless generations Rosmersholm has been a stronghold of discipline and order—of all those precious things that are most revered and highly respected in our Society. The whole district has always taken its stamp from Rosmersholm. It would cause the most deplorable, the most irreparable confusion, if it became known that you of all people had broken away from what might be called the Rosmer Way of Life.

ROSMER: That's not the way I see things,

Kroll. It seems to me my duty is to spread a little light and happiness here, where former Rosmers spread only gloom and despotism.

KROLL (*Looks at him sternly*): That indeed would be a worthy mission for the last of the Rosmers to perform! No. Leave such things alone—they are not for you. You were born to live the quiet life of a scholar.

ROSMER: Perhaps. But all the same, I feel compelled to take part in the present crisis.

KROLL: You realize it will mean a life and death struggle with all your former friends?

ROSMER (*Quietly*): I can't believe they are all as fanatical as you.

KROLL: You are a simple-hearted soul, Rosmer; a naive soul. You have no conception of the powerful storm that will sweep over you.

(MRS. HELSETH *looks in at the door.*)

MRS. HELSETH: Miss West would like to know—

ROSMER: What is it?

MRS. HELSETH: There's a man downstairs who wants a few words with you, Sir.

ROSMER: Is it the one who was here yesterday?

MRS. HELSETH: No; it's that Mortensgaard.

ROSMER: Mortensgaard!

KROLL: Aha! I see. So it's already come to this!

ROSMER: Why should be want to see me? Why didn't you send him away?

MRS. HELSETH: Miss West told me to ask if he might come upstairs a minute.

ROSMER: Tell him I'm busy—

KROLL (*To* MRS. HELSETH): No! No! By all means let him come up, Mrs. Helseth. (MRS. HELSETH *goes;* KROLL *takes up hat*) I shall leave the field to him—for the moment. But the main battle has yet to be fought.

ROSMER: I give you my word of honor, Kroll —I have nothing whatever to do with Mortensgaard.

KROLL: I no longer believe anything you say, Rosmer. I can no longer take your word on any subject. It's war to the death now. We shall make every effort to disarm you.

ROSMER: That you should have sunk so low, Kroll!

KROLL: You dare say that to me! A man who—! Remember Beata?

ROSMER: Are you going to harp on that again?

KROLL: No. I shall leave you to solve the mystery of Beata's death after your own conscience—if you still possess anything of the sort.

(PEDER MORTENSGAARD *enters slowly and quietly by the door left. He is a small, wiry man with thin reddish hair and beard.*)

KROLL (*With a look of hatred*): I never thought I'd live to see *The Beacon* burning at Rosmersholm! (*Buttons his coat*) That settles it! I no longer have any doubt which course to take.

MORTENSGAARD (*Deferentially*): *The Beacon* may always be relied upon to light the Professor home.

KROLL: Yes; your good will has been apparent for some time. There is, to be sure, a commandment about bearing false-witness against your neighbor—

MORTENSGAARD: There is no need for Professor Kroll to teach me the commandments.

KROLL: Not even the seventh?

ROSMER: Kroll—!

MORTENSGAARD: Were that necessary, it would surely be the Pastor's business.

KROLL (*With covert sarcasm*): The Pastor's? Oh, of course! Pastor Rosmer is unquestionably the man for that— Good luck to your conference, gentlemen! (*Goes out, slams door behind him.*)

ROSMER (*Keeps eyes fixed on closed door and says to himself*): So be it, then. (*Turns*) Now, Mr. Mortensgaard; what brings you here?

MORTENSGAARD: I really came to see Miss West. I wanted to thank her for the nice note she sent me yesterday.

ROSMER: Yes, I know she wrote to you. Did you get a chance to talk to her?

MORTENSGAARD: Yes, for a little while. (*With a faint smile*) I understand there has been a certain change of views at Rosmersholm.

ROSMER: Yes. My views have changed on many subjects. On all subjects, perhaps.

MORTENSGAARD: So Miss West told me. She suggested that I come up and talk things over with you.

ROSMER: Talk what over, Mr. Mortensgaard?

MORTENSGAARD: I should like to make an announcement in *The Beacon*. May I say that your views have changed, and that you are now ready to support the cause of progress—the cause of Freedom?

ROSMER: Announce it, by all means. In fact I urge you to do so.

MORTENSGAARD: It will be in tomorrow morning. It will cause quite a sensation: Pastor Rosmer of Rosmersholm stands ready to guide people toward the Light— in this sense too.

ROSMER: I don't quite understand you.

MORTENSGAARD: It's always a good thing for us to gain the approval of men like you—men well-known for their strict Christian principles; the moral support it gives our Cause is much needed—and invaluable.

ROSMER (*With some surprise*): Then, you don't know—? Didn't Miss West tell you about that, too?

MORTENSGAARD: About what, Pastor Rosmer? Miss West seemed in a great hurry; she said I'd better come upstairs and hear the rest from you.

ROSMER: I'd better tell you myself, then. You see—I've freed myself in every way: I no longer have any connection with the church, or with its doctrines; they no longer concern me in the least.

MORTENSGAARD (*Looks at him in amazement*): What! If the skies were to fall I couldn't be more—! Pastor Rosmer! Is this true?

ROSMER: Yes. So, you see—I am now in full accord with you. In this too I share the opinions you have held for many years. And this too you may announce tomorrow in *The Beacon*.

MORTENSGAARD: No. Forgive me, my dear Pastor, but I don't think it would be wise to touch on that side of the question.

ROSMER: How do you mean?

MORTENSGAARD: Not at first—at all events.

ROSMER: I don't quite understand—

MORTENSGAARD: Let me explain; you naturally don't know the circumstances as well as I do. Since you've come over to the cause of freedom—and I gather from Miss West you intend to take an active part in the Progressive movement—I presume you would wish to help the cause to the fullest possible extent.

ROSMER: Yes, I'm most anxious to do so.

MORTENSGAARD: Then I think I should point out, that if your defection from the church is publicly announced, it will prove a serious handicap to you from the start.

ROSMER: You think so?

MORTENSGAARD: Undoubtedly. You could accomplish very little—particularly in this part of the country. We've a great many free-thinkers in our ranks already—too many, I was about to say. What the party lacks is the Christian element, Pastor Rosmer—something that commands respect. That is our greatest need. So—in matters that do not directly concern the general public—it would seem wiser to be discreet. That's my opinion, at any rate.

ROSMER: In other words, if I make known my break with the church, you dare not have anything to do with me?

MORTENSGAARD (*Shaking his head*): I shouldn't like to risk it, Pastor Rosmer. In recent years I have made it a point never to lend support to anything or anyone antagonistic to the church.

ROSMER: Have you, yourself, returned to the fold, then?

MORTENSGAARD: That is a purely personal matter.

ROSMER: So that's it. Now I understand you.

MORTENSGAARD: You should understand, Pastor Rosmer, that my hands are tied more than most people's.

ROSMER: How so?

MORTENSGAARD: I am a marked man, you should know that.

ROSMER: Indeed?

MORTENSGAARD: A marked man, yes. Surely you've not forgotten? You were mainly responsible for that.

ROSMER: If I'd seen things then as I do now, I should have shown more understanding.

MORTENSGAARD: I dare say, but it's too late now. You branded me for good—branded me for life—I don't suppose you quite realize what that means. You soon may, though.

ROSMER: I?

MORTENSGAARD: Yes. You surely don't think Professor Kroll and his set will ever forgive a desertion like yours? They say the *County News* will be most sanguinary in future. You may find yourself a marked man, too.

ROSMER: They can't possibly harm me in personal matters, Mr. Mortensgaard. My private life has always been beyond reproach.

MORTENSGAARD (*With a sly smile*): That's a bold statement, Mr. Rosmer.

ROSMER: Perhaps, but I feel I have the right to make it.

MORTENSGAARD: Even if you were to examine your own conduct as thoroughly as you once examined mine?

ROSMER: Your tone is very curious. What are you hinting at? Anything definite?

MORTENSGAARD: Yes, quite definite. It's only a little thing. But it could prove quite nasty, if the wrong people were to get wind of it.

ROSMER: Then be good enough to tell me what it is.

MORTENSGAARD: Can't you guess that for yourself?

ROSMER: Certainly not. I've no idea.

MORTENSGAARD: Then I suppose I'd better tell you. I have a rather curious letter in my possession—one that was written here at Rosmersholm.

ROSMER: Miss West's letter, you mean? Is there anything curious about that?

MORTENSGAARD: No, there's nothing curious about that one. But I once received another letter from this house.

ROSMER: Was that from Miss West too?

MORTENSGAARD: No, Pastor Rosmer.

ROSMER: From whom do you mean then? Tell me!

MORTENSGAARD: From the late Mrs. Rosmer.

ROSMER: From my wife! You received a letter from my wife?

MORTENSGAARD: Yes, I did.

ROSMER: When?

MORTENSGAARD: Not long before Mrs. Rosmer died—about a year and a half ago, perhaps. That is the letter I find curious.

ROSMER: I suppose you know my wife's mind was affected at that time.

MORTENSGAARD: Yes, I know many people thought so. But the letter gave no indication of anything like that. No—when I called the letter "curious," I meant it in quite a different sense.

ROSMER: What on earth could my poor wife have written to you about?

MORTENSGAARD: She begins by saying something to the effect that she is living in great fear and anguish. There are so many malicious people in this neighborhood, she writes, whose only thought is to do you every possible harm.

ROSMER: Me?

MORTENSGAARD: That's what she says. Then comes the most curious part of all. Shall I go on?

ROSMER: Of course! By all means.

MORTENSGAARD: Your late wife then begs me to be magnanimous. She knows, she says, that it was you who had me dismissed from my position as a teacher and she humbly implores me not to take revenge.

ROSMER: What did she mean? In what way take revenge?

MORTENSGAARD: She says in the letter, that if I should hear scandalous rumors about certain things at Rosmersholm, I must discount them; that they are slanders spread by evil-minded people to do you injury.

ROSMER: Is all this in the letter?

MORTENSGAARD: You're welcome to read it yourself, Pastor Rosmer, at your convenience.

ROSMER: But I don't understand—! What scandalous rumors could she have been referring to?

MORTENSGAARD: First that you had deserted the Faith. She denied this absolutely—then. And next—h'm—

ROSMER: Well?

MORTENSGAARD: Next she writes—and this is rather confused—that to her knowledge there has been no breach of morals at Rosmersholm; that she has never been wronged in any way. And if rumors of that sort should reach me, she begs me to say nothing of the matter in *The Beacon*.

ROSMER: No name is mentioned?

MORTENSGAARD: None.

ROSMER: Who brought you this letter?

MORTENSGAARD: I promised not to say. It was brought to me one evening, after dark.

ROSMER: If you had made inquiries at the time, you would have found out that my poor wife was not fully responsible for her actions.

MORTENSGAARD: I did make inquiries, Pastor Rosmer. But that was not the impression I received.

ROSMER: Indeed? And what made you choose this particular moment to tell me about this letter?

MORTENSGAARD: I felt I should warn you to be exceedingly cautious, Pastor Rosmer.

ROSMER: In my personal life, you mean?

MORTENSGAARD: Yes; you're no longer entirely your own master. Remember—you've ceased to be a neutral.

ROSMER: Then you are quite convinced I have something to conceal?

MORTENSGAARD: There's no reason why a man of liberal views shouldn't be able to live his life to the full—live it exactly as he chooses; however, I repeat, this is a time for caution. If certain rumors were to get about concerning you—rumors that might offend current prejudices, shall we say?—the whole Liberal Movement might be seriously affected. Good-bye, Pastor Rosmer.

ROSMER: Good-bye.

MORTENSGAARD: I'll go straight back to the office. This is important news; I'll have it in *The Beacon* by tomorrow.

ROSMER: Be sure to include everything.

MORTENSGAARD: Don't worry! I shall include everything that respectable people need to know. (*He bows and goes out.* ROSMER *remains standing in doorway while*

*he goes down the stairs. The outer door is
heard to close.*)

ROSMER (*In doorway, calls softly*): Rebekka,
Re— H'm. (*Aloud*) Mrs. Helseth—isn't
Miss West down there?

MRS. HELSETH (*From the hall below*): No;
she's not here, Sir.

(*The curtain in the background is drawn
aside.* REBEKKA *appears in doorway.*)

REBEKKA: Rosmer!

ROSMER (*Turns*): Rebekka! What are you
doing there? Have you been in my room
all the time?

REBEKKA (*Goes up to him*): Yes, Rosmer. I
was listening.

ROSMER: How could you do such a thing,
Rebekka!

REBEKKA: I had to. He was so disgusting
when he said that about my dressing-
gown—

ROSMER: Then you were in there when
Kroll—?

REBEKKA: Yes, I had to know what he meant
by all those things he said—

ROSMER: I would have told you.

REBEKKA: You'd scarcely have told me
everything. And certainly not in his words.

ROSMER: You heard the whole conversation,
then?

REBEKKA: Most of it, I think. I had to go
downstairs a moment when Mortensgaard
came.

ROSMER: Then you came up again?

REBEKKA: Don't be angry with me; please,
Rosmer, dear!

ROSMER: You're perfectly free to do whatever seems right to you, you know that.
What do you make of it all, Rebekka—?
Oh, I don't know when I've ever needed
you as much as I do now!

REBEKKA: After all, we knew this would have
to come some day; we've been prepared
for it.

ROSMER: But, not for this.

REBEKKA: Why not for this?

ROSMER: I knew of course that sooner or
later our friendship would be misunderstood—would be dragged down into the
mud. Not by Kroll—I never expected that
of him—but by all those others; those

coarse-grained, insensitive people who are
blind to everything but evil. I had good
reason to guard our relationship so
jealously. It was a dangerous secret.

REBEKKA: Why should we care what all
those people think! We know we've done
no wrong.

ROSMER: No wrong, you say? I? Yes, until
today I was convinced of that. But now,
Rebekka—?

REBEKKA: What?

ROSMER: How am I to explain Beata's dreadful accusation?

REBEKKA (*Vehemently*): Don't talk about
Beata— Don't *think* about Beata any
more! You were just beginning to escape
from her—she's dead!

ROSMER: After what I've heard, she seems in
a ghastly sort of way to be alive again.

REBEKKA: Not that, Rosmer! Please—not
that!

ROSMER: Yes, I tell you. Somehow we must
get to the bottom of it all. How could
she possibly have misinterpreted things
in such a hideous way?

REBEKKA: She was on the verge of madness!
Surely you're not beginning to doubt that?

ROSMER: That's just it—I no longer feel quite
sure; besides—even if she was—

REBEKKA: Even if she was—?

ROSMER: I mean—if her sick mind was on
the borderline, what was it that gave the
final impetus—that drove her to actual
madness?

REBEKKA: What possible good can it do, to
torment yourself with questions that have
no answers?

ROSMER: I cannot help it, Rebekka. Much
as I'd like to, I can't shake off these
doubts.

REBEKKA: Don't you see how dangerous it
is to keep on dwelling on this one morbid
subject?

ROSMER (*Walks about restlessly in thought*):
I must have given myself away somehow.
She must have noticed how much happier
I was after you came to live with us.

REBEKKA: Well—even if she did—?

ROSMER: She must have noticed how many
things we had in common; how we were

drawn together by our interest in the same books—in all the new ideas and theories. Yet I can't understand it! I was so careful to spare her feelings. I went out of my way, it seems to me, to keep her from knowing just how many interests we shared. Isn't that so, Rebekka?

REBEKKA: Yes, it is.

ROSMER: And you did the same. Yet in spite of that—! Oh, it's awful to think of! All that time she must have been watching us, observing us, noticing everything in silence; and her morbid love of me made her see it all in a false light.

REBEKKA (*Clenching her hands*): I should never have come to Rosmersholm!

ROSMER: The agony she must have gone through in silence! The sordid images her sick brain must have conjured up! Did she never say anything to you? Give any indication of her feelings, that might have warned you?

REBEKKA (*As if startled*): Do you think I'd have stayed here a moment longer if she had?

ROSMER: No, no, of course not— Oh, how she must have struggled, Rebekka—and all alone! To be so desperate, and quite alone! And then, the final triumph—the heartbreaking, silent accusation—of the mill-race. (*Throws himself into the chair by the writing-table, puts his elbows on the table and buries his face in his hands.*)

REBEKKA (*Approaches him cautiously from behind*): Tell me something, Rosmer. If it were in your power to call Beata back— to you—to Rosmersholm—would you do it?

ROSMER: How do I know what I would do, or wouldn't do? I can't tear my thoughts away from this one thing—this one irrevocable thing.

REBEKKA: You were just beginning to live, Rosmer. You *had* begun to live. You had freed yourself—in every way. You were feeling so buoyant, so happy—

ROSMER: It's true—I was. And now, to have to face all this!

REBEKKA (*Behind him, rests her arms on the back of his chair*): We were so happy sitting downstairs in the old room together, in the twilight—don't you remember?

Talking over our new plans; helping one another to see life with new eyes. You wanted to take part in life, at last—to be really *alive* in life—you used to say. You wanted to go from house to house spreading the word of freedom, winning over men's hearts and minds, awakening in them a sense of the nobility of life—of their *own* nobility; you wanted to create a noble race of men—

ROSMER: Noble—and happy, yes.

REBEKKA: Yes—happy, too.

ROSMER: For minds are ennobled through happiness, Rebekka.

REBEKKA: Don't you think—through suffering, too. Great suffering, I mean?

ROSMER: Yes; if one can live through it, conquer it, and go beyond it.

REBEKKA: That's what *you* must do.

ROSMER (*Shakes his head gloomily*): I shall never quite get over this. There'll always be a doubt—a question in my mind. I'll never again experience the joy that fills life with such sweetness.

REBEKKA (*Bends over his chair-back and says more softly*): What joy do you mean, Rosmer?

ROSMER (*Looking up at her*): Peaceful joy— The confidence of innocence.

REBEKKA (*Recoils a step*): Ah! Innocence; yes.

(*A short pause.*)

ROSMER (*With elbow on table, leaning his head on his hand, and looking straight before him*): And how cleverly she worked the whole thing out. How systematically she put it all together! First she began to doubt the soundness of my faith—At that time how could she have suspected that? But she did suspect it; and later she became convinced of it. And then, of course, it was easy enough for her to believe in the possibility of all the rest. (*Sits up in his chair and runs his hands through his hair*) All these wild imaginings! I shall never get rid of them. I feel it. I know it. Suddenly, at any moment, they'll come sweeping through my mind—bringing back the thought of the dead.

REBEKKA: Like the White Horse of Rosmersholm.

ROSMER: Yes—just like that. Sweeping

through the darkness—through the silence.

REBEKKA: And because of this wretched hallucination, you'd be willing to give up being alive in life!

ROSMER: It's hard—it's hard, Rebekka. But I have no choice. How can I ever recover from all this?

REBEKKA (*Behind his chair*): You must take up new interests; you must enter into new relationships—

ROSMER (*Surprised, looks up*): New relationships?

REBEKKA: Yes—with the world at large. You must live, work, *act*—instead of sitting here brooding over insoluble enigmas.

ROSMER (*Rises*): New relationships? (*Walks across the floor, stops at the door and then comes back*) One question occurs to me, Rebekka; has it never occurred to you?

REBEKKA (*Scarcely breathing*): Tell me—what it is.

ROSMER: What future is there for our relationship—after today?

REBEKKA: I believe our friendship will endure—in spite of everything.

ROSMER: That's not quite what I meant. The thing that first brought us together and that unites us so closely—our faith in the possibility of a pure comradeship between a man and a woman—

REBEKKA: What of that—?

ROSMER: A relationship such as ours, I mean —shouldn't that presuppose a happy, peaceful life—?

REBEKKA: Well—?

ROSMER: But the life I face is one of struggle, unrest and violent agitation. For I intend to live my life, Rebekka! I will not be crushed by these gloomy speculations. I refuse to have a way of life imposed upon me, either by the living or by—anyone else.

REBEKKA: No! That must not happen, Rosmer. You must be free in every way!

ROSMER: Then—can you guess my thoughts? Can you guess them, Rebekka? There's only one way that I can free myself—rid myself of these haunting memories—this loathsome, tragic past.

REBEKKA: What way is that?

ROSMER: It must be stamped out, and replaced by something alive and real—

REBEKKA (*Groping for the chair-back*): Alive and real—? You mean—?

ROSMER (*Comes nearer*): If I were to ask you—? Oh, Rebekka! Will you be my wife?

REBEKKA (*For a moment, speechless, then cries out with joy*): Your wife! Your—! I!

ROSMER: Yes, let us truly belong to one another—let us be as one. The empty place must remain empty no longer.

REBEKKA: I—take Beata's place—?

ROSMER: Then it will be as though she'd never been.

REBEKKA (*Softly, trembling*): You believe that, Rosmer?

ROSMER: It must be so! It must! I refuse to live my life chained to a corpse; help me to free myself, Rebekka! Together we will conquer all memories of the past; in freedom, in joy, in passion. You shall be to me my first, my only, wife.

REBEKKA (*With self-control*): You must never speak of this again! I can never be your wife.

ROSMER: Never! You mean—you could never come to love me? But we love each other already, Rebekka! Our friendship has already turned to love.

REBEKKA (*Puts her hands over her ears as if in terror*): No, no! Don't talk like that! Don't say such things!

ROSMER (*Seizes her arm*): But it has! Our relationship is full of promise. You must feel that too—you must, Rebekka!

REBEKKA (*Once more firm and calm*): Listen to me. If you speak of this again—I shall go away from Rosmersholm. I mean it.

ROSMER: You! Go away! But that's impossible.

REBEKKA: It's still more impossible that I should ever be your wife. I can't be. I can never marry you.

ROSMER (*Looks at her in surprise*): You *can't* be? You say that so strangely. Why can't you be?

REBEKKA (*Seizes both his hands*): For your sake, as well as mine—don't ask me why. (*Lets go his hands*) Don't ask me, Rosmer. (*Goes towards door.*)

ROSMER: From now on I shall never cease to ask that question—why?

REBEKKA (*Turns and looks at him*): Then it's all over.

ROSMER: Between us, you mean?

REBEKKA: Yes.

ROSMER: It will never be over between us; and you will never go away from Rosmersholm.

REBEKKA (*With her hand on the door handle*): Perhaps not. But if you ask that question again, it will be over all the same.

ROSMER: How do you mean?

REBEKKA: Because then I shall go, the way Beata went. I've warned you, Rosmer—

ROSMER: Rebekka—?

REBEKKA (*In the doorway, nods slowly*): I've warned you. (*She goes out.*)

ROSMER (*Stares thunderstruck at the door, and says to himself*): What does this mean?

CURTAIN

ACT III

SCENE: *The sitting-room at Rosmersholm. The window and the hall door are open. A bright sunny morning.* REBEKKA WEST, *dressed as in the first act, stands at the window, watering and arranging the flowers. Her crochet work lies in the arm-chair.* MRS. HELSETH *moves about the room, dusting the furniture with a feather duster.*

REBEKKA (*After a short silence*): It's strange that Mr. Rosmer should stay upstairs so late today.

MRS. HELSETH: He often does. He'll be down soon, I expect.

REBEKKA: Have you seen him yet this morning?

MRS. HELSETH: I caught a glimpse of him when I took his coffee up; he was in his bedroom, dressing.

REBEKKA: He didn't seem to feel well yesterday, that's why I asked.

MRS. HELSETH: No; he didn't look well. I was wondering if there was anything wrong between him and his brother-in-law.

REBEKKA: What do you think it could be?

MRS. HELSETH: I really couldn't say. Perhaps it's that Mortensgaard that's made trouble between them.

REBEKKA: It's possible. Do you know anything about this Peder Mortensgaard?

MRS. HELSETH: No indeed, Miss. How could you think that? A person like him!

REBEKKA: You mean because of that newspaper of his?

MRS. HELSETH: Not just because of that; but you must have heard about him, Miss. He had a child by a married woman whose husband had deserted her.

REBEKKA: Yes, I've heard it mentioned. But that must have been long before I came here.

MRS. HELSETH: Lord, yes! He was quite young at the time; and she should have known better. He wanted to marry her too; but of course that was impossible. He paid dearly for it, they say. But he's gone up in the world since then. Plenty of people run after him now.

REBEKKA: Yes, I hear most of the poor people go to him when they're in any trouble.

MRS. HELSETH: Oh, not just the poor people, Miss. There've been others too—

REBEKKA (*Looks at her furtively*): Really?

MRS. HELSETH (*By the sofa, dusting away vigorously*): Oh, yes, Miss. Perhaps the very last people you'd ever dream of.

REBEKKA (*Busy with the flowers*): That's just one of your ideas, Mrs. Helseth. You can't be sure about a thing like that.

MRS. HELSETH: That's what you think, Miss. But I am sure all the same. I may as well tell you—I once took a letter to Mortensgaard myself.

REBEKKA (*Turning*): *You* did?

MRS. HELSETH: Yes indeed I did. And what's more, that letter was written here at Rosmersholm.

REBEKKA: Really, Mrs. Helseth?

MRS. HELSETH: Yes indeed, Miss. And it was written on fine note paper, too; and sealed with fine red sealing wax.

REBEKKA: And you were asked to deliver it? Then, my dear Mrs. Helseth, it's not very hard to guess who wrote it.

MRS. HELSETH: Well?

REBEKKA: It was poor Mrs. Rosmer, I suppose—

MRS. HELSETH: I never said so, Miss.

REBEKKA: What was in the letter? But, of course, you couldn't very well know that.

MRS. HELSETH: Suppose I did know, all the same?

REBEKKA: You mean she told you?

MRS. HELSETH: No, not exactly. But after Mortensgaard had read it, he began asking me questions—kept on and on at me; it wasn't hard to guess what it was all about.

REBEKKA: What do you think it was? Dear, darling Mrs. Helseth, do tell me!

MRS. HELSETH: Certainly not, Miss. Not for the world!

REBEKKA: But surely you can tell *me!* After all, we're such good friends.

MRS. HELSETH: The good Lord preserve me from telling you anything about that, Miss. No! All I can say is that it was a horrible thing they'd got the poor sick lady to believe.

REBEKKA: Who got her to believe it?

MRS. HELSETH: Wicked people, Miss West. Wicked people.

REBEKKA: Wicked—?

MRS. HELSETH: Yes, and I say it again; real wicked people!

REBEKKA: Who do you suppose it could have been?

MRS. HELSETH: Oh, I know well enough what I think. But Lord forbid I should say anything. To be sure, there's a certain lady in town who—hm!

REBEKKA: You mean Mrs. Kroll, don't you?

MRS. HELSETH: She's a fine one, she is, with her airs and graces! She was always on her high horse with me. And I don't think she's ever had any too much love for you, either.

REBEKKA: Do you think Mrs. Rosmer was in her right mind when she wrote that letter?

MRS. HELSETH: A person's mind is a queer thing, Miss; not *clear* out of her mind, I wouldn't say.

REBEKKA: She seemed to go all to pieces when she found out she could never have children; that's when she first showed signs of madness.

MRS. HELSETH: Yes, that was a dreadful blow to her, poor lady.

REBEKKA (*Takes up her crochet work and sits in the chair by the window*): Still—it may have been the best thing for Mr. Rosmer.

MRS. HELSETH: What, Miss?

REBEKKA: That there were no children. Don't you think so?

MRS. HELSETH: I don't quite know what to say to that.

REBEKKA: I think it was. He could never have put up with a house full of children; they'd have disturbed him with their crying.

MRS. HELSETH: But children don't cry at Rosmersholm, Miss.

REBEKKA (*Looks at her*): Don't cry?

MRS. HELSETH: No. As long as people can remember, children have never been known to cry in this house.

REBEKKA: How very strange.

MRS. HELSETH: Yes, isn't it? It runs in the family. And then there's another strange thing. When they grow up, they never laugh. Never—as long as they live.

REBEKKA: Why, how queer—

MRS. HELSETH: Do you ever remember hearing or seeing Pastor Rosmer laugh, Miss?

REBEKKA: No—I don't believe I ever have, come to think of it. You're right, Mrs. Helseth. But then nobody laughs much in this part of the country, it seems to me.

MRS. HELSETH: No, they don't. It began at Rosmersholm, they say. And I suppose it spread round about, like one of those contagions.

REBEKKA: You're a very wise woman, Mrs. Helseth.

MRS. HELSETH: Don't you go making fun of me, Miss! (*Listens*) Hush—here's the Pastor coming down. He doesn't like to see me dusting. (*She goes out.*)

(JOHANNES ROSMER, *with hat and stick in his hand, enters from the hall.*)

ROSMER: Good morning, Rebekka.

REBEKKA: Good morning, dear. (*A moment after—crocheting*) Are you going out?

ROSMER: Yes.

REBEKKA: It's such beautiful weather.

ROSMER: You didn't come in to see me this morning.

REBEKKA: No, I didn't. Not today.

ROSMER: Aren't you going to in the future?

REBEKKA: I don't know yet, dear.

ROSMER: Has anything come for me?

REBEKKA: The *County News* came, yes.

ROSMER: The *County News?*

REBEKKA: There it is—on the table.

ROSMER (*Puts down his hat and cane*): Is there anything in it—?

REBEKKA: Yes.

ROSMER: Why didn't you send it up?

REBEKKA: I thought you'd see it soon enough.

ROSMER: Indeed? (*Takes the paper and reads, standing by the table*) Good heavens! ". . . We feel it our duty to issue a solemn warning against unprincipled renegades." (*Looks at her*) They call me a renegade, Rebekka.

REBEKKA: They mention no names.

ROSMER: It's obvious enough. (*Reads on*) "Men who secretly betray the cause of righteousness . . ." "Brazen Judases who seize the opportunity to proclaim their apostasy as soon as they feel it will work to their advantage."—". . . wanton defamation of a name honored through generations."—". . . in expectation of suitable rewards from the party momentarily in power." (*Lays down the paper on the table*) How dare they—? Men who have known me intimately for years! They know there's not a word of truth in all this—they themselves can't possibly believe it— Yet they write it all the same.

REBEKKA: That's not all of it.

ROSMER (*Takes up the paper again*): "Inexperience and lack of judgment the only excuse"—"pernicious influence—possibly extending to certain matters which, for the present, we prefer not to make public." (*Looks at her*) What do they mean by that?

REBEKKA: It is aimed at me—obviously.

ROSMER (*Lays down the paper*): It's an outrage—the work of thoroughly dishonorable men.

REBEKKA: Yes, I don't think they need throw stones at Mortensgaard!

ROSMER (*Walks about the room*): This has got to stop. If this kind of thing continues, all that is best in human nature will be destroyed. It must be stopped. It must! If only I could find some way to bring a little light into all this hideous darkness —how happy I should be!

REBEKKA (*Rises*): Yes, that would be a cause worth living for!

ROSMER: If I could only make them see themselves! Make them repent and feel ashamed! If I could only make them see that they must work together for the common good—in charity and tolerance!

REBEKKA: Try it, Rosmer, try! You could do it—I *know* you could!

ROSMER: I believe it might be possible. And then—how glorious life would be! Instead of all this hideous discord—universal aspiration. A common goal. Each man in his own way contributing his best to further progress and enlightenment. Happiness for all—through all. (*Happens to look out of the window, shudders and says sadly*) But it could never come through me, Rebekka.

REBEKKA: Why not through you?

ROSMER: Nor could I ever have a share in it.

REBEKKA: Stop doubting yourself, Rosmer!

ROSMER: There can be no happiness where there is guilt.

REBEKKA (*Looks straight before her*): Stop talking about guilt—!

ROSMER: You know nothing about guilt, Rebekka. But I—

REBEKKA: You least of all.

ROSMER (*Points out the window*): The mill-race.

REBEKKA: Oh, Rosmer—!

(MRS. HELSETH *looks in at the door.*)

MRS. HELSETH: Miss West!

REBEKKA: Not just now, Mrs. Helseth— presently!

MRS. HELSETH: Just one word, Miss.

(REBEKKA *goes to the door.* MRS. HELSETH *tells her something. They whisper together for a few moments.* MRS. HELSETH *nods and goes out.*)

ROSMER (*Uneasily*): Was it anything for me?

REBEKKA: No, just household matters. Why don't you go out into the fresh air, dear Rosmer. Take a good, long walk.

ROSMER (*Takes up his hat*): Very well. Let's go together.

REBEKKA: I can't just now. You go alone. Throw off these gloomy thoughts. Promise me that.

ROSMER: I'm afraid I'll never be able to do that.

REBEKKA: But this is a mere delusion, Rosmer! You must not let it gain a hold on you—

ROSMER: It's no mere delusion. I brooded over it all night. Perhaps Beata was right after all.

REBEKKA: In what?

ROSMER: When she suspected me of being in love with you.

REBEKKA: Ah! I see.

ROSMER (*Lays his hat on the table*): I keep asking myself—weren't we deceiving ourselves when we called our feeling friendship?

REBEKKA: Should we have called it—?

ROSMER: Love— Yes. Even while Beata was alive, it was always you I thought of—you I longed for. It was with you that I found peace and happiness. Thinking back—it seems to me we fell in love from the very first—as two children might; sweetly, mysteriously—untroubled by dreams of passion or desire. Don't you think that's true, Rebekka? Tell me.

REBEKKA (*Struggling with herself*): I don't know what to answer.

ROSMER: And we imagined this communion was merely friendship, when all the time it was a spiritual marriage. That is why I say I'm guilty. I had no right to it. No right—for Beata's sake.

REBEKKA: No right to happiness? Is that what you believe, Rosmer?

ROSMER: She watched us with the eyes of love—and judged us accordingly. What else could she have done? That judgment was inevitable.

REBEKKA: But since she was wrong, why should you blame yourself?

ROSMER: She killed herself for love of me. That fact remains. I shall never get over that, Rebekka.

REBEKKA: You *must* get over it. You've devoted your life to a great cause—you must think only of that.

ROSMER (*Shakes his head*): It can never be accomplished. Not by me. Not now that I know.

REBEKKA: Why not by you?

ROSMER: Because no victory was ever truly won by guilty men.

REBEKKA (*Vehemently*): Oh, all these doubts, these fears, these scruples! They're all ancestral relics come to haunt you. It's like this myth about the dead returning in the shape of galloping white horses— it's all part of the same thing!

ROSMER: That may be so—but if I can't escape these things, what difference does it make? And what I say is true, Rebekka; only a happy man—a blameless man—can bring a cause to lasting victory.

REBEKKA: Does happiness mean so much to you, Rosmer?

ROSMER:—Yes, it does.

REBEKKA: And yet you don't know how to laugh!

ROSMER: In spite of that, I have a great capacity for happiness.

REBEKKA: You must go for your walk now, dear. A good long walk. Do you hear? There—here is your hat. And here is your stick.

ROSMER (*Takes them from her*): Thanks. You're sure you won't come with me?

REBEKKA: No, I can't just now.

ROSMER: Very well; you're always with me, anyhow.

(*He goes out by the entrance door.* REBEKKA *waits a moment, cautiously watching his departure from behind the open door; then she goes to the door on right.*)

REBEKKA (*Opens the door and says in a low tone*): Mrs. Helseth! You may show him in, now. (*Goes toward the window; a moment after* PROFESSOR KROLL *enters. He bows silently and formally, and keeps his hat in his hand.*)

KROLL: Has he gone?

REBEKKA: Yes.

KROLL: Does he usually stay out for some time?

REBEKKA: Yes, usually. But one can't count on him today. So if you prefer not to see him—

KROLL: No; it's you I want to see; and quite alone.

REBEKKA: Then we had better not waste time. Sit down, Professor. (*Sits in the easy chair by window;* KROLL *sits on chair beside her.*)

KROLL: I don't suppose you quite realize, Miss West, how deeply this change in Johannes Rosmer has affected me.

REBEKKA: We expected that would be so— at first.

KROLL: Only at first?

REBEKKA: Rosmer was so confident that sooner or later you would join him.

KROLL: I?

REBEKKA: Yes, you—and all his other friends as well.

KROLL: There you see! That only goes to show how faulty his judgment has become, where men and practical matters are concerned.

REBEKKA: Well, after all—since he's chosen to be free—to stand completely on his own—

KROLL: But wait—you see, I don't believe that for a moment.

REBEKKA: Oh. Then what do you believe?

KROLL: I believe *you* are at the bottom of it all.

REBEKKA: Your wife put that into your head, Professor.

KROLL: Never mind who put it into my head; the fact remains that I have a strong suspicion—an exceedingly strong suspicion—the more I think things over, and piece together what I know of your behavior ever since you came here.

REBEKKA (*Looks at him*): I seem to recall a time when you felt an exceedingly strong faith in me, dear Professor. I might almost call it a *warm* faith.

KROLL (*In a subdued voice*): Whom could you not bewitch, if you set your mind to it?

REBEKKA: You think I set my mind to—?

KROLL: Yes, I do. I'm no longer such a fool as to imagine you had any feelings in the matter. You simply wanted to worm your way in here—to become firmly entrenched at Rosmersholm; and I was to help you do it. I see through your little game quite clearly now.

REBEKKA: You seem to forget that it was Beata who begged and implored me to come and live out here.

KROLL: Yes, when you had bewitched her too. For surely one could never call her feeling for you friendship? It was worship—idolatry. It developed into a kind of—I don't know what to call it—a kind of frenzied passion—Yes, that's the only word for it.

REBEKKA: Be so good as to remember your sister's condition. So far as I am concerned, I don't think anyone can accuse me of being hysterical.

KROLL: No, that's true enough; and that makes you doubly dangerous to those you wish to get into your power. It's easy enough for you; you weigh each action with cold deliberation and accurately calculate each consequence; you're able to do this because you have no heart.

REBEKKA: Are you so sure of that?

KROLL: Yes; now I'm quite convinced of it. Otherwise how could you have lived here year after year pursuing your aim so ruthlessly? Well—you've succeeded in your purpose; you've gained full power over him and over everything around him. And in order to do this, you didn't hesitate to rob him of his happiness.

REBEKKA: That is not true. I did no such thing—you, yourself, did that!

KROLL: *I* did!

REBEKKA: Yes, when you led him to imagine he was responsible for Beata's tragic death.

KROLL: Has that really affected him so deeply?

REBEKKA: Well, naturally. A mind as sensitive as his—

KROLL: I thought a so-called emancipated man would be above such scruples— But I'm not surprised—in fact I anticipated something of the sort. Look at his ancestors—these men that stare out at us from all these portraits; the heritage they've handed down to him in an unbroken line through generations is not so easily discounted.

REBEKKA (*Looks down thoughtfully:*) It's true; Johannes Rosmer's family roots go deep.

KROLL: Yes, and you should have taken that

into account; especially if you had any real affection for him. But such a thing would be difficult for you to grasp. Your background is so entirely different.

REBEKKA: What do you mean by background?

KROLL: I am speaking of your origin—your family background, Miss West.

REBEKKA: Oh, I see! It's true I come of very humble people; but still—

KROLL: I am not referring to rank or social position. I was thinking of your moral background.

REBEKKA: Moral—? In what sense?

KROLL: The circumstances of your birth.

REBEKKA: What do you mean by that?

KROLL: I mention it only because I feel it accounts for your whole conduct.

REBEKKA: I don't understand this. I demand an explanation!

KROLL: I shouldn't have thought an explanation would be necessary. If you didn't know the facts, doesn't it seem rather odd that you should have let Dr. West adopt you?

REBEKKA (*Rises*): Ah! Now I understand.

KROLL: —and that you should have taken his name? Your mother's name was Gamvik.

REBEKKA (*Walks across the room*): My father's name was Gamvik, Professor Kroll.

KROLL: Your mother's work must have kept her in constant touch with the doctor of the district—

REBEKKA: Yes, it did.

KROLL: And at your mother's death he immediately adopts you and takes you to live with him. He treats you with the greatest harshness, yet you make no attempt to get away. You're well aware that he won't leave you a penny—actually, all he left you was a trunk full of books—and yet you stay on; you put up with him and nurse him to the end.

REBEKKA (*Stands by the table, looking scornfully at him*): And because I did all this, you assume there must be something improper—something immoral about my birth?

KROLL: I believe your care of him was the result of involuntary filial instinct. As a matter of fact I attribute your entire conduct to the circumstances of your birth.

REBEKKA (*Vehemently*): But there is not a word of truth in what you say! And I can prove it! Dr. West didn't come to Finmark till after I was born.

KROLL: I beg your pardon, Miss West, I've made inquiries. He was there the year before.

REBEKKA: You're wrong! You're utterly wrong, I tell you!

KROLL: The day before yesterday you told me yourself that you were twenty-nine—in your thirtieth year, you said.

REBEKKA: Really! Did I say that?

KROLL: Yes, you did. And I calculate from that—

REBEKKA: Stop! You needn't. You might as well know—I'm a year older than I say I say I am.

KROLL (*Smiles incredulously*): Indeed! You surprise me! What motive have you for that?

REBEKKA: After I'd passed twenty-five I felt I was getting a little old for an unmarried woman, so I began to lie about my age.

KROLL: I should have thought an emancipated woman like you would be above such conventions!

REBEKKA: I know it was absurd and idiotic of me—but there you are! It's one of those silly ideas one clings to in spite of oneself.

KROLL: Be that as it may; but that still does not refute my theory; for Dr. West paid a brief visit to Finmark the year before his appointment there.

REBEKKA (*With a vehement outburst*): That's not true!

KROLL: Not true, Miss West?

REBEKKA: No. My mother never mentioned such a thing.

KROLL: She didn't—eh?

REBEKKA: No, never. Nor Dr. West either; he never said a word about it.

KROLL: Mightn't that have been because they both had good reason to wish to skip a year, just as you have done? Perhaps it runs in the family, Miss West.

REBEKKA (*Walks about clenching and wringing*

her hands): What you say is quite impossible. You simply want to trick me into believing it! But it's not true—it can't be true! It can't! It can't—!

KROLL (*Rises*): My dear Miss West—why in Heaven's name are you so upset about it? You quite terrify me! What am I to think —to believe—?

REBEKKA: Nothing! You must think and believe nothing.

KROLL: Then you really must explain this agitation. Why should this matter—this possibility—affect you in this way?

REBEKKA (*Controlling herself*): It is perfectly simple, Professor Kroll. I don't choose to be considered illegitimate.

KROLL: I see! Well—I suppose I shall have to be satisfied with that explanation—at least for the time being. But then, am I to conclude that you still have certain prejudices on this point too?

REBEKKA: Yes, I suppose I have.

KROLL: I don't think this so-called Emancipation of yours goes very deep! You've steeped yourself in a lot of new ideas and new opinions. You've picked up a lot of theories out of books—theories that claim to overthrow certain irrefutable and unassailable principles—principles that form the bulwark of our Society. But this has been no more than a superficial, intellectual exercise, Miss West. It has never really been absorbed into your bloodstream.

REBEKKA (*Thoughtfully*): Perhaps you are right.

KROLL: Just put yourself to the test—you'll see! And if this is true of you, how much truer must it be of Johannes Rosmer. For him all this is sheer, unmitigated madness —it's running blindfold to destruction! Do you suppose a man of his sensitive retiring nature could bear to be an outcast—to be persecuted by all his former friends— exposed to ruthless attacks from all the best elements in the community? Of course not! He's not the man to endure that.

REBEKKA: He must endure it! It's too late for him to turn back now.

KROLL: No, it's not too late—not by any means; it's still possible to hush the matter up—or it can be attributed to a mere temporary aberration, however deplorable. But one thing is essential.

REBEKKA: What might that be?

KROLL: You must persuade him to legalize this relationship, Miss West.

REBEKKA: His relationship with me?

KROLL: Yes. You must insist on his doing that.

REBEKKA: You still cling to the belief that our relationship requires to be legalized, as you call it?

KROLL: I prefer not to examine the situation too closely. But I seem to have noticed that the usual cause for lightly disregarding the so-called conventions is—

REBEKKA: A relationship between man and woman, you mean?

KROLL: Frankly—yes. That is my opinion.

REBEKKA (*Wanders across the room and looks out the window*): I might almost say—I wish you were right, Professor Kroll.

KROLL: What do you mean? You say that very strangely.

REBEKKA: Oh, never mind—don't let's discuss it any more. Listen! Here he comes.

KROLL: So soon! I must go, then.

REBEKKA (*Goes towards him*): No—please stay. There's something I want you to hear.

KROLL: Not just now. I don't think I could bear to see him.

REBEKKA: Please—I beg you! You'll regret it later, if you don't. It's the last time I shall ever ask anything of you.

KROLL (*Looks at her in surprise and puts down his hat*): Very well, Miss West—if you insist.

(*A short silence. Then* JOHANNES ROSMER *enters from the hall.*)

ROSMER (*Sees the Professor and stops in the doorway*): What! You here!

REBEKKA: He would have preferred not to meet you, dearest.

KROLL (*Involuntarily*): "Dearest!"

REBEKKA: Yes, Professor; Rosmer and I sometimes call each other "dearest." That's another result of our relationship.

KROLL: Was this what you wanted me to hear?

REBEKKA: That—and a good deal more.

ROSMER (*Comes forward*): What is the purpose of this visit?

KROLL: I wanted to make one last effort to stop you—to win you back.

ROSMER (*Points to the newspaper*): After what's printed there?

KROLL: I did not write it.

ROSMER: Did you take any steps to prevent it?

KROLL: I should not have felt justified in doing that. It was not in my power, in any case.

REBEKKA (*Tears the paper into shreds, crushes up the pieces and throws them behind the stove*): There! Now it's out of sight; let it be out of mind, too. There'll be no more of that sort of thing, Rosmer.

KROLL: If you use your influence, you can make sure of that!

REBEKKA: Come and sit down, Rosmer. Let's all sit down. I'm going to tell you everything.

ROSMER (*Seats himself mechanically*): What has come over you, Rebekka? Why this peculiar calm? What is it?

REBEKKA: It's the calm of decision. (*Seats herself*) Sit down—you too, Professor. (KROLL *seats himself.*)

ROSMER: Decision? What decision?

REBEKKA: I've come to a decision, Rosmer. I'm going to give you back what to you makes life worth living: your confidence of innocence.

ROSMER: What are you talking about!

REBEKKA: Just listen to me—then you'll know.

ROSMER: Well?

REBEKKA: When I first came here from Finmark—with Dr. West—I felt as if a great, new, wonderful world was opening up before me. Doctor West had taught me many things—in fact, all the scattered knowledge I had of life in those days, I'd learned from him. (*With a struggle and in a scarcely audible voice*) And then—

KROLL: And then?

ROSMER: But, Rebekka—I already know all this.

REBEKKA (*Mastering herself*): Yes, of course; I suppose you do.

KROLL (*Looks hard at her*): Perhaps I had better go.

REBEKKA: No, stay where you are, Professor. (*To* ROSMER) So, you see—I wanted to be a part of this new world; I wanted to belong to it—to share in all these new ideas. One day Professor Kroll was telling me of the great influence Ulrik Brendel had over you, when you were still a boy; I suddenly thought it might be possible for me to carry on his work.

ROSMER: You came here with a hidden purpose—?

REBEKKA: I wanted us to join hands and work for this new Freedom; we were to be in the very front ranks and march on side by side; forward—always forward. But I soon found there was a gloomy, insurmountable barrier standing in your way.

ROSMER: Barrier? What barrier?

REBEKKA: I knew there could be no freedom for you unless you could break loose—get out into the clear bright sunshine. I saw you pining away here; defeated—stultified by your disastrous marriage.

ROSMER: You've never before spoken of my marriage in such terms.

REBEKKA: No—I did not dare; I didn't want to frighten you.

KROLL (*Nods to* ROSMER): Do you hear that?

REBEKKA (*Goes on*): I could see where your salvation lay—your only salvation. And so I set to work.

ROSMER: Set to work? How?

KROLL: Do you mean by that—?

REBEKKA: Yes, Rosmer—(*Rises*) No! Stay where you are! You too, Professor Kroll. Now you must know the truth. It wasn't you, Rosmer. You are entirely innocent. It was *I* who worked on Beata and deliberately lured her into madness.

ROSMER (*Springs up*): Rebekka!

KROLL (*Rises from sofa*): —into madness!

REBEKKA: Yes, the madness that led her to the mill-race. That is the truth. Now you know all about it.

ROSMER (*As if stunned*): I don't understand— What is it she's saying? I don't understand a word—!

KROLL: But I'm beginning to.

ROSMER: But what did you do? What could you possibly have said to her? There was nothing to tell—absolutely nothing!

REBEKKA: She was given to understand that you were gradually working yourself free from all your former beliefs and prejudices.

ROSMER: Yes, but that was not true at the time.

REBEKKA: I knew it soon would be.

KROLL (*Nods to* ROSMER): Aha!

ROSMER: Well? And what else? I must know everything.

REBEKKA: Shortly after that—I begged and implored her to let me go away from Rosmersholm.

ROSMER: What made you want to go—then?

REBEKKA: I didn't want to. I wanted to stay here. But I led her to believe it would be wisest for me to go—for all our sakes—before it was too late. I hinted that if I were to remain here, something—anything—might happen.

ROSMER: You actually did all this!

REBEKKA: Yes, Rosmer.

ROSMER: So that is what you meant by "setting to work"!

REBEKKA (*In a broken voice*): That's what I meant—yes.

ROSMER (*After a pause*): Have you confessed everything now, Rebekka?

REBEKKA: Yes.

KROLL: No, not quite.

REBEKKA (*Looks at him in fear*): What more could there be?

KROLL: Didn't you finally persuade Beata that it was necessary—not merely that it would be wisest—but that it was definitely necessary for you to go away as soon as possible—for yours and Rosmer's sake? Well? Didn't you?

REBEKKA (*Low and indistinctly*): I may have—Yes, perhaps.

ROSMER (*Sinks into armchair by window*): And she was deceived by all these lies! Poor, wretched, bewildered little thing—she actually believed them; firmly believed them! (*Looks up at* REBEKKA) Oh! Why didn't she come to me! But she didn't—

she never said a word. You persuaded her not to, didn't you, Rebekka? I see it in your face.

REBEKKA: She had become obsessed by the fact that she was childless—and never could have children; because of that she felt she had no right here. She was convinced it was her duty to efface herself—her duty to you, I mean.

ROSMER: And you did nothing to dissuade her from that thought?

REBEKKA: No.

KROLL: Perhaps you confirmed her in it? Answer me! Didn't you?

REBEKKA: I dare say that's how she understood it.

ROSMER: She always gave way to you in everything; you dominated her completely. And then—she *did* efface herself! (*Springs up*) How could you play this horrible game, Rebekka?

REBEKKA: I had to choose between your life and hers.

KROLL (*Severely and impressively*): What right had you to make such a choice!

REBEKKA (*Vehemently*): You seem to think I acted with shrewd deliberation—that I was cold and calm about it all; but I was a very different person then. And, anyway—most people's minds are divided, it seems to me. I wanted Beata out of the way—somehow; but at the same time it never occurred to me that the thing would really happen. A voice inside me kept crying out "Stop! No further!"—but I couldn't resist the impulse to go on. And I went on—step by step—in spite of myself. I thought: a little further—just a little further; a tiny step more—and then another; I couldn't stop! And suddenly—there it was! That's the way these things happen, you see. (*A short silence.*)

ROSMER (*To* REBEKKA): What will become of you now? After this?

REBEKKA: I don't know. It doesn't greatly matter.

KROLL: Not a single word of remorse! I dare say you feel none?

REBEKKA (*Coldly putting aside his question*):

You must excuse me, Professor Kroll—that concerns no one but myself. I shall deal with that in my own way.

KROLL (*To* ROSMER): So this is the woman you've been sharing your life with—in the closest intimacy! (*Looks round at the portraits*) I wonder what all these good souls would say, if they could see us now!

ROSMER: Are you going back to town?

KROLL (*Takes up his hat*): Yes. The sooner, the better.

ROSMER (*Does the same*): Then I'll go with you.

KROLL: You will! There—you see! I was sure we hadn't really lost you.

ROSMER: Come, Kroll! Let us go. (*Both go out through the hall without looking at* RE-BEKKA.)

(*After a moment* REBEKKA *goes cautiously to the window and looks out through the flowers.*)

REBEKKA (*Speaks to herself under her breath*): And still he won't venture over the bridge—he's taking the upper-road again. He never will cross by the mill-race. Never. (*Leaves the window*) Ah, well! (*Goes and pulls bell-rope—a moment after,* MRS. HELSETH *enters.*)

MRS. HELSETH: Yes, Miss?

REBEKKA: Mrs. Helseth, would you be so kind as to have my trunk brought down from the attic?

MRS. HELSETH: Your trunk, Miss?

REBEKKA: Yes, you know, the brown sealskin trunk.

MRS. HELSETH: I know the one, Miss. Are you going on a journey?

REBEKKA: Yes, Mrs. Helseth—I'm going on a journey.

MRS. HELSETH: You mean—at once?

REBEKKA: As soon as I've packed.

MRS. HELSETH: Well—I must say! You'll be back soon, won't you, Miss?

REBEKKA: I'm never coming back, Mrs. Helseth.

MRS. HELSETH: *Never*, Miss! But how shall we manage at Rosmersholm without you? And just when the poor master was beginning to be happy and comfortable, too!

REBEKKA: I had a bad fright today, Mrs. Helseth.

MRS. HELSETH: Good gracious, Miss! How?

REBEKKA: I thought I caught a glimpse of the white horses.

MRS. HELSETH: The white horses! In broad daylight!

REBEKKA: I expect they're around both day and night—the white horses of Rosmersholm. (*With a change of tone*) And now—would you see to the trunk, Mrs. Helseth?

MRS. HELSETH: Yes, of course, Miss; the trunk.

(*They both go out by the door right.*)

CURTAIN

ACT IV

SCENE: *The sitting-room at Rosmersholm. Late evening. A lighted lamp, with a lampshade, on the table.* REBEKKA WEST *stands by the table, packing some small articles in a handbag. Her cloak, hat and the white crocheted shawl are hanging over the back of the sofa.*

MRS. HELSETH *enters from the door right.*

MRS. HELSETH (*Speaks in a low voice and appears ill at ease*): All your things are down now, Miss. They're in the kitchen hallway.

REBEKKA: Thank you. You've ordered the carriage?

MRS. HELSETH. Yes. What time will you want it, Miss? The coachman wants to know.

REBEKKA: About eleven o'clock, I should think. The steamer sails at midnight.

MRS. HELSETH (*Hesitates a little*): But what about Mr. Rosmer? Supposing he's not back by then?

REBEKKA: I'll have to leave all the same. If I don't see him, say I'll write to him—a long letter, tell him.

MRS. HELSETH: Letters may be all very well—
But, poor Miss West— Don't you think
you should try and have another talk with
him?

REBEKKA: Perhaps. And yet—perhaps I'd
better not.

MRS. HELSETH: To think I should live to see
this! I certainly never thought a thing like
this would happen!

REBEKKA: What *did* you think then, Mrs.
Helseth?

MRS. HELSETH: I thought Pastor Rosmer
would be more dependable.

REBEKKA: Dependable?

MRS. HELSETH: That's what I said, Miss.

REBEKKA: But, my dear Mrs. Helseth, what
do you mean by that?

MRS. HELSETH: I mean what's right and proper, Miss. He shouldn't be allowed to get
out of it like this.

REBEKKA (*Looks at her*): Listen to me, Mrs.
Helseth—I want you to be quite honest
with me; why do you think I am going
away?

MRS. HELSETH: I suppose it can't be helped,
Miss. But it's not right of Pastor Rosmer
all the same. There was some excuse for
Mortensgaard; her husband was still alive,
you see—so they couldn't marry, however
much they wanted to. But in Pastor
Rosmer's case—!

REBEKKA (*With a faint smile*): Did you actually believe such a thing of Pastor Rosmer
and me?

MRS. HELSETH: No, never, Miss! That is, I
mean—not until today.

REBEKKA: And what made you change your
mind?

MRS. HELSETH: I'm told the papers are saying
dreadful things about the Pastor—

REBEKKA: Aha!

MRS. HELSETH: I wouldn't put anything past
a man who would take up Mortensgaard's
religion!

REBEKKA: I see. But what about me? What
have you to say of me?

MRS. HELSETH: Lord bless me, Miss—I can't
think you're to blame. We're all of us
human—and it's not easy for a single
woman to be always on her guard.

REBEKKA: That is very true, Mrs. Helseth—
We are all of us human—Did you hear
something?

MRS. HELSETH (*In a low voice*): I thought—I
do believe he's coming, Miss.

REBEKKA (*Starts*): In that case—? (*Resolutely*) Well—so be it.
(ROSMER *enters from hall.*)

ROSMER (*Sees handbag, etc.—turns to* RE-
BEKKA *and asks*): What does this mean?

REBEKKA: I am going.

ROSMER: At once?

REBEKKA Yes. (*To* MRS. HELSETH) Eleven
o'clock, then.

MRS. HELSETH: Very well, Miss. (*Goes out by
the door right.*)

ROSMER (*After a short pause*): Where are you
going, Rebekka?

REBEKKA: North; by the steamer.

ROSMER: Why North?

REBEKKA: That's where I came from.

ROSMER: What do you plan to do?

REBEKKA: I don't know. I just want to put
an end to the whole business.

ROSMER: Put an end to it?

REBEKKA: Rosmersholm has crushed me.

ROSMER (*His attention aroused*): How can you
say that?

REBEKKA: Crushed me utterly—completely.
When I came here I had a healthy, fearless
spirit—but I've had to bow before an alien
law. I no longer have the courage to face
anything.

ROSMER: Why not? What law do you mean?

REBEKKA: Don't let's talk about it, Rosmer.
What happened between you and Kroll?

ROSMER: We have made peace.

REBEKKA: I see. So that is how it ended.

ROSMER: All our old friends were gathered
at his house. They convinced me that the
kind of work I had in mind was not for
me. And anyway—the rehabilitation of
mankind—! How hopeless it all seems! I
shall give up all thought of that.

REBEKKA: Perhaps it's for the best.

ROSMER: Have you come to think that too?

REBEKKA: These past few days I've come to
think it; yes.

ROSMER: You're lying.

REBEKKA: Lying—!

ROSMER: Yes, you're lying. You never really had faith in me. You never really believed I would succeed.

REBEKKA: I believed we might succeed together.

ROSMER: That's not true, either. You believed yourself destined for great things; you believed you could use me as an instrument —as a means to serve your ends. That's what you believed.

REBEKKA: Listen to me, Rosmer—

ROSMER (*Seats himself listlessly on the sofa*): Oh, what is the use? I know the truth now. I've been nothing but clay in your hands.

REBEKKA: You *must* listen to me, Rosmer. We must talk this thing through. It'll be the last time we'll ever talk together. (*Sits in chair close to sofa*) I was going to write you all about it—once I'd got away—but perhaps it's best that I should tell you now.

ROSMER: Have you still more to confess?

REBEKKA: Yes. The most vital thing of all.

ROSMER: Vital—?

REBEKKA: Something you've never suspected for a moment—and yet it's the key to all the rest.

ROSMER (*Shakes his head*): I don't understand.

REBEKKA: It is true that I did everything to worm my way in here—I had a feeling it would be to my advantage whichever way things went.

ROSMER: And you succeeded in your purpose.

REBEKKA: In those days I believe I could have succeeded in absolutely anything—my spirit was still free and fearless then. I had no scruples; no personal ties stood in my way. Then I began to be possessed by the thing that was to crush me—the thing that broke my spirit and warped my life forever.

ROSMER: Why can't you speak plainly?

REBEKKA: I became possessed by a wild, uncontrollable passion, Rosmer—

ROSMER: Passion? You—! For what? For whom?

REBEKKA: For you.

ROSMER (*Tries to spring up*): What—?

REBEKKA: (*Stops him*): No—stay where you are! Let me go on.

ROSMER: You mean to tell me you loved me —in that way?

REBEKKA: At that time I called it love. Yes, I thought it was love, then. But now I know it wasn't. It was what I just said: a a wild, uncontrollable passion.

ROSMER (*With difficulty*): Can this be true, Rebekka? Is it possible that you're really speaking of *yourself?*

REBEKKA: It's hard for you to believe it of me, isn't it?

ROSMER: So this was the cause—this was the reason—that you "set to work" as you call it?

REBEKKA: It swept over me like a storm at sea—like one of those winter-storms we have up in the North. It seizes hold of you and carries you off with it—wherever it will. Resistance is impossible.

ROSMER: And you let this storm carry poor Beata to her death.

REBEKKA: Yes. It was a death-struggle between us at that time, you see.

ROSMER: You were certainly the strongest; stronger than Beata and me together.

REBEKKA: I knew you well enough to realize that I had no hope of reaching you until you were a free man—not only in spirit, but in fact.

ROSMER: But I don't understand you, Rebekka. You—your whole conduct—is incomprehensible to me. I am free now— both in spirit and in fact. You have reached the very goal you aimed at from the first. And yet—in spite of that—

REBEKKA: I have never been further from my goal than I am now.

ROSMER: And yet in spite of that, I say— yesterday when I asked you, begged you, to be my wife—you cried out, as if in terror, that that could never be!

REBEKKA: I cried out in despair, Rosmer.

ROSMER: But why?

REBEKKA: Because Rosmersholm has robbed me of my strength. My spirit that was once so fearless has become warped and crippled here—as though its wings had been clipped. I no longer have any daring,

Rosmer—I've lost the power of action.

ROSMER: How did this happen to you?

REBEKKA: Through living with you.

ROSMER: But how? How?

REBEKKA: When I found myself alone with you—and you began to be yourself again—

ROSMER: Yes, yes?

REBEKKA: —for you were never quite yourself while Beata was alive—

ROSMER: No—I'm afraid that's true.

REBEKKA: Then I was able to live here with you in peace, in solitude; you confided your thoughts to me without reserve; I became aware of your slightest mood— of all the tenderness and delicacy of your nature; and gradually—little by little—a great change came over me. At first it was almost imperceptible—but it grew and grew—until at last it dominated my whole being.

ROSMER: What *is* all this, Rebekka!

REBEKKA: And all that other thing—that evil, sensual thing—seemed to fade into the distance. All violent passion subsided —conquered by silence. My mind was filled with peace. My spirit became still; it was like the stillness on one of our northern birdcliffs under the midnight sun.

ROSMER: Tell me more about this, Rebekka. Everything you know about it—tell me!

REBEKKA: There's not much more to tell. Only this: I knew then that love had come to me; real love—love that asks nothing for itself—that is content with life together —just as we have known it.

ROSMER: If I'd only had an inkling of all this—!

REBEKKA: It's perhaps best as it is. Yesterday when you asked me to be your wife—I cried out with joy—

ROSMER: Yes, you did, didn't you, Rebekka? It sounded so to me.

REBEKKA: For a moment—yes! For a moment I forgot myself! It was my former fearless spirit trying to assert itself—struggling for freedom. But it no longer has any power—no power to endure.

ROSMER: How do you account for this change in you?

REBEKKA: My will has become infected by the Rosmer view on life—your view on life at any rate.

ROSMER: Infected?

REBEKKA: Yes! It has grown weak and sickly. It's become a slave to laws that it despised before. Living with you, Rosmer, has exalted and purified my spirit—

ROSMER: How I wish I could believe that, Rebekka—!

REBEKKA: You *can* believe it. The Rosmer view on life exalts—but—but—!

ROSMER: Well?

REBEKKA: —it kills happiness!

ROSMER: You really think that?

REBEKKA: I know it does, for me.

ROSMER: How can you be so sure? If I were to ask you again, now, Rebekka—if I were to beg you—to entreat you—

REBEKKA: My dearest—you must never speak of this again! There's something—in my past—that makes it quite impossible!

ROSMER: Something beyond what you've already told me?

REBEKKA: Yes. It has to do with something else—something quite different.

ROSMER: I've sometimes thought—isn't it strange, Rebekka? — I've sometimes thought I knew.

REBEKKA: And yet—? In spite of that—?

ROSMER: I never really believed it. I used to speculate on it sometimes—play with it— in my thoughts—

REBEKKA: I'll tell you about it—if you want me to—

ROSMER: No—not a word! Whatever it may be—I can forget it.

REBEKKA: But I can't, you see.

ROSMER: Rebekka—!

REBEKKA: That's what's so dreadful, Rosmer! Happiness is here; I've only to stretch out my hand to seize it. But now I've changed, and this—thing in my past, stands in the way.

ROSMER: Your past is dead, Rebekka. It can no longer touch you—it no longer has any claim on you, as you are now.

REBEKKA: You know those are just phrases! What about innocence? Can I ever find that again?

ROSMER (*Wearily*): Innocence—!

REBEKKA: Innocence, yes. Happiness and joy

cannot exist without it—you said that yourself, Rosmer. That was the truth you wanted to instill in those noble men you dreamed of—

ROSMER: Don't remind me of that, Rebekka. It was an immature dream, a nebulous fancy—I no longer believe in it myself. Nobility cannot be imposed upon us from without.

REBEKKA (*Quietly*): Not even by love, Rosmer? Quiet, unselfish love?

ROSMER (*Thoughtfully*): Yes—what a great power that could be! How glorious—if only it existed! But does it? If I were only sure—if I could only convince myself of that.

REBEKKA: You don't believe me, Rosmer?

ROSMER: How can I believe you fully—when I think of all these incredible things you've concealed from me for years? And now —this new approach—how do I know what secret purpose lies behind it? Is there something you wish to gain by it? Be honest with me! You know I'll do anything in my power to give you what you want.

REBEKKA (*Wringing her hands*): Oh these doubts—these morbid doubts! Rosmer, Rosmer!

ROSMER: I know! But what can I do? I'll never be able to get rid of them. How can I ever be quite certain of your love?

REBEKKA: But you must know in your heart how truly changed I am—and that this change has come to me through you— because of you!

ROSMER: I no longer believe in my power to change others, Rebekka. I no longer believe in myself in any way. I have no faith in myself, and I have no faith in you.

REBEKKA (*Looks at him sadly*): How will you be able to endure life, Rosmer?

ROSMER: I don't know. I can't imagine how. I don't think I will be able to endure it. I can think of nothing in this world worth living for.

REBEKKA: Still—life renews itself continually. Let's cling to it, Rosmer. We shall leave it soon enough.

ROSMER (*Jumps up restlessly*): Then give me back my faith. My faith in your love, Rebekka! My faith in you! Give me proof! I must have proof!

REBEKKA: Proof! How can I give you proof?

ROSMER: You must! I can't endure this desolation—this dreadful emptiness—this —this—

(*A loud knock at the hall door.*)

REBEKKA (*Starts from her chair*): What was that?

(*The door opens.* ULRIK BRENDEL *enters. He wears a dress shirt, a black coat and a good pair of high shoes, with his trousers tucked into them. Otherwise he is dressed as in the first act. He looks excited.*)

ROSMER: Oh—it's you, Mr. Brendel!

BRENDEL: Johannes, my boy—hail and fare-well!

ROSMER: Where are you going so late at night?

BRENDEL: Downhill.

ROSMER: How do you mean?

BRENDEL: I am going home, beloved pupil. I am homesick for the great Nothingness.

ROSMER: Something has happened to you, Mr. Brendel; what is it?

BRENDEL: So, you notice the change in me, eh? I'm not surprised! When last I entered these halls, I was a prosperous man—full of self-confidence—

ROSMER: I don't quite understand—

BRENDEL: But tonight you see me a deposed monarch, squatting on the ash-heap that was once my palace.

ROSMER: If there's anything I can do to help you—

BRENDEL: You have managed to retain your good child-like heart, Johannes. Could you oblige me with a loan?

ROSMER: Of course! Gladly.

BRENDEL: Could you spare me an ideal or two?

ROSMER: What did you say?

BRENDEL: A couple of cast-off ideals? You'd be doing a good deed, I assure you. For I'm broke, my boy. Cleaned out. Stripped.

REBEKKA: Didn't you give your lecture, Mr. Brendel?

BRENDEL: No, entrancing lady. Only think! Just as I stood there ready to empty my horn of plenty, I made the painful discovery that I was bankrupt.

REBEKKA: But what about all those unwritten works of yours?

BRENDEL: I've sat for twenty-five years like a miser on his money-bags. And yesterday—when I went to open them, intending to pour forth the treasure—I found there was none! The Teeth of Time had ground it into dust. It all amounted to *nichts* and nothing!

ROSMER: Are you quite sure of that?

BRENDEL: There is no room for doubt, my boy. The President convinced me.

ROSMER: The President?

BRENDEL: Well—his Excellency, then. *Ganz nach Belieben.*

ROSMER: But whom do you mean?

BRENDEL: Peder Mortensgaard, of course.

ROSMER: What!

BRENDEL (*Mysteriously*): Hush! Peder Mortensgaard is Lord and Master of the Future. Never have I stood in a more august presence. Peder Mortensgaard has divine power; he is omnipotent; he can do anything he wills!

ROSMER: You don't really believe that!

BRENDEL: Yes, my boy! For Peder Mortensgaard never *wills* more than he can do. Peder Mortensgaard is capable of living without ideals. And that, you see, is the secret of action and success. It is the sum of worldly wisdom. *Basta!*

ROSMER (*In a low voice*): I understand now why you're leaving poorer than you came.

BRENDEL: *Bien!* So just take a *Beispiel* from your old teacher. Throw out everything he tried to impress upon your mind. Don't build your house on shifting sand. And be wary—be very sure—before you build too many hopes on this charming creature who fills your life wih sweetness.

REBEKKA: Is that meant for me?

BRENDEL: Yes, my fascinating mermaid.

REBEKKA: Why shouldn't he build hopes on me?

BRENDEL (*Comes a step nearer*): It seems my former pupil has chosen to fight for a great cause.

REBEKKA: Well—?

BRENDEL: His Victory is certain, but—remember this—on one irrevocable condition.

REBEKKA: What condition?

BRENDEL (*Taking her gently by the wrist*): That the woman who loves him, will gladly go out into the kitchen and hack off her sweet, rosy, little finger—here—right at the middle joint. Item: that the aforesaid loving woman will—with equal gladness—chop off her incomparable, exquisite, left ear. (*Lets her go, and turns to* ROSMER) Farewell, my victorious Johannes.

ROSMER: Are you going now? In the dark? In the middle of the night?

BRENDEL: The dark is best. Peace be with you. (*He goes. There is a short silence in the room.*)

REBEKKA (*Breathes heavily*): It's so close in here—it's stifling! (*Goes to the window, opens it, and remains standing by it.*)

ROSMER (*Sits down in arm-chair by stove*): There's nothing else to do, Rebekka—I see that now. You'll have to go away.

REBEKKA: Yes, I see no choice.

ROSMER: Let's make the most of these last moments. Come over here and sit with me.

REBEKKA (*Goes and sits on the sofa*): What have you to say to me, Rosmer?

ROSMER: First I want to tell you this; you needn't have any anxiety about your future.

REBEKKA (*Smiles*): Ha—my future!

ROSMER: I took care of that long ago. Whatever happens, you will be looked after.

REBEKKA: You thought of that too—my dearest!

ROSMER: I should think you'd have known that.

REBEKKA: It's a long time since I've concerned myself with things of that sort.

ROSMER: I suppose you thought things could never change between us.

REBEKKA: Yes, I did.

ROSMER: So did I. But if I were to go—

REBEKKA: You will live longer than I will, Rosmer—

ROSMER: This wretched life of mine! At least I have the power to end it when I choose.

REBEKKA: What do you mean? You'd never think of—?

ROSMER: Would that be so strange? I've allowed myself to be defeated—miserably, ignominiously defeated. I turned my back on the work I had to do; I surrendered

—gave up the fight before it had actually begun!

REBEKKA: You must take it up again, Rosmer! You'll win—you'll see! You have the power to change men's spirits; to fill their minds with hope and aspiration—to bring nobility into their lives. Try! Don't give up the fight!

ROSMER: I no longer have faith, Rebekka!

REBEKKA: But you've already proved your power. You've changed my spirit. As long as I live I can never go back to being what I was.

ROSMER: If I could only believe that.

REBEKKA (*Pressing her hands together*): Oh, Rosmer! Do you know of nothing—nothing, that could make you believe that?

ROSMER (*Starts as if in fear*) Don't ask me that, Rebekka! This must go no further. Don't say another word!

REBEKKA: But it must go further! Tell me! Do you know of anything that could remove this doubt? I can think of nothing.

ROSMER: It's best that you shouldn't—best for us both.

REBEKKA: No! I won't be put off with that. Do you know of anything that would absolve me in your eyes? If you do—I have the right to know it.

ROSMER (*As if impelled against his will to speak*): Very well—let's see. You say you're filled with a great love—a pure, transcendent love. That through me your spirit has been changed—your life transformed. Is this really true, Rebekka? You're sure of that? Shall we put it to the test?

REBEKKA: I am ready to do that.

ROSMER: At any time?

REBEKKA: Now, if you like. The sooner the better.

ROSMER: Then would you be willing, Rebekka—now—this evening—for my sake —to— (*Breaks off*) Oh—no, no!

REBEKKA: Yes, Rosmer—yes! Tell me, and you'll see!

ROSMER: Have you the courage to—are you willing to—gladly, as Ulrik Brendel said —for my sake, now tonight—gladly—to go the same way Beata went?

REBEKKA (*Rises slowly from the sofa; almost voiceless*): Rosmer!

ROSMER: That question will go on haunting me after you're gone; I shan't be able to get away from it. Over and over again I shall come back to it. I can picture it so clearly: You're standing out on the bridge, right in the very center. Now you're leaning far out over the railing, as though hypnotized by the rushing stream below. But then—you turn away. You dare not do—what she did.

REBEKKA: And supposing I *did* dare? Dared to do it—gladly? What then?

ROSMER: I should *have* to believe you then. My faith would be restored to me; faith in my vision of life—faith in my power to make men see that vision.

REBEKKA (*Takes up her shawl slowly, and puts it over her head; says with composure*): You shall have your faith again.

ROSMER: Have you the courage, have you the will—to do this, Rebekka?

REBEKKA: You'll know that tomorrow—or later—when they find my body.

ROSMER (*Puts his hand to his forehead*): There's a ghastly fascination about this—

REBEKKA: For I don't want to be left down there—any longer than necessary. You must see that they find me.

ROSMER (*Springs up*): This is sheer madness! Go—or stay, if you will! I'll believe anything you tell me—just as I always have.

REBEKKA: These are just words, Rosmer! This time, there can be no escape in cowardice. After today—how can you ever believe in me again?

ROSMER: But I don't want to see you fail, Rebekka.

REBEKKA: I shall not fail.

ROSMER: You won't be able to help it. You'd never have the courage Beata had.

REBEKKA: Don't you think so?

ROSMER: No—never. You're not like Beata. You're not under the spell of madness.

REBEKKA: No. But I've fallen under another spell—the spell of Rosmersholm; and now I know that if I've sinned, then I must pay the penalty.

ROSMER (*Looks at her fixedly*): Is that what you've come to believe, Rebekka?

REBEKKA: Yes.

ROSMER (*With resolution*): Well, I still believe that man is a free spirit. There is no

judge above us; we must each judge ourselves.

REBEKKA (*Misunderstanding him*): That's
true, too. My going will save what's best
in you.

ROSMER: There's nothing left in me to save.

REBEKKA: Oh, yes there is! But as for me—I
should be nothing but a kind of sea-troll,
clinging to the ship on which you must
sail forward—pulling it back. I must go
overboard. Why should I stay on in this
world dragging out a stunted life? Pondering and brooding over a happiness that
my past forbids me to enjoy? No—I must
get out of the game.

ROSMER: If you go—then I go with you.

REBEKKA (*Smiles almost imperceptibly, looks
at him, and says more softly*): Yes, you
come too—you shall be witness—

ROSMER: I will go with you, I say.

REBEKKA: As far as the bridge, yes. You
know you never dare set foot on it.

ROSMER: You've noticed that?

REBEKKA (*Sadly and brokenly*): Yes; that's
how I knew my love was hopeless.

ROSMER: I lay my hand upon your head,
Rebekka—and take you in marriage as
my true wife.

REBEKKA (*Takes both his hands, and bows her
head towards his breast*): Thank you,
Rosmer. (*Lets him go*) Now I can go—
gladly!

ROSMER: Man and wife should go together.

REBEKKA: Only as far as the bridge, Rosmer.

ROSMER: Out onto the bridge too; I have the
courage now. However far you go—I shall
go with you.

REBEKKA: Are you quite certain, Rosmer?
Is this the best way for you?

ROSMER: I'm quite certain it's the only way.

REBEKKA: What if you were deceiving yourself? Supposing this were only a delusion
— One of those White Horses that prey
on Rosmersholm?

ROSMER: It may be so. The White Horses!
We Rosmers can never escape them!

REBEKKA: Then stay, Rosmer!

ROSMER: The husband belongs with his wife,
as the wife with her husband.

REBEKKA: Tell me this first: Is it you who go
with me? Or is it I who go with you?

ROSMER: We shall never know the answer
to that question, Rebekka.

REBEKKA: I should so like to know—

ROSMER: We go together, Rebekka. I with
you, and you with me.

REBEKKA: Yes—I believe that's true—

ROSMER: For now we two are *one*.

REBEKKA: Yes, now we are *one*. Come! Let
us go—gladly! (*They go out hand in hand
through the hall, and are seen to turn to
the left. The door remains open. The room
stands empty for a little while. Then the
door to the right is opened by* MRS.
HELSETH.)

MRS. HELSETH: Miss West—the carriage is—
(*Looks around*) No one here? They must
have gone out together—at this time of
night too! (*Goes out into hall, looks round,
and comes in again*) They're not out on
the bench. Ah, well—(*Goes to the window
and looks out*) Lord bless me! What's that
white thing out there—! It's them—out on
the bridge, and in each other's arms!
(*Shrieks aloud*) Ah! Over the railing—both
of them—down into the mill-race! Help!
Help! (*Her knees tremble; she leans on
the chair-back, shaking all over; she can
scarcely get the words out*) No! No one
can help them now. It's the dead wife—
the dead wife has taken them.

CURTAIN

Part Two

COMEDY

COMEDY

It may be true in life that what appears comic to one man will seem tragic to the next. But in the drama, no such confusion is possible; a comedy always announces itself, and everybody knows it for what it is. If a play makes you laugh, and if it has a happy ending, it is called a comedy. Define laughter to include the superior smile and the less pleasant smirk, as well as the hearty guffaw; recognize the ambiguity of "happy"; and the definition has some empiric validity. For we do laugh at most comedies, and most comedies do have happy endings—the hero does not die but gets what he appears to want, the girl. The definition also tells us that plays are classified as comedies in part by how the audience reacts to them and in part by how the conflict in them is resolved.

A comedy is readily distinguished by its plot. True, the stories of comedies are as infinite and various as the activities of men and women, for the subjects of comedies are the all-too-common follies of men. But comic plots are, generally speaking, much the same in their basic pattern; they tend to be circular or concentric, often ending up where they began, or turning back on themselves. Further, there is usually minimal character exposition in comedy, for the yesterdays of characters in comedies need concern us very little. In effect, these *personae* wear masks that reveal all we need to know about them—not unlike the actors in Greek plays who wore actual masks that established their characters. The masks for the characters in comedies, as Aristotle noted, revealed their deformities without distorting them so much as to cause the spectator pain. There must be in comedy, as Bergson has suggested, an anesthesia of the heart; we must be able to maintain sufficient distance from the character to be able to laugh at him without injuring ourselves.

The comic vision of the dramatist, like the sense of humor, develops out of the perspective of maturity; comedy is, after all, an adult and sophisticated thing. Like the man with a sense of humor, the dramatist with the comic vision looks into the human situation and decides that all is not hopeless; though apparently hopelessly entangled in frustrations resulting from his own follies and errors, man is not in reality doomed to defeat. By emphasizing the wonder and the possibility of fruitful *being*, comedies free men from the pain of brooding about *becoming*, a burden that so frequently makes the human condition seem intolerable. Unlike tragedy, which places the reader at the heart of the human situation, comedy removes him to a distance from which he can look at the absurdities of characters who often turn out to be very like himself. The experience may chasten him, but it does not defeat him.

Comedy may not plumb the same depths that tragedy does; nevertheless, the comic vision is at least the equal of pity and terror as the liberator of souls. For comedy on the stage, like the sense of humor in life, helps us to see that life is livable; it suggests a road to survival for the group and, even more significantly, for the individuals that constitute the group. Paradoxically, as the socializing, indeed the civilizing form of literature, comedy exalts the group in order to preserve the individual.

It is this concept of comedy as a cleansing agent, as a mode of drama that is primarily curative in nature, that is emphasized in the essays that follow. First, the famous statement by George Meredith that the purpose of comedy is to provoke "thoughtful laughter" establishes this theme. Meredith's playful tribute to the Comic Spirit, which he sees hovering over man and keeping a friendly but critical eye on his affairs, is elaborated in the next essay, by Louis Kronenberger. Mr. Kronenberger explains in fuller detail that comedy is not only a kind of entertainment found in the theater, but is also a way of surveying life, a means by which man comes to grip with his own imperfections, and finds them bearable. He points out that, inevitably, the subject matter of comedy is the individual's role as part of a group; and he shows how comedy chastens and corrects man when he strays from the accepted mores of his group.

The forms comedy may take is Northrup Frye's subject. He too finds in comedy "the integration of society," and in laughter a kind of "deliverance." He shows how these features of comedy emerge through irony, satire, the comedy of manners, and other comic modes.

The final statement is that of the philosopher James K. Feibleman, who prepares for a contrast between the aims of comedy and those of tragedy by showing that, paradoxically, the latter lead to contentment with man's lot, while the former are always rooted in dissatisfaction and lead to an awareness of limitations. Mr. Feibleman speaks for all his fellows when he calls comedy "revolutionary," when he cites its ability to "release" man, to chastise him and then return him to his group.

THE COMIC SPIRIT

George Meredith

To touch and kindle the mind through laughter demands more than sprightliness, a most subtle delicacy. That must be a natal gift in the comic poet. The substance he deals with will show him a startling exhibition of the dyer's hand, if he is without it. People are ready to surrender themselves to witty thumps on the back, breast, and sides; all except the head: and it is there that he aims. He must be subtle to penetrate. A corresponding acuteness must exist to welcome him. The necessity for the two conditions will explain how it is that we count him during centuries in the singular number. . . .

The comic poet is in the narrow field, or enclosed square, of the society he depicts; and he addresses the still narrower enclosure of men's intellects, with reference to the operation of the social world upon their characters. He is not concerned with beginnings or endings or surroundings, but with what you are now weaving. To understand his work and value it, you must have a sober liking of your kind, and a sober estimate of our civilized qualities. The aim and business of the comic poet are misunderstood, his meaning is not seized nor his point of view taken, when he is accused of dishonoring our nature and being hostile to sentiment, tending to spitefulness and making an unfair use of laughter. Those who detect irony in comedy do so because they choose to see it in life. Poverty, says the satirist, has nothing harder in itself than that it makes men ridiculous. But poverty is never ridiculous to comic perception until it attempts to make its rags conceal its bareness in a forlorn attempt at decency, or foolishly to rival ostentation. . . .

One excellent test of the civilization of a country, as I have said, I take to be the flourishing of the comic idea and comedy; and the test of true comedy is that it shall awaken thoughtful laughter.

If you believe that our civilization is founded in common sense (and it is the first condition of sanity to believe it), you will, when contemplating men, discern a Spirit overhead; not more heavenly than the light flashed upward from glassy surfaces, but luminous and watchful; never shooting beyond them, nor lagging in the rear, so closely attached to them that it may be taken for a slavish reflex, until its features are studied. It has the sage's brows, and the sunny malice of a faun lurks at the corners of the half-closed lips drawn in an idle wariness of half-tension. That slim feasting smile, shaped like the long-bow, was once a big round satyr's laugh, that flung up the brows like a fortress lifted by gunpowder. The laugh will come again, but it will be of the order of the smile, finely tempered, showing sunlight of the mind, mental richness rather than noisy enormity. Its common aspect is one of unsolicitous observation, as if surveying a full field and having leisure to dart on its chosen morsels, without any fluttering eagerness. Men's future upon earth does not attract it; their honesty and shapeliness in the present does; and whenever they wax out of proportion, overblown, affected, pretentious, bombastical, hypocritical, pedantic, fantastically delicate; whenever it sees them self-deceived or hoodwinked, given to run riot in idolatries, drifting into vanities, congregating in absurdities, planning short-sightedly, plotting dementedly; whenever they are at variance with their professions, and violate the unwritten but perceptible laws binding them in consideration one to another; whenever they offend sound reason, fair justice; are false in humility or mined with conceit, individually, or in the bulk—the Spirit overhead will look humanely malign and cast an oblique light on them, followed by volleys of silvery laughter. That is the Comic Spirit.

SOME PREFATORY WORDS ON COMEDY

Louis Kronenberger

Comedy is not just a happy as opposed to an unhappy ending, but a way of surveying life so that happy endings must prevail. But it is not to be confused, on that account, with optimism, any more than a happy ending is to be confused with happiness. Comedy is much more reasonably associated with pessimism—with at any rate a belief in the smallness that survives as against the greatness that is scarred or destroyed. In mortal affairs it is tragedy, like forgiveness, that seems divine; and comedy, like error, that is human.

One might perhaps begin by talking about comedy in its philosophic sense, as an attitude toward life, rather than as a mere technical aspect of the theater. One might begin, in other words, by speaking of the comedy that unites such writers and writings as Lucian and Aristophanes, the *Decameron* and *Candide*, Congreve and Peacock and Sterne, *Pride and Prejudice* and *Le Bourgeois Gentilhomme*, rather than of the comedy that is the official label for such diverse plays as *Measure for Measure* and *The Man of Mode*, or *All's Well That Ends Well* and *The Importance of Being Earnest*, or *The Misanthrope* and *Private Lives*. For obviously—despite immense differences—the same spirit animates an Aristophanes and a Jane Austen; whereas a vastly different spirit separates *Measure for*

Measure from *The Importance of Being Earnest*. *Measure for Measure*, we feel, is not really comedy; and *The Misanthrope*, again, is something more than comedy. But coarse as Aristophanes can be and genteel as Jane Austen, broadly as Aristophanes can clown and exquisitely as Jane Austen can annihilate, the two have much the same vision of life, much the same eye for its absurdities. They have in full measure the comic point of view, as other writers have the tragic point of view. In the theater, comedy and tragedy are forms that can be used with some purity. Much Restoration comedy was indeed written with some purity. Today, when the theater is debased by the naturalistic drama, when the drama itself is three parts play to seven parts production, when the only comedy that most playwrights try for is standing-room comedy—today very little in the theater really expresses the comic sense of life. Far from probing, it seldom even honestly paints the surface. And the real trouble is not that the contemporary stage aims at artifice, but that it professes to aim at naturalness. It was one of the real virtues of the Restoration stage that it never sought—and never managed—to be "natural." It lied its head off about a good many of the appurtenances of life, but it managed to capture a surprising amount of the thing itself; and even its lies squared with the partial truth that life is a masquerade.

Comedy appeals to the laughter, which is in part at least the malice, in us; for comedy is concerned with human imperfection, with people's failure to measure up either to the world's or to their own conception of excellence. All tragedy is idealistic and says in effect, "The pity of it"—that owing to this fault of circumstance or that flaw of character, a man who is essentially good does evil, a man who is essentially great is toppled from the heights. But all comedy tends to be skeptical and says in effect, "The absurdity of it"—that in spite of his fine talk or noble resolutions, a man is the mere creature of pettiness and vanity and folly. Tragedy is always lamenting the Achilles tendon, the destructive flaw in man; but comedy, in a sense, is always looking for it. Not cheaply, out of malevolence or cynicism; but rather because even at his greatest, man offers some touch of the fatuous and small, just as a murderer, even at his cleverest, usually makes some fatal slip. In tragedy men aspire to more than they can achieve; in comedy, they pretend to more.

The difference, again, between the two is the very question of difference. A great tragic hero—an Oedipus or Lear—strikes us as tremendously far removed from common humanity. But comedy, stripping off the war-paint and the feathers, the college degrees or the military medals, shows how very like at bottom the hero is to everybody else. Tragedy cannot flourish without giving its characters a kind of aura of poetry, or idealism, or doom; comedy scarcely functions till the aura has been dispelled. And as it thrives on a revelation of the true rather than the trumped-up motive, as it is in one way sustained by imposture, so in another it is sustained by incongruity. Here is the celebrated philosopher cursing the universe because he has mislaid a book. Here are all those who, like King Canute, would bid the clock go backward or the waves stand still. Here is not only the cheat, but the victim who but for his own dishonest desires could never be cheated.

Comedy, in brief, is criticism. If through laughing at others we purge ourselves of certain spiteful and ungenerous instincts—as through tragedy we achieve a higher and more publicized catharsis—that is not quite the whole of it. Comedy need not be hostile to idealism; it need only show how far human beings fall short of the ideal. The higher comedy mounts, the airier and more brilliant its forms, the more are we aware of man's capacity for being foolish or self-deluded or complacent; in the very highest comedy, such as the finale of Mozart's *Marriage of Figaro*, we are in a very paradise of self-deceptions and misunderstandings and cross-purposes. At the heart of high comedy there is always a strain of melancholy, as round the edges there is all gaiety and ebullience and glitter; and Schiller was perhaps right in regarding high comedy as the greatest of all literary forms.

Comedy is criticism, then, because it exposes human beings for what they are in contrast to what they profess to be. How much idealism, it asks, shall we find entirely free from self-love? How much beneficence is born of guilt, how much affection is produced by flattery? At its most severe, doubtless, comedy is not just skeptical but cynical; and asks many of the same questions, returning many of the same answers, as that prince—or at any rate duke—of cynics, La Rochefoucauld. "Pride," La Rochefoucauld remarked, "does not wish to owe, and vanity does not wish to pay." Or again: "To establish oneself in the world, one does all one can to seem established there." Of these and many similar maxims, a play or story might easily be written; from each much cold and worldly comedy, or harsh and worldly farce, might be contrived. But comedy need not be so harsh, and seldom is: though it can be harsher still, can be—as in Ben Jonson—gloating and sardonic. But always it is the enemy, not of virtue or idealism, but of hypocrisy and pretense; and what it does in literature is very much, I suppose, what experience does for most of us in life: it knocks the bloom off the peach, the gilt off the gingerbread.

But though the comic spirit is, in Meredith's phrase, "humanely malign," it is also kindly and even companionable, in the sense that it brings men together as fellow-fools and sinners, and is not only criticism but understanding. Comedy is always jarring us with the evidence that we are no better than other people, and always comforting us with the knowledge that most other people are no better than we are. It makes us more critical but it leaves us more tolerant; and to that extent it performs a very notable social function. Its whole character, indeed—quite aside from that point—is rather social than individual.

The social basis rests in the very subject-matter of comedy—in all that has to do with one's life as part of a group; with one's wish to charm or persuade or deceive or dazzle others. Thus no exhibitionist can exist in solitude, no hypocrite or poseur can work without an audience. There are indeed so many social situations that engender comedy that many of them are notably hackneyed. There are all kinds of classic family jokes—the mother-in-law joke pre-eminently; but equally the rich-uncle theme, or the country cousin, or the visiting relative who forgets to leave, or the one that proffers advice, or the one that prophesies disaster. Right in the home there is the precocious brat or the moping adolescent; there are countless varieties of comic servants; and there is finally the question, though it perhaps belongs in a different category, of who heads the family—the husband or the wife.

The idea of husband and wife more likely belongs with the social aspects of sex, with the War Between the Sexes as it is fought out in the drawing room. As a purely sexual conflict, this war would not be social; but by the same token it would not be comedy. The question whether man really makes the decisions—including the decision to marry—or is merely permitted to think he does, is, whatever the answer, thoroughly social in nature. Or there is the business of how men and women perform in society for one another's benefit: being the fearless protector or the clinging vine, the woman who always understands or the man who is never understood. We have social comedy again when we pit one nationality as well as one sex against another, when the American puritan is ensnared by a continental siren, or when the suitor is German and humorless, and the besought one is French and amused. There is still another social aspect when we add a third person to the situation, a mistress as well as a wife, or a lover as well as a husband; or—for the situation need not be illicit, it need only be triangular—when the wife's old beau or the husband's old flame reappears on the scene. Or there is the man who does not know which of two sisters, or two heiresses, or two widows to marry; or the girl which of a half dozen suitors.

Comedy, indeed, must gain admittance into any part of the world—including prisons and sickrooms and funerals—where people are thrown together. Any institution involving hierarchies and rivalries—for example, a university—is a perfect hotbed of it. There will be everybody's relation to the President or the President's wife; or the President's relation to the President's wife; or to his trustees; all the struggles for precedence and the problems of protocol; the progressives on the faculty and the die-hards; the wives who can't help looking dowdy, the wives who suppose they look chic. For obviously any institution, whether a college or a department store, an artist colony or a country club, provides a cross-section of social types and traits, and brings us face to face with a hundred things out of which comedy is distilled: ambition and pride, arrogance and obsequiousness; a too-slavish following or a too-emphatic flouting of convention; all the stratagems men use in order to outwit or get their way.

And of course comedy becomes purely social in that best known and perhaps best liked of all its higher forms—the comedy of manners. Here we have hardly less than a picture of society itself; here the men and women are but parts of a general whole, and what survives—if we have it from the past—is likely to be known as the Restoration Scene, or Regency London, or Victorian Family Life. Here the drawing room is not merely the setting of the play or novel, but the subject and even the hero; here enter all the prejudices, the traditions, the taboos, the aspirations, the absurdities, the snobberies, of a group. The group, to constitute itself one, must partake of a common background and accept a similar view of life: though there will usually exist some outsider, some rebel, some nonconformist who, as the case may be, is ringing the doorbell or shattering the window panes; trying desperately to get in or desperately to get out; bending the knee or thumbing his nose. Or the comedy of manners will contrast one social milieu with another—the urban and the rustic, the capital and the provinces, Philistia and Bohemia, America and Europe. And in the comedy of manners, ignorance of good form has much the same value that, in straight drama, ignorance of some vital fact has.

And with ignorance of one kind or another we begin coming close to the very mainspring of comedy, or at any rate of comedy in action. For most comedy is born of ignorance or false knowledge; is based on misunderstanding. (Obviously not knowing the truth—though here one might add "until it is too late"—applies to much tragedy also.) At the level of ordinary farce or romantic comedy, the lovers are estranged until a quarter of eleven because the young man misunderstood why the young lady was walking with Sir Robert in the garden. At a higher level, it will not be mere circumstance or coincidence, but qualities of character that block the way. Envy proves an obstruction, or arrogance; or a too-great tendency to be suspicious or to take offense. In *Pride and Prejudice* the very title makes this clear. In Jane Austen's finest novel, *Emma*, there is every variety of misunderstanding, but the greatest misunderstanding of all, and the one that leads to so many of the others, is Emma's concerning her own nature. Emma—so high-handed and so wrongheaded, so often reasonable and so seldom right—is herself a wonderfully modulated comic character. And what

matters is not so much the realistic consequences of her mistakes as the assured and benevolent air with which she commits them. And now moving higher still, to Meredith's *The Egoist*, we see self-deluded character constituting, really, the whole book. Sir Willoughby Patterne is the supreme example of self-centeredness in literature—the man who, in his absorption with the creature he is and the role he plays and the impression he makes, can care about nobody else. He tramples on the emotions and even the liberties of all who come his way, only cherishing such people so far as they cherish or pay homage to him. He is stunned by what seems to him *their* selfishness when, appalled by his, they walk out or turn away. And as we watch Meredith's great demonstration of human egoism, as we see with what comic flourishes and farcical leaps and wild extravagant motions it proceeds—as we smile and even laugh—we become increasingly uncomfortable. The more monstrous Sir Willoughby seems, the more we realize that in some sense this man is ourselves. If no one ever misunderstood his own nature worse, no one has ever pointed a moral better. Comedy at its greatest is criticism indeed; is nothing less, in fact, than a form of moral enlightenment.

The Egoist is sometimes declared to be comedy in name only, to be at bottom tragic. I would myself disagree—Meredith carries his theme to so extreme a length as to transform his hero from a man into a sort of sublime caricature, and gives him a purely comic intensity, an intensity quite disproportionate to what it is intense about. If just this is the "tragedy" of most human beings, it must yet serve to expose rather than exalt them; otherwise what shall we call genuine tragedy when we encounter it? Malvolio in *Twelfth Night*, who has also been looked upon as tragic, comes somewhat closer to being so. For pretension with him does partake a little of aspiration; his vanity, moreover, is stung because he is a servant, and stimulated by the mischievousness of others. But Malvolio, like Sir Willoughby, is really too trivial for tragedy, as he is also too priggish. What happens to him seems painful rather than tragic; it is not quite our modern idea of fun.

And this brings up the point that though Comedy has its permanent subject-matter and even its body of laws, it is liable, like everything else, to changes in fashion and taste, to differences of sensibility. One generation's pleasure is the next generation's embarrassment: much that the Victorians shuddered at merely makes us laugh, much that they laughed at might well make us shudder. One always reacts—and quite fortunately—from the vantage-point of one's own age; and it is probably a mistake, and certainly a waste of breath, to be arrogant or snobbish or moral about what amuses or does not amuse one: we may fancy we are less callous than our grandfathers and only be less callous about different things. The cuckold was clearly, in Restoration comedy, a figure to hoot at. Simply for being cuckolded we do not today find a man so comic, or even comic at all: though the moment we add an extra element to his role, such as his elation over cuckolding others, he becomes a comic figure for us. To what extent sex itself is a comic theme must naturally vary with the morality of a particular age: there are times when it seems shocking for a man ever to have a mistress; there are times when it seems even more shocking for a man never to have one. Right in the same age, what is considered virtue by the parson may be termed repression by the psychiatrist; and in such an age, which is usually one of moral transition, we may well find conflicting comedy values. The pendulum-swing of taste always makes it hard for people to know what they really like: if they are in revolt against gentility, they are likely to confuse what is funny with what is merely bold or obscene; if they are converts to gentility, they will be too much outraged by the indecent to inquire whether it is funny. There is nothing at which the Comic Spirit must smile more than our fickle and inconstant notions as to what constitutes comedy. We need not always look back to Shakespeare's drearier clowns as an instance of how tastes change: sometimes we need only attend a revival of what convulsed us ten years before.

COMIC FICTIONAL MODES

Northrup Frye

The theme of the comic is the integration of society, which usually takes the form of incorporating a central character into it. The mythical comedy corresponding to the death of the Dionysiac god is Apollonian, the story of how a hero is accepted by a society of gods. In Classical literature the theme of acceptance forms part of the stories of Hercules, Mercury, and other deities who had a probation to go through, and in Christian literature it is the theme of salvation, or, in a more concentrated form, of assumption: the comedy that stands just at the end of Dante's *Commedia*. The mode of romantic comedy corresponding to the elegiac is best described as idyllic, and its chief vehicle is the pastoral. Because of the social interest of comedy, the idyllic cannot equal the introversion of the elegiac, but it preserves the theme of escape from society to the extent of idealizing a simplified life in the country or on the frontier (the pastoral of popular modern literature is the Western story). The close association with animal and vegetable nature that we noted in the elegiac recurs in the sheep and pleasant pastures (or the cattle and ranches) of the idyllic, and the same easy connection with myth recurs in the fact that such imagery is often used, as it is in the Bible, for the theme of salvation.

The clearest example of high mimetic comedy is the Old Comedy of Aristophanes. The New Comedy of Menander is closer to the low mimetic, and through Plautus and Terence its formulas were handed down to the Renaissance, so that there has always been a strongly low mimetic bias to social comedy. In Aristophanes there is usually a central figure who constructs his (or her) own society in the teeth of strong opposition, driving off one after another all the people who come to prevent or exploit him, and eventually achieving a heroic triumph, complete with mistresses, in which he is sometimes assigned the honors of a reborn god. We notice that just as there is a catharsis of pity and fear in tragedy, so there is a catharsis of the corresponding comic emotions, which are sympathy and ridicule, in Old Comedy. The comic hero will get his triumph whether what he has done is sensible or silly, honest or rascally. Thus Old Comedy, like the tragedy contemporary with it, is a blend of the heroic and the ironic. In some plays this fact is partly concealed by Aristophanes' strong desire to get his own opinion of what the hero is doing into the record, but his greatest comedy, *The Birds*, preserves an exquisite balance between comic heroism and comic irony.

New Comedy normally presents an erotic intrigue between a young man and a young woman which is blocked by some kind of opposition, usually paternal, and resolved by a twist in the plot which is the comic form of Aristotle's "discovery," and is more manipulated than its tragic counterpart. At the beginning of the play the forces thwarting the hero are in control of the play's society, but after a discovery in which the hero becomes wealthy or the heroine respectable, a new society crystallizes on the stage around the hero and his bride. The action of the comedy thus moves towards the incorporation of the hero into the society that he naturally fits. The hero himself is seldom a very interesting person: in conformity with low mimetic decorum, he is ordinary in his virtues, but socially attractive. In Shakespeare and in the kind of romantic comedy that most closely resembles his there is a development of these formulas in a more distinctively high mimetic direction. In the figure of Prospero we have one of the few approaches to the Aristophanic technique of having the whole comic action projected by a central character. Usually Shakespeare achieves his high mimetic pattern by making the struggle of the repressive and the desirable societies a struggle between two levels of existence, the former like our own world or worse, the latter enchanted and idyllic. This point will be dealt with more fully later.

For the reasons given above the domestic comedy of later fiction carries on with much the same conventions as were used in the Renaissance. Domestic comedy is usually based on the Cinderella archetype, the kind of thing that happens when Pamela's virtue is rewarded, the incorporation of an individual very like the reader into the society aspired to by both, a society ushered in with a happy rustle of bridal gowns and banknotes. Here again, Shakespearean comedy may marry off eight or ten people of approximately equal dramatic interest, just as a high mimetic tragedy may kill the same number, but in domestic comedy such diffusion of sexual energy is more rare. The chief difference between high and low mimetic comedy, however, is that the resolution of the latter more frequently involves a social promotion. More sophisticated writers of low mimetic comedy often present the same success-story formula with the moral ambiguities that we have found in Aristophanes. In Balzac or Stendhal a clever and ruthless scoundrel may achieve the same kind of success as the virtuous heroes of Samuel Smiles and Horatio Alger. Thus the comic counterpart of the *alazon* seems to be the clever, likeable, unprincipled *picaro* of the picaresque novel.

In studying ironic comedy we must start with the theme of driving out the *pharmakos* from the point of view of society. This appeals to the kind of relief we are expected to feel when we see Jonson's Volpone condemned to the galleys, Shylock stripped of his wealth, or Tartuffe taken off to prison. Such a theme, unless touched very lightly, is difficult to make convincing, for the reasons suggested in connection with ironic tragedy. Insisting on the theme of social revenge on an individual, however great a rascal he may be, tends to make him look less involved in guilt and the society more so. This is particularly true of characters who have been trying to amuse either the actual or the internal audience, and who are the comic counterparts of the tragic hero as artist. The rejection of the entertainer, whether fool, clown, buffoon, or simpleton, can be one of the most terrible ironies known to art, as the rejection of Falstaff shows, and certain scenes in Chaplin.

In some religious poetry, for example at the end of the *Paradiso*, we can see that literature has an upper limit, a point at which an imaginative vision of an eternal world becomes an experience of it. In ironic comedy we begin to see that art has also a lower limit in actual life. This is the condition of savagery, the world in which comedy consists of inflicting pain on a helpless victim, and tragedy in enduring it. Ironic comedy brings us to the figure of the scapegoat ritual and the nightmare dream, the human symbol that concentrates our fears and hates. We pass the boundary of art when this symbol becomes existential, as it does in the black man of a lynching, the Jew of a pogrom, the old woman of a witch hunt, or anyone picked up at random by a mob, like Cinna the poet in *Julius Caesar*. In Aristophanes the irony sometimes edges very close to mob violence because the attacks are personal: one thinks of all the easy laughs he gets, in play after play, at the pederasty of Cleisthenes or the cowardice of Cleonymus. In Aristophanes the word *pharmakos* means simply scoundrel, with no nonsense about it. At the conclusion of *The Clouds*, where the poet seems almost to be summoning a lynching party to go and burn down Socrates' house, we reach the comic counterpart of one of the greatest masterpieces of tragic irony in literature, Plato's *Apology*.

But the element of *play* is the barrier that separates art from savagery, and playing at human sacrifice seems to be an important theme of ironic comedy. Even in laughter itself some kind of deliverance from the unpleasant, even the horrible, seems to be very important. We notice this particularly in all forms of art in which a large number of auditors are simultaneously present, as in drama, and, still more obviously, in games. We notice too that playing at sacrifice has nothing to do with any historical descent from sacrificial ritual, such as has been suggested for Old Comedy. All the features of such ritual, the king's son, the mimic death, the executioner, the substituted victim, are far more explicit in Gilbert and Sullivan's *Mikado* than they are in Aristophanes. There is certainly no evidence that baseball has descended from a ritual of human sacrifice, but the umpire is quite as much of a *pharmakos* as if it had: he is an abandoned scoundrel, a greater robber than Barabbas; he has the evil eye; the supporters of the losing team scream for his death. At play, mob emotions are boiled in an open pot, so to speak; in the lynching mob they are in a sealed furnace of what Blake would call moral virtue. The gladiatorial combat, in which the audience has the actual power of life and death over the people who are entertaining them, is perhaps the most concentrated of all the savage or demonic parodies of drama.

The fact that we are now in an ironic phase of literature largely accounts for the popularity of the detective story, the formula of how a man-hunter locates a *pharmakos* and gets rid of him. The detective story begins in the Sherlock Holmes period as an intensification of low mimetic, in the sharpening of attention to details that makes the dullest and most neglected trivia of daily living leap into mysterious and fateful significance. But as we move further away from this we move toward a ritual drama around a corpse in which a wavering finger of social condemnation passes over a group of "suspects" and finally settles on one. The sense of a victim chosen by lot is very strong, for the case against him is only plausibly manipulated. If it were really inevitable, we should have tragic irony, as in *Crime and Punishment*, where Raskolnikoff's crime is so interwoven with his character that there can be no question of any "whodunit" mystery. In the growing brutality of the crime story (a brutality protected by the convention of the form, as it is conventionally impossible that the man-hunter can be mistaken in believing that one of his suspects is a murderer), detection begins to merge with the thriller as one of the forms of melodrama. In melodrama two themes are important: the triumph of moral virtue over villainy, and the consequent idealizing of the moral views assumed to be held by the audience. In the melodrama of the brutal thriller we come as close as it is normally possible for art to come to the pure self-righteousness of the lynching mob.

We should have to say, then, that all forms of melodrama, the detective story in particular, were advance propaganda for the police state, in so far as that represents the regularizing of mob violence, if it were possible to take them seriously. But it seems not to be possible. The protecting wall of play is still there. Serious melodrama soon gets entangled with its own pity and fear: the more serious it is, the more likely it is to be looked at ironically by the reader, its pity and fear seen as sentimental drivel and owlish solemnity, respectively. One pole of ironic comedy is the recognition of the absurdity of naive melodrama, or, at least, of the absurdity of its attempt to define the enemy of society as a person outside that society. From there it develops toward the opposite pole, which is true comic irony or satire, and which defines the enemy of society as a spirit within that society. Let us arrange the forms of ironic comedy from this point of view.

Cultivated people go to a melodrama to hiss the villain with an air of condescension: they are making a point of the fact that they cannot take his villainy seriously. We have here a type of irony which exactly corresponds to that of two other major arts of the ironic age, advertising and propaganda. These arts pretend to address themselves seriously to a subliminal audience of cretins, an audience that may not even exist, but which is assumed to be simpleminded enough to accept at their face value the statements made about the purity of a soap or a government's motives. The rest of us, realizing that irony never says precisely what it means, take these arts ironically, or, at least, regard them as a kind of ironic game. Similarly, we read murder stories with a strong sense of the unreality of the villainy involved. Murder is doubtless a serious crime, but if private murder really were a major threat to our civilization it would not be relaxing to read about it. We may compare the abuse showered on the pimp in Roman comedy, which was similarly based on the indisputable ground that brothels are immoral.

The next step is an ironic comedy addressed to the people who can realize that murderous violence is less an attack on a virtuous society by a malignant individual than a symptom of that society's own viciousness. Such a comedy would be the kind of intellectualized parody of melodramatic formulas represented by, for instance, the novels of Graham Greene. Next comes the ironic comedy directed at the melodramatic spirit itself, an astonishingly persistent tradition in all comedy in which there is a large ironic admixture. One notes a recurring tendency on the part of ironic comedy to ridicule and scold an audience assumed to be hankering after sentiment, solemnity, and the triumph of fidelity and approved moral standards. The arrogance of Jonson and Congreve, the mocking of bourgeois sentiment in Goldsmith, the parody of melodramatic situations in Wilde and Shaw, belong to a consistent tradition. Molière had to please his king, but was not temperamentally an exception. To comic drama one may add the ridicule of melodramatic romance in the novelists, from Fielding to Joyce.

Finally comes the comedy of manners, the portrayal of a chattering-monkey society devoted to snobbery and slander. In this kind of irony the characters who are opposed to or excluded from the fictional society have the sympathy of the audience. Here we are close to a parody of tragic irony, as we can see in the appalling fate of the relatively harmless hero of Evelyn Waugh's A Handful of Dust. Or we may have a character who, with the sympathy of the author or audience, repudiates such a society to the point of deliberately walking out of it, becoming thereby a kind of *pharmakos* in reverse. This happens for instance at the conclusion of Aldous Huxley's *Those Barren Leaves*. It is more usual, however, for the artist to present an ironic deadlock in which the hero is regarded as a fool or worse by the fictional society, and yet impresses the real audience as having something more valuable than his society has. The obvious example, and certainly one of the greatest, is Dostoievsky's *The Idiot*, but there are many others. *The Good Soldier Schweik*, *Heaven's My Destination* and *The Horse's Mouth* are instances that will give some idea of the range of the theme.

What we have said about the return of irony to myth in tragic modes thus holds equally well for comic ones. Even popular literature appears to be slowly shifting its center of gravity from murder stories to science fiction—or at any rate a rapid growth of science fiction is certainly a fact about contemporary popular literature. Science fiction frequently tries to imagine what life would be like on a plane as far above us as we are above savagery; its setting is often of a kind that appears to us as technologically miraculous. It is thus a mode of romance with a strong inherent tendency to myth.

THE MEANING OF COMEDY

James K. Feibleman

There are many points on which comedy and tragedy may be contrasted, which will serve to explain them both in a more thorough manner. Comedy is an intellectual affair, and deals chiefly with logic. Tragedy is an emotional affair, and deals chiefly with value. Comedy is negative; it is a criticism of limitations and an unwillingness to accept them. Tragedy is positive; it is an uncritical acceptance of the positive content of that which is delimited. Since comedy deals with the limitations of actual situations and tragedy with their positive content, comedy must ridicule and tragedy must endorse. Comedy affirms the direction toward infinite value by insisting upon the absurdly final claims of finite things and events. Tragedy strives to serve this same purpose, but through a somewhat different method. For tragedy also affirms the direction toward infinite value, but does so by indicating that no matter how limited the value of finite things and events may be, it is still a real part of infinite value. Logic being after all the only formal limitation of value which is the positive stuff of existence, tragedy which affirms that positive stuff is greater than comedy which can affirm it only indirectly by denying its limitations.

Comedy is by its very nature a more revolutionary affair than tragedy. Through the glasses of tragedy, the positive aspect of actuality always yields a glimpse of infinite value. Thus tragedy leads to a state of contentment with the actual world just as it is found. According to tragedy, whatever in this finite world could be substituted for the actuality we experience, would still have to be actual and therefore to some extent limited. It would have to be finite to be available for experience, and would not be the infinite value toward which we always are working. The historical order of actuality, wherever and whenever it is sampled, yields a small amount of positive content which must be a fragmentary part of actuality. Thus, tragedy seems to say, since any segment of actuality is bound to be a fragmentary part of infinite value, why change one for another? Better to stress the fact that whatever small fragment of value we have, it is as much value (though not as much *of* value) as any other fragment? Why then, it asks, be dissatisfied?

Comedy, however, is occupied with the termini of things and events, their formal limitations, as opposed to tragedy, which is occupied with their positive stuff or content. If it is only the limitations of actuality which prevent actuality from containing infinite value, those limitations should not be suffered. To justify the demand for their elimination, it is only necessary to point out that they are limitations. Comedy leads to dissatisfaction and the overthrow of all reigning theories and practices in favor of those less limited. It thus works against current customs and institutions; hence its inherently revolutionary nature. Actuality may contain value, so comedy seems to argue, but it is capable of containing more of value; and it is necessary to dissolve those things and events which have some value in order to procure others which have a greater amount. Better to stress the fact that however much value any actual situation may have, it is prevented from having more only by its limitations. Why, then, be satisfied? In periods of social change, we may expect to see the role of comedy assume an increasing importance, although, to be sure, both the comic and the tragic aspects of being are always and eternally omnipresent.

It has been pointed out by Bergson and others that comedy bears a closer resemblance to real life than does tragedy. This is true, and it is very obvious why it should be so. The contradictions and disvalues of actuality wear a greater vividity than do truths and values. In our daily occupations, we are confronted more frequently with the intense aspects of existence than we are with the diffused aspects. Error, ugliness and evil, are, after all, colorful. Truth and value, as found, for example, in the systems of mathematics and the feelings of ecstasy, are wonderful; but they are likewise rare. Everyday life knows much more of the partial and extremely limited side of existence, and it is only a truism to say that this side is more familiar. Fortunately for the progress of humanity, familiarity is no index to value; what we are forever condemned to pursue are just those fleeting glimpses of infinite value which come to us so seldom. But it is comedy which wears the common dress.

Comedy, then, criticizes the finite for not being infinite. It witnesses the limitations of actuality, just as tragedy witnesses the fragmentary exemplifications of the logical order. Tragedy affirms continuity by showing how it exists in every actual thing and event. Tragedy shows the worth of every actual, down to the most ephemeral, and so is always close to the permanent value of the worshipful. Comedy comes to the same affirmation, but inversely and by indirection, just as one might affirm beauty by criticizing the ugly. Comedy catches the principle of unity in every finite thing; tragedy attends to the principle of infinity.

It should be remembered that our contrast of comedy with tragedy tends toward a misleading oversimplification, as all analysis, of necessity, must. There are subtle relations between comedy and tragedy which reveal them to have more in common than do the rough comparisons we have had to make. Often indeed the connection between comedy and tragedy is so close as to render them hardly distinguishable.

An excellent example of comedy in this sense is afforded by the episode of Alice and the Cheshire Cat, in Carroll's *Alice in Wonderland*. Alice had been nursing a baby, when suddenly, much to her dismay, it turns into a pig. She puts it down and it trots off into the woods. Alice walks through the forest, "getting well used to queer things happening," when with no warning the Cheshire Cat reappears exactly where it had been before. In the midst of this series of marvels, the Cat's conversation assumes the most casual, conversational tone.

" 'By-the-by, what became of the baby?' said the Cat. 'I'd nearly forgotten to ask.'

" 'It turned into a pig,' Alice answered very quietly, just as if the Cat had come back in a natural way.

" 'I thought it would,' said the Cat, and vanished again."

Here comedy, too, turns upon the logical order of events, but what events! Through the exposition of their connectivity, limitations are unexpectedly exposed and the comic aspect brought into predominant relief. Or the connectivity is emphasized as one of continuous value, and the tragic aspect triumphs. There is comedy in actual situations whose limitations have been laid bare. There is tragedy in the inexorable march of actual situations, because what value is contained in them will not be denied. Both comedy and tragedy emerge from the same ontological problem: the relation of the logical to the historical order. We may see the actual situation as comedy or as tragedy; for in fact it is both.

It is appropriate that a study of comedy should begin with a work by the Greek dramatist Aristophanes, who lived from about 450 B.C. to 380 B.C., for the very word *comedy* is itself Greek in origin and grows out of the Dionysian festivals that were still celebrated in Aristophanes' time. The word derives from the Greek *komos* (a banquet or festival) and *oidos* (singer); the etymology suggests the origin of comedy in a celebration or festival at which the gods were invoked in friendly terms and joy was expressed through song and dance.

Whatever its source in ritual, comedy for Aristophanes was not always a matter of joy and good will; it was a weapon, a vehicle for his polemics. He was the first writer in the Western world to show us how to use laughter as a means of exposing political chicanery and academic pretensions, and as a goad to bring about reform. He turned his barbs against the rulers, the manipulators, and those people in power who ran the state for their own advantage. As might be expected, he won many enemies by his invective and the boldness of his attack. But since he was a writer of comedies, the laughter triumphs over the invective, and all means at his disposal—including bawdy action and indecent dialogue—served one clear purpose: to compel his audience into the acceptance of reason rather than emotion as a guiding principle.

Growing up during the time of the Peloponnesian War (431–404 B.C.) between Athens and Sparta, he observed what seemed a bitter and unnecessary struggle between the two leading Greek city-states, a struggle begun by politicians and protracted by opportunists. This is the problem of *Lysistrata* (the name means Madame Demobilizer): how to end such a war and, by extension, to expose the folly of all wars. Aristophanes' military strategy—the strike by the wives of soldiers—may not receive much consideration by generals and chiefs-of-staff in these days of atom bombs and intercontinental missiles; but if Aristophanes' point were understood and applied, perhaps the threat of nuclear disaster could be diminished.

The determined ladies of the play are too much concerned with ending an unwanted war to worry about the niceties of polite society, and so to modern audiences the play sometimes seems audacious for its sexual candor. But its real audacity is its recourse to common sense; and this is, after all, the perennial solution that comedy offers.

LYSISTRATA

Aristophanes

Translated by
Charles T. Murphy

LYSISTRATA⎤
CALONICE ⎬ *Athenian women*
MYRRHINE ⎦
LAMPITO, *a Spartan woman*
LEADER *of the Chorus of Old Men*
CHORUS *of Old Men*
LEADER *of the Chorus of Old Women*
CHORUS *of Old Women*
ATHENIAN MAGISTRATE
THREE ATHENIAN WOMEN
CINESIAS, *an Athenian, husband of*
  Myrrhine
SPARTAN HERALD
SPARTAN AMBASSADORS
ATHENIAN AMBASSADORS
TWO ATHENIAN CITIZENS
CHORUS *of Athenians*
CHORUS *of Spartans*

(As is usual in ancient comedy, the leading characters have significant names. LYSISTRATA is "She who disbands the armies"; MYRRHINE'S name is chosen to suggest *myrton*, a Greek word meaning *pudenda muliebria;* LAMPITO is a celebrated Spartan name; CINESIAS, although a real name in Athens, is chosen to suggest a Greek verb *kinein, to move,* then *to make love, to have intercourse,* and the name of his deme, Paionidai, suggests the verb *paiein,* which has about the same significance.)

(SCENE: *In Athens, beneath the Acropolis. In the center of the stage is the Propylaea, or gate-way to the Acropolis; to one side is a small grotto, sacred to Pan. The Orchestra represents a slope leading up to the gate-way.*

It is early in the morning. LYSISTRATA *is pacing impatiently up and down.*)

LYSISTRATA: If they'd been summoned to worship the God of Wine, or Pan, or to visit the Queen of Love, why, you couldn't have pushed your way through the streets for all the timbrels. But now there's not a single woman here—except my neighbour; here she comes.

(*Enter* CALONICE.)

Good day to you, Calonice.

CALONICE: And to you, Lysistrata. (*noticing* LYSISTRATA's *impatient air*) But what ails you? Don't scowl, my dear; it's not becoming to you to knit your brows like that.

LYSISTRATA (*sadly*): Ah, Calonice, my heart aches; I'm so annoyed at us women. For among men we have a reputation for sly trickery—

CALONICE: And rightly too, on my word!

LYSISTRATA: —but when they were told to meet here to consider a matter of no small importance, they lie abed and don't come.

CALONICE: Oh, they'll come all right, my dear. It's not easy for a woman to get out, you know. One is working on her husband, another is getting up the maid, another has to put the baby to bed, or wash and feed it.

LYSISTRATA: But after all, there are other matters more important than all that.

CALONICE: My dear Lysistrata, just what is this matter you've summoned us women to consider? What's up? Something big?

LYSISTRATA: Very big.

CALONICE (*interested*): Is it stout, too?

LYSISTRATA (*smiling*): Yes indeed—both big and stout.

CALONICE: What? And the women still haven't come?

LYSISTRATA: It's not what you suppose; they'd have come soon enough for *that*. But I've worked up something, and for many a sleepless night I've turned it this way and that.

CALONICE (*in mock disappointment*): Oh, I guess it's pretty fine and slender, if you've turned it this way and that.

LYSISTRATA: So fine that the safety of the whole of Greece lies in us women.

CALONICE: In us women? It depends on a very slender reed then.

LYSISTRATA: Our country's fortunes are in our hands; and whether the Spartans shall perish—

CALONICE: Good! Let them perish, by all means.

LYSISTRATA: —and the Boeotians shall be completely annihilated.

CALONICE: Not completely! Please spare the eels.

LYSISTRATA: As for Athens, I won't use any such unpleasant words. But you understand what I mean. But if the women will meet here—the Spartans, the Boeotians, and we Athenians—then all together we will save Greece.

CALONICE: But what could women do that's clever or distinguished? We just sit around all dolled up in silk robes, looking pretty in our sheer gowns and evening slippers.

LYSISTRATA: These are just the things I hope will save us: these silk robes, perfumes, evening slippers, rouge, and our chiffon blouses.

CALONICE: How so?

LYSISTRATA: So never a man alive will lift a spear against the foe—

CALONICE: I'll get a silk gown at once.

LYSISTRATA: —or take up his shield—

CALONICE: I'll put on my sheerest gown!

LYSISTRATA: —or sword.

CALONICE: I'll buy a pair of evening slippers.

LYSISTRATA: Well then, shouldn't the women have come?

CALONICE: Come? Why, they should have *flown* here.

LYSISTRATA: Well, my dear, just watch: they'll act in true Athenian fashion— everything too late! And now there's not a woman here from the shore or from Salamis.

CALONICE: They're coming, I'm sure; at daybreak they were laying—to their oars to cross the straits.

LYSISTRATA: And those I expected would be the first to come—the women of Acharnae—they haven't arrived.

CALONICE: Yet the wife of Theagenes means to come: she consulted Hecate about it. (*seeing a group of women approaching*) But look! Here come a few. And there are some more over here. Hurrah! Where do they come from?

LYSISTRATA: From Anagyra.

CALONICE: Yes indeed! We've raised up quite a stink from Anagyra anyway.

(*Enter* MYRRHINE *in haste, followed by several other women.*)

MYRRHINE (*breathlessly*): Have we come in time, Lysistrata? What do you say? Why so quiet?

LYSISTRATA: I can't say much for you, Myrrhine, coming at this hour on such important business.

MYRRHINE: Why, I had trouble finding my girdle in the dark, But if it's so important, we're here now; tell us.

LYSISTRATA: No. Let's wait a little for the women from Boeotia and the Peloponnesus.

MYRRHINE: That's a much better suggestion. Look! Here comes Lampito now.

(*Enter* LAMPITO *with two other women.*)

LYSISTRATA: Greetings, my dear Spartan friend. How pretty you look, my dear. What a smooth complexion and well-developed figure! You could throttle an ox.

LAMPITO: Faith, yes, I think I could. I take exercises and kick my heels against my bum. (*She demonstrates with a few steps of the Spartan "bottom-kicking" dance.*)

LYSISTRATA: And what splendid breasts you have.

LAMPITO: La! You handle me like a prize steer.

LYSISTRATA: And who is this young lady with you?

LAMPITO: Faith, she's an Ambassadress from Boeotia.

LYSISTRATA: Oh yes, a Boeotian, and blooming like a garden too.

CALONICE (*lifting up her skirt*): My word! How neatly her garden's weeded!

LYSISTRATA: And who is the other girl?

LAMPITO: Oh, she's a Corinthian swell.

MYRRHINE (*after a rapid examination*): Yes indeed. She swells very nicely (*pointing*) here and here.

LAMPITO: Who has gathered together this company of women?

LYSISTRATA: I have.

LAMPITO: Speak up, then. What do you want?

MYRRHINE: Yes, my dear, tell us what this important matter is.

LYSISTRATA: Very well, I'll tell you. But before I speak, let me ask you a little question.

MYRRHINE: Anything you like.

LYSISTRATA (*earnestly*): Tell me: don't you yearn for the fathers of your children, who are away at the wars? I know you all have husbands abroad.

CALONICE: Why, yes; mercy me! my husband's been away for five months in Thrace keeping guard on—Eucrates.

MYRRHINE: And mine for seven whole months in Pylus.

LAMPITO: And mine, as soon as ever he returns from the fray, readjusts his shield and flies out of the house again.

LYSISTRATA: And as for lovers, there's not even a ghost of one left. Since the Milesians revolted from us, I've not even seen an eight-inch dingus to be a leather consolation for us widows. Are you willing, if I can find a way, to help me end the war?

MYRRHINE: Goodness, yes! I'd do it, even if I had to pawn my dress and—get drunk on the spot!

CALONICE: And I, even if I had to let myself be split in two like a flounder.

LAMPITO: I'd climb up Mt. Taygetus if I could catch a glimpse of peace.

LYSISTRATA: I'll tell you, then, in plain and simple words. My friends, if we are going to force our men to make peace, we must do without—

MYRRHINE: Without what? Tell us.

LYSISTRATA: Will you do it?

MYRRHINE: We'll do it, if it kills us.

LYSISTRATA: Well then, we must do without sex altogether. (*general consternation*) Why do you turn away? Where go you? Why turn so pale? Why those tears? Will you do it or not? What means this hesitation?

MYRRHINE: I won't do it! Let the war go on.

CALONICE: Nor I! Let the war go on.

LYSISTRATA: So, my little flounder? Didn't you say just now you'd split yourself in half?

CALONICE: Anything else you like. I'm

willing, even if I have to walk through fire. Anything rather than sex. There's nothing like it, my dear.

LYSISTRATA (*to* MYRRHINE): What about you?

MYRRHINE (*sullenly*): I'm willing to walk through fire, too.

LYSISTRATA: Oh vile and cursed breed! No wonder they make tragedies about us: we're naught but "love-affairs and bassinets." But you, my dear Spartan friend, if you alone are with me, our enterprise might yet succeed. Will you vote with me?

LAMPITO: 'Tis cruel hard, by my faith, for a woman to sleep alone without her nooky; but for all that, we certainly do need peace.

LYSISTRATA: O my dearest friend! You're the only real woman here.

CALONICE (*wavering*): Well, if we do refrain from—(*shuddering*) what you say (God forbid!), would that bring peace?

LYSISTRATA: My goodness, yes! If we sit at home all rouged and powdered, dressed in our sheerest gowns, and neatly depilated, our men will get excited and want to take us; but if you don't come to them and keep away, they'll soon make a truce.

LAMPITO: Aye; Menelaus caught sight of Helen's naked breast and dropped his sword, they say.

CALONICE: What if the men give us up?

LYSISTRATA: "Flay a skinned dog," as Pherecrates says.

CALONICE: Rubbish! These make-shifts are no good. But suppose they grab us and drag us into the bedroom?

LYSISTRATA: Hold on to the door.

CALONICE: And if they beat us?

LYSISTRATA: Give in with a bad grace. There's no pleasure in it for them when they have to use violence. And you must torment them in every possible way. They'll give up soon enough; a man gets no joy if he doesn't get along with his wife.

MYRRHINE: If this is your opinion, we agree.

LAMPITO: As for our own men, we can persuade them to make a just and fair peace; but what about the Athenian rabble? Who will persuade them not to start any more monkey-shines?

LYSISTRATA: Don't worry. We guarantee to convince them.

LAMPITO: Not while their ships are rigged so well and they have that mighty treasure in the temple of Athene.

LYSISTRATA: We've taken good care for that too: we shall seize the Acropolis today. The older women have orders to do this, and while we are making our arrangements, they are to pretend to make a sacrifice and occupy the Acropolis.

LAMPITO: All will be well then. That's a very fine idea.

LYSISTRATA: Let's ratify this, Lampito, with the most solemn oath.

LAMPITO: Tell us what oath we shall swear.

LYSISTRATA: Well said. Where's our Police-woman? (*to a Scythian slave*) What are you gaping at? Set a shield upside-down here in front of me, and give me the sacred meats.

CALONICE: Lysistrata, what sort of an oath are we to take?

LYSISTRATA: What oath? I'm going to slaughter a sheep over the shield, as they do in Aeschylus.

CALONICE: Don't, Lysistrata! No oaths about peace over a shield.

LYSISTRATA: What shall the oath be, then?

CALONICE: How about getting a white horse somewhere and cutting out its entrails for the sacrifice?

LYSISTRATA: White horse indeed!

CALONICE: Well then, how shall we swear?

MYRRHINE: I'll tell you: let's place a large black bowl upside-down and then slaughter—a flask of Thasian wine. And then let's swear—not to pour in a single drop of water.

LAMPITO: Lord! How I like that oath!

LYSISTRATA: Someone bring out a bowl and a flask.

(*A slave brings the utensils for the sacrifice.*)

CALONICE: Look, my friends! What a big jar! Here's a cup that 'twould give me joy to handle. (*She picks up the bowl.*)

LYSISTRATA: Set it down and put your

hands on our victim. (*as* CALONICE *places her hands on the flask*) O Lady of Persuasion and dear Loving Cup, graciously vouchsafe to receive this sacrifice from us women. (*She pours the wine into the bowl.*)

CALONICE: The blood has a good colour and spurts out nicely.

LAMPITO: Faith, it has a pleasant smell, too.

MYRRHINE: Oh, let me be the first to swear, ladies!

CALONICE: No, by our Lady! Not unless you're allotted the first turn.

LYSISTRATA: Place all your hands on the cup, and one of you repeat on behalf of what I say. Then all will swear and ratify the oath. *I will suffer no man, be he husband or lover,*

CALONICE: *I will suffer no man, be he husband or lover,*

LYSISTRATA: *To approach me all hot and horny.* (*as* CALONICE *hesitates*) Say it!

CALONICE (*slowly and painfully*): *To approach me all hot and horny.* O Lysistrata, I feel so weak in the kness!

LYSISTRATA: *I will remain at home unmated,*

CALONICE: *I will remain at home unmated,*

LYSISTRATA: *Wearing my sheerest gown and carefully adorned,*

CALONICE: *Wearing my sheerest gown and carefully adorned,*

LYSISTRATA: *That my husband may burn with desire for me.*

CALONICE: *That my husband may burn with desire for me.*

LYSISTRATA: *And if he takes me by force against my will,*

CALONICE: *And if he takes me by force against my will,*

LYSISTRATA: *I shall do it badly and keep from moving.*

CALONICE: *I shall do it badly and keep from moving.*

LYSISTRATA: *I will not stretch my slippers toward the ceiling,*

CALONICE: *I will not stretch my slippers toward the ceiling,*

LYSISTRATA: *Nor will I take the posture of the lioness on the knife-handle.*

CALONICE: *Nor will I take the posture of the lioness on the knife-handle.*

LYSISTRATA: *If I keep this oath, may I be permitted to drink from this cup,*

CALONICE: *If I keep this oath, may I be permitted to drink from this cup,*

LYSISTRATA: *But if I break it, may the cup be filled with water.*

CALONICE: *But if I break it, may the cup be filled with water.*

LYSISTRATA: Do you all swear to this?

ALL: I do, so help me!

LYSISTRATA: Come then, I'll just consummate this offering.

(*She takes a long drink from the cup.*)

CALONICE (*snatching the cup away*): Shares, my dear! Let's drink to our continued friendship.

(*A shout is heard from off-stage.*)

LAMPITO: What's that shouting?

LYSISTRATA: That's what I was telling you: the women have just seized the Acropolis. Now, Lampito, go home and arrange matters in Sparta; and leave these two ladies here as hostages. We'll enter the Acropolis to join our friends and help them lock the gates.

CALONICE: Don't you suppose the men will come to attack us?

LYSISTRATA: Don't worry about them. Neither threats nor fire will suffice to open the gates, except on the terms we've stated.

CALONICE: I should say not! Else we'd belie our reputation as unmanageable pests.

(LAMPITO *leaves the stage. The other women retire and enter the Acropolis through the Propylaea.*)

(*Enter the* CHORUS OF OLD MEN, *carrying fire-pots and a load of heavy sticks.*)

LEADER OF MEN: Onward, Draces, step by step, though your shoulder's aching.
  Cursèd logs of olive-wood, what a load you're making!

FIRST SEMI-CHORUS OF OLD MEN (*singing*):
  Aye, many surprises await a man who lives to a ripe old age;
  For who could suppose, Strymodorus my

lad, that the women we've nourished (alas!),
Who sat at home to vex our days,
Would seize the holy image here,
And occupy this sacred shrine,
With bolts and bars, with fell design,
To lock the Propylaea?

LEADER OF MEN: Come with speed, Philourgus, come! to the temple hast'ning.
There we'll heap these logs about in a circle round them,
And whoever has conspired, raising this rebellion,
Shall be roasted, scorched, and burnt, all without exception,
Doomed by one unanimous vote—but first the wife of Lycon.

SECOND SEMI-CHORUS (*singing*):
No, no! by Demeter, while I'm alive, no woman shall mock at me.
Not even the Spartan Cleomenes, our citadel first to seize,
Got off unscathed; for all his pride
And haughty Spartan arrogance,
He left his arms and sneaked away,
Stripped to his shirt, unkempt, unshav'd
With six years' filth still on him.

LEADER OF MEN: I besieged that hero bold, sleeping at my station,
Marshalled at these holy gates sixteen deep against him.
Shall I not these cursèd pests punish for their daring,
Burning these Euripides-and-God-detested women?
Aye! or else may Marathon overturn my trophy.

FIRST SEMI-CHORUS (*singing*):
There remains of my road
Just this brow of the hill;
There I speed on my way.
Drag the logs up the hill, though we've got no ass to help.
(God! my shoulder's bruised and sore!)
Onward still must we go.
Blow the fire! Don't let it go out
Now we're near the end of our road.

ALL (*blowing on the fire-pots*):
Whew! Whew! Drat the smoke!

SECOND SEMI-CHORUS (*singing*):
Lord, what smoke rushing forth
From the pot, like a dog
Running mad, bites my eyes!
This must be Lemnos-fire. What a sharp and stinging smoke!
Rushing onward to the shrine
Aid the gods. Once for all
Show your mettle, Laches my boy!
To the rescue hastening all!

ALL (*blowing on the fire-pots*): Whew! Whew! Drat the smoke!

(*The chorus has now reached the edge of the Orchestra nearest the stage, in front of the Propylaea. They begin laying their logs and fire-pots on the ground.*)

LEADER OF MEN: Thank heaven, this fire is still alive. Now let's first put down these logs here and place our torches in the pots to catch; then let's make a rush for the gates with a battering-ram. If the women don't unbar the gate at our summons, we'll have to smoke them out.

Let me put down my load. Ouch! That hurts! (*to the audience*) Would any of the generals in Samos like to lend a hand with this log? (*throwing down a log*) Well, *that* won't break my back any more, at any rate. (*turning to his fire-pot*) Your job, my little pot, is to keep those coals alive and furnish me shortly with a red-hot torch.

O mistress Victory, be my ally and grant me to rout these audacious women in the Acropolis.

(*While the men are busy with their logs and fires, the* CHORUS OF OLD WOMEN *enters, carrying pitchers of water.*)

LEADER OF WOMEN: What's this I see? Smoke and flames? Is that a fire ablazing?
Let's rush upon them. Hurry up! They'll find us women ready.

FIRST SEMI-CHORUS OF OLD WOMEN (*singing*):
With wingèd foot onward I fly,
Ere the flames consume Neodice;
Lest Critylla be overwhelmed
By a lawless, accurst herd of old men.
I shudder with fear. Am I too late to aid them?

At break of the day filled we our jars
with water
Fresh from the spring, pushing our way
straight through the crowds. Oh, what
a din!
Mid crockery crashing, jostled by
slave-girls,
Sped we to save them, aiding our
neighbours,
Bearing this water to put out the flames.

SECOND SEMI-CHORUS OF OLD WOMEN (*singing*):
Such news I've heard: doddering
fools
Come with logs, like furnace-at-
tendants,
Loaded down with three hundred
pounds,
Breathing many a vain, blustering
threat,
That all these abhorred sluts will be
burnt to charcoal.
O goddess, I pray never may they be
kindled;
Grant them to save Greece and our men;
madness and war help them to end.
With this as our purpose, golden-
plumed Maiden,
Guardian of Athens, seized we thy
precinct.
Be my ally, Warrior-maiden,
'Gainst these old men, bearing water
with me.

(*The women have now reached their position
in the Orchestra, and their* LEADER *advances toward the* LEADER OF THE MEN.)

LEADER OF WOMEN: Hold on there! What's
this, you utter scoundrels? No decent,
God-fearing citizens would act like this.

LEADER OF MEN: Oho! Here's something
unexpected: a swarm of women have
come out to attack us.

LEADER OF WOMEN: What, do we frighten
you? Surely you don't think we're too
many for you. And yet there are ten
thousand times more of us whom you
haven't even seen.

LEADER OF MEN: What say, Phaedria? Shall
we let these women wag their tongues?
Shan't we take our sticks and break
them over their backs?

LEADER OF WOMEN: Let's set our pitchers on
the ground; then if anyone lays a hand
on us, they won't get in our way.

LEADER OF MEN: By God! If someone gave
them two or three smacks on the jaw,
like Bupalus, they wouldn't talk so much!

LEADER OF WOMEN: Go on, hit me, somebody! Here's my jaw! But no other
bitch will bite a piece out of you before me.

LEADER OF MEN: Silence! or I'll knock out
your—senility!

LEADER OF WOMEN: Just lay one finger on
Stratyllis, I dare you!

LEADER OF MEN: Suppose I dust you off
with this first? What will you do?

LEADER OF WOMEN: I'll tear the living guts
out of you with my teeth.

LEADER OF MEN: No poet is more clever
than Euripides: "There is no beast so
shameless as a woman."

LEADER OF WOMEN: Let's pick up our jars
of water, Rhodippe.

LEADER OF MEN: Why have you come here
with water, you detestable slut?

LEADER OF WOMEN: And why have you
come with fire, you funeral vault? To
cremate yourself?

LEADER OF MEN: To light a fire and singe
your friends.

LEADER OF WOMEN: And I've brought water
to put out your fire.

LEADER OF MEN: What? You'll put out my
fire?

LEADER OF WOMEN: Just try and see!

LEADER OF MEN: I wonder: shall I scorch
you with this torch of mine?

LEADER OF WOMEN: If you've got any soap,
I'll give you a bath.

LEADER OF MEN: Give *me* a bath, you stinking hag?

LEADER OF WOMEN: Yes—a bridal bath!

LEADER OF MEN: Just listen to her! What
crust!

LEADER OF WOMEN: Well, I'm a free citizen.

LEADER OF MEN: I'll put an end to your
bawling. (*The men pick up their torches.*)

LEADER OF WOMEN: You'll never do jury-
duty again. (*The women pick up their
pitchers.*)

LEADER OF MEN: Singe her hair for her!

LEADER OF WOMEN: Do your duty, water!

(The women empty their pitchers on the men.)

LEADER OF MEN: Ow! Ow! For heaven's sake!

LEADER OF WOMEN: Is it too hot?

LEADER OF MEN: What do you mean "hot"? Stop! What are you doing?

LEADER OF WOMEN: I'm watering you, so you'll be fresh and green.

LEADER OF MEN: But I'm all withered up with shaking.

LEADER OF WOMEN: Well, you've got a fire; why don't you dry yourself?

(Enter an Athenian MAGISTRATE, *accompanied by four Scythian policemen.)*

MAGISTRATE: Have these wanton women flared up again with their timbrels and their continual worship of Sabazius? Is this another Adonis-dirge upon the roof-tops—which we heard not long ago in the Assembly? That confounded Demostratus was urging us to sail to Sicily, and the whirling women shouted, "Woe for Adonis!" And then Demostratus said we'd best enroll the infantry from Zacynthus, and a tipsy woman on the roof shrieked, "Beat your breasts for Adonis!" And that vile and filthy lunatic forced his measure through. Such license do our women take.

LEADER OF MEN: What if you heard of the insolence of these women here? Besides their other violent acts, they threw water all over us, and we have to shake out our clothes just as if we'd leaked in them.

MAGISTRATE: And rightly, too, by God! For we ourselves lead the women astray and teach them to play the wanton; from these roots such notions blossom forth. A man goes into the jeweler's shop and says, "About that necklace you made for my wife, goldsmith: last night, while she was dancing, the fastening-bolt slipped out of the hole. I have to sail over to Salamis today; if you're free, do come around tonight and fit in a new bolt for her." Another goes to the shoe-maker, a strapping young fellow with manly parts, and says, "See here, cobbler, the sandal-strap chafes my wife's little—toe; it's so

tender. Come around during the siesta and stretch it a little, so she'll be more comfortable." Now we see the results of such treatment: here I'm a special Councillor and need money to procure oars for the galleys; and I'm locked out of the Treasury by these women.

But this is no time to stand around. Bring up crow-bars there! I'll put an end to their insolence. (*to one of the policemen*) What are you gaping at, you wretch? What are you staring at? Got an eye out for a tavern, eh? Set your crow-bars here to the gates and force them open. (*retiring to a safe distance*) I'll help from over here.

(The gates are thrown open and LYSISTRATA *comes out followed by several other women.)*

LYSISTRATA: Don't force the gates; I'm coming out of my own accord. We don't need crow-bars here; what we need is good sound common-sense.

MAGISTRATE: Is that so, you strumpet? Where's my policeman? Officer, arrest her and tie her arms behind her back.

LYSISTRATA: By Artemis, if he lays a finger on me, he'll pay for it, even if he is a public servant.

(The policeman retires in terror.)

MAGISTRATE: You there, are you afraid? Seize her round the waist—and you, too. Tie her up, both of you!

FIRST WOMAN (*as the second policeman approaches* LYSISTRATA): By Pandrosus, if you but touch her with your hand, I'll kick the stuffings out of you.

(The second policeman retires in terror.)

MAGISTRATE: Just listen to that: "kick the stuffings out." Where's another policeman? Tie *her* up first, for her chatter.

SECOND WOMAN: By the Goddess of the Light, if you lay the tip of your finger on her, you'll soon need a doctor.

(The third policeman retires in terror.)

MAGISTRATE: What's this? Where's my policeman? Seize *her* too. I'll soon stop your sallies.

THIRD WOMAN: By the Goddess of Tauros, if you go near her, I'll tear out your hair until it shrieks with pain.

(*The fourth policeman retires in terror.*)

MAGISTRATE: Oh, damn it all! I've run out of policemen. But women must never defeat us. Officers, let's charge them all together. Close up your ranks!

(*The policemen rally for a mass attack.*)

LYSISTRATA: By heaven, you'll soon find out that we have four companies of warrior-women, all fully equipped within!

MAGISTRATE (*advancing*): Twist their arms off, men!

LYSISTRATA (*shouting*): To the rescue, my valiant women!

O sellers-of-barley-green-stuffs-and-eggs,

O sellers-of-garlic, ye keepers-of-taverns, and vendors-of-bread,

Grapple! Smite! Smash!

Won't you heap filth on them? Give them a tongue-lashing!

(*The women beat off the policemen.*)

Halt! Withdraw! No looting on the field.

MAGISTRATE: Damn it! My police-force has put up a very poor show.

LYSISTRATA: What did you expect? Did you think you were attacking slaves? Didn't you know that women are filled with passion?

MAGISTRATE: Aye, passion enough—for a good strong drink!

LEADER OF MEN: O chief and leader of this land, why spend your words in vain?

Don't argue with these shameless beasts. You know not how we've fared:

A soapless bath they've given us; our clothes are soundly soaked.

LEADER OF WOMEN: Poor fool! You never should attack or strike a peaceful girl.

But if you do, your eyes must swell. For I am quite content

To sit unmoved, like modest maids, in peace and cause no pain;

But let a man stir up my hive, he'll find me like a wasp.

CHORUS OF MEN (*singing*):

O God, whatever shall we do with creatures like Womankind?

This can't be endured by any man alive. Question them!

Let us try to find out what this means. To what end have they seized on this shrine,

This steep and rugged, high and holy, Undefiled Acropolis?

LEADER OF MEN: Come, put your questions; don't give in, and probe her every statement.

For base and shameful it would be to leave this plot untested.

MAGISTRATE: Well then, first of all I wish to ask her this: for what purpose have you barred us from the Acropolis?

LYSISTRATA: To keep the treasure safe, so you won't make war on account of it.

MAGISTRATE: What? Do we make war on account of the treasure?

LYSISTRATA: Yes, and you cause all our other troubles for it, too. Peisander and those greedy office-seekers keep things stirred up so they can find occasions to steal. Now let them do what they like: they'll never again make off with any of this money.

MAGISTRATE: What will you do?

LYSISTRATA: What a question! We'll administer it ourselves.

MAGISTRATE: *You* will administer the treasure?

LYSISTRATA: What's so strange in that? Don't we administer the household money for you?

MAGISTRATE: That's different.

LYSISTRATA: How is it different?

MAGISTRATE: We've got to make war with this money.

LYSISTRATA: But that's the very first thing: you mustn't make war.

MAGISTRATE: How else can we be saved?

LYSISTRATA: We'll save you.

MAGISTRATE: *You*?

LYSISTRATA: Yes, we!

MAGISTRATE: God forbid!

LYSISTRATA: We'll save you, whether you want it or not.

MAGISTRATE: Oh! This is terrible!

LYSISTRATA: You don't like it, but we're going to do it none the less.

MAGISTRATE: Good God! it's illegal!

LYSISTRATA: We *will* save you, my little man!

MAGISTRATE: Suppose I don't want you to?

LYSISTRATA: That's all the more reason.

MAGISTRATE: What business have you with war and peace?

LYSISTRATA: I'll explain.

MAGISTRATE: (*shaking his fist*): Speak up, or you'll smart for it.

LYSISTRATA: Just listen, and try to keep your hands still.

MAGISTRATE: I can't. I'm so mad I can't stop them.

FIRST WOMAN: Then you'll be the one to smart for it.

MAGISTRATE: Croak to yourself, old hag! (*to* LYSISTRATA) Now then, speak up.

LYSISTRATA: Very well. Formerly we endured the war for a good long time with our usual restraint, no matter what you men did. You wouldn't let us say "boo," although nothing you did suited us. But we watched you well, and though we stayed at home we'd often hear of some terribly stupid measure you'd proposed. Then, though grieving at heart, we'd smile sweetly and say, "What was passed in the Assembly today about writing on the treaty-stone?" "What's that to you?" my husband would say. "Hold your tongue!" And I held my tongue.

FIRST WOMAN: But I wouldn't have—not I!

MAGISTRATE: You'd have been soundly smacked, if you hadn't kept still.

LYSISTRATA: So I kept still at home. Then we'd hear of some plan still worse than the first; we'd say, "Husband, how could you pass such a stupid proposal?" He'd scowl at me and say, "If you don't mind your spinning, your head will be sore for weeks. *War shall be the concern of Men.*"

MAGISTRATE: And he was right, upon my word!

LYSISTRATA: Why right, you confounded fool, when your proposals were so stupid and we weren't allowed to make suggestions?

"There's not a *man* left in the country," says one. "No, not one," says another.

Therefore all we women have decided in council to make a common effort to save Greece. How long should we have waited? Now, if you're willing to listen to our excellent proposals and keep silence for us in your turn, we still may save you.

MAGISTRATE: We men keep silence for you? That's terrible; I won't endure it!

LYSISTRATA: Silence!

MAGISTRATE: Silence for *you*, you wench, when you're wearing a snood? I'd rather die!

LYSISTRATA: Well, if that's all that bothers you—here! take my snood and tie it round your head. (*During the following words the women dress up the* MAGISTRATE *in women's garments.*) And *now* keep quiet! Here, take this spinning-basket, too, and card your wool with robes tucked up, munching on beans. *War shall be the concern of Women!*

LEADER OF WOMEN: Arise and leave your pitchers, girls; no time is this to falter.

We too must aid our loyal friends; our turn has come for action.

CHORUS OF WOMEN (*singing*):

I'll never tire of aiding them with song and dance; never may

Faintness keep my legs from moving to and fro endlessly.

For I yearn to do all for my friends;

They have charm, they have wit, they have grace,

With courage, brains, and best of virtues—

Patriotic sapience.

LEADER OF WOMEN: Come, child of manliest ancient dames, offspring of stinging nettles,

Advance with rage unsoftened; for fair breezes speed you onward.

LYSISTRATA: If only sweet Eros and the Cyprian Queen of Love shed charm over our breasts and limbs and inspire our men with amorous longing and priapic spasms, I think we may soon be called Peacemakers among the Greeks.

MAGISTRATE: What will you do?

LYSISTRATA: First of all, we'll stop those fellows who run madly about the Marketplace in arms.

FIRST WOMAN: Indeed we shall, by the Queen of Paphos.

LYSISTRATA: For now they roam about the market, amid the pots and greenstuffs, armed to the teeth like Corybantes.

MAGISTRATE: That's what manly fellows ought to do!

LYSISTRATA: But it's so silly: a chap with a Gorgon-emblazoned shield buying pickled herring.

FIRST WOMAN: Why, just the other day I saw one of those long-haired dandies who command our cavalry ride up on horseback and pour into his bronze helmet the egg-broth he'd bought from an old dame. And there was a Thracian slinger too, shaking his lance like Tereus; he'd scared the life out of the poor fig-peddler and was gulping down all her ripest fruit.

MAGISTRATE: How can you stop all the confusion in the various states and bring them together?

LYSISTRATA: Very easily.

MAGISTRATE: Tell me how.

LYSISTRATA: Just like a ball of wool, when it's confused and snarled: we take it thus, and draw out a thread here and a thread there with our spindles; thus we'll unsnarl this war, if no one prevents us, and draw together the various states with embassies here and embassies there.

MAGISTRATE: Do you suppose you can stop this dreadful business with balls of wool and spindles, you nit-wits?

LYSISTRATA: Why, if *you* had any wits, you'd manage all affairs of state like our wool-working.

MAGISTRATE: How so?

LYSISTRATA: First you ought to treat the city as we do when we wash the dirt out of a fleece: stretch it out and pluck and thrash out of the city all those prickly scoundrels; aye, and card out those who conspire and stick together to gain office, pulling off their heads. Then card the wool, all of it, into one fair basket of good-will, mingling in the aliens residing here, any loyal foreigners, and anyone who's in debt to the Treasury; and consider that all our colonies lie scattered round about like remnants; from all of these collect the wool and gather it together here, wind up a great ball, and then weave a good stout cloak for the democracy.

MAGISTRATE: Dreadful! Talking about thrashing and winding balls of wool, when you haven't the slightest share in the war!

LYSISTRATA: Why, you dirty scoundrel, we bear more than twice as much as you. First, we bear children and send off our sons as soldiers.

MAGISTRATE: Hush! Let bygones be bygones!

LYSISTRATA: Then, when we ought to be happy and enjoy our youth, we sleep alone because of your expeditions abroad. But never mind us married women: I grieve most for the maids who grow old at home unwed.

MAGISTRATE: Don't men grow old too?

LYSISTRATA: For heaven's sake! That's not the same thing. When a man comes home, no matter how grey he is, he soon finds a girl to marry. But woman's bloom is short and fleeting; if she doesn't grasp her chance, no man is willing to marry her and she sits at home a prey to every fortune-teller.

MAGISTRATE (*coarsely*): But if a man can still get it up—

LYSISTRATA: See here, you: what's the matter? Aren't you dead yet? There's plenty of room for you. Buy yourself a shroud and I'll bake you a honey-cake. (*handing him a copper coin for his passage across the Styx*) Here's your fare! Now get yourself a wreath.

(*During the following dialogue the women dress up the* MAGISTRATE *as a corpse.*)

FIRST WOMAN: Here, take these fillets.

SECOND WOMAN: Here, take this wreath.

LYSISTRATA: What do you want? What's lacking? Get moving; off to the ferry! Charon is calling you; don't keep him from sailing.

MAGISTRATE: Am I to endure these insults?

By God! I'm going straight to the mag-
istrates to show them how I've been
treated.

LYSISTRATA: Are you grumbling that you
haven't been properly laid out? Well,
the day after tomorrow we'll send around
all the usual offerings early in the morning.

(*The* MAGISTRATE *goes out still wearing his
funeral decorations.* LYSISTRATA *and the
women retire into the Acropolis.*)

LEADER OF MEN: Wake, ye sons of freedom,
wake! 'Tis no time for sleeping. Up and
at them, like a man! Let us strip for
action.

(*The* CHORUS OF MEN *remove their outer
cloaks.*)

CHORUS OF MEN (*singing*):
Surely there is something here greater
than meets the eye;
For without a doubt I smell Hippias'
tyranny.
Dreadful fear assails me lest certain
bands of Spartan men,
Meeting here with Cleisthenes, have
inspired through treachery
All these god-detested women secretly
to seize
Athens' treasure in the temple, and to
stop that pay
Whence I live at my ease.

LEADER OF MEN: Now isn't it terrible for
them to advise the state and chatter about
shields, being mere women?

And they think to reconcile us with
the Spartans—men who hold nothing
sacred any more than hungry wolves.
Surely this is a web of deceit, my friends,
to conceal an attempt at tyranny. But
they'll never lord it over me; I'll be on
my guard and from now on,
"The blade I bear
A myrtle spray shall wear."
I'll occupy the market under arms and
stand next to Aristogeiton.

Thus I'll stand beside him. (*He strikes
the pose of the famous statue of the
tyrannicides, with one arm raised.*) And

here's my chance to take this accurst old
hag and—(*striking the* LEADER OF WOMEN)
smack her on the jaw!

LEADER OF WOMEN: You'll go home in such
a state your Ma won't recognize you!
Ladies all, upon the ground let us place
these garments.

(*The* CHORUS OF WOMEN *remove their outer
garments.*)

CHORUS OF WOMEN (*singing*):
Citizens of Athens, hear useful words
for the state.
Rightly; for it nurtured me in my youth
royally.
As a child of seven years carried I the
sacred box;
Then I was a Miller-maid, grinding at
Athene's shrine;
Next I wore the saffron robe and played
Brauronia's Bear;
And I walked as Basket-bearer, wearing
chains of figs,
As a sweet maiden fair.

LEADER OF WOMEN: Therefore, am I not
bound to give good advice to the city?

Don't take it ill that I was born a
woman, if I contribute something better
than our present troubles. I pay my share;
for I contribute MEN. But you miserable
old fools contribute nothing, and after
squandering our ancestral treasure, the
fruit of the Persian Wars, you make no
contribution in return. And now, all on
account of you, we're facing ruin.

What, muttering, are you? If you
annoy me, I'll take this hard, rough
slipper and— (*striking the* LEADER OF
MEN) smack you on the jaw!

CHORUS OF MEN (*singing*):
This is outright insolence! Things go
from bad to worse.
If you're men with any guts, prepare to
meet the foe.
Let us strip our tunics off! We need the
smell of male
Vigour. And we cannot fight all swad-
dled up in clothes.

(*They strip off their tunics.*)

Come then, my comrades, on to the battle,
ye who once to Leipsydrion came;
Then ye were MEN. Now call back your
youthful vigour.
With light, wingèd footstep advance,
Shaking old age from your frame.
LEADER OF MEN: If any of us give these
wenches the slightest hold, they'll stop
at nothing: such is their cunning.
They will even build ships and sail
against us, like Artemisia. Or if they turn
to mounting, I count our Knights as
done for: a woman's such a tricky jockey
when she gets astraddle, with a good firm
seat for trotting. Just look at those
Amazons that Micon painted, fighting
on horseback against men!
But we must throw them all in the
pillory— (*seizing and choking the* LEADER
OF WOMEN) grabbing hold of yonder neck!

CHORUS OF WOMEN (*singing*):
'Ware my anger! Like a boar 'twill rush
upon you men.
Soon you'll bawl aloud for help, you'll
be so soundly trimmed!
Come, my friends, let's strip with speed,
and lay aside these robes;
Catch the scent of women's rage. Attack
with tooth and nail!

(*They strip off their tunics.*)

Now then, come near me, you miserable
man! you'll never eat garlic or black
beans again.
And if you utter a single hard word, in
rage I will "nurse" you as once
The beetle requited her foe.
LEADER OF WOMEN: For you don't worry
me; no, not so long as my Lampito lives
and our Theban friend, the noble Ismenia.
You can't do anything, not even if
you pass a dozen—decrees! You miserable
fool, all our neighbours hate you. Why,
just the other day when I was holding a
festival for Hecate, I invited as playmate
from our neighbours the Boeotians

a charming, wellbred Copaic—eel. But
they refused to send me one on account
of your decrees.
And you'll never stop passing decrees
until I grab your foot and— (*tripping
up the* LEADER OF MEN) toss you down
and break your neck!

(*Here an interval of five days is supposed to
elapse.* LYSISTRATA *comes out from the
Acropolis.*)

LEADER OF WOMEN (*dramatically*): Empress
of this great emprise and undertaking,
Why come you forth, I pray, with frown-
ing brow?
LYSISTRATA: Ah, these cursèd women!
Their deeds and female notions make me
pace up and down in utter despair.
LEADER OF WOMEN: Ah, what sayest thou?
LYSISTRATA: The truth, alas! the truth.
LEADER OF WOMEN: What dreadful tale hast
thou to tell thy friends?
LYSISTRATA: 'Tis shame to speak, and not
to speak is hard.
LEADER OF WOMEN: Hide not from me
whatever woes we suffer.
LYSISTRATA: Well then, to put it briefly,
we want—laying!
LEADER OF WOMEN: O Zeus, Zeus!
LYSISTRATA: Why call on Zeus? That's the
way things are. I can no longer keep
them away from the men, and they're
all deserting. I caught one wriggling
through a hole near the grotto of Pan,
another sliding down a rope, another
deserting her post; and yesterday I found
one getting on a sparrow's back to fly
off to Orsilochus and had to pull her
back by the hair. They're digging up
all sorts of excuses to get home. Look,
here comes one of them now. (*A woman
comes hastily out of the Acropolis.*) Here
you! Where are you off to in such a hurry?
FIRST WOMAN: I want to go home. My very
best wool is being devoured by moths.
LYSISTRATA: Moths? Nonsense! Go back
inside.
FIRST WOMAN: I'll come right back; I swear
it. I just want to lay it out on the bed.

LYSISTRATA: Well, you won't lay it out, and you won't go home, either.

FIRST WOMAN: Shall I let my wool be ruined?

LYSISTRATA: If necessary, yes. (*Another woman comes out.*)

SECOND WOMAN: Oh dear! Oh dear! My precious flax! I left it at home all unpeeled.

LYSISTRATA: Here's another one, going home for her "flax." Come back here!

SECOND WOMAN: But I just want to work it up a little and then I'll be right back.

LYSISTRATA: No indeed! If you start this, all the other women will want to do the same. (*A third woman comes out.*)

THIRD WOMAN: O Eilithyia, goddess of travail, stop my labour till I come to a lawful spot!

LYSISTRATA: What's this nonsense?

THIRD WOMAN: I'm going to have a baby— right now!

LYSISTRATA: But you weren't even pregnant yesterday.

THIRD WOMAN: Well, I am today. O Lysistrata, do send me home to see a midwife, right away.

LYSISTRATA: What are you talking about? (*putting her hand on her stomach*) What's this hard lump here?

THIRD WOMAN: A little boy.

LYSISTRATA: My goodness, what have you got there? It seems hollow; I'll just find out. (*pulling aside her robe*) Why, you silly goose, you've got Athene's sacred helmet there. And you said you were having a baby!

THIRD WOMAN: Well, I *am* having one, I swear!

LYSISTRATA: Then what's this helmet for?

THIRD WOMAN: If the baby starts coming while I'm still in the Acropolis, I'll creep into this like a pigeon and give birth to it there.

LYSISTRATA: Stuff and nonsense! It's plain enough what you're up to. You just wait here for the christening of this—helmet.

THIRD WOMAN: But I can't sleep in the Acropolis since I saw the sacred snake.

FIRST WOMAN: And I'm dying for lack of sleep: the hooting of the owls keeps me awake.

LYSISTRATA: Enough of these shams, you wretched creatures. You want your husbands, I suppose. Well, don't you think they want us? I'm sure they're spending miserable nights. Hold out, my friends, and endure for just a little while. There's an oracle that we shall conquer, if we don't split up. (*producing a roll of paper*) Here it is.

FIRST WOMAN: Tell us what it says.

LYSISTRATA: Listen.

"When in the length of time the Swallows shall gather together,
Fleeing the Hoopoe's amorous flight and the Cockatoo shunning,
Then shall your woes be ended and Zeus who thunders in heaven
Set what's below on top—"

FIRST WOMAN: What? Are we going to be on top?

LYSISTRATA: "But if the Swallows rebel and flutter away from the temple,
Never a bird in the world shall seem more wanton and worthless."

FIRST WOMAN: That's clear enough, upon my word!

LYSISTRATA: By all that's holy, let's not give up the struggle now. Let's go back inside. It would be a shame, my dear friends, to disobey the oracle.

(*The women all retire to the Acropolis again.*)

CHORUS OF MEN (*singing*):
I have a tale to tell,
Which I know full well.
    It was told me
    In the nursery.

Once there was a likely lad,
    Melanion they name him;
The thought of marriage made him mad,
    For which I cannot blame him.

So off he went to mountains fair;
    (No women to upbraid him!)
A mighty hunter of the hare,
    He had a dog to aid him.

He never came back home to see
    Detested women's faces.
He showed a shrewd mentality.
    With him I'd fain change places!

ONE OF THE MEN (*to one of the women*):
Come here, old dame; give me a kiss.
WOMAN: You'll ne'er eat garlic, if you dare!
MAN: I want to kick you—just like this!
WOMAN: Oh, there's a leg with bushy hair!
MAN: Myronides and Phormio
Were hairy—and they thrashed the foe.

CHORUS OF WOMEN (*singing*):
I have another tale,
With which to assail
Your contention
'Bout Melanion.

Once upon a time a man
Named Timon left our city,
To live in some deserted land.
(We thought him rather witty.)

He dwelt alone amidst the thorn;
In solitude he brooded.
From some grim Fury he was born:
Such hatred he exuded.

He cursed you men, as scoundrels
through
And through, till life he ended.
He couldn't stand the sight of YOU!
But women he befriended.

WOMAN (*to one of the men*): I'll smash your
face in, if you like.
MAN: Oh no, please don't! You frighten me.
WOMAN: I'll lift my foot—and thus I'll strike.
MAN: Aha! Look there! What's that I see?
WOMAN: Whate'er you see, you cannot say
That I'm not neatly trimmed today.

(LYSISTRATA *appears on the wall of the
Acropolis.*)

LYSISTRATA: Hello! Hello! Girls, come
here quick!

(*Several women appear beside her.*)

WOMAN: What is it? Why are you calling?
LYSISTRATA: I see a man coming: he's in
a dreadful state. He's mad with passion.
O Queen of Cyprus, Cythera, and Paphos,
just keep on this way!
WOMAN: Where is the fellow?
LYSISTRATA: There, beside the shrine of
Demeter.

WOMAN: Oh yes, so he is. Who is he?
LYSISTRATA: Let's see. Do any of you know
him?
MYRRHINE: Yes indeed. That's my husband,
Cinesias.
LYSISTRATA: It's up to you, now: roast him,
rack him, fool him, love him—and leave
him! Do everything, except what our
oath forbids.
MYRRHINE: Don't worry; I'll do it.
LYSISTRATA: I'll stay here to tease him and
warm him up a bit. Off with you.

(*The other women retire from the wall. Enter*
CINESIAS *followed by a slave carrying a
baby.* CINESIAS *is obviously in great pain
and distress.*)

CINESIAS (*groaning*): Oh-h! Oh-h-h! This
is killing me! O God, what tortures
I'm suffering!
LYSISTRATA (*from the wall*): Who's that
within our lines?
CINESIAS: Me.
LYSISTRATA: A *man*?
CINESIAS (*pointing*): A *man*, indeed!
LYSISTRATA: Well, go away!
CINESIAS: Who are you to send me away?
LYSISTRATA: The captain of the guard.
CINESIAS: Oh, for heaven's sake, call out
Myrrhine for me.
LYSISTRATA: Call Myrrhine? Nonsense!
Who are you?
CINESIAS: Her husband, Cinesias of
Paionidai.
LYSISTRATA (*appearing much impressed*):
Oh, greetings, friend. Your name is not
without honour here among us. Your
wife is always talking about you, and
whenever she takes an egg or an apple,
she says, "Here's to my dear Cinesias!"
CINESIAS (*quivering with excitement*): Oh, ye
gods in heaven!
LYSISTRATA: Indeed she does! And whenever
our conversations turn to men, your wife
immediately says, "All others are mere
rubbish compared with Cinesias."
CINESIAS (*groaning*): Oh! Do call her for me.
LYSISTRATA: Why should I? What will you
give me?
CINESIAS: Whatever you want. All I have is
yours—and you see what I've got.

LYSISTRATA: Well then, I'll go down and call her. (*She descends.*)

CINESIAS: And hurry up! I've had no joy of life ever since she left home. When I go in the house, I feel awful: everything seems so empty and I can't enjoy my dinner. I'm in such a state all the time!

MYRRHINE (*from behind the wall*): I *do* love him so. But he won't let me love him. No, no! Don't ask me to see him!

CINESIAS: O my darling, O Myrrhine honey, why do you do this to me? (MYRRHINE *appears on the wall.*) Come down here!

MYRRHINE: No, I won't come down.

CINESIAS: Won't you come, Myrrhine, when *I* call you?

MYRRHINE: No; you don't want me.

CINESIAS: *Don't want you*? I'm in agony!

MYRRHINE: I'm going now.

CINESIAS: Please don't! At least, listen to your baby. (*to the baby*) Here you, call your mamma! (*pinching the baby*)

BABY: Ma-ma! Ma-ma! Ma-ma!

CINESIAS (*to* MYRRHINE): What's the matter with you? Have you no pity for your child, who hasn't been washed or fed for five whole days?

MYRRHINE: Oh, poor child; your father pays no attention to you.

CINESIAS: Come down then, you heartless wretch, for the baby's sake.

MYRRHINE: Oh, what it is to be a mother! I've got to come down, I suppose. (*She leaves the wall and shortly reappears at the gate.*)

CINESIAS (*to himself*): She seems much younger, and she has such a sweet look about her. Oh, the way she teases me! And her pretty, provoking ways make me burn with longing.

MYRRHINE (*coming out of the gate and taking the baby*): O my sweet little angel. Naughty papa! Here, let Mummy kiss you, Mamma's little sweetheart! (*She fondles the baby lovingly.*)

CINESIAS (*in despair*): You heartless creature, why do you do this? Why follow these other women and make both of us suffer so? (*He tries to embrace her.*)

MYRRHINE: Don't touch me!

CINESIAS: You're letting all our things at home go to wrack and ruin.

MYRRHINE: I don't care.

CINESIAS: You don't care that your wool is being plucked to pieces by the chickens?

MYRRHINE: Not in the least.

CINESIAS: And you haven't celebrated the rites of Aphrodite for ever so long. Won't you come home?

MYRRHINE: Not on your life, unless you men make a truce and stop the war.

CINESIAS: Well then, if that pleases you, we'll do it.

MYRRHINE: Well then, if that pleases *you*, I'll come home—afterwards! Right now I'm on oath not to.

CINESIAS: Then just lie down here with me for a moment.

MYRRHINE: No— (*in a teasing voice*) and yet, I won't say I don't love you.

CINESIAS: You love me? Oh, do lie down here, Myrrhine dear!

MYRRHINE: What, you silly fool! in front of the baby?

CINESIAS (*hastily thrusting the baby at the slave*): Of course not. Here—home! Take him, Manes! (*The slave goes off with the baby.*) See, the baby's out of the way. Now won't you lie down?

MYRRHINE: But where, my dear?

CINESIAS: Where? The grotto of Pan's a lovely spot.

MYRRHINE: How could I purify myself before returning to the shrine?

CINESIAS: Easily: just wash here in the Clepsydra.

MYRRHINE: And then, shall I go back on my oath?

CINESIAS: On my head be it! Don't worry about the oath.

MYRRHINE: All right, then, Just let me bring out a bed.

CINESIAS: No, don't. The ground's all right.

MYRRHINE: Heavens, no! Bad as you are, I won't let you lie on the bare ground. (*She goes into the Acropolis.*)

CINESIAS: Why, she really loves me; it's plain to see.

MYRRHINE (*returning with a bed*): There! Now hurry up and lie down. I'll just slip off this dress. But—let's see: oh yes, I must fetch a mattress.

CINESIAS: Nonsense! No mattress for me.

MYRRHINE: Yes indeed! It's not nice on the bare springs.

CINESIAS: Give me a kiss.

MYRRHINE (*giving him a hasty kiss*): There! (*She goes.*)

CINESIAS (*in mingled distress and delight*): Oh-h! Hurry back!

MYRRHINE (*returning with a mattress*): Here's the mattress; lie down on it. I'm taking my things off now—but—let's see: you have no pillow.

CINESIAS: I don't *want* a pillow!

MYRRHINE: But I do. (*She goes.*)

CINESIAS: Cheated again, just like Heracles and his dinner!

MYRRHINE (*returning with a pillow*): Here, lift your head. (*to herself, wondering how else to tease him*) Is that all?

CINESIAS: Surely that's all! Do come here, precious!

MYRRHINE: I'm taking off my girdle. But remember: don't go back on your promise about the truce.

CINESIAS: Hope to die, if I do.

MYRRHINE: You don't have a blanket.

CINESIAS (*shouting in exasperation*): *I don't want one!* I WANT TO—

MYRRHINE: Sh-h! There, there, I'll be back in a minute. (*She goes.*)

CINESIAS: She'll be the death of me with these bed-clothes.

MYRRHINE (*returning with a blanket*): Here, get up.

CINESIAS: I've got *this* up!

MYRRHINE: Would you like some perfume?

CINESIAS: Good heavens, no! I won't have it!

MYRRHINE: Yes, you shall, whether you want it or not. (*She goes.*)

CINESIAS: O lord! Confound all perfumes anyway!

MYRRHINE (*returning with a flask*): Stretch out your hand and put some on.

CINESIAS (*suspiciously*): By God, I don't much like this perfume. It smacks of shilly-shallying, and has no scent of the marriage-bed.

MYRRHINE: Oh dear! This is Rhodian perfume I've brought.

CINESIAS: It's quite all right, dear. Never mind.

MYRRHINE: Don't be silly! (*She goes out with the flask.*)

CINESIAS: Damn the man who first concocted perfumes!

MYRRHINE (*returning with another flask*): Here, try this flask.

CINESIAS: I've got another one all ready for you. Come, you wretch, lie down and stop bringing me things.

MYRRHINE: All right; I'm taking off my shoes. But, my dear, see that you vote for peace.

CINESIAS (*absently*): I'll consider it. (MYRRHINE *runs away to the Acropolis.*) I'm ruined! The wench has skinned me and run away! (*chanting, in tragic style*) Alas! Alas! Deceived, deserted by this fairest of women, whom shall I—lay? Ah, my poor little child, how shall I nurture thee? Where's Cynalopex? I needs must hire a nurse!

LEADER OF MEN (*chanting*): Ah, wretched man, in dreadful wise beguiled, bewrayed, thy soul is sore distressed. I pity thee, alas! alas! What soul, what loins, what liver could stand this strain? How firm and unyielding he stands, with naught to aid him of a morning.

CINESIAS: O lord! O Zeus! What tortures I endure!

LEADER OF MEN: This is the way she's treated you, that vile and cursèd wanton.

LEADER OF WOMEN: Nay, not vile and cursèd, but sweet and dear.

LEADER OF MEN: Sweet, you say? Nay, hateful, hateful!

CINESIAS: Hateful indeed! O Zeus, Zeus!
Seize her and snatch her away,
Like a handful of dust, in a mighty,
Fiery tempest! Whirl her aloft, then let her drop
Down to the earth, with a crash, as she falls—

On the point of this waiting
   Thingummybob! (*He goes out.*)

(*Enter a Spartan* HERALD, *in an obvious state of excitement, which he is doing his best to conceal.*)

HERALD: Where can I find the Senate or the Prytanes? I've got an important message. (*The Athenian* MAGISTRATE *enters.*)

MAGISTRATE: Say there, are you a man or Priapus?

HERALD (*in annoyance*): I'm a herald, you lout! I've come from Sparta about the truce.

MAGISTRATE: Is that a spear you've got under your cloak?

HERALD: No, of course not!

MAGISTRATE: Why do you twist and turn so? Why hold your cloak in front of you? Did you rupture yourself on the trip?

HERALD: By gum, the fellow's an old fool.

MAGISTRATE (*pointing*): Why, you dirty rascal, you're all excited.

HERALD: Not at all. Stop this tom-foolery.

MAGISTRATE: Well, what's that I see?

HERALD: A Spartan message-staff.

MAGISTRATE: Oh, certainly! That's just the kind of message-staff I've got. But tell me the honest truth: how are things going in Sparta?

HERALD: All the land of Sparta is up in arms—and our allies are up, too. We need Pellene.

MAGISTRATE: What brought this trouble on you? A sudden Panic?

HERALD: No, Lampito started it and then all the other women in Sparta with one accord chased their husbands out of their beds.

MAGISTRATE: How do you feel?

HERALD: Terrible. We walk around the city bent over like men lighting matches in a wind. For our women won't let us touch them until we all agree and make peace throughout Greece.

MAGISTRATE: This is a general conspiracy of the women; I see it now. Well, hurry back and tell the Spartans to send ambassadors here with full powers to arrange a truce. And I'll go tell the Council to choose ambassadors from here; I've got a little something here that will soon persuade them!

HERALD: I'll fly there; for you've made an excellent suggestion.

(*The* HERALD *and the* MAGISTRATE *depart on opposite sides of the stage.*)

LEADER OF MEN: No beast or fire is harder than womankind to tame,
Nor is the spotted leopard so devoid of shame.

LEADER OF WOMEN: Knowing this, you dare provoke us to attack? I'd be your steady friend, if you'd but take us back.

LEADER OF MEN: I'll never cease my hatred keen of womankind.

LEADER OF WOMEN: Just as you will. But now just let me help you find
That cloak you threw aside. You look so silly there
Without your clothes. Here, put it on and don't go bare.

LEADER OF MEN: That's very kind, and shows you're not entirely bad.
But I threw off my things when I was good and mad.

LEADER OF WOMEN: At last you seem a man, and won't be mocked, my lad.
If you'd been nice to me, I'd take this little gnat
That's in your eye and pluck it out for you, like that.

LEADER OF MEN: So that's what's bothered me and bit my eye so long!
Please dig it out for me. I own that I've been wrong.

LEADER OF WOMEN: I'll do so, though you've been a most ill-natured brat.
Ye gods! See here! A huge and monstrous little gnat!

LEADER OF MEN: Oh, how that helps! For it was digging wells in me.
And now it's out, my tears can roll down hard and free.

LEADER OF WOMEN: Here, let me wipe them off, although you're such a knave,
And kiss me.

LEADER OF MEN: No!

LEADER OF WOMEN: Whate'er you say, a kiss I'll have. (*She kisses him.*)

LEADER OF MEN: Oh, confound these women!
  They've a coaxing way about them.
  He was wise and never spoke a truer
  word, who said,
  "We can't live with women, but we
  cannot live without them."
  Now I'll make a truce with you. We'll
  fight no more; instead,
    I will not injure you if you do me no
    wrong.
    And now let's join our ranks and then
    begin a song.
COMBINED CHORUS (singing):
  Athenians, we're not prepared,
  To say a single ugly word
  About our fellow-citizens.
  Quite the contrary: we desire but to say
  and to do
  Naught but good. Quite enough are the
  ills now on hand.

    Men and women, be advised:
    If anyone requires
    Money—minae two or three—
    We've got what he desires.

    My purse is yours, on easy terms:
    When Peace shall reappear,
    Whate'er you've borrowed will be due.
    So speak up without fear.

    You needn't pay me back, you see,
    If you can get a cent from me!

    We're about to entertain
    Some foreign gentlemen;
    We've soup and tender, fresh-killed
    pork.
    Come round to dine at ten.

    Come early; wash and dress with care,
    And bring the children, too.
    Then step right in, no "by your leave."
    We'll be expecting you.

    Walk in as if you owned the place.
    You'll find the door—shut in your face!

(*Enter a group of Spartan Ambassadors;
they are in the same desperate condition as
the Herald in the previous scene.*)

LEADER OF CHORUS: Here come the envoys
  from Sparta, sprouting long beards and
  looking for all the world as if they were
  carrying pig-pens in front of them.
    Greetings, gentlemen of Sparta. Tell
  me, in what state have you come?
SPARTAN: Why waste words? You can
  plainly see what state we've come in!
LEADER OF CHORUS: Wow! You're in a
  pretty high-strung condition, and it
  seems to be getting worse.
SPARTAN: It's indescribable. Won't someone
  please arrange a peace for us—in any
  way you like.
LEADER OF CHORUS: Here come our own,
  native ambassadors, crouching like
  wrestlers and holding their clothes in
  front of them; this seems an athletic kind
  of malady.

(*Enter several Athenian Ambassadors.*)

ATHENIAN: Can anyone tell us where Lysistrata is? You see our condition.
LEADER OF CHORUS: Here's another case
  of the same complaint. Tell me, are the
  attacks worse in the morning?
ATHENIAN: No, we're always afflicted this
  way. If someone doesn't soon arrange
  this truce, you'd better not let me get
  my hands on—Cleisthenes!
LEADER OF CHORUS: If you're smart, you'll
  arrange your cloaks so none of the fellows
  who smashed the Hermae can see you.
ATHENIAN: Right you are; a very good
  suggestion.
SPARTAN: Aye, by all means. Here, let's
  hitch up our clothes.
ATHENIAN: Greetings, Spartan. We've
  suffered dreadful things.
SPARTAN: My dear fellow, we'd have suffered still worse if one of those fellows
  had seen us in this condition.
ATHENIAN: Well, gentlemen, we must get
  down to business. What's your errand
  here?
SPARTAN: We're ambassadors about peace.
ATHENIAN: Excellent; so are we. Only
  Lysistrata can arrange things for us; shall
  we summon her?
SPARTAN: Aye, and Lysistratus too, if you
  like.

LEADER OF CHORUS: No need to summon her, it seems. She's coming out of her own accord.

(*Enter* LYSISTRATA *accompanied by a statue of a nude female figure, which represents Reconciliation.*)

Hail, noblest of women; now must thou be
A judge shrewd and subtle, mild and severe,
Be sweet yet majestic: all manners employ.
The leaders of Hellas, caught by thy love-charms,
Have come to thy judgment, their charges submitting.

LYSISTRATA: This is no difficult task, if one catch them still in amorous passion, before they've resorted to each other. But I'll soon find out. Where's Reconciliation? Go, first bring the Spartans here, and don't seize them rudely and violently, as our tactless husbands used to do, but as befits a woman, like an old, familiar friend; if they won't give you their hands, take them however you can. Then go fetch these Athenians here, taking hold of whatever they offer you. Now then, men of Sparta, stand here beside me, and you Athenians on the other side, and listen to my words.

I am a woman, it is true, but I have a mind; I'm not badly off in native wit, and by listening to my father and my elders, I've had a decent schooling.

Now I intend to give you a scolding which you both deserve. With one common font you worship at the same altars, just like brothers, at Olympia, at Thermopylae, at Delphi—how many more might I name, if time permitted;—and the Barbarians stand by waiting with their armies; yet you are destroying the men and towns of Greece.

ATHENIAN: Oh, this tension is killing me!

LYSISTRATA: And now, men of Sparta,—to turn to you—don't you remember how the Spartan Pericleidas came here once as a suppliant, and sitting at our altar, all pale with fear in his crimson cloak, begged us for an army? For all Messene had attacked you and the god sent an earthquake too? Then Cimon went forth with four thousand hoplites and saved all Lacedaemon. Such was the aid you received from Athens, and now you lay waste the country which once treated you so well.

ATHENIAN (*hotly*): They're in the wrong, Lysistrata, upon my word, they are!

SPARTAN (*absently, looking at the statue of Reconciliation*): We're in the wrong. What hips! How lovely they are!

LYSISTRATA: Don't think I'm going to let you Athenians off. Don't you remember how the Spartans came in arms when you were wearing the rough, sheepskin cloak of slaves and slew the host of Thessalians, the comrades and allies of Hippias? Fighting with you on that day, alone of all the Greeks, they set you free and instead of a sheepskin gave your folk a handsome robe to wear.

SPARTAN (*looking at* LYSISTRATA): I've never seen a more distinguished woman.

ATHENIAN (*looking at Reconciliation*): I've never seen a more voluptuous body!

LYSISTRATA: Why then, with these many noble deeds to think of, do you fight each other? Why don't you stop this villainy? Why not make peace? Tell me, what prevents it?

SPARTAN (*waving vaguely at Reconciliation*): We're willing, if you're willing to give up your position on yonder flank.

LYSISTRATA: What position, my good man?

SPARTAN: Pylus; we've been panting for it for ever so long.

ATHENIAN: No, by God! You shan't have it!

LYSISTRATA: Let them have it, my friend.

ATHENIAN: Then what shall we have to rouse things up?

LYSISTRATA: Ask for another place in exchange.

ATHENIAN: Well, let's see: first of all (*pointing to various parts of Reconciliation's anatomy*) give us Echinus here, this Maliac Inlet in back there, and these two Megarian legs.

SPARTAN: No, by heavens! You can't have *everything*, you crazy fool!

LYSISTRATA: Let it go. Don't fight over a pair of legs.

ATHENIAN (*taking off his cloak*): I think I'll strip and do a little planting now.

SPARTAN (*following suit*): And I'll just do a little fertilizing, by gosh!

LYSISTRATA: Wait until the truce is concluded. Now if you've decided on this course, hold a conference and discuss the matter with your allies.

ATHENIAN: Allies? Don't be ridiculous! They're in the same state we are. Won't all our allies want the same thing we do—to jump in bed with their women?

SPARTAN: Ours will, I know.

ATHENIAN: Especially the Carystians, by God!

LYSISTRATA: Very well. Now purify yourselves, that your wives may feast and entertain you in the Acropolis; we've provisions by the basketfull. Exchange your oaths and pledges there, and then each of you may take his wife and go home.

ATHENIAN: Let's go at once.

SPARTAN: Come on, where you will.

ATHENIAN: For God's sake, let's hurry!

(*They all go into the Acropolis.*)

CHORUS (*singing*):

Whate'er I have of coverlets
  And robes of varied hue
And golden trinkets,—without stint
  I offer them to you.

Take what you will and bear it home,
  Your children to delight,
Or if your girl's a Basket-maid;
  Just choose whate'er's in sight.

There's naught within so well secured
  You cannot break the seal
And bear it off; just help yourselves;
  No hesitation feel.

But you'll see nothing, though you try,
Unless you've sharper eyes than I!

If anyone needs bread to feed
  A growing family,
I've lots of wheat and full-grown loaves;
  So just apply to me.

Let every poor man who desires
  Come round and bring a sack
To fetch the grain; my slave is there
  To load it on his back.

But don't come near my door, I say:
Beware the dog, and stay away!

(*An* ATHENIAN *enters carrying a torch; he knocks at the gate.*)

ATHENIAN: Open the door! (*to the* CHORUS, *which is clustered around the gate*) Make way, won't you! What are you hanging around for? Want me to singe you with this torch? (*to himself*) No; it's a stale trick, I won't do it! (*to the audience*) Still, if I've got to do it to please *you*, I suppose I'll have to take the trouble.

(*A* SECOND ATHENIAN *comes out of the gate.*)

SECOND ATHENIAN: And I'll help you.

FIRST ATHENIAN (*waving his torch at the* CHORUS): Get out! Go bawl your heads off! Move on there, so the Spartans can leave in peace when the banquet's over.

(*They brandish their torches until the* CHORUS *leaves the Orchestra.*)

SECOND ATHENIAN: I've never seen such a pleasant banquet: the Spartans are charming fellows, indeed they are! And we Athenians are very witty in our cups.

FIRST ATHENIAN: Naturally: for when we're sober we're never at our best. If the Athenians would listen to me, we'd always get a little tipsy on our embassies. As things are now, we go to Sparta when we're sober and look around to stir up trouble. And then we don't hear what they say—and as for what they *don't* say, we have all sorts of suspicions. And then we bring back varying reports about the mission. But this time everything is pleasant; even if a man should sing the Telamon-song when he ought to sing "Cleitagoras," we'd praise him and swear it was excellent.

(*The two* CHORUSES *return, as a* CHORUS OF ATHENIANS *and a* CHORUS OF SPARTANS.)

Here they come back again. Go to the devil, you scoundrels!

SECOND ATHENIAN: Get out, I say! They're coming out from the feast.

(*Enter the Spartan and Athenian envoys, followed by* LYSISTRATA *and all the women.*)

SPARTAN (*to one of his fellow-envoys*): My good fellow, take up your pipes; I want to do a fancy two-step and sing a jolly song for the Athenians.

ATHENIAN: Yes, do take your pipes, by all means. I'd love to see you dance.

SPARTAN (*singing and dancing with the* CHORUS OF SPARTANS): These youths inspire

> To song and dance, O Memory;
> Stir up my Muse, to tell how we
> And Athens' men, in our galleys clash-
>   ing
> At Artemisium, 'gainst foemen dashing
> In godlike ire,
> Conquered the Persian and set Greece
>   free.
> Leonidas

Led on his valiant warriors
Whetting their teeth like angry boars.
Abundant foam on their lips was
    flow'ring,
A stream of sweat from their limbs
    was show'ring.
The Persian was
Numberless as the sand on the shores.

O Huntress who slayest the beasts in
    the glade,
O Virgin divine, hither come to our
    truce,
Unite us in bonds which all time will
    not loose.
Grant us to find in this treaty, we pray,
An unfailing source of true friendship
    today,
And all of our days, helping us to refrain
From weaseling tricks which bring
    war in their train.
> Then hither, come hither! O huntress
>   maid.

LYSISTRATA: Come then, since all is fairly done, men of Sparta, lead away your wives, and you, Athenians, take yours. Let every man stand beside his wife, and every wife beside her man, and then, to celebrate our fortune, let's dance. And in the future, let's take care to avoid these misunderstandings.

CHORUS OF ATHENIANS (*singing and dancing*):
> Lead on the dances, your graces reveal-
>   ing.
> Call Artemis hither, call Artemis' twin,
> Leader of dances, Apollo the Healing,
> Kindly God—hither! let's summon
>   him in!

> Nysian Bacchus call,
> Who with his Maenads, his eyes flash-
>   ing fire,
> Dances, and last of all
> Zeus of the thunderbolt flaming, the
>   Sire,
> And Hera in majesty,
> Queen of prosperity.

> Come, ye Powers who dwell above
> Unforgetting, our witnesses be
> Of Peace with bonds of harmonious
>   love—
> The Peace which Cypris has wrought
>   for me.
> Alleluia! Io Paean!
> Leap in joy—hurrah! hurrah!
> 'Tis victory—hurrah! hurrah!
> Euoi! Euoi! Euai! Euai!

LYSISTRATA (*to the Spartans*): Come now, sing a new song to cap ours.

CHORUS OF SPARTANS (*singing and dancing*):
> Leaving Taygetus fair and renown'd
> Muse of Laconia, hither come:
> Amyclae's god in hymns resound,
> Athene of the Brazen Home,
> And Castor and Pollux, Tyndareus'
>   sons,
> Who sport where Eurotas murmuring
>   runs.

> On with the dance! Heia! Ho!
>   All leaping along,
> Mantles a-swinging as we go!
>   Of Sparta our song.
> There the holy chorus ever gladdens,
> There the beat of stamping feet,
> As our winsome fillies, lovely maidens,
> Dance, beside Eurotas' banks a-skip-
>   ping,—

Nimbly go to and fro
Hast'ning, leaping feet in measures
  tripping,
Like the Bacchae's revels, hair a-
  streaming.
Leda's child, divine and mild,
Leads the holy dance, her fair face
  beaming.
  On with the dance! as your hand
  Presses the hair
Streaming away unconfined.

Leap in the air
Light as the deer; footsteps resound
Aiding our dance, beating the ground.
Praise Athene, Maid divine, unrivalled
  in her might,
Dweller in the Brazen Home, uncon-
  quered in the fight.

(*All go out singing and dancing.*)

THE END

In Bernard Shaw's *Caesar and Cleopatra*, written in 1898 and first performed in 1907, the humor derives not from overt physical action or clever schemes, but from the ironic viewpoint of its central character. Shaw has here created a Caesar who is not only a world-conqueror but also a wise visionary, a comic seer: though he is fully successful in worldly terms and is a master of the scene in which he appears, he is also able to stand apart from the world's madness and confusion.

Reportedly dissatisfied with Shakespeare's conception of Julius Caesar in the play of that name, Shaw wrote his play partly to correct what he thought was an erroneous view, partly to construct a portrait of a genius who combines action and thought. In *Caesar and Cleopatra* Shaw permits Caesar to retain some of the authority and grandeur of his imposing historical image, but he also makes him the ironic observer of the pomp and ceremony of his own life. He endows him with the knowledge that, great as he now may be, he is nevertheless like all other men: he is little, and he will die. This is the knowledge that the Sun god Ra speaks of in the prologue; it is the knowledge that permits Caesar to smile in condescension and in secret understanding as he watches the vain struggles for power that go on around him; it is the knowledge that Shaw wishes to impart to his audience, writing the play as he did at the end of England's imperialist century.

This Caesar, this visionary who sees through men's pretensions, has a childlike, almost saintly, directness—the ability to get to essentials that is the mark of the hero of a comedy. He is not bewildered by his environment nor confused by the masks other people may wear. He is the asker of simple questions, those that bring us up short and make us examine the whole foundation of our lives. He is a supreme realist; he knows that in the Egypt he leaves at the end of the play, as in the world it symbolizes, the same mad race for power and vengeance will go on when his steadying influence is withdrawn. In terms of its plot, the play consists of a series of quasi-historical events, and it does follow Caesar as he walks through the world; but it is concerned primarily with what he sees, with what Cleopatra learns from him, not with where he is going. Its real subject is not Caesar's destiny or Cleopatra's, but the human folly his presence reveals. This revelation is, again, one of the great functions of comedy.

CAESAR AND CLEOPATRA

Bernard Shaw

CÆSAR	IRAS
CLEOPATRA	CHARMIAN
FTATATEETA	BELZANOR
POTHINUS	PERSIAN
THEODOTUS	CENTURION
PTOLEMY	SENTINEL
ACHILLAS	RA
RUFIO	BEL AFFRIS
BRITANNUS	NUBIAN SENTINEL
LUCIUS SEPTIMIUS	COURTIERS, SOLDIERS, SLAVES,
APOLLODORUS	LADIES, *et al.*

PROLOGUE

In the doorway of the temple of RA *in Memphis. Deep gloom. An august personage with a hawk's head is mysteriously visible by his own light in the darkness within the temple. He surveys the modern audience with great contempt; and finally speaks the following words to them.*

Peace! Be silent and hearken unto me, ye quaint little islanders. Give ear, ye men with white paper on your breasts and nothing written thereon (to signify the innocency of your minds). Hear me, ye women who adorn yourselves alluringly and conceal your thoughts from your men, leading them to believe that ye deem them wondrous strong and masterful whilst in truth ye hold them in your hearts as children without judgment. Look upon my hawk's head; and know that I am Ra, who was once in Egypt a mighty god. Ye cannot kneel nor prostrate yourselves; for ye are packed in rows without freedom to move, obstructing one another's vision; neither do any of ye regard it as seemly to do aught until ye all the rest do so too; wherefore it commonly happens that in great emergencies ye do nothing, though each telleth his fellow that something must be done. I ask you not for worship, but for silence. Let not your men speak nor your women cough; for I am come to draw you back two thousand years over the graves of sixty generations. Ye poor posterity,

think not that ye are the first. Other fools
before ye have seen the sun rise and set, and
the moon change her shape and her hour.
As they were so ye are; and yet not so great;
for the pyramids my people built stand to
this day; whilst the dustheaps on which ye
slave, and which ye call empires, scatter in
the wind even as ye pile your dead sons'
bodies on them to make yet more dust.

Hearken to me then, oh ye compulsorily
educated ones. Know that even as there is
an old England and a new, and ye stand
perplexed between the twain; so in the days
when I was worshipped was there an old
Rome and a new, and men standing perplexed between them. And the old Rome
was poor and little, and greedy and fierce,
and evil in many ways; but because its mind
was little and its work was simple, it knew
its own mind and did its own work; and
the gods pitied it and helped it and strengthened it and shielded it; for the gods are
patient with littleness. Then the old Rome,
like the beggar on horseback, presumed on
the favor of the gods, and said, "Lo! there
is neither riches nor greatness in our littleness: the road to riches and greatness is
through robbery of the poor and slaughter
of the weak." So they robbed their own
poor until they became great masters of
that art, and knew by what laws it could be
made to appear seemly and honest. And
when they had squeezed their own poor dry,
they robbed the poor of other lands, and
added those lands to Rome until there came
a new Rome, rich and huge. And I, Ra,
laughed; for the minds of the Romans
remained the same size whilst their dom-
inion spread over the earth.

Now mark me, that ye may understand
what ye are presently to see. Whilst the
Romans still stood between the old Rome
and the new, there arose among them a
mighty soldier: Pompey the Great. And the
way of the soldier is the way of death; but
the way of the gods is the way of life; and
so it comes that a god at the end of his way
is wise and a soldier at the end of his way is
a fool. So Pompey held by the old Rome,
in which only soldiers could become great;
but the gods turned to the new Rome, in

which any man with wit enough could
become what he would. And Pompey's
friend Julius Cæsar was on the side of the
gods; for he saw that Rome had passed
beyond the control of the little old Romans.
This Cæsar was a great talker and a politician: he bought men with words and with
gold, even as ye are bought. And when
they would not be satisfied with words and
gold, and demanded also the glories of war,
Cæsar in his middle age turned his hand to
that trade; and they that were against him
when he sought their welfare, bowed down
before him when he became a slayer and a
conqueror; for such is the nature of you
mortals. And as for Pompey, the gods
grew tired of his triumphs and his airs of
being himself a god; for he talked of law
and duty and other matters that concerned
not a mere human worm. And the gods
smiled on Cæsar; for he lived the life they
had given him boldly, and was not forever
rebuking us for our indecent ways of creation, and hiding our handiwork as a shameful
thing. Ye know well what I mean; for this
is one of your own sins.

And thus it fell out between the old Rome
and the new, that Cæsar said, "Unless I
break the law of old Rome, I cannot take
my share in ruling her; and the gift of ruling
that the gods gave me will perish without
fruit." But Pompey said, "The law is above
all; and if thou break it thou shalt die."
Then said Cæsar, "I will break it: kill me
who can." And he broke it. And Pompey
went for him, as ye say, with a great army
to slay him and uphold the old Rome. So
Cæsar fled across the Adriatic sea; for the
high gods had a lesson to teach him, which
lesson they shall also teach you in due time
if ye continue to forget them and to worship
that cad among gods, Mammon. Therefore
before they raised Cæsar to be master of
the world, they were minded to throw him
down into the dust, even beneath the feet
of Pompey, and blacken his face before the
nations. And Pompey they raised higher
than ever, he and his laws and his high
mind that aped the gods, so that his fall
might be the more terrible. And Pompey
followed Cæsar, and overcame him with all

the majesty of old Rome, and stood over him and over the whole world even as ye stand over it with your fleet that covers thirty miles of the sea. And when Cæsar was brought down to utter nothingness, he made a last stand to die honorably, and did not despair; for he said, "Against me there is Pompey, and the old Rome, and the law and the legions: all, all against me; but high above these are the gods; and Pompey is a fool." And the gods laughed and approved; and on the field of Pharsalia the impossible came to pass; the blood and iron ye pin your faith on fell before the spirit of man; for the spirit of man is the will of the gods; and Pompey's power crumbled in his hand, even as the power of imperial Spain crumbled when it was set against your fathers in the days when England was little, and knew her own mind, and had a mind to know instead of a circulation of newspapers. Wherefore look to it, lest some little people whom ye would enslave rise up and become in the hand of God the scourge of your boastings and your injustices and your lusts and stupidities.

And now, would ye know the end of Pompey, or will ye sleep while a god speaks? Heed my words well; for Pompey went where ye are gone, even to Egypt, where there was a Roman occupation even as there was but now a British one. And Cæsar pursued Pompey to Egypt: a Roman fleeing, and a Roman pursuing: dog eating dog. And the Egyptians said, "Lo: these Romans which have lent money to our kings and levied a distraint upon us with their arms, call for ever upon us to be loyal to them by betraying our own country to them. But now behold two Romes! Pompey's Rome and Cæsar's Rome! To which of the twain shall we pretend to be loyal?" So they turned in their perplexity to a soldier that had once served Pompey, and that knew the way of Rome and was full of her lusts. And they said to him, "Lo: in thy country dog eats dog; and both dogs are coming to eat us: what counsel hast thou to give us?" And this soldier, whose name was Lucius Septimius, and whom ye shall presently see before ye, replied, "Ye shall diligently consider which is the bigger dog of the two; and ye shall kill the other dog for his sake and thereby earn his favor." And the Egyptians said, "Thy counsel is expedient; but if we kill a man outside the law we set ourselves in the place of the gods; and this we dare not do. But thou, being a Roman, art accustomed to this kind of killing; for thou hast imperial instincts. Wilt thou therefore kill the lesser dog for us?" And he said, "I will; for I have made my home in Egypt; and I desire consideration and influence among you." And they said, "We knew well thou wouldst not do it for nothing: thou shalt have thy reward." Now when Pompey came, he came alone in a little galley, putting his trust in the law and the constitution. And it was plain to the people of Egypt that Pompey was now but a very small dog. So when he set his foot on the shore he was greeted by his old comrade Lucius Septimius, who welcomed him with one hand and with the other smote off his head, and kept it as it were a pickled cabbage to make a present to Cæsar. And mankind shuddered; but the gods laughed; for Septimius was but a knife that Pompey had sharpened; and when it turned against his own throat they said that Pompey had better have made Septimius a ploughman than so brave and ready-handed a slayer. Therefore again I bid you beware, ye who would all be Pompeys if ye dared; for war is a wolf that may come to your own door.

Are ye impatient with me? Do ye crave for a story of an unchaste woman? Hath the name of Cleopatra tempted ye hither? Ye foolish ones; Cleopatra is as yet but a child that is whipped by her nurse. And what I am about to shew you for the good of your souls is how Cæsar, seeking Pompey in Egypt, found Cleopatra; and how he received that present of a pickled cabbage that was once the head of Pompey; and what things happened between the old Cæsar and the child queen before he left Egypt and battled his way back to Rome to be slain there as Pompey was slain, by men in whom the spirit of Pompey still lived. All this ye shall see; and ye shall marvel, after your ignorant manner, that men twenty centuries ago were already just such as you, and spoke and lived as ye speak and live, no worse and no better, no wiser and no sillier. And the two thousand years that have past are to me, the god Ra, but a moment; nor is this day any other than the day in which Cæsar set foot in the land of my people. And now I leave you; for ye are a dull folk, and instruction is wasted on you; and I had not spoken so much but that it is in the nature of a god to struggle for ever with the dust and the darkness, and to drag from them, by the force of his longing for the divine, more life and more light. Settle ye therefore in your seats and keep silent; for ye are about to hear a man speak, and a great man he was, as ye count greatness. And fear not that I shall speak to you again: the rest of the story must ye learn from them that lived it. Farewell; and do not presume to applaud me. [*The temple vanishes in utter darkness.*]

An Alternative to the Prologue

An October night on the Syrian border of Egypt towards the end of XXXIII Dynasty, in the year 706 by Roman computation, afterwards reckoned by Christian computation as 48 B.C. A great radiance of silver fire, the dawn of a moonlit night, is rising in the east. The stars and the cloudless sky are our own contemporaries, nineteen and a half centuries younger than we know them; but you would not guess that from their appearance. Below them are two notable drawbacks of civilization: a palace, and soldiers. The palace, an old, low, Syrian building of whitened mud, is not so ugly as Buckingham Palace; and the officers in the courtyard are more highly civilized than modern English officers: for example, they do not dig up the corpses of their dead enemies and mutilate them, as we dug up Cromwell and the Mahdi. They are in two groups: one intent on the gambling of their captain Belzanor, a warrior of fifty, who, with his spear on the ground beside his knee, is stooping to throw dice with a sly-looking young Persian recruit; the other gathered about a guardsman who has just finished telling a naughty story (still current in English barracks) at which they are laughing uproariously. They are about a dozen in number, all highly aristocratic young Egyptian guardsmen, handsomely equipped with weapons and armor, very un-English in point of not being ashamed of and uncomfortable in their professional dress; on the contrary, rather ostentatiously and arrogantly warlike, as valuing themselves on their military caste.

Belzanor is a typical veteran, tough and wilful; prompt, capable and crafty where brute force will serve; helpless and boyish when it will not: an active sergeant, an incompetent general, a deplorable dictator. Would, if influentially connected, be employed in the two last capacities by a modern European State on the strength of his success in the first. Is rather to be pitied just now in view of the fact that Julius Cæsar is invading his country. Not knowing this, is intent on his game with the Persian, whom, as a foreigner, he considers quite capable of cheating him.

His subalterns are mostly handsome young fellows whose interest in the game and the story symbolize with tolerable completeness the main interests in life of which they are conscious. Their spears are leaning against the walls, or lying on the ground ready to their hands. The corner of the courtyard forms a triangle of which one side is the front of the palace, with a doorway, the other a wall with a gateway. The storytellers are on the palace side: the gamblers, on the gateway side. Close to the gateway, against the wall, is a stone block high enough to enable a Nubian sentinel, standing on it, to look over the wall. The yard is lighted by a torch stuck in the wall. As the laughter from the group round the storyteller dies away, the kneeling Persian, winning the throw, snatches up the stake from the ground.

BELZANOR. By Apis, Persian, thy gods are good to thee.

THE PERSIAN. Try yet again, O captain. Double or quits!

BELZANOR. No more. I am not in the vein.

THE SENTINEL. [*Poising his javelin as he peers over the wall.*] Stand. Who goes there? [*They all start, listening. A strange* VOICE *replies from without.*]

VOICE. The bearer of evil tidings.

BELZANOR. [*Calling to the sentry.*] Pass him.

THE SENTINEL. [*Grounding his javelin.*] Draw near, O bearer of evil tidings.

BELZANOR. [*Pocketing the dice and picking up his spear.*] Let us receive this man with honor. He bears evil tidings. [*The* GUARDS-MEN *seize their spears and gather about the gate, leaving a way through for the newcomer.*]

PERSIAN. [*Rising from his knee.*] Are evil tidings, then, so honorable?

BELZANOR. O barbarous Persian, hear my instruction. In Egypt the bearer of good tidings is sacrificed to the gods as a thank offering; but no god will accept the blood of the messenger of evil. When we have good tidings, we are careful to send them in the mouth of the cheapest slave we can find. Evil tidings are borne by young noblemen who desire to bring themselves into notice. [*They join the rest at the gate.*]

THE SENTINEL. Pass. O young captain; and bow the head in the House of the Queen.

VOICE. Go anoint thy javelin with fat of swine, O Blackamoor: for before morning the Romans will make thee eat it to the very butt. [*The owner of the* VOICE, *a fairhaired dandy, dressed in a different fashion from that affected by the* GUARDS-MEN, *but no less extravagantly, comes through the gateway laughing. He is somewhat battlestained; and his left forearm, bandaged, comes through a torn sleeve. In his right hand he carries a Roman sword in its sheath. He swaggers down the courtyard, the* PERSIAN *on his right,* BEL-ZANOR *on his left, and the* GUARDSMEN *crowding down behind him.*]

BELZANOR. Who are thou that laughest in the House of Cleopatra the Queen, and in the teeth of Belzanor, the captain of her guard?

THE NEW COMER. I am Bel Affris, descended from the gods.

BELZANOR. [*Ceremoniously.*] Hail, cousin!

ALL. [*Except the* PERSIAN.] Hail, cousin!

PERSIAN. All the Queen's guards are descended from the gods, O stranger, save myself. I am Persian, and descended from many kings.

BEL AFFRIS. [*To the* GUARDSMEN.] Hail, cousins! [*To the* PERSIAN, *condescendingly.*] Hail, mortal!

BELZANOR. You have been in battle, Bel Affris; and you are a soldier among soldiers. You will not let the Queen's women have the first of your tidings.

BEL AFFRIS. I have no tidings, except that we shall have our throats cut presently, women, soldiers, and all.

PERSIAN. [*To* BELZANOR.] I told you so.

THE SENTINEL. [*Who has been listening.*] Woe, alas!

BEL AFFRIS. [*Calling to him.*] Peace, peace, poor Ethiop: destiny is with the gods who painted thee black. [*To* BELZANOR.] What has this mortal [*Indicating the* PERSIAN.] told you?

BELZANOR. He says that the Roman Julius Cæsar, who has landed on our shores with a handful of followers, will make himself master of Egypt. He is afraid of the Roman soldiers. [*The* GUARDSMEN *laugh with boisterous scorn.*] Peasants, brought up to scare crows and follow the plough! Sons of smiths and millers and tanners! And we nobles, consecrated to arms, descended from the gods!

PERSIAN. Belzanor: the gods are not always good to their poor relations.

BELZANOR. [*Hotly, to the* PERSIAN.] Man to man, are we worse than the slaves of Cæsar?

BEL AFFRIS. [*Stepping between them.*] Listen, cousin. Man to man, we Egyptians are as gods above the Romans.

THE GUARDSMEN. [*Exultantly.*] Aha!

BEL AFFRIS. But this Cæsar does not pit man against man: he throws a legion at you where you are weakest as he throws a stone from a catapult; and that legion is as a man with one head, a thousand arms, and no religion. I have fought against them; and I know.

BELZANOR. [*Derisively.*] Were you frightened, cousin? [*The* GUARDSMEN *roar with laughter, their eyes sparkling at the wit of their captain.*]

BEL AFFRIS. No, cousin; but I was beaten. They were frightened (perhaps); but they scattered us like chaff. [*The* GUARDSMEN, *much damped, utter a growl of contemptuous disgust.*]

BELZANOR. Could you not die?

BEL AFFRIS. No: that was too easy to be worthy of a descendant of the gods. Besides, there was no time: all was over in a moment. The attack came just where we least expected it.

BELZANOR. That shews that the Romans are cowards.

BEL AFFRIS. They care nothing about cowardice, these Romans: they fight to win. The pride and honor of war are nothing to them.

PERSIAN. Tell us the tale of the battle. What befell?

THE GUARDSMEN. [*Gathering eagerly round* BEL AFFRIS.] Ay: the tale of the battle.

BEL AFFRIS. Know then, that I am a novice in the guard of the temple of Ra in Memphis, serving neither Cleopatra nor her brother Ptolemy, but only the high gods. We went a journey to inquire of Ptolemy why he had driven Cleopatra into Syria, and how we of Egypt should deal with the Roman Pompey, newly come to our shores after his defeat by Cæsar at Pharsalia. What, think ye, did we learn? Even that Cæsar is coming also in hot pursuit of his foe, and that Ptolemy has slain Pompey, whose severed head he holds in readiness to present to the conqueror. [*Sensation among the* GUARDSMEN.] Nay, more: we found that Cæsar is already come; for we had not made half a day's journey on our way back when we came upon a city rabble flying from his legions, whose landing they had gone out to withstand.

BELZANOR. And ye, the temple guard! did ye not withstand these legions?

BEL AFFRIS. What man could, that we did.

But there came the sound of a trumpet whose voice was as the cursing of a black mountain. Then saw we a moving wall of shields coming towards us. You know how the heart burns when you charge a fortified wall; but how if the fortified wall were to charge you?

THE PERSIAN. [*Exulting in having told them so.*] Did I not say it?

BEL AFFRIS. When the wall came nigh, it changed into a line of men—common fellows enough, with helmets, leather tunics, and breastplates. Every man of them flung his javelin: the one that came my way drove through my shield as through a papyrus—lo there! [*He points to the bandage on his left arm.*] and would have gone through my neck had I not stooped. They were charging at the double then, and were upon us with short swords almost as soon as their javelins. When a man is close to you with such a sword, you can do nothing with our weapons: they are all too long.

THE PERSIAN. What did you do?

BEL AFFRIS. Doubled my fist and smote my Roman on the sharpness of his jaw. He was but mortal after all: he lay down in a stupor; and I took his sword and laid it on. [*Drawing the sword.*] Lo! a Roman sword with Roman blood on it!

THE GUARDSMEN. [*Approvingly.*] Good!

[*They take the sword and hand it round, examining it curiously.*]

THE PERSIAN. And your men?

BEL AFFRIS. Fled. Scattered like sheep.

BELZANOR. [*Furiously.*] The cowardly slaves! Leaving the descendants of the gods to be butchered!

BEL AFFRIS. [*With acid coolness.*] The descendants of the gods did not stay to be butchered, cousin. The battle was not to the strong; but the race was to the swift. The Romans, who have no chariots, sent a cloud of horsemen in pursuit, and slew multitudes. Then our high priest's captain rallied a dozen descendants of the gods and exhorted us to die fighting. I said to myself: surely it is safer to stand than to lose my breath and be stabbed in the back; so I joined our captain and stood.

Then the Romans treated us with respect; for no man attacks a lion when the field is full of sheep, except for the pride and honor of war, of which these Romans know nothing. So we escaped with our lives; and I am come to warn you that you must open your gates to Cæsar; for his advance guard is scarce an hour behind me; and not an Egyptian warrior is left standing between you and his legions.

THE SENTINEL. Woe, alas! [*He throws down his javelin and flies into the palace.*]

BELZANOR. Nail him to the door, quick! [*The* GUARDSMEN *rush for him with their spears; but he is too quick for them.*] Now this news will run through the palace like fire through stubble.

BEL AFFRIS. What shall we do to save the women from the Romans?

BELZANOR. Why not kill them?

PERSIAN. Because we should have to pay blood money for some of them. Better let the Romans kill them: it is cheaper.

BELZANOR. [*Awestruck at his brain power.*] O subtle one! O serpent!

BEL AFFRIS. But your Queen?

BELZANOR. True: we must carry off Cleopatra.

BEL AFFRIS. Will ye not await her command?

BELZANOR. Command! a girl of sixteen! Not we. At Memphis ye deem her a Queen: here we know better. I will take her on the crupper of my horse. When we soldiers have carried her out of Cæsar's reach, then the priests and the nurses and the rest of them can pretend she is a Queen again, and put their commands into her mouth.

PERSIAN. Listen to me, Belzanor.

BELZANOR. Speak, O subtle beyond thy years.

THE PERSIAN. Cleopatra's brother Ptolemy is at war with her. Let us sell her to him.

THE GUARDSMEN. O subtle one! O serpent!

BELZANOR. We dare not. We are descended from the gods; but Cleopatra is descended from the river Nile; and the lands of our fathers will grow no grain if the Nile rises not to water them. Without our father's gifts we should live the lives of dogs.

PERSIAN. It is true: the Queen's guard cannot live on its pay. But hear me further, O ye kinsmen of Osiris.

THE GUARDSMEN. Speak, O subtle one. Hear the serpent begotten!

PERSIAN. Have I heretofore spoken truly to you of Cæsar, when you thought I mocked you?

GUARDSMEN. Truly, truly.

BELZANOR. [*Reluctantly admitting it.*] So Bel Affris says.

PERSIAN. Hear more of him, then. This Cæsar is a great lover of women: he makes them his friends and counsellors.

BELZANOR. Faugh! This rule of women will be the ruin of Egypt.

THE PERSIAN. Let it rather be the ruin of Rome! Cæsar grows old now: he is past fifty and full of labors and battles. He is too old for the young women; and the old women are too wise to worship him.

BEL AFFRIS. Take heed, Persian. Cæsar is by this time almost within earshot.

PERSIAN. Cleopatra is not yet a woman: neither is she wise. But she already troubles men's wisdom.

BELZANOR. Ay: that is because she is descended from the river Nile and a black kitten of the sacred White Cat. What then?

PERSIAN. Why, sell her secretly to Ptolemy, and then offer ourselves to Cæsar as volunteers to fight for the overthrow of her brother and the rescue of our Queen, the Great Granddaughter of the Nile.

THE GUARDSMEN. O serpent!

PERSIAN. He will listen to us if we come with her picture in our mouths. He will conquer and kill her brother, and reign in Egypt with Cleopatra for his Queen. And we shall be her guard.

GUARDSMEN. O subtlest of all the serpents! O admiration! O wisdom!

BEL AFFRIS. He will also have arrived before you have done talking, O word spinner.

BELZANOR. That is true. [*An affrighted uproar in the palace interrupts him.*] Quick: the flight has begun: guard the door. [*They rush to the door and form a cordon before it with their spears. A mob of women-servants and nurses surges out. Those in front recoil from the spears, screaming to those behind to keep back.* BELZANOR'S *voice dominates the disturbance as he shouts.*] Back there. In again, unprofitable cattle.

THE GUARDSMEN. Back, unprofitable cattle.

BELZANOR. Send us out Ftatateeta, the Queen's chief nurse.

THE WOMEN. [*Calling into the palace.*] Ftatateeta, Ftatateeta. Come, come. Speak to Belzanor.

A WOMAN. Oh, keep back. You are thrusting me on the spearheads. [*A huge grim woman, her face covered with a network of tiny wrinkles, and her eyes old, large, and wise; sinewy handed, very tall, very strong; with the mouth of a bloodhound and the jaws of a bulldog, appears on the threshold. She is dressed like a person of consequence in the palace, and confronts the* GUARDSMEN *insolently.*]

FTATATEETA. Make way for the Queen's chief nurse.

BELZANOR. [*With solemn arrogance.*] Ftatateeta: I am Belzanor, the captain of the Queen's guard, descended from the gods.

FTATATEETA. [*Retorting his arrogance with interest.*] Belzanor: I am Ftatateeta, the Queen's chief nurse; and your divine ancestors were proud to be painted on the wall in the pyramids of the kings whom my fathers served. [*The women laugh triumphantly.*]

BELZANOR. [*With grim humor.*] Ftatateeta: daughter of a long-tongued, swivel-eyed chameleon, the Romans are at hand. [*A cry of terror from* THE WOMEN: *they would fly but for the spears.*] Not even the descendants of the gods can resist them; for they have each man seven arms, each carrying seven spears. The blood in their veins is boiling quicksilver; and their wives become mothers in three hours, and are slain and eaten the next day. [*A shudder of horror from* THE WOMEN. FTATATEETA, *despising them and scorning the soldiers, pushes her way through the crowd and confronts the spear points undismayed.*]

FTATATEETA. Then fly and save yourselves, O cowardly sons of the cheap clay gods that are sold to fish porters; and leave us to shift for ourselves.

BELZANOR. Not until you have first done our bidding, O terror of manhood. Bring out Cleopatra the Queen to us; and then go whither you will.

FTATATEETA. [*With a derisive laugh.*] Now I know why the gods have taken her out of our hands. [*The* GUARDSMEN *start and look at one another.*] Know, thou foolish soldier, that the Queen has been missing since an hour past sundown.

BELZANOR. [*Furiously.*] Hag: you have hidden her to sell to Cæsar or her brother. [*He grasps her by the left wrist, and drags her, helped by a few of the guard, to the middle of the courtyard, where, as they fling her on her knees, he draws a murderous looking knife.*] Where is she? Where is she? or—[*He threatens to cut her throat.*]

FTATATEETA. [*Savagely.*] Touch me, dog; and the Nile will not rise on your fields for seven times seven years of famine.

BELZANOR. [*Frightened, but desperate.*] I will sacrifice: I will pay. Or stay. [*To the* PERSIAN.] You, O subtle one: your father's lands lie far from the Nile. Slay her.

PERSIAN. [*Threatening her with his knife.*] Persia has but one god; yet he loves the blood of old women. Where is Cleopatra?

FTATATEETA. Persian: as Osiris lives, I do not know. I chid her for bringing evil days upon us by talking to the sacred cats of the priests, and carrying them in her arms. I told her she would be left alone here when the Romans came as a punishment for her disobedience. And now she is gone—run away—hidden. I speak the truth. I call Osiris to witness—

THE WOMEN. [*Protesting officiously.*] She speaks the truth, Belzanor.

BELZANOR. You have frightened the child: she is hiding. Search—quick—into the palace—search every corner. [*The* GUARDS, *led by* BELZANOR, *shoulder their way into the palace through the flying crowd of women, who escape through the courtyard gate.*]

FTATATEETA. [*Screaming.*] Sacrilege! Men in the Queen's chambers! Sa— [*Her voice dies away as the Persian puts his knife to her throat.*]

BEL AFFRIS. [*Laying a hand on* FTATATEETA'S *left shoulder.*] Forbear her yet a moment, Persian. [*To* FTATATEETA, *very significantly.*] Mother: your gods are asleep or away hunting; and the sword is at your throat. Bring us to where the Queen is hid, and you shall live.

FTATATEETA. [*Contemptuously.*] Who shall stay the sword in the hand of a fool, if the high gods put it there? Listen to me, ye young men without understanding. Cleopatra fears me; but she fears the Romans more. There is but one power greater in her eyes than the wrath of the Queen's nurse and the cruelty of Cæsar; and that is the power of the Sphinx that sits in the desert watching the way to the sea. What she would have it know, she tells into the ears of the sacred cats; and on her birthday she sacrifices to it and decks it with poppies. Go ye therefore into the desert and seek Cleopatra in the shadow of the Sphinx; and on your heads see to it that no harm comes to her.

BEL AFFRIS. [*To the* PERSIAN.] May we believe this, O subtle one?

PERSIAN. Which way come the Romans?

BEL AFFRIS. Over the desert, from the sea, by this very Sphinx.

PERSIAN. [*To* FTATATEETA.] O mother of guile! O aspic's tongue! You have made up this tale so that we two may go into the desert and perish on the spears of the Romans. [*Lifting his knife.*] Taste death.

FTATATEETA. Not from thee, baby. [*She snatches his ankle from under him and flies stooping along the palace wall, vanishing in the darkness within its precinct.* BEL AFFRIS *roars with laughter as the* PERSIAN *tumbles. The* GUARDSMEN *rush out of the palace with* BELZANOR *and a mob of fugitives, mostly carrying bundles.*]

PERSIAN. Have you found Cleopatra?

BELZANOR. She is gone. We have searched every corner.

THE NUBIAN SENTINEL. [*Appearing at the door of the palace.*] Woe! Alas! Fly, fly!

BELZANOR. What is the matter now?

THE NUBIAN SENTINEL. The sacred white cat has been stolen.

ALL. Woe! woe! [*General panic. They all fly with cries of consternation. The torch is thrown down and extinguished in the rush. The noise of the fugitives dies away. Darkness and dead silence.*]

ACT I

The same darkness into which the temple of Ra and the Syrian palace vanished. The same silence. Suspense. Then the blackness and stillness break softly into silver mist and strange airs as the windswept harp of Memnon plays at the dawning of the moon. It rises full over the desert; and a vast horizon comes into relief, broken by a huge shape which soon reveals itself in the spreading radiance as a Sphinx pedestalled on the sands. The light still clears, until the upraised eyes of the image are distinguished looking straight forward and upward in infinite fearless vigil, and a mass of color between its great paws defines itself as a heap of red poppies on which a girl lies motionless, her silken vest heaving gently and regularly with the breathing of a dream-less sleeper, and her braided hair glittering in a shaft of moonlight like a bird's wing.

Suddenly there comes from afar a vaguely fearful sound (it might be the bellow of a Minotaur softened by great distance) and Memnon's music stops. Silence: then a few faint high-ringing trumpet notes. Then silence again. Then a man comes from the south with stealing steps, ravished by the mystery of the night, all wonder, and halts, lost in contemplation, opposite the left flank of the Sphinx, whose bosom, with its burden, is hidden from him by its massive shoulder.

THE MAN. Hail, Sphinx: salutation from Julius Cæsar! I have wandered in many lands, seeking the lost regions from which my birth into this world exiled me, and the company of creatures such as I myself. I have found flocks and pastures, men and cities, but no other Cæsar, no air native to me, no man kindred to me, none who can do my day's deed, and think my night's thought. In the little world yonder, Sphinx, my place is as high as yours in this great desert; only I wander, and you sit still; I conquer, and you endure; I work and wonder, you watch and wait; I look up and am dazzled, look down and am darkened, look round and am puzzled, whilst your eyes never turn from looking out—out of the world— to the lost region—the home from which we have strayed. Sphinx, you and I, strangers to the race of men, are no strangers to one another: have I not been conscious of you and of this place since I was born? Rome is a madman's dream: this is my Reality. These starry lamps of yours I have seen from afar in Gaul, in Britain, in Spain, in Thessaly, signalling great secrets to some eternal sentinel below, whose post I never could find. And here at last is their sentinel—an image of the constant and immortal part of my life, silent, full of thoughts, alone in the silver desert. Sphinx, Sphinx: I have climbed mountains at night to hear in the distance the stealthy footfall of the winds that case your sands in forbidden play— our invisible children, O Sphinx, laughing in whispers. My way hither was the way of destiny; for I am he of whose genius you are the symbol: part brute, part woman, and part god—nothing of man in me at all. Have I read your riddle, Sphinx?

THE GIRL. [*Who has wakened, and peeped cautiously from her nest to see who is speaking.*] Old gentleman.

CÆSAR. [*Starting violently, and clutching his sword.*] Immortal gods!

THE GIRL. Old gentleman: dont run away.

CÆSAR. [*Stupefied.*] "Old gentleman: dont run away"! ! ! This! to Julius Cæsar!

THE GIRL. [*Urgently.*] Old gentleman.

CÆSAR. Sphinx: you presume on your centuries. I am younger than you, though your voice is but a girl's voice as yet.

THE GIRL. Climb up here, quickly; or the Romans will come and eat you.

CÆSAR. [*Running forward past the Sphinx's shoulder, and seeing her.*] A child at its breast! a divine child!

THE GIRL. Come up quickly. You must get up at its side and creep round.

CÆSAR. [*Amazed.*] Who are you?

THE GIRL. Cleopatra, Queen of Egypt.

CÆSAR. Queen of the Gypsies, you mean.

CLEOPATRA. You must not be disrespectful to me, or the Sphinx will let the Romans eat you. Come up. It is quite cosy here.

CÆSAR. [*To himself.*] What a dream! What a magnificent dream! Only let me not wake, and I will conquer ten continents to pay for dreaming it out to the end. [*He climbs to the Sphinx's flank, and presently reappears to her on the pedestal, stepping round to its right shoulder.*]

CLEOPATRA. Take care. That's right. Now sit down: you may have its other paw. [*She seats herself comfortably on its left paw.*] It is very powerful and will protect us; but [*Shivering, and with plaintive loneliness.*] it would not take any notice of me or keep me company. I am glad you have come: I was very lonely. Did you happen to see a white cat anywhere?

CÆSAR. [*Sitting slowly down on the right paw in extreme wonderment.*] Have you lost one?

CLEOPATRA. Yes: the sacred white cat: is it not dreadful? I brought him here to sacrifice him to the Sphinx; but when we got a little way from the city a black cat called him, and he jumped out of my arms and ran away to it. Do you think that the black cat can have been my great-great-great-grandmother?

CÆSAR. [*Staring at her.*] Your great-great-great-grandmother! Well, why not? Nothing would surprise me on this night of nights.

CLEOPATRA. I think it must have been. My great-grandmother's great-grandmother was a black kitten of the sacred white cat; and the river Nile made her his seventh wife. That is why my hair is so wavy. And I always want to be let do as I like, no matter whether it is the will of the gods or not: that is because my blood is made with Nile water.

CÆSAR. What are you doing here at this time of night? Do you live here?

CLEOPATRA. Of course not: I am the Queen; and I shall live in the palace at Alexandria when I have killed my brother, who drove me out of it. When I am old enough I shall do just what I like. I shall be able to poison the slaves and see them wriggle, and pretend to Ftatateeta that she is going to be put into the fiery furnace.

CÆSAR. Hm! Meanwhile why are you not at home and in bed?

CLEOPATRA. Because the Romans are coming to eat us all. You are not at home and in bed either.

CÆSAR. [With conviction.] Yes I am. I live in a tent; and I am now in that tent, fast asleep and dreaming. Do you suppose that I believe you are real, you impossible little dream witch?

CLEOPATRA. [Giggling and leaning trustfully towards him.] You are a funny old gentleman. I like you.

CÆSAR. Ah that spoils the dream. Why dont you dream that I am young?

CLEOPATRA. I wish you were; only I think I should be more afraid of you. I like men, especially young men with round strong arms; but I am afraid of them. You are old and rather thin and stringy; but you have a nice voice; and I like to have somebody to talk to, though I think you are a little mad. It is the moon that makes you talk to yourself in that silly way.

CÆSAR. What! you heard that, did you? I was saying my prayers to the great Sphinx.

CLEOPATRA. But this isn't the great Sphinx.

CÆSAR. [Much disappointed, looking up at the statue.] What!

CLEOPATRA. This is only a dear little kitten of a Sphinx. Why, the great Sphinx is so big that it has a temple between its paws. This is my pet Sphinx. Tell me: do you think the Romans have any sorcerers who could take us away from the Sphinx by magic?

CÆSAR. Why? Are you afraid of the Romans?

CLEOPATRA. [Very seriously.] Oh, they would eat us if they caught us. They are barbarians. Their chief is called Julius Cæsar. His father was a tiger and his mother a burning mountain; and his nose is like an elephant's trunk. [Cæsar involuntarily rubs his nose.] They all have long noses, and ivory tusks, and little tails, and seven arms with a hundred arrows in each; and they live on human flesh.

CÆSAR. Would you like me to shew you a real Roman?

CLEOPATRA. [Terrified.] No. You are frightening me.

CÆSAR. No matter: this is only a dream—

CLEOPATRA. [Excitedly.] It is not a dream: it is not a dream. See, see. [She plucks a pin from her hair and jabs it repeatedly into his arm.]

CÆSAR. Ffff—Stop. [Wrathfully.] How dare you?

CLEOPATRA. [Abashed.] You said you were dreaming. [Whimpering.] I only wanted to shew you—

CÆSAR. [Gently.] Come, come: dont cry. A queen mustnt cry. [He rubs his arm, wondering at the reality of the smart.] Am I awake? [He strikes his hand against the Sphinx to test its solidity. It feels so real that he begins to be alarmed, and says perplexedly.] Yes, I— [Quite panicstricken.] No: impossible: madness, madness! [Desperately.] Back to camp—to camp. [He rises to spring down from the pedestal.]

CLEOPATRA. [Flinging her arms in terror round him.] No: you shant leave me. No, no, no: dont go. I'm afraid—afraid of the Romans.

CÆSAR. [As the conviction that he is really awake forces itself on him.] Cleopatra: can you see my face well?

CLEOPATRA. Yes. It is so white in the moonlight.

CÆSAR. Are you sure it is the moonlight that makes me look whiter than an Egyptian? [Grimly.] Do you notice that I have a rather long nose?

CLEOPATRA. [Recoiling, paralysed by a terrible suspicion.] Oh!

CÆSAR. It is a Roman nose, Cleopatra.

CLEOPATRA. Ah! [*With a piercing scream she springs up; darts round the left shoulder of the Sphinx; scrambles down to the sand; and falls on her knees in frantic supplication, shrieking.*] Bite him in two, Sphinx: bite him in two. I meant to sacrifice the white cat—I did indeed—I [*Cæsar, who has slipped down from the pedestal, touches her on the shoulder.*] —Ah! [*She buries her head in her arms.*]

CÆSAR. Cleopatra: shall I teach you a way to prevent Cæsar from eating you?

CLEOPATRA. [*Clinging to him piteously.*] Oh do, do, do. I will steal Ftatateeta's jewels and give them to you. I will make the river Nile water your lands twice a year.

CÆSAR. Peace, peace, my child. Your gods are afraid of the Romans: you see the Sphinx dare not bite me, nor prevent me carrying you off to Julius Cæsar.

CLEOPATRA. [*In pleading murmurings.*] You wont, you wont. You said you wouldnt.

CÆSAR. Cæsar never eats women.

CLEOPATRA. [*Springing up full of hope.*] What!

CÆSAR. [*Impressively.*] But he eats girls [*She relapses.*] and cats. Now you are a silly little girl; and you are descended from the black kitten. You are both a girl and a cat.

CLEOPATRA. [*Trembling.*] And will he eat me?

CÆSAR. Yes; unless you make him believe that you are a woman.

CLEOPATRA. Oh, you must get a sorcerer to make a woman of me. Are you a sorcerer?

CÆSAR. Perhaps. But it will take a long time; and this very night you must stand face to face with Cæsar in the palace of your fathers.

CLEOPATRA. No, no. I darent.

CÆSAR. Whatever dread may be in your soul—however terrible Cæsar may be to you—you must confront him as a brave woman and a great queen; and you must feel no fear. If your hand shakes: if your voice quavers; then—night and death! [*She moans.*] But if he thinks you worthy to rule, he will set you on the throne by his side and make you the real ruler of Egypt.

CLEOPATRA. [*Despairingly.*] No: he will find me out: he will find me out.

CÆSAR. [*Rather mournfully.*] He is easily deceived by women. Their eyes dazzle him; and he sees them not as they are but as he wishes them to appear to him.

CLEOPATRA. [*Hopefully.*] Then we will cheat him. I will put on Ftatateeta's headdress. and he will think me quite an old woman;

CÆSAR. If you do that he will eat you at one mouthful.

CLEOPATRA. But I will give him a cake with my magic opal and seven hairs of the white cat baked in it; and—

CÆSAR. [*Abruptly.*] Pah! you are a little fool. He will eat your cake and you too. [*He turns contemptuously from her.*]

CLEOPATRA. [*Running after him and clinging to him.*] Oh please, please! I will do whatever you tell me. I will be good. I will be your slave. [*Again the terrible bellowing note sounds across the desert, now closer at hand. It is the bucina, the Roman war trumpet.*]

CÆSAR. Hark!

CLEOPATRA. [*Trembling.*] What was that?

CÆSAR. Cæsar's voice.

CLEOPATRA. [*Pulling at his hand.*] Let us run away. Come. Oh, come.

CÆSAR. You are safe with me until you stand on your throne to receive Cæsar. Now lead me thither.

CLEOPATRA. [*Only too glad to get away.*] I will, I will. [*Again the bucina.*] Oh come, come, come: the gods are angry. Do you feel the earth shaking?

CÆSAR. It is the tread of Cæsar's legions.

CLEOPATRA. [*Drawing him away.*] This way, quickly. And let us look for the white cat as we go. It is he that has turned you into a Roman.

CÆSAR. Incorrigible, oh, incorrigible! Away! [*He follows her, the bucina sounding louder as they steal across the desert. The moonlight wanes: the horizon again shews black against the sky, broken only by the fantastic silhouette of the Sphinx. The sky itself vanishes in darkness, from which there is no relief until the gleam of a distant torch falls on great Egyptian pillars supporting the roof of a majestic corridor.*]

At the further end of this corridor a Nubian slave appears carrying the torch. CÆSAR, *still led by* CLEOPATRA, *follows him. They come down the corridor,* CÆSAR, *peering keenly about at the strange architecture, and at the pillar shadows between which, as the passing torch makes them hurry noiselessly backwards, figures of men with wings and hawks' heads, and vast black marble cats, seem to flit in and out of ambush. Further along, the wall turns a corner and makes a spacious transept in which* CÆSAR *sees, on his right, a throne, and behind the throne a door. On each side of the throne is a slender pillar with a lamp on it.*]

CÆSAR. What place is this?

CLEOPATRA. This is where I sit on the throne when I am allowed to wear my crown and robes. [*The slave holds his torch to shew the throne.*]

CÆSAR. Order the slave to light the lamps.

CLEOPATRA. [*Shyly.*] Do you think I may?

CÆSAR. Of course. You are the Queen. [*She hesitates.*] Go on.

CLEOPATRA. [*Timidly, to the slave.*] Light all the lamps.

FTATATEETA. [*Suddenly coming from behind the throne.*] Stop. [*The slave stops. She turns sternly to* CLEOPATRA, *who quails like a naughty child.*] Who is this you have with you; and how dare you order the lamps to be lighted without my permission? [CLEOPATRA *is dumb with apprehension.*]

CÆSAR. Who is she?

CLEOPATRA. Ftatateeta.

FTATATEETA. [*Arrogantly.*] Chief nurse to—

CÆSAR. [*Cutting her short.*] I speak to the Queen. Be silent. [*To* CLEOPATRA.] Is this how your servants know their places? Send her away; and do you [*to the slave*] do as the Queen has bidden. [*The slave lights the lamps. Meanwhile* CLEOPATRA *stands hesitating, afraid of* FTATATEETA.] You are the Queen: send her away.

CLEOPATRA. [*Cajoling.*] Ftatateeta, dear: you must go away—just for a little.

CÆSAR. You are not commanding her to go away: you are begging her. You are no Queen. You will be eaten. Farewell. [*He turns to go.*]

CLEOPATRA. [*Clutching him.*] No, no, no. Dont leave me.

CÆSAR. A Roman does not stay with queens who are afraid of their slaves.

CLEOPATRA. I am not afraid. Indeed I am not afraid.

FTATATEETA. We shall see who is afraid here. [*Menacingly.*] Cleopatra—

CÆSAR. On your knees, woman: am I also a child that you dare trifle with me? [*He points to the floor at* CLEOPATRA'S *feet.* FTATATEETA, *half cowed, half savage, hesitates.* CÆSAR *calls to the* NUBIAN.] Slave. [*The* NUBIAN *comes to him.*] Can you cut off a head? [*The* NUBIAN *nods and grins ecstatically, showing all his teeth.* CÆSAR *takes his sword by the scabbard, ready to offer the hilt to the* NUBIAN, *and turns again to* FTATATEETA, *repeating his gesture.*] Have you remembered yourself, mistress? [FTATATEETA, *crushed, kneels before* CLEOPATRA, *who can hardly believe her eyes.*]

FTATATEETA. [*Hoarsely.*] O Queen, forget not thy servant in the days of thy greatness.

CLEOPATRA. [*Blazing with excitement.*] Go. Begone. Go away. [FTATATEETA *rises with stooped head, and moves backwards towards the door.* CLEOPATRA *watches her submission eagerly, almost clapping her hands, which are trembling. Suddenly she cries.*] Give me something to beat her with. [*She snatches a snake-skin from the throne and dashes after* FTATATEETA, *whirling it like a scourge in the air.* CÆSAR *makes a bound and manages to catch her and hold her while* FTATATEETA *escapes.*]

CÆSAR. You scratch, kitten, do you?

CLEOPATRA. [*Breaking from him.*] I will beat somebody. I will beat him. [*She attacks the slave.*] There, there, there! [*The slave flies for his life up the corridor and vanishes. She throws the snakeskin away and jumps on the step of the throne with her arms waving, crying.*] I am a real Queen at last—a real, real Queen! Cleopatra the Queen! [CÆSAR *shakes his head dubiously, the advantage of the change seeming open to question from the point of view of the general welfare of Egypt. She turns and looks at him exultantly. Then she jumps*

*down from the steps, runs to him, and flings
her arms round him rapturously, crying.*]
Oh, I love you for making me a Queen.

CÆSAR. But queens love only kings.

CLEOPATRA. I will make all the men I love
kings. I will make you a king. I will have
many young kings, with round, strong
arms; and when I am tired of them I will
whip them to death; but you shall always
be my king: my nice, kind, wise, good
old king.

CÆSAR. Oh, my wrinkles, my wrinkles!
And my child's heart! You will be the
most dangerous of all Cæsar's conquests.

CLEOPATRA. [*Appalled.*] Cæsar! I forgot
Cæsar. [*Anxiously.*] You will tell him that
I am a Queen, will you not?—a real
Queen. Listen! [*Stealthily coaxing him.*]
let us run away and hide until Cæsar is
gone.

CÆSAR. If you fear Cæsar, you are no true
queen; and though you were to hide
beneath a pyramid, he would go straight
to it and lift it with one hand. And then
—! [*He chops his teeth together.*]

CLEOPATRA. [*Trembling.*] Oh!

CÆSAR. Be afraid if you dare. [*The note of
the bucina resounds again in the distance.
She moans with fear. CÆSAR exults in it,
exclaiming.*] Aha! Cæsar approaches the
throne of Cleopatra. Come: take your
place. [*He takes her hand and leads her
to the throne. She is too downcast to speak.*]
Ho, there, Teetatota. How do you call
your slaves?

CLEOPATRA. [*Spiritlessly, as she sinks on
the throne and cowers there, shaking.*]
Clap your hands. [*He claps his hands.
FTATATEETA returns.*]

CÆSAR. Bring the Queen's robes, and her
crown, and her women; and prepare her.

CLEOPATRA. [*Eagerly—recovering herself a
little.*] Yes, the crown, Ftatateeta: I shall
wear the crown.

FTATATEETA. For whom must the Queen
put on her state?

CÆSAR. For a citizen of Rome. A king of
kings, Totateeta.

CLEOPATRA. [*Stamping at her.*] How dare
you ask questions? Go and do as you
are told. [FTATATEETA *goes out with a*

grim smile. CLEOPATRA *goes on eagerly,
to* CÆSAR.] Cæsar will know that I am a
Queen when he sees my crown and robes,
will he not?

CÆSAR. No. How shall he know that you
are not a slave dressed up in the Queen's
ornaments?

CLEOPATRA. You must tell him.

CÆSAR. He will not ask me. He will know
Cleopatra by her pride, her courage, her
majesty, and her beauty. [*She looks very
doubtful.*] Are you trembling?

CLEOPATRA. [*Shivering with dread.*] No,
I—I— [*In a very sickly voice.*] No.

[FTATATEETA *and* THREE WOMEN *come in
with the regalia.*]

FTATATEETA. Of all the Queen's women,
these three alone are left. The rest are
fled. [*They begin to deck* CLEOPATRA, *who
submits, pale and motionless.*]

CÆSAR. Good, good. Three are enough.
Poor Cæsar generally has to dress himself.

FTATATEETA. [*Contemptuously.*] The queen
of Egypt is not a Roman barbarian.
[*To* CLEOPATRA.] Be brave, my nursling.
Hold up your head before this stranger.

CÆSAR. [*Admiring* CLEOPATRA, *and placing
the crown on her head.*] Is it sweet or
bitter to be a Queen, Cleopatra?

CLEOPATRA. Bitter.

CÆSAR. Cast out fear; and you will conquer
Cæsar. Tota: are the Romans at hand?

FTATATEETA. They are at hand; and the
guard has fled.

THE WOMEN. [*Wailing subduedly.*] Woe to us!
[*The* NUBIAN *comes running down the hall.*]

NUBIAN. The Romans are in the courtyard.
[*He bolts through the door. With a shriek,
the* WOMEN *fly after him.* FTATATEETA'S
*jaw expresses savage resolution: she does
not budge.* CLEOPATRA *can hardly restrain
herself from following them.* CÆSAR *grips
her wrist, and looks steadfastly at her.
She stands like a martyr.*]

CÆSAR. The Queen must face Cæsar alone.
Answer "So be it."

CLEOPATRA. [*White.*] So be it.

CÆSAR. [*Releasing her.*] Good. [*A tramp and
tumult of armed men is heard.* CLEOPATRA'S
*terror increases. The bucina sounds close
at hand, followed by a formidable clangor*

of trumpets. This is too much for CLEOPATRA: *she utters a cry and darts towards the door.* FTATATEETA *stops her ruthlessly.*]

FTATATEETA. You are my nursling. You have said "So be it"; and if you die for it, you must make the Queen's word good. [*She hands* CLEOPATRA *to* CÆSAR, *who takes her back, almost beside herself with apprehension, to the throne.*]

CÆSAR. Now, if you quail—! [*He seats himself on the throne.*]

[*She stands on the step, all but unconscious, waiting for death. The Roman soldiers troop in tumultuously through the corridor, headed by their ensign with his eagle, and their bucinator, a burly fellow with his instrument coiled round his body, its brazen bell shaped like the head of a howling wolf. When they reach the transept, they stare in amazement at the throne; dress into ordered rank opposite; draw their swords and lift them in the air with a shout of* Hail, CÆSAR. CLEOPATRA *turns and stares wildly at* CÆSAR; *grasps the situation; and, with a great sob of relief, falls into his arms.*]

ACT II

Alexandria. A hall on the first floor of the Palace, ending in a loggia approached by two steps. Through the arches of the loggia the Mediterranean can be seen, bright in the morning sun. The clean lofty walls, painted with a procession of the Egyptian theocracy, presented in profile as flat ornament, and the absence of mirrors, sham perspectives, stuffy upholstery and textiles, make the place handsome, wholesome, simple and cool, or, as a rich English manufacturer would express it, poor, bare, ridiculous and unhomely. For Tottenham Court Road civilization is to this Egyptian civilization as glass bead and tattoo civilization is to Tottenham Court Road.

The young king PTOLEMY DIONYSUS (aged ten) is at the top of the steps, on his way in through the loggia, led by his guardian POTHINUS, who has him by the hand. The court is assembled to receive him. It is made up of men and women (some of the women being officials) of various complexions and races, mostly Egyptian; some of them, comparatively fair, from lower Egypt, some, much darker, from upper Egypt; with a few Greeks and Jews. Prominent in a group on PTOLEMY's right hand is THEODOTUS, PTOLEMY's tutor. Another group, on PTOLEMY's left, is headed by ACHILLAS, the general of PTOLEMY's troops. THEODOTUS is a little old man, whose features are as cramped and wizened as his limbs, except his tall straight forehead, which occupies more space than all the rest of his face. He maintains an air of magpie keenness and profundity, listening to what the others say with the sarcastic vigilance of a philosopher listening to the exercises of his disciples. ACHILLAS is a tall handsome man of thirty-five, with a fine black beard curled like the coat of a poodle. Apparently not a clever man, but distinguished and dignified. POTHINUS is a vigorous man of fifty, a eunuch, passionate, energetic and quick witted, but of common mind and character; impatient and unable to control his temper. He has fine tawny hair, like fur. PTOLEMY, the King, looks much older than an English boy of ten; but he has the childish air, the habit of being in leading strings, the mixture of impotence and petulance, the appearance of being excessively washed, combed and dressed by other hands, which is exhibited by court-bred princes of all ages.

All receive the King with reverences. He comes down the steps to a chair of state which stands a little to his right, the only seat in the hall. Taking his place before it, he looks nervously for instructions to POTHINUS, who places himself at his left hand.

POTHINUS. The king of Egypt has a word to speak.

THEODOTUS. [*In a squeak which he makes impressive by sheer self-opinionativeness.*] Peace for the King's word!

PTOLEMY. [*Without any vocal inflexions: he is evidently repeating a lesson.*] Take notice of this all of you. I am the first-born son of Auletes the Flute Blower who was your King. My sister Berenice drove him from his throne and reigned in his stead but—but—[*He hesitates.*]—

POTHINUS. [*Stealthily prompting.*]—but the gods would not suffer—

PTOLEMY. Yes—the gods would not suffer—not suffer—[*He stops; then, crestfallen.*] I forgot what the gods would not suffer.

THEODOTUS. Let Pothinus, the King's guardian, speak for the King.

POTHINUS. [*Suppressing his impatience with difficulty.*] The King wished to say that the gods would not suffer the impiety of his sister to go unpunished.

PTOLEMY. [*Hastily.*] Yes: I remember the rest of it. [*He resumes his monotone.*] Therefore the gods sent a stranger one Mark Antony a Roman captain of horsemen across the sands of the desert and he set my father again upon the throne. And my father took Berenice my sister and struck her head off. And now that my father is dead yet another of his daughters my sister Cleopatra would snatch the kingdom from me and reign in my place. But the gods would not suffer—[POTHINUS *coughs admonitorily.*]—the gods—the gods would not suffer—

POTHINUS. [*Prompting.*]—will not maintain—

PTOLEMY. Oh yes—will not maintain such iniquity they will give her head to the axe even as her sister's. But with the help of the witch Ftatateeta she hath cast a spell on the Roman Julius Cæsar to make him uphold her false pretence to rule in Egypt. Take notice then that I will not suffer—that I will not suffer—[*Pettishly, to* POTHINUS.] What is it that I will not suffer?

POTHINUS. [*Suddenly exploding with all the force and emphasis of political passion.*] The King will not suffer a foreigner to take from him the throne of our Egypt. [*A shout of applause.*] Tell the King,

Achillas, how many soldiers and horsemen follow the Roman?

THEODOTUS. Let the King's general speak!

ACHILLAS. But two Roman legions, O King, Three thousand soldiers and scarce a thousand horsemen. [*The court breaks into derisive laughter; and a great chattering begins, amid which* RUFIO, *a Roman officer, appears in the loggia. He is a burly, black-bearded man of middle age, very blunt, prompt and rough, with small clear eyes, and plump nose and cheeks, which, however, like the rest of his flesh, are in ironhard condition.*]

RUFIO. [*From the steps.*] Peace, ho! [*The laughter and chatter cease abruptly.*] Cæsar approaches.

THEODOTUS. [*With much presence of mind.*] The King permits the Roman commander to enter! [CÆSAR, *plainly dressed, but wearing an oak wreath to conceal his baldness, enters from the loggia, attended by* BRITANNUS, *his secretary, a Briton, about forty, tall, solemn, and already slightly bald, with a heavy, drooping, hazel-colored moustache trained so as to lose its ends in a pair of trim whiskers. He is carefully dressed in blue, with portfolio, inkhorn, and reed pen at his girdle. His serious air and sense of the importance of the business in hand is in marked contrast to the kindly interest of* CÆSAR, *who looks at the scene, which is new to him, with the frank curiosity of a child, and then turns to the king's chair:* BRITANNUS *and* RUFIO *posting themselves near the steps at the other side.*]

CÆSAR. [*Looking at* POTHINUS *and* PTOLEMY.] Which is the King? the man or the boy?

POTHINUS. I am Pothinus, the guardian of my lord the King.

CÆSAR. [*Patting* PTOLEMY *kindly on the shoulder.*] So you are the King. Dull work at your age, eh? [*To* POTHINUS.] Your servant, Pothinus. [*He turns away unconcernedly and comes slowly along the middle of the hall, looking from side to side at the courtiers until he reaches* ACHILLAS.] And this gentleman?

THEODOTUS. Achillas, the King's general.

CÆSAR. [*To* ACHILLAS, *very friendly.*] A

general, eh? I am a general myself. But I began too old, too old. Health and many victories, Achillas!

ACHILLAS. As the gods will, Cæsar.

CÆSAR. [*Turning to* THEODOTUS.] And you, sir, are—?

THEODOTUS. Theodotus, the King's tutor.

CÆSAR. You teach men how to be kings, Theodotus. That is very clever of you. [*Looking at the gods on the walls as he turns away from* THEODOTUS *and goes up again to* POTHINUS.] And this place?

POTHINUS. The council chamber of the chancellors of the King's treasury, Cæsar.

CÆSAR. Ah! that reminds me. I want some money.

POTHINUS. The King's treasury is poor, Cæsar.

CÆSAR. Yes: I notice that there is but one chair in it.

RUFIO. [*Shouting gruffly.*] Bring a chair there, some of you, for Cæsar.

PTOLEMY. [*Rising shyly to offer his chair.*] Cæsar—

CÆSAR. [*Kindly.*] No, no, my boy: that is your chair of state. Sit down. [*He makes* PTOLEMY *sit down again. Meanwhile* RUFIO, *looking about him, sees in the nearest corner an image of the god* RA, *represented as a seated man with the head of a hawk. Before the image is a bronze tripod, about as large as a threelegged stool, with a stick of incense burning on it.* RUFIO, *with Roman resourcefulness and indifference to foreign superstitions, promptly seizes the tripod; shakes off the incense; blows away the ash; and dumps it down behind* CÆSAR, *nearly in the middle of the hall.*]

RUFIO. Sit on that, Cæsar. [*A shiver runs through the court, followed by a hissing whisper of* Sacrilege!]

CÆSAR. [*Seating himself.*] Now, Pothinus, to business. I am badly in want of money.

BRITANNUS. [*Disapproving of these informal expressions.*] My master would say that there is a lawful debt due to Rome by Egypt, contracted by the King's deceased father to the Triumvirate; and that it is Cæsar's duty to his country to require immediate payment.

CÆSAR. [*Blandly.*] Ah, I forgot. I have not made my companions known here. Pothinus: this is Britannus, my secretary. He is an islander from the western end of the world, a day's voyage from Gaul. [BRITANNUS *bows stiffly.*] This gentleman is Rufio, my comrade in arms. [RUFIO *nods.*] Pothinus: I want 1,600 talents. [*The courtiers, appalled, murmur loudly, and* THEODOTUS *and* ACHILLAS *appeal mutely to one another against so monstrous a demand.*]

POTHINUS. [*Aghast.*] Forty million sesterces! Impossible. There is not so much money in the King's treasury.

CÆSAR. [*Encouragingly.*] Only sixteen hundred talents, Pothinus. Why count it in sesterces? A sestertius is only worth a loaf of bread.

POTHINUS. And a talent is worth a racehorse. I say it is impossible. We have been at strife here, because the King's sister Cleopatra falsely claims his throne. The King's taxes have not been collected for a whole year.

CÆSAR. Yes they have, Pothinus. My officers have been collecting them all morning. [*Renewed whisper and sensation, not without some stifled laughter, among the courtiers.*]

RUFIO. [*Bluntly.*] You must pay, Pothinus. Why waste words? You are getting off cheaply enough.

POTHINUS. [*Bitterly.*] Is it possible that Cæsar, the conqueror of the world, has time to occupy himself with such a trifle as our taxes?

CÆSAR. My friend: taxes are the chief business of a conqueror of the world.

POTHINUS. Then take warning, Cæsar. This day, the treasures of the temple and the gold of the King's treasury shall be sent to the mint to be melted down for our ransom in the sight of the people. They shall see us sitting under bare walls and drinking from wooden cups. And their wrath be on your head, Cæsar, if you force us to this sacrilege!

CÆSAR. Do not fear, Pothinus: the people know how well wine tastes in wooden cups. In return for your bounty, I will settle this dispute about the throne for you, if you will. What say you?

POTHINUS. If I say no, will that hinder you?

RUFIO. [*Defiantly.*] No.

CÆSAR. You say the matter has been at issue for a year, Pothinus. May I have ten minutes at it?

POTHINUS. You will do your pleasure, doubtless.

CÆSAR. Good! But first, let us have Cleopatra here.

THEODOTUS. She is not in Alexandria: she is fled into Syria.

CÆSAR. I think not. [*To* RUFIO.] Call Totateeta.

RUFIO. [*Calling.*] Ho there, Teetatota. [FTATATEETA *enters the loggia, and stands arrogantly at the top of the step.*]

FTATATEETA. Who pronounces the name of Ftatateeta, the Queen's chief nurse?

CÆSAR. Nobody can pronounce it, Tota, except yourself. Where is your mistress? [CLEOPATRA, *who is hiding behind* FTATATEETA, *peeps out at them, laughing.* CÆSAR *rises.*]

CÆSAR. Will the Queen favor us with her presence for a moment?

CLEOPATRA. [*Pushing* FTATATEETA *aside and standing haughtily on the brink of the steps.*] Am I to behave like a Queen?

CÆSAR. Yes. [CLEOPATRA *immediately comes down to the chair of state; seizes* PTOLEMY; *drags him out of his seat; then takes his place in the chair.* FTATATEETA *seats herself on the step of the loggia, and sits there, watching the scene with sibylline intensity.*]

PTOLEMY. [*Mortified, and struggling with his tears.*] Cæsar: this is how she treats me always. If I am King why is she allowed to take everything from me?

CLEOPATRA. You are not to be King, you little cry-baby. You are to be eaten by the Romans.

CÆSAR. [*Touched by* PTOLEMY'S *distress.*] Come here, my boy, and stand by me. [PTOLEMY *goes over to* CÆSAR, *who, resuming his seat on the tripod, takes the boy's hand to encourage him.* CLEOPATRA, *furiously jealous, rises and glares at them.*]

CLEOPATRA. [*With flaming cheeks.*] Take your throne: I dont want it. [*She flings away from the chair, and approaches* PTOLEMY, *who shrinks from her.*] Go this instant and sit down in your place.

CÆSAR. Go, Ptolemy. Always take a throne when it is offered to you.

RUFIO. I hope you will have the good sense to follow your own advice when we return to Rome, Cæsar. [PTOLEMY *slowly goes back to the throne, giving* CLEOPATRA *a wide berth, in evident fear of her hands. She takes his place beside* CÆSAR.]

CÆSAR. Pothinus—

CLEOPATRA. [*Interrupting him.*] Are you not going to speak to me?

CÆSAR. Be quiet. Open your mouth again before I give you leave; and you shall be eaten.

CLEOPATRA. I am not afraid. A queen must not be afraid. Eat my husband there, if you like: he is afraid.

CÆSAR. [*Starting.*] You husband! What do you mean?

CLEOPATRA. [*Pointing to* PTOLEMY.] That little thing. [*The two Romans and the Briton stare at one another in amazement.*]

THEODOTUS. Cæsar: you are a stranger here, and not conversant with our laws. The kings and queens of Egypt may not marry except with their own royal blood. Ptolemy and Cleopatra are born king and consort just as they are born brother and sister.

BRITANNUS. [*Shocked.*] Cæsar: this is not proper.

THEODOTUS. [*Outraged.*] How!

CÆSAR. [*Recovering his self-possession.*] Pardon him, Theodotus: he is a barbarian, and thinks that the customs of his tribe and island are the laws of nature.

BRITANNUS. On the contrary, Cæsar, it is these Egyptians who are barbarians; and you do wrong to encourage them. I say it is a scandal.

CÆSAR. Scandal or not, my friend, it opens the gate of peace. [*He addresses* POTHINUS *seriously.*] Pothinus: hear what I propose.

RUFIO. Hear Cæsar there.

CÆSAR. Ptolemy and Cleopatra shall reign jointly in Egypt.

ACHILLAS. What of the King's younger brother and Cleopatra's younger sister?

RUFIO. [*Explaining.*] There is another little Ptolemy, Cæsar: so they tell me.

CÆSAR. Well, the little Ptolemy can marry the other sister; and we will make them both a present of Cyprus.

POTHINUS. [*Impatiently.*] Cyprus is of no use to anybody.

CÆSAR. No matter: you shall have it for the sake of peace.

BRITANNUS. [*Unconsciously anticipating a later statesman.*] Peace with honor, Pothinus.

POTHINUS. [*Mutinously.*] Cæsar: be honest. The money you demand is the price of our freedom. Take it; and leave us to settle our own affairs.

THE BOLDER COURTIERS. [*Encouraged by* POTHINUS's *tone and* CÆSAR's *quietness.*] Yes, yes. Egypt for the Egyptians! [*The conference now becomes an altercation, the Egyptians becoming more and more heated.* CÆSAR *remains unruffled; but* RUFIO *grows fiercer and doggeder, and* BRITANNUS *haughtily indignant.*]

RUFIO. [*Contemptuously.*] Egypt for the Egyptians! Do you forget that there is a Roman army of occupation here, left by Aulus Gabinius when he set up your toy king for you?

ACHILLAS. [*Suddenly asserting himself.*] And now under my command. *I* am the Roman general here, Cæsar.

CÆSAR. [*Tickled by the humor of the situation.*] And also the Egyptian general, eh?

POTHINUS. [*Triumphantly.*] That is so, Cæsar.

CÆSAR. [*To* ACHILLAS.] So you can make war on the Egyptians in the name of Rome, and on the Romans—on me, if necessary—in the name of Egypt?

ACHILLAS. That is so, Cæsar.

CÆSAR. And which side are you on at present, if I may presume to ask, general?

ACHILLAS. On the side of the right and of the gods.

CÆSAR. Hm! How many men have you?

ACHILLAS. That will appear when I take the field.

RUFIO. [*Truculently.*] Are your men Romans? If not, it matters not how many there

are, provided you are no stronger than 500 to ten.

POTHINUS. It is useless to try to bluff us, Rufio. Cæsar has been defeated before and may be defeated again. A few weeks ago Cæsar was flying for his life before Pompey: a few months hence he may be flying for his life before Cato and Juba of Numidia, the African King.

ACHILLAS. [*Following up* POTHINUS's *speech menacingly.*] What can you do with 4,000 men?

THEODOTUS. [*Following up* ACHILLAS's *speech with a raucous squeak.*] And without money? Away with you.

ALL THE COURTIERS. [*Shouting fiercely and crowding towards* CÆSAR.] Away with you. Egypt for the Egyptians! Be gone. [RUFIO *bites his beard, too angry to speak.* CÆSAR *sits as comfortably as if he were at breakfast, and the cat were clamoring for a piece of Finnan-haddie.*]

CLEOPATRA. Why do you let them talk to you like that, Cæsar? Are you afraid?

CÆSAR. Why, my dear, what they say is quite true.

CLEOPATRA. But if you go away, I shall not be Queen.

CÆSAR. I shall not go away until you are Queen.

POTHINUS. Achillas: if you are not a fool, you will take that girl whilst she is under your hand.

RUFIO. [*Daring them.*] Why not take Cæsar as well, Achillas?

POTHINUS. [*Retorting the defiance with interest.*] Well said, Rufio. Why not?

RUFIO. Try, Achillas. [*Calling.*] Guard there. [*The loggia immediately fills with* CÆSAR's *soldiers, who stand, sword in hand, at the top of the steps, waiting the word to charge from their centurion, who carries a cudgel. For a moment the Egyptians face them proudly: then they retire sullenly to their former places.*]

BRITANNUS. You are Cæsar's prisoners, all of you.

CÆSAR. [*Benevolently.*] Oh no, no, no. By no means. Cæsar's guests, gentlemen.

CLEOPATRA. Wont you cut their heads off?

CÆSAR. What! Cut off your brother's head?

CLEOPATRA. Why not? He would cut off mine, if he got the chance. Wouldnt you, Ptolemy?

PTOLEMY. [*Pale and obstinate.*] I would. I will, too, when I grow up. [CLEOPATRA *is rent by a struggle between her newly-acquired dignity as a queen, and a strong impulse to put out her tongue at him. She takes no part in the scene which follows, but watches it with curiosity and wonder, fidgeting with the restlessness of a child, and sitting down on* CÆSAR'S *tripod when he rises.*]

POTHINUS. Cæsar: if you attempt to detain us—

RUFIO. He will succeed, Egyptian: make up your mind to that. We hold the palace, the beach, and the eastern harbor. The road to Rome is open; and you shall travel it if Cæsar chooses.

CÆSAR. [*Courteously.*] I could do no less, Pothinus, to secure the retreat of my own soldiers. I am accountable for every life among them. But you are free to go. So are all here, and in the palace.

RUFIO. [*Aghast at this clemency.*] What! Renegades and all?

CÆSAR. [*Softening the expression.*] Roman army of occupation and all, Rufio.

POTHINUS. [*Bewildered.*] But—but—but—

CÆSAR. Well, my friend?

POTHINUS. You are turning us out of our own palace into the streets; and you tell us with a grand air that we are free to go! It is for you to go.

CÆSAR. Your friends are in the street, Pothinus. You will be safer there.

POTHINUS. This is a trick. I am the King's guardian: I refuse to stir. I stand on my right here. Where is your right?

CÆSAR. It is in Rufio's scabbard, Pothinus. I may not be able to keep it there if you wait too long. [*Sensation.*]

POTHINUS. [*Bitterly.*] And this is Roman justice!

THEODOTUS. But not Roman gratitude, I hope.

CÆSAR. Gratitude! Am I in your debt for any service, gentlemen?

THEODOTUS. Is Cæsar's life of so little account to him that he forgets that we have saved it?

CÆSAR. My life! Is that all?

THEODOTUS. Your life. Your laurels. Your future.

POTHINUS. It is true. I can call a witness to prove that but for us, the Roman army of occupation, led by the greatest soldier in the world, would now have Cæsar at its mercy. [*Calling through the loggia.*] Ho, there, Lucius Septimius [CÆSAR *starts, deeply moved.*] If my voice can reach you, come forth and testify before Cæsar.

CÆSAR. [*Shrinking.*] No, no.

THEODOTUS. Yes, I say. Let the military tribune bear witness. [LUCIUS SEPTIMIUS, *a clean shaven, trim athlete of about 40, with symmetrical features, resolute mouth, and handsome, thin Roman nose, in the dress of a Roman officer, comes in through the loggia and confronts* CÆSAR, *who hides his face with his robe for a moment; then, mastering himself, drops it, and confronts the tribune with dignity.*]

POTHINUS. Bear witness, Lucius Septimius. Cæsar came hither in pursuit of his foe. Did we shelter his foe?

LUCIUS. As Pompey's foot touched the Egyptian shore, his head fell by the stroke of my sword.

THEODOTUS. [*With viperish relish.*] Under the eyes of his wife and child! Remember that, Cæsar! They saw it from the ship he had just left. We have given you a full and sweet measure of vengeance.

CÆSAR. [*With horror.*] Vengeance!

POTHINUS. Our first gift to you, as your galley came into the roadstead, was the head of your rival for the empire of the world. Bear witness, Lucius Septimius: is it not so?

LUCIUS. It is so. With this hand, that slew Pompey, I placed his head at the feet of Cæsar.

CÆSAR. Murderer! So would you have slain Cæsar, had Pompey been victorious at Pharsalia.

LUCIUS. Woe to the vanquished, Cæsar! When I served Pompey, I slew as good men as he, only because he conquered them. His turn came at last.

THEODOTUS. [*Flatteringly.*] The deed was not yours, Cæsar, but ours—nay, mine; for it was done by my counsel. Thanks to us, you keep your reputation for clemency, and have your vengeance too.

CÆSAR. Vengeance! Vengeance!! Oh, if I could stoop to vengeance, what would I not exact from you as the price of this murdered man's blood? [*They shrink back, appalled and disconcerted.*] Was he not my son-in-law, my ancient friend, for 20 years the master of great Rome, for 30 years the compeller of victory? Did not I, as a Roman, share his glory? Was the Fate that forced us to fight for the mastery of the world, of our making? Am I Julius Cæsar, or am I a wolf, that you fling to me the grey head of the old soldier, the laurelled conqueror, the mighty Roman, treacherously struck down by this callous ruffian, and then claim my gratitude for it! [*To* LUCIUS SEPTIMIUS.] Begone: you fill me with horror.

LUCIUS. [*Cold and undaunted.*] Pshaw! You have seen severed heads before, Cæsar, and severed right hands too, I think; some thousands of them, in Gaul, after you vanquished Vercingetorix. Did you spare him, with all your clemency? Was that vengeance?

CÆSAR. No, by the gods! would that it had been! Vengeance at least is human. No, I say: those severed right hands, and the brave Vercingetorix basely strangled in a vault beneath the Capitol were [*With shuddering satire.*] a wise severity, a necessary protection to the commonwealth, a duty of statesmanship—follies and fictions ten times bloodier than honest vengeance! What a fool was I then! To think that men's lives should be at the mercy of such fools! [*Humbly.*] Lucius Septimius, pardon me: why should the slayer of Vercingetorix rebuke the slayer of Pompey? You are free to go with the rest. Or stay if you will: I will find a place for you in my service.

LUCIUS. The odds are against you, Cæsar. I go. [*He turns to go out through the loggia.*]

RUFIO. [*Full of wrath at seeing his prey escaping.*] That means that he is a Republican.

LUCIUS. [*Turning defiantly on the loggia steps.*] And what are you?

RUFIO. A Cæsarian, like all Cæsar's soldiers.

CÆSAR. [*Courteously.*] Lucius: believe me, Cæsar is no Cæsarian. Were Rome a true republic, then were Cæsar the first of Republicans. But you have made your choice. Farewell.

LUCIUS. Farewell. Come, Achillas, whilst there is yet time. [CÆSAR, *seeing that* RUFIO's *temper threatens to get the worse of him, puts his hand on his shoulder and brings him down the hall out of harm's way,* BRITANNUS *accompanying them and posting himself on* CÆSAR's *right hand. This movement brings the three in a little group to the place occupied by* ACHILLAS, *who moves haughtily away and joins* THEODOTUS *on the other side.* LUCIUS SEPTIMIUS *goes out through the soldiers in the loggia.* POTHINUS, THEODOTUS *and* ACHILLAS *follow him with the* COURTIERS, *very mistrustful of the* SOLDIERS, *who close up in their rear and go out after them, keeping them moving without much ceremony. The King is left in his chair, piteous, obstinate, with twitching face and fingers. During these movements* RUFIO *maintains an energetic grumbling, as follows.*]

RUFIO. [*As* LUCIUS *departs.*] Do you suppose he would let us go if he had our heads in his hands?

CÆSAR. I have no right to suppose that his ways are any baser than mine.

RUFIO. Psha!

CÆSAR. Rufio: if I take Lucius Septimius for my model, and become exactly like him, ceasing to be Cæsar, will you serve me still?

BRITANNUS. Cæsar: this is not good sense. Your duty to Rome demands that her enemies should be prevented from doing further mischief. [CÆSAR, *whose delight in the moral eye-to-business of his British secretary is inexhaustible, smiles indulgently.*]

RUFIO. It is no use talking to him, Britannus: you may save your breath to cool your porridge. But mark this, Cæsar. Clemency is very well for you; but what is it for your soldiers, who have to fight tomorrow the men you spared yesterday? You may give what orders you please; but I tell you that your next victory will be a massacre, thanks to your clemency. *I,*

for one, will take no prisoners. I will kill
my enemies in the field; and then you
can preach as much clemency as you
please: I shall never have to fight them
again. And now, with your leave, I will
see these gentry off the premises. [*He
turns to go.*]

CÆSAR. [*Turning also and seeing* PTOLEMY.]
What! have they left the boy alone! Oh
shame, shame!

RUFIO. [*Taking* PTOLEMY'S *hand and making
him rise.*] Come, your majesty!

PTOLEMY. [*To* CÆSAR, *drawing away his
hand from* RUFIO.] Is he turning me out
of my palace?

RUFIO. [*Grimly.*] You are welcome to stay
if you wish.

CÆSAR. [*Kindly.*] Go, my boy. I will not
harm you; but you will be safer away,
among your friends. Here you are in the
lion's mouth.

PTOLEMY. [*Turning to go.*] It is not the lion
I fear, but [*Looking at* RUFIO.] the jackal.
[*He goes out through the loggia.*]

CÆSAR. [*Laughing approvingly.*] Brave boy!

CLEOPATRA. [*Jealous of* CÆSAR'S *approbation,
calling after* PTOLEMY.] Little silly. You
think that very clever.

CÆSAR. Britannus: attend the King. Give
him in charge to that Pothinus fellow.
[BRITANNUS *goes out after* PTOLEMY.]

RUFIO. [*Pointing to* CLEOPATRA.] And this
piece of goods? What is to be done with
her? However, I suppose I may leave
that to you. [*He goes out through the
loggia.*]

CLEOPATRA. [*Flushing suddenly and turning
on* CÆSAR.] Did you mean me to go with
the rest?

CÆSAR. [*A little preoccupied, goes with a
sigh to* PTOLEMY'S *chair, whilst she waits
for his answer with red cheeks and clenched
fists.*] You are free to do just as you please,
Cleopatra.

CLEOPATRA. Then you do not care whether
I stay or not?

CÆSAR. [*Smiling.*] Of course I had rather
you stayed.

CLEOPATRA. Much, much rather?

CÆSAR. [*Nodding.*] Much, much rather.

CLEOPATRA. Then I consent to stay, because
I am asked. But I do not want to, mind.

CÆSAR. That is quite understood. [*Calling.*]
Totateeta. [FTATATEETA, *still seated, turns
her eyes on him with a sinister expression,
but does not move.*]

CLEOPATRA. [*With a splutter of laughter.*]
Her name is not Totateeta: it is Ftatateeta.
[*Calling.*] Ftatateeta. [FTATATEETA *instantly
rises and comes to* CLEOPATRA.]

CÆSAR. [*Stumbling over the name.*] Tfatafeeta
will forgive the erring tongue of a Roman.
Tota: the Queen will hold her state here
in Alexandria. Engage women to attend
upon her; and do all that is needful.

FTATATEETA. Am I then the mistress of the
Queen's household?

CLEOPATRA. [*Sharply.*] No: *I* am the mistress
of the Queen's household. Go and do
as you are told, or I will have you thrown
into the Nile this very afternoon, to
poison the poor crocodiles.

CÆSAR. [*Shocked.*] Oh no, no.

CLEOPATRA. Oh yes, yes. You are very
sentimental, Cæsar; but you are clever;
and if you do as I tell you, you will soon
learn to govern. [CÆSAR, *quite dumb-
founded by this impertinence, turns in his
chair and stares at her.* FTATATEETA,
*smiling grimly, and shewing a splendid set
of teeth, goes, leaving them alone together.*]

CÆSAR. Cleopatra: I really think I must
eat you, after all.

CLEOPATRA. [*Kneeling beside him and looking
at him with eager interest, half real, half
affected to shew how intelligent she is.*]
You must not talk to me now as if I
were a child.

CÆSAR. You have been growing up since
the sphinx introduced us the other night;
and you think you know more than I
do already.

CLEOPATRA. [*Taken down, and anxious to
justify herself.*] No: that would be very
silly of me: of course I know that. But—
[*Suddenly.*] are you angry with me?

CÆSAR. No.

CLEOPATRA. [*Only half believing him.*] Then
why are you so thoughtful?

CÆSAR. [*Rising.*] I have work to do, Cleopatra.

CLEOPATRA. [*Drawing back.*] Work! [*Offended.*] You are tired of talking to me; and
that is your excuse to get away from me.

CÆSAR. [*Sitting down again to appease her.*] Well, well: another minute. But then —work!

CLEOPATRA. Work! what nonsense! You must remember that you are a king now: I have made you one. Kings dont work.

CÆSAR. Oh! Who told you that, little kitten? Eh?

CLEOPATRA. My father was King of Egypt; and he never worked. But he was a great king, and cut off my sister's head because she rebelled against him and took the throne from him.

CÆSAR. Well; and how did he get his throne back again?

CLEOPATRA. [*Eagerly, her eyes lighting up.*] I will tell you. A beautiful young man, with strong round arms, came over the desert with many horsemen, and slew my sister's husband and gave my father back his throne. [*Wistfully.*] I was only twelve then. Oh, I wish he would come again, now that I am queen. I would make him my husband.

CÆSAR. It might be managed, perhaps; for it was I who sent that beautiful young man to help your father.

CLEOPATRA. [*Enraptured.*] You know him!

CÆSAR. [*Nodding.*] I do.

CLEOPATRA. Has he come with you? [CÆSAR *shakes his head: she is cruelly disappointed.*] Oh, I wish he had, I wish he had. If only I were a little older; so that he might not think me a mere kitten, as you do! But perhaps that is because you are old. He is many many years younger than you, is he not?

CÆSAR. [*As if swallowing a pill.*] He is somewhat younger.

CLEOPATRA. Would he be my husband, do you think, if I asked him?

CÆSAR. Very likely.

CLEOPATRA. But I should not like to ask him. Could you not persuade him to ask me—without knowing that I wanted him to?

CÆSAR. [*Touched by her innocence of the beautiful young man's character.*] My poor child!

CLEOPATRA. Why do you say that as if you were sorry for me? Does he love anyone else?

CÆSAR. I am afraid so.

CLEOPATRA. [*Tearfully.*] Then I shall not be his first love.

CÆSAR. Not quite the first. He is greatly admired by women.

CLEOPATRA. I wish I could be the first. But if he loves me, I will make him kill all the rest. Tell me: is he still beautiful? Do his strong round arms shine in the sun like marble?

CÆSAR. He is in excellent condition—considering how much he eats and drinks.

CLEOPATRA. Oh, you must not say common, earthly things about him; for I love him. He is a god.

CÆSAR. He is a great captain of horsemen, and swifter of foot than any other Roman.

CLEOPATRA. What is his real name?

CÆSAR. [*Puzzled.*] His real name?

CLEOPATRA. Yes, I always call him Horus, because Horus is the most beautiful of our gods. But I want to know his real name.

CÆSAR. His name is Mark Antony.

CLEOPATRA. [*Musically.*] Mark Antony, Mark Antony, Mark Antony! What a beautiful name! [*She throws her arms round* CÆSAR's *neck.*] Oh, how I love you for sending him to help my father! Did you love my father very much?

CÆSAR. No, my child; but your father, as you say, never worked. I always work. So when he lost his crown he had to promise me 16,000 talents to get it back for him.

CLEOPATRA. Did he ever pay you?

CÆSAR. Not in full.

CLEOPATRA. He was quite right: it was too dear. The whole world is not worth 16,000 talents.

CÆSAR. That is perhaps true, Cleopatra. Those Egyptians who work paid as much of it as he could drag from them. The rest is still due. But as I most likely shall not get it, I must go back to my work. So you must run away for a little and send my secretary to me.

CLEOPATRA. [*Coaxing.*] No: I want to stay and hear you talk about Mark Antony.

CÆSAR. But if I do not get to work, Pothinus and the rest of them will cut us off from the harbor; and then the way from Rome will be blocked.

CLEOPATRA. No matter: I dont want you to go back to Rome.

CÆSAR. But you want Mark Antony to come from it.

CLEOPATRA. [*Springing up.*] Oh, yes, yes, yes: I forgot. Go quickly and work, Cæsar; and keep the way over the sea open for my Mark Antony. [*She runs out through the loggia, kissing her hand to Mark Antony across the sea.*]

CÆSAR. [*Going briskly up the middle of the hall to the loggia steps.*] Ho, Britannus. [*He is startled by the entry of a wounded Roman* SOLDIER, *who confronts him from the upper step.*] What now?

SOLDIER. [*Pointing to his bandaged head.*] This, Cæsar; and two of my comrades killed in the market place.

CÆSAR. [*Quiet, but attending.*] Ay. Why?

SOLDIER. There is an army come to Alexandria, calling itself the Roman army.

CÆSAR. The Roman army of occupation. Ay?

SOLDIER. Commanded by one Achillas.

CÆSAR. Well?

SOLDIER. The citizens rose against us when the army entered the gates. I was with two others in the market place when the news came. They set upon us. I cut my way out; and here I am.

CÆSAR. Good. I am glad to see you alive. [RUFIO *enters the loggia hastily, passing behind the* SOLDIER *to look out through one of the arches at the quay beneath.*] Rufio: we are besieged.

RUFIO. What! Already?

CÆSAR. Now or tomorrow: what does it matter? We shall be besieged. [BRITANNUS *runs in.*]

BRITANNUS. Cæsar—

CÆSAR. [*Anticipating him.*] Yes: I know. [RUFIO *and* BRITANNUS *come down the hall from the loggia at opposite sides, past* CÆSAR, *who waits for a moment near the step to say to the* SOLDIER.] Comrade: give the word to turn out on the beach and stand by the boats. Get your wound attended to. Go. [*The* SOLDIER *hurries out.* CÆSAR *comes down the hall between*

RUFIO *and* BRITANNUS.] Rufio: we have some ships in the west harbor. Burn them.

RUFIO. [*Staring.*] Burn them!!

CÆSAR. Take every boat we have in the east harbor, and seize the Pharos—that island with the lighthouse. Leave half our men behind to hold the beach and the quay outside this palace: that is the way home.

RUFIO. [*Disapproving strongly.*] Are we to give up the city?

CÆSAR. We have not got it, Rufio. This palace we have; and—what is that building next door?

RUFIO. The theatre.

CÆSAR. We will have that too: it commands the strand. For the rest, Egypt for the Egyptians!

RUFIO. Well, you know best, I suppose. Is that all?

CÆSAR. That is all. Are those ships burnt yet?

RUFIO. Be easy: I shall waste no more time. [*He runs out.*]

BRITANNUS. Cæsar: Pothinus demands speech of you. In my opinion he needs a lesson. His manner is most insolent.

CÆSAR. Where is he?

BRITANNUS. He waits without.

CÆSAR. Ho there! admit Pothinus. [POTHINUS *appears in the loggia, and comes down the hall very haughtily to* CÆSAR's *left hand.*]

CÆSAR. Well, Pothinus?

POTHINUS. I have brought you our ultimatum, Cæsar.

CÆSAR. Ultimatum! The door was open: you should have gone out through it before you declared war. You are my prisoner now. [*He goes to the chair and loosens his toga.*]

POTHINUS. [*Scornfully.*] I your prisoner! Do you know that you are in Alexandria, and that King Ptolemy, with an army outnumbering your little troop a hundred to one, is in possession of Alexandria?

CÆSAR. [*Unconcernedly taking off his toga and throwing it on the chair.*] Well, my friend, get out if you can. And tell your friends not to kill any more Romans in the market place. Otherwise my soldiers, who do not share my celebrated clemency, will probably kill you. Britannus: pass the word to the guard; and fetch my armor. [BRITANNUS *runs out.* RUFIO *returns.*] Well?

RUFIO. [*Pointing from the loggia to a cloud of smoke drifting over the harbor.*] See there! [POTHINUS *runs eagerly up the steps to look out.*]

CÆSAR. What, ablaze already! Impossible!

RUFIO. Yes, five good ships, and a barge laden with oil grappled to each. But it is not my doing: the Egyptians have saved me the trouble. They have captured the west harbor.

CÆSAR. [*Anxiously.*] And the east harbor? The lighthouse, Rufio?

RUFIO. [*With a sudden splutter of raging ill usage, coming down to* CÆSAR *and scolding him.*] Can I embark a legion in five minutes? The first cohort is already on the beach. We can do no more. If you want faster work, come and do it yourself.

CÆSAR. [*Soothing him.*] Good, good. Patience, Rufio, patience.

RUFIO. Patience! Who is impatient here, you or I? Would I be here, if I could not oversee them from that balcony?

CÆSAR. Forgive me, Rufio; and [*Anxiously.*] hurry them as much as—[*He is interrupted by an outcry as of an old man in the extremity of misfortune. It draws near rapidly; and* THEODOTUS *rushes in, tearing his hair, and squeaking the most lamentable exclamations.* RUFIO *steps back to stare at him, amazed at his frantic condition.* POTHINUS *turns to listen.*]

THEODOTUS. [*On the steps, with uplifted arms.*] Horror unspeakable! Woe, alas! Help!

RUFIO. What now?

CÆSAR. [*Frowning.*] Who is slain?

THEODOTUS. Slain! Oh, worse than the death of ten thousand men! Loss irreparable to mankind!

RUFIO. What has happened, man?

THEODOTUS. [*Rushing down the hall between them.*] The fire has spread from your ships. The first of the seven wonders of the world perishes. The library of Alexandria is in flames.

RUFIO. Psha! [*Quite relieved, he goes up to the loggia and watches the preparations of the troops on the beach.*]

CÆSAR. Is that all?

THEODOTUS. [*Unable to believe his senses.*] All! Cæsar: will you go down to posterity as a barbarous soldier too ignorant to know the value of books?

CÆSAR. Theodotus: I am an author myself; and I tell you it is better that the Egyptians should live their lives than dream them away with the help of books.

THEODOTUS. [*Kneeling, with genuine literary emotion: the passion of the pedant.*] Cæsar: once in ten generations of men, the world gains an immortal book.

CÆSAR. [*Inflexible.*] If it did not flatter mankind, the common executioner would burn it.

THEODOTUS. Without history, death will lay you beside your meanest soldier.

CÆSAR. Death will do that in any case. I ask no better grave.

THEODOTUS. What is burning there is the memory of mankind.

CÆSAR. A shameful memory. Let it burn.

THEODOTUS. [*Wildly.*] Will you destroy the past?

CÆSAR. Ay, and build the future with its ruins. [THEODOTUS, *in despair, strikes himself on the temples with his fists.*] But harken, Theodotus, teacher of kings: you who valued Pompey's head no more than a shepherd values an onion, and who now kneel to me, with tears in your old eyes, to plead for a few sheepskins scrawled with errors. I cannot spare you a man or a bucket of water just now; but you shall pass freely out of the palace. Now, away with you to Achillas; and borrow his legions to put out the fire. [*He hurries him to the steps.*]

POTHINUS. [*Significantly.*] You understand, Theodotus: I remain a prisoner.

THEODOTUS. A prisoner!

CÆSAR. Will you stay to talk whilst the memory of mankind is burning? [*Calling through the loggia.*] Ho there! Pass Theodotus out. [*To* THEODOTUS.] Away with you.

THEODOTUS. [*To* POTHINUS.] I must go to save the library. [*He hurries out.*]

CÆSAR. Follow him to the gate, Pothinus. Bid him urge your people to kill no more of my soldiers, for your sake.

POTHINUS. My life will cost you dear if you take it, Cæsar. [*He goes out after* THEODOTUS. RUFIO, *absorbed in watching the embarkation, does not notice the departure of the two Egyptians.*]

RUFIO. [*Shouting from the loggia to the beach.*] All ready, there?

A CENTURION. [*From below.*] All ready. We wait for Cæsar.

CÆSAR. Tell them Cæsar is coming—the rogues! [*Calling.*] Britannicus. [*This magniloquent version of his secretary's name is one of* CÆSAR's *jokes. In later years it would have meant, quite seriously and officially, Conqueror of Britain.*]

RUFIO. [*Calling down.*] Push off, all except the longboat. Stand by it to embark, Cæsar's guard there. [*He leaves the balcony and comes down into the hall.*] Where are those Egyptians? Is this more clemency? Have you let them go?

CÆSAR. [*Chuckling.*] I have let Theodotus go to save the library. We must respect literature, Rufio.

RUFIO. [*Raging.*] Folly on folly's head! I believe if you could bring back all the dead of Spain, Gaul, and Thessaly to life, you would do it that we might have the trouble of fighting them over again.

CÆSAR. Might not the gods destroy the world if their only thought were to be at peace next year? [RUFIO, *out of all patience, turns away in anger.* CÆSAR *suddenly grips his sleeve, and adds slyly in his ear.*] Besides, my friend: every Egyptian we imprison means imprisoning two Roman soldiers to guard him. Eh?

RUFIO. Agh! I might have known there was some fox's trick behind your fine talking. [*He gets away from* CÆSAR *with an ill-humored shrug, and goes to the balcony for another look at the preparations; finally goes out.*]

CÆSAR. Is Britannus asleep? I sent him for my armor an hour ago. [*Calling.*] Britannicus, thou British islander. Britannicus! [CLEOPATRA *runs in through the loggia with* CÆSAR's *helmet and sword, snatched from* BRITANNUS, *who follows her with a cuirass and greaves. They come down to* CÆSAR, *she to his left hand,* BRITANNUS *to his right.*]

CLEOPATRA. I am going to dress you, Cæsar. Sit down. [*He obeys.*] These Roman helmets are so becoming! [*She takes off his wreath.*] Oh! [*She bursts out laughing at him.*]

CÆSAR. What are you laughing at?

CLEOPATRA. *Youre bald.* [*Beginning with a big B, and ending with a splutter.*]

CÆSAR. [*Almost annoyed.*] Cleopatra! [*He rises, for the convenience of* BRITANNUS, *who puts the cuirass on him.*]

CLEOPATRA. So that is why you wear the wreath—to hide it.

BRITANNUS. Peace, Egyptian: they are the bays of the conqueror. [*He buckles the cuirass.*]

CLEOPATRA. Peace, thou: islander! [*To* CÆSAR.] You should rub your head with strong spirits of sugar, Cæsar. That will make it grow.

CÆSAR. [*With a wry face.*] Cleopatra: do you like to be reminded that you are very young?

CLEOPATRA. [*Pouting.*] No.

CÆSAR. [*Sitting down again, and setting out his leg for* BRITANNUS, *who kneels to put on his greaves.*] Neither do I like to be reminded that I am—middle aged. Let me give you ten of my superfluous years. That will make you 26, and leave me only—no matter. Is it a bargain?

CLEOPATRA. Agreed. 26, mind. [*She puts the helmet on him.*] Oh! How nice! You look only about 50 in it!

BRITANNUS. [*Looking up severely at* CLEOPATRA.] You must not speak in this manner to Cæsar.

CLEOPATRA. Is it true that when Cæsar caught you on that island, you were painted all over blue?

BRITANNUS. Blue is the color worn by all Britons of good standing. In war we stain our bodies blue; so that though our enemies may strip us of our clothes and our lives, they cannot strip us of our respectability. [*He rises.*]

CLEOPATRA. [*With* CÆSAR's *sword.*] Let me

hang this on. Now you look splendid. Have they made any statues of you in Rome?

CÆSAR. Yes, many statues.

CLEOPATRA. You must send for one and give it to me.

RUFIO. [Coming back into the loggia, more impatient than ever.] Now Cæsar: have you done talking? The moment your foot is aboard there will be no holding our men back: the boats will race one another for the lighthouse.

CÆSAR. [Drawing his sword and trying the edge.] Is this well set today, Britannicus? At Pharsalia it was as blunt as a barrel-hoop.

BRITANNUS. It will split one of the Egyptian's hairs today, Cæsar. I have set it myself.

CLEOPATRA. [Suddenly throwing her arms in terror round CÆSAR.] Oh, you are not really going into battle to be killed?

CÆSAR. No, Cleopatra. No man goes to battle to be killed.

CLEOPATRA. But they do get killed. My sister's husband was killed in battle. You must not go. Let him go. [Pointing to RUFIO. They all laugh at her.] Oh please, please dont go. What will happen to me if you never come back?

CÆSAR. [Gravely.] Are you afraid?

CLEOPATRA. [Shrinking.] No.

CÆSAR. [With quiet authority.] Go to the balcony; and you shall see us take the Pharos. You must learn to look on battles. Go. [She goes, downcast, and looks out from the balcony.] That is well. Now, Rufio. March.

CLEOPATRA. [Suddenly clapping her hands.] Oh, you will not be able to go!

CÆSAR. Why? What now?

CLEOPATRA. They are drying up the harbor with buckets—a multitude of soldiers—over there [Pointing out across the sea to her left.]—they are dipping up the water.

RUFIO. [Hastening to look.] It is true. The Egyptian army! Crawling over the edge of the west harbor like locusts. [With sudden anger he strides down to CÆSAR.] This is your accursed clemency, Cæsar. Theodotus has brought them.

CÆSAR. [Delighted at his own cleverness.] I meant him to, Rufio. They have come to put out the fire. The library will keep them busy whilst we seize the lighthouse. Eh? [He rushes out buoyantly through the loggia, followed by BRITANNUS.]

RUFIO. [Disgustedly.] More foxing! Agh! [He rushes off. A shout from the soldiers announces the appearance of CÆSAR below.]

CENTURION. [Below.] All aboard. Give way there. [Another shout.]

CLEOPATRA. [Waving her scarf through the loggia arch.] Goodbye, goodbye, dear Cæsar. Come back safe. Goodbye!

ACT III

The edge of the quay in front of the palace, looking out west over the east harbor of Alexandria to Pharos island, just to the end of which, and connected with it by a narrow mole, is the famous lighthouse, a gigantic square tower of white marble diminishing in size storey by storey to the top, on which stands a cresset beacon. The island is joined to the main land by the Heptastadium, a great mole or causeway five miles long bounding the harbor on the south.

In the middle of the quay a Roman SENTINEL stands on guard, pilum in hand, looking out to the lighthouse with strained attention, his left hand shading his eyes. The pilum is a stout wooden shaft $4\frac{1}{2}$ feet long, with an iron spit about three feet long fixed in it. The SENTINEL is so absorbed that he does not notice the approach from the north end of the quay of four Egyptian market porters carrying rolls of carpet, preceded by FTATATEETA and APOLLODORUS the Sicilian. APOLLODORUS is a dashing young man of about 24, handsome and debonair, dressed with deliberate æstheticism in the most delicate purples and dove greys, with ornaments of bronze, oxydized silver, and stones of jade and agate. His sword, designed as carefully as a medieval cross, has a blued blade shewing through an openwork scabbard of purple leather and filigree. The porters, conducted by FTATA-TEETA, pass along the quay behind the SENTINEL to the steps of the palace, where they put down their bales and squat on the ground. APOLLODORUS does not pass along with them: he halts, amused by the preoccupation of the SENTINEL.

APOLLODORUS. [*Calling to the* SENTINEL.] Who goes there, eh?

SENTINEL. [*Starting violently and turning with his pilum at the charge, revealing himself as a small, wiry, sandy-haired, conscientious young man with an elderly face.*] What's this? Stand. Who are you?

APOLLODORUS. I am Apollodorus the Sicilian. Why, man, what are you dreaming of? Since I came through the lines beyond the theatre there, I have brought my caravan past three sentinels, all so busy staring at the lighthouse that not one of them challenged me. Is this Roman discipline?

SENTINEL. We are not here to watch the land but the sea. Cæsar has just landed on the Pharos. [*Looking at* FTATATEETA.] What have you here? Who is this piece of Egyptian crockery?

FTATATEETA. Apollodorus: rebuke this Roman dog; and bid him bridle his tongue in the presence of Ftatateeta, the mistress of the Queen's household.

APOLLODORUS. My friend: this is a great lady, who stands high with Cæsar.

SENTINEL. [*Not at all impressed, pointing to the carpets.*] And what is all this truck?

APOLLODORUS. Carpets for the furnishing of the Queen's apartments in the palace. I have picked them from the best carpets in the world; and the Queen shall choose the best of my choosing.

SENTINEL. So you are the carpet merchant?

APOLLODORUS. [*Hurt.*] My friend: I am a patrician.

SENTINEL. A patrician! A patrician keeping a shop instead of following arms!

APOLLODORUS. I do not keep a shop. Mine is a temple of the arts. I am a worshipper of beauty. My calling is to choose beautiful things for beautiful queens. My motto is Art for Art's sake.

SENTINEL. That is not the password.

APOLLODORUS. It is a universal password.

SENTINEL. I know nothing about universal passwords. Either give me the password for the day or get back to your shop. [FTATATEETA, *roused by his hostile tone, steals towards the edge of the quay with the step of a panther, and gets behind him.*]

APOLLODORUS. How if I do neither?

SENTINEL. Then I will drive this pilum through you.

APOLLODORUS. At your service, my friend. [*He draws his sword, and springs to his guard with unruffled grace.*]

FTATATEETA. [*Suddenly seizing the* SENTINEL'S *arms from behind.*] Thrust your knife into the dog's throat, Apollodorus. [*The chivalrous* APOLLODORUS *laughingly shakes his head; breaks ground away from the* SENTINEL *towards the palace; and lowers his point.*]

SENTINEL. [*Struggling vainly.*] Curse on you! Let me go. Help ho!

FTATATEETA. [*Lifting him from the ground.*] Stab the little Roman reptile. Spit him on your sword. [*A couple of Roman* SOLDIERS, *with a* CENTURION, *come running along the edge of the quay from the north end. They rescue their comrade, and throw off* FTATATEETA, *who is sent reeling away on the left hand of the* SENTINEL.]

CENTURION. [*An unattractive man of fifty, short in his speech and manners, with a vinewood cudgel in his hand.*] How now? What is all this?

FTATATEETA. [*To* APOLLODORUS.] Why did you not stab him? There was time!

APOLLODORUS. Centurion: I am here by order of the Queen to—

CENTURION. [*Interrupting him.*] The Queen! Yes, yes: [*To the* SENTINEL.] pass him in. Pass all these bazaar people in to the Queen, with their goods. But mind you pass no one out that you have not passed in—not even the Queen herself.

SENTINEL. This old woman is dangerous: she is as strong as three men. She wanted the merchant to stab me.

APOLLODORUS. Centurion: I am not a merchant. I am a patrician and a votary of art.

CENTURION. Is the woman your wife?

APOLLODORUS. [*Horrified.*] No, no! [*Correcting himself politely.*] Not that the lady is not a striking figure in her own way. But [*Emphatically.*] she is not my wife.

FTATATEETA. [*To the* CENTURION.] Roman: I am Ftatateeta, the mistress of the Queen's household.

CENTURION. Keep your hands off our men, mistress; or I will have you pitched into the harbor, though you were as strong as ten men. [*To his men.*] To your posts: march! [*He returns with his men the way they came.*]

FTATATEETA. [*Looking malignantly after him.*] We shall see whom Isis loves best: her servant Ftatateeta or a dog of a Roman.

SENTINEL. [*To* APOLLODORUS, *with a wave of his pilum towards the palace.*] Pass in there; and keep your distance. [*Turning to* FTATATEETA.] Come within a yard of me, you old crocodile; and I will give you this [*The pilum.*] in your jaws.

CLEOPATRA. [*Calling from the palace.*] Ftatateeta, Ftatateeta.

FTATATEETA. [*Looking up, scandalized.*] Go from the window, go from the window. There are men here.

CLEOPATRA. I am coming down.

FTATATEETA. [*Distracted.*] No, no. What are you dreaming of? O ye gods, ye gods! Apollodorus: bid your men pick up your bales; and in with me quickly.

APOLLODORUS. Obey the mistress of the Queen's household.

FTATATEETA. [*Impatiently, as the porters stoop to lift the bales.*] Quick, quick: she will be out upon us. [CLEOPATRA *comes from the palace and runs across the quay to* FTATATEETA.] Oh that ever I was born!

CLEOPATRA. [*Eagerly.*] Ftatateeta: I have thought of something. I want a boat—at once.

FTATATEETA. A boat! No, no: you cannot. Apollodorus: speak to the Queen.

APOLLODORUS. [*Gallantly.*] Beautiful queen: I am Apollodorus the Sicilian, your servant, from the bazaar. I have brought you the three most beautiful Persian carpets in the world to choose from.

CLEOPATRA. I have no time for carpets today. Get me a boat.

FTATATEETA. What whim is this? You cannot go on the water except in the royal barge.

APOLLODORUS. Royalty, Ftatateeta, lies not in the barge but in the Queen. [*To* CLEOPATRA.] The touch of your majesty's foot on the gunwale of the meanest boat in the harbor will make it royal. [*He turns to the harbor and calls seaward.*] Ho there, boatman! Pull in to the steps.

CLEOPATRA. Apollodorus: you are my perfect knight; and I will always buy my carpets through you. [APOLLODORUS *bows joyously. An oar appears above the quay; and the* BOATMAN, *a bullet-headed, vivacious, grinning fellow, burnt almost black by the sun, comes up a flight of steps from the water on the* SENTINEL'S *right, oar in hand, and waits at the top.*] Can you row, Apollodorus?

APOLLODORUS. My oars shall be your majesty's wings. Whither shall I row my Queen?

CLEOPATRA. To the lighthouse. Come. [*She makes for the steps.*]

SENTINEL. [*Opposing her with his pilum at the charge.*] Stand. You cannot pass.

CLEOPATRA. [*Flushing angrily.*] How dare you? Do you know that I am the Queen?

SENTINEL. I have my orders. You cannot pass.

CLEOPATRA. I will make Cæsar have you killed if you do not obey me.

SENTINEL. He will do worse to me if I disobey my officer. Stand back.

CLEOPATRA. Ftatateeta: strangle him.

SENTINEL. [*Alarmed—looking apprehensively at* FTATATEETA, *and brandishing his pilum.*] Keep off, there.

CLEOPATRA. [*Running to* APOLLODORUS.]

Apollodorus: make your slaves help us.

APOLLODORUS. I shall not need their help, lady. [*He draws his sword.*] Now, soldier: choose which weapon you will defend yourself with. Shall it be sword against pilum, or sword against sword?

SENTINEL. Roman against Sicilian, curse you. Take that. [*He hurls his pilum at* APOLLODORUS, *who drops expertly on one knee. The pilum passes whizzing over his head and falls harmless.* APOLLODORUS, *with a cry of triumph, springs up and attacks the* SENTINEL, *who draws his sword and defends himself, crying.*] Ho there, guard. Help! [CLEOPATRA, *half frightened, half delighted, takes refuge near the palace, where the porters are squatting among the bales. The* BOATMAN, *alarmed, hurries down the steps out of harm's way, but stops, with his head just visible above the edge of the quay, to watch the fight. The* SENTINEL *is handicapped by his fear of an attack in the rear from* FTATATEETA. *His swordsmanship, which is of rough and ready sort, is heavily taxed, as he has occasionally to strike at her to keep her off between a blow and a guard with* APOLLODORUS. *The* CENTURION *returns with several* SOLDIERS. APOLLODORUS *springs back towards* CLEOPATRA *as this reinforcement confronts him.*]

CENTURION. [*Coming to the* SENTINEL'S *right hand.*] What is this? What now?

SENTINEL. [*Panting.*] I could do well enough by myself if it werent for the old woman. Keep her off me: that is all the help I need.

CENTURION. Make your report, soldier. What has happened?

FTATATEETA. Centurion: he would have slain the Queen.

SENTINEL. [*Bluntly.*] I would, sooner than let her pass. She wanted to take boat, and go—so she said—to the lighthouse. I stopped her, as I was ordered to; and she set this fellow on me. [*He goes to pick up his pilum and returns to his place with it.*]

CENTURION. [*Turning to* CLEOPATRA.] Cleopatra: I am loth to offend you; but without Cæsar's express order we dare not let you pass beyond the Roman lines.

APOLLODORUS. Well, Centurion; and has not the lighthouse been within the Roman lines since Cæsar landed there?

CLEOPATRA. Yes, yes. Answer that, if you can.

CENTURION. [*To* APOLLODORUS.] As for you, Apollodorus, you may thank the gods that you are not nailed to the palace door with a pilum for your meddling.

APOLLODORUS. [*Urbanely.*] My military friend, I was not born to be slain by so ugly a weapon. When I fall, it will be [*Holding up his sword.*] by this white queen of arms, the only weapon fit for an artist. And now that you are convinced that we do not want to go beyond the lines, let me finish killing your sentinel and depart with the Queen.

CENTURION. [*As the* SENTINEL *makes an angry demonstration.*] Peace there, Cleopatra: I must abide by my orders, and not by the subtleties of this Sicilian. You must withdraw into the palace and examine your carpets there.

CLEOPATRA. [*Pouting.*] I will not: I am the Queen. Cæsar does not speak to me as you do. Have Cæsar's centurions changed manners with his scullions?

CENTURION. [*Sulkily.*] I do my duty. That is enough for me.

APOLLODORUS. Majesty: when a stupid man is doing something he is ashamed of, he always declares that it is his duty.

CENTURION. [*Angry.*] Apollodorus—

APOLLODORUS. [*Interrupting him with defiant elegance.*] I will make amends for that insult with my sword at fitting time and place. Who says artist, says duellist. [*To* CLEOPATRA.] Hear my counsel, star of the east. Until word comes to these soldiers from Cæsar himself, you are a prisoner. Let me go to him with a message from you, and a present; and before the sun has stooped half way to the arms of the sea, I will bring you back Cæsar's order of release.

CENTURION. [*Sneering at him.*] And you will sell the Queen the present, no doubt.

APOLLODORUS. Centurion: the Queen shall have from me, without payment, as the unforced tribute of Sicilian taste to Egyptian beauty, the richest of these carpets for her present to Cæsar.

CLEOPATRA. [*Exultantly, to the* CENTURION.] Now you see what an ignorant common creature you are!

CENTURION. [*Curtly.*] Well, a fool and his wares are soon parted. [*He turns to his* MEN.] Two more men to this post here; and see that no one leaves the palace but this man and his merchandise. If he draws his sword again inside the lines, kill him. To your posts. March. [*He goes out, leaving two auxiliary* SENTINELS *with the other.*]

APOLLODORUS. [*With polite goodfellowship.*] My friends: will you not enter the palace and bury our quarrel in a bowl of wine? [*He takes out his purse, jingling the coins in it.*] The Queen has presents for you all.

SENTINEL. [*Very sulky.*] You heard our orders. Get about your business.

FIRST AUXILIARY. Yes: you ought to know better. Off with you.

SECOND AUXILIARY. [*Looking longingly at the purse—this* SENTINEL *is a hooknosed man, unlike his comrade, who is squab faced.*] Do not tantalize a poor man.

APOLLODORUS. [*To* CLEOPATRA.] Pearl of Queens: the centurion is at hand; and the Roman soldier is incorruptible when his officer is looking. I must carry your word to Cæsar.

CLEOPATRA. [*Who has been meditating among the carpets.*] Are these carpets very heavy?

APOLLODORUS. It matters not how heavy. There are plenty of porters.

CLEOPATRA. How do they put the carpets into boats? Do they throw them down?

APOLLODORUS. Not into small boats, majesty. It would sink them.

CLEOPATRA. Not into that man's boat, for instance? [*Pointing to the* BOATMAN.]

APOLLODORUS. No. Too small.

CLEOPATRA. But you can take a carpet to Cæsar in it if I send one?

APOLLODORUS. Assuredly.

CLEOPATRA. And you will have it carried gently down the steps and take great care of it?

APOLLODORUS. Depend on me.

CLEOPATRA. Great, great care?

APOLLODORUS. More than of my own body.

CLEOPATRA. You will promise me not to let the porters drop it or throw it about?

APOLLODORUS. Place the most delicate glass goblet in the palace in the heart of the roll, Queen; and if it be broken, my head shall pay for it.

CLEOPATRA. Good. Come, Ftatateeta. [FTATATEETA *comes to her.* APOLLODORUS *offers to squire them into the palace.*] No, Apollodorus, you must not come. I will choose a carpet for myself. You must wait here. [*She runs into the palace.*]

APOLLODORUS. [*To the* PORTERS.] Follow this lady [*Indicating* FTATATEETA.] and obey her. [*The* PORTERS *rise and take up their bales.*]

FTATATEETA. [*Addressing the* PORTERS *as if they were vermin.*] This way. And take your shoes off before you put your feet on those stairs. [*She goes in, followed by the* PORTERS *with the carpets. Meanwhile* APOLLODORUS *goes to the edge of the quay and looks out over the harbor. The* SENTINELS *keep their eyes on him malignantly.*]

APOLLODORUS. [*Addressing the* SENTINEL.] My friend—

SENTINEL. [*Rudely.*] Silence there.

FIRST AUXILIARY. Shut your muzzle, you.

SECOND AUXILIARY. [*In a half whisper, glancing apprehensively towards the north end of the quay.*] Cant you wait a bit?

APOLLODORUS. Patience, worthy three-headed donkey. [*They mutter ferociously; but he is not at all intimidated.*] Listen: were you set here to watch me, or to watch the Egyptians?

SENTINEL. We know our duty.

APOLLODORUS. Then why dont you do it? There is something going on over there. [*Pointing southwestward to the mole.*]

SENTINEL. [*Sulkily.*] I do not need to be told what to do by the like of you.

APOLLODORUS. Blockhead. [*He begins shouting.*] Ho there, Centurion. Hoiho!

SENTINEL. Curse your meddling. [*Shouting.*] Hoiho! Alarm! Alarm!

FIRST AND SECOND AUXILIARIES. Alarm! Alarm! Hoiho! [*The* CENTURION *comes running in with his* GUARD.]

CENTURION. What now? Has the old woman attacked you again? [*Seeing* APOLLODORUS.] Are you here still?

APOLLODORUS. [*Pointing as before.*] See there. The Egyptians are moving. They are going to recapture the Pharos. They will attack by sea and land: by land along the great mole; by sea from the west harbor. Stir yourselves, my military friends: the hunt is up. [*A clangor of trumpets from several points along the quay.*] Aha! I told you so.

CENTURION. [*Quickly.*] The two extra men pass the alarm to the south posts. One man keep guard here. The rest with me— quick. [*The two* AUXILIARY SENTINELS *run off to the south. The* CENTURION *and his* GUARD *run off northward; and immediately afterwards the bucina sounds. The four* PORTERS *come from the palace carrying a carpet, followed by* FTATATEETA.]

SENTINEL. [*Handling his pilum apprehensively.*] You again! [*The* PORTERS *stop.*]

FTATATEETA. Peace, Roman fellow: you are now single-handed. Apollodorus: this carpet is Cleopatra's present to Cæsar. It has rolled up in it ten precious goblets of the thinnest Iberian crystal, and a hundred eggs of the sacred blue pigeon. On your honor, let not one of them be broken.

APOLLODORUS. On my head be it! [*To the* PORTERS.] Into the boat with them carefully. [*The* PORTERS *carry the carpet to the steps.*]

FIRST PORTER. [*Looking down at the boat.*] Beware what you do, sir. Those eggs of which the lady speaks must weigh more than a pound apiece. This boat is too small for such a load.

BOATMAN. [*Excitedly rushing up the steps.*] Oh thou injurious porter! Oh thou unnatural son of a she-camel! [*To* APOLLODORUS.] My boat, sir, hath often carried five men. Shall it not carry your lordship and a bale of pigeon's eggs? [*To the* PORTER.] Thou mangey dromedary, the gods shall punish thee for this envious wickedness.

FIRST PORTER. [*Stolidly.*] I cannot quit this bale now to beat these; but another day I will lie in wait for thee.

APOLLODORUS. [*Going between them.*] Peace there. If the boat were but a single plank, I would get to Cæsar on it.

FTATATEETA. [*Anxiously.*] In the name of the gods, Apollodorus, run no risks with that bale.

APOLLODORUS. Fear not, thou venerable grotesque: I guess its great worth. [*To the* PORTERS.] Down with it, I say; and gently; or ye shall eat nothing but stick for ten days. [*The* BOATMAN *goes down the steps, followed by the* PORTERS *with the bale:* FTATATEETA *and* APOLLODORUS *watching from the edge.*]

APOLLODORUS. Gently, my sons, my children—[*With sudden alarm.*] gently, ye dogs. Lay it level in the stern—so—tis well.

FTATATEETA. [*Screaming down at one of the* PORTERS.] Do not step on it, do not step on it. Oh thou brute beast!

FIRST PORTER. [*Ascending.*] Be not excited, mistress: all is well.

FTATATEETA. [*Panting.*] All well! Oh, thou hast given my heart a turn! [*She clutches her side, gasping. The four* PORTERS *have now come up and are waiting at the stairhead to be paid.*]

APOLLODORUS. Here, ye hungry ones. [*He gives money to the first* PORTER, *who holds it in his hand to shew to the others. They crowd greedily to see how much it is, quite prepared, after the Eastern fashion, to protest to heaven against their patron's stinginess. But his liberality overpowers them.*]

FIRST PORTER. O bounteous prince!

SECOND PORTER. O lord of the bazaar!

THIRD PORTER. O favored of the gods!

FOURTH PORTER. O father to all the porters of the market.

SENTINEL. [*Enviously, threatening them fiercely with his pilum.*] Hence, dogs: off. Out of this. [*They fly before him northward along the quay.*]

APOLLODORUS. Farewell. Ftatateeta. I shall be at the lighthouse before the Egyptians. [*He descends the steps.*]

FTATATEETA. The gods speed thee and protect my nursling! [*The* SENTRY *returns from chasing the* PORTERS *and looks down*

*at the boat, standing near the stairhead
lest* FTATATEETA *should attempt to escape.*]

APOLLODORUS. [*From beneath, as the boat
moves off.*] Farewell, valiant pilum pitcher.

SENTINEL. Farewell, shopkeeper.

APOLLODORUS. Ha, ha! Pull, thou brave
boatman, pull. Soho-o-o-o-o! [*He begins
to sing in barcarolle measure to the
rhythm of the oars.*]

My heart, my heart, spread out thy wings:
Shake off thy heavy load of love—
Give me the oars, O son of a snail.

SENTINEL. [*Threatening* FTATATEETA.] Now
mistress: back to your henhouse. In with
you.

FTATATEETA. [*Falling on her knees and
stretching her hands over the waters.*]
Gods of the seas, bear her safely to the
shore!

SENTINEL. Bear who safely? What do you
mean?

FTATATEETA. [*Looking darkly at him.*] Gods
of Egypt and of Vengeance, let this
Roman fool be beaten like a dog by his
captain for suffering her to be taken over
the waters.

SENTINEL. Accursed one: is she then in the
boat? [*He calls over the sea.*] Hoiho,
there, boatman! Hoiho!

APOLLODORUS. [*Singing in the distance.*]
My heart, my heart, be whole and free:
Love is thine only enemy.

[*Meanwhile* RUFIO, *the morning's fighting
done, sits munching dates on a faggot of
brushwood outside the door of the lighthouse, which towers gigantic to the clouds
on his left. His helmet, full of dates, is
between his knees; and a leathern bottle
of wine is by his side. Behind him the
great stone pedestal of the lighthouse is
shut in from the open sea by a low stone
parapet, with a couple of steps in the
middle to the broad coping. A huge chain
with a hook hangs down from the lighthouse
crane above his head. Faggots like the one
he sits on lie beneath it ready to be drawn
up to feed the beacon.* CÆSAR *is standing
on the step at the parapet looking out
anxiously, evidently ill at ease.* BRITANNUS
comes out of the lighthouse door.*]

RUFIO. Well, my British islander. Have you
been up to the top?

BRITANNUS. I have. I reckon it at 200 feet
high.

RUFIO. Anybody up there?

BRITANNUS. One elderly Tyrian to work the
crane; and his son, a well conducted
youth of 14.

RUFIO. [*Looking at the chain.*] What! An old
man and a boy work that! Twenty men,
you mean.

BRITANNUS. Two only, I assure you. They
have counter-weights, and a machine
with boiling water in it which I do not
understand: it is not of British design.
They use it to haul up barrels of oil and
faggots to burn in the brazier on the roof.

RUFIO. But—

BRITANNUS. Excuse me: I came down because there are messengers coming along
the mole to us from the island. I must
see what their business is. [*He hurries
out past the lighthouse.*]

CÆSAR. [*Coming away from the parapet,
shivering and out of sorts.*] Rufio: this has
been a mad expedition. We shall be
beaten. I wish I knew how our men
are getting on with that barricade across
the great mole.

RUFIO. [*Angrily.*] Must I leave my food and
go starving to bring you a report?

CÆSAR. [*Soothing him nervously.*] No, Rufio,
no. Eat, my son, eat. [*He takes another
turn,* RUFIO *chewing dates meanwhile.*]
The Egyptians cannot be such fools as
not to storm the barricade and swoop
down on us here before it is finished.
It is the first time I have ever run an
avoidable risk. I should not have come
to Egypt.

RUFIO. An hour ago you were all for
victory.

CÆSAR. [*Apologetically.*] Yes: I was a fool—
rash, Rufio—boyish.

RUFIO. Boyish! Not a bit of it. Here [*Offering
him a handful of dates.*]

CÆSAR. What are these for?

RUFIO. To eat. Thats whats the matter with
you. When a man comes to your age,
he runs down before his midday meal.

Eat and drink; and then have another look at our chances.

CÆSAR. [*Taking the dates.*] My age! [*He shakes his head and bites a date.*] Yes, Rufio: I am an old man—worn out now—true, quite true. [*He gives way to melancholy contemplation, and eats another date.*] Achillas is still in his prime: Ptolemy is a boy. [*He eats another date, and plucks up a little.*] Well, every dog has his day; and I have had mine: I cannot complain. [*With sudden cheerfulness.*] These dates are not bad, Rufio. [BRITANNUS *returns, greatly excited, with a leathern bag.* CÆSAR *is himself again in a moment.*] What now?

BRITANNUS. [*Triumphantly.*] Our brave Rhodian mariners have captured a treasure. There! [*He throws the bag down at* CÆSAR's *feet.*] Our enemies are delivered into our hands.

CÆSAR. In that bag?

BRITANNUS. Wait till you hear, Cæsar. This bag contains all the letters which have passed between Pompey's party and the army of occupation here.

CÆSAR. Well?

BRITANNUS. [*Impatient of* CÆSAR's *slowness to grasp the situation.*] Well, we shall now know who your foes are. The name of every man who has plotted against you since you crossed the Rubicon may be in these papers, for all we know.

CÆSAR. Put them in the fire.

BRITANNUS. Put them—[*He gasps.*] ! ! !

CÆSAR. In the fire. Would you have me waste the next three years of my life of proscribing and condemning men who will be my friends when I have proved that my friendship is worth more than Pompey's was—than Cato's is. O incorrigible British islander: am I a bull dog, to seek quarrels merely to shew how stubborn my jaws are?

BRITANNUS. But your honor—the honor of Rome—

CÆSAR. I do not make human sacrifices to my honor, as your Druids do. Since you will not burn these, at least I can drown them. [*He picks up the bag and throws it over the parapet into the sea.*]

BRITANNUS. Cæsar: this is mere eccentricity. Are traitors to be allowed to go free for the sake of a paradox?

RUFIO. [*Rising.*] Cæsar: when the islander has finished preaching, call me again. I am going to have a look at the boiling water machine. [*He goes into the lighthouse.*]

BRITANNUS. [*With genuine feeling.*] O Cæsar, my great master, if I could but persuade you to regard life seriously, as men do in my country!

CÆSAR. Do they truly do so, Britannus?

BRITANNUS. Have you not been there? Have you not seen them? What Briton speaks as you do in your moments of levity? What Briton neglects to attend the services at the sacred grove? What Briton wears clothes of many colors as you do, instead of plain blue, as all solid, well esteemed men should? These are moral questions with us.

CÆSAR. Well, well, my friend: some day I shall settle down and have a blue toga, perhaps. Meanwhile, I must get on as best I can in my flippant Roman way. [APOLLODORUS *comes past the lighthouse.*] What now?

BRITANNUS. [*Turning quickly, and challenging the stranger with official haughtiness.*] What is this? Who are you? How did you come here?

APOLLODORUS. Calm yourself, my friend: I am not going to eat you. I have come by boat, from Alexandria, with precious gifts for Cæsar.

CÆSAR. From Alexandria!

BRITANNUS. [*Severely.*] This is Cæsar, sir.

RUFIO. [*Appearing at the lighthouse door.*] Whats the matter now?

APOLLODORUS. Hail, great Cæsar! I am Apollodorus the Sicilian, an artist.

BRITANNUS. An artist! Why have they admitted this vagabond?

CÆSAR. Peace, man. Apollodorus is a famous patrician amateur.

BRITANNUS. [*Disconcerted.*] I crave the gentleman's pardon. [*To* CÆSAR.] I understood him to say that he was a professional. [*Somewhat out of countenance, he allows* APOLLODORUS *to approach* CÆSAR, *changing places with him.* RUFIO, *after looking* APOLLODORUS *up and down with marked disparagement, goes to the other side of the platform.*]

CÆSAR. You are welcome, Apollodorus. What is your business?

APOLLODORUS. First, to deliver to you a present from the Queen of Queens.

CÆSAR. Who is that?

APOLLODORUS. Cleopatra of Egypt.

CÆSAR. [*Taking him into his confidence in his most winning manner.*] Apollodorus: this is no time for playing with presents. Pray you, go back to the Queen, and tell her that if all goes well I shall return to the palace this evening.

APOLLODORUS. Cæsar: I cannot return. As I approached the lighthouse, some fool threw a great leathern bag into the sea. It broke the nose of my boat; and I had hardly time to get myself and my charge to the shore before the poor little cockleshell sank.

CÆSAR. I am sorry, Apollodorus. The fool shall be rebuked. Well, well: what have you brought me? The Queen will be hurt if I do not look at it.

RUFIO. Have we time to waste on this trumpery? The Queen is only a child.

CÆSAR. Just so: that is why we must not disappoint her. What is the present, Apollodorus?

APOLLODORUS. Cæsar: it is a Persian carpet—a beauty! And in it are—so I am told—pigeons' eggs and crystal goblets and fragile precious things. I dare not for my head have it carried up that narrow ladder from the causeway.

RUFIO. Swing it up by the crane, then. We will send the eggs to the cook; drink our wine from the goblets; and the carpet will make a bed for Cæsar.

APOLLODORUS. The crane! Cæsar: I have sworn to tender this bale of carpet as I tender my own life.

CÆSAR. [*Cheerfully.*] Then let them swing you up at the same time; and if the chain breaks, you and the pigeons' eggs will perish together. [*He goes to the chain and looks up along it, examining it curiously.*]

APOLLODORUS. [*To* BRITANNUS.] Is Cæsar serious?

BRITANNUS. His manner is frivolous because he is an Italian; but he means what he says.

APOLLODORUS. Serious or not, he spake well. Give me a squad of soldiers to work the crane.

BRITANNUS. Leave the crane to me. Go and await the descent of the chain.

APOLLODORUS. Good. You will presently see me there [*Turning to them all and pointing with an eloquent gesture to the sky above the parapet.*] rising like the sun with my treasure. [*He goes back the way he came.* BRITANNUS *goes into the lighthouse.*]

RUFIO. [*Ill-humoredly.*] Are you really going to wait here for this foolery, Cæsar?

CÆSAR. [*Backing away from the crane as it gives signs of working.*] Why not?

RUFIO. The Egyptians will let you know why not if they have the sense to make a rush from the shore end of the mole before our barricade is finished. And here we are waiting like children to see a carpet full of pigeons' eggs. [*The chain rattles, and is drawn up high enough to clear the parapet. It then swings round out of sight behind the lighthouse.*]

CÆSAR. Fear not, my son Rufio. When the first Egyptian takes his first step along the mole, the alarm will sound; and we two will reach the barricade from our end before the Egyptians reach it from their end—we two, Rufio: I, the old man, and you, his biggest boy. And the old man will be there first. So peace; and give me some more dates.

APOLLODORUS. [*From the causeway below.*] Soho, haul away. So-ho-o-o-o! [*The chain is drawn up and comes round again from behind the lighthouse.* APOLLODORUS *is swinging in the air with his bale of carpet at the end of it. He breaks into song as he soars above the parapet.*]

Aloft, aloft, behold the blue
That never shone in woman's eyes—

Easy there: stop her. [*He ceases to rise.*] Further round! [*The chain comes forward above the platform.*]

RUFIO. [*Calling up.*] Lower away there.

[The chain and its load begin to descend.]

APOLLODORUS. *[Calling up.]* Gently—slowly —mind the eggs.

RUFIO. *[Calling up.]* Easy there—slowly— slowly. [APOLLODORUS *and the bale are deposited safely on the flags in the middle of the platform.* RUFIO *and* CÆSAR *help* APOLLODORUS *to cast off the chain from the bale.]*

RUFIO. Haul up. *[The chain rises clear of their heads with a rattle.* BRITANNUS *comes from the lighthouse and helps them to uncord the carpet.]*

APOLLODORUS. *[When the cords are loose.]* Stand off, my friends: let Cæsar see. *[He throws the carpet open.]*

RUFIO. Nothing but a heap of shawls. Where are the pigeons' eggs?

APOLLODORUS. Approach, Cæsar; and search for them among the shawls.

RUFIO. *[Drawing his sword.]* Ha, treachery! Keep back, Cæsar: I saw the shawl move: there is something alive there.

BRITANNUS. *[Drawing his sword.]* It is a serpent.

APOLLODORUS. Dares Cæsar thrust his hand into the sack where the serpent moves?

RUFIO. *[Turning on him.]* Treacherous dog—

CÆSAR. Peace. Put up your swords. Apollodorus: your serpent seems to breathe very regularly. *[He thrusts his hand under the shawls and draws out a bare arm.]* This is a pretty little snake.

RUFIO. *[Drawing out the other arm.]* Let us have the rest of you. *[They pull* CLEOPATRA *up by the wrists into a sitting position.* BRITANNUS, *scandalized, sheathes his sword with a drive of protest.]*

CLEOPATRA. *[Gasping.]* Oh, I'm smothered. Oh, Cæsar, a man stood on me in the boat; and a great sack of something fell upon me out of the sky; and then the boat sank; and then I was swung up into the air and bumped down.

CÆSAR. *[Petting her as she rises and takes refuge on his breast.]* Well, never mind: here you are safe and sound at last.

RUFIO. Ay; and now that she is here, what are we to do with her?

BRITANNUS. She cannot stay here, Cæsar, without the companionship of some matron.

CLEOPATRA. *[Jealously, to* CÆSAR, *who is obviously perplexed.]* Arnt you glad to see me?

CÆSAR. Yes, yes; *I* am very glad. But Rufio is very angry; and Britannus is shocked.

CLEOPATRA. *[Contemptuously.]* You can have their heads cut off, can you not?

CÆSAR. They would not be so useful with their heads cut off as they are now, my sea bird.

RUFIO. *[To* CLEOPATRA.] We shall have to go away presently and cut some of your Egyptians' heads off. How will you like being left here with the chance of being captured by that little brother of yours if we are beaten?

CLEOPATRA. But you mustnt leave me alone. Cæsar: you will not leave me alone, will you?

RUFIO. What! not when the trumpet sounds and all our lives depend on Cæsar's being at the barricade before the Egyptians reach it? Eh?

CLEOPATRA. Let them lose their lives: they are only soldiers.

CÆSAR. *[Gravely.]* Cleopatra: when that trumpet sounds, we must take every man his life in his hand, and throw it in the face of Death. And of my soldiers who have trusted me there is not one whose hand I shall not hold more sacred than your head. [CLEOPATRA *is overwhelmed. Her eyes fill with tears.]* Apollodorus: you must take her back to the palace.

APOLLODORUS. Am I a dolphin, Cæsar, to cross the seas with young ladies on my back? My boat is sunk: all yours are either at the barricade or have returned to the city. I will hail one if I can: that is all I can do. *[He goes back to the causeway.]*

CLEOPATRA. *[Struggling with her tears.]* It does not matter. I will not go back. Nobody cares for me.

CÆSAR. Cleopatra—

CLEOPATRA. You want me to be killed.

CÆSAR. *[Still more gravely.]* My poor child: your life matters little here to anyone but yourself. *[She gives way altogether at this, casting herself down on the faggots weeping. Suddenly a great tumult is heard in the distance, bucinas and trumpets sounding through a storm of shouting.* BRITANNUS *rushes to the parapet and looks along the mole.* CÆSAR *and* RUFIO *turn to one another with quick intelligence.*]

CÆSAR. Come, Rufio.

CLEOPATRA. [*Scrambling to her knees and clinging to him.*] No no. Do not leave me, Cæsar. [*He snatches his skirt from her clutch.*] Oh!

BRITANNUS. [*From the parapet.*] Cæsar: we are cut off. The Egyptians have landed from the west harbor between us and the barricade! ! !

RUFIO. [*Running to see.*] Curses! It is true. We are caught like rats in a trap.

CÆSAR. [*Ruthfully.*] Rufio, Rufio: my men at the barricade are between the sea party and the shore party. I have murdered them.

RUFIO. [*Coming back from the parapet to* CÆSAR'S *right hand.*] Ay: that comes of fooling with this girl here.

APOLLODORUS. [*Coming up quickly from the causeway.*] Look over the parapet, Cæsar.

CÆSAR. We have looked, my friend. We must defend ourselves here.

APOLLODORUS. I have thrown the ladder into the sea. They cannot get in without it.

RUFIO. Ay; and we cannot get out. Have you thought of that?

APOLLODORUS. Not get out! Why not? You have ships in the east harbor.

BRITANNUS. [*Hopefully, at the parapet.*] The Rhodian galleys are standing in towards us already. [CÆSAR *quickly joins* BRITANNUS *at the parapet.*]

RUFIO. [*To* APOLLODORUS, *impatiently.*] And by what road are we to walk to the galleys, pray?

APOLLODORUS. [*With gay, defiant rhetoric.*] By the road that leads everywhere—the diamond path of the sun and moon. Have you never seen a child's shadow play of The Broken Bridge? "Ducks and geese with ease get over"—eh? [*He throws away his cloak and cap, and binds his sword on his back.*]

RUFIO. What are you talking about?

APOLLODORUS. I will shew you. [*Calling to* BRITANNUS.] How far off is the nearest galley?

BRITANNUS. Fifty fathom.

CÆSAR. No, no: they are further off than they seem in this clear air to your British eyes. Nearly quarter of a mile, Apollodorus.

APOLLODORUS. Good. Defend yourselves here until I send you a boat from that galley.

RUFIO. Have you wings, perhaps?

APOLLODORUS. Water wings, soldier. Behold! [*He runs up the steps between* CÆSAR *and* BRITANNUS *to the coping of the parapet; springs into the air; and plunges head foremost into the sea.*]

CÆSAR. [*Like a schoolboy—wildly excited.*] Bravo, bravo! [*Throwing off his cloak.*] By Jupiter, I will do that too.

RUFIO. [*Seizing him.*] You are mad. You shall not.

CÆSAR. Why not? Can I not swim as well as he?

RUFIO. [*Frantic.*] Can an old fool dive and swim like a young one? He is twenty-five and you are fifty.

CÆSAR. [*Breaking loose from* RUFIO.] Old! ! !

BRITANNUS. [*Shocked.*] Rufio: you forget yourself.

CÆSAR. I will race you to the galley for a week's pay, father Rufio.

CLEOPATRA. But me! me!! me!!! what is to become of me?

CÆSAR. I will carry you on my back to the galley like a dolphin. Rufio: when you see me rise to the surface, throw her in: I will answer for her. And then in with you after her, both of you.

CLEOPATRA. No, no, NO. I shall be drowned.

BRITANNUS. Cæsar: I am a man and a Briton, not a fish. I must have a boat. I cannot swim.

CLEOPATRA. Neither can I.

CÆSAR. [*To* BRITANNUS.] Stay here, then, alone, until I recapture the lighthouse. I will not forget you. Now, Rufio.

RUFIO. You have made up your mind to this folly?

CÆSAR. The Egyptians have made it up for me. What else is there to do? And mind where you jump: I do not want to get your fourteen stone in the small of my back as I come up. [*He runs up the steps and stands on the coping.*]

BRITANNUS. [*Anxiously.*] One last word, Cæsar. Do not let yourself be seen in the fashionable part of Alexandria until you have changed your clothes.

CÆSAR. [*Calling over the sea.*] Ho, Apollodorus: [*He points skyward and quotes the barcarolle.*]

The white upon the blue above—

APOLLODORUS. [*Swimming in the distance.*] Is purple on the green below—

CÆSAR. [*Exultantly.*] Aha! [*He plunges into the sea.*]

CLEOPATRA. [*Running excitedly to the steps.*] Oh, let me see. He will be drowned.

[RUFIO *seizes her.*]—Ah—ah—ah—ah! [*He pitches her screaming into the sea.* RUFIO *and* BRITANNUS *roar with laughter.*]

RUFIO. [*Looking down after her.*] He has got her. [*To* BRITANNUS.] Hold the fort, Briton. Cæsar will not forget you. [*He springs off.*]

BRITANNUS. [*Running to the steps to watch them as they swim.*] All safe, Rufio?

RUFIO. [*Swimming.*] All safe.

CÆSAR. [*Swimming further off.*] Take refuge up there by the beacon; and pile the fuel on the trap door, Britannus.

BRITANNUS. [*Calling in reply.*] I will first do so, and then commend myself to my country's gods. [*A sound of cheering from the sea.* BRITANNUS *gives full vent to his excitement.*] The boat has reached him: Hip, hip, hip, hurrah!

ACT IV

CLEOPATRA'S sousing in the east harbor of Alexandria was in October 48 B.C. In March 47 she is passing the afternoon in her boudoir in the palace, among a bevy of her ladies, listening to a slave girl who is playing the harp in the middle of the room. The harpist's master, an old musician, with a lined face, prominent brows, white beard, moustache and eyebrows twisted and horned at the ends, and a consciously keen and pretentious expression, is squatting on the floor close to her on her right, watching her performance. FTATATEETA is in attendance near the door, in front of a group of female slaves. Except the harp player all are seated: CLEOPATRA in a chair opposite the door on the other side of the room; the rest on the ground. CLEOPATRA'S ladies are all young, the most conspicuous being CHARMIAN and IRAS, her favorites. CHARMIAN is a hatchet faced, terra cotta colored little goblin, swift in her movements, and neatly finished at the hands and feet. IRAS is a plump, goodnatured creature, rather fatuous, with a profusion of red hair, and a tendency to giggle on the slightest provocation.

CLEOPATRA. Can I—

FTATATEETA. [*Insolently, to the player.*] Peace, thou! The Queen speaks. [*The player stops.*]

CLEOPATRA. [*To the old musician.*] I want to learn to play the harp with my own hands. Cæsar loves music. Can you teach me?

MUSICIAN. Assuredly I and no one else can teach the queen. Have I not discovered the lost method of the ancient Egyptians, who could make a pyramid tremble by touching a bass string? All the other teachers are quacks: I have exposed them repeatedly.

CLEOPATRA. Good: you shall teach me. How long will it take?

MUSICIAN. Not very long: only four years. Your Majesty must first become proficient in the philosophy of Pythagoras.

CLEOPATRA. Has she [*Indicating the slave.*] become proficient in the philosophy of Pythagoras?

MUSICIAN. Oh, she is but a slave. She learns as a dog learns.

CLEOPATRA. Well, then, I will learn as a dog learns; for she plays better than you.

You shall give me a lesson every day for a fortnight. [*The* MUSICIAN *hastily scrambles to his feet and bows profoundly.*] After that, whenever I strike a false note you shall be flogged; and if I strike so many that there is not time to flog you, you shall be thrown into the Nile to feed the crocodiles. Give the girl a piece of gold; and send them away.

MUSICIAN. [*Much taken aback.*] But true art will not be thus forced.

FTATATEETA. [*Pushing him out.*] What is this? Answering the Queen, forsooth. Out with you. [*He is pushed out by* FTATATEETA, *the girl following with her harp, amid the laughter of the ladies and slaves.*]

CLEOPATRA. Now, can any of you amuse me? Have you any stories or any news?

IRAS. Ftatateeta—

CLEOPATRA. Oh, Ftatateeta, Ftatateeta, always Ftatateeta. Some new tale to set me against her.

IRAS. No: this time Ftatateeta has been virtuous. [*All the ladies laugh—not the slaves.*] Pothinus has been trying to bribe her to let him speak with you.

CLEOPATRA. [*Wrathfully.*] Ha! you all sell audiences with me, as if I saw whom you please, and not whom I please. I should like to know how much of her gold piece that harp girl will have to give up before she leaves the palace.

IRAS. We can easily find out that for you. [*The ladies laugh.*]

CLEOPATRA. [*Frowning.*] You laugh; but take care, take care. I will find out some day how to make myself served as Cæsar is served.

CHARMIAN. Old hooknose! [*They laugh again.*]

CLEOPATRA. [*Revolted.*] Silence. Charmian: do not you be a silly little Egyptian fool. Do you know why I allow you all to chatter impertinently just as you please, instead of treating you as Ftatateeta would treat you if she were Queen?

CHARMIAN. Because you try to imitate Cæsar in everything; and he lets everybody say what they please to him.

CLEOPATRA. No; but because I asked him one day why he did so; and he said "Let your women talk; and you will learn something from them." What have I to learn from them? I said. "What they are," said he; and oh! you should have seen his eye as he said it. You would have curled up, you shallow things. [*They laugh. She turns fiercely on* IRAS.] At whom are you laughing—at me or at Cæsar?

IRAS. At Cæsar.

CLEOPATRA. If you were not a fool, you would laugh at me; and if you were not a coward you would not be afraid to tell me so. [FTATATEETA *returns.*] Ftatateeta: they tell me that Pothinus has offered you a bribe to admit him to my presence.

FTATATEETA. [*Protesting.*] Now by my father's gods—

CLEOPATRA. [*Cutting her short despotically.*] Have I not told you not to deny things? You would spend the day calling your father's gods to witness to your virtues if I let you. Go take the bribe; and bring in Pothinus. [FTATATEETA *is about to reply.*] Dont answer me. Go. [FTATATEETA *goes out; and* CLEOPATRA *rises and begins to prowl to and fro between her chair and the door, meditating. All rise and stand.*]

IRAS. [*As she reluctantly rises.*] Heigho! I wish Cæsar were back in Rome.

CLEOPATRA. [*Threateningly.*] It will be a bad day for you all when he goes. Oh, if I were not ashamed to let him see that I am as cruel at heart as my father, I would make you repent that speech! Why do you wish him away?

CHARMIAN. He makes you so terribly prosy and serious and learned and philosophical. It is worse than being religious, at our ages. [*The* LADIES *laugh.*]

CLEOPATRA. Cease that endless cackling, will you. Hold your tongues.

CHARMIAN. [*With mock resignation.*] Well, well: we must try to live up to Cæsar. [*They laugh again.* CLEOPATRA *rages silently as she continues to prowl to and fro.* FTATATEETA *comes back with* POTHINUS, *who halts on the threshold.*]

FTATATEETA. [*At the door.*] Pothinus craves the ear of the—

CLEOPATRA. There, there: that will do: let him come in. [*She resumes her seat. All sit down except* POTHINUS, *who advances to the middle of the room.* FTATATEETA *takes her former place.*] Well, Pothinus: what is the latest news from your rebel friends?

POTHINUS. [*Haughtily.*] I am no friend of rebellion. And a prisoner does not receive news.

CLEOPATRA. You are no more a prisoner than I am—than Cæsar is. These six months we have been besieged in this palace by my subjects. You are allowed to walk on the beach among the soldiers. Can I go further myself, or can Cæsar?

POTHINUS. You are but a child, Cleopatra, and do not understand these matters. [*The* LADIES *laugh.* CLEOPATRA *looks inscrutably at him.*]

CHARMIAN. I see you do not know the latest news, Pothinus.

POTHINUS. What is that?

CHARMIAN. That Cleopatra is no longer a child. Shall I tell you how to grow much older, and much, much wiser in one day?

POTHINUS. I should prefer to grow wiser without growing older.

CHARMIAN. Well, go up to the top of the lighthouse; and get somebody to take you by the hair and throw you into the sea. [*The* LADIES *laugh.*]

CLEOPATRA. She is right, Pothinus: you will come to the shore with much conceit washed out of you. [*The* LADIES *laugh.* CLEOPATRA *rises impatiently.*] Begone, all of you. I will speak with Pothinus alone. Drive them out, Ftatateeta. [*They run out laughing.* FTATATEETA *shuts the door on them.*] What are you waiting for?

FTATATEETA. It is not meet that the Queen remain alone with—

CLEOPATRA. [*Interrupting her.*] Ftatateeta: must I sacrifice you to your father's gods to teach you that *I* am Queen of Egypt, and not you?

FTATATEETA. [*Indignantly.*] You are like the rest of them. You want to be what these Romans call a New Woman. [*She goes out, banging the door.*]

CLEOPATRA. [*Sitting down again.*] Now,

Pothinus: why did you bribe Ftatateeta to bring you hither?

POTHINUS. [*Studying her gravely.*] Cleopatra: what they tell me is true. You are changed.

CLEOPATRA. Do you speak with Cæsar every day for six months: and you will be changed.

POTHINUS. It is the common talk that you are infatuated with this old man.

CLEOPATRA. Infatuated? What does that mean? Made foolish, is it not? Oh no: I wish I were.

POTHINUS. You wish you were made foolish! How so?

CLEOPATRA. When I was foolish, I did what I liked, except when Ftatateeta beat me; and even then I cheated her and did it by stealth. Now that Cæsar has made me wise, it is no use my liking or disliking: I do what must be done, and have no time to attend to myself. That is not happiness; but it is greatness. If Cæsar were gone, I think I could govern the Egyptians; for what Cæsar is to me, I am to the fools around me.

POTHINUS. [*Looking hard at her.*] Cleopatra: this may be the vanity of youth.

CLEOPATRA. No, no: it is not that I am so clever, but that the others are so stupid.

POTHINUS. [*Musingly.*] Truly, that is the great secret.

CLEOPATRA. Well, now tell me what you came to say?

POTHINUS. [*Embarrassed.*] I! Nothing.

CLEOPATRA. Nothing!

POTHINUS. At least—to beg for my liberty: that is all.

CLEOPATRA. For that you would have knelt to Cæsar. No, Pothinus: you came with some plan that depended on Cleopatra being a little nursery kitten. Now that Cleopatra is a Queen, the plan is upset.

POTHINUS. [*Bowing his head submissively.*] It is so.

CLEOPATRA. [*Exultant.*] Aha!

POTHINUS. [*Raising his eyes keenly to hers.*] Is Cleopatra then indeed a Queen, and no longer Cæsar's prisoner and slave?

CLEOPATRA. Pothinus: we are all Cæsar's slaves—all we in this land of Egypt—

whether we will or no. And she who is wise enough to know this will reign when Cæsar departs.

POTHINUS. You harp on Cæsar's departure.

CLEOPATRA. What if I do?

POTHINUS. Does he not love you?

CLEOPATRA. Love me! Pothinus: Cæsar loves no one. Who are those we love? Only those whom we do not hate: all people are strangers and enemies to us except those we love. But it is not so with Cæsar. He has no hatred in him: he makes friends with everyone as he does with dogs and children. His kindness to me is a wonder: neither mother, father, nor nurse have ever taken so much care for me, or thrown open their thoughts to me so freely.

POTHINUS. Well: is not this love?

CLEOPATRA. What! when he will do as much for the first girl he meets on his way back to Rome? Ask his slave, Britannus: he has been just as good to him. Nay, ask his very horse! His kindness is not for anything in me: it is in his own nature.

POTHINUS. But how can you be sure that he does not love you as men love women?

CLEOPATRA. Because I cannot make him jealous. I have tried.

POTHINUS. Hm! Perhaps I should have asked, then, do you love him?

CLEOPATRA. Can one love a god? Besides, I love another Roman: one whom I saw long before Cæsar—no god, but a man—one who can love and hate—one whom I can hurt and who would hurt me.

POTHINUS. Does Cæsar know this?

CLEOPATRA. Yes.

POTHINUS. And he is not angry?

CLEOPATRA. He promises to send him to Egypt to please me!

POTHINUS. I do not understand this man.

CLEOPATRA. [With superb contempt.] You understand Cæsar! How could you? [Proudly.] I do—by instinct.

POTHINUS. [Deferentially, after a moment's thought.] Your Majesty caused me to be admitted today. What message has the Queen for me?

CLEOPATRA. This. You think that by making

my brother king, you will rule in Egypt because you are his guardian and he is a little silly.

POTHINUS. The Queen is pleased to say so.

CLEOPATRA. The Queen is pleased to say this also. That Cæsar will eat up you, and Achillas, and my brother, as a cat eats up mice; and that he will put on this land of Egypt as a shepherd puts on his garment. And when he has done that, he will return to Rome, and leave Cleopatra here as his viceroy.

POTHINUS. [Breaking out wrathfully.] That he shall never do. We have a thousand men to his ten; and we will drive him and his beggarly legions into the sea.

CLEOPATRA. [With scorn, getting up to go.] You rant like any common fellow. Go, then, and marshal your thousands; and make haste; for Mithridates of Pergamus is at hand with reinforcements for Cæsar. Cæsar has held you at bay with two legions: we shall see what he will do with twenty.

POTHINUS. Cleopatra—

CLEOPATRA. Enough, enough: Cæsar has spoiled me for talking to weak things like you. [She goes out. POTHINUS, with a gesture of rage, is following, when FTATA-TEETA enters and stops him.]

POTHINUS. Let me go forth from this hateful place.

FTATATEETA. What angers you?

POTHINUS. The curse of all the gods of Egypt be upon her! She sold her country to the Roman, that she may buy it back from him with her kisses.

FTATATEETA. Fool: did she not tell you that she would have Cæsar gone?

POTHINUS. You listened?

FTATATEETA. I took care that some honest woman should be at hand whilst you were with her.

POTHINUS. Now by the gods—

FTATATEETA. Enough of your gods! Cæsar's gods are all powerful here. It is no use you coming to Cleopatra: you are only an Egyptian. She will not listen to any of her own race: she treats us all as children.

POTHINUS. May she perish for it!

FTATATEETA. [*Balefully.*] May your tongue wither for that wish! Go! send for Lucius Septimius, the slayer of Pompey. He is a Roman: may be she will listen to him. Begone!

POTHINUS. [*Darkly.*] I know to whom I must go now.

FTATATEETA. [*Suspiciously.*] To whom, then?

POTHINUS. To a greater Roman than Lucius. And mark this, mistress. You thought, before Cæsar came, that Egypt should presently be ruled by you and your crew in the name of Cleopatra. I set myself against it—

FTATATEETA. [*Interrupting him—wrangling.*] Ay; that it might be ruled by you and your crew in the name of Ptolemy.

POTHINUS. Better me, or even you, than a woman with a Roman heart; and that is what Cleopatra is now become. Whilst I live, she shall never rule. So guide yourself accordingly. [*He goes out.*]

[*It is by this time drawing on to dinner time. The table is laid on the roof of the palace; and thither* RUFIO *is now climbing, ushered by a majestic palace official, wand of office in hand, and followed by a slave carrying an inlaid stool. After many stairs they emerge at last into a massive colonnade on the roof. Light curtains are drawn between the columns on the north and east to soften the westering sun.* THE OFFICIAL *leads* RUFIO *to one of these shaded sections. A cord for pulling the curtains apart hangs down between the pillars.*]

THE OFFICIAL. [*Bowing.*] The Roman commander will await Cæsar here. [*The slave sets down the stool near the southernmost column, and slips out through the curtains.*]

RUFIO. [*Sitting down, a little blown.*] Pouf! That was a climb. How high have we come?

THE OFFICIAL. We are on the palace roof, O Beloved of Victory!

RUFIO. Good! the Beloved of Victory has no more stairs to get up. [*A* SECOND OFFICIAL *enters from the opposite end, walking backwards.*]

THE SECOND OFFICIAL. Cæsar approaches. [CÆSAR, *fresh from the bath, clad in a new tunic of purple silk, comes in, beaming and festive, followed by two slaves carrying a light couch, which is hardly more than an elaborately designed bench. They place it near the northmost of the two curtained columns. When this is done they slip out through the curtains; and the two* OFFICIALS, *formally bowing, follow them.* RUFIO *rises to receive* CÆSAR.]

CÆSAR. [*Coming over to him.*] Why, Rufio! [*Surveying his dress with an air of admiring astonishment.*] A new baldrick! A new golden pommel to your sword! And you have had your hair cut! But not your beard—? impossible! [*He sniffs at* RUFIO's *beard.*] Yes, perfumed, by Jupiter Olympus!

RUFIO. [*Growling.*] Well: is it to please myself?

CÆSAR. [*Affectionately.*] No, my son Rufio, but to please me—to celebrate my birthday.

RUFIO. [*Contemptuously.*] Your birthday! You always have a birthday when there is a pretty girl to be flattered or an ambassador to be conciliated. We had seven of them in ten months last year.

CÆSAR. [*Contritely.*] It is true, Rufio! I shall never break myself of these petty deceits.

RUFIO. Who is to dine with us—besides Cleopatra?

CÆSAR. Apollodorus the Sicilian.

RUFIO. That popinjay!

CÆSAR. Come! the popinjay is an amusing dog—tells a story; sings a song; and saves us the trouble of flattering the Queen. What does she care for old politicians and camp-fed bears like us? No, Apollodorus is good company, Rufio, good company.

RUFIO. Well, he can swim a bit and fence a bit: he might be worse, if he only knew how to hold his tongue.

CÆSAR. The gods forbid he should ever learn! Oh, this military life! this tedious, brutal life of action! That is the worst of us Romans: we are mere doers and drudgers: a swarm of bees turned into men. Give me a good talker—one with wit and imagination enough to live without continually doing something!

RUFIO. Ay! a nice time he would have of it with you when dinner was over! Have you noticed that I am before my time?

CÆSAR. Aha! I thought that meant something. What is it?

RUFIO. Can we be overheard here?

CÆSAR. Our privacy invites eavesdropping. I can remedy that. [*He claps his hands twice. The curtains are drawn, revealing the roof garden with a banqueting table set across in the middle for four persons, one at each end, and two side by side. The side next* CÆSAR *and* RUFIO *is blocked with golden wine vessels and basins. A gorgeous major-domo is superintending the laying of the table by a staff of slaves. The colonnade goes round the garden at both sides to the further end, where a gap in it, like a great gateway, leaves the view open to the sky beyond the western edge of the roof, except in the middle, where a life size image of* RA, *seated on a huge plinth, towers up, with hawk and crown of asp and disk. His altar, which stands at his feet, is a single white stone.*] Now everybody can see us, nobody will think of listening to us. [*He sits down on the bench left by the two slaves.*]

RUFIO. [*Sitting down on his stool.*] Pothinus wants to speak to you. I advise you to see him: there is some plotting going on here among the women.

CÆSAR. Who is Pothinus?

RUFIO. The fellow with hair like squirrel's fur—the little King's bear leader, whom you kept prisoner.

CÆSAR. [*Annoyed.*] And has he not escaped?

RUFIO. No.

CÆSAR. [*Rising imperiously.*] Why not? You have been guarding this man instead of watching the enemy. Have I not told you always to let prisoners escape unless there are special orders to the contrary? Are there not enough mouths to be fed without him?

RUFIO. Yes; and if you would have a little sense and let me cut his throat, you would save his rations. Anyhow he wont escape. Three sentries have told him they would put a pilum through him if they saw him again. What more can they do? He prefers to stay and spy on us. So would I if I had to do with generals subject to fits of clemency.

CÆSAR. [*Resuming his seat, argued down.*] Hm! And so he wants to see me.

RUFIO. Ay. I have brought him with me. He is waiting there [*Jerking his thumb over his shouder.*] under guard.

CÆSAR. And you want me to see him?

RUFIO. [*Obstinately.*] I dont want anything. I daresay you will do what you like. Dont put it on to me.

CÆSAR. [*With an air of doing it expressly to indulge* RUFIO.] Well, well: let us have him.

RUFIO. [*Calling.*] Ho there, guard! Release your man and send him up. [*Beckoning.*] Come along! [POTHINUS *enters and stops mistrustfully between the two, looking from one to the other.*]

CÆSAR. [*Graciously.*] Ah, Pothinus! You are welcome. And what is the news this afternoon?

POTHINUS. Cæsar: I come to warn you of a danger, and to make you an offer.

CÆSAR. Never mind the danger. Make the offer.

RUFIO. Never mind the offer. Whats the danger?

POTHINUS. Cæsar: you think that Cleopatra is devoted to you.

CÆSAR. [*Gravely.*] My friend: I already know what I think. Come to your offer.

POTHINUS. I will deal plainly. I know not by what strange gods you have been enabled to defend a palace and a few yards of beach against a city and an army. Since we cut you off from Lake Mareotis, and you dug wells in the salt sea sand and brought up buckets of fresh water from them, we have known that your gods are irresistible, and that you are a worker of miracles. I no longer threaten you—

RUFIO. [*Sarcastically.*] Very handsome of you, indeed.

POTHINUS. So be it: you are the master. Our gods sent the northwest winds to keep you in our hands; but you have been too strong for them.

CÆSAR. [*Gently urging him to come to the point.*] Yes, yes, my friend. But what then?

RUFIO. Spit it out, man. What have you to say?

POTHINUS. I have to say that you have a traitress in your camp. Cleopatra—

THE MAJOR-DOMO. [*At the table, announcing.*] The Queen! [CÆSAR *and* RUFIO *rise.*]

RUFIO. [*Aside to* POTHINUS.] You should have spat it out sooner, you fool. Now it is too late. [CLEOPATRA, *in gorgeous raiment, enters in state through the gap in the colonnade, and comes down past the image of* RA *and past the table to* CÆSAR. *Her retinue, headed by* FTATATEETA, *joins the staff at the table.* CÆSAR *gives* CLEOPATRA *his seat, which she takes.*]

CLEOPATRA. [*Quickly, seeing* POTHINUS.] What is he doing here?

CÆSAR. [*Seating himself beside her, in the most amiable of tempers.*] Just going to tell me something about you. You shall hear it. Proceed, Pothinus.

POTHINUS. [*Disconcerted.*] Cæsar—[*He stammers.*]

CÆSAR. Well, out with it.

POTHINUS. What I have to say is for your ear, not for the Queen's.

CLEOPATRA. [*With subdued ferocity.*] There are means of making you speak. Take care.

POTHINUS. [*Defiantly.*] Cæsar does not employ those means.

CÆSAR. My friend: when a man has anything to tell in this world, the difficulty is not to make him tell it, but to prevent him from telling it too often. Let me celebrate my birthday by setting you free. Farewell: we shall not meet again.

CLEOPATRA. [*Angrily.*] Cæsar: this mercy is foolish.

POTHINUS. [*To* CÆSAR.] Will you not give me a private audience? Your life may depend on it. [CÆSAR *rises loftily.*]

RUFIO. [*Aside to* POTHINUS.] Ass! Now we shall have some heroics.

CÆSAR. [*Oratorically.*] Pothinus—

RUFIO. [*Interrupting him.*] Cæsar: the dinner will spoil if you begin preaching your favorite sermon about life and death.

CLEOPATRA. [*Priggishly.*] Peace, Rufio. I desire to hear Cæsar.

RUFIO. [*Bluntly.*] Your Majesty has heard it before. You repeated it to Apollodorus last week; and he thought it was all your own. [CÆSAR'S *dignity collapses. Much tickled, he sits down again and looks roguishly at* CLEOPATRA, *who is furious.* RUFIO *calls as before.*] Ho there, guard! Pass the prisoner out. He is released. [*To* POTHINUS.] Now off with you. You have lost your chance.

POTHINUS. [*His temper overcoming his prudence.*] I will speak.

CÆSAR. [*To* CLEOPATRA.] You see. Torture would not have wrung a word from him.

POTHINUS. Cæsar: you have taught Cleopatra the arts by which the Romans govern the world.

CÆSAR. Alas! they cannot even govern themselves. What then?

POTHINUS. What then? Are you so besotted with her beauty that you do not see that she is impatient to reign in Egypt alone, and that her heart is set on your departure?

CLEOPATRA. [*Rising.*] Liar!

CÆSAR. [*Shocked.*] What! Protestations! Contradictions!

CLEOPATRA. [*Ashamed, but trembling with suppressed rage.*] No. I do not deign to contradict. Let him talk. [*She sits down again.*]

POTHINUS. From her own lips I have heard it. You are to be her catspaw: you are to tear the crown from her brother's head and set it on her own, delivering us all into her hand—delivering yourself also. And then Cæsar can return to Rome, or depart through the gate of death, which is nearer and surer.

CÆSAR. [*Calmly.*] Well, my friend; and is not this very natural?

POTHINUS. [*Astonished.*] Natural! Then you do not resent treachery?

CÆSAR. Resent! O thou foolish Egyptian, what have I to do with resentment? Do I resent the wind when it chills me, or the night when it makes me stumble in darkness? Shall I resent youth when it turns from age, and ambition when it turns from servitude? To tell me such a story as this is but to tell me that the sun will rise tomorrow.

CLEOPATRA. [*Unable to contain herself.*] But it is false—false. I swear it.

CÆSAR. It is true, though you swore it a thousand times, and believed all you swore. [*She is convulsed with emotion. To screen her, he rises and takes* POTHINUS *to* RUFIO, *saying.*] Come, Rufio: let us see Pothinus past the guard. I have a word to say to him. [*Aside to them.*] We must give the Queen a moment to recover herself. [*Aloud.*] Come. [*He takes* POTHINUS *and* RUFIO *out with him, conversing with them meanwhile.*] Tell your friends, Pothinus, that they must not think I am opposed to a reasonable settlement of the country's affairs—[*They pass out of hearing.*]

CLEOPATRA. [*In a stifled whisper.*] Ftatateeta, Ftatateeta.

FTATATEETA. [*Hurrying to her from the table and petting her.*] Peace, child: be comforted—

CLEOPATRA. [*Interrupting her.*] Can they hear us?

FTATATEETA. No, dear heart, no.

CLEOPATRA. Listen to me. If he leaves the Palace alive, never see my face again.

FTATATEETA. He? Poth—

CLEOPATRA. [*Striking her on the mouth.*] Strike his life out as I strike his name from your lips. Dash him down from the wall. Break him on the stones. Kill, kill, kill him.

FTATATEETA. [*Shewing all her teeth.*] The dog shall perish.

CLEOPATRA. Fail in this, and you go out from before me for ever.

FTATATEETA. [*Resolutely.*] So be it. You shall not see my face until his eyes are darkened. [CÆSAR *comes back, with* APOLLODORUS, *exquisitely dressed, and* RUFIO.]

CLEOPATRA. [*To* FTATATEETA.] Come soon— soon. [FTATATEETA *turns her meaning eyes for a moment on her mistress; then goes grimly away past* RA *and out.* CLEOPATRA *runs like a gazelle to* CÆSAR.] So you have come back to me, Cæsar. [*Caressingly.*] I thought you were angry. Welcome,

Apollodorus. [*She gives him her hand to kiss, with her other arm about* CÆSAR.]

APOLLODORUS. Cleopatra grows more womanly beautiful from week to week.

CLEOPATRA. Truth, Apollodorus?

APOLLODORUS. Far, far short of the truth! Friend Rufio threw a pearl into the sea: Cæsar fished up a diamond.

CÆSAR. Cæsar fished up a touch of rheumatism, my friend. Come: to dinner! to dinner! [*They move towards the table.*]

CLEOPATRA. [*Skipping like a young fawn.*] Yes, to dinner. I have ordered such a dinner for you, Cæsar!

CÆSAR. Ay? What are we to have?

CLEOPATRA. Peacocks' brains.

CÆSAR. [*As if his mouth watered.*] Peacocks' brains, Apollodorus!

APOLLODORUS. Not for me. I prefer nightingales' tongues. [*He goes to one of the two covers set side by side.*]

CLEOPATRA. Roast boar, Rufio!

RUFIO. [*Gluttonously.*] Good! [*He goes to the seat next* APOLLODORUS, *on his left.*]

CÆSAR. [*Looking at his seat, which is at the end of the table, to* RA'S *left hand.*] What has become of my leathern cushion?

CLEOPATRA. [*At the opposite end.*] I have got new ones for you.

THE MAJOR-DOMO. These cushions, Cæsar, are of Maltese gauze, stuffed with rose leaves.

CÆSAR. Rose leaves! Am I a caterpillar? [*He throws the cushions away and seats himself on the leather mattress underneath.*]

CLEOPATRA. What a shame! My new cushions!

THE MAJOR-DOMO. [*At* CÆSAR'S *elbow.*] What shall we serve to whet Cæsar's appetite?

CÆSAR. What have you got?

THE MAJOR-DOMO. Sea hedgehogs, black and white sea acorns, sea nettles beccaficoes, purple shellfish—

CÆSAR. Any oysters?

THE MAJOR-DOMO. Assuredly.

CÆSAR. British oysters?

THE MAJOR-DOMO. [*Assenting.*] British oysters, Cæsar.

CÆSAR. Oysters, then. [THE MAJOR-DOMO *signs to a slave at each order; and the slave goes out to execute it.*] I have been in Britain—that western land of romance—the last piece of earth on the edge of the ocean that surrounds the world. I went there in search of its famous pearls. The British pearl was a fable; but in searching for it I found the British oyster.

APOLLODORUS. All posterity will bless you for it. [*To* THE MAJOR-DOMO.] Sea hedgehogs for me.

RUFIO. Is there nothing solid to begin with?

THE MAJOR-DOMO. Fieldfares with asparagus—

CLEOPATRA. [*Interrupting.*] Fattened fowls! have some fattened fowls, Rufio.

RUFIO. Ay, that will do.

CLEOPATRA. [*Greedily.*] Fieldfares for me.

THE MAJOR-DOMO. Cæsar will deign to choose his wine? Sicilian, Lesbian, Chian—

RUFIO. [*Contemptuously.*] All Greek.

APOLLODORUS. Who would drink Roman wine when he could get Greek. Try the Lesbian, Cæsar.

CÆSAR. Bring me my barley water.

RUFIO. [*With intense disgust.*] Ugh! Bring me my Falernian. [*The Falernian is presently brought to him.*]

CLEOPATRA. [*Pouting.*] It is waste of time giving you dinners, Cæsar. My scullions would not condescend to your diet.

CÆSAR. [*Relenting.*] Well, well: let us try the Lesbian. [THE MAJOR-DOMO *fills* CÆSAR'S *goblet; then* CLEOPATRA'S *and* APOLLODORUS'S.] But when I return to Rome, I will make laws against these extravagances. I will even get the laws carried out.

CLEOPATRA. [*Coaxingly.*] Never mind. Today you are to be like other people: idle, luxurious, and kind. [*She stretches her hand to him along the table.*]

CÆSAR. Well, for once I will sacrifice my comfort—[*Kissing her hand.*] there! [*He takes a draught of wine.*] Now are you satisfied?

CLEOPATRA. And you no longer believe that I long for your departure for Rome?

CÆSAR. I no longer believe anything. My brains are asleep. Besides, who knows whether I shall return to Rome?

RUFIO. [*Alarmed.*] How? Eh? What?

CÆSAR. What has Rome to shew me that I have not seen already? One year of Rome is like another, except that I grow older, whilst the crowd in the Appian Way is always the same age.

APOLLODORUS. It is no better here in Egypt. The old men, when they are tired of life, say "We have seen everything except the source of the Nile."

CÆSAR. [*His imagination catching fire.*] And why not see that? Cleopatra: will you come with me and track the flood to its cradle in the heart of the regions of mystery? Shall we leave Rome behind us—Rome, that has achieved greatness only to learn how greatness destroys nations of men who are not great! Shall I make you a new kingdom, and build you a holy city there in the great unknown?

CLEOPATRA. [*Rapturously.*] Yes, yes. You shall.

RUFIO. Ay: now he will conquer Africa with two legions before we come to the roast boar.

APOLLODORUS. Come: no scoffing. This is a noble scheme: in it Cæsar is no longer merely the conquering soldier, but the creative poet-artist. Let us name the holy city, and consecrate it with Lesbian wine.

CÆSAR. Cleopatra shall name it herself.

CLEOPATRA. It shall be called Cæsar's Gift to his Beloved.

APOLLODORUS. No, no. Something vaster than that—something universal, like the starry firmament.

CÆSAR. [*Prosaically.*] Why not simply The Cradle of the Nile?

CLEOPATRA. No: the Nile is my ancestor; and he is a god. Oh! I have thought of something. The Nile shall name it himself. Let us call upon him. [*To* THE MAJOR-DOMO.] Send for him. [*The three men stare at one another; but* THE MAJOR-DOMO *goes out as if he had received the most matter-of-fact order.*] And [*To the retinue.*] away with you all. [*The retinue withdraws, making obeisance. A* PRIEST *enters, carrying a miniature sphinx with a tiny tripod before it. A morsel of incense is smoking* in the tripod. The PRIEST *comes to the table and places the image in the middle of it. The light begins to change to the magenta purple of the Egyptian sunset, as if the god had brought a strange colored shadow with him. The three men are determined not to be impressed; but they feel curious in spite of themselves.*]

CÆSAR. What hocus-pocus is this?

CLEOPATRA. You shall see. And it is not hocus-pocus. To do it properly, we should kill something to please him; but perhaps he will answer Cæsar without that if we spill some wine to him.

APOLLODORUS. [*Turning his head to look up over his shoulder at* RA.] Why not appeal to our hawkheaded friend here?

CLEOPATRA. [*Nervously.*] Sh! He will hear you and be angry.

RUFIO. [*Phlegmatically.*] The source of the Nile is out of his district, I expect.

CLEOPATRA. No: I will have my city named by nobody but my dear little sphinx, because it was in its arms that Cæsar found me asleep. [*She languishes at* CÆSAR *then turns curtly to the* PRIEST.] Go. I am a priestess, and have power to take your charge from you. [*The* PRIEST *makes a reverence and goes out.*] Now let us call on the Nile all together. Perhaps he will rap on the table.

CÆSAR. What! table rapping! Are such superstitions still believed in this year 707 of the Republic?

CLEOPATRA. It is no superstition: our priests learn lots of things from the tables. Is it not so, Apollodorus?

APOLLODORUS. Yes: I profess myself a converted man. When Cleopatra is priestess, Apollodorus is a devotee. Propose the conjuration.

CLEOPATRA. You must say with me "Send us thy voice, Father Nile."

ALL FOUR. [*Holding their glasses together before the idol.*] Send us thy voice, Father Nile. [*The death cry of a man in mortal terror and agony answers them. Appalled, the men set down their glasses, and listen. Silence. The purple deepens in the sky.* CÆSAR, *glancing at* CLEOPATRA, *catches her pouring out her wine before the god, with*

gleaming eyes, and mute assurances of gratitude and worship. APOLLODORUS *springs up and runs to the edge of the roof to peer down and listen.*]

CÆSAR. [*Looking piercingly at* CLEOPATRA.] What was that?

CLEOPATRA. [*Petulantly.*] Nothing. They are beating some slave.

CÆSAR. Nothing.

RUFIO. A man with a knife in him, I'll swear.

CÆSAR. [*Rising.*] A murder!

APOLLODORUS. [*At the back, waving his hand for silence.*] S-sh! Silence. Did you hear that?

CÆSAR. Another cry?

APOLLODORUS. [*Returning to the table.*] No, a thud. Something fell on the beach, I think.

RUFIO. [*Grimly, as he rises.*] Something with bones in it, eh?

CÆSAR. [*Shuddering.*] Hush, hush, Rufio. [*He leaves the table and returns to the colonnade:* RUFIO *following at his left elbow, and* APOLLODORUS *at the other side.*]

CLEOPATRA. [*Still in her place at the table.*] Will you leave me, Cæsar? Apollodorus: are you going?

APOLLODORUS. Faith, dearest Queen, my appetite is gone.

CÆSAR. Go down to the courtyard, Apollodorus; and find out what has happened. [APOLLODORUS *nods and goes out, making for the staircase by which* RUFIO *ascended.*]

CLEOPATRA. Your soldiers have killed somebody, perhaps. What does it matter? [*The murmur of a crowd rises from the beach below.* CÆSAR *and* RUFIO *look at one another.*]

CÆSAR. This must be seen to. [*He is about to follow* APOLLODORUS *when* RUFIO *stops him with a hand on his arm as* FTATATEETA *comes back by the far end of the roof, with dragging steps, a drowsy satiety in her eyes and in the corners of the bloodhound lips. For a moment* CÆSAR *suspects that she is drunk with wine. Not so* RUFIO: *he knows well the red vintage that has inebriated her.*]

RUFIO. [*In a low tone.*] There is some mischief between these two.

FTATATEETA. The Queen looks again on the

face of her servant. [CLEOPATRA *looks at her for a moment with an exultant reflection of her murderous expression. Then she flings her arms round her; kisses her repeatedly and savagely; and tears off her jewels and heaps them on her. The two men turn from the spectacle to look at one another.* FTATATEETA *drags herself sleepily to the altar; kneels before* RA; *and remains there in prayer.* CÆSAR *goes to* CLEOPATRA, *leaving* RUFIO *in the colonnade.*]

CÆSAR. [*With searching earnestness.*] Cleopatra: what has happened?

CLEOPATRA. [*In mortal dread of him, but with her utmost cajolery.*] Nothing, dearest Cæsar. [*With sickly sweetness, her voice almost failing.*] Nothing. I am innocent. [*She approaches him affectionately.*] Dear Cæsar: are you angry with me? Why do you look at me so? I have been here with you all the time. How can I know what has happened?

CÆSAR. [*Reflectively.*] That is true.

CLEOPATRA. [*Greatly relieved, trying to caress him.*] Of course it is true. [*He does not respond to the caress.*] You know it is true, Rufio. [*The murmur without suddenly swells to a roar and subsides.*]

RUFIO. I shall know presently. [*He makes for the altar in the burly trot that serves him for a stride, and touches* FTATATEETA *on the shoulder.*] Now, mistress: I shall want you. [*He orders her, with a gesture, to go before him.*]

FTATATEETA. [*Rising and glowering at him.*] My place is with the Queen.

CLEOPATRA. She has done no harm, Rufio.

CÆSAR. [*To* RUFIO.] Let her stay.

RUFIO. [*Sitting down on the altar.*] Very well. Then my place is here too; and you can see what is the matter for yourself. The city is in a pretty uproar, it seems.

CÆSAR. [*With grave displeasure.*] Rufio: there is a time for obedience.

RUFIO. And there is a time for obstinacy. [*He folds his arms doggedly.*]

CÆSAR. [*To* CLEOPATRA.] Send her away.

CLEOPATRA. [*Whining in her eagerness to propitiate him.*] Yes, I will. I will do whatever you ask me, Cæsar, always,

because I love you. Ftatateeta: go away.

FTATATEETA. The Queen's word is my will. I shall be at hand for the Queen's call. [*She goes out past* RA, *as she came.*]

RUFIO. [*Following her.*] Remember, Cæsar, your bodyguard is also within call. [*He follows her out.* CLEOPATRA, *presuming upon* CÆSAR'S *submission to* RUFIO, *leaves the table and sits down on the bench in the colonnade.*]

CLEOPATRA. Why do you allow Rufio to treat you so? You should teach him his place.

CÆSAR. Teach him to be my enemy, and to hide his thoughts from me as you are now hiding yours?

CLEOPATRA. [*Her fears returning.*] Why do you say that, Cæsar? Indeed, indeed, I am not hiding anything. You are wrong to treat me like this. [*She stifles a sob.*] I am only a child; and you turn into stone because you think some one has been killed. I cannot bear it. [*She purposely breaks down and weeps. He looks at her with profound sadness and complete coldness. She looks up to see what effect she is producing. Seeing that he is unmoved, she sits up, pretending to struggle with her emotion and to put it bravely away.*] But there: I know you hate tears: you shall not be troubled with them. I know you are not angry, but only sad; only I am so silly, I cannot help being hurt when you speak coldly. Of course you are quite right: it is dreadful to think of anyone being killed or even hurt; and I hope nothing really serious has—[*Her voice dies away under his contemptuous penetration.*]

CÆSAR. What has frightened you into this? What have you done? [*A trumpet sounds on the beach below.*] Aha! that sounds like the answer.

CLEOPATRA. [*Sinking back trembling on the bench and covering her face with her hands.*] I have not betrayed you, Cæsar: I swear it.

CÆSAR. I know that. I have not trusted you. [*He turns from her, and is about to go out when* APOLLODORUS *and* BRITANNUS *drag in* LUCIUS SEPTIMIUS *to him.* RUFIO *follows.* CÆSAR *shudders.*] Again, Pompey's murderer!

RUFIO. The town has gone mad, I think. They are for tearing the palace down and driving us into the sea straight away. We laid hold of this renegade in clearing them out of the courtyard.

CÆSAR. Release him. [*They let go his arms.*] What has offended the citizens, Lucius Septimius?

LUCIUS. What did you expect, Cæsar? Pothinus was a favorite of theirs.

CÆSAR. What has happened to Pothinus? I set him free, here, not half an hour ago. Did they not pass him out?

LUCIUS. Ay, through the gallery arch sixty feet above ground, with three inches of steel in his ribs. He is as dead as Pompey. We are quits now, as to killing—you and I.

CÆSAR. [*Shocked.*] Assassinated!—our prisoner, our guest! [*He turns reproachfully on* RUFIO.] Rufio—

RUFIO. [*Emphatically—anticipating the question.*] Whoever did it was a wise man and a friend of yours [CLEOPATRA *is greatly emboldened.*] but none of us had a hand in it. So it is no use to frown at me. [CÆSAR *turns and looks at* CLEOPATRA.]

CLEOPATRA. [*Violently—rising.*] He was slain by order of the Queen of Egypt. I am not Julius Cæsar the dreamer, who allows every slave to insult him. Rufio has said I did well: now the others shall judge me too. [*She turns to the others.*] This Pothinus sought to make me conspire with him to betray Cæsar to Achillas and Ptolemy. I refused; and he cursed me and came privily to Cæsar to accuse me of his own treachery. I caught him in the act; and he insulted me—me, the Queen! to my face. Cæsar would not avenge me: he spoke him fair and set him free. Was I right to avenge myself? Speak, Lucius.

LUCIUS. I do not gainsay it. But you will get little thanks from Cæsar for it.

CLEOPATRA. Speak, Apollodorus. Was I wrong?

APOLLODORUS. I have only one word of blame, most beautiful. You should have called upon me, your knight; and in a fair duel I should have slain the slanderer.

CLEOPATRA. [*Passionately.*] I will be judged by your very slave, Cæsar. Britannus: speak. Was I wrong?

BRITANNUS. Were treachery, falsehood, and disloyalty left unpunished, society must become like an arena full of wild beasts, tearing one another to pieces. Cæsar is in the wrong.

CÆSAR. [*With quiet bitterness.*] And so the verdict is against me, it seems.

CLEOPATRA. [*Vehemently.*] Listen to me, Cæsar. If one man in all Alexandria can be found to say that I did wrong, I swear to have myself crucified on the door of the palace by my own slaves.

CÆSAR. If one man in all the world can be found, now or forever, to know that you did wrong, that man will have either to conquer the world as I have, or be crucified by it. [*The uproar in the streets again reaches them.*] Do you hear? These knockers at your gate are also believers in vengeance and in stabbing. You have slain their leader: it is right that they shall slay you. If you doubt it, ask your four counsellors here. And then in the name of that right [*He emphasizes the word with great scorn.*] shall I not slay them for murdering their Queen, and be slain in my turn by their countrymen as the invader of their fatherland? Can Rome do less then than slay these slayers, too, to shew the world how Rome avenges her sons and her honor. And so, to the end of history, murder shall breed murder, always in the name of right and honor and peace, until the gods are tired of blood and create a race that can understand. [*Fierce uproar.* CLEOPATRA *becomes white with terror.*] Hearken, you who must not be insulted. Go near enough to catch their words: you will find them bitterer than the tongue of Pothinus. [*Loftily, wrapping himself up in an impenetrable dignity.*] Let the Queen of Egypt now give her orders for vengeance, and take her measures for defence; for she has renounced Cæsar. [*He turns to go.*]

CLEOPATRA. [*Terrified, running to him and falling on her knees.*] You will not desert me, Cæsar. You will defend the palace.

CÆSAR. You have taken the powers of life and death upon you. I am only a dreamer.

CLEOPATRA. But they will kill me.

CÆSAR. And why not?

CLEOPATRA. In pity—

CÆSAR. Pity! What! has it come to this so suddenly, that nothing can save you now but pity? Did it save Pothinus? [*She rises, wringing her hands, and goes back to the bench in despair.* APOLLODORUS *shews his sympathy with her by quietly posting himself behind the bench. The sky has by this time become the most vivid purple, and soon begins to change to a glowing pale orange, against which the colonnade and the great image shew darklier and darklier.*]

RUFIO. Cæsar: enough of preaching. The enemy is at the gate.

CÆSAR. [*Turning on him and giving way to his wrath.*] Ay; and what has held him baffled at the gate all these months? Was it my folly, as you deem it, or your wisdom? In this Egyptian Red Sea of blood, whose hand has held all your heads above the waves? [*Turning on* CLEOPATRA.] And yet, when Cæsar says to such an one, "Friend, go free," you, clinging for your little life to my sword, dare steal out and stab him in the back? And you, soldiers and gentlemen, and honest servants as you forget that you are, applaud this assassination, and say "Cæsar is in the wrong." By the gods, I am tempted to open my hand and let you all sink into the flood.

CLEOPATRA. [*With a ray of cunning hope.*] But, Cæsar, if you do, you will perish yourself. [CÆSAR'S *eyes blaze.*]

RUFIO. [*Greatly alarmed.*] Now, by great Jove, you filthy little Egyptian rat, that is the very word to make him walk out alone into the city and leave us here to be cut to pieces. [*Desperately, to* CÆSAR.] Will you desert us because we are a parcel of fools? I mean no harm by kill-ing: I do it as a cat, by instinct. We are all dogs at your heels; but we have served you faithfully.

CÆSAR. [*Relenting.*] Alas, Rufio, my son, my son: as dogs we are like to perish now in the streets.

APOLLODORUS. [*At his post behind* CLEOPATRA's *seat.*] Cæsar: what you say has an Olympian ring in it: it must be right; for it is fine art. But I am still on the side of Cleopatra. If we must die, she shall not want the devotion of a man's heart nor the strength of a man's arm.

CLEOPATRA. [*Sobbing.*] But I dont want to die.

CÆSAR. [*Sadly.*] Oh, ignoble, ignoble!

LUCIUS. [*Coming forward between* CÆSAR *and* CLEOPATRA.] Hearken to me, Cæsar. It may be ignoble; but I also mean to live as long as I can.

CÆSAR. Well, my friend, you are likely to outlive Cæsar. Is it any magic of mine, think you, that has kept your army and this whole city at bay for so long? Yesterday, what quarrel had they with me that they should risk their lives against me? But today we have flung them down their hero, murdered; and now every man of them is set upon clearing out this nest of assassins—for such we are and no more. Take courage then; and sharpen your sword. Pompey's head has fallen; and Cæsar's head is ripe.

APOLLODORUS. Does Cæsar despair?

CÆSAR. [*With infinite pride.*] He who has never hoped can never despair. Cæsar, in good or bad fortune, looks his fate in the face.

LUCIUS. Look it in the face, then; and it will smile as it always has on Cæsar.

CÆSAR. [*With involuntary haughtiness.*] Do you presume to encourage me?

LUCIUS. I offer you my services. I will change sides if you will have me.

CÆSAR. [*Suddenly coming down to earth again, and looking sharply at him, divining that there is something behind the offer.*] What! At this point?

LUCIUS. [*Firmly.*] At this point.

RUFIO. Do you suppose Cæsar is mad, to trust you?

LUCIUS. I do not ask him to trust me until he is victorious. I ask for my life, and for a command in Cæsar's army. And since Cæsar is a fair dealer, I will pay in advance.

CÆSAR. Pay! How?

LUCIUS. With a piece of good news for you. [CÆSAR *divines the news in a flash.*]

RUFIO. What news?

CÆSAR. [*With an elate and buoyant energy which makes* CLEOPATRA *sit up and stare.*] What news! What news, did you say, my son Rufio? The relief has arrived: what other news remains for us? Is it not so, Lucius Septimius? Mithridates of Pergamos is on the march.

LUCIUS. He has taken Pelusium.

CÆSAR. [*Delighted.*] Lucius Septimius: you are henceforth my officer. Rufio: the Egyptians must have sent every soldier from the city to prevent Mithridates crossing the Nile. There is nothing in the streets now but mob—mob!

LUCIUS. It is so. Mithridates is marching by the great road to Memphis to cross above the Delta. Achillas will fight him there.

CÆSAR. [*All audacity.*] Achillas shall fight Cæsar there. See, Rufio. [*He runs to the table; snatches a napkin; and draws a plan on it with his finger dipped in wine, whilst* RUFIO *and* LUCIUS SEPTIMIUS *crowd about him to watch, all looking closely, for the light is now almost gone.*] Here is the palace [*Pointing to his plan.*]; here is the theatre. You [*To* RUFIO.] take twenty man and pretend to go by that street [*Pointing it out.*]; and whilst they are stoning you, out go the cohorts by this and this. My streets are right, are they, Lucius?

LUCIUS. Ay, that is the fig market—

CÆSAR. [*Too much excited to listen to him.*] I saw them the day we arrived. Good! [*He throws the napkin on the table, and comes down again into the colonnade.*] Away, Britannus: tell Petronius that within an hour half our forces must take ship for the western lake. See to my horse and armor. [BRITANNUS *runs out.*] With the rest, *I* shall march round the lake and up the Nile to meet Mithridates. Away, Lucius; and give the word. [LUCIUS *hurries out after* BRITANNUS.] Apollodorus: lend me your sword and your right arm for this campaign.

APOLLODORUS. Ay, and my heart and life to boot.

CÆSAR. [*Grasping his hand.*] I accept both. [*Mighty handshake.*] Are you ready for work?

APOLLODORUS. Ready for Art—the Art of War. [*He rushes out after* LUCIUS, *totally forgetting* CLEOPATRA.]

RUFIO. Come! this is something like business.

CÆSAR. [*Buoyantly.*] Is it not, my only son? [*He claps his hands. The slaves hurry in to the table.*] No more of this mawkish revelling: away with all this stuff: shut it out of my sight and be off with you. [*The slaves begin to remove the table; and the curtains are drawn, shutting in the colonnade.*] You understand about the streets, Rufio?

RUFIO. Ay, I think I do. I will get through them, at all events. [*The bucina sounds busily in the courtyard beneath.*]

CÆSAR. Come, then: we must talk to the troops and hearten them. You down to the beach: I to the courtyard. [*He makes for the staircase.*]

CLEOPATRA. [*Rising from her seat, where she has been quite neglected all this time, and stretching out her hands timidly to him.*] Cæsar.

CÆSAR. [*Turning.*] Eh?

CLEOPATRA. Have you forgotten me?

CÆSAR. [*Indulgently.*] I am busy now, my child, busy. When I return your affairs shall be settled. Farewell; and be good and patient. [*He goes, preoccupied and quite indifferent. She stands with clenched fists, in speechless rage and humiliation.*]

RUFIO. That game is played and lost, Cleopatra. The woman always gets the worst of it.

CLEOPATRA. [*Haughtily.*] Go. Follow your master.

RUFIO. [*In her ear, with rough familiarity.*] A word first. Tell your executioner that if Pothinus had been properly killed—in

the throat—he would not have called out.
Your man bungled his work.

CLEOPATRA. [*Enigmatically.*] How do you
know it was a man?

RUFIO. [*Startled, and puzzled.*] It was not
you: you were with us when it happened.
[*She turns her back scornfully on him.
He shakes his head, and draws the curtains
to go out. It is now a magnificent moonlit
night. The table has been removed.
FTATATEETA is seen in the light of the moon
and stars, again in prayer before the white
altar-stone of RA. RUFIO starts; closes the
curtains again softly; and says in a low
voice to CLEOPATRA.*] Was it she? with
her own hand?

CLEOPATRA. [*Threateningly.*] Whoever it
was, let my enemies beware of her. Look
to it, Rufio, you who dare make the

Queen of Egypt a fool before Cæsar.

RUFIO. [*Looking grimly at her.*] I will look to
it, Cleopatra. [*He nods in confirmation of
the promise, and slips out through the
curtains, loosening his sword in its sheath
as he goes.*]

ROMAN SOLDIERS. [*In the courtyard below.*]
Hail, Cæsar! Hail, hail! [CLEOPATRA
listens. The bucina sounds again, followed
by several trumpets.]

CLEOPATRA. [*Wringing her hands and calling.*]
Ftatateeta. Ftatateeta. It is dark; and I
am alone. Come to me. [*Silence.*] Ftatateeta. [*Louder.*] Ftatateeta. [*Silence. In a
panic she snatches the cord and pulls the
curtains apart.* FTATATEETA *is lying dead
on the altar of* RA, *with her throat cut.
Her blood deluges the white stone.*]

ACT V

High noon. Festival and military pageant
on the esplanade before the palace. In the
east harbor CÆSAR's galley, so gorgeously
decorated that it seems to be rigged with
flowers, is alongside the quay, close to the
steps APOLLODORUS descended when he
embarked with the carpet. A Roman guard
is posted there in charge of a gangway,
whence a red floorcloth is laid down the
middle of the esplanade, turning off to the
north opposite the central gate in the palace
front, which shuts in the esplanade on the
south side. The broad steps of the gate,
crowded with CLEOPATRA's ladies, all in
their gayest attire, are like a flower garden.
The façade is lined by her guard, officered
by the same gallants to whom BEL AFFRIS
announced the coming of CÆSAR six months
before in the old palace on the Syrian
border. The north side is lined by Roman
soldiers, with the townsfolk on tiptoe
behind them, peering over their heads at
the cleared esplanade, in which the officers
stroll about, chatting. Among these are
BELZANOR and the PERSIAN; also the
CENTURION, vinewood cudgel in hand, battle
worn, thick-booted, and much outshone,
both socially and decoratively, by the
Egyptian officers.

APOLLODORUS makes his way through the
townsfolk and calls to the officers from
behind the Roman line.

APOLLODORUS. Hullo! May I pass?

CENTURION. Pass Apollodorus the Sicilian
there! [*The* SOLDIERS *let him through.*]

BELZANOR. Is Cæsar at hand?

APOLLODORUS. Not yet. He is still in the
market place. I could not stand any more
of the roaring of the soldiers! After half
an hour of the enthusiasm of an army,
one feels the need of a little sea air.

PERSIAN. Tell us the news. Hath he slain
the priests?

APOLLODORUS. Not he. They met him in
the market place with ashes on their
heads and their gods in their hands. They
placed the gods at his feet. The only one
that was worth looking at was Apis: a
miracle of gold and ivory work. By my
advice he offered the chief priest two
talents for it.

BELZANOR. [*Appalled.*] Apis the all-knowing
for two talents! What said the chief
Priest?

APOLLODORUS. He invoked the mercy of
Apis, and asked for five.

BELZANOR. Pooh! Why did not Apis cause
Cæsar to be vanquished by Achillas?

Any fresh news from the war, Apollodorus?

APOLLODORUS. The little King Ptolemy was drowned.

BELZANOR. Drowned! How?

APOLLODORUS. With the rest of them. Cæsar attacked them from three sides at once and swept them into the Nile. Ptolemy's barge sank.

BELZANOR. A marvellous man, this Cæsar! Will he come soon, think you?

APOLLODORUS. He was settling the Jewish question when I left. [*A flourish of trumpets from the north and commotion among the townsfolk announce the approach of* CÆSAR.]

PERSIAN. He has made short work of them. Here he comes. [*He hurries to his post in front of the Egyptian lines.*]

BELZANOR. [*Following him.*] Ho there! Cæsar comes. [*The* SOLDIERS *stand at attention, and dress their lines.* APOLLODORUS *goes to the Egyptian line.*]

CENTURION. [*Hurrying to the gangway guard.*] Attention there! Cæsar comes. [CÆSAR *arrives in state with* RUFIO: BRITANNUS *following. The* SOLDIERS *receive him with enthusiastic shouting.*]

CÆSAR. I see my ship awaits me. The hour of Cæsar's farewell to Egypt has arrived. And now, Rufio, what remains to be done before I go?

RUFIO. [*At his left hand.*] You have not yet appointed a Roman governor for this province.

CÆSAR. [*Looking whimsically at him, but speaking with perfect gravity.*] What say you to Mithridates of Pergamos, my reliever and rescuer, the great son of Eupator?

RUFIO. Why, that you will want him elsewhere. Do you forget that you have some three or four armies to conquer on your way home?

CÆSAR. Indeed! Well, what say you to yourself?

RUFIO. [*Incredulously.*] I! I a governor! What are you dreaming of? Do you not know that I am only the son of a freedman?

CÆSAR. [*Affectionately.*] Has not Cæsar called you his son? [*Calling to the whole assembly.*] Peace awhile there; and hear me.

THE ROMAN SOLDIERS. Hear Cæsar.

CÆSAR. Hear the service, quality, rank and name of the Roman governor. By service, Cæsar's shield; by quality, Cæsar's friend; by rank, a Roman soldier. [THE ROMAN SOLDIERS *give a triumphant shout.*] By name, Rufio. [*They shout again.*]

RUFIO. [*Kissing* CÆSAR'S *hand.*] Ay: I am Cæsar's shield; but of what use shall I be when I am no longer on Cæsar's arm? Well, no matter—[*He becomes husky, and turns away to recover himself.*]

CÆSAR. Where is that British Islander of mine?

BRITANNUS. [*Coming forward on* CÆSAR'S *right hand.*] Here, Cæsar

CÆSAR. Who bade you, pray, thrust yourself into the battle of the Delta, uttering the barbarous cries of your native land, and affirming yourself a match for any four of the Egyptians, to whom you applied unseemly epithets?

BRITANNUS. Cæsar: I ask you to excuse the language that escaped me in the heat of the moment.

CÆSAR. And how did you, who cannot swim, cross the canal with us when we stormed the camp?

BRITANNUS. Cæsar: I clung to the tail of your horse.

CÆSAR. These are not the deeds of a slave, Britannicus, but of a free man.

BRITANNUS. Cæsar: I was born free.

CÆSAR. But they call you Cæsar's slave.

BRITANNUS. Only as Cæsar's slave have I found real freedom.

CÆSAR. [*Moved.*] Well said. Ungrateful that I am, I was about to set you free; but now I will not part from you for a million talents. [*He claps him friendlily on the shoulder.* BRITANNUS, *gratified, but a trifle shamefaced, takes his hand and kisses it sheepishly.*]

BELZANOR. [*To the* PERSIAN.] This Roman knows how to make men serve him.

PERSIAN. Ay: men too humble to become dangerous rivals to him.

BELZANOR. O subtle one! O cynic!

CÆSAR. [*Seeing* APOLLODORUS *in the Egyptian corner, and calling to him.*] Apollodorus:

I leave the art of Egypt in your charge. Remember: Rome loves art and will encourage it ungrudgingly.

APOLLODORUS. I understand, Cæsar. Rome will produce no art itself; but it will buy up and take away whatever the other nations produce.

CÆSAR. What! Rome produce no art! Is peace not an art? is war not an art? is government not an art? is civilization not an art? All these we give you in exchange for a few ornaments. You will have the best of the bargain. [*Turning to* RUFIO.] And now, what else have I to do before I embark? [*Trying to recollect.*] There is something I cannot remember: what can it be? Well, well: it must remain undone: we must not waste this favorable wind. Farewell, Rufio.

RUFIO. Cæsar: I am loth to let you go to Rome without your shield. There are too many daggers there.

CÆSAR. It matters not: I shall finish my life's work on my way back; and then I shall have lived long enough. Besides: I have always disliked the idea of dying: I had rather be killed. Farewell.

RUFIO. [*With a sigh, raising his hands and giving* CÆSAR *up as incorrigible.*] Farewell. [*They shake hands.*]

CÆSAR. [*Waving his hand to* APOLLODORUS.] Farewell, Apollodorus, and my friends, all of you. Aboard! [*The gangway is run out from the quay to the ship. As* CÆSAR *moves toward it,* CLEOPATRA, *cold and tragic, cunningly dressed in black, without ornaments or decoration of any kind, and thus making a striking figure among the brilliantly dressed bevy of ladies as she passes through it, comes from the palace and stands on the steps.* CÆSAR *does not see her until she speaks.*]

CLEOPATRA. Has Cleopatra no part in this leavetaking?

CÆSAR. [*Enlightened.*] Ah, I knew there was something. [*To* RUFIO.] How could you let me forget her, Rufio? [*Hastening to her.*] Had I gone without seeing you, I should never have forgiven myself. [*He takes her hands, and brings her into the middle of the esplanade. She submits stonily.*] Is this mourning for me?

CLEOPATRA. No.

CÆSAR. [*Remorsefully.*] Ah, that was thoughtless of me! It is for your brother.

CLEOPATRA. No.

CÆSAR. For whom, then?

CLEOPATRA. Ask the Roman governor whom you have left us.

CÆSAR. Rufio?

CLEOPATRA. Yes: Rufio. [*She points at him with deadly scorn.*] He who is to rule here in Cæsar's name, in Cæsar's way, according to Cæsar's boasted laws of life.

CÆSAR. [*Dubiously.*] He is to rule as he can, Cleopatra. He has taken the work upon him, and will do it in his own way.

CLEOPATRA. Not in your way, then?

CÆSAR. [*Puzzled.*] What do you mean by my way?

CLEOPATRA. Without punishment. Without revenge. Without judgment.

CÆSAR. [*Approvingly.*] Ay: that is the right way, the great way, the only possible way in the end. [*To* RUFIO.] Believe it, Rufio, if you can.

RUFIO. Why, I believe it, Cæsar. You have convinced me of it long ago. But look you. You are sailing for Numidia today. Now tell me: if you meet a hungry lion there, you will not punish it for wanting to eat you?

CÆSAR. [*Wondering what he is driving at.*] No.

RUFIO. Nor revenge upon it the blood of those it has already eaten.

CÆSAR. No.

RUFIO. Nor judge it for its guiltiness.

CÆSAR. No.

RUFIO. What, then, will you do to save your life from it?

CÆSAR. [*Promptly.*] Kill it, man, without malice, just as it would kill me. What does this parable of the lion mean?

RUFIO. Why, Cleopatra had a tigress that killed men at her bidding. I thought she might bid it kill you some day. Well, had I not been Cæsar's pupil, what pious things might I not have done to that tigress! I might have punished it. I might have revenged Pothinus on it.

CÆSAR. [*Interjects.*] Pothinus!

RUFIO. [*Continuing.*] I might have judged it. But I put all these follies behind me; and, without malice, only cut its throat.

And that is why Cleopatra comes to you in mourning.

CLEOPATRA. [*Vehemently.*] He has shed the blood of my servant Ftatateeta. On your head be it as upon his, Cæsar, if you hold him free of it.

CÆSAR. [*Energetically.*] On my head be it, then; for it was well done. Rufio: had you set yourself in the seat of the judge, and with hateful ceremonies and appeals to the gods handed that woman over to some hired executioner to be slain before the people in the name of justice, never again would I have touched your hand without a shudder. But this was natural slaying: I feel no horror at it. [RUFIO, *satisfied, nods at* CLEOPATRA, *mutely inviting her to mark that.*]

CLEOPATRA. [*Pettish and childish in her impotence.*] No: no when a Roman slays an Egyptian. All the world will now see how unjust and corrupt Cæsar is.

CÆSAR. [*Taking her hands coaxingly.*] Come: do not be angry with me. I am sorry for that poor Totateeta. [*She laughs in spite of herself.*] Aha! you are laughing. Does that mean reconciliation?

CLEOPATRA. [*Angry with herself for laughing.*] No, no, NO!! But it is so ridiculous to hear you call her Totateeta.

CÆSAR. What! As much a child as ever, Cleopatra! Have I not made a woman of you after all?

CLEOPATRA. Oh, it is you who are a great baby: you make me seem silly because you will not behave seriously. But you have treated me badly; and I do not forgive you.

CÆSAR. Bid me farewell.

CLEOPATRA. I will not.

CÆSAR. [*Coaxing.*] I will send you a beautiful present from Rome.

CLEOPATRA. [*Proudly.*] Beauty from Rome to Egypt indeed! What can Rome give me that Egypt cannot give me?

APOLLODORUS. That is true, Cæsar. If the present is to be really beautiful, I shall have to buy it for you in Alexandria.

CÆSAR. You are forgetting the treasures for which Rome is most famous, my friend. You cannot buy them in Alexandria.

APOLLODORUS. What are they, Cæsar?

CÆSAR. Her sons. Come, Cleopatra: forgive me and bid me farewell; and I will send you a man, Roman from head to heel and Roman of the noblest; not old and ripe for the knife; not lean in the arms and cold in the heart; not hiding a bald head under his conqueror's laurels; not stooped with the weight of the world on his shoulders; but brisk and fresh, strong and young, hoping in the morning, fighting in the day, and revelling in the evening. Will you take such an one in exchange for Cæsar?

CLEOPATRA. [*Palpitating.*] His name, his name?

CÆSAR. Shall it be Mark Antony? [*She throws herself into his arms.*]

RUFIO. You are a bad hand at a bargain, mistress, if you will swop Cæsar for Antony.

CÆSAR. So now you are satisfied.

CLEOPATRA. You will not forget.

CÆSAR. I will not forget. Farewell: I do not think we shall meet again. Farewell. [*He kisses her on the forehead. She is much affected and begins to sniff. He embarks.*]

THE ROMAN SOLDIERS. [*As he sets his foot on the gangway.*] Hail, Cæsar; and farewell! [*He reaches the ship and returns* RUFIO'S *wave of the hand.*]

APOLLODORUS. [*To* CLEOPATRA.] No tears, dearest Queen: they stab your servant to the heart. He will return some day.

CLEOPATRA. I hope not. But I cant help crying, all the same. [*She waves her handkerchief to* CÆSAR; *and the ship begins to move.*]

THE ROMAN SOLDIERS. [*Drawing their swords and raising them in the air.*] Hail, Cæsar!

The third of our comedies, Jean Giraudoux's *The Madwoman of Chaillot*, is a product of the dark days of World War II. It was completed in 1944, just before the death of its author, who did not live to see it performed. *The Madwoman* combines poetic fantasy with elements of broad farce; yet the delightfully eccentric characters—perhaps in fact so sane that the world can cope with them only by calling them "mad"—and the apparently inconsequential dialogue never obscure, but rather underline, a coruscating exposure of the modern political and economic worlds that Giraudoux presents to us.

Internationally, Giraudoux is less well known for his somber tragedies that reflect his observation of the ascendancy of force and greed, than for fanciful comedies like *Ondine* and *The Madwoman*. Though the latter plays may also have, as has been said, their serious side, and are firmly rooted in the author's perception of the darker areas of man's nature, they still offer a glittering and scintillating *surface* that immediately catches the eye. *The Madwoman* is a kind of fairy-tale: we know this as soon as we learn that the play takes place "a little before noon in the Spring of next year." But the wonderland to which it introduces us is not unrelated to that of Lewis Carroll's Alice or Swift's Gulliver; it soon reveals a curious and disturbing resemblance to the everyday world we inhabit. The trouble is that, as the comedy becomes more delirious, we are uncertain whether the mad world of this play is our ordinary world with a few distortions grafted on—or whether it is the real world as it could be if some of the existing and accepted distortions were cut away.

For this is a comic fairy-tale in external appearance only. We soon recognize that it pits easily identifiable representatives of good—the innocent, the happy, the free—against equally obvious forces of evil—the exploiters, the craven and ruthless seekers of power. The representatives of the forces of good, the Countess Aurelia and her friends, may be eccentric by just those standards we are here led to question; but in the comic world they inhabit, their virtue shines clear. For what act more pious than the removal of evil from the world could any man accomplish? let alone a crazy old woman anxious to get back to her cats. Yet, unhappily, such accomplishment seems improbable, except in the sane and sober world of comedy.

THE MADWOMAN OF CHAILLOT

Jean Giraudoux

Translated by
Maurice Valency

THE WAITER
THE LITTLE MAN
THE PROSPECTOR
THE PRESIDENT
THE BARON
THERESE
THE STREET SINGER
THE FLOWER GIRL
THE RAGPICKER
PAULETTE
THE DEAF-MUTE
IRMA
THE SHOE-LACE PEDDLER
THE BROKER
THE STREET JUGGLER
DR. JADIN
COUNTESS AURELIA, *Madwoman of*
   Chaillot
THE DOORMAN

THE POLICEMAN
PIERRE
THE SERGEANT
THE SEWER-MAN
MME. CONSTANCE, *Madwoman of*
   Passy
MLLE. GABRIELLE, *Madwoman of*
   St. Sulpice
MME. JOSEPHINE, *Madwoman of*
   La Concorde
THE PRESIDENTS
THE PROSPECTORS
THE PRESS AGENTS
THE LADIES
THE ADOLPHE BERTAUTS

ACT ONE: *The Café Terrace of* Chez
   Francis.
ACT TWO: *The Countess' Cellar—21*
   Rue de Chaillot.

ACT I

SCENE: *The café terrace at* Chez Francis, *on the Place de l'Alma in Paris. The Alma is in the stately quarter of Paris* *known as Chaillot, between the Champs Élysées and the Seine, across the river from the Eiffel Tower.*

171

Chez Francis *has several rows of tables set out under its awning, and, as it is lunch time, a good many of them are occupied. At a table, downstage, a somewhat obvious* BLONDE *with ravishing legs is sipping a vermouth-cassis and trying hard to engage the attention of the* PROSPECTOR, *who sits at an adjacent table taking little sips of water and rolling them over his tongue with the air of a connoisseur. Downstage right, in front of the tables on the sidewalk, is the usual Paris bench, a stout and uncomfortable affair provided by the municipality for the benefit of those who prefer to sit without drinking. A* POLICEMAN *lounges about, keeping the peace without unnecessary exertion.*

TIME: *It is a little before noon in the Spring of next year.*

AT RISE. *The* PRESIDENT *and the* BARON *enter with importance, and are ushered to a front table by the* WAITER.

PRES. Baron, sit down. This is a historic occasion. It must be properly celebrated. The waiter is going to bring out my special port.

BAR. Splendid.

PRES. (*Offers his cigar case.*) Cigar? My private brand.

BAR. Thank you. You know, this all gives me the feeling of one of those enchanted mornings in the *Arabian Nights* when thieves foregather in the market place. Thieves—pashas . . .

(*He sniffs the cigar judiciously, and begins lighting it.*)

PRES. (*Chuckles.*) Tell me about yourself.

BAR. Well, where shall I begin?

(*The* STREET SINGER *enters. He takes off a battered black felt with a flourish and begins singing an ancient mazurka.*)

ST. SING. (*Sings.*)
"Do you hear, Mademoiselle,
Those musicians of hell?"

PRES. Waiter! Get rid of that man.

WAIT. He is singing *La Belle Polonaise.*

PRES. I didn't ask for the program. I asked you to get rid of him. (*The* WAITER *doesn't budge. The* SINGER *goes by himself.*) As you were saying, Baron . . . ?

BAR. Well, until I was fifty . . . (*The* FLOWER GIRL *enters through the café door, center.*) my life was relatively uncomplicated. It consisted of selling off one by one the various estates left me by my father. Three years ago, I parted with my last farm. Two years ago, I lost my last mistress. And now—all that is left me is . . .

FLOW. GIRL. (*To the* BARON.) Violets, sir?

PRES. Run along.

(*The* FLOWER GIRL *moves on.*)

BAR. (*Staring after her.*) So that, in short, all I have left now is my name.

PRES. Your name is precisely the name we need on our board of directors.

BAR. (*With an inclination of his head.*) Very flattering.

PRES. You will understand when I tell you that mine has been a very different experience. I came up from the bottom. My mother spent most of her life bent over a washtub in order to send me to school. I'm eternally grateful to her, of course, but I must confess that I no longer remember her face. It was no doubt beautiful—but when I try to recall it, I see only the part she invariably showed me—her rear.

BAR. Very touching.

PRES. When I was thrown out of school for the fifth and last time, I decided to find out for myself what makes the world go round. I ran errands for an editor, a movie star, a financier. . . . I began to understand a little what life is. Then, one day, in the subway, I saw a face. . . . My rise in life dates from that day.

BAR. Really?

PRES. One look at that face, and I knew. One look at mine, and he knew. And so I made my first thousand—passing a boxful of counterfeit notes. A year later, I saw another such face. It got me a nice berth in the narcotics business. Since then, all I do is to look out for such faces. And now here I am—president of eleven corporations, director of fifty-two companies, and, beginning today, chairman of the board of the international combine in which you have been so good as to accept a post. (*The* RAGPICKER

passes, sees something under the PRE-
SIDENT'S *table, and stoops to pick it up.*)
Looking for something?

RAG. Did you drop this?

PRES. I never drop anything.

RAG. Then this hundred-franc note isn't
yours?

PRES. Give it here. (*The* RAGPICKER *gives
him the note, and goes out.*)

BAR. Are you sure it's yours?

PRES. All hundred-franc notes, Baron, are
mine.

BAR. Mr. President, there's something I've
been wanting to ask you. What exactly
is the purpose of our new company?
Or is that an indiscreet question . . . ?

PRES. Indiscreet? Not a bit. Merely unusual.
As far as I know, you're the first member
of a board of directors ever to ask such
a question.

BAR. Do we plan to exploit a commodity?
A utility?

PRES. My dear sir, I haven't the faintest idea.

BAR. But if you don't know—who does?

PRES. Nobody. And at the moment, it's
becoming just a trifle embarrassing.
Yes, my dear Baron, since we are now
close business associates, I must confess
that for the time being we're in a little
trouble.

BAR. I was afraid of that. The stock issue
isn't going well?

PRES. No, no—on the contrary. The stock
issue is going beautifully. Yesterday
morning at ten o'clock we offered 500,000
shares to the general public. By 10:05
they were all snapped up at par. By 10:20,
when the police finally arrived, our offices
were a shambles. . . . Windows smashed—
doors torn off their hinges—you never
saw anything so beautiful in your life!
And this morning our stock is being
quoted over the counter at 124 with no
sellers, and the orders are still pouring in.

BAR. But in that case—what is the trouble?

PRES. The trouble is we have a tremendous
capital, and not the slightest idea of
what to do with it.

BAR. You mean all those people are fighting
to buy stock in a company that has no
object?

PRES. My dear Baron, do you imagine that
when a subscriber buys a share of stock,
he has any idea of getting behind a counter
or digging a ditch? A stock certificate is
not a tool, like a shovel, or a commodity,
like a pound of cheese. What we sell a
customer is not a share in a business, but
a view of the Elysian Fields. A financier
is a creative artist. Our function is to
stimulate the imagination. We are poets!

BAR. But in order to stimulate the imagination, don't you need some field of
activity?

PRES. Not at all. What you need for that is
a name. A name that will stir the pulse
like a trumpet call, set the brain awhirl
like a movie star, inspire reverence like
a cathedral. *United General International
Consolidated*! Of course that's been used.
That's what a corporation needs.

BAR. And do we have such a name?

PRES. So far we have only a blank space.
In that blank space a name must be
printed. This name must be a masterpiece.
And if I seem a little nervous today,
it's because—somehow—I've racked my
brains, but it hasn't come to me. Oho!
Look at that! Just like the answer to a
prayer . . . ! (*The* BARON *turns and stares
in the direction of the* PROSPECTOR.) You
see? There's one. And what a beauty!

BAR. You mean that girl?

PRES. No, no, not the girl. That face. You
see . . . ? The one that's drinking water.

BAR. You call that a face? That's a tomb-
stone.

PRES. It's a milestone. It's a signpost. But is
it pointing the way to steel, or wheat,
or phosphates? That's what we have to
find out. Ah! He sees me. He understands. He will be over.

BAR. And when he comes . . . ?

PRES. He will tell me what to do.

BAR. You mean business is done this way?
You mean, you would trust a stranger
with a matter of this importance?

PRES. Baron, I trust neither my wife, nor my
daughter, nor my closest friend. My
confidential secretary has no idea where
I live. But a face like that I would trust
with my inmost secrets. Though we have

never laid eyes on each other before, that man and I know each other to the depths of our souls. He's no stranger—he's my brother, he's myself. You'll see. He'll be over in minute. (*The* DEAF MUTE *enters and passes slowly among the tables, placing a small envelope before each customer. He comes to the* PRESIDENT'S *table.*) What is this anyway? A conspiracy? We don't want your envelopes. Take them away. (*The* DEAF MUTE *makes a short but pointed speech in sign language.*) Waiter, what the devil's he saying?

WAIT. Only Irma understands him.

PRES. Irma? Who's Irma?

WAIT. (*Calls.*) Irma! It's the waitress inside, sir. Irma!

(IRMA *comes out. She is twenty. She has the face and figure of an angel.*)

IRMA. Yes?

WAIT. These gentlemen would . . .

PRES. Tell this fellow to get out of here, for God's sake! (*The* DEAF MUTE *makes another manual oration.*) What's he trying to say, anyway?

IRMA. He says it's an exceptionally beautiful morning, sir. . . .

PRES. Who asked him?

IRMA. But, he says, it was nicer before the gentleman stuck his face in it.

PRES. Call the manager!

(IRMA *shrugs. She goes back into the restaurant. The* DEAF MUTE *walks off, Left. Meanwhile a* SHOELACE PEDDLER *has arrived.*)

PED. Shoelaces? Postcards?

BAR. I think I could use a shoelace.

PRES. No, no . . .

PED. Black? Tan?

BAR. (*Showing his shoes.*) What would you recommend?

PED. Anybody's guess.

BAR. Well, give me one of each.

PRES. (*Putting a hand on the* BARON'S *arm.*) Baron, although I am your chairman, I have no authority over your personal life—none, that is, except to fix the amount of your director's fees, and eventually to assign a motor car for your use. Therefore, I am asking you, as a personal favor to me, not to purchase anything from this fellow.

BAR. How can I resist so gracious a request? (*The* PEDDLER *shrugs, and passes on.*) But I really don't understand. . . . What difference would it make?

PRES. Look here, Baron. Now that you're with us, you must understand that between this irresponsible riff-raff and us there is an impenetrable barrier. *We* have no dealings whatever with *them.*

BAR. But without us, the poor devil will starve.

PRES. No, he won't. He expects nothing from us. He has a clientele of his own. He sells shoelaces exclusively to those who have no shoes. Just as the necktie peddler sells only to those who wear no shirts. And that's why these street hawkers can afford to be insolent, disrespectful and independent. They don't need us. They have a world of their own. Ah! My broker. Splendid. He's beaming.

(*The* BROKER *walks up and grasps the* PRESIDENT'S *hand with enthusiasm.*)

BRO. Mr. President! My heartiest congratulations! What a day! What a day!

(*The* STREET JUGGLER *appears, Right. He removes his coat, folds it carefully, and puts it on the bench. Then he opens a suitcase, from which he extracts a number of colored clubs.*)

PRES. (*Presenting the* BROKER.) Baron Tommard, of our Board of Directors. My broker. (*The* BROKER *bows. So does the* JUGGLER. *The* BROKER *sits down and signals for a drink. The* JUGGLER *prepares to juggle.*) What's happened?

BRO. Listen to this. Ten o'clock this morning. The market opens. (*As he speaks, the* JUGGLER *provides a visual counterpart to the* BROKER'S *lines, his clubs rising and falling in rhythm to the* BROKER'S *words.*) Half million shares issued at par, par value a hundred, quoted on the curb at 124 and we start buying at 126, 127, 129—and it's going up—up—up—(*The* JUGGLER'S *clubs rise higher and higher.*)— 132—133—138—141—141—141—141 . . .

BAR. May I ask . . . ?

PRES. No, no—any explanation would only confuse you.

BRO. Ten forty-five we start selling short on rumors of a Communist plot, market bearish. . . .   141—138—133—132—and it's down—down—down—102—and we start buying back at 93. Eleven o'clock, rumors denied—95—98—101—106—124 —141—and by 11:30 we've got it all back—net profit three and a half million francs.

PRES. Classical. Pure. (*The* JUGGLER *bows again. A* LITTLE MAN *leans over from a near-by table, listening intently, and trembling with excitement.*) And how many shares do we reserve to each member of the board?

BRO. Fifty, as agreed.

PRES. Bit stingy, don't you think?

BRO. All right—three thousand.

PRES. That's a little better. (*To the* BARON.) You get the idea?

BAR. I'm beginning to get it.

BRO. And now we come to the exciting part . . . (*The* JUGGLER *prepares to juggle with balls of fire.*) Listen carefully: With 35 percent of our funded capital under Section 32 I buy 50,000 United at 36 which I immediately reconvert into 32,000 National Amalgamated two's preferred which I set up as collateral on 150,000 General Consols which I deposit against a credit of fifteen billion to buy Eastern Hennequin which I immediately turn into Argentine wheat realizing 136 percent of the original investment which naturally accrues as capital gain and not as corporate income thus saving twelve millions in taxes, and at once convert the 25 percent cotton reserve into lignite, and as our people swing into action in London and New York, I beat up the price on greige goods from 26 to 92— 114—203—306—(*The* JUGGLER *by now is juggling his fireballs in the sky. The balls no longer return to his hands.*) 404 . . . (*The* LITTLE MAN *can stand no more. He rushes over and dumps a sackful of money on the table.*)

L. MAN. Here—take it—please, take it!

BRO. (*Frigidly.*) Who is this man? What is this money?

L. MAN. It's my life's savings. Every cent. I put it all in your hands.

BRO. Can't you see we're busy?

L. MAN. But I beg you . . . It's my only chance . . . Please don't turn me away.

BRO. Oh, all right. (*He sweeps the money into his pocket.*) Well?

L. MAN. I thought—perhaps you'd give me a little receipt. . . .

PRES. My dear man, people like us don't give receipts for money. We take them.

L. MAN. Oh, pardon. Of course. I was confused. Here it is. (*Scribbles a receipt.*) Thank you—thank you—thank you. (*He rushes off joyfully. The* STREET SINGER *reappears.*)

ST. SING. (*Sings.*)
  "Do you hear, Mademoiselle,
  Those musicians of hell?"

PRES. What, again? Why does he keep repeating those two lines like a parrot?

WAIT. What else can he do? He doesn't know any more and the song's been out of print for years.

BAR. Couldn't he sing a song he knows?

WAIT. He likes this one. He hopes if he keeps singing the beginning someone will turn up to teach him the end.

PRES. Tell him to move on. We don't know the song.

(*The* PROFESSOR *strolls by, swinging his cane. He overhears.*)

PROF. (*Stops and addresses the* PRESIDENT *politely.*) Nor do I, my dear sir. Nor do I. And yet, I'm in exactly the same predicament. I remember just two lines of my favorite song, as a child. A mazurka also, in case you're interested. . . .

PRES. I'm not.

PROF. Why is it, I wonder, that one always forgets the words of a mazurka? I suppose they just get lost in that damnable rhythm. All I remember is: (*He sings.*)
  "From England to Spain
  I have drunk, it was bliss . . ."

ST. SING. (*Walks over, and picks up the tune.*)
  "Red wine and champagne
  And many a kiss."

PROF. Oh, God! It all comes back to me
... ! (*He sings.*)
  "Red lips and white hands I have
  known
  Where the nightingales dwell. . . ."
PRES. (*Holding his hands to his ears.*) Please—
please . . .
ST. SING.
  "And to each one I've whispered,
  'My own,'
  And to each one, I've murmured:
  'Farewell.'"
PRES. Farewell. Farewell.
ST. SING. ⎫
PROF.   ⎬ (*duo*)
  "But there's one I shall never forget.
  . . ."
PRES. This isn't a café. It's a circus!
(*The two go off, still singing:* "There is one
  that's engraved in my heart." *The* PROS-
  PECTOR *gets up slowly and walks toward
  the* PRESIDENT'S *table. He looks down
  without a word. There is a tense silence.*)
PROS. Well?
PRES. I need a name.
PROS. (*Nods, with complete comprehension.*)
  I need fifty thousand.
PRES. For a corporation.
PROS. For a woman.
PRES. Immediately.
PROS. Before evening.
PRES. Something . . .
PROS. Unusual?
PRES. Something . . .
PROS. Provocative?
PRES. Something . . .
PROS. Practical.
PRES. Yes.
PROS. Fifty thousand. Cash.
PRES. I'm listening.
PROS. *International Substrate of Paris, Inc.*
PRES. (*Snaps his fingers.*) That's it! (*To the*
  BROKER.) Pay him off. (*The* BROKER *pays
  with the* LITTLE MAN'S *money.*) Now—
  what does it mean?
PROS. It means what it says. I'm a prospector.
PRES. (*rises*). A prospector! Allow me to
  shake your hand. Baron. You are in the
  presence of one of nature's noblemen.
  Shake his hand. This is Baron Tommard.
  (*They shake hands.*) It is this man, my

dear Baron, who smells out in the
bowels of the earth those deposits of
metal or liquid on which can be founded
the only social unit of which our age
is capable—the corporation. Sit down,
please. (*They all sit.*) And now that we
have a name . . .
PROS. You need a property.
PRES. Precisely.
PROS. I have one.
PRES. A claim?
PROS. Terrific.
PRES. Foreign?
PROS. French.
BAR. In Indo-China?
BRO. Morocco?
PRES. In France?
PROS. (*Matter of fact.*) In Paris.
PRES. In Paris? You've been prospecting
  in Paris?
BAR. For women, no doubt.
PRES. For art?
BRO. For gold?
PROS. Oil.
BRO. He's crazy.
PRES. Sh! He's inspired.
PROS. You think I'm crazy. Well, they
  thought Columbus was crazy.
BAR. Oil in Paris?
BRO. But how is it possible?
PROS. It's not only possible. It's certain.
PRES. Tell us.
PROS. You don't know, my dear sir, what
  treasures Paris conceals. Paris is the least
  prospected place in the world. We've
  gone over the rest of the planet with a
  fine-tooth comb. But has anyone ever
  thought of looking for oil in Paris?
  Nobody. Before me, that is.
PRES. Genius!
PROS. No. Just a practical man. I use my
  head.
BAR. But why has nobody ever thought of
  this before?
PROS. The treasures of the earth, my dear
  sir, are not easy to find nor to get at.
  They are invariably guarded by dragons.
  Doubtless there is some reason for this.
  For once we've dug out and consumed
  the internal ballast of the planet, the
  chances are it will shoot off on some

irresponsible tangent and smash itself up in the sky. Well, that's the risk we take. Anyway, that's not my business. A prospector has enough to worry about.

BAR. I know—snakes—tarantulas—fleas . . .

PROS. Worse than that, sir. Civilization.

PRES. Does that annoy you?

PROS. Civilization gets in our way all the time. In the first place, it covers the earth with cities and towns which are damned awkward to dig up when you want to see what's underneath. It's not only the real-estate people—you can always do business with them—it's human sentimentality. How do you do business with that?

PRES. I see what you mean.

PROS. They say that where we pass, nothing ever grows again. What of it? Is a park any better than a coal mine? What's a mountain got that a slag pile hasn't? What would you rather have in your garden—an almond tree or an oil well?

PRES. Well . . .

PROS. Exactly. But what's the use of arguing with these fools? Imagine the choicest place you ever saw for an excavation, and what do they put there? A playground for children! Civilization!

PRES. Just show us the point where you want to start digging. We'll do the rest. Even if it's in the middle of the Louvre. Where's the oil?

PROS. Perhaps you think it's easy to make an accurate fix in an area like Paris where everything conspires to put you off the scent? Women—perfume—flowers—history. You can talk all you like about geology, but an oil deposit, gentlemen, has to be smelled out. I have a good nose. I go further. I have a phenomenal nose. But the minute I get the right whiff—the minute I'm on the scent—a fragrance rises from what I take to be the spiritual deposits of the past—and I'm completely at sea. Now take this very point, for example, this very spot.

BAR. You mean—right here in Chaillot?

PROS. Right under here.

PRES. Good heavens! (*He looks under his chair.*)

PROS. It's taken me months to locate this spot.

BAR. But what in the world makes you think . . . ?

PROS. Do you know this place, Baron?

BAR. Well, I've been sitting here for thirty years.

PROS. Did you ever taste the water?

BAR. The water? Good God, no!

PROS. It's plain to see that you are no prospector! A prospector, Baron, is addicted to water as a drunkard to wine. Water, gentlemen, is the one substance from which the earth can conceal nothing. It sucks out its innermost secrets and brings them to our very lips. Well—beginning at Notre Dame, where I first caught the scent of oil three months ago, I worked my way across Paris, glassful by glassful, sampling the water, until at last I came to this café. And here—just two days ago—I took a sip. My heart began to thump. Was it possible that I was deceived? I took another, a third, a fourth, a fifth. I was trembling like a leaf. But there was no mistake. Each time that I drank, my taste-buds thrilled to the most exquisite flavor known to a prospector—the flavor of—(*with utmost lyricism*) petroleum!

PRES. Waiter! Some water and four glasses. Hurry. This round, gentlemen, is on me. And as a toast—I shall propose International Substrate of Paris, Incorporated. (*The* WAITER *brings a decanter and the glasses. The* PRESIDENT *pours out the water amid profound silence. They taste it with the air of connoisseurs savoring something that has never before passed human lips. Then they look at each other doubtfully. The* PROSPECTOR *pours himself a second glass and drinks it off.*) Well . . .

BRO. Ye-es . . .

BAR. Mm . . .

PROS. Get it?

BAR. Tastes queer.

PROS. That's it. To the unpracticed palate it tastes queer. But to the taste-buds of the expert—ah!

BAR. Still, there's one thing I don't quite understand . . .

PROS. Yes?

BAR. This café doesn't have its own well, does it?

PROS. Of course not. This is Paris water.

BRO. Then why should it taste different here than anywhere else?

PROS. Because, my dear sir, the pipes that carry this water pass deep through the earth, and the earth just here is soaked with oil, and this oil permeates the pores of the iron and flavors the water it carries. Ever so little, yes—but quite enough to betray its presence to the sensitive tongue of the specialist.

BAR. I see.

PROS. I don't say everyone is capable of tasting it. No. But I—I can detect the presence of oil in water that has passed within fifteen miles of a deposit. Under special circumstances, twenty.

PRES. Phenomenal!

PROS. And so here I am with the greatest discovery of the age on my hands—but the blasted authorities won't let me drill a single well unless I show them the oil! Now how can I show them the oil unless they let me dig? Completely stymied! Eh?

PRES. What? A man like you?

PROS. That's what they think. That's what they want. Have you noticed the strange glamor of the women this morning? And the quality of the sunshine? And this extraordinary convocation of vagabonds buzzing about protectively like bees around a hive? Do you know why it is? Because they know. It's a plot to distract us, to turn us from our purpose. Well, let them try. I know there's oil here. And I'm going to dig it up, even if I . . . (*He smiles.*) Shall I tell you my little plan?

PRES. By all means.

PROS. Well . . . For heaven's sake, what's that?

(*At this point, the* MADWOMAN *enters. She is dressed in the grand fashion of 1885, a taffeta skirt with an immense train—which she has gathered up by means of a clothespin —ancient button shoes, and a hat in the style of Marie Antoinette. She wears a* lorgnette *on a chain, and an enormous cameo pin at her throat. In her hand she carries a small basket. She walks in with great dignity, extracts a dinner bell from the bosom of her dress, and rings it sharply.* IRMA *appears.*)

COUNT. Are my bones ready, Irma?

IRMA. There won't be much today, Countess. We had broilers. Can you wait? While the gentleman inside finishes eating?

COUNT. And my gizzard?

IRMA. I'll try to get it away from him.

COUNT. If he eats my gizzard, save me the giblets. They will do for the tomcat that lives under the bridge. He likes a few giblets now and again.

IRMA. Yes, Countess. (IRMA *goes back into the café. The* COUNTESS *takes a few steps and stops in front of the* PRESIDENT's *table. She examines him with undisguised disapproval.*)

PRES. Waiter. Ask that woman to move on.

WAIT. Sorry, sir. This is her café.

PRES. Is she the manager of the café?

WAIT. She's the Madwoman of Chaillot.

PRES. A Madwoman? She's mad?

WAIT. Who says she's mad?

PRES. You just said so yourself.

WAIT. Look, sir. You asked me who she was. And I told you. What's mad about her? She's the Madwoman of Chaillot.

PRES. Call a policeman.

(*The* COUNTESS *whistles through her fingers. At once, the* DOORMAN *runs out of the café. He has three scarves in his hands.*)

COUNT. Have you found it? My feather boa?

DOOR. Not yet, Countess. Three scarves. But no boa.

COUNT. It's five years since I lost it. Surely you've had time to find it.

DOOR. Take one of these, Countess. Nobody's claimed them.

COUNT. A boa like that doesn't vanish, you know. A feather boa nine feet long!

DOOR. How about this blue one?

COUNT. With my pink ruffle and my green veil? You're joking! Let me see the yellow. (*She tries it on.*) How does it look?

DOOR. Terrific.

(*With a magnificent gesture, she flings the scarf about her, upsetting the* PRESIDENT'S *glass and drenching his trousers with water. She stalks off without a glance at him.*)

PRES. Waiter! I'm making a complaint.

WAIT. Against whom?

PRES. Against her! Against you! The whole gang of you! That singer! The shoelace peddler! That female lunatic! Or whatever you call her!

BAR. Calm yourself, Mr. President. . . .

PRES. I'll do nothing of the sort! Baron, the first thing we have to do is to get rid of these people! Good heavens, look at them! Every size, shape, color and period of history imaginable. It's utter anarchy! I tell you, sir, the only safeguard of order and discipline in the modern world is a standardized worker with interchangeable parts. That would solve the entire problem of management. Here, the manager . . . And there—one composite drudge grunting and sweating all over the world. Just we two. Ah, how beautiful! How easy on the eyes! How restful for the conscience!

BAR. Yes, yes—of course.

PRES. Order. Symmetry. Balance. But instead of that, what? Here in Chaillot, the very citadel of management, these insolent phantoms of the past come to beard us with their raffish individualism— with the right of the voiceless to sing, of the dumb to make speeches, of trousers to have no seats and bosoms to have dinner bells!

BAR. But, after all, do these people matter?

PRES. My dear sir, wherever the poor are happy, and the servants are proud, and the mad are respected, our power is at an end. Look at that! That waiter! That madwoman! That flower girl! Do I get that sort of service? And suppose that I—president of twelve corporations and ten times a millionaire—were to stick a gladiolus in my buttonhole and start yelling—(*He tinkles his spoon in a glass violently, yelling.*) Are my bones ready, Irma?

BAR. (*Reprovingly.*) Mr. President . . .

(*People at the adjoining tables turn and stare with raised eyebrows. The* WAITER *starts to come over.*)

PRES. You see? Now.

PROS. We were discussing my plan.

PRES. Ah yes, your plan. (*He glances in the direction of the* MADWOMAN'S *table.*) Careful—she's looking at us.

PROS. Do you know what a bomb is?

PRES. I'm told they explode.

PROS. Exactly. You see that white building across the river. Do you happen to know what that is?

PRES. I do not.

PROS. That's the office of the City Architect. That man has stubbornly refused to give me a permit to drill for oil anywhere within the limits of the city of Paris. I've tried everything with him—influence, bribes, threats. He says I'm crazy. And now . . .

PRES. Oh, my God! What is this one trying to sell us?

(*A little* OLD MAN *enters Left, and doffs his hat politely. He is somewhat ostentatiously respectable—gloved, pomaded, and carefully dressed, with a white handkerchief peeping out of his breast pocket.*)

DR. JAD. Nothing but health, sir. Or rather the health of the feet. But remember—as the foot goes, so goes the man. May I present myself . . . ? Dr. Gaspard Jadin, French Navy, retired. Former specialist in the extraction of ticks and chiggers. At present specializing in the extraction of bunions and corns. In case of sudden emergency, Martial the waiter will furnish my home address. My office is here, second row, third table, week days, twelve to five. Thank you very much. (*He sits at his table.*)

WAIT. Your vermouth, Doctor?

DR. JAD. My vermouth. My vermouths. How are your gallstones today, Martial?

WAIT. Fine. Fine. They rattle like anything.

DR. JAD. Splendid. (*He spies the* COUNTESS.) Good morning, Countess. How's the floating kidney? Still afloat? (*She nods graciously.*) Splendid. Splendid. So long as it floats, it can't sink.

PRES. This is impossible! Let's go somewhere else.

PROS. No. It's nearly noon.

PRES. Yes. It is. Five to twelve.

PROS. In five minutes' time you're going to see that City Architect blown up, building and all—boom!

BRO. Are you serious?

PROS. That imbecile has no one to blame but himself. Yesterday noon, he got my ultimatum—he's had twenty-four hours to think it over. No permit? All right. Within two minutes my agent is going to drop a little package in his coal bin. And three minutes after that, precisely at noon . . .

BAR. You prospectors certainly use modern methods.

PROS. The method may be modern. But the idea is old. To get at the treasure, it has always been necessary to slay the dragon. I guarantee that after this, the City Architect will be more reasonable. The new one, I mean.

PRES. Don't you think we're sitting a little close for comfort?

PROS. Oh no, no. Don't worry. And, above all, don't stare. We may be watched. (*A clock strikes.*) Why, that's noon. Something's wrong! Good God! What's this? (*A* POLICEMAN *staggers in bearing a lifeless body on his shoulders in the manner prescribed as "The Fireman's Lift."*) It's Pierre! My agent! (*He walks over with affected nonchalance.*) I say, Officer, what's that you've got?

POLICE. Drowned man. (*He puts him down on the bench.*)

WAIT. He's not drowned. His clothes are dry. He's been slugged.

POLICE. Slugged is also correct. He was just jumping off the bridge when I came along and pulled him back. I slugged him, naturally, so he wouldn't drag me under. Life Saving Manual, Rule 5: "In cases where there is danger of being dragged under, it is necessary to render

the subject unconscious by means of a sharp blow." He's had that. (*He loosens the clothes and begins applying artificial respiration.*)

PROS. The stupid idiot! What the devil did he do with the bomb? That's what comes of employing amateurs!

PRES. You don't think he'll give you away?

PROS. Don't worry. (*He walks over to the* POLICEMAN.) Say, what do you think you're doing?

POLICE. Lifesaving. Artificial respiration. First aid to the drowning.

PROS. But he's not drowning.

POLICE. But he thinks he is.

PROS. You'll never bring him round that way, my friend. That's meant for people who drown in water. It's no good at all for those who drown without water.

POLICE. What am I supposed to do? I've just been sworn in. It's my first day on the beat. I can't afford to get in trouble. I've got to go by the book.

PROS. Perfectly simple. Take him back to the bridge where you found him and throw him in. Then you can save his life and you'll get a medal. This way, you'll only get fined for slugging an innocent man.

POLICE. What do you mean, innocent? He was just going to jump when I grabbed him.

PROS. Have you any proof of that?

POLICE. Well, I saw him.

PROS. Written proof? Witnesses?

POLICE. No, but . . .

PROS. Then don't waste time arguing. You're in trouble. Quick—before anybody notices —throw him in and dive after him. It's the only way out.

POLICE. But I don't swim.

PRES. You'll learn how on the way down. Before you were born, did you know how to breathe?

POLICE. (*Convinced.*) All right. Here we go. (*He starts lifting the body.*)

DR. JAD. One moment, please. I don't like to interfere, but it's my professional duty to point out that medical science has definitely established the fact of intra-uterine respiration. Consequently, this policeman, even before he was born, knew not only how to breathe but also how to cough, hiccup and belch.

PRES. Suppose he did—how does it concern you?

DR. JAD. On the other hand, medical science has never established the fact of intra-uterine swimming or diving. Under the circumstances, we are forced to the opinion, Officer, that if you dive in you will probably drown.

POLICE. You think so?

PROS. Who asked you for an opinion?

PRES. Pay no attention to that quack, Officer.

DR. JAD. Quack, sir?

PROS. This is not a medical matter. It's a legal problem. The officer has made a grave error. He's new. We're trying to help him.

BRO. He's probably afraid of the water.

POLICE. Nothing of the sort. Officially, I'm afraid of nothing. But I always follow doctor's orders.

DR. JAD. You see, Officer, when a child is born . . .

PROS. Now, what does he care about when a child is born? He's got a dying man on his hands. . . . Officer, if you want my advice . . .

POLICE. It so happens, I care a lot about when a child is born. It's part of my duty to aid and assist any woman in childbirth or labor.

PRES. Can you imagine!

POLICE. Is it true, Doctor, what they say, that when you have twins, the first born is considered to be the youngest?

DR. JAD. Quite correct. And what's more, if the twins happen to be born at midnight on December 31st, the older is a whole year younger. He does his military service a year later. That's why you have to keep your eyes open. And that's the reason why a queen always gives birth before witnesses. . . .

POLICE. God! The things a policeman is supposed to know! Doctor, what does it mean if, when I get up in the morning sometimes . . .

PROS. (*Nudging the* PRESIDENT *meaningfully.*) The old woman . . .

BRO. Come on, Baron.

PRES. I think we'd better all run along.

PROS. Leave him to me.

PRES. I'll see you later. (*The* PRESIDENT *steals off with the* BROKER *and the* BARON.)

POLICE. (*Still in conference with* DR. JADIN.) But what's really worrying me, Doctor, is this—don't you think it's a bit risky for a man to marry after forty-five?

(*The* BROKER *runs in breathlessly.*)

BRO. Officer! Officer!

POLICE. What's the trouble?

BRO. Quick! Two women are calling for help—on the sidewalk—Avenue Wilson!

POLICE. Two women at once? Standing up or lying down?

BRO. You'd better go and see. Quick!

PROS. You'd better take the Doctor with you.

POLICE. Come along, Doctor, come along. . . . (*Pointing to* PIERRE.) Tell him to wait till I get back. Come along, Doctor. (*He runs out, the* DOCTOR *following. The* PROSPECTOR *moves over toward* PIERRE, *but* IRMA *crosses in front of him and takes the boy's hand.*)

IRMA. How beautiful he is! Is he dead, Martial?

WAIT. (*Handing her a pocket mirror.*) Hold this mirror to his mouth. If it clouds over . . .

IRMA. It clouds over.

WAIT. He's alive. (*He holds out his hand for the mirror.*)

IRMA. Just a sec—(*She rubs it clean and looks at herself intently. Before handing it back, she fixes her hair and applies her lipstick. Meanwhile the* PROSPECTOR *tries to get around the other side, but the* COUNTESS' *eagle eye drives him off. He shrugs his shoulders and exits with the* BARON.) Oh, look—he's opened his eyes! (PIERRE *opens his eyes, stares intently at* IRMA *and closes them again with the expression of a man who is among the angels.*)

PIERRE (*Murmurs.*) Oh! How beautiful!

VOICE (*From within the café.*) Irma!

IRMA. Coming. Coming. (*She goes in, not without a certain reluctance. The* COUNTESS *at once takes her place on the bench, and also the* YOUNG MAN'S *hand.* PIERRE *sits up suddenly, and finds himself staring, not at* IRMA, *but into the very peculiar face of the* COUNTESS. *His expression changes.*)

COUNT. You're looking at my iris? Isn't it beautiful?

PIERRE. Very. (*He drops back, exhausted.*)

COUNT. The Sergeant was good enough to say it becomes me. But I no longer trust his taste. Yesterday, the flower girl gave me a lily, and he said it didn't suit me.

PIERRE (*Weakly.*) It's beautiful.

COUNT. He'll be very happy to know that you agree with him. He's really quite sensitive. (*She calls.*) Sergeant!

PIERRE. No, please—don't call the police.

COUNT. But I must. I think I hurt his feelings.

PIERRE. Let me go, Madame.

COUNT. No, no. Stay where you are. Sergeant! (PIERRE *struggles weakly to get up.*)

PIERRE. Please let me go.

COUNT. I'll do nothing of the sort. When you let someone go, you never see him again. I let Charlotte Mazumet go. I never saw her again.

PIERRE. Oh, my head.

COUNT. I let Adolphe Bertaut go. And I was holding him. And I never saw him again.

PIERRE. Oh, God!

COUNT. Except once. Thirty years later. In the market. He had changed a great deal —he didn't know me. He sneaked a melon from right under my nose, the only good one of the year. Ah, here we are. Sergeant! (*The* POLICE SERGEANT *comes in with importance.*)

SERG. I'm in a hurry, Countess.

COUNT. With regard to the iris. This young man agrees with you. He says it suits me.

SERG. (*Going.*) There's a man drowning in the Seine.

COUNT. He's not drowning in the Seine. He's drowning here. Because I'm holding him tight—as I should have held Adol-phe Bertaut. But if I let him go, I'm sure he will go and drown in the Seine. He's a lot better looking than Adolphe Bertaut, wouldn't you say? (PIERRE *sighs deeply.*)

SERG. How would I know?

COUNT. I've shown you his photograph. The one with the bicycle.

SERG. Oh, yes. The one with the harelip.

COUNT. I've told you a hundred times! Adolphe Bertaut had no harelip. That was a scratch in the negative. (*The* SERGEANT *takes out his notebook and pencil.*) What are you doing?

SERG. I am taking down the drowned man's name, given name and date of birth.

COUNT. You think that's going to stop him from jumping in the river? Don't be silly, Sergeant. Put that book away and try to console him.

SERG. I should try and console him?

COUNT. When people want to die, it is your job as a guardian of the state to speak out in praise of life. Not mine.

SERG. I should speak out in praise of life?

COUNT. I assume you have some motive for interfering with people's attempts to kill each other, and rob each other, and run each other over? If you believe that life has some value, tell him what it is. Go on.

SERG. Well, all right. Now look, young man . . .

COUNT. His name is Roderick.

PIERRE. My name is not Roderick.

COUNT. Yes, it is. It's noon. At noon all men become Roderick.

SERG. Except Adolphe Bertaut.

COUNT. In the days of Adolphe Bertaut, we were forced to change the men when we got tired of their names. Nowadays, we're more practical—each hour on the hour all names are automatically changed. The men remain the same. But you're not here to discuss Adolphe Bertaut, Sergeant. You're here to convince the young man that life is worth living.

PIERRE. It isn't.

SERG. Quiet. Now then—what was the idea of jumping off the bridge, anyway?

COUNT. The idea was to land in the river.

Roderick doesn't seem to be at all confused about that.

SERG. Now how can I convince anybody that life is worth living if you keep interrupting all the time?

COUNT. I'll be quiet.

SERG. First of all, Mr. Roderick, you have to realize that suicide is a crime against the state. And why is it a crime against the state? Because every time anybody commits suicide, that means one soldier less for the army, one taxpayer less for the . . .

COUNT. Sergeant, isn't there something about life that you really enjoy?

SERG. That I enjoy?

COUNT. Well, surely, in all these years, you must have found something worth living for. Some secret pleasure, or passion. Don't blush. Tell him about it.

SERG. Who's blushing? Well, naturally, yes—I have my passions—like everybody else. The fact is, since you ask me—I love—to play—casino. And if the gentleman would like to join me, by and by when I go off duty, we can sit down to a nice little game in the back room with a nice cold glass of beer. If he wants to kill an hour, that is.

COUNT. He doesn't want to kill an hour. He wants to kill himself. Well? Is that all the police force has to offer by way of earthly bliss?

SERG. Huh? You mean— (*He jerks a thumb in the direction of the pretty* BLONDE, *who has just been joined by a* BRUNETTE *of the same stamp.*) Paulette? (*The young man groans.*)

COUNT. You're not earning your salary, Sergeant. I defy anybody to stop dying on your account.

SERG. Go ahead, if you can do any better. But you won't find it easy.

COUNT. Oh, this is not a desperate case at all. A young man who has just fallen in love with someone who has fallen in love with him!

PIERRE. She hasn't. How could she?

COUNT. Oh, yes, she has. She was holding your hand, just as I'm holding it, when

all of a sudden . . . Did you ever know Marshal Canrobert's niece?

SERG. How could he know Marshal Canrobert's niece?

COUNT. Lots of people knew her—when she was alive. (PIERRE *begins to struggle energetically.*) No, no, Roderick—stop—stop!

SERG. You see? You won't do any better than I did.

COUNT. No? Let's bet. I'll bet my iris against one of your gold buttons. Right?— Roderick, I know very well why you tried to drown yourself in the river.

PIERRE. You don't at all.

COUNT. It's because that Prospector wanted you to commit a horrible crime.

PIERRE. How did you know that?

COUNT. He stole my boa, and now he wants you to kill me.

PIERRE. Not exactly.

COUNT. It wouldn't be the first time they've tried it. But I'm not so easy to get rid of, my boy, oh, no . . . Because . . .

(*The* DOORMAN *rides in on his bicycle. He winks at the* SERGEANT, *who has now seated himself while the* WAITER *serves him a beer.*)

DOOR. Take it easy, Sergeant.

SERG. I'm busy saving a drowning man.

COUNT. They can't kill me because—I have no desire to die.

PIERRE. You're fortunate.

COUNT. To be alive is to be fortunate, Roderick. Of course, in the morning, when you first awake, it does not always seem so very gay. When you take your hair out of the drawer, and your teeth out of the glass, you are apt to feel a little out of place in this world. Especially if you've just been dreaming that you're a little girl on a pony looking for strawberries in the woods. But all you need to feel the call of life once more is a letter in your mail giving you your schedule for the day—your mending, your shopping, that letter to your grandmother that you never seem to get around to. And so, when you've washed your face in rosewater, and powdered it—not with this awful rice-powder they sell nowadays, which does nothing for the skin, but with a cake of pure white starch—and put on your pins, your rings, your brooches, bracelets, earrings and pearls—in short, when you are dressed for your morning coffee—and have had a good look at yourself—not in the glass, naturally—it lies—but in the side of the brass gong that once belonged to Admiral Courbet—then, Roderick, then you're armed, you're strong, you're ready—you can begin again. (PIERRE *is listening now intently. There are tears in his eyes.*)

PIERRE. Oh, Madame . . . ! Oh, Madame . . . !

COUNT. After that, everything is pure delight. First the morning paper. Not, of course, these current sheets full of lies and vulgarity. I always read the *Gaulois*, the issue of March 22, 1903. It's by far the best. It has some delightful scandal, some excellent fashion notes, and, of course, the last-minute bulletin on the death of Leonide Leblanc. She used to live next door, poor woman, and when I learn of her death every morning, it gives me quite a shock. I'd gladly lend you my copy, but it's in tatters.

SERG. Couldn't we find him a copy in some library?

COUNT. I doubt it. And so, when you've taken your fruit salts—not in water, naturally—no matter what they say, it's water that gives you gas—but with a bit of spiced cake—then in sunlight or rain, Chaillot calls. It is time to dress for your morning walk. This takes much longer, of course—without a maid, impossible to do it under an hour, what with your corset, corset-cover and drawers all of which lace or button in the back. I asked Madame Lanvin, a while ago, to fit the drawers with zippers. She was quite charming, but she declined. She thought it would spoil the style.

(*The* DEAF-MUTE *comes in.*)

WAIT. I know a place where they put zippers on anything.

(*The* RAGPICKER *enters.*)

COUNT. I think Lanvin knows best. But I really manage very well, Martial. What I do now is, I lace them up in front, then twist them around to the back. It's quite simple, really. Then you choose a lorgnette, and then the usual fruitless search for the feather boa that the prospector stole—I know it was he: he didn't dare look me in the eye—and then all you need is a rubber band to slip around your parasol—I lost the catch the day I struck the cat that was stalking the pigeon—it was worth it—ah, that day I earned my wages!

RAG. Countess, if you can use it, I found a nice umbrella catch the other day with a cat's eye in it.

COUNT. Thank you, Ragpicker. They say these eyes sometimes come to life and fill with tears. I'd be afraid . . .

PIERRE. Go on, Madame, go on . . .

COUNT. Ah! So life is beginning to interest you, is it? You see how beautiful it is?

PIERRE. What a fool I've been!

COUNT. Then, Roderick, I begin my rounds. I have my cats to feed, my dogs to pet, my plants to water. I have to see what the evil ones are up to in the district—those who hate people, those who hate plants, those who hate animals. I watch them sneaking off in the morning to put on their disguises—to the beauty parlors, to the barbers. But they can't deceive me. And when they come out again with blonde hair and false whiskers, to pull up my flowers and poison my dogs, I'm there, and I'm ready. All you have to do to break their power is to cut across their path from the left. That isn't always easy. Vice moves swiftly. But I have a good long stride and I generally manage. . . . Right, my friends? (*The* WAITER *and the* RAGPICKER *nod their heads with evident approval.*) Yes, the flowers have been marvelous this year. And the butcher's dog on the Rue Bizet, in spite of that wretch that tried to poison him, is friskier than ever. . . .

SERG. That dog had better look out. He has no license.

COUNT. He doesn't seem to feel the need for one.

RAG. The Duchess de la Rochefoucauld's whippet is getting awfully thin. . . .

COUNT. What can I do? She bought that dog full grown from a kennel where they didn't know his right name. A dog without his right name is bound to get thin.

RAG. I've got a friend who knows a lot about dogs—an Arab . . .

COUNT. Ask him to call on the Duchess. She receives Thursdays, five to seven. You see, then, Roderick. That's life. Does it appeal to you now?

PIERRE. It seems marvelous.

COUNT. Ah! Sergeant. My button. (*The* SERGEANT *gives her his button and goes off. At this point the* PROSPECTOR *enters.*) That's only the morning. Wait till I tell you about the afternoon!

PROS. All right, Pierre. Come along now.

PIERRE. I'm perfectly all right here.

PROS. I said, come along now.

PIERRE (*To the* COUNTESS.) I'd better go, Madame.

COUNT. No.

PIERRE. It's no use. Please let go my hand.

PROS. Madame, will you oblige me by letting my friend go?

COUNT. I will not oblige you in any way.

PROS. All right. Then I'll oblige you . . . ! (*He tries to push her away. She catches up a soda water siphon and squirts it in his face.*)

PIERRE. Countess . . .

COUNT. Stay where you are. This man isn't going to take you away. In the first place, I shall need you in a few minutes to take me home. I'm all alone here and I'm very easily frightened.

(*The* PROSPECTOR *makes a second attempt to drag* PIERRE *away. The* COUNTESS *cracks him over the skull with the siphon. They join battle. The* COUNTESS *whistles. The* DOORMAN *comes, then the other* VAGABONDS, *and lastly the* POLICE SERGEANT.)

PROS. Officer! Arrest this woman!

SERG. What's the trouble here?

PROS. She refuses to let this man go.

SERG. Why should she?

PROS. It's against the law for a woman to detain a man on the street.

IRMA. Suppose it's her son whom she's found again after twenty years?

RAG. (*Gallantly.*) Or her long-lost brother? The Countess is not so old.

PROS. Officer, this is a clear case of disorderly conduct.

(*The* DEAF-MUTE *interrupts with frantic signals.*)

COUNT. Irma, what is the Deaf-Mute saying?

IRMA (*Interpreting.*) The young man is in danger of his life. He mustn't go with him.

PROS. What does he know?

IRMA. He knows everything.

PROS. Officer, I'll have to take your number.

COUNT. Take his number. It's 2133. It adds up to nine. It will bring you luck.

SERG. Countess, between ourselves, what are you holding him for, anyway?

COUNT. I'm holding him because it's very pleasant to hold him. I've never really held anybody before, and I'm making the most of it. And because so long as *I* hold him, he's free.

PROS. Pierre, I'm giving you fair warning. . . .

COUNT. And I'm holding him because Irma wants me to hold him. Because if I let him go, it will break her heart.

IRMA. Oh, Countess!

SERG. (*To the* PROSPECTOR.) All right, you— move on. Nobody's holding you. You're blocking traffic. Move on.

PROS. (*Menacingly.*) I have your number. (*And murderously, to* PIERRE.) You'll regret this, Pierre.   (*Exit* PROSPECTOR.)

PIERRE. Thank you, Countess.

COUNT. They're blackmailing you, are they? (PIERRE *nods.*) What have you done? Murdered somebody?

PIERRE. No.

COUNT. Stolen something?

PIERRE. No.

COUNT. What then?

PIERRE. I forged a signature.

COUNT. Whose signature?

PIERRE. My father's. To a note.

COUNT. And this man has the paper, I suppose?

PIERRE. He promised to tear it up, if I did what he wanted. But I couldn't do it.

COUNT. But the man is mad! Does he really want to destroy the whole neighborhood?

PIERRE. He wants to destroy the whole city.

COUNT. (*Laughs.*) Fantastic.

PIERRE. It's not funny, Countess. He can do it. He's mad, but he's powerful, and he has friends. Their machines are already drawn up and waiting. In three months' time you may see the city covered by a forest of derricks and drills.

COUNT. But what are they looking for? Have they lost something?

PIERRE. They're looking for oil. They're convinced that Paris is sitting on a lake of oil.

COUNT. Suppose it is. What harm does it do?

PIERRE. They want to bring the oil to the surface, Countess.

COUNT. (*Laughs.*) How silly! Is that a reason to destroy a city? What do they want with this oil?

PIERRE. They want to make war, Countess.

COUNT. Oh, dear, let's forget about these horrible men. The world is beautiful. It's happy. That's how God made it. No man can change it.

WAIT. Ah, Countess, if you only knew . . .

COUNT. If I only knew what?

WAIT. Shall we tell her now? Shall we tell her?

COUNT. What is it you are hiding from me?

RAG. Nothing, Countess. It's you who are hiding.

WAIT. You tell her. You've been a pitchman. You can talk.

ALL. Tell her. Tell her. Tell her.

COUNT. You're frightening me, my friends. Go on. I'm listening.

RAG. Countess, there was a time when old clothes were as good as new—in fact, they were better. Because when people wore clothes, they gave something to them. You may not believe it, but right this minute, the highest-priced shops in Paris are selling clothes that were thrown away thirty years ago. They're selling them for new. That's how good they were.

COUNT. Well?

RAG. Countess, there was a time when garbage was a pleasure. A garbage can was not what it is now. If it smelled a little strange, it was because it was a little confused—there was everything there— sardines, cologne, iodine, roses. An amateur might jump to a wrong conclusion. But to a professional—it was the smell of God's plenty.

COUNT. Well?

RAG. Countess, the world has changed.

COUNT. Nonsense. How could it change? People are the same, I hope.

RAG. No, Countess. The people are not the same. The people are different. There's been an invasion. An infiltration. From another planet. The world is not beautiful any more. It's not happy.

COUNT. Not happy? Is that true? Why didn't you tell me this before?

RAG. Because you live in a dream, Countess. And we don't like to disturb you.

COUNT. But how could it have happened?

RAG. Countess, there was a time when you could walk around Paris, and all the people you met were just like yourself. A little cleaner, maybe, or dirtier, per- haps, or angry, or smiling—but you knew them. They were you. Well, Countess, twenty years ago, one day, on the street, I saw a face in the crowd. A face, you might say, without a face. The eyes— empty. The expression—not human. Not a human face. It saw me staring, and when it looked back at me with its gelatine eyes, I shuddered. Because I knew that to make room for this one, one of us must have left the earth. A while after, I saw another. And another. And since then, I've seen hundreds come in—yes—thousands.

COUNT. Describe them to me.

RAG. You've seen them yourself, Countess. Their clothes don't wrinkle. Their hats don't come off. When they talk, they don't look at you. They don't perspire.

COUNT. Have they wives? Have they children?

RAG. They buy the models out of shop windows, furs and all. They animate them by a secret process. Then they marry them. Naturally, they don't have children.

COUNT. What work do they do?

RAG. They don't do any work. Whenever they meet, they whisper, and then they pass each other thousand-franc notes. You see them standing on the corner by the Stock Exchange. You see them at auctions—in the back. They never raise a finger—they just stand there. In theater lobbies, by the box office—they never go inside. They don't do anything, but wherever you see them things are not the same. I remember well the time when a cabbage could sell itself just by being a cabbage. Nowadays it's no good being a cabbage—unless you have an agent and pay him a commission. Nothing is free any more to sell itself or give itself away. These days, Countess, every cabbage has its pimp.

COUNT. I can't believe that.

RAG. Countess, little by little, the pimps have taken over the world. They don't do anything, they don't make anything—they just stand there and take their cut. It makes a difference. Look at the shop-keepers. Do you ever see one smiling at a customer any more? Certainly not. Their smiles are strictly for the pimps. The butcher has to smile at the meat-pimp, the florist at the rose-pimp, the grocer at the fresh-fruit-and-vegetable pimp. It's all organized down to the slightest detail. A pimp for bird-seed. A pimp for fishfood. That's why the cost of living keeps going up all the time. You buy a glass of beer—it costs twice as much as it used to. Why? 10 per cent for the glass-pimp, 10 per cent for the beer-pimp, 20 per cent for the glass-of-beer-pimp—that's where our money goes. Personally, I prefer the old-fashioned type. Some of those men at least were loved by the women they sold. But what feelings can a pimp arouse in a leg of lamb? Pardon my language, Irma.

COUNT. It's all right. She doesn't understand it.

RAG. So now you know, Countess, why the world is no longer happy. We are the last of the free people of the earth. You saw them looking us over today. Tomorrow,

the street-singer will start paying the song-pimp, and the garbage-pimp will be after me. I tell you, Countess, we're finished. It's the end of free enterprise in this world!

COUNT. Is this true, Roderick?

PIERRE. I'm afraid it's true.

COUNT. Did you know about this, Irma?

IRMA. All I know is the doorman says that faith is dead.

DOOR. I've stopped taking bets over the phone.

JUG. The very air is different, Countess. You can't trust it any more. If I throw my torches up too high, they go out.

RAG. The sky-pimp puts them out.

FLOW. GIRL. My flowers don't last over night now. They wilt.

JUG. Have you noticed, the pigeons don't fly any more?

RAG. They can't afford to. They walk.

COUNT. They're a lot of fools and so are you! You should have told me at once! How can you bear to live in a world where there is unhappiness? Where a man is not his own master? Are you cowards? All we have to do is to get rid of these men.

PIERRE. How can we get rid of them? They're too strong.

(*The* SERGEANT *walks up again.*)

COUNT. (*Smiling.*) The Sergeant will help us.

SERG. Who? Me?

IRMA. There are a great many of them, Countess. The Deaf-Mute knows them all. They employed him once, years ago, because he was deaf. (*The* DEAF-MUTE *wigwags a short speech.*) They fired him because he wasn't blind. (*Another flash of sign language.*) They're all connected like the parts of a machine.

COUNT. So much the better. We shall drive the whole machine into a ditch.

SERG. It's not that easy, Countess. You never catch these birds napping. They change before your very eyes. I remember when I was in the detectives. . . . You catch a president, pfft! He turns into a trustee. You catch him as trustee, and pfft! he's not a trustee—he's an honorary vice-chairman. You catch a Senator dead to rights: he becomes Minister of Justice. You get after the Minister of Justice—he is Chief of Police. And there you are—no longer in the detectives.

PIERRE. He's right, Countess. They have all the power. And all the money. And they're greedy for more.

COUNT. They're greedy? Ah, then, my friends, they're lost. If they're greedy, they're stupid. If they're greedy—don't worry, I know exactly what to do. Roderick, by tonight you will be an honest man. And, Juggler, your torches will stay lit. And your beer will flow freely again, Martial. And the world will be saved. Let's get to work.

RAG. What are you going to do?

COUNT. Have you any kerosene in the house, Irma?

IRMA. Yes. Would you like some?

COUNT. I want just a little. In a dirty bottle. With a little mud. And some mange-cure, if you have it. (*To the* DEAF-MUTE.) Deaf-Mute! Take a letter. (IRMA *interprets in sign language. To the* SINGER.) Singer, go and find Madame Constance. (IRMA *and the* WAITER *go into the café.*)

ST. SING. Yes, Countess.

COUNT. Ask her to be at my house by two o'clock. I'll be waiting for her in the cellar. You may tell her we have to discuss the future of humanity. That's sure to bring her.

ST. SING. Yes, Countess.

COUNT. And ask her to bring Mademoiselle Gabrielle and Madame Josephine with her. Do you know how to get in to speak to Madame Constance? You ring twice, and then meow three times like a cat. Do you know how to meow?

ST. SING. I'm better at barking.

COUNT. Better practise meowing on the way. Incidentally, I think Madame Constance knows all the verses of your mazurka. Remind me to ask her.

ST. SING. Yes, Countess.

(IRMA *comes in. She is shaking the oily concoction in a little perfume vial, which she now hands the* COUNTESS.)

IRMA. Here you are, Countess.

COUNT. Thanks, Irma. (*She assumes a presidential manner.*) Deaf-Mute! Ready?

(IRMA *interprets in sign language. The* WAITER *has brought out a portfolio of letter paper and placed it on a table. The* DEAF-MUTE *sits down before it, and prepares to write.*)

IRMA. (*Speaking for the* DEAF-MUTE.) I'm ready.

COUNT. My dear Mr.—What's his name?

(IRMA *wigwags the question to the* DEAF-MUTE, *who answers in the same manner. It is all done so deftly that it is as if the* DEAF-MUTE *were actually speaking.*)

IRMA. They are all called Mr. President.

COUNT. My dear Mr. President: I have personally verified the existence of a spontaneous outcrop of oil in the cellar of Number 21 Rue de Chaillot, which is at present occupied by a dignified person of unstable mentality. (*The* COUNTESS *grins knowingly.*) This explains why, fortunately for us, the discovery has so long been kept secret. If you should wish to verify the existence of this outcrop for yourself, you may call at the above address at three P.M. today. I am herewith enclosing a sample so that you may judge the quality and consistency of the crude. Yours very truly. Roderick, can you sign the prospector's name?

PIERRE. You wish me to?

COUNT. One forgery wipes out the other. (PIERRE *signs the letter. The* DEAF-MUTE *types the address on an envelope.*)

IRMA. Who is to deliver this?

COUNT. The Doorman, of course. On his bicycle. And as soon as you have delivered it, run over to the prospector's office. Leave word that the President expects to see him at my house at three.

DOOR. Yes, Countess.

COUNT. I shall leave you now. I have many pressing things to do. Among others, I must press my red gown.

RAG. But this only takes care of two of them, Countess.

COUNT. Didn't the Deaf-Mute say they are all connected like the works of a machine?

IRMA. Yes.

COUNT. Then, if one comes, the rest will follow. And we shall have them all. My boa, please.

DOOR. The one that's stolen, Countess?

COUNT. Naturally. The one the prospector stole.

DOOR. It hasn't turned up yet, Countess. But someone has left an ermine collar.

COUNT. Real ermine?

DOOR. Looks like it.

COUNT. Ermine and iris were made for each other. Let me see it.

DOOR. Yes, Countess.   (*Exit* DOORMAN.)

COUNT. Roderick, you shall escort me. You still look pale. I have some old Chartreuse at home. I always take a glass each year. Last year I forgot. You shall have it.

PIERRE. If there is anything I can do, Countess . . . ?

COUNT. There is a great deal you can do. There are all the things that need to be done in a room that no man has been in for twenty years. You can untwist the cord on the blind and let in a little sunshine for a change. You can take the mirror off the wardrobe door, and deliver me once and for all from the old harpy that lives in the mirror. You can let the mouse out of the trap. I'm tired of feeding it. (*To her friends.*) Each man to his post. See you later, my friends. (*The* DOORMAN *puts the ermine collar around her shoulders.*) Thank you, my boy. It's rabbit. (*One o'clock strikes.*) Your arm, Valentine.

PIERRE. Valentine?

COUNT. It's just struck one. At one, all men become Valentine.

PIERRE. (*He offers his arm.*) Permit me.

COUNT. Or Valentino. It's obviously far from the same, isn't it, Irma? But they have that much choice. (*She sweeps out majestically with* PIERRE. *The others disperse. All but* IRMA.)

IRMA. (*Clearing off the table.*) I hate ugliness. I love beauty. I hate meanness. I adore kindness. It may not seem so grand to some to be a waitress in Paris. I love it. A waitress meets all sorts of people. She observes life. I hate to be alone. I love people. But I have never said I love you to a man. Men try to make me say it. They put their arms around me—I pretend I don't see it. They pinch me—I pretend I don't feel it. They kiss me—I pretend I don't know it. They take me out in the evening and make me drink— but I'm careful, I never say it. If they don't like it, they can leave me alone. Because when I say I love you to Him, He will know just by looking in my eyes that many have held me and pinched me and kissed me, but I have never said I love you to anyone in the world before. Never. No. (*Looking off in the direction in* which PIERRE *has gone, she whispers softly:*) I love you.

VOICE. (*From within the café.*) Irma!

IRMA. Coming.   (*Exits.*)

(CURTAIN)

ACT II

SCENE: *The cellar of the* COUNTESS' *house. An ancient vault set deep in the ground, with walls of solid masonry, part brick and part great ashlars, mossy and sweating. A staircase of medieval pattern is built into the thickness of the wall, and leads up to the street level from a landing halfway down. In the corners of the cellar are piled casks, packing cases, bird cages, and other odds and ends—the accumulation of* centuries—*the whole effect utterly fantastic. In the center of the vast underground room, some furniture has been arranged to give an impression of a sitting-room of the 1890's. There is a venerable chaise-longue piled with cushions that once were gay, three armchairs, a table with an oil lamp and a bowl of flowers, a shaggy rug. It is two P.M., the same day.*

AT RISE: *The* COUNTESS *is sitting over a bit*

of mending, in one of the armchairs. IRMA *appears on the landing and calls down.*

IRMA. Countess! The Sewer Man is here.

COUNT. Thank goodness, Irma. Send him down. (*The* SEWER MAN *enters. He carries his hip-boots in his hand.*) How do you do, Mr. Sewer Man? (*The* SEWER MAN *bows.*) But why do you have your boots in your hand instead of on your feet?

SEWER MAN. Etiquette, Countess. Etiquette.

COUNT. How very American! I'm told that Americans nowadays apologize for their gloves if they happen to take one's hand. As if the skin of a human were nicer to touch than the skin of a sheep! And particularly if they have sweaty hands ... !

SEWER MAN. My feet never sweat, Countess.

COUNT. How very nice! But please don't stand on ceremony here. Put your boots on. Put them on.

SEWER MAN. (*Complying.*) Thanks very much, Countess.

COUNT. (*While he draws on his boots.*) I'm sure you must have a very poor opinion of the upper world, from what you see of it. The way people throw their filth into your territory is absolutely scandalous! I burn all my refuse, and I scatter the ashes. All I ever throw in the drain is flowers. Did you happen to see a lily float by this morning? Mine. But perhaps you didn't notice?

SEWER MAN. We notice a lot more down there, Countess, than you might think. You'd be surprised the things we notice. There's lots of things come along that were obviously intended for us—little gifts, you might call them—sometimes a brand-new shaving brush—sometimes, *The Brothers Karamazov....* Thanks for the lily, Countess. A very sweet thought.

COUNT. Tomorrow you shall have this iris. But now, let's come to the point. I have two questions to ask you.

SEWER MAN. Yes, Countess?

COUNT. First—and this has nothing to do with our problem—it's just something that has been troubling me.... Tell me, is it true that the sewer men of Paris have a king?

SEWER MAN. Oh, now, Countess, that's another of those fairy tales out of the Sunday supplements. It just seems those writers can't keep their minds off the sewers! It fascinates them. They keep thinking of us moving around in our underground canals like gondoliers in Venice, and it sends them into a fever of romance! The things they say about us! They say we have a race of girls down there who never see the light of day! It's completely fantastic! The girls naturally come out— every Christmas and Easter. And orgies by torchlight with gondolas and guitars! With troops of rats that dance as they follow the piper! What nonsense! The rats are not allowed to dance. No, no, no. Of course we have no king. Down in the sewers, you'll find nothing but good Republicans.

COUNT. And no queen?

SEWER MAN. No. We may run a beauty contest down there once in a while. Or crown a mermaid Queen of the May. But no queen what you'd call a queen. And, as for these swimming races they talk so much about ... possibly once in a while—in the summer—in the dog days ...

COUNT. I believe you. I believe you. And now tell me. Do you remember that night I found you here in my cellar— looking very pale and strange—you were half-dead as a matter of fact—and I gave you some brandy....

SEWER MAN. Yes, Countess.

COUNT. That night you promised if ever I should need it—you would tell me the secret of this room.

SEWER MAN. The secret of the moving stone?

COUNT. I need it now.

SEWER MAN. Only the King of the Sewer Men knows this secret.

COUNT. I'm sure of it. I know most secrets, of course. As a matter of fact, I have three magic words that will open any door that words can open. I have tried them all—in various tones of voice. They don't seem to work. And this is a matter of life and death.

SEWER MAN. Look, Countess. (*He locates a brick in the masonry, and pushes it. A huge block of stone slowly pivots and uncovers a trap from which a circular staircase winds into the bowels of the earth.*)

COUNT. Good heavens! Where do those stairs lead?

SEWER MAN. Nowhere.

COUNT. But they must go somewhere.

SEWER MAN. They just go down.

COUNT. Let's go and see.

SEWER MAN. No, Countess. Never again. That time you found me, I had a pretty close shave. I kept going down and around, and down and around for an hour, a year—I don't know. There's no end to it, Countess. Once you start you can't stop. . . . Your head begins to turn —you're lost. No—once you start down, there's no coming up.

COUNT. You came up.

SEWER MAN. I—I am a special case. Besides, I had my tools, my ropes. And I stopped in time.

COUNT. You could have screamed—shouted.

SEWER MAN. You could fire off a cannon.

COUNT. Who could have built a thing like this?

SEWER MAN. Paris is old, you know. Paris is very old.

COUNT. You don't suppose, by any chance, there is oil down there?

SEWER MAN. There's only death down there.

COUNT. I should have preferred a little oil too—or a vein of gold—or emeralds. You're quite sure there is nothing?

SEWER MAN. Not even rats.

COUNT. How does one lower this stone?

SEWER MAN. Simple. To open, you press here. And to close it, you push there. (*He presses the brick. The stone descends.*) Now there's two of us in the world that know it.

COUNT. I won't remember long. Is it all right if I repeat my magic words while I press it?

SEWER MAN. It's bound to help.

(IRMA *enters.*)

IRMA. Countess, Madame Constance and Mademoiselle Gabrielle are here.

COUNT. Show them down, Irma. Thank you very much, Mr. Sewer Man.

SEWER MAN. Like that story about the steam laundry that's supposed to be running day and night in my sewer . . . I can assure you. . . .

COUNT. (*Edging him toward the door.*) Thank you very much.

SEWER MAN. Pure imagination! They never work nights. (*He goes off, bowing graciously.*)

(CONSTANCE, *the Madwoman of Passy, and* GABRIELLE, *the Madwoman of St. Sulpice, come down daintily.* CONSTANCE *is all in white. She wears an enormous hat graced with ostrich plumes, and a lavender veil.* GABRIELLE *is costumed with the affected simplicity of the 1880's. She is atrociously made up in a remorseless parody of blushing innocence, and she minces down the stairs with macabre coyness.*)

CON. Aurelia! Don't tell us they've found your feather boa?

GAB. You don't mean Adolphe Bertaut has proposed at last! I knew he would.

COUNT. How are you, Constance? (*She shouts.*) How are you, Gabrielle?

GAB. You needn't shout today, my dear. It's Wednesday. Wednesdays, I hear perfectly.

CON. It's Thursday.

GAB. Oh, dear. Well, never mind. I'm going to make an exception just this once.

CON. (*To an imaginary dog who has stopped on the landing.*) Come along, Dickie. Come along. And stop barking. What a racket you're making! Come on, darling —we've come to see the longest boa and the handsomest man in Paris. Come on.

COUNT. Constance, it's not a question of my boa today. Nor of poor Adolphe. It's a question of the future of the human race.

CON. You think it has a future?

COUNT. Please don't make silly jokes. Sit down and listen to me. Today we must make a decision which may alter the fate of the world.

CON. Couldn't we do it tomorrow? I want to wash my slippers. Now, Dickie—please!

COUNT. We haven't a moment to waste. Where is Josephine? Well, we'd best have our tea, and the moment Josephine comes . . .

GAB. Josephine is sitting on her bench in front of the palace waiting for President Wilson to come out. She says she's sorry, but she positively must see him today.

CON. Dickie!

COUNT. What a pity! (*She gets the tea things from the side table, pours tea and serves cake and honey.*) I wish she were here to help us. She has a first-class brain.

CON. Go ahead, dear. We're listening. (*To* DICKIE.) What is it, Dickie? You want to sit in Aunt Aurelia's lap. All right, darling. Go on. Jump, Dickie.

COUNT. Constance, we love you, as you know. And we love Dickie. But this is a serious matter. So let's stop being childish for once.

CON. And what does that mean, if you please?

COUNT. It means Dickie. You know perfectly well that we love him and fuss over him just as if he were still alive. He's a sacred memory and we wouldn't hurt his feelings for the world. But please don't plump him in my lap when I'm settling the future of mankind. His basket is in the corner—he knows where it is, and he can just go and sit in it.

CON. So you're against Dickie too! You too!

COUNT. Constance! I'm not in the least against Dickie! I adore Dickie. But you know as well as I that Dickie is only a convention with us. It's a beautiful convention—but it doesn't have to bark all the time. Besides, it's you that spoil him. The time you went to visit your niece and left him with me, we got on marvelously together. He didn't bark, he didn't tear things, he didn't even eat. But when you're with him, one can pay attention to nothing else. I'm not going to take Dickie in my lap at a solemn moment like this, no, not for anything in the world. And that's that!

GAB. (*Very sweetly.*) Constance, dear, I don't mind taking him in my lap. He loves to sit in my lap, don't you, darling?

CON. Kindly stop putting on angelic airs, Gabrielle. I know you very well. You're much too sweet to be sincere. There's plenty of times that I make believe that Dickie is here, when really I've left him home, and you cuddle and pet him just the same.

GAB. I adore animals.

CON. If you adore animals, you shouldn't pet them when they're not there. It's a form of hypocrisy.

COUNT. Now, Constance, Gabrielle has as much right as you . . .

CON. Gabrielle has no right to do what she does. Do you know what she does? She invites *people* to come to tea with us. *People* whom we know nothing about. *People* who exist only in her imagination.

COUNT. You think that's not an existence?

GAB. I don't invite them at all. They come by themselves. What can I do?

CON. You might introduce us.

COUNT. If you think they're only imaginary, there's no point in your meeting them, is there?

CON. Of course they're imaginary. But who likes to have imaginary people staring at one? Especially strangers.

GAB. Oh, they're really very nice. . . .

CON. Tell me just one thing, Gabrielle—are they here now?

COUNT. Am I to be allowed to speak? Or is this going to be the same as the argument about inoculating Josephine's cat, when we didn't get to the subject at all?

CON. Never! Never! Never! I'll never give my consent to that. (*To* DICKIE.) I'd never do a thing like that to you, Dickie sweet. . . . Oh, no! Oh, no! (*She begins to weep softly.*)

COUNT. Good heavens! Now we have her in tears. What an impossible creature! With the fate of humanity hanging in the balance! All right, all right, stop crying. I'll take him in my lap. Come, Dickie, Dickie.

CON. No. He won't go now. Oh, how can you be so cruel? Don't you suppose I know about Dickie? Don't you think I'd rather have him here alive and woolly and frisking around the way he used to? You have your Adolphe. Gabrielle has her birds. But I have only Dickie. Do you think I'd be so silly about him if it wasn't that it's only by pretending that he's here all the time that I get him to come sometimes, really? Next time I won't bring him!

COUNT. Now let's not get ourselves worked up over nothing. Come here, Dickie. . . . Irma is going to take you for a nice walk. (*She rings her bell.*) Irma!

(IRMA *appears on the landing.*)

CON. No. He doesn't want to go. Besides, I didn't bring him today. So there!

COUNT. Very well, then. Irma, make sure the door is locked.

IRMA. Yes, Countess.   (IRMA *exits.*)

CON. What do you mean? Why locked? Who's coming?

COUNT. If you'd let me get a word in, you'd know by now. A terrible thing has happened. This morning, this very morning, exactly at noon . . .

CON. (*Thrilled.*) Oh, how exciting!

COUNT. Be quiet. This morning, exactly at noon, thanks to a young man who drowned himself in the Seine . . . Oh, yes, while I think of it—do you know a mazurka called *La Belle Polonaise*?

CON. Yes, Aurelia.

COUNT. Could you sing it now? This very minute?

CON. Yes, Aurelia.

COUNT. All of it?

CON. Yes, Aurelia. But who's interrupting now, Aurelia?

COUNT. You're right. Well, this morning, exactly at noon, I discovered a horrible plot. There is a group of men who intend to tear down the whole city!

CON. Is that all?

GAB. But I don't understand, Aurelia. Why should men want to tear down the city? It was they themselves who put it up.

COUNT. You are so innocent, my poor Gabrielle. There are people in the world who want to destroy everything. They have the fever of destruction. Even when they pretend that they're building, it is only in order to destroy. When they put up a new building, they quietly knock down two old ones. They build cities so

that they can destroy the countryside. They destroy space with telephones and time with airplanes. Humanity is now dedicated to the task of universal destruction. I am speaking, of course, primarily of the male sex.

GAB. (*Shocked.*) Oh . . . !

CON. Aurelia! Must you talk sex in front of Gabrielle?

COUNT. There *are* two sexes.

CON. Gabrielle is a virgin, Aurelia!

COUNT. Oh, she can't be as innocent as all that. She keeps canaries.

GAB. I think you're being very cruel about men, Aurelia. Men are big and beautiful, and as loyal as dogs. I preferred not to marry, it's true. But I hear excellent reports from friends who have had an opportunity to observe them closely.

COUNT. My poor darling! You are still living in a dream. But one day, you will wake up as I have, and then you will see what is happening in the world. The tide has turned, my dear. Men are changing back into beasts. They know it. They no longer try to hide it. There was once such a thing as manners. I remember a time when the hungriest was the one who took the longest to pick up his fork. The one with the broadest grin was the one who needed most to go to the . . . It was such fun to keep them grinning like that for hours. But now they no longer pretend. Just look at them—snuffling their soup like pigs, tearing their meat like tigers, crunching their lettuce like crocodiles! A man doesn't take your hand nowadays. He gives you his paw.

CON. Would that trouble you so much if they turned into animals? Personally, I think it's a good idea.

GAB. Oh, I'd love to see them like that. They'd be sweet.

CON. It might be the salvation of the human race.

COUNT. (*To* CONSTANCE.) You'd make a fine rabbit, wouldn't you?

CON. I?

COUNT. Naturally. You don't think it's only the men who are changing? You change along with them. Husbands and wives together. We're all one race, you know.

CON. You think so? And why would my poor husband have to be a rabbit if he were alive?

COUNT. Remember his front teeth? When he nibbled his celery?

CON. I'm happy to say, I remember absolutely nothing about him. All I remember on that subject is the time that Father Lacordaire tried to kiss me in the park.

COUNT. Yes, yes, of course.

CON. And what does that mean, if you please, "Yes, yes, of course"?

COUNT. Constance, just this once, look us in the eye and tell us truly—did that really happen or did you read about it in a book?

CON. Now I'm being insulted!

COUNT. We promise you faithfully that we'll believe it all over again afterwards, won't we, Gabrielle? But tell us the truth this once.

CON. How dare you question my memories? Suppose I said your pearls were false!

COUNT. They were.

CON. I'm not asking what they were. I'm asking what they are. Are they false or are they real?

COUNT. Everyone knows that little by little, as one wears pearls, they become real.

CON. And isn't it exactly the same with memories?

COUNT. Now do not let us waste time. I must go on.

CON. I think Gabrielle is perfectly right about men. There are still plenty who haven't changed a bit. There's an old Senator who bows to Gabrielle every day when he passes her in front of the palace. And he takes off his hat each time.

GAB. That's perfectly true, Aurelia. He's always pushing an empty baby carriage, and he always stops and bows.

COUNT. Don't be taken in, Gabrielle. It's all make-believe. And all we can expect from these make-believe men is itself make-believe. They give us face powder made of stones, sausages made of sawdust, shirts made of glass, stockings made of milk. It's all a vulgar pretense. And if

that is the case, imagine what passes, these days, for virtue, sincerity, generosity and love! I warn you, Gabrielle, don't let this Senator with the empty baby carriage pull the wool over your eyes.

GAB. He's really the soul of courtesy. He seems very correct.

COUNT. Those are the worst. Gabrielle, beware! He'll make you put on black riding boots, while he dances the can-can around you, singing God knows what filth at the top of his voice. The very thought makes one's blood run cold!

GAB. You think that's what he has in mind?

COUNT. Of course. Men have lost all sense of decency. They are all equally disgusting. Just look at them in the evening, sitting at their tables in the café, working away in unison with their toothpicks, hour after hour, digging up roast beef, veal, onion . . .

CON. They don't harm anyone that way.

COUNT. Then why do you barricade your door, and make your friends meow before you let them come up? Incidentally, we must make an interesting sight, Gabrielle and I, yowling together on your doorstep like a couple of tomcats!

CON. There's no need at all for you to yowl together. One would be quite enough. And you know perfectly well why I have to do it. It's because there are murderers.

COUNT. I don't quite see what prevents murderers from meowing like anybody else. But why are there murderers?

CON. Why? Because there are thieves.

COUNT. And why are there thieves? Why is there almost nothing but thieves?

CON. Because they worship money. Because money is king.

COUNT. Ah—now we've come to it. Because we live in the reign of the Golden Calf. Did you realize that, Gabrielle? Men now publicly worship the Golden Calf!

GAB. How awful! Have the authorities been notified?

COUNT. The authorities do it themselves, Gabrielle.

GAB. Oh! Has anyone talked to the bishop?

COUNT. Nowadays only money talks to the bishop. And so you see why I asked you to come here today. The world has gone out of its mind. Unless we do something, humanity is doomed! Constance, have you any suggestions?

CON. I know what I always do in a case like this. . . .

COUNT. You write to the Prime Minister.

CON. He always does what I tell him.

COUNT. Does he ever answer your letters?

CON. He knows I prefer him not to. It might excite gossip. Besides, I don't always write. Sometimes I wire. The time I told him about the Archbishop's frigidaire, it was by wire. And they sent a new one the very next day.

COUNT. There was probably a commission in it for someone. And what do you suggest, Gabrielle?

CON. Now, how can she tell you until she's consulted her voices?

GAB. I could go right home and consult them, and we could meet again after dinner.

COUNT. There's no time for that. Besides, your voices are not real voices.

GAB. (*Furious.*) How dare you say a thing like that?

COUNT. Where do your voices come from? Still from your sewing-machine?

GAB. Not at all. They've passed into my hot-water bottle. And it's much nicer that way. They don't chatter any more. They gurgle. But they haven't been a bit nice to me lately. Last night they kept telling me to let my canaries out. "Let them out. Let them out. Let them out."

CON. Did you?

GAB. I opened the cage. They wouldn't go.

COUNT. I don't call that *voices*. Objects talk—everyone knows that. It's the principle of the phonograph. But to ask a hot-water bottle for advice is silly. What does a hot-water bottle know? No, all we have to consult here is our own judgment.

CON. Very well then, tell us what you have decided. Since you're asking our opinion, you've doubtless made up your mind.

COUNT. Yes, I've thought the whole thing out. All I really needed to discover was the source of the infection. Today I found it.

CON. Where?

COUNT. You'll see soon enough. I've baited a trap. In just a few minutes, the rats will be here.

GAB. (*In alarm*). Rats!

COUNT. Don't be alarmed. They're still in human form.

GAB. Heavens! What are you going to do with them?

COUNT. That's just the question. Suppose I get these wicked men all here at once—in my cellar—have I the right to exterminate them?

GAB. To kill them?

(COUNTESS *nods.*)

CON. That's not a question for us. You'll have to ask Father Bridet.

COUNT. I have asked him. Yes. One day, in confession, I told him frankly that I had a secret desire to destroy all wicked people. He said: "By all means, my child. And when you're ready to go into action, I'll lend you the jawbone of an ass."

CON. That's just talk. You get him to put that in writing.

GAB. What's your scheme, Aurelia?

COUNT. That's a secret.

CON. It's not so easy to kill them. Let's say you had a tank full of vitriol all ready for them. You could never get them to walk into it. There's nothing so stubborn as a man when you want him to do something.

COUNT. Leave that to me.

CON. But if they're killed, they're bound to be missed, and then we'll be fined. They fine you for every little thing these days.

COUNT. They won't be missed.

GAB. I wish Josephine were here. Her sister's husband was a lawyer. She knows all about these things.

COUNT. Do you miss a cold when it's gone? Or the germs that caused it? When the world feels well again, do you think it will regret its illness? No, it will stretch itself joyfully, and it will smile—that's all.

CON. Just a moment! Gabrielle, are they here now? Yes or no?

COUNT. What's the matter with you now?

CON. I'm simply asking Gabrielle if her friends are in the room or not. I have a right to know.

GAB. I'm not allowed to say.

CON. I know very well they are. I'm sure of it. Otherwise you wouldn't be making faces.

COUNT. May I ask what difference it makes to you if her friends are in the room?

CON. Just this: If they're here, I'm not going to say another word! I'm certainly not going to commit myself in a matter involving the death sentence in the presence of third parties, whether they exist or not.

GAB. That's not being very nice to my guests, is it?

COUNT. Constance, you must be mad! Or are you so stupid as to think that just because we're alone, there's nobody with us? Do you consider us so boring or repulsive that of all the millions of beings, imaginary or otherwise, who are prowling about in space, there's not one who might possibly enjoy spending a little time with us? On the contrary, my dear—my house is full of guests always. They know that here they have a place in the universe where they can come when they're lonely and be sure of a welcome. For my part, I'm delighted to have them.

GAB. Thank you, Aurelia.

CON. You know perfectly well, Aurelia ...

COUNT. I know perfectly well that at this moment the whole universe is listening to us—and that every word we say echoes to the remotest star. To pretend otherwise is the sheerest hypocrisy.

CON. Then why do you insult me in front of everybody? I'm not mean. I'm shy. I feel timid about giving an opinion in front of such a crowd. Furthermore, if you think I'm so bad and so stupid, why did you invite me, in the first place?

COUNT. I'll tell you. And I'll tell you why, disagreeable as you are, I always give you the biggest piece of cake and my best honey. It's because when you come there's always someone with you—and I don't mean Dickie—I mean someone who resembles you like a sister, only she's young and lovely, and she sits modestly to one side and smiles at me tenderly all the time you're bickering and quarreling, and never says a word. That's the Constance to whom I give the cake that you gobble, and it's because of her that you're here today, and it's her vote that I'm asking you to cast in this crucial moment. And not yours, which is of no importance whatever.

CON. I'm leaving.

COUNT. Be so good as to sit down. I can't let her go yet.

CON. (Crossing toward the stairs.) No. This is too much. I'm taking her with me.

(IRMA enters.)

IRMA. Madame Josephine.

COUNT. Thank heaven!

GAB. We're saved.

(JOSEPHINE, the Madwoman of La Concorde, sweeps in majestically in a get-up somewhere between the regal and the priestly.)

JOS. My dear friends, today once again, I waited for President Wilson—but he didn't come out.

COUNT. You'll have to wait quite a while longer before he does. He's been dead since 1924.

JOS. I have plenty of time.

COUNT. In anyone else, Josephine, these extravagances might seem a little childish. But a person of your judgment doubtless has her reasons for wanting to talk to a man to whom no one would listen when he was alive. We have a legal problem for you. Suppose you had all the world's criminals here in this room. And suppose you had a way of getting rid of them forever. Would you have the right to do it?

JOS. Why not?

COUNT. Exactly my point.

GAB. But, Josephine, so many people!

JOS. De minimis non curat lex! The more there are, the more legal it is. It's impersonal. It's even military. It's the cardinal principle of battle—you get all your enemies in one place, and you kill them all together at one time. Because if you had to track them down one by one in their houses and offices, you'd get tired, and sooner or later you'd stop. I believe your idea is very practical, Aurelia. I can't imagine why we never thought of it before.

GAB. Well, if you think it's all right to do it. . . .

JOS. By all means. Your criminals have had a fair trial, I suppose?

COUNT. Trial?

JOS. Certainly. You can't kill anybody without a trial. That's elementary. "No man shall be deprived of his life, liberty and property without due process of law."

COUNT. They deprive us of ours.

JOS. That's not the point. You're not accused of anything. Every accused—man, woman or child—has the right to defend himself at the bar of justice. Even animals. Before the Deluge, you will recall, the Lord permitted Noah to speak in defense of his fellow mortals. He evidently stuttered. You know the result. On the other hand, Captain Dreyfus was not only innocent —he was defended by a marvelous orator. The result was precisely the same. So you see, in having a trial, you run no risk whatever.

COUNT. But if I give them the slightest cause for suspicion—I'll lose them.

JOS. There's a simple procedure prescribed in such cases. You can summon the defendants by calling them three times— mentally, if you like. If they don't appear, the court may designate an attorney who will represent them. This attorney can then argue their case to the court, *in absentia*, and a judgment can then be rendered, *in contumacio*.

COUNT. But I don't know any attorneys. And we have only ten minutes.

GAB. Hurry, Josephine, hurry!

JOS. In case of emergency, it is permissible for the court to order the first passer-by to act as attorney for the defense. A defense is like a baptism. Absolutely indispensable, but you don't have to know anything to do it. Ask Irma to get you somebody. Anybody.

COUNT. The Deaf-Mute?

JOS. Well—that's getting it down a bit fine. That might be questionable on appeal.

COUNT. (*Calls.*) Irma! What about the Police Sergeant?

JOS. He won't do. He's under oath to the state.

(IRMA *appears.*)

IRMA. Yes, Countess?

COUNT. Who's out there, Irma?

IRMA. All our friends, Countess. There's the Ragpicker and . . .

COUNT. Send down the Ragpicker.

CON. Do you think it's wise to have all those millionaires represented by a rag-picker?

JOS. It's a first-rate choice. Criminals are always represented by their opposites. Murderers, by someone who obviously wouldn't hurt a fly. Rapists, by a member of the League for Decency. Experience shows it's the only way to get an acquittal.

COUNT. But we must not have an acquittal. That would mean the end of the world!

JOS. Justice is justice, my dear.

(*The* RAGPICKER *comes down, with a stately air. Behind him, on the landing, appear the other* VAGABONDS.)

RAG. Greetings, Countess. Greetings, ladies. My most sincere compliments.

COUNT. Has Irma told you . . . ?

RAG. She said something about a trial.

COUNT. You have been appointed attorney for the defense.

RAG. Terribly flattered, I'm sure.

COUNT. You realize, don't you, how much depends on the outcome of this trial?

JOS. Do you know the defendants well enough to undertake the case?

RAG. I know them to the bottom of their souls. I go through their garbage every day.

CON. And what do you find there?

RAG. Mostly flowers.

GAB. It's true, you know, the rich are always surrounded with flowers.

CON. How beautiful!

COUNT. Are you trying to prejudice the court?

RAG. Oh no, Countess, no.

COUNT. We want a completely impartial defense.

RAG. Of course, Countess, of course. Permit me to make a suggestion.

COUNT. Will you preside, Josephine?

RAG. Instead of speaking as attorney, suppose you let me speak directly as defendant. It will be more convincing, and I can get into it more.

JOS. Excellent idea. Motion granted.

COUNT. We don't want you to be too convincing, remember.

RAG. Impartial, Countess, impartial.

JOS. Well? Have you prepared your case?

RAG. How rich am I?

JOS. Millions. Billions.

RAG. How did I get them? Theft? Murder? Embezzlement?

COUNT. Most likely.

RAG. Do I have a wife? A mistress?

COUNT. Everything.

RAG. All right. I'm ready.

GAB. Will you have some tea?

RAG. Is that good?

CON. Very good for the voice. The Russians drink nothing but tea. And they talk like anything.

RAG. All right. Tea.

JOS. (*To the* VAGABONDS.) Come in. Come in. All of you. You may take places. The trial is public. (*The* VAGABONDS *dispose themselves on the steps and elsewhere.*) Your bell, if you please, Aurelia.

COUNT. But what if I should need to ring for Irma?

JOS. Irma will sit here, next to me. If you need her, she can ring for herself. (*To the* POLICE SERGEANT *and the* POLICEMAN.) Conduct the accused to the bar. (*The officers conduct the* RAGPICKER *to a bar improvised with a rocking chair and a packing case marked* "Fragile." *The* RAGPICKER *mounts the box. She rings the bell.*) The court is now in session. (*All sit.*) Counsel for the defense, you may take the oath.

RAG. I swear to tell the truth, the whole truth, and nothing but the truth, so help me God.

JOS. Nonsense! You're not a witness. You're an attorney. It's your duty to lie, conceal and distort everything, and slander everybody.

RAG. All right. I swear to lie, conceal and distort everything, and slander everybody.

(JOSEPHINE *rings stridently.*)

JOS. Quiet! Begin.

RAG. May it please the honorable, august and elegant Court . . .

JOS. Flattery will get you nowhere. That will do. The defense has been heard. Cross-examination.

COUNT. Mr. President . . .

RAG. (*Bowing with dignity.*) Madame.

COUNT. Do you know what you are charged with?

RAG. I can't for the life of me imagine. My life is an open book. My ways are known to all. I am a pillar of the church and the sole support of the Opera. My hands are spotless.

COUNT. What an atrocious lie! Just look at them!

CON. You don't have to insult the man. He's only lying to please you.

COUNT. Be quiet, Constance! You don't get the idea at all. (*To the* RAGPICKER.) You are charged with the crime of worshipping money.

RAG. Worshipping money? Me?

JOS. Do you plead guilty or not guilty? Which is it?

RAG. Why, Your Honor . . .

JOS. Yes or no?

RAG. Yes or no? No! I don't worship money, Countess. Heavens, no! Money worships me. It adores me. It won't let me alone. It's damned embarrassing, I can tell you.

JOS. Kindly watch your language.

COUNT. Defendant, tell the Court how you came by your money.

RAG. The first time money came to me, I was a mere boy, a little golden-haired child in the bosom of my dear family. It came to me suddenly in the guise of a gold brick which, in my innocence, I picked out of a garbage can one day while playing. I was horrified, as you can imagine. I immediately tried to get rid of it by swapping it for a little rundown one-track railroad which, to my consternation, at once sold itself for a hundred times its value. In a desperate effort to get rid of this money, I began to buy things. I bought the Northern Refineries, the Galeries Lafayette, and the Schneider-Creusot Munition Works. And now I'm stuck with them. It's a horrible fate—but I'm resigned to it. I don't ask for your sympathy, I don't ask for your pity—all I ask for is a little common human understanding. . . . (*He begins to cry.*)

COUNT. I object. This wretch is trying to play on the emotions of the Court.

JOS. The Court has no emotions.

RAG. Everyone knows that the poor have no one but themselves to blame for their poverty. It's only just that they should suffer the consequences. But how is it the fault of the rich if they're rich?

COUNT. Dry your tears. You're deceiving nobody. If, as you say, you're ashamed of your money, why is it you hold onto it with such a death-grip?

RAG. Me?

ST. PED. You never part with a franc!

JUG. You wouldn't even give the poor Deaf-Mute a sou!

RAG. Me, hold onto money? What slander! What injustice! What a thing to say to me in the presence of this honorable, august and elegant Court! I spend all my time trying to spend my money. If I have tan shoes, I buy black ones. If I have a bicycle, I buy a motor car. If I have a wife, I buy . . .

JOS. (*Rings.*) Order!

RAG. I dispatch a plane to Java for a bouquet of flowers. I send a steamer to Egypt for a basket of figs. I send a special representative to New York to fetch me an ice-cream cone. And if it's not just exactly right, back it goes. But no matter what I do, I can't get rid of my money! If I play a hundred to one shot, the horse comes in by twenty lengths. If I throw a diamond in the Seine, it turns up in the trout they serve me for lunch. Ten diamonds—ten trout. Well, now, do you suppose I can get rid of forty millions by giving a sou to a deaf-mute? Is it even worth the effort?

CON. He's right.

RAG. Ah! You see, my dear? At last, there is somebody who understands me! Somebody who is not only beautiful, but extraordinarily sensitive and intelligent.

COUNT. I object!

JOS. Overruled!

RAG. I should be delighted to send you some flowers, Miss—directly I'm acquitted. What flowers do you prefer?

CON. Roses.

RAG. You shall have a bale every morning for the next five years. Money means nothing to me.

CON. And amaryllis.

RAG. I'll make a note of the name. (*In his best lyrical style.*) The lady understands, ladies and gentlemen. The lady is no fool. She's been around and she knows what's what. If I gave the Deaf-Mute a franc, twenty francs, twenty million francs—I still wouldn't make a dent in the forty times a thousand million francs that I'm afflicted with! Right, little lady?

CON. Right.

JOS. Proceed.

RAG. Like on the Stock Exchange. If *you* buy a stock, it sinks at once like a plummet. But if *I* buy a stock, it turns around and soars like an eagle. If I buy it at 33 . . .

PED. It goes up to a thousand.

RAG. It goes to twenty thousand! That's how I bought my twelve chateaux, my twenty villas, my 234 farms. That's how I endow the Opera and keep my twelve ballerinas.

FLOW. GIRL. I hope every one of them deceives you every moment of the day!

RAG. How can they deceive me? Suppose they try to deceive me with the male chorus, the general director, the assistant electrician or the English horn—I own them all, body and soul. It would be like deceiving me with my big toe.

CON. Don't listen, Gabrielle.

GAB. Listen to what?

RAG. No. I am incapable of jealousy. I have all the women—or I can have them, which is the same thing. I get the thin ones with caviar—the fat ones with pearls . . .

COUNT. So you think there are no women with morals?

RAG. I mix morals with mink—delicious combination. I drip pearls into protests. I adorn resistance with rubies. My touch is jeweled; my smile, a motor car. What woman can withstand me? I lift my little finger—and do they fall?—Like leaves in autumn—like tin cans from a second-story window.

CON. That's going a little too far!

COUNT. You see where money leads.

RAG. Of course. When you have no money, nobody trusts you, nobody believes you, nobody likes you. Because to have money is to be virtuous, honest, beautiful and witty. And to be without is to be ugly and boring and stupid and useless.

COUNT. One last question. Suppose you find this oil you're looking for. What do you propose to do with it?

RAG. I propose to make war! I propose to conquer the world!

COUNT. You have heard the defense, such as it is. I demand a verdict of guilty.

RAG. What are you talking about? Guilty? I? I am never guilty!

JOS. I order you to keep quiet.

RAG. I am never quiet!

JOS. Quiet, in the name of the law!

RAG. I am the law. When I speak, that is the law. When I present my backside, it is etiquette to smile and to apply the lips respectfully. It is more than etiquette—it is a cherished national privilege, guaranteed by the Constitution.

JOS. That's contempt of court. The trial is over.

COUNT. And the verdict?

ALL. Guilty!

JOS. Guilty as charged.

COUNT. Then I have full authority to carry out the sentence?

ALL. Yes!

COUNT. I can do what I like with them?

ALL. Yes!

COUNT. I have the right to exterminate them?

ALL. Yes!

JOS. Court adjourned!

COUNT. (*To the* RAGPICKER.) Congratulations, Ragpicker. A marvelous defense. Absolutely impartial.

RAG. Had I known a little before, I could have done better. I could have prepared a little speech, like the time I used to sell the Miracle Spot Remover. . . .

JOS. No need for that. You did very well, extempore. The likeness was striking and the style reminiscent of Clemenceau. I predict a brilliant future for you. Goodbye, Aurelia. I'll take our little Gabrielle home.

CON. I'm going to walk along the river. (*To* DICKIE.) Oh! So here you are. And your ear all bloody! Dickie! Have you been fighting again? Oh, dear . . . !

COUNT. (*To the* RAGPICKER.) See that she gets home all right, won't you? She loses everything on the way. And in the queerest places. Her prayer book in the butcher shop. And her corset in church.

RAG. (*Bowing and offering his arm.*) Permit me, Madame.

ST. SING. Oh, Countess—my mazurka. Remember?

COUNT. Oh, yes. Constance, wait a moment. (*To the* SINGER.) Well? Begin.

ST. SING. (*Sings.*)
  "Do your hear, Mademoiselle,
  Those musicians of hell?"

CON. Why, of course, it's *La Belle Polonaise.* . . . (*She sings.*)
  "From Poland to France
  Comes this marvelous dance,
    So gracious,
    Audacious,
  Will you foot it, perchance?"

ST. SING. I'm saved!

JOS. (*Reappearing at the head of the stairs.*)
  "Now my arm I entwine
  Round these contours divine,
  So pure, so impassioned,
  Which Cupid has fashioned. . . ."

GAB. (*Reappearing also, she sings a quartet with the others.*)
  "Come, let's dance the mazurka, that devilish measure,
  'Tis a joy that's reserved to the gods for their pleasure—
    Let's gallop, let's hop,
    With never a stop,
    My blonde Polish miss,
  Let our heads spin and turn

As the dance-floor we spurn—
There was never such pleasure as this!"
(*They all exit, dancing.*)

IRMA. It's time for your afternoon nap.

COUNT. But suppose they come, Irma!

IRMA. I'll watch out for them.

COUNT. Thank you, Irma. I *am* tired. (*She smiles.*) Did you ever see a trial end more happily in your life?

IRMA. Lie down and close your eyes a moment.

(*The* COUNTESS *stretches out on the chaise-longue and shuts her eyes.* IRMA *tiptoes out. In a moment,* PIERRE *comes down softly, the feather boa in his hands. He stands over the chaise-longue, looking tenderly down at the sleeping woman, then kneels beside her and takes her hand.*)

COUNT. (*Without opening her eyes.*) Is it you, Adolphe Bertaut?

PIERRE. It's only Pierre.

COUNT. Don't lie to me, Adolphe Bertaut. These are your hands. Why do you complicate things always? Say that it's you.

PIERRE. Yes. It is I.

COUNT. Would it cost you so much to call me Aurelia?

PIERRE. It's I, Aurelia.

COUNT. Why did you leave me, Adolphe Bertaut? Was she so very lovely, this Georgette of yours?

PIERRE. No. You are a thousand times lovelier.

COUNT. But she was clever.

PIERRE. She was stupid.

COUNT. It was her soul, then, that drew you? When you looked into her eyes, you saw a vision of heaven, perhaps?

PIERRE. I saw nothing.

COUNT. That's how it is with men. They love you because you are beautiful and clever and soulful—and at the first opportunity they leave you for someone who is plain and dull and soulless. But why does it have to be like that, Adolphe Bertaut? Why?

PIERRE. Why, Aurelia?

COUNT. I know very well she wasn't rich. Because when I saw you that time at the grocer's, and you snatched the only good melon from right under my nose, your cuffs, my poor friend, were badly frayed. . . .

PIERRE. Yes. She was poor.

COUNT. "Was" poor? Is she dead then? If it's because she's dead that you've come back to me—then no. Go away. I will not take their leavings from the dead. I refuse to inherit you. . . .

PIERRE. She's quite well.

COUNT. Your hands are still the same, Adolphe Bertaut. Your touch is young and firm. Because it's the only part of you that has stayed with me. The rest of you is pretty far gone, I'm afraid. I can see why you'd rather not come near me when my eyes are open. It's thoughtful of you.

PIERRE. Yes. I've aged.

COUNT. Not I. I am young because I haven't had to live down my youth, like you. I have it with me still, as fresh and beautiful as ever. But when you walk now in the park at Colombes with Georgette, I'm sure . . .

PIERRE. There is no longer a park at Colombes.

COUNT. Is there a park still at St. Cloud? Is there a park at Versailles? I've never gone back to see. But I think, if they could move, those trees would have walked away in disgust the day you went there with Georgette. . . .

PIERRE. They did. Not many are left.

COUNT. You take her also, I suppose, to hear *Denise*?

PIERRE. No one hears *Denise* any more.

COUNT. It was on the way home from *Denise*, Adolphe Bertaut, that I first took your arm. Because it was windy and it was late. I have never set foot in that street again. I go the other way round. It's not easy, in the winter, when there's ice. One is quite apt to fall. I often do.

PIERRE. Oh, my darling—forgive me.

COUNT. No, never. I will never forgive you. It was very bad taste to take her to the very places where we'd been together.

PIERRE. All the same, I swear, Aurelia . . .

COUNT. Don't swear. I know what you did. You gave her the same flowers. You bought her the same chocolates. But has she any left? No. I have all your flowers still. I have twelve chocolates. No, I will never forgive you as long as I live.

PIERRE. I always loved you, Aurelia.

COUNT. You "loved" me? Then you too are dead, Adolphe Bertaut?

PIERRE. No. I love you. I shall always love you, Aurelia.

COUNT. Yes. I know. That much I've always known. I knew it the moment you went away, Adolphe, and I knew that nothing could ever change it. Georgette is in his arms now—yes. But he loves me. Tonight he's taken Georgette to hear *Denise*—yes. But he loves me. . . . I know it. You never loved her. Do you think I believed for one moment that absurd story about her running off with the osteopath? Of course not. Since you didn't love her, obviously she stayed with you. And, after that, when she came back, and I heard about her going off with the surveyor—I knew that couldn't be true, either. You'll never get rid of her, Adolphe Bertaut—never. Because you don't love her.

PIERRE. I need your pity, Aurelia. I need your love. Don't forget me. . . .

COUNT. Farewell, Adolphe Bertaut. Farewell. Let go my hand, and give it to little Pierre. (PIERRE *lets go her hand, and after a moment takes it again. The* COUNTESS *opens her eyes.*) Pierre? Ah, it's you. Has he gone?

PIERRE. Yes, Countess.

COUNT. I didn't hear him go. Oh, he knows how to make a quick exit, that one. (*She sees the boa.*) Good heavens! Wherever did you find it?

PIERRE. In the wardrobe, Countess. When I took off the mirror.

COUNT. Was there a purple felt shopping bag with it?

PIERRE. Yes, Countess.

COUNT. And a little child's sewing box?

PIERRE. No, Countess.

COUNT. Oh, they're frightened now. They're trembling for their lives. You see what they're up to? They're quietly putting back all the things they have stolen. I

never open that wardrobe, of course, on account of the old woman in the mirror. But I have sharp eyes. I don't need to open it to see what's in it. Up to this morning, that wardrobe was empty. And now—you see? But, dear me, how stupid they are! The one thing I really miss is my little sewing box. It's something they stole from me when I was a child. They haven't put it back? You're quite sure?

PIERRE. What was it like?

COUNT. Green cardboard with paper lace and gold stamping. I got it for Christmas when I was seven. They stole it the very next day. I cried my eyes out every time I thought of it—until I was eight.

PIERRE. It's not there, Countess.

COUNT. The thimble was gilt. I swore I'd never use any other. Look at my poor fingers. . . .

PIERRE. They've kept the thimble too.

COUNT. Splendid! Then I'm under no obligation to be merciful. Put the boa around my neck, Pierre. I want them to see me wearing it. They'll think it's a real boa. (IRMA *runs in excitedly.*)

IRMA. Here they come, Countess! You were right—it's a procession. The street is full of limousines and taxis!

COUNT. I will receive them. (*As* PIERRE *hesitates to leave her.*) Don't worry. There's nothing to be frightened of. (PIERRE *goes out.*) Irma, did you remember to stir the kerosene into the water?

IRMA. Yes, Countess. Here it is.

COUNT. (*Looking critically at the bottle.*) You might as well pour in what's left of the tea. (IRMA *shakes up the liquid.*) Don't forget, I'm supposed to be deaf. I want to hear what they're thinking.

IRMA. Yes, Countess.

COUNT. (*Putting the finishing touches to her make-up.*) I don't have to be merciful— but, after all, I do want to be just. . . .

(IRMA *goes up to the landing and exits. As soon as she is alone, the* COUNTESS *presses the brick, and the trap door opens. There is a confused sound of auto horns in the street above, and the noise of an approaching crowd.*)

IRMA (*Offstage.*) Yes, Mr. President. Come in, Mr. President. You're expected, Mr. President. This way, Mr. President. (*The* PRESIDENTS *come down, led by the* PRESIDENT. *They all look alike, are dressed alike, and all have long cigars.*) The Countess is quite deaf, gentlemen. You'll have to shout. (*She announces.*) The presidents of the boards of directors!

PRES. I had a premonition, Madame, when I saw you this morning, that we should meet again. (*The* COUNTESS *smiles vaguely. He continues, a tone louder.*) I want to thank you for your trust. You may place yourself in our hands with complete confidence.

2ND. PRES. Louder. The old trot can't hear you.

PRES. I have a letter here, Madame, in which . . .

2ND. PRES. Louder. Louder.

3RD. PRES. (*Shouting.*) Is it true that you've located . . . ? (*The* COUNTESS *stares at him blankly. He shouts at the top of his voice.*) Oil? (*The* COUNTESS *nods with a smile, and points down. The* PRESIDENT *produces a legal paper and a fountain pen.*) Sign here.

COUNT. What is it? I haven't my glasses.

PRES. Your contract. (*He offers the pen.*)

COUNT. Thank you.

2ND. PRES. (*Normal voice.*) What is it?

3RD. PRES. Waiver of all rights. (*He takes it back signed.*) Thank you. (*He hands it to the* SECOND PRESIDENT.) Witness. (*The* SECOND PRESIDENT *witnesses it. The* PRESIDENT *passes it on to the* THIRD PRESIDENT.) Notarize. (*The paper is notarized. The* PRESIDENT *turns to the* COUNTESS *and shouts.*) My congratulations. And now, Madame— (*He produces a gold brick wrapped in tissue paper.*) If you'll show us the well, this package is yours.

COUNT. What is it?

PRES. Pure gold. Twenty-four karat. For you.

COUNT. Thank you very much. (*She takes it.*) It's heavy.

2ND. PRES. Are you going to give her that?

PRES. Don't worry. We'll pick it up again on the way out. (*He shouts at the* COUNTESS, *pointing at the trap door.*) Is this the way?

COUNT. That's the way.

(*The* SECOND PRESIDENT *tries to slip in first. The* PRESIDENT *pulls him back.*)

PRES. Just a minute, Mr. President. After me, if you don't mind. And watch those cigars. It's oil, you know. (*But as he is about to descend, the* COUNTESS *steps forward.*)

COUNT. Just one moment . . .

PRES. Yes?

COUNT. Did any of you happen to bring along a little sewing box?

PRES. Sewing box? (*He pulls back another impatient* PRESIDENT.) Take it easy.

COUNT. Or a little gold thimble?

PRES. Not me.

PRESIDENTS. Not us.

COUNT. What a pity!

PRES. Can we go down now?

COUNT. Yes. You may go down now. Watch your step!

(*They hurry down eagerly. When they have quite disappeared,* IRMA *appears on the landing and announces the next echelon.*)

IRMA. Countess, the Prospectors.

COUNT. Heavens! Are there more than one?

IRMA. There's a whole delegation.

COUNT. Send them down.

(*The* PROSPECTOR *comes in, following his nose.*)

IRMA. Come in, please.

PROS. (*Sniffing the air like a bloodhound.*) I smell something. . . . Who's that?

IRMA. The Countess. She is very deaf.

PROS. Good.

(*The* PROSPECTORS *also look alike. Sharp clothes, Western hats and long noses. They crowd down the stairs after the* PROSPECTOR, *sniffing in unison. The* PROSPECTOR *is especially talented. He casts about on the scent until it leads him to the decanter on the table. He pours himself a glass, drinks it off, and belches with much satisfaction. The others join him at once, and follow his example. They all belch in unison.*)

PROSPECTORS. Oil?

PROS. Oil!

COUNT. Oil.

PROS. Traces? Puddles?

COUNT. Pools. Gushers.

2ND. PROS. Characteristic odor? (*He sniffs.*)

PROS. Chanel Number 5. Nectar! Undoubtedly—the finest—rarest! (*He drinks.*) Sixty gravity crude: straight gasoline! (*To the* COUNTESS.) How found? By blast? Drill?

COUNT. By finger.

PROS. (*Whipping out a document.*) Sign here, please.

COUNT. What is it?

PROS. Agreement for dividing the profits. . . . (*The* COUNTESS *signs.*)

2ND. PROS. (*To* 1ST. PROSPECTOR.) What is it?

PROS. (*Pocketing the paper.*) Application to enter a lunatic asylum. Down there?

COUNT. Down there. (*The* PROSPECTORS *go down, sniffing.*)

(IRMA *enters.*)

IRMA. The gentlemen of the press are here.

COUNT. The rest of the machine! Show them in.

IRMA. The Public Relations Counsellors! (*They enter, all shapes and sizes, all in blue pin-striped suits and black homburg hats.*) The Countess is very deaf, gentlemen. You'll have to shout!

1ST. PR. AGENT. You don't say—Delighted to make the acquaintance of so charming and beautiful a lady. . . .

2ND. PR. AGENT. Louder. She can't hear you.

1ST. PR. AGENT. What a face! (*Shouts.*) Madame, we are the press. You know our power. We fix all values. We set all standards. Your entire future depends on us.

COUNT. How do you do?

1ST. PR. AGENT. What will we charge the old trull? The usual thirty?

2ND. PR. AGENT. Forty.

3RD. PR. AGENT. Sixty.

1ST. PR. AGENT. All right—seventy-five. (*He fills in a form and offers it to the* COUNTESS.) Sign here, Countess. This contract really gives you a break.

COUNT. That is the entrance.

1ST. PR. AGENT. Entrance to what?

COUNT. The oil well.

1ST. PR. AGENT. Oh, we don't need to see that, Madame.

COUNT. Don't need to see it?

1ST. PR. AGENT. No, no—we don't have to see it to write about it. We can imagine it. An oil well is an oil well. "That's oil we know on earth, and oil we need to know." (*He bows.*)

COUNT. But if you don't see it, how can you be sure the oil is there?

1ST. PR. AGENT. If it's there, well and good. If it's not, by the time we get through, it will be. You underestimate the creative aspect of our profession, Madame. (*The* COUNTESS *shakes her head, handing back the papers.*) I warn you, if you insist on rubbing our noses in this oil, it will cost you 10 per cent extra.

COUNT. It's worth it. (*She signs. They cross toward the trap door.*)

2ND. PR. AGENT. (*Descending.*) You see, Madame, we of the press can refuse a lady nothing.

3RD. PR. AGENT. Especially, such a lady. (THIRD PRESS AGENT *starts going down.*)

2ND. PR. AGENT. (*Going down. Gallantly.*) It's plain to see, Madame, that even fountains of oil have their nymphs. . . . I can use that somewhere. That's copy!

(*The* PRESS AGENTS *go down. As he disappears, the* FIRST PRESS AGENT *steals the gold brick and blows a kiss gallantly to the* COUNTESS, *who blows one back.*)

(*There is a high-pitched chatter offstage, and* IRMA *comes in, trying hard to hold back* THREE WOMEN *who pay no attention to her whatever. These* WOMEN *are tall, slender, and as soulless as if they were molded of wax. They march down the steps, erect and abstracted like animated window models, but chattering incessantly.*)

IRMA. But, ladies, please—you have no business here—you are not expected. (*To the* COUNTESS.) There are some strange ladies coming. . . .

COUNT. Show them in, Irma. (*The* WOMEN *come down, without taking the slightest interest in their surroundings.*) Who are you?

1ST. WOM. Madame, we are the most powerful pressure group in the world.

2ND. WOM. We are the ultimate dynamic.

3RD. WOM. The mainspring of all combinations.

1ST. WOM. Nothing succeeds without our assistance. Is that the well, Madame?

COUNT. That is the well.

1ST. WOM. Put out your cigarettes, girls. We don't want any explosions. Not with my brand-new eyelashes. (*They go down, still chattering. The* COUNTESS *crosses to the wall to close the trap. As she does so, there is a commotion on the landing.*)

IRMA. Countess . . .

(*A* MAN *rushes in breathlessly.*)

MAN. Just a minute! Just a minute! (*He rushes for the trap door.*)

COUNT. Wait! Who are you?

MAN. I'm in a hurry. Excuse me. It's my only chance! (*He rushes down.*)

COUNT. But . . . (*But he is gone. She shrugs her shoulders, and presses the brick. The trap closes. She rings the bell for* IRMA.) My gold brick! Why, they've stolen my gold brick! (*She moves toward the trap. It is now closed.*) Well, let them take their god with them.

(IRMA *enters and sees with astonishment that the stage is empty of all but the* COUNTESS. *Little by little, the scene is suffused with light, faint at first, but increasing as if the very walls were glowing with the quiet radiance of universal joy. Only around the closed trap a shadow lingers.*)

IRMA. But what's happened? They've gone! They've vanished!

COUNT. They've evaporated, Irma. They were wicked. Wickedness evaporates.

(PIERRE *enters. He is followed by the* VAGABONDS, *all of them. The new radiance of the world is now very perceptible. It glows from their faces.*)

PIERRE. Oh, Countess . . . !

WAIT. Countess, everything's changed. Now you can breathe again. Now you can see.

PIERRE. The air is pure! The sky is clear!

IRMA. Life is beautiful again.

RAG. (*Rushes in.*) Countess—the pigeons! The pigeons are flying!

FLOW. GIRL. They don't have to walk any more.

RAG. They're flying. . . . The air is like crystal. And young grass is sprouting on the pavements.

COUNT. Is it possible?

IRMA (*Interpreting for the* DEAF-MUTE.) Now,

Juggler, you can throw your fireballs up as high as you please—they won't go out.

SERG. On the street, utter strangers are shaking hands, they don't know why, and offering each other almond bars!

COUNT. Oh, my friends . . .

WAIT. Countess, we thank you. . . .

(*They go on talking with happy and animated gestures, but we no longer hear them, for their words blend into a strain of unearthly music which seems to thrill from the uttermost confines of the universe. And out of this music comes a voice.*)

1ST. VOICE. Countess . . . (*Only the* COUNTESS *hears it. She turns from the group of* VAGABONDS *in wonder.*)

2ND. VOICE. Countess . . .

3RD. VOICE. Countess . . . (*As she looks up in rapture, the* FIRST VOICE *speaks again.*)

1ST. VOICE. Countess, we thank you. We are the friends of animals.

2ND. VOICE. We are the friends of people.

3RD. VOICE. We are the friends of friendship.

1ST. VOICE. You have freed us!

2ND. VOICE. From now on, there will be no hungry cats. . . .

3RD. VOICE. And we shall tell the Duchess her dog's right name!

(*The* VOICES *fade off. And now another group of voices is heard.*)

1ST. VOICE. Countess, we thank you. We are the friends of flowers.

2ND. VOICE. From now on, every plant in Paris will be watered. . . .

3RD. VOICE. And the sewers will be fragrant with jasmine!

(*These voices, too, are silent. For an instant, the stage is vibrant with music. Then the* DEAF-MUTE *speaks, and his voice is the most beautiful of all.*)

DEAF-MUTE. Sadness flies on the wings of the morning, and out of the heart of darkness comes the light.

(*Suddenly a group of figures detaches itself from the shadows. These are exactly similar in face and figure and in dress. They are shabby in the fashion of 1900 and their cuffs are badly frayed. Each bears in his hand a ripe melon.*)

1ST. ADOLPHE BERTAUT. Countess, we thank

you. We, too, are freed at last. We are the Adolphe Bertauts of the world.

2ND. ADOLPHE BERTAUT. We are no longer timid.

3RD. ADOLPHE BERTAUT. We are no longer weak.

1ST. ADOLPHE BERTAUT. From this day on, we shall hold fast to what we love. For your sake, henceforth, we shall be handsome, and our cuffs forever immaculate and new. Countess, we bring you this melon and with it our hearts . . . ! (*They all kneel.*) Will you do us the honor to be our wife?

COUNT. (*Sadly.*) Too late! Too late! (*She waves them aside. They take up their melons sadly and vanish. The voices of the* VAGABONDS *are heard again, and the music dies.*) Too late! Too late!

PIERRE. Too late, Countess?

IRMA. Too late for what?

COUNT. I say that it's too late for them. On the twenty-fourth of May, 1881, the most beautiful Easter in the memory of man, it was not too late. And on the fifth of September, 1887, the day they caught the trout and broiled it on the open fire by the brook at Villeneuve, it was not too late. And it was even not too late for them on the twenty-first of August, 1897, the day the Czar visited Paris with his guard. But they did nothing and they said nothing, and now—kiss each other, you two, this very instant!

IRMA. You mean . . . ?

PIERRE. You mean . . . ?

IRMA. But, Countess . . .

COUNT. It's three hours since you've met and known and loved each other. Kiss each other quickly. (PIERRE *hesitates.*) Look at him. He hesitates. He trembles. Happiness frightens him. . . . How like a man! Oh, Irma, kiss him, kiss him! If two people who love each other let a single instant wedge itself between them, it grows—it becomes a month, a year, a century; it becomes too late. Kiss him, Irma, kiss him while there is time, or in a moment his hair will be white and there will be another madwoman in Paris! Oh, make her kiss him, all of you! (*They kiss.*) Bravo! Oh, if only you'd had the courage to do that thirty years ago, how different I would be today! Dear Deaf-Mute, be still—your words dazzle our eyes! And Irma is too busy to translate for you. (*They kiss once more.*) Well, there we are. The world is saved. And you see how simple it all was? Nothing is ever so wrong in this world that a sensible woman can't set it right in the course of an afternoon. Only, the next time, don't wait until things begin to look black. The minute you notice anything, tell me at once.

RAG. We will, Countess. We will.

COUNT. (*Puts on her hat. Her tone becomes businesslike.*) Irma. My bones. My gizzard.

IRMA. I have them ready, Countess.

COUNT. Good. (*She puts the bones into her basket and starts for the stairs.*) Well, let's get on to more important things. Four o'clock. My poor cats must be starved. What a bore for them if humanity had to be saved every afternoon. They don't think much of it, as it is.

(CURTAIN)

Part Three

TRAGEDY

TRAGEDY

It is easy to understand why tragedy so frequently dominates the discussion of drama. Problem plays force us to consider serious social issues; historical drama uses the past to teach us political lessons for our own day; melodrama excites and thrills us; comedies alert us to the follies and vices of others; but only tragedy involves us directly in death—in the deaths of heroes and in our own deaths. In the simplest (and most popular) view, tragedies seem to teach us either wisdom or prudence: when to die, or how to avoid those traps that lead men to untimely destruction. Examined more closely, tragedies suggest that passionate lives lead inevitably to violent deaths: inevitably but also justifiably. For after a closer look, we notice that tragic plays ensure our seeing such deaths as the only possible terminus for the journeys undertaken. Death indeed, for the tragic writer, means annihilation, and therefore his patterns of action and character-development are of a kind that force us to confront and question the cosmos. Yet this questioning does not lead us to despair: the emergent tragic sense reflects not only the sufferings and evil of life, but also its goodness, and the power of man to endure. Indeed, the delicate balance of these polarities—of evil and goodness, of suffering and endurance—has led some critics to speak of tragedy as a life-rhythm, rather than simply as a literary genre or a set of dramatic conventions.

So strongly do we recoil from the unexplained and inexplicable death that we have come to label all sudden disasters as tragedies, as if we might in this way impose the order of art on the seeming disorder of life. But can we in fact equate the "accident-riddled" with the "tragedy-ridden"? Professor Lerner's recent effort to make sense of the series of afflictions visited on the Kennedy family suggests otherwise: unlike the individuals *we* see cut down, every day, around us, who die against a background of highway-intersection or hospital ward, the characters the *dramatist* sets in motion move against a background of large-scaled forces engaged in struggles vital not only to the individuals immediately concerned but also to all mankind. Moreover, at the center of tragedy there stand, not the problems of man's daily being, but the limiting conditions of his becoming. Comedy asks: How can the social fabric be mended? tragedy asks: Can man preserve his private values and yet escape annihilation?

True, accident, affliction, and the malevolent act occur frequently in our own lives; but in tragedies they dominate the scene and appear, at least, to fall cumulatively into place as parts of a pattern. They stand, that is, as milestones on the hero's journey toward destruction, even though *he* cannot read them until the end. To us who have the insight and wisdom of spectators, the milestones seem more like recurring road signs that both record and direct the hero's progress to his doom. The perceived pattern terrifies us with its inevitability; through its apparent rationality we are released.

To meet the demands of his plot and of the tragic situation, the dramatist must create a hero fit to contest the forces of darkness. Consider the tragic situation. Man, by no choice of his own, inhabits a universe only fitfully under his control—a fact never more apparent than in the middle of the twentieth century. He appears to be a creature uniquely endowed to enjoy the fruits of his world; he is gifted with reason, even with a degree of wisdom. Yet he is constantly subject not only to the winds of chance, but to fundamental instabilities in his own nature—instabilities which, moreover, inevitably carry over into the society he constructs. In the unequal struggle he goes down to defeat. Nevertheless, his *endowments* must never be taken as negligible. For only man is at the same time able to endure his fate and to comprehend it. Before the moment of his destruction arrives, he demonstrates his capacity for endurance, but also his expanding awareness of the human situation. These qualities make him both the representative of his fellow men, and their spokesman.

The question "what is a tragedy, a tragic hero, a tragic plot?" continues to tempt the critic into generalizing from the observed characteristics. The essays that follow offer such generalizations. To begin with, there is the problem of the tragedian. The attempt to convey the sense of tragedy lays upon the actor the burden of projecting both the power of Man and the weakness of men. Mr. Carnovsky * recorded his effort to discover a voice proper both to Lear's indomitability and to his anguish, which is to say that he had to discover how Lear could outshout the Elements without deafening his fellow-men: *they* must be convinced that the voice will endure even after the speaker has died. Oscar Mandel's *A Definition of Tragedy*, perhaps the best sustained analysis of definition in our time, emphasizes the essential characteristics of the tragic mode, freed, as Professor Mandel suggests, from speculations about emotional effects and ethical aims. Nevertheless, it is necessary and fruitful to ask *why* we enjoy tragic dramas, when the horror and affliction that dominate them sicken us as we meet them in everyday life. Roy Morrell's essay on the "Psychology of Tragic Pleasure" uses psychoanalytic tools to probe our responses.

Such primary questions do not, of course, exhaust the possibilities of discussion. Speculations about the origin and social role of tragedy have led men to ask whether special conditions of social organization, of belief or skepticism, of tradition and convention, must prevail for the flourishing of tragedy as an art. Is "the tragic moment" a moment in every age?

Specifically, it is necessary to ask whether tragedy is possible in our time, as it was in Periclean Athens and Elizabethan England; whether deterministic science and pseudoscience, and equalitarian democracy, have denied us the sense of tragedy. Louis Bredvold's "The Modern Temper and Tragic Drama" summarizes current answers to such arguments—as they appeared

---

* See page 25 above.

in the 1920's in J.W. Krutch's famous essay, "The Tragic Fallacy"—and projects a hopeful reply based on extensive historical background and impressive dramatic insight. Arthur Miller's more polemical defense of the common man as potential hero proclaims that men like his own Willy Loman (Low-man) carry the tragic tradition forward, changed but not degraded, in terms appropriate to their own times.

A FATED FAMILY

Max Lerner

The Kennedy family has been gathering in affliction, where it once gathered in rejoicing at triumphs. Yet the afflictions are not new. Their count (as everyone has been noting) goes far back to a daughter mentally retarded, a brilliant son killed in the war, and a daughter killed in a plane crash; it goes on to the father paralyzed by a stroke, a young president blossoming into greatness and killed by an assassin, and now a young senator with his back broken in another plane crash.

Things happen to the Kennedys. One might argue that they are bound to happen to any large brood, especially one that has been so active and mobile, exposed to all risks; in one case there was the ultimate exposure, in the target seat atop the greatest pyramid of power in world history. Granted the numbers and the risks this may be a case in sheer probability theory.

Yet few will be satisfied with that. These may all be accidents. But where we see a family so accident-riddled we also see one tragedy-ridden, and we cannot help wondering whether the tragedy may not have a source in some principle which is part of the scheme of things beyond our understanding.

Luck and unluck? That is only a way of covering over our ignorance. God and His design? That was the problem in the Job story, in the Old Testament, and it is a problem that after many generations of theologians and philosophers still remains unresolved. You had to reconcile a family affliction with a God who—however implacable toward the unjust—was hard to conceive as implacable also toward the just. I happened to be in a hospital in Boston the night when the news of the plane crash came. Speaking of what had happened to the Kennedy family a young Negro nurse said, "And they are so good. It doesn't pay to be good." It was the Job problem.

The Greeks had a different approach. It was the idea of "hubris," the sin of overreaching which was resented by the gods. For the Greeks no man, no family, was good if it had attained a summit place in life. If you reach out for wealth and power you are bound to ride roughshod over others in getting there. And the gods are angry at mortals who lay claim, as if as a matter of right, to what only the gods can assign on their own terms, however whimsical. The Greeks understood this when they saw their great tragic plays and watched a man, a family, tangled in a net of tragic involvement.

There was another approach the Greeks and Romans had, especially in their later divine myths. It was to turn their gods into very human beings, with jealousies and passions like the human. Thus you could always attribute a man's or family's misfortunes to the persistent hostility of some god or goddess, without attaching the blame to the whole circle of gods. When a storm arose to batter the ships of Aeneas it was due to the jealousy of a god; when it died down it was because his protecting deity had prevailed.

When many gods were replaced by one God, the problem—as the Job story shows—became harder. For the single principle or design ruling the universe had to become responsible for explaining not only the ordered justice of life but injustice, accident, blind and brutal chance. Men had to find in a single God somehow not only the principle of reason in life, but the reason of unreason as well.

How shall I explain these things to my son, Adam? That the gods are jealous? That there is a principle of order even in disorder, and that whatever happens, happens for the best? That we must carry on a heartbroken Job-like dialogue with God, which we can never win? A little of each of these, yes.

But mainly I shall tell him that the universe doesn't make sense morally, however much sense the scientists may make of it; that built into its very constitution is a principle of tragedy which none of us can escape; that it strikes wildly and often unjustly, but that the tragic heights are reached by those—a man, a woman, a family—whose humanity is not destroyed by what happens, but deepened by it.

A DEFINITION OF TRAGEDY

Oscar Mandel

So far, then, we walk in the footsteps of Aristotle: our definition is to be purely aesthetic; it is to depend for its existence on no other discipline, and on no fact undiscoverable in the texts themselves; it is to emerge, like Aristotle's, simply from experience with the texts, as though we had never thought about "higher questions." Again, this definition will set tragedy at liberty to exhibit any ontological or ethical order which is not directly incompatible with the terms of tragedy; and the field, as we shall see, is large.

The following, then, is a substantive definition by situation. It purports to be perfectly economical, admitting not a single word which is not absolutely required by the case.

A work of art is tragic if it substantiates the following situation: *A protagonist who commands our earnest good will is impelled in a given world by a purpose, or undertakes an action, of a certain seriousness and magnitude; and by that very purpose or action, subject to that same given world, necessarily and inevitably meets with grave spiritual or physical suffering.*

This definition is not meant to startle; in one or two respects it repeats the unpretentious Aristotelian concept. But what is worth stressing once more is that the statement represents the *whole* definition; that, what-ever else the tragic work may say, only this is properly tragic, only this exhausts the identity among all tragedies. By the same token, whatever the statement omits—and it is quiet on many subjects—is therefore not properly an ingredient in the essence of tragedy. Tragedy, as we have seen already, has been an ideal site for lofty intellectual constructions, but the builders have more than once been tempted to build high rather than well. The modesty of the definition proposed here must justify itself in the sequel: we are to explore the possibility of maintaining a view of tragedy which does not slip into rhapsody.

It may be useful at this point to present Aristotle's concept as well as the modified concept suggested by S. H. Butcher, though the latter intends to be faithful to his master.

What follows is a *composite* definition drawn from Butcher's and Bywater's translations of the *Poetics*. It makes use of various portions of Aristotle's analysis instead of limiting itself to the well-known central paragraph (1449 b), and it attempts to distinguish with great care between what Aristotle seems to regard as essential—that is to say, as part of the definition—and elements which he regards as merely useful or commendable.

"Tragedy, then, is an imitation of a single, unified action that is serious, complete, probable [we might say "plausible" nowadays] and of a certain magnitude; concerning the fall of a man whose character is good (though not pre-eminently just or virtuous), appropriate, believable and consistent; whose misfortune is brought about not by vice or depravity but by some error or frailty; in language embellished with each kind of artistic ornament, the several kinds being found in separate parts of the play; in the form of an action, not of narrative; with incidents arousing pity and fear, wherewith to accomplish the catharsis of these emotions.

Let us set beside this Butcher's own view, though it too, like so many modern definitions, is given rather casually, in this case in the midst of a discussion of the martyr as a tragic hero.

"Tragedy, in its pure idea, shows us a mortal will engaged in an unequal struggle with destiny, whether that destiny be represented by the forces within or without the mind. The conflict reaches its tragic issue when the individual perishes, but through his ruin the disturbed order of the world is restored and the moral forces reassert their sway."

The chief point to be observed in connection with the three definitions is that Aristotle includes an emotional effect, Butcher an ethical direction, and the proposed definition neither. We will return to these points in later sections, and turn our attention for the moment to the center of the proposed definition.

The Kernel of the Definition

The idea of tragedy proposed here is not a literary artifact, like the three unities, but a reality. It is very seldom, of course, that we encounter in life the completeness and the purity of literature. Perhaps Brunetière is right: "Of all dramatic forms, tragedy is the least realistic, in a sense the most symbolic, and, as such, in its masterpieces, the least *contingent* or the closest neighbor of absolute beauty. In life, all seems at first sight to be made up of contingencies. The curtain does not fall at a climactic moment,

we splutter occasionally in what should be fine situations, bricks do break our heads at awkward and ridiculous times, and more than once we are surprised by a *deus ex machina* who liberates us without regard for artistic nicety. And yet, for all this, the tragic idea, as it represents the search for happiness by means or under conditions which themselves defeat that search, is one of the lasting and important ideas concerning human existence. From Leonidas in the Thermopylae to Peter renouncing his Lord, from the heresiarch who burns for a creed to the man who must choose between mother and wife, the tragic idea reaffirms a particular phase of the stirring platitude that "the world appears to be so constituted, that the greatness of men leads only too easily to misery and ruin." But tragedy asserts more than "that men die and are not happy"; it asserts that they die and are not happy through their own efforts. And not as a mere outcome of their own efforts, but *necessarily* as a condition contained in the effort. Tragedy, taken all in all, exposes an original and fatal defect in the relation between a purpose and a something within or without. Here we leave Aristotle to name the precise condition of downfall: *inevitability* impresses us as the kernel of the definition. No work can be tragic without it. Tragedy is always ironic, but it is not because an action *eventually* leads to the opposite of its intention, but because that opposite is grafted into the action from the very beginning. If this austere view of tragedy seems narrow, the pattern is nevertheless repeated time after time, in work after work. No other precise concept will bind the literature of so many years and so many nations together. The ironic idea that man's destruction can be occasioned by his very aspiration is obviously perennial and perennially fascinating, and it turns up in the guise of a thousand dramatic situations. The concrete applications of this idea—the plots which express it—are inexhaustible.

In naming inevitability as the *sine qua non* of tragedy, we do not discover something which had escaped the notice of critics these two thousand years; and indeed, it would be alarming had we done so. We are merely giving this concept the eminence which it has not achieved so far. Aristotle, for one, merely hints in our direction: "Thus a person of a given character should speak or act in a given way, by the rule either of necessity or of probability; just as this event should follow that by necessary or probable sequence. It is therefore evident that the unravelling of the plot, no less than the complication, must arise out of the plot itself, it must not be brought about by the *Deus ex Machina*." Or again: reversal and recognition "should arise from the internal structure of the plot, so that what follows should be the necessary or probable result of the preceding action." But Aristotle seems to be dealing here with the scenes or episodes of the play rather than, in all clarity, with the initial tragic purpose. Nor is inevitability at the center of his thoughts on tragedy. Still, if we feel the need for his authority, that authority can be invoked from such passages as tending to support absolute inevitability at the very inception of the purpose.

In the work of contemporary critics too, the idea of finality occurs sporadically. It is not our purpose to catalogue authors and to parade allies, but a few critics may be cited here. Mr. Frye, for example, speaks of tragedy as residing "in the inevitability of the consequences of the [hero's] act, not in its moral significance as an act"; Jaspers applies to tragedy his concept of the permanence along with the permanent limitation of the philosophic quest: "Man's mind fails and breaks down in the very wealth of its potentialities. Every one of these potentialities, as it becomes fulfilled, provokes and reaps disaster"; while Miss Langer describes comedy as the image of Fortune, and tragedy as the image of Fate, by which she means that the latter, in abstracting the pattern of essential human behavior, shows man as aware of death and giving himself a career, a destiny, "shaped essentially in advance and only incidentally by chance happenings."

Among the Romantic critics, the idea of inevitability assumed the more exalted names of Fate and Destiny. We dispense with these inflated terms at the risk of a certain dryness The word inevitability is unevocative, but it has the advantage of "meaning business" and of being clear; and the still more important advantage of being suitable for any species of tragedy, whether Greek, Christian, atheistic, or merely secular.

THE PSYCHOLOGY OF TRAGIC PLEASURE

Roy Morrell

Mine is a hackneyed subject, and I should like to say at once that some obvious points which may appear heavily labored in the first part of this paper, are included not in order to instruct, but to facilitate reference when I come to a psychoanalytical analogy at the end.

I have little room, in my theory, for the jargon of psychological pleasure terms such as sadism and masochism. The masochistic element in literature is familiar and it appears distinct from tragedy. The Romantic mood which finds pleasure in "swooning to death" has, I know, been called tragic, but this is, I believe, a confusion. When tragedy appears in nineteenth century literature, it seems alien and even shocking to the Romantic sensibility. The argument that the appeal of tragedy is sadistic is likewise unconvincing: the critic argues—rightly, I think—that literature or drama which openly relishes cruelty repels those of us who are not sadists, yet those of us who are not sadists can find pleasure in tragedy.

The argument in favour of sadism might, however, be pressed in a different way: it might be said that some "censorship" mechanism enables us to derive sadistic pleasure—those of us who deny that we are sadists—only from something not *too* sadistic, from something not recognizable as sadism. Psychologists do, in fact, extend the term sadism to include not only sexual violence or a relish in inflicting pain inexplicable except through some sexual analogy, but also a more general satisfaction in the discomfiture of others. At one time it seemed to me that tragic pleasure must be explicable in this way. Are not all but the best of men moved to envy the lot of their more energetic or more successful fellows? We may think we are unselfish, or good sportsmen, rejoicing in our friend's success, his windfall, his prize in the sweepstake—he bought only one ticket, lucky fellow, and we had bought ten—we may rejoice in his fat legacy. We cannot blame ourselves, we blame only him, when we quickly detect signs of "uppishness" in him; and we leave him to go his superior way. How quickly and virtuously, on the other hand, do we rally round with demonstrations of friendship and pity, refraining from the least mention of "poetic justice," should he lose his wealth as quickly as he acquired it. Nor is it entirely petty thus to wish for an assurance that Fate is not too unfair, that if she withholds from us her special favors, she does not deal us her worst blows. To see disaster befalling a great and fortunate person dwarfs our own worries and troubles, and makes them more easily bearable. Fate, great personages, disasters befalling them—these are the stuff of tragedy, and that pity should be seen as

217

something related to envy, and therefore undesirable, perhaps indicates that Aristotle was thinking partly along these lines.

Reflection will show us, however, that any such theory is incomplete. It assumes a detachment on the part of the audience; it ignores the fact that most spectators and readers sympathize, or perhaps actually identify themselves with the hero. We may be more sophisticated than the schoolboy who forgets that Jim Hawkins is not himself, but we sympathize with Oedipus, Lear, Othello, Tess and Hugo actively enough to wish to avert the disasters which await them. In short, tragic pleasure does not arise through the gratification of a wish, but in a wish's frustration. This reminder should prevent our toying with psychological pleasure terms, masochism or sadism, dilute them as we may, or with any conception of "poetic justice." Tragedy does not "please" in this sense; it does not please our palate, nor awaken pleasurable anticipation. On the contrary, we resist tragedy, and try to avert it. The pleasure arises only afterwards, and no small part of the pleasure is the discovery that we have the strength to face a world which is larger than the mere creation of our wishes.

There remain the anthropologists' data of the magical origins of tragedy. We all know that pain, mutilation, sacrifice, ritual burial, once implied renewal, resurrection, the germination of the seed. But what have such things to do with us today? Having outgrown the magical view of the world, why have we not outgrown tragedy? It is true that primitive impulses still move us unconsciously. Freud has shown that accidents, breakages, and the like, are sometimes instinctive sacrifices, sops to Nemesis. We may not use the word *Hubris*, but we dislike and fear boasting; we touch wood, and hang up mistletoe; and in the same way the tragic experience, in which we suffer vicariously, may still be "good magic" and seem to appease the Fates.

The Fates indeed are merely projections of our anxieties, and if the Fates have gone, the anxieties remain. And it is in this way, I think, that we usually find the appeal of tragedy defined today. If art is man's method of imposing a pattern on the disorderly material of life, tragedy's function is to get under control life's most chaotic and difficult parts. Gilbert Murray said, "In its primitive form, drama was doing beforehand the thing you longed or dreaded to do; doing afterwards the thing that lived in your mind and could not be exorcised."

Modern warfare has shown that man has not outgrown this need for anticipating or exorcising. In Freud's account of war neuroses, he pointed out that the anxious individuals, whose imaginations pictured the horrors of battle in advance, were least liable to shell-shock. He also pointed out that recovery from shock was necessarily accompanied by dreams of the shocking experience. Attempts to cure the patient by diverting his mind always failed; his injured psyche was set on rehearsing and rehearsing the horror in daydreams and in sleep until gradually the experience was brought under control; and cures were accelerated not by removing the patients to the quiet of the country, trying to make them forget, but rather by reminding them of the battlefield, supplementing their imaginings by noises of bombardment and by additional shocks.

All this is well known, but it is interesting because, first, it suggests why surprise is unimportant in tragedy. Indeed, as Mr. Lucas says, dramatic irony and suspense— with their hints of what is about to happen —far from detracting from the effect of tragedy, only enhance the horror. We can, moreover, see a great tragedy again and again, without diminution of effect: it is, indeed, as if, within our own minds, tragedy were never a performance, always a rehearsal. Second, Freudian psychology corroborates our previous impression that "tragic pleasure" is a phrase which can be used only with reserve, in inverted commas. We are not "pleased" by the destruction of the hero, any more than the soldier is "pleased" either by the shock which penetrates his illusions, or by the dreams by which he seeks to control or exorcise the terror. Pleasure there is indeed, but only afterwards, in the feeling of having gained control, partial or complete, over the chaotic experience.

In the book where Freud develops this theme—that certain human behavior can be explained only by going, as the title puts it, "Beyond the Pleasure Principle," he analyzes examples of play in children, where sometimes, by persistent repetition, the child's psyche obtains control over a painful experience. Freud then compares the psyche to a cell. He sees it as having a highly sensitive interior protected by a hard rind from the cruel shock-laden wind of the real world. Some objective reality may be absorbed into layers of the rind, and defences may be strengthened by marshalling energies from within to resist specific attacks—just as our soldier who was full of "horrible imaginings" before the battle, saved himself from shell-shock. Some adaptation is possible, but the psyche tries to "make do" with the simplest set of illusions which seems as if it might, with luck, work. Except that "work" is hardly the word: the psyche is essentially lazy, seeking to economize effort. Sooner or later, however, an unexpected disaster may break through these too simple defences, and the whole equilibrium of the psyche may be upset until the new experience has been absorbed and brought under control, and a more complex, a less dangerously sensitive, composition established.

There is nothing new in this: it is Gilbert Murray's theory of rehearsing and exorcising, in metaphor. But, as Freud explains, the metaphor of the cell economizing its energy in pursuit of a "pleasure principle" (its little labor-saving ideal home is really the home of the death instincts), but being forced to reorganize itself into more complex life—this metaphor refers these "unpleasure processes," of which the tragic experience is one, to the very principle of life itself. It is thus that the sperm forces the ovum to live, repeating in every individual the process by which organic life began. Whatever disturbances occurred during the cooling of the globe, one imagines life—not real life at first, but merely the potentiality of life—coming into being not once but many times,

and fading out again, until some further disturbances intervened, enforcing a readjustment, a complication of the cell, the beginning of a cycle of life, before the simplicity of death could be re-attained.

In this view, then, there are two sets of impulses, one set which can be termed "death instincts," which are innate; and the other set, reacting to disturbing stimulation from the outside, which enable the individual to adapt and to reorganize and to live more complexly—tragedy exciting the second set. I am simplifying, perhaps; for instance I omit the possibility of innate disturbances which may complicate the life of the psyche by fifth-column activity within. With Freud's name on one's lips one is not likely to forget such impulses as complicated the life of Oedipus, for example. But on the whole I am not misrepresenting Freud, for in this book he does make mention—a single passing mention, but unambiguous—of tragedy.

By "death instincts" Freud explains that he doesn't mean "suicide instincts." Death is not their immediate, only their ultimate aim; their immediate aim is the preservation of the established life-cycle to death, with the least possible interference or tension. Tragedy's preoccupation with death indicates no alliance with these "death instincts" but rather a desire to rid us of the numbing effect of its terror. But there are obvious reservations to be made here: in many tragedies we are reminded that death is not the worst that can happen to the hero, and I hope to show later that his death has, in addition, a special function to perform.

For the moment the essential function of tragedy would appear to be the complicating and strengthening of the psyche by means of shocks from outside: not, of course, violent and disorganizing shocks, but mild, preventive, reorganizing ones. The participation in "tragic conflicts" may be a part of such reorganizing; though I am thinking of a toughening less crude than that which some German philosophers have thought desirable. Theoretically it would, I suppose, be possible to present a tragedy so horrible that there resulted a real shock—like shell-

shock—from which the patient would have
to be cured. In practice, however, we can
usually protect ourselves by recalling, if we
are forced, that what is happening on the
stage is not "real." There is probably a
level of tragedy, involving not too drastic
a reorganization of the psyche, at which
tragedy is most effective.

But when we come to define this level,
and to consider the mechanism by which
the tragic experience is conveyed to the
audience, it seems to me that we are inevitably defining characteristics in the tragic
hero. In Elizabethan tragedy, we are at once
aware of the hero's position—Faustus's,
Hamlet's, Clermont's, Othello's—a step or
so ahead of his age. He develops fine sensi-
bilities at heavy cost; he suffers and fails.
The audience follow the hero's aspirations,
his explorations in new realms of feeling;
they face the possibility that such noble
struggles will be thwarted by the insensibility
and evil of the men around them, by the
weight of the past, by blind chance. Despite
the hero's defeat, however, the experience
is, for the audience, a reorganization from
the old life to the new fuller one; the cell is
hindered in its easy acceptance of the old
instinctive life cycle, and compelled to live
more complexly. I believe great tragedy
always has this effect of bringing the consciousness to a threshold between the old
and the new, although it may have other
methods of doing this than by representing
the hero as thus stepping to a threshold or
beyond. Nor is the representation of such a
hero alone sufficient: the nobility of Clermont is not enough, for instance, to make a
great tragedy out of *The Revenge of Bussy
D'Ambois*.

None the less, a great hero—one human
enough for the audience's sympathy, and
remarkable enough to lift their imaginations
—is important. It is mainly through the
hero's thoughts and feelings that we judge
the truth of the world which the dramatist
asks us to accept, its "values," its relevance
to the possibilities of our own existence.
I have already said we feel more than a
detached sympathy for the hero; we feel
more than "there, but for the grace of God,

go I"; we identify ourselves, and go, with
him. The extent of the identification varies
in different members of the audience, and
with different types of tragedy. Some
identification occurs even in comedy; but
the essence of comedy is that identification
is partial and temporary and that we are
continually dissociating ourselves in laughter. Stephen Haggard and Athene Seyler tell
us in *The Craft of Comedy* that actors
recognize this, keeping slightly "outside"
the parts, self-dramatizing and slightly
overcharacterizing, in comedy, but acting
realistically and "straight," identifying
themselves with their parts and trying to
"live" them, empathizing—if I may use this
word in a more limited sense than it is
normally used in criticism—empathizing in
the characters in a serious play. I used the
word "realistically" inaccurately as a para-
phrase of the actors' word "straight." In
fact, too great a degree of realism with its
reminders of the particular and commonplace can be distressing to the audience. If
the audience too are to empathize in the
hero, we should probably agree that a
slightly stylized and remote production is
more effective; indeed, this matter of "psychological distance" in drama has been
explored by philosophers and critics.

My emphasis on the reality of the hero is
unfashionable, and went out with Bradley.
But although I am willing to defend this
emphasis, I realise that the position has its
dangers; particularly if adopted by actors.
If an actor believes that a play exists for
the sake of character, and for his acting of
it, the result is frequently disastrous. Nothing repels an audience so much as finding
that an actor, with a strong and perhaps
highly mannered personality, has "got in"
first. I am not arguing that personalities
should dominate the play, least of all the
personalities of actors. Such domination
defeats the whole end of drama, which is
not to give scope for actors or actresses
(pace M. Cocteau), nor to impress the
audience, but to enable the audience to
respond and react themselves. And they can
only respond naturally and unselfconsciously
if the actor has the tact to leave a little of

the initiative to them, if he underacts a little, perhaps. And, needless to say, they can only respond if the whole play, the whole action, rings true. Only then can they also be convinced by the hero's part in it. I certainly do not believe that the play should be subordinated to character; none the less I do believe that for the full functioning—the purging—of tragedy, our credulity, our four-dimensional acceptance, our ability to empathize in the tragic hero, or bovarize—as Huxley and others have called it—is always relevant. I need hardly distinguish here between bad bovarism and good: if we are tempted to identify ourselves with some hero of less intelligence and capacity for living than ourselves, it is probably to satisfy some dream of affluence or success; in short, to escape. Empathy in a character of a different kind, with a mind and soul larger than our own, requires effort and imagination, and, apart from any ordeal, any adjustment to the harsher realities which may be forced upon us by the tragic development of the plot, the greater awareness into which we are led tallies with the experience we derive from other great art.

Before considering whether this is the whole truth, I should like to recapitulate briefly and add to what I've said about the tragic hero. We have argued that whatever pleasure-principle factors enter, the distinctive appeal of tragedy can only be explained by going "beyond the pleasure principle"; we suffer an ordeal, face life at its most difficult and complex, but derive pleasure in the new readiness and power we have gained thereby. To enable us to live more complexly and to persuade us that what we are getting is true to life—for it is important that we should not feel that the dramatist is either cheating us or sparing us, treating us as children who cannot be told the truth—we are invited to empathize in a hero of a certain type. We feel more deeply and subtly, act more courageously, more passionately, in him, and all the time with the conviction that it is true to life, a fuller life than our own. We may add that as drama has to work quickly, superficial superiorities, such as those of rank and fortune mentioned by

classical critics, may predispose some of us to empathize, though modern class-conscious audiences may prefer other qualities. Whatever else the tragic hero is, however, he should not be dull: some conscientiously proletarian modern writers make a mistake, I think, when they solemnly present a drab little hero—unless they succeed in making out of him a twentieth-century Everyman. That may be as successful occasionally as the great character who lifts our imaginations, and it may invite our empathy no less.

Edith Sitwell has remarked that tragedy always opens on a question, "Who?"—Who is the tragic hero? what is his significance? The answer is seldom given as explicitly as in the closing lines of *The Great God Brown:* the Police Captain, you may remember, has given Cybel a few minutes alone with the dying Brown to make him talk; he then comes in and asks, "Well, what's his name?" Cybel answers, "Man," and the Police Officer, his notebook open, asks "How d'yuh spell it?"

The spelling is not difficult: it is either "Everyman," ourselves, whose fate we must endure; or it is "Potential Man," whose powers of living it would be well for the species if we could assimilate.

Nothing of what I have said so far is new, and little, I hope, is controversial. But one point is unexplained: If tragedy is, as I have described it, a vicarious ordeal, why is the unhappy ending essential? Why cannot the ordeal be provided by a serious and terrifying depiction of the sufferings of the hero, if he recovers from an almost mortal wound to live "happily ever after"? Death, as we know, is not essential. Oedipus lives on for a while; but in his despair, blood streaming from his eyesockets, he is a more terrible symbol of defeat than the hanged Jocasta. Defeat, the end of effective life, the end of hope for the hero—these are essential. His death, in fact, is convenient; but why?

It is true that the death of the hero is occasionally accompanied by the suggestion of a new start. Before the death of Henchard, some of our interest has been transferred to Elizabeth-Jane; Macbeth's death is followed by the coronation of Malcolm; there is even mention of the succession in *Hamlet;* but these are not "happy endings." Between the effect of *Hamlet* and that of *The Winter's Tale* there is a difference of kind not of degree: I know this difference depends not merely on the ending, but differences in the texture of the play throughout; and a key difference, in my view, is that in the tragicomedy our sympathies are not centered to the same extent on a single person. In this, it seems to me there is a special propriety: that the audience should not be asked to empathize seriously and deeply in a hero who is going, not to die, but to live "happily ever after."

Still, there is this difference in texture and it would be fairer to compare the effect of *Villette* with that of *Jane Eyre*, or the two versions of a Shakespeare tragedy, before and after it had been doctored to "please" Restoration or eighteenth-century audiences. I don't think there can be serious doubt that, despite Aristotle's contrary opinion, the unhappy ending is indispensable for tragic effect, and the ordeal theory is incomplete. Indeed nothing would seem to fit the ordeal theory better than some modern crime fiction. Raymond Chandler does not spare his readers when he describes his hero being taught by some thug to mind his own business, but I have yet to encounter a critic who calls this literature tragic.

The effect of tragedy is courage; not mere toughness, nor bravado, nor the will to display power, but simply calmness and readiness, the discovery that even in the harshest experiences there is, to quote Richards, "no difficulty"; the difficulty arises from the illusions and subterfuges by which we seek to dodge reality, and which we unconsciously fear are going to betray us.

But how does this change come about? How is it that for a time we are personally participating in the fears and difficulties of the hero, our need to dodge increased; and then that we are, almost suddenly sometimes, freed from these apprehensions, having achieved an impersonal objective attitude?

Freudian psychology helped us with a corroboration before; can it now provide us with an answer? We are again up against the difficulty of providing generalizations which are valid for all types of individuals —I recall a member of the Cambridge English Faculty who claimed that he had never experienced tragic catharsis: clearly my generalizations cannot include him. I put forward no chain of proof, tested at every link, only a kind of analogy which seems to me more plausible at some times than at others.

In pathological "fixations," when the psyche shrinks from developing into maturity, it often turns aside into a fantasy world comparable to the empathizing or bovarizing fantasies which we have been discussing. It is permissible to compare normal with pathological processes, for, as the example of Mme Bovary reminds us, no sharp line divides the two. It is a matter of better or of worse adjustment, and both possibilities are open to all of us.

At all events, with the conception of psychological fixation in mind, we can reframe our question thus, "Does tragedy provide the individual in the audience with a means of expansion through empathy, through good 'bovarism,' and then, *but only in the destruction of the hero*, free the individual, break his empathy at the point where it is in danger of becoming a fixation, where his fantasies might otherwise usurp the energies required for real life?" If this question is framed correctly, we could say simply that the individual adjusts himself to real life because his fantasy life has died with the hero.

I do not know how general these fixation fantasies are, however, and I should like to establish an analogy between the tragic "empathy-ordeal-disaster" process and some more general fantasy process. But meanwhile one point is worth noting. Freud in dealing with fixations has concentrated mainly on infantile incest fantasies; the tragic function—of enabling one to grow and adjust oneself—might therefore be expressed as breaking free from a fixation, if one had no more to explain than *Oedipus*

Tyrannus. But the main point hangs on Freud's reminder that an elaborate fantasy-living is *normal* in children. In their "endless imitation," they enter into fantasies, change them, discard them to meet the demands of real life, return to fantasy play at a moment's notice—they cease being soldiers or Red Indians and rush in to their real dinner, then rush out again to be pirates or shipwrecked mariners—doing safely, easily and normally what no adult can do without serious risk to his sanity. The explanation of this links up with what we said earlier about good and bad empathy: the whole principle of a child's life is growth, expansion; and his normal fantasies are informed inevitably with this expansion; they are, mainly, fantasies of growing up; and he is indeed growing minute by minute; except for the pathological case, the child with the infantile fixation, the child has no past, but only a future which he is constantly realizing. For the adult it is a different matter; every fantasy has the danger of becoming a fixation, a mental cancer growing inward when the normal expansive organic growth has slowed down, a step aside, a turn back to the past—unless, as we have suggested, the fantasy is of a special kind, derived from outside impact, demanding new effort, offering new opportunities of creative, imaginative, expansion.

But we were seeking in the realms of psychology for a more general type of fantasy, for comparison with tragic empathy. Is this not found in the artificially induced fantasy of the "transference," a part of the mechanism by which all psycho-therapeutic analysis was at one time attempted? An account of this mechanism is given in Jung's *Modern Man in Search of a Soul*. Jung describes the failure of Breuer's early therapeutic treatment, which Breuer with deliberate but, as it turned out, most unfortunate reference to Aristotle, called "Catharsis." Breuer's "Catharsis" was simply free confession aided by the probings of the physician, and Jung explains that it "consisted of putting the patient in touch with the hinterland of his mind." It failed

because one of two kinds of fixation followed treatment and caused a relapse. In fact, though of course Breuer did not realize it at this stage, it did not purge effectively; the term "Catharsis" had been usurped.

Breuer's treatment seemed to promise success; the patient always improved at first; but then one of two things happened: in some cases, to use Jung's words, "The patient goes away apparently cured—but he is now so fascinated by the hinterland of his own mind, that he continues to practice catharsis to himself at the expense of his adaptation to life. He is bound to the unconscious—to himself." In other cases, as is well known, the patient develops a sense of complete dependence on the physician, and collapses if the connection is severed. Both reactions are in the nature of fantasy-fixations: in the first case, the patient's fantasies are self-contained, they are fantasies about himself; in the second case a fantasy of child-parent dependence—the patient is the child; the physician the parent—is set up, and persists. In short, all Breuer had discovered or rediscovered was the relief and comfort of confession, and the helpless dependence which followed it.

Freud's system of analysis which superseded Breuer's made use of a similar relationship of dependence—the dependence of child-patient on father-confessor-physician—in the preliminary stages, but strove to break this "transference" later. This break was always regarded, of course, as indispensable for a cure; and, when properly successful, it effected something much more in the nature of a real catharsis. The important difference between Freud's analytical "transference" and Breuer's was that Freud's did not merely bring to light a few repressed thoughts and impulses from the "hinterland of the patient's mind," it strove also to bring the patient face to face with some terror, forced him to experience in his fantasy something which had been evaded in the past, something which provided a key to later conduct with its evasions and suppressions. Only if the psychoanalyst is able to lead the patient to a climax of resistance ending in painful temporary collapse, does this treatment end successfully and lead to the eventual readjustment of the patient. This process is different from that of tragedy mainly in the fact that the patient is led back to a point where a wrong turning had been taken in his past development, where he takes the hurdle he had evaded then, and leaves his old self behind; whereas in tragedy, the individual is led forward. But there are points of comparison too: there is the initial fantasy, there is the postponed and resisted pain, eventually faced either in the death of the hero, or in what may be regarded as the death of the old incomplete self; there is also that oft-discussed, perhaps essential tragic element, "recognition," the "anagnorisis" of Aristotle, which is akin to, perhaps leads to, self-revelation.

I had hoped to explain tragedy in terms of psychoanalysis and instead find myself expressing the analytical process in terms of tragedy. We can, however, add a few more bricks which seem to fit into the wall of this circular argument. If the effect of tragedy depends, as I believe, upon the end, not merely upon any earlier ordeal; if, not indeed the death of the hero, but the end of what he stands for is essential to release the audience and enable them to adjust themselves to reality; if purgation depends not merely upon the intensity of the transference but indispensably also upon the way it is broken, then we might expect, as a result of empathizing in heroes who do not fail tragically, but instead live "happily ever afterwards," a pathological state of dependence similar to the pathological condition of Breuer's patients. But this is not unlike Mme Bovary's state; and those people who, not making the mistake of Mme Bovary and attempting to live their daydreams, do nonetheless seek wish-fulfilment dreams in novels and films, are often called, with justice, film or fiction "addicts." Their first need after reading the average novel, or seeing the average film, seems to be to return to the cinema or the fiction library for another one. Whatever exciting or dangerous "ordeals" the addict has experienced vicariously, "purgation" is not

one of them, and he attempts no adjustment but remains dependent on his fantasies. He could not continue to empathize in a person who is dead, but he is glad to do so in one who lives happily ever afterwards; and the more he gets from Hollywood or the bestseller-writer, the more dependent he becomes, upon his own fantasies, or upon the dispenser of them. I make the distinction because the tone of certain writers—talking down to the reader, flattering him, comforting him, encouraging his prejudices— has not escaped critical comment. It seems to me not impossible that a reader may get to the point of feeling that the favorite author knows him and his weaknesses and secrets so well that the author is almost in the reader's confidence; and as a sales device, ensuring the complete dependence of the reader upon the physician-confessor-guardian-parent of an author who continually dispenses absolution to the reader for not growing up, it is unrivalled.

Referring to *Hamlet* and *The Winter's Tale* earlier, I suggested that in a tragicomedy there was a propriety in not inviting so deep and serious an empathy in the hero, as would be proper in tragedy. The reason is implied in what I have just said: empathy does not break itself, and an author whose theme gives him no opportunity of breaking it, should not—if he intends to deal honestly with his public—invite it very deeply and intensely in the first place. Good tragicomedy —and perhaps most of us would agree that tragicomedy is not commonly entirely convincing—but the best tragicomedy has some of the critical detachment of comedy; or else it distributes the empathy among several characters.

Had I the time I should have liked to mention one or two other points. I think, for instance, that those moments to which Mr. Eliot has called attention, when the hero dramatizes himself and his lonely struggle against the Fates, find a place in my scheme. Such self-dramatization in real life is not amiable; we forgive it, in moments of exceptional stress, in those we know and love, but we take it as weakness. The heroes who do this kind of thing continually from the rise of the curtain on Act I are, as serious tragic heroes, intolerable. In great tragedy we forgive it, as we forgive it in ourselves and in our friends; but the dramatic effect lies in the fact that at such moments, when the audience know the limits of the hero's strength, the nearness of his end, and the hero too knows it, but is desperately hiding the knowledge from himself—at such moments our critical faculty is stirring to waken, and our empathy is, as it were, being worked loose.

I should also have liked to discuss those tragedies which the audience approaches quite detachedly, their critical sense awake throughout. In my view such tragedies are a different species, and to regard them as the same leads only to confusion in theatrical production and in criticism.

But it is possible here to offer only a brief summary.

Tragedy is man's rehearsal of the harsher realities of life; by it the psyche's cell is forced out of its lethargy, its conservative instinctive life-cycle where it is only delusively secure, and it adapts itself to a more complex readiness for life.

The tragic hero is usually, as Aristotle said, uncommonly great and alive: only if he is great (but we mean by this not merely great in rank) does his downfall impress us with the insignificance of our own petty anxieties and mishaps; only if he is great—better than ourselves—does our attempt to share his experiences increase our own capacity for living. The place of the great hero is sometimes, however, successfully supplied by the figure of "Everyman" or by the representative not of all mankind but of a large group. Exceptionally our empathy may even be elicited by an idea, a "cause," with the success of which the fates of numerous individuals are bound up. This could be said not only of a few modern plays, but also of *Antigone*. Character, or some figure or idea in which the audience can identify themselves exactly as in a great character, is indispensable to tragedy; it must not dominate the action, but it is, despite Aristotle, as indispensable as action. In certain modern plays—*A Streetcar Named Desire*, *Lottie Dundass*, and others—the action is adequate, the end is disastrous, but the persons are not tragic characters: their place is not in drama, but in a psychoanalyst's case-book; they are tawdry and second-rate persons with whom no audience can with advantage identify themselves, and their failure, whatever else it may be, is not tragic.

Finally, despite Aristotle, Mr. Lucas and others, the general seriousness of the theme is not enough: the action must end in disaster. More than a bare hint of the "rebirth" or renewal theme is dangerous. A production of *Macbeth*, for instance, which allowed all our sympathy for Macbeth to ebb before the desperate scenes in Acts IV and V, and encouraged us to identify ourselves and our interests in Malcolm, would transform the play into melodrama. But in the tragic end of the hero, and of the hopes we had in him, there is nothing defeatist; for only in his failure is some connection, some "transference" between us and our fantasy life in the play, broken, and our own energies set free.

THE MODERN TEMPER AND TRAGIC DRAMA

Louis I. Bredvold

Just twenty-five years ago Mr. Joseph Wood Krutch published a volume of essays on *The Modern Temper*, a devastating analysis which has enjoyed enormous prestige and influence among thoughtful people, young and old. It continues even now to find readers who regard it as a sort of classic for our times, and who cannot but admire the courage and candor with which Mr. Krutch has exposed our modern disillusionment. It is still read by college students, who, recognizing the brilliance and the persuasiveness of the writing, defer to it as to an unquestionable authority. The unequal battle between the unprepared college student and *The Modern Temper* has for years been one of the major crises facing undergraduates.

One of the essays, on "The Tragic Fallacy," is particularly troublesome to students of literature. It is a pitiless explanation of why "we read but we do not write tragedies." It admits that "when we turn the pages of a Sophoclean or a Shakespearean tragedy we participate faintly in the experience which created it," but the truth is, we learn, that even when we are most moved by such tragedy "we perceive a Sophocles or a Shakespeare soaring in an air which we can never hope to breathe." The great tragic dramas of the past have faded for us; "we no longer live in the world which they

represent, but we can half imagine it, and we can measure the distance which we have moved away." As moderns we would be incapable of even forming by ourselves any conception of "the tragic spirit," and we can think about it only as we find it exemplified in these half-comprehended dramas left us from earlier ages.

The difficulty, says Mr. Krutch, is not a problem of art, but of two worlds, of a mind in the modern world trying to understand a mind from another world. We are separated from Shakespeare and Sophocles by our discovery of "the meanness of human life." A tragedy must have a hero, but "from the universe, as we see it, both the Glory of God and the Glory of Man have departed. Our cosmos may be farcical or it may be pathetic, but it has not the dignity of tragedy and we cannot accept it as such." We have lost the faith that makes possible the tragic vision; we can never recapture that faith because we live in the modern world. For that faith, says Mr. Krutch, was born "out of an instinctive confidence in life which is nearer to the animal's unquestioning allegiance to the scheme of nature than it is to that critical intelligence characteristic of a full developed humanism." The modern reader of tragic drama is therefore in a dilemma: either he enjoys the drama and gives up his critical intelligence, or he gives up the drama as naive and adolescent.

All this argument is sweeping in its generality. But one may gather from the essay some more specific statements as to how the great tragedy of the past was generated by a view of the world and of man no longer tenable by the modern critical intelligence. First, the moderns have learned that the cosmos is indifferent to them. "They cannot believe that the universe trembles when their love is, like Romeo's, cut off, or when the place where they, small as they are, have gathered up their trivial treasure is, like Othello's sanctuary, defiled." But the man contemporary with Sophocles or Shakespeare, believing that he occupied "the exact centre of the universe which would have no meaning except for him," could naturally assume that "each of his acts reverberates through the universe." Such cosmic importance imparts dignity to the tragic hero. In the second place, "the tragic spirit is in reality the product of a religious faith," whether it be in "God, Nature, or that still vaguer thing called a Moral Order," and because this faith is an "assumption" and not valid for us, we cannot feel that the struggles of the tragic hero are important. It is more modern to conceive of the catastrophe of the tragic hero as not differing essentially from the destruction of bacteria in a test tube. Finally, the modern world has turned from the hero to the common man, as is so evident in our novels as well as in drama. "We can no longer tell tales of the fall of noble men, because we do not believe that noble men exist. The best that we can achieve is pathos, and the most that we can do is to feel sorry for ourselves. Man has put off his royal robes, and it is only in sceptred pomp that tragedy can come sweeping by." We may summarize the argument thus: modern science has destroyed the old illusions regarding the cosmos; consequently, as the older tragedy was written in this obsolete "world," we can no longer be moved by its representation of human life and destiny. . . .

When Mr. Krutch says that a Shakespear-ean hero perishes with dignity because "a God leans out from infinity to strike him down," he speaks strangely and apparently in momentary forgetfulness of the plays. Those grand figures perished because they struck themselves down, not without more or less assistance, it is true, from those around them. The moving forces in their destinies were in the human, not a superhuman, sphere and therefore universally understandable as experiences that are possible, alas, to us all . . . .

. . . The story that unfolds in a great tragedy, rooted though it must be in human nature, presents a view of human destiny that raises issues beyond the power of a stage play to resolve. There are emotional upheavals, insights adumbrating into mystery, awesome revelations, that have the power to shake the complacency, one might think, of even the most hardened materialist, who might well leave the theater in a momentary mood to say with Hamlet, "for mine own poor part, look you, I'll go pray." For the great theme of tragedy is the problem of evil, from which even the materialist is not immune, the greatest problem mankind has to face, and the inspiration of the greatest literature mankind has so far produced. The tragedian raises metaphysical and religious issues which pass beyond the limits of his art, and on which it is impossible for him as a playwright to commit himself. As has been pointed out, he cannot resolve the problem of evil by assuming an existence after death in which rewards and punishments will balance the accounts of justice. Even if scenes of that sort were feasible in the theatre, they would have to be rejected as inharmonious with the tragic experience. No one wants an afterpiece showing Othello and Desdemona united happily in heaven. Tragedy must limit itself to showing heaven and hell as extreme possibilities of our destiny here on earth. The tragic hero is great, not because of any extraterrestrial relationships, but in himself. It is the depths of human nature, not the cosmos, that the dramatist must explore. He must have the creative power to plummet those depths and the dramatic technique to convey his tragic vision to his audience. The essential requirement for reading and writing great tragedy is therefore not a prescribed view of the universe, but a profound, imaginative, and sympathetic insight into human nature.

This, it seems, is where the modern dramatist falls short. He is unable to find in man the dignity and greatness necessary to true tragedy. He is unable, as Mr. Krutch says, to "tell the tales of the fall of noble men, because we do not believe that noble men exist." Against this proposition it must be permissible to expostulate. Are we to receive this universal negative as a scientific finding of the modern sociologist or the modern psychologist? Is this desperate generalization now become an obligatory creed? Is it the truth that "all contemporary minds" feel "that man is relatively trivial"? Our dramatists themselves might possibly have seen not so long ago some commonplace sewing-machine salesman (let us say) descend from the skies over Normandy and with his fellow troopers do heroic battle like the heroes of old. They have greater opportunity, if they can use it, to observe nobility and heroism in other commonplace people less spectacularly employed. It seems a very heavy ideology, indeed, that so dehumanizes a creative artist as to blind him to the very humanity which it is his mission to interpret. Mr. Krutch, like others afflicted with the "modern temper," falls back upon the cosmos as the explanation. "Our cosmos," he says, "may be farcical or it may be pathetic, but it has not the dignity of tragedy and we cannot accept it as such." If the humanity of man can be validly dismissed on such a priori grounds, the modern dramatist has of course only one problem to solve: how to utilize the highly developed technical expertness of the modern theater to exploit the meanness and triviality of human life into a box-office success.

Because he chooses such limited contacts with human nature the modern dramatist produces a monotony of effect, tense though his play may be with suspense, which contrasts with the rich and variegated patterns of Shakespeare. As a matter of fact, it could be argued plausibly that Shakespeare was master of all the stock in trade of the modern dramatist, but used it in such a way as to justify Dryden's remark that of all ancients and moderns he had the most comprehensive mind. The tragic street battles in *Romeo and Juliet* take their rise in each case in trivial buffoonery by servants; in such a complex pattern even farce may suddenly take on a serious significance. In *Hamlet* Shakespeare created an atmosphere as depressing as can be found in any modern play; Hamlet speaks of Denmark as a prison, or as an "unweeded garden, things rank and gross infest it merely"; a moral miasma has settled over it, more death-dealing and blinding than a smog. And Hamlet is not incapable of some quite "modern" utterances about the farcical aspects of man. He can observe, for instance, that "we fat all creatures else to fat us, and we fat ourselves for maggots." What modern dramatist wouldn't envy Shakespeare that pitiless cynicism! But in *Hamlet* such moods are passing, mere aspects of a complex personality, falling into their proper place in a larger and nobler view of life. And the modern lament about the indifference of the cosmos to the destinies of men is in fact not something new; on that point the older tragedy anticipated the moderns. What Prossor Hall Frye has observed about Greek tragedy is equally applicable to Shakespeare's: "the tragic qualm is perhaps nothing more or less than a sudden and appalling recognition of our desperate plight in a universe apparently indiscriminate of good and evil as of happiness and misery."

It is because he cherishes so dearly a pinched and starved view of human nature that the modern dramatist finds himself incapable of rising above sordid misery and achieving the truly tragic vision. Mr. Krutch himself gives us a good statement of what is lacking in the moderns. We rise from reading the old tragedy, he says, with a feeling of "elation"; more specifically, the old tragedians understood that "it is only in calamity that the human spirit has the opportunity to reveal itself triumphant over the outward universe which fails to conquer it." The statement needs some minor qualification: the triumph of Othello or King Lear was not primarily over "the outward universe." But some sort of triumph there is in great tragedy, and the audience shares in it. For if the tragic vision is to impress us with a sense of profound loss, it must at the same time bring home to us an equally profound sense of the values without which the loss would not be real. As we participate sympathetically in the tragic role of the hero, we clutch more and more firmly certain values which the action of the play reveals to us as infinitely precious to us as human beings. These values appear concretely in the nobility of the characters, especially in the erring hero, and in a Lear, an Othello, an Oedipus they operate as a redemptive power. Matthew Arnold praised Sophocles for seeing life steadily and seeing it whole. This steady vision led Sophocles to a tragical self-knowledge; and, in the words of Werner Jaeger, "to know oneself is for Sophocles to know man's powerlessness; but it is also to know the indestructible and conquering majesty of suffering humanity." Perhaps no Greek drama impresses a modern reader more profoundly and powerfully than Sophocles' treatment of the Oedipus story, in spite of its oracle and sphinx and gods. Oedipus found himself unwittingly guilty of patricide and incest.

When he is forced to acknowledge his guilt, he begins his expiation; he blinds himself, wanders many years as an outcast old man, in the deepest misery and agony, his one loyal daughter his only friend and support. But the strength and nobility of his character help him through his long ordeal, and as he ages he grows into a venerable figure. Like Lear, he reaches wisdom through suffering; his nobility is tested by his agony. And therefore even we, moderns as we are, agree that it is right that the gods themselves should at last give Oedipus mysterious release and sepulture. "No mortal eye," says Jaeger, a modern interpreter, "may see the mystery; only he who is consecrated by suffering may take part in it. Hallowed by pain, Oedipus is in some mysterious way brought near to divinity: his agonies have set him apart from other men. Now he rests on the hill of Colonus, in the poet's own dear homeland, in the eternally green grove of the Kind Spirits where the nightingale sings from the branches. No human foot may tread in that place, but from it there goes out a blessing over all the land of Attica."

Is it possible for the modern world to produce great tragic drama? No doubt it is, if dramatists with sufficient ability will give up their a priori inhibitions and see human nature steadily and see it whole. If they can do that, they will find a large and receptive audience awaiting them.

TRAGEDY AND THE COMMON MAN

Arthur Miller

In this age few tragedies are written. It has often been held that the lack is due to a paucity of heroes among us, or else that modern man has had the blood drawn out of his organs of belief by the skepticism of science, and the heroic attack on life cannot feed on an attitude of reserve and circumspection. For one reason or another, we are often held to be below tragedy—or tragedy above us. The inevitable conclusion is, of course, that the tragic mode is archaic, fit only for the very highly placed, the kings or the kingly, and where this admission is not made in so many words it is most often implied.

I believe that the common man is as apt a subject for tragedy in its highest sense as kings were. On the face of it this ought to be obvious in the light of modern psychiatry, which bases its analysis upon classific formulations, such as the Oedipus and Orestes complexes, for instance, which were enacted by royal beings, but which apply to everyone in similar emotional situations.

More simply, when the question of tragedy in art is not at issue, we never hesitate to attribute to the well-placed and the exalted the very same mental processes as the lowly. And finally, if the exaltation of tragic action were truly a property of the high-bred character alone, it is inconceivable that the mass of mankind should cherish tragedy above all other forms, let alone be capable of understanding it.

As a general rule, to which there may be exceptions unknown to me, I think the tragic feeling is evoked in us when we are in the presence of a character who is ready to lay down his life, if need be, to secure one thing—his sense of personal dignity. From Orestes to Hamlet, Medea to Macbeth, the underlying struggle is that of the individual attempting to gain his "rightful" position in his society.

Sometimes he is one who has been displaced from it, sometimes one who seeks to attain it for the first time, but the fateful wound from which the inevitable events spiral is the wound of indignity, and its dominant force is indignation. Tragedy, then, is the consequence of a man's total compulsion to evaluate himself justly.

In the sense of having been initiated by the hero himself, the tale always reveals what has been called his "tragic flaw," a failing that is not peculiar to grand or elevated characters. Nor is it necessarily a weakness. The flaw, or crack in the character, is really nothing—and need be nothing —but his inherent unwillingness to remain passive in the face of what he conceives to be a challenge to his dignity, his image of his rightful status. Only the passive, only those who accept their lot without active retaliation, are "flawless." Most of us are in that category.

But there are among us today, as there always have been, those who act against the scheme of things that degrades them, and in the process of action, everything we have accepted out of fear or insensitivity or ignorance is shaken before us and examined, and from this total onslaught by an individual against the seemingly stable cosmos surrounding us—from this total examination of the "unchangeable" environment—comes the terror and the fear that is classically associated with tragedy.

More important, from this total questioning of what has been previously unquestioned, we learn. And such a process is not beyond the common man. In revolutions around the world, these past thirty years, he has demonstrated again and again this inner dynamic of all tragedy.

Insistence upon the rank of the tragic hero, or the so-called nobility of his character, is really but a clinging to the outward forms of tragedy. If rank or nobility of character was indispensable, then it would follow that the problems of those with rank were the particular problems of tragedy. But surely the right of one monarch to capture the domain from another no longer raises our passions, nor are our concepts of justice what they were to the mind of an Elizabethan king.

The quality in such plays that does shake us, however, derives from the underlying fear of being displaced, the disaster inherent in being torn away from our chosen image of what and who we are in this world. Among us today this fear is as strong, and perhaps stronger, than it ever was. In fact, it is the common man who knows this fear best.

Now, if it is true that tragedy is the consequence of a man's total compulsion to evaluate himself justly, his destruction in the attempt posits a wrong or an evil in his environment. And this is precisely the morality of tragedy and its lesson. The discovery of the moral law, which is what the enlightenment of tragedy consists of, is not the discovery of some abstract or metaphysical quantity.

The tragic right is a condition of life, a condition in which the human personality is able to flower and realize itself. The wrong is the condition which suppresses man, perverts the flowing out of his love and creative instinct. Tragedy enlightens—and it must, in that it points the heroic finger at the enemy of man's freedom. The thrust for freedom is the quality in tragedy which exalts. The revolutionary questioning of the stable environment is what terrifies. In no way is the common man debarred from such thoughts or such actions.

Seen in this light, our lack of tragedy may be partially accounted for by the turn which modern literature has taken toward the purely psychiatric view of life, or the purely sociological. If all our miseries, our indignities, are born and bred within our minds, then all action, let alone the heroic action, is obviously impossible.

And if society alone is responsible for the cramping of our lives, then the protagonist must needs be so pure and faultless as to force us to deny his validity as a character. From neither of these views can tragedy derive, simply because neither represents a balanced concept of life. Above all else, tragedy requires the finest appreciation by the writer of cause and effect.

No tragedy can therefore come about when its author fears to question absolutely everything, when he regards any institution, habit or custom as being either everlasting, immutable or inevitable. In the tragic view the need of man to wholly realize himself is the only fixed star, and whatever it is that hedges his nature and lowers it is ripe for attack and examination. Which is not to say that tragedy must preach revolution.

The Greeks could probe the very heavenly origin of their ways and return to confirm the rightness of laws. And Job could face God in anger, demanding his right, and end in submission. But for a moment everything is in suspension, nothing is accepted, and in this stretching and tearing apart of the cosmos, in the very action of so doing, the character gains "size," the tragic stature which is spuriously attached to the royal or the high born in our minds. The commonest of men may take on that stature to the extent of his willingness to throw all he has into the contest, the battle to secure his rightful place in his world.

There is a misconception of tragedy with which I have been struck in review after review, and in many conversations with writers and readers alike. It is the idea that tragedy is of necessity allied to pessimism. Even the dictionary says nothing more about the word than that it means a story with a sad or unhappy ending. This impression is so firmly fixed that I almost hesitate to claim that in truth tragedy implies more optimism in its author than does comedy, and that its final result ought to be the reinforcement of the onlooker's brightest opinions of the human animal.

For, if it is true to say that in essence the tragic hero is intent upon claiming his whole due as a personality, and if this struggle must be total and without reservation, then it automatically demonstrates the indestructible will of man to achieve his humanity.

The possibility of victory must be there in tragedy. Where pathos rules, where pathos is finally derived, a character has fought a battle he could not possibly have won. The pathetic is achieved when the protagonist is, by virtue of his witlessness, his insensitivity, or the very air he gives off, incapable of grappling with a much superior force.

Pathos truly is the mode for the pessimist. But tragedy requires a nicer balance between what is possible and what is impossible. And it is curious, although edifying, that the plays we revere, century after century, are the tragedies. In them, and in them alone, lies the belief—optimistic, if you will—in the perfectibility of man.

It is time, I think, that we who are without kings, took up this bright thread of our history and followed it to the only place it can possibly lead in our time—the heart and spirit of the average man.

No subsequent tragedy can match for terror the story of Oedipus, tyrant of Thebes, a tale of murder, incest, suicide, and self-mutilation. Writing in post-Periclean Athens, Sophocles used the story not for its suspense or melodramatic excitement—the story was already universally known—but to "imitate" the actions of men grown proud. Oedipus' pride arose from his belief that human knowledge could not only measure the ways of men, but also probe the secrets of the universe; that men could not only master the riddles of Nature, but also direct their own destinies. Driven by the oracle of Apollo, Oedipus undertakes to discover and expel the polluter of plague-ridden Thebes and thus to free his city; his quest leads first to self-discovery, and then to self-destruction. However, reading *Oedipus* does not leave us with the feeling that ignorance is preferable to knowledge, nor even that self-knowledge leads necessarily to self-destruction. Sophocles is not simply antirationalist. He does, however, create a world that suggests the limits of man's rational capacity. What Oedipus learns from his travail is that man is not the measure of all things; above all, that he is not the measurer of the gods. Parricide, lover of his mother, brother to his own children, over-proud ruler, and a man blindest in his clearest visions, Oedipus nevertheless achieves magnificence of stature. For what is measured in this play is the greatness of his soul; despite his pride, his ambition, and his impetuosity, greatness of soul emerges as the crowning attribute of the Theban tyrant; he is the proper measure of what man may become.

Yet Sophocles does not exalt either Oedipus or man. Perhaps even more important for understanding this tragedy, Sophocles does not tell a story of human error, of a man who simply makes the wrong choice. Oedipus *has* no choice—except to be Oedipus. To be Oedipus is to be man of knowledge and power; in a word, to be singled out from ordinary men. To be Oedipus is to be exposed to forces no man can contend with successfully. Such forces, in Sophocles' view, dominate the universe; confronting them, man can either hide and shrink back to mediocrity, or stand forth, achieve greatness, but also be destroyed. These are the only alternatives. Oedipus is offered no choice between good acts and evil; in spite of his tendency to rash acts and words, he is always seen undertaking good, or at least justifiable, deeds. The deeds themselves fail; and in the end it is only Oedipus' spirit, symbolic of human endurance, that gives them meaning.

Central to any discussion of this drama are the conditions that limit Oedipus the man. First, it is not he who calls down the curse the operation of which we see acted out; he is only its instrument, the son fated to kill his father and mate with his mother. Second, though Oedipus is distinguished among men by his knowledge and power, his name begins as a synonym for lameness and ends as a symbol for human blindness. Finally, though the tyrant is destroyed, the man lives on; the human spirit endures. Indeed, many years later Sophocles, in a sequel (*Oedipus at Colonnus*), portrayed the admission of this greatest of heroes—though not a god—to the company of the gods themselves.

These conditions define Oedipus' tragic situation; they suggest further the vision that underlies all tragedy: the paradox that man, who is so clearly suited to enjoy the fruits of this earth, who touches sublimity in action as well as in thought, is nevertheless hedged in, is ultimately subservient, and in the end must surrender his life for the possession of those very things that make his life meaningful.

OEDIPUS REX

Sophocles

Translated by
Dudley Fitts and Robert Fitzgerald

OEDIPUS
A PRIEST
CREON
TEIRESIAS
IOCASTE

MESSENGER
SHEPHERD OF LAIOS
SECOND MESSENGER
CHORUS OF THEBAN ELDERS

THE SCENE. *Before the palace of Oedipus, King of Thebes. A central door and two lateral doors open onto a platform which runs the length of the façade. On the platform, right and left, are altars; and three steps lead down into the* orchestra, *or chorus-ground.*

The steps are crowded by suppliants who have brought branches and chaplets of olive leaves and who lie in various attitudes of despair. OEDIPUS *enters.*

OEDIPUS. My children, generations of the living
In the line of Kadmos, nursed at his ancient hearth:
Why have you strewn yourselves before these altars
In supplication, with your boughs and garlands?
The breath of incense rises from the city
With a sound of prayer and lamentation.
                              Children,
I would not have you speak through messengers,
And therefore I have come myself to hear you—
I, Oedipus, who bear the famous name.
[*To a* PRIEST.] You, there, since you are eldest in the company,
Speak for them all, tell me what preys upon you,
Whether you come in dread, or crave some blessing:
Tell me, and never doubt that I will help you
In every way I can; I should be heartless
Were I not moved to find you suppliant here.
PRIEST. Great Oedipus, O powerful King of Thebes!

You see how all the ages of our people
Cling to your altar steps: here are boys
Who can barely stand alone, and here
  are priests
By weight of age, as I am a priest of God,
And young men chosen from those yet
  unmarried;
As for the others, all that multitude,
They wait with olive chaplets in the
  squares,
At the two shrines of Pallas, and where
  Apollo
Speaks in the glowing embers.
                              Your own eyes
Must tell you: Thebes is in her extremity
And can not lift her head from the surge
  of death.
A rust consumes the buds and fruits of
  the earth;
The herds are sick; children die unborn,
And labor is vain. The god of plague
  and pyre
Raids like detestable lightning through
  the city,
And all the house of Kadmos is laid
  waste,
All emptied, and all darkened: Death
  alone
Battens upon the misery of Thebes.
You are not one of the immortal gods,
  we know;
Yet we have come to you to make our
  prayer
As to the man of all men best in adversity
And wisest in the ways of God. You
  saved us
From the Sphinx, that flinty singer, and
  the tribute
We paid to her so long; yet you were
  never
Better informed than we, nor could we
  teach you:
It was some god breathed in you to set
  us free.
Therefore, O mighty King, we turn to
  you:
Find us our safety, find us a remedy,
Whether by counsel of the gods or men.
A king of wisdom tested in the past
Can act in a time of troubles, and act
  well.

Noblest of men, restore
Life to your city! Think how all men
  call you
Liberator for your triumph long ago;
Ah, when your years of kingship are
  remembered,
Let them not say *We rose, but later fell*—
Keep the State from going down in the
  storm!
Once, years ago, with happy augury,
You brought us fortune; be the same
  again!
No man questions your power to rule
  the land:
But rule over men, not over a dead city!
Ships are only hulls, citadels are nothing,
When no life moves in the empty pas-
  sageways.

OEDIPUS. Poor children! You may be sure
  I know
All that you longed for in your coming
  here.
I know that you are deathly sick; and yet,
Sick as you are, not one is as sick as I.
Each of you suffers in himself alone
His anguish, not another's; but my spirit
Groans for the city, for myself, for you.
  I was not sleeping, you are not waking
  me.
No, I have been in tears for a long while
And in my restless thought walked many
  ways.
In all my search, I found one helpful
  course,
And that I have taken: I have sent Creon,
Son of Menoikeus, brother of the Queen,
To Delphi, Apollo's place of revelation,
To learn there, if he can,
What act or pledge of mine may save
  the city.
I have counted the days, and now, this
  very day,
I am troubled, for he has overstayed
  his time.
What is he doing? He has been gone
  too long.
Yet whenever he comes back, I should
  do ill
To scant whatever hint the god may give.

PRIEST. It is a timely promise. At this instant
They tell me Creon is here.

OEDIPUS.   O Lord Apollo!
May his news be fair as his face is radiant!
PRIEST. It could not be otherwise: he is
crowned with bay,
The chaplet is thick with berries.
OEDIPUS.   We shall soon know;
He is near enough to hear us now.
                    [*Enter* CREON.]
                                O Prince:
Brother: son of Menoikeus:
What answer do you bring us from the
god?
CREON. It is favorable. I can tell you, great
afflictions
Will turn out well, if they are taken well.
OEDIPUS. What was the oracle? These vague
words
Leave me still hanging between hope
and fear.
CREON. Is it your pleasure to hear me with
all these
Gathered around us? I am prepared to
speak,
But should we not go in?
OEDIPUS.   Let them all hear it.
It is for them I suffer, more than for
myself.
CREON. Then I will tell you what I heard
at Delphi.
In plain words
The god commands us to expel from the
land of Thebes
An old defilement that it seems we shelter.
It is a deathly thing, beyond expiation.
We must not let it feed upon us longer.
OEDIPUS. What defilement? How shall we
rid ourselves of it?
CREON. By exile or death, blood for blood.
It was
Murder that brought the plague-wind on
the city.
OEDIPUS. Murder of whom? Surely the god
has named him?
CREON. My lord: long ago Laïos was our
king,
Before you came to govern us.
OEDIPUS.   I know;
I learned of him from others; I never
saw him.
CREON. He was murdered; and Apollo
commands us now

To take revenge upon whoever killed
him.
OEDIPUS. Upon whom? Where are they?
Where shall we find a clue
To solve that crime, after so many years?
CREON. Here in this land, he said. If we
make enquiry,
We may touch things that otherwise
escape us.
OEDIPUS. Tell me: Was Laïos murdered in
his house,
Or in the fields, or in some foreign coun-
try?
CREON. He said he planned to make a pil-
grimage.
He did not come home again.
OEDIPUS. And was there no one,
No witness, no companion, to tell what
happened?
CREON. They were all killed but one, and
he got away
So frightened that he could remember
one thing only.
OEDIPUS. What was that one thing? One
may be the key
To everything, if we resolve to use it.
CREON. He said that a band of highwaymen
attacked them,
Outnumbered them, and overwhelmed
the King.
OEDIPUS. Strange, that a highwayman
should be so daring—
Unless some faction here bribed him to
do it.
CREON. We thought of that. But after Laïos'
death
New troubles arose and we had no
avenger.
OEDIPUS. What troubles could prevent your
hunting down the killers?
CREON. The riddling Sphinx's song
Made us deaf to all mysteries but her own.
OEDIPUS. Then once more I must bring what
is dark to light.
It is most fitting that Apollo shows,
As you do, this compunction for the dead.
You shall see how I stand by you, as
I should,
To avenge the city and the city's god,
And not as though it were for some
distant friend,

But for my own sake, to be rid of evil.
Whoever killed King Laïos might—who
  knows?—
Decide at any moment to kill me as well.
By avenging the murdered king I protect
  myself.
Come, then, my children: leave the altar
  steps,
Lift up your olive boughs!
                          One of you go
And summon the people of Kadmos to
  gather here.
I will do all that I can; you may tell them
  that. [*Exit a* PAGE.]
So, with the help of God,
We shall be saved—or else indeed we are
  lost.

PRIEST. Let us rise, children. It was for this
  we came,
And now the King has promised it himself.
Phoibos has sent us an oracle; may he
  descend
Himself to save us and drive out the
  plague.
  [*Exeunt* OEDIPUS *and* CREON *into the
  palace by the central door. The* PRIEST
  and the SUPPLIANTS *disperse R and L.
  After a short pause the* CHORUS *enters
  the* orchestra.]

CHORUS. What is the god singing in his
  profound
Delphi of gold and shadow?
What oracle for Thebes, the sunwhipped
  city?
Fear unjoints me, the roots of my heart
  tremble.
Now I remember, O Healer, your power,
  and wonder:
Will you send doom like a sudden cloud,
  or weave it
Like nightfall of the past?
Ah no: be merciful, issue of holy sound:
Dearest to our expectancy: be tender!
Let me pray to Athenê, the immortal
  daughter of Zeus,
And to Artemis her sister
Who keeps her famous throne in the
  market ring,
And to Apollo, bowman at the far butts
  of heaven—

O gods, descend! Like three streams
  leap against
The fires of our grief, the fires of dark-
  ness;
Be swift to bring us rest!
  As in the old time from the brilliant
  house
Of air you stepped to save us, come
  again!
Now our afflictions have no end,
Now all our stricken host lies down
And no man fights off death with his
  mind;
  The noble plowland bears no grain,
And groaning mothers can not bear—
  See, how our lives like birds take wing,
Like sparks that fly when a fire soars,
To the shore of the god of evening.
  The plague burns on, it is pitiless,
Though pallid children laden with death
Lie unwept in the stony ways,
  And old gray women by every path
Flock to the strand about the altars
There to strike their breasts and cry
Worship of Zeus in wailing prayers:
Be kind, God's golden child!
There are no swords in this attack by fire,
No shields, but we are ringed with cries.
  Send the besieger plunging from our
  homes
Into the vast sea-room of the Atlantic
Or into the waves that foam eastward of
  Thrace—
  For the day ravages what the night
  spares—
  Destroy our enemy, lord of the thunder!
Let him be riven by lightning from
  heaven!
  Phoibos Apollo, stretch the sun's bow-
  string,
That golden cord, until it sing for us,
Flashing arrows in heaven!
                          Artemis, Huntress,
Race with flaring lights upon our moun-
  tains!
  O scarlet god, O golden-banded brow,
O Theban Bacchos in a storm of Maenads,
[*Enter* OEDIPUS, *from the palace.*]
  Whirl upon Death, that all the Undy-
  ing hate!
Come with blinding cressets, come in joy!

OEDIPUS. Is this your prayer? It may be answered. Come,

Listen to me, act as the crisis demands,

And you shall have relief from all these evils.

Until now I was a stranger to this tale,

As I had been a stranger to the crime.

Could I track down the murderer without a clue?

But now, friends,

As one who became a citizen after the murder,

I make this proclamation to all Thebans:

If any man knows by whose hand Laïos, son of Labdakos,

Met his death, I direct that man to tell me everything,

No matter what he fears for having so long withheld it.

Let it stand as promised that no further trouble

Will come to him, but he may leave the land in safety.

Moreover: If anyone knows the murderer to be foreign,

Let him not keep silent: he shall have his reward from me.

However, if he does conceal it; if any man

Fearing for his friend or for himself disobeys this edict,

Hear what I propose to do:

I solemnly forbid the people of this country,

Where power and throne are mine, ever to receive that man

Or speak to him, no matter who he is, or let him

Join in sacrifice, lustration, or in prayer.

I decree that he be driven from every house,

Being, as he is, corruption itself to us: the Delphic

Voice of Zeus has pronounced this revelation.

Thus I associate myself with the oracle

And take the side of the murdered king.

As for the criminal, I pray to God—

Whether it be a lurking thief, or one of a number—

I pray that that man's life be consumed in evil and wretchedness.

And as for me, this curse applies no less

If it should turn out that the culprit is my guest here,

Sharing my hearth.

        You have heard the penalty.

I lay it on you now to attend to this

For my sake, for Apollo's, for the sick

Sterile city that heaven has abandoned.

Suppose the oracle had given you no command:

Should this defilement go uncleansed for ever?

You should have found the murderer: your king,

A noble king, had been destroyed!

           Now I,

Having the power that he held before me,

Having his bed, begetting children there

Upon his wife, as he would have, had he lived—

Their son would have been my children's brother

If Laïos had had luck in fatherhood!

(But surely ill luck rushed upon his reign)—

I say I take the son's part, just as though

I were his son, to press the fight for him

And see it won! I'll find the hand that brought

Death to Labdakos' and Polydoros' child,

Heir of Kadmos' and Agenor's line.

And as for those who fail me,

May the gods deny them the fruit of the earth,

Fruit of the womb, and may they rot utterly!

Let them be wretched as we are wretched, and worse!

For you, for loyal Thebans, and for all

Who find my actions right, I pray the favor

Of justice, and of all the immortal gods.

CHORAGOS. Since I am under oath, my lord, I swear

I did not do the murder, I can not name

The murderer. Might not the oracle

That has ordained the search tell where to find him?

OEDIPUS. An honest question. But no man in the world

Can make the gods do more than the gods will.

CHORAGOS. There is one last expedient—

OEDIPUS.   Tell me what it is.
Though it seem slight, you must not hold it back.

CHORAGOS. A lord clairvoyant to the lord Apollo,
As we all know, is the skilled Teiresias.
One might learn much about this from him, Oedipus.

OEDIPUS. I am not wasting time:
Creon spoke of this, and I have sent for him—
Twice, in fact; it is strange that he is not here.

CHORAGOS. The other matter—that old report—seems useless.

OEDIPUS. Tell me. I am interested in all reports.

CHORAGOS. The King was said to have been killed by highwaymen.

OEDIPUS. I know. But we have no witnesses to that.

CHORAGOS. If the killer can feel a particle of dread,
Your curse will bring him out of hiding!

OEDIPUS.   No.
The man who dared that act will fear no curse.

[*Enter the blind seer* TEIRESIAS, *led by a* PAGE.]

CHORAGOS. But there is one man who may detect the criminal.
This is Teiresias, this is the holy prophet
In whom, alone of all men, truth was born.

OEDIPUS. Teiresias: seer: student of mysteries,
Of all that's taught and all that no man tells,
Secrets of Heaven and secrets of the earth:
Blind though you are, you know the city lies
Sick with plague; and from this plague, my lord,
We find that you alone can guard or save us.
Possibly you did not hear the messengers?
Apollo, when we sent to him,
Sent us back word that this great pestilence

Would lift, but only if we established clearly
The identity of those who murdered Laïos.
They must be killed or exiled.
                                              Can you use
Birdflight or any art of divination
To purify yourself, and Thebes, and me
From this contagion? We are in your hands.
There is no fairer duty
Than that of helping others in distress.

TEIRESIAS. How dreadful knowledge of the truth can be
When there's no help in truth! I knew this well,
But did not act on it: else I should not have come.

OEDIPUS. What is troubling you? Why are your eyes so cold?

TEIRESIAS. Let me go home. Bear your own fate, and I'll
Bear mine. It is better so: trust what I say.

OEDIPUS. What you say is ungracious and unhelpful
To your native country. Do not refuse to speak.

TEIRESIAS. When it comes to speech, your own is neither temperate
Nor opportune. I wish to be more prudent.

OEDIPUS. In God's name, we all beg you—

TEIRESIAS.   You are all ignorant.
No; I will never tell you what I know.
Now it is my misery; then, it would be yours.

OEDIPUS. What! You do know something, and will not tell us?
You would betray us all and wreck the State?

TEIRESIAS. I do not intend to torture myself, or you.
Why persist in asking? You will not persuade me.

OEDIPUS. What a wicked old man you are! You'd try a stone's
Patience! Out with it! Have you no feeling at all?

TEIRESIAS. You call me unfeeling. If you could only see
The nature of your own feelings . . .

OEDIPUS.   Why,
Who would not feel as I do? Who could
endure
Your arrogance toward the city?

TEIRESIAS.   What does it matter!
Whether I speak or not, it is bound to
come.

OEDIPUS. Then, if "it" is bound to come,
you are bound to tell me.

TEIRESIAS. No, I will not go on. Rage as
you please.

OEDIPUS. Rage? Why not!
                And I'll tell you what I think:
You planned it, you had it done, you
all but
Killed him with your own hands: if you
had eyes,
I'd say the crime was yours, and yours
alone.

TEIRESIAS. So? I charge you, then,
Abide by the proclamation you have
made:
From this day forth
Never speak again to these men or to me;
You yourself are the pollution of this
country.

OEDIPUS. You dare say that! Can you possibly think you have
Some way of going free, after such insolence?

TEIRESIAS. I have gone free. It is the truth
sustains me.

OEDIPUS. Who taught you shamelessness?
It was not your craft.

TEIRESIAS. You did. You made me speak.
I did not want to.

OEDIPUS. Speak what? Let me hear it again
more clearly.

TEIRESIAS. Was it not clear before? Are you
tempting me?

OEDIPUS. I did not understand it. Say it
again.

TEIRESIAS. I say that you are the murderer
whom you seek.

OEDIPUS. Now twice you have spat out
infamy. You'll pay for it!

TEIRESIAS. Would you care for more? Do
you wish to be really angry?

OEDIPUS. Say what you will. Whatever you
say is worthless.

TEIRESIAS. I say that you live in hideous
love with her
Who is nearest you in blood. You are
blind to the evil.

OEDIPUS. It seems you can go on mouthing
like this for ever.

TEIRESIAS. I can, if there is power in truth.

OEDIPUS.   There is:
But not for you, not for you,
You sightless, witless, senseless, mad old
man!

TEIRESIAS. You are the madman. There is
no one here
Who will not curse you soon, as you
curse me.

OEDIPUS. You child of endless night! You
cannot hurt me
Or any other man who sees the sun.

TEIRESIAS. True: it is not from me your
fate will come.
That lies within Apollo's competence,
As it is his concern.

OEDIPUS.   Tell me:
Are you speaking for Creon, or for
yourself?

TEIRESIAS. Creon is no threat. You weave
your own doom.

OEDIPUS. Wealth, power, craft of states-
manship!
Kingly position, everywhere admired!
What savage envy is stored up against
these,
If Creon, whom I trusted, Creon my
friend,
For this great office which the city once
Put in my hands unsought—if for this
power
Creon desires in secret to destroy me!
He has bought this decrepit fortune-
teller, this
Collector of dirty pennies, this prophet
fraud—
Why, he is no more clairvoyant than
I am!
                                Tell us:
Has your mystic mummery ever ap-
proached the truth?
When that hellcat the Sphinx was per-
forming here,
What help were you to these people?

Her magic was not for the first man who
  came along:
It demanded a real exorcist. Your birds—
What good were they? or the gods, for
  the matter of that?
But I came by,
Oedipus, the simple man, who knows
  nothing—
I thought it out for myself, no birds
  helped me!
And this is the man you think you can
  destroy,
That you may be close to Creon when
  he's king!
Well, you and your friend Creon, it seems
  to me,
Will suffer most. If you were not an old
  man,
You would have paid already for your
  plot.

CHORAGOS. We cannot see that his words
  or yours
Have been spoken except in anger, Oedi-
  pus,
And of anger we have no need. How can
  God's will
Be accomplished best? That is what most
  concerns us.

TEIRESIAS. You are a king. But where ar-
  gument's concerned
I am your man, as much a king as you.
I am not your servant, but Apollo's.
I have no need of Creon to speak for me.
  Listen to me. You mock my blindness,
  do you?
But I say that you, with both your eyes,
  are blind:
You can not see the wretchedness of
  your life,
Nor in whose house you live, no, nor
  with whom.
Who are your father and mother? Can
  you tell me?
You do not even know the blind wrongs
That you have done them, on earth and
  in the world below.
But the double lash of your parents' curse
  will whip you
Out of this land some day, with only
  night
Upon your precious eyes.

Your cries then—where will they not be
  heard?
What fastness of Kithairon will not
  echo them?
And that bridal-descant of yours—you'll
  know it then,
The song they sang when you came here
  to Thebes
And found your misguided berthing.
All this, and more, that you can not
  guess at now,
Will bring you to yourself among your
  children.
  Be angry, then. Curse Creon. Curse
  my words.
I tell you, no man that walks upon the
  earth
Shall be rooted out more horribly than
  you.

OEDIPUS. Am I to bear this from him?—
  Damnation
Take you! Out of this place! Out of
  my sight!

TEIRESIAS. I would not have come at all if
  you had not asked me.

OEDIPUS. Could I have told that you'd talk
  nonsense, that
You'd come here to make a fool of yourself, and of me?

TEIRESIAS. A fool? Your parents thought me
  sane enough.

OEDIPUS. My parents again!—Wait: who
  were my parents?

TEIRESIAS. This day will give you a father,
  and break your heart.

OEDIPUS. Your infantile riddles! Your
  damned abracadabra!

TEIRESIAS. You were a great man once at
  solving riddles.

OEDIPUS. Mock me with that if you like;
  you will find it true.

TEIRESIAS. It was true enough. It brought
  about your ruin.

OEDIPUS. But if it saved this town?

TEIRESIAS. [To the PAGE.] Boy, give me
  your hand.

OEDIPUS. Yes, boy; lead him away.
                              —While you are here
  We can do nothing. Go; leave us in peace.

TEIRESIAS. I will go when I have said what
  I have to say.

How can you hurt me? And I tell you
     again:
The man you have been looking for all
     this time,
The damned man, the murderer of Laïos,
That man is in Thebes. To your mind he
     is foreign-born,
But it will soon be shown that he is a
     Theban,
A revelation that will fail to please.
                              A blind man,
Who has his eyes now; a penniless man,
     who is rich now;
And he will go tapping the strange earth
     with his staff.
To the children with whom he lives now
     he will be
Brother and father—the very same; to her
Who bore him, son and husband—the
     very same
Who came to his father's bed, wet with
     his father's blood.
     Enough. Go think that over.
If later you find error in what I have said,
You may say that I have no skill in
     prophecy.

          [*Exit* TEIRESIAS, *led by his* PAGE.
          OEDIPUS *goes into the palace.*]

CHORUS. The Delphic stone of prophecies
     Remembers ancient regicide
     And a still bloody hand.
     That killer's hour of flight has come.
     He must be stronger than riderless
     Coursers of untiring wind,
     For the son of Zeus armed with his
          father's thunder
     Leaps in lightning after him;
     And the Furies follow him, the sad
          Furies.
     Holy Parnassos' peak of snow
     Flashes and blinds that secret man,
     That all shall hunt him down:
     Though he may roam the forest shade
     Like a bull gone wild from pasture
     To rage through glooms of stone.
     Doom comes down on him; flight will
          not avail him;
     For the world's heart calls him desolate,
     And the immortal Furies follow, for-
          ever follow.
     But now a wilder thing is heard

From the old man skilled at hearing Fate
     in the wingbeat of a bird.
Bewildered as a blown bird, my soul
     hovers and can not find
Foothold in this debate, or any reason or
     rest of mind.
But no man ever brought—none can
     bring
Proof of strife between Thebes' royal
     house,
Labdakos' line, and the son of Polybos;
And never until now has any man brought
     word
Of Laïos' dark death staining Oedipus the
     King.
Divine Zeus and Apollo hold
Perfect intelligence alone of all tales
     ever told;
And well though this diviner works, he
     works in his own night;
No man can judge that rough unknown
     or trust in second sight,
For wisdom changes hands among the wise.
Shall I believe my great lord criminal
At a raging word that a blind old man
     let fall?
I saw him, when the carrion woman faced
     him of old,
Prove his heroic mind! These evil words
     are lies.

CREON. Men of Thebes:
     I am told that heavy accusations
     Have been brought against me by King
          Oedipus.
          I am not the kind of man to bear this
               tamely.
          If in these present difficulties
     He holds me accountable for any harm
          to him
     Through anything I have said or done—
          why, then,
     I do not value life in this dishonor.
     It is not as though this rumor touched
          upon
     Some private indiscretion. The matter is
          grave.
     The fact is that I am being called disloyal
     To the State, to my fellow citizens, to
          my friends.
CHORAGOS. He may have spoken in anger,
     not from his mind.

CREON. But did you not hear him say I was
the one
Who seduced the old prophet into lying?
CHORAGOS. The thing was said; I do not
know how seriously.
CREON. But you were watching him! Were
his eyes steady?
Did he look like a man in his right mind?
CHORAGOS.   I do not know.
I can not judge the behavior of great men.
But here is the King himself.
[*Enter* OEDIPUS.]
OEDIPUS.   So you dared come back.
Why? How brazen of you to come to
my house,
You murderer!
                       Do you think I do not know
That you plotted to kill me, plotted to
steal my throne?
Tell me, in God's name: am I coward,
a fool,
That you should dream you could ac-
complish this?
A fool who could not see your slippery
game?
A coward, not to fight back when I saw
it?
You are the fool, Creon, are you not?
hoping
Without support or friends to get a
throne?
Thrones may be won or bought: you
could do neither.
CREON. Now listen to me. You have talked;
let me talk, too.
You can not judge unless you know
the facts.
OEDIPUS. You speak well: there is one fact;
but I find it hard
To learn from the deadliest enemy I have.
CREON. That above all I must dispute with
you.
OEDIPUS. That above all I will not hear
you deny.
CREON. If you think there is anything good
in being stubborn
Against all reason, then I say you are
wrong.
OEDIPUS. If you think a man can sin against
his own kind

And not be punished for it, I say you are
mad.
CREON. I agree. But tell me: what have
I done to you?
OEDIPUS. You advised me to send for that
wizard, did you not?
CREON. I did. I should do it again.
OEDIPUS.   Very well. Now tell me:
How long has it been since Laïos—
CREON.   What of Laïos?
OEDIPUS. Since he vanished in that onset by
the road?
CREON. It was long ago, a long time.
OEDIPUS.   And this prophet,
Was he practicing here then?
CREON. He was; and with honor, as now.
OEDIPUS. Did he speak of me at that time?
CREON.   He never did;
At least, not when I was present.
OEDIPUS.   But . . . the enquiry?
I suppose you held one?
CREON. We did, but we learned nothing.
OEDIPUS. Why did the prophet not speak
against me then?
CREON. I do not know; and I am the kind
of man
Who holds his tongue when he has no
facts to go on.
OEDIPUS. There's one fact that you know,
and you could tell it.
CREON. What fact is that? If I know it, you
shall have it.
OEDIPUS. If he were not involved with you,
he could not say
That it was I who murdered Laïos.
CREON. If he says that, you are the one that
knows it!—
But now it is my turn to question you.
OEDIPUS. Put your questions. I am no mur-
derer.
CREON. First, then: You married my sister?
OEDIPUS.   I married your sister.
CREON. And you rule the kingdom equally
with her?
OEDIPUS. Everything that she wants she has
from me.
CREON. And I am the third, equal to both
of you?
OEDIPUS. That is why I call you a bad
friend.

CREON. No. Reason it out, as I have done.
Think of this first: Would any sane man prefer
Power, with all a king's anxieties,
To that same power and the grace of sleep?
Certainly not I.
I have never longed for the king's power
—only his rights.
Would any wise man differ from me in this?
As matters stand, I have my way in everything
With your consent, and no responsibilities.
If I were king, I should be a slave to policy.
How could I desire a scepter more
Than what is now mine—untroubled influence?
No, I have not gone mad; I need no honors,
Except those with the perquisites I have now.
I am welcome everywhere; every man salutes me,
And those who want your favor seek my ear,
Since I know how to manage what they ask.
Should I exchange this ease for that anxiety?
Besides, no sober mind is treasonable.
I hate anarchy
And never would deal with any man who likes it.
Test what I have said. Go to the priestess
At Delphi, ask if I quoted her correctly.
And as for this other thing: if I am found
Guilty of treason with Teiresias,
Then sentence me to death! You have my word
It is a sentence I should cast my vote for—
But not without evidence!
                        You do wrong
When you take good men for bad, bad men for good.
A true friend thrown aside—why, life itself
Is not more precious!

In time you will know this well:
For time, and time alone, will show the just man,
Though scoundrels are discovered in a day.
CHORAGOS. This is well said, and a prudent man would ponder it.
Judgments too quickly formed are dangerous.
OEDIPUS. But is he not quick in his duplicity?
And shall I not be quick to parry him?
Would you have me stand still, hold my peace, and let
This man win everything, through my inaction?
CREON. And you want—what is it, then? To banish me?
OEDIPUS. No, not exile. It is your death I want,
So that all the world may see what treason means.
CREON. You will persist, then? You will not believe me?
OEDIPUS. How can I believe you?
CREON.   Then you are a fool.
OEDIPUS. To save myself?
CREON.   In justice, think of me.
OEDIPUS. You are evil incarnate.
CREON. But suppose that you are wrong?
OEDIPUS. Still I must rule.
CREON.   But not if you rule badly.
OEDIPUS. O city, city!
CREON.   It is my city, too!
CHORAGOS. Now, my lords, be still. I see the Queen,
Iocastê, coming from her palace chambers;
And it is time she came, for the sake of you both.
This dreadful quarrel can be resolved through her.
                [*Enter* IOCASTE.]
IOCASTE. Poor foolish men, what wicked din is this?
With Thebes sick to death, is it not shameful
That you should rake some private quarrel up?
[*To* OEDIPUS.] Come into the house.
                —And you, Creon, go now:

Let us have no more of this tumult over
  nothing.
CREON. Nothing? No, sister: what your
  husband plans for me
Is one of two great evils: exile or death.
OEDIPUS. He is right.
  Why, woman, I have caught him squarely
  Plotting against my life.
CREON.   No! Let me die
Accurst if ever I have wished you harm!
IOCASTE. Ah, believe it, Oedipus!
  In the name of the gods, respect this
  oath of his
For my sake, for the sake of these people
  here!
CHORAGOS. Open your mind to her, my lord.
  Be ruled by her, I beg you!
OEDIPUS. What would you have me do?
CHORAGOS. Respect Creon's word. He has
  never spoken like a fool,
And now he has sworn an oath.
OEDIPUS.   You know what you ask?
CHORAGOS.   I do.
OEDIPUS.   Speak on, then.
CHORAGOS. A friend so sworn should not
  be baited so,
In blind malice, and without final proof.
OEDIPUS. You are aware, I hope, that what
  you say
Means death for me, or exile at the least.
CHORAGOS. No, I swear by Helios, first in
  Heaven!
May I die friendless and accurst,
The worst of deaths, if ever I meant that!
  It is the withering fields
    That hurt my sick heart:
  Must we bear all these ills,
  And now your bad blood as well?
OEDIPUS. Then let him go. And let me die,
  if I must,
Or be driven by him in shame from the
  land of Thebes.
It is your unhappiness, and not his talk,
That touches me.
                    As for him—
Wherever he is, I will hate him as long
  as I live.
CREON. Ugly in yielding, as you were ugly
  in rage!
Natures like yours chiefly torment them-
  selves.

OEDIPUS. Can you not go? Can you not
  leave me?
CREON.   I can.
  You do not know me; but the city knows
  me,
And in its eyes I am just, if not in yours.
  [Exit CREON.]
CHORAGOS. Lady Iocastê, did you not ask
  the King to go to his chambers?
IOCASTE. First tell me what has happened.
CHORAGOS. There was suspicion without
  evidence; yet it rankled
As even false charges will.
IOCASTE.   On both sides?
CHORAGOS.   On both.
IOCASTE.   But what was said?
CHORAGOS. Oh let it rest, let it be done with!
  Have we not suffered enough?
OEDIPUS. You see to what your decency has
  brought you:
  You have made difficulties where my
  heart saw none.
CHORAGOS. Oedipus, it is not once only
  I have told you—
  You must know I should count myself
  unwise
To the point of madness, should I now
  forsake you—
    You, under whose hand,
      In the storm of another time,
    Our dear land sailed out free.
    But now stand fast at the helm!
IOCASTE. In God's name, Oedipus, inform
  your wife as well:
Why are you so set in this hard anger?
OEDIPUS. I will tell you, for none of these
  men deserves
My confidence as you do. It is Creon's
  work,
His treachery, his plotting against me.
IOCASTE. Go on, if you can make this clear
  to me.
OEDIPUS. He charges me with the murder
  of Laïos.
IOCASTE. Has he some knowledge? Or does
  he speak from hearsay?
OEDIPUS. He would not commit himself to
  such a charge,
But he has brought in that damnable
  soothsayer
To tell his story.

IOCASTE.   Set your mind at rest.
If it is a question of soothsayers, I tell you
That you will find no man whose craft
gives knowledge
Of the unknowable.
                           Here is my proof:
An oracle was reported to Laïos once
(I will not say from Phoibos himself but
from
His appointed ministers, at any rate)
That his doom would be death at the
hands of his own son—
His son, born of his flesh and of mine!
Now, you remember the story: Laïos
was killed
By marauding strangers where three
highways meet;
But his child had not been three days
in this world
Before the King had pierced the baby's
ankles
And had him left to die on a lonely
mountain.
Thus, Apollo never caused that child
To kill his father, and it was not Laïos'
fate
To die at the hands of his son, as he had
feared.
This is what prophets and prophecies are
worth!
Have no dread of them.
                           It is God himself
Who can show us what he wills, in his
own way.
OEDIPUS. How strange a shadowy memory
crossed my mind,
Just now while you were speaking; it
chilled my heart.
IOCASTE. What do you mean? What memory
do you speak of?
OEDIPUS. If I understand you, Laïos was
killed
At a place where three roads meet.
IOCASTE.   So it was said;
We have no later story.
OEDIPUS.   Where did it happen?
IOCASTE. Phokis, it is called: at a place
where the Theban Way
Divides into the roads toward Delphi and
Daulia.
OEDIPUS. When?

IOCASTE. We had the news not long before
you came
And proved the right to your succession
here.
OEDIPUS. Ah, what net has God been weav-
ing for me?
IOCASTE. Oedipus! Why does this trouble
you?
OEDIPUS.   Do not ask me yet.
First, tell me how Laïos looked, and tell
me
How old he was.
IOCASTE.
                    He was tall, his hair just touched
With white; his form was not unlike
your own.
OEDIPUS. I think that I myself may be accurst
By my own ignorant edict.
IOCASTE.   You speak strangely.
It makes me tremble to look at you, my
King.
OEDIPUS. I am not sure that the blind man
can not see.
But I should know better if you were to
tell me—
IOCASTE. Anything—though I dread to hear
you ask it.
OEDIPUS. Was the King lightly escorted, or
did he ride
With a large company, as a ruler should?
IOCASTE. There were five men with him in
all: one was a herald;
And a single chariot, which he was driving.
OEDIPUS. Alas, that makes it plain enough!
                           But who—
Who told you how it happened?
IOCASTE.   A household servant,
The only one to escape.
OEDIPUS.   And is he still
A servant of ours?
IOCASTE. No; for when he came back at
last
And found you enthroned in the place of
the dead king,
He came to me, touched my hand with
his, and begged
That I would send him away to the fron-
tier district
Where only the shepherds go—
As far away from the city as I could send
him.

I granted his prayer; for although the man
was a slave,
He had earned more than this favor at
my hands.

OEDIPUS. Can he be called back quickly?

IOCASTE.   Easily.
But why?

OEDIPUS.
                I have taken too much upon myself
Without enquiry; therefore I wish to
consult him.

IOCASTE. Then he shall come.
                                    But am I not one also
To whom you might confide these fears
of yours?

OEDIPUS. That is your right; it will not be
denied you,
Now least of all; for I have reached a
pitch
Of wild foreboding. Is there anyone
To whom I should sooner speak?
Polybos of Corinth is my father.
My mother is a Dorian: Meropê.
I grew up chief among the men of Corinth
Until a strange thing happened—
Not worth my passion, it may be, but
strange.
            At a feast, a drunken man maundering
in his cups
Cries out that I am not my father's son!
I contained myself that night, though
I felt anger
And a sinking heart. The next day I
visited
My father and mother, and questioned
them. They stormed,
Calling it all the slanderous rant of a
fool;
And this relieved me. Yet the suspicion
Remained always aching in my mind;
I knew there was talk; I could not rest;
And finally, saying nothing to my parents,
I went to the shrine at Delphi.
The god dismissed my question without
reply;
He spoke of other things.
                                    Some were clear,
Full of w.etchedness, dreadful, unbear-
able:
As, that I should lie with my own mother,
breed

Children from whom all men would turn
their eyes;
And that I should be my father's mur-
derer.
            I heard all this, and fled. And from that
day
Corinth to me was only in the stars
Descending in that quarter of the sky,
As I wandered farther and farther on
my way
To a land where I should never see the evil
Sung by the oracle. And I came to this
country
Where, so you say, King Laïos was killed.
I will tell you all that happened there,
my lady.
            There were three highways
Coming together at a place I passed;
And there a herald came towards me,
and a chariot
Drawn by horses, with a man such as
you describe
Seated in it. The groom leading the horses
Forced me off the road at his lord's
command;
But as this charioteer lurched over to-
wards me
I struck him in my rage. The old man
saw me
And brought his double goad down upon
my head
As I came abreast.
                              He was paid back, and more!
Swinging my club in this right hand I
knocked him
Out of his car, and he rolled on the
ground.
                                                I killed him.
I killed them all.
Now if that stranger and Laïos were—kin,
Where is a man more miserable than I?
More hated by the gods? Citizen and
alien alike
Must never shelter me or speak to me—
I must be shunned by all.
                                          And I myself
Pronounced this malediction upon myself!
Think of it: I have touched you with
these hands,
These hands that killed your husband.
What defilement!

Am I all evil, then? It must be so,
Since I must flee from Thebes, yet never
again
See my own countrymen, my own country,
For fear of joining my mother in marriage
And killing Polybos, my father.
                                        Ah,
If I was created so, born to this fate,
Who could deny the savagery of God?
O holy majesty of heavenly powers!
May I never see that day! Never!
Rather let me vanish from the race of
men
Than know the abomination destined me!

CHORAGOS. We too, my lord, have felt
dismay at this.
But there is hope: you have yet to hear
the shepherd.

OEDIPUS. Indeed, I fear no other hope is
left me.

IOCASTE. What do you hope from him when
he comes?

OEDIPUS.   This much:
If his account of the murder tallies with
yours,
Then I am cleared.

IOCASTE.   What was it that I said
Of such importance?

OEDIPUS. Why, "marauders," you said,
Killed the King, according to this man's
story.
If he maintains that still, if there were
several,
Clearly the guilt is not mine: I was alone.
But if he says one man, singlehanded, did
it,
Then the evidence all points to me.

IOCASTE. You may be sure that he said there
were several;
And can he call back that story now?
He can not.
The whole city heard it as plainly as I.
But suppose he alters some detail of it:
He can not ever show that Laïos' death
Fulfilled the oracle: for Apollo said
My child was doomed to kill him; and
my child—
Poor baby!—it was my child that died
first.
No. From now on, where oracles are
concerned,

I would not waste a second thought
on any.

OEDIPUS. You may be right.
                        But come: let someone go
For the shepherd at once. This matter
must be settled.

IOCASTE. I will send for him.
I would not wish to cross you in anything,
And surely not in this.—Let us go in.

[Exeunt into the palace, the CHORUS
                                        remaining.]

CHORUS. Let me be reverent in the ways
of right,
Lowly the paths I journey on;
Let all my words and actions keep
The laws of the pure universe
From highest Heaven handed down.
For Heaven is their bright nurse,
Those generations of the realms of light;
Ah, never of mortal kind were they
begot,
Nor are they slaves of memory, lost in
sleep:
Their Father is greater than Time and
ages not.
    The tyrant is a child of Pride
Who drinks from his great sickening cup
Recklessness and vanity,
Until from his high crest headlong
He plummets to the dust of hope.
That strong man is not strong.
But let no fair ambition be denied;
May God protect the wrestler for the
State
In government, in comely policy,
Who will fear God, and on His ordinance
wait.
    Haughtiness and the high hand of dis-
dain
Tempt and outrage God's holy law;
And any mortal who dares hold
No immortal Power in awe
Will be caught up in a net of pain:
The price for which his levity is sold.
Let each man take due earnings, then,
And keep his hands from holy things,
And from blasphemy stand apart—
Else the crackling blast of heaven
Blows on his head, and on his desperate
heart;
Though fools will honor impious men,

In their cities no tragic poet sings.
    Shall we lose faith in Delphi's obscuri-
    ties,
We who have heard the world's core
Discredited, and the sacred wood
Of Zeus at Elis praised no more?
The deeds and the strange prophecies
Must make a pattern yet to be understood.
Zeus, if indeed you are lord of all,
Throned in light over night and day,
Mirror this in your endless mind:
Our masters call the oracle
Words on the wind, and the Delphic
    vision blind!
Their hearts no longer know Apollo,
And reverence for the gods has died away.

             [*Enter* IOCASTE.]

IOCASTE. Princes of Thebes, it has occurred
    to me
To visit the altars of the gods, bearing
These branches as a suppliant, and this
    incense.
Our King is not himself: his noble soul
Is overwrought with fantasies of dread,
Else he would consider
The new prophecies in the light of the old.
He will listen to any voice that speaks
    disaster,
And my advice goes for nothing.

        [*She approaches the altar.*]

             To you, then, Apollo,
Lycean lord, since you are nearest, I turn
    in prayer.
Receive these offerings, and grant us
    deliverance
From defilement. Our hearts are heavy
    with fear
When we see our leader distracted, as
    helpless sailors
Are terrified by the confusion of their
    helmsman.

          [*Enter* MESSENGER.]

MESSENGER. Friends, no doubt you can
    direct me:
Where shall I find the house of Oedipus,
Or, better still, where is the King himself?

CHORAGOS. It is this very place, stranger;
    he is inside.
This is his wife and mother of his chil-
    dren.

MESSENGER. I wish her happiness in a happy
    house,
Blest in all the fulfillment of her marriage.

IOCASTE. I wish as much for you: your
    courtesy
Deserves a like good fortune. But now,
    tell me:
Why have you come? What have you to
    say to us?

MESSENGER. Good news, my lady, for your
    house and your husband.

IOCASTE. What news? Who sent you here?

MESSENGER.   I am from Corinth.
The news I bring ought to mean joy for
    you,
Though it may be you will find some
    grief in it.

IOCASTE. What is it? How can it touch us
    in both ways?

MESSENGER. The people of Corinth, they
    say,
Intend to call Oedipus to be their king.

IOCASTE. But old Polybos—is he not reigning
    still?

MESSENGER. No. Death holds him in his
    sepulchre.

IOCASTE. What are you saying? Polybos
    is dead?

MESSENGER. If I am not telling the truth,
    may I die myself.

IOCASTE. [*To a* MAIDSERVANT.] Go in, go
    quickly; tell this to your master.
O riddlers of God's will, where are you
    now!
This was the man whom Oedipus, long
    ago,
Feared so, fled so, in dread of destroying
    him—
But it was another fate by which he died.

      [*Enter* OEDIPUS, *from palace.*]

OEDIPUS. Dearest Iocastê, why have you
    sent for me?

IOCASTE. Listen to what this man says, and
    then tell me
What has become of the solemn pro-
    phecies.

OEDIPUS. Who is this man? What is his
    news for me?

IOCASTE. He has come from Corinth to
    announce your father's death!

OEDIPUS. Is it true, stranger? Tell me in your own words.

MESSENGER. I can not say it more clearly: the King is dead.

OEDIPUS. Was it by treason? Or by an attack of illness?

MESSENGER. A little thing brings old men to their rest.

OEDIPUS. It was sickness, then?

MESSENGER.   Yes, and his many years.

OEDIPUS. Ah!

Why should a man respect the Pythian hearth, or
Give heed to the birds that jangle above his head?
They prophesied that I should kill Polybos,
Kill my own father; but he is dead and buried,
And I am here—I never touched him, never,
Unless he died of grief for my departure,
And thus, in a sense, through me. No. Polybos
Has packed the oracles off with him underground.
They are empty words.

IOCASTE.   Had I not told you so?

OEDIPUS. You had; it was my faint heart that betrayed me.

IOCASTE. From now on never think of those things again.

OEDIPUS. And yet—must I not fear my mother's bed?

IOCASTE. Why should anyone in this world be afraid,
Since Fate rules us and nothing can be foreseen?
A man should live only for the present day.
Have no more fear of sleeping with your mother:
How many men, in dreams, have lain with their mothers!
No reasonable man is troubled by such things.

OEDIPUS. That is true; only—
If only my mother were not still alive!
But she is alive. I cannot help my dread.

IOCASTE. Yet this news of your father's death is wonderful.

OEDIPUS. Wonderful. But I fear the living woman.

MESSENGER. Tell me, who is this woman that you fear?

OEDIPUS. It is Meropê, man; the wife of King Polybos.

MESSENGER. Meropê? Why should you be afraid of her?

OEDIPUS. An oracle of the gods, a dreadful saying.

MESSENGER. Can you tell me about it or are you sworn to silence?

OEDIPUS. I can tell you, and I will.
Apollo said through his prophet that I was the man
Who should marry his own mother, shed his father's blood
With his own hands. And so, for all these years
I have kept clear of Corinth, and no harm has come—
Though it would have been sweet to see my parents again.

MESSENGER. And is this the fear that drove you out of Corinth?

OEDIPUS. Would you have me kill my father?

MESSENGER.   As for that
You must be reassured by the news I gave you.

OEDIPUS. If you could reassure me, I would reward you.

MESSENGER. I had that in mind, I will confess: I thought
I could count on you when you returned to Corinth.

OEDIPUS. No: I will never go near my parents again.

MESSENGER. Ah, son, you still do not know what you are doing—

OEDIPUS. What do you mean? In the name of God tell me!

MESSENGER. —If these are your reasons for not going home.

OEDIPUS. I tell you, I fear the oracle may come true.

MESSENGER. And guilt may come upon you through your parents?

OEDIPUS. That is the dread that is always in my heart.

MESSENGER. Can you not see that all your fears are groundless?

OEDIPUS. How can you say that? They are my parents, surely?

MESSENGER. Polybos was not your father.

OEDIPUS.   Not my father?

MESSENGER. No more your father than the man speaking to you.

OEDIPUS. But you are nothing to me!

MESSENGER.   Neither was he.

OEDIPUS. Then why did he call me son?

MESSENGER.   I will tell you:
Long ago he had you from my hands, as a gift.

OEDIPUS. Then how could he love me so, if I was not his?

MESSENGER. He had no children, and his heart turned to you.

OEDIPUS. What of you? Did you buy me? Did you find me by chance?

MESSENGER. I came upon you in the crooked pass of Kithairon.

OEDIPUS. And what were you doing there?

MESSENGER.   Tending my flocks.

OEDIPUS. A wandering shepherd?

MESSENGER. But your savior, son, that day.

OEDIPUS. From what did you save me?

MESSENGER.
               Your ankles should tell you that.

OEDIPUS. Ah, stranger, why do you speak of that childhood pain?

MESSENGER. I cut the bonds that tied your ankles together.

OEDIPUS. I have had the mark as long as I can remember.

MESSENGER. That was why you were given the name you bear.

OEDIPUS. God! Was it my father or my mother who did it?
Tell me!

MESSENGER. I do not know. The man who gave you to me
Can tell you better than I.

OEDIPUS. It was not you that found me, but another?

MESSENGER. It was another shepherd gave you to me.

OEDIPUS. Who was he? Can you tell me who he was?

MESSENGER. I think he was said to be one of Laïos' people.

OEDIPUS. You mean the Laïos who was king here years ago?

MESSENGER. Yes; King Laïos; and the man was one of his herdsmen.

OEDIPUS. Is he still alive? Can I see him?

MESSENGER.   These men here
Know best about such things.

OEDIPUS.   Does anyone here
Know this shepherd that he is talking about?
Have you seen him in the fields, or in the town?
If you have, tell me. It is time things were made plain.

CHORAGOS. I think the man he means is that same shepherd
You have already asked to see. Iocastê perhaps
Could tell you something.

OEDIPUS.   Do you know anything
About him, Lady? Is he the man we have summoned?
Is that the man this shepherd means?

IOCASTE.   Why think of him?
Forget this herdsman. Forget it all.
This talk is a waste of time.

OEDIPUS.   How can you say that,
When the clues to my true birth are in my hands?

IOCASTE. For God's love, let us have no more questioning!
Is your life nothing to you?
My own is pain enough for me to bear.

OEDIPUS. You need not worry. Suppose my mother a slave,
And born of slaves: no baseness can touch you.

IOCASTE. Listen to me, I beg you: do not do this thing!

OEDIPUS. I will not listen; the truth must be made known.

IOCASTE. Everything that I say is for your own good!

OEDIPUS.   My own good
Snaps my patience, then; I want none of it.

IOCASTE. You are fatally wrong! May you never learn who you are!

OEDIPUS. Go, one of you, and bring the shepherd here.
Let us leave this woman to brag of her royal name.

IOCASTE. Ah, miserable!
   That is the only word I have for you now.
   That is the only word I can ever have.
   [*Exit into the palace.*]
CHORAGOS. Why has she left us, Oedipus?
   Why has she gone
   In such a passion of sorrow? I fear this
   silence:
   Something dreadful may come of it.
OEDIPUS.   Let it come!
   However base my birth, I must know
   about it.
   The Queen, like a woman, is perhaps
   ashamed
   To think of my low origin. But I
   Am a child of Luck; I can not be dis-
   honored.
   Luck is my mother; the passing months,
   my brothers,
   Have seen me rich and poor.
                                           If this is so,
   How could I wish that I were someone
   else?
   How could I not be glad to know my
   birth?
CHORUS. If ever the coming time were
   known
   To my heart's pondering,
   Kithairon, now by Heaven I see the
   torches
   At the festival of the next full moon,
   And see the dance, and hear the choir
   sing
   A grace to your gentle shade:
   Mountain where Oedipus was found,
   O mountain guard of a noble race!
   May the god who heals us lend his aid,
   And let that glory come to pass
   For our king's cradling-ground.
      Of the nymphs that flower beyond the
      years,
   Who bore you, royal child,
   To Pan of the hills or the timberline
   Apollo,
   Cold in delight where the upland clears,
   Or Hermês for whom Kyllenê's heights
   are piled?
   Or flushed as evening cloud,
   Great Dionysos, roamer of mountains,
   He—was it he who found you there,
   And caught you up in his own proud

Arms from the sweet god-ravisher
Who laughed by the Muses' fountains?
OEDIPUS. Sirs: though I do not know the
   man,
   I think I see him coming, this shepherd
   we want:
   He is old, like our friend here, and the
   men
   Bringing him seem to be servants of
   my house.
   But you can tell, if you have ever seen
   him.
   [*Enter* SHEPHERD *escorted by servants.*]
CHORAGOS. I know him, he was Laïos' man.
   You can trust him.
OEDIPUS. Tell me first, you from Corinth:
   is this the shepherd
   We were discussing?
MESSENGER.   This is the very man.
OEDIPUS. [*To* SHEPHERD.] Come here. No,
   look at me. You must answer
   Everything I ask.—You belonged to
   Laios?
SHEPHERD. Yes: born his slave, brought up
   in his house.
OEDIPUS. Tell me: what kind of work did
   you do for him?
SHEPHERD. I was a shepherd of his, most
   of my life.
OEDIPUS. Where mainly did you go for
   pasturage?
SHEPHERD. Sometimes Kithairon, sometimes
   the hills near-by.
OEDIPUS. Do you remember ever seeing this
   man out there?
SHEPHERD. What would he be doing there?
   This man?
OEDIPUS. This man standing here. Have you
   ever seen him before?
SHEPHERD. No. At least, not to my recol-
   lection.
MESSENGER. And that is not strange, my
   lord. But I'll refresh
   His memory: he must remember when
   we two
   Spent three whole seasons together,
   March to September,
   On Kithairon or thereabouts. He had two
   flocks;
   I had one. Each autumn I'd drive mine
   home

And he would go back with his to Laïos'
sheepfold.—

Is this not true, just as I have described it?

SHEPHERD. True, yes; but it was all so long
ago.

MESSENGER. Well, then: do you remember,
back in those days,

That you gave me a baby boy to bring up
as my own?

SHEPHERD. What if I did? What are you
trying to say?

MESSENGER. King Oedipus was once that
little child.

SHEPHERD. Damn you, hold your tongue!

OEDIPUS.   No more of that!
It is your tongue needs watching, not
this man's.

SHEPHERD. My King, my Master, what is it
I have done wrong?

OEDIPUS. You have not answered his question about the boy.

SHEPHERD. He does not know . . . He is
only making trouble . . .

OEDIPUS. Come, speak plainly, or it will go
hard with you.

SHEPHERD. In God's name, do not torture
an old man!

OEDIPUS. Come here, one of you; bind his
arms behind him.

SHEPHERD. Unhappy king! What more do
you wish to learn?

OEDIPUS. Did you give this man the child
he speaks of?

SHEPHERD.   I did.
And I would to God I had died that
very day.

OEDIPUS. You will die now unless you
speak the truth.

SHEPHERD. Yet if I speak the truth, I am
worse than dead.

OEDIPUS. Very well; since you insist upon
delaying—

SHEPHERD. No! I have told you already that
I gave him the boy.

OEDIPUS. Where did you get him? From
your house? From somewhere else?

SHEPHERD. Not from mine, no. A man gave
him to me.

OEDIPUS. Is that man here? Do you know
whose slave he was?

SHEPHERD. For God's love, my King, do
not ask me any more!

OEDIPUS. You are a dead man if I have to
ask you again.

SHEPHERD. Then . . . Then the child was
from the palace of Laïos.

OEDIPUS. A slave child? or a child of his
own line?

SHEPHERD. Ah, I am on the brink of dreadful
speech!

OEDIPUS. And I of dreadful hearing. Yet
I must hear.

SHEPHERD. If you must be told, then . . .
They said it was Laïos' child;

But it is your wife who can tell you
about that.

OEDIPUS. My wife!—Did she give it to you?

SHEPHERD.   My lord, she did.

OEDIPUS. Do you know why?

SHEPHERD.   I was told to get rid of it.

OEDIPUS. An unspeakable mother!

SHEPHERD.
                    There had been prophecies . . .

OEDIPUS. Tell me.

SHEPHERD. It was said that the boy would
kill his own father.

OEDIPUS. Then why did you give him over
to this old man?

SHEPHERD. I pitied the baby, my King,

And I thought that this man would take
him far away

To his own country.

          He saved him—but for what a fate!
For if you are what this man says you
are,

No man living is more wretched than
Oedipus.

OEDIPUS. Ah God!
It was true!

          All the prophecies!

                                    —Now,
O Light, may I look on you for the last
time!

I, Oedipus,

Oedipus, damned in his birth, in his
marriage damned,

Damned in the blood he shed with his
own hand!

          [He rushes into the palace.]

CHORUS. Alas for the seed of men.

What measure shall I give these genera-
tions
That breathe on the void and are void
And exist and do not exist?
    Who bears more weight of joy
Than mass of sunlight shifting in images,
Or who shall make his thoughts stay on
That down time drifts away?
    Your splendor is all fallen.
    O naked brow of wrath and tears,
O change of Oedipus!
I who saw your days call no man blest—
Your great days like ghósts góne.

    That mind was a strong bow.
    Deep, how deep you drew it then, hard
archer,
At a dim fearful range,
And brought dear glory down!
    You overcame the stranger—
The virgin with her hooking lion claws—
And though death sang, stood like a tower
To make pale Thebes take heart.

    Fortress against our sorrow!
    Divine king, giver of laws,
Majestic Oedipus!
No prince in Thebes had ever such re-
nown,
No prince won such grace of power.

    And now of all men ever known
Most pitiful is this man's story:
His fortunes are most changed, his state
Fallen to a low slave's
Ground under bitter fate.

    O Oedipus, most royal one!
The great door that expelled you to the
light
Gave at night—ah, gave night to your
glory:
As to the father, to the fathering son.

    All understood too late.
    How could that queen whom Laïos
won,
The garden that he harrowed at his
height,
Be silent when that act was done?

    But all eyes fail before time's eye,
All actions come to justice there.
Though never willed, though far down
the deep past,
Your bed, your dread sirings,

Are brought to book at last.
    Child by Laïos doomed to die,
Then doomed to lose that fortunate little
death,
Would God you never took breath in
this air
That with my wailing lips I take to cry:
    For I weep the world's outcast.

    Blind I was, and can not tell why;
Asleep, for you had given ease of breath;
A fool, while the false years went by.

[*Enter, from the palace,* SECOND MESSENGER.]

SECOND MESSENGER. Elders of Thebes, most
    honored in this land,
What horrors are yours to see and hear,
    what weight
Of sorrow to be endured, if, true to your
    birth,
You venerate the line of Labdakos!
I think neither Istros nor Phasis, those
    great rivers,
Could purify this place of the corruption
It shelters now, or soon must bring to
    light—
Evil not done unconsciously, but willed.
    The greatest griefs are those we cause
    ourselves.

CHORAGOS. Surely, friend, we have grief
    enough already;
What new sorrow do you mean?

SECOND MESSENGER. The Queen is dead.

CHORAGOS. Iocastê? Dead? But at whose
    hand?

SECOND MESSENGER.   Her own.
The full horror of what happened you
    can not know,
For you did not see it; but I, who did,
    will tell you
As clearly as I can how she met her
    death.
    When she had left us,
In passionate silence, passing through the
    court,
She ran to her apartment in the house,
Her hair clutched by the fingers of both
    hands.
She closed the doors behind her; then,
    by that bed
Where long ago the fatal son was con-
    ceived—

That son who should bring about his
father's death—
We heard her call upon Laïos, dead so
many years,
And heard her wail for the double fruit
of her marriage,
A husband by her husband, children by
her child.
Exactly how she died I do not know:
For Oedipus burst in moaning and would
not let us
Keep vigil to the end: it was by him
As he stormed about the room that our
eyes were caught.
From one to another of us he went, beg-
ging a sword,
Cursing the wife who was not his wife,
the mother
Whose womb had carried his own chil-
dren and himself.
I do not know: it was none of us aided
him,
But surely one of the gods was in control!
For with a dreadful cry
He hurled his weight, as though wrenched
out of himself,
At the twin doors: the bolts gave, and he
rushed in.
And there we saw her hanging, her body
swaying
From the cruel cord she had noosed
about her neck.
A great sob broke from him, heartbreak-
ing to hear,
As he loosed the rope and lowered her
to the ground.
I would blot out from my mind what
happened next!
For the King ripped from her gown the
golden brooches
That were her ornament, and raised them,
and plunged them down
Straight into his own eyeballs, crying,
"No more,
No more shall you look on the misery
about me,
The horrors of my own doing! Too long
you have known
The faces of those whom I should never
have seen,

Too long been blind to those for whom
I was searching!
From this hour, go in darkness!" And as
he spoke,
He struck at his eyes—not once, but
many times;
And the blood spattered his beard,
Bursting from his ruined sockets like red
hail.
So from the unhappiness of two this
evil has sprung,
A curse on the man and woman alike.
The old
Happiness of the house of Labdakos
Was happiness enough: where is it today?
It is all wailing and ruin, disgrace, death
—all
The misery of mankind that has a name—
And it is wholly and for ever theirs.

CHORAGOS. Is he in agony still? Is there no
rest for him?

SECOND MESSENGER. He is calling for some-
one to lead him to the gates
So that all the children of Kadmos may
look upon
His father's murderer, his mother's—no,
I can not say it!
            And then he will leave Thebes,
Self-exiled, in order that the curse
Which he himself pronounced may depart
from the house.
He is weak, and there is none to lead him,
So terrible is his suffering.
                        But you will see:
Look, the doors are opening; in a moment
You will see a thing that would crush
a heart of stone.

[The central door is opened; OEDIPUS,
            blinded, is led in.]

CHORAGOS. Dreadful indeed for men to see.
Never have my own eyes
Looked on a sight so full of fear.
Oedipus!
What madness came upon you, what
daemon
Leaped on your life with heavier
Punishment than a mortal man can bear?
No: I can not even
Look at you, poor ruined one.
And I would speak, question, ponder,

If I were able. No.
You make me shudder.
OEDIPUS. God.   God.
Is there a sorrow greater?
Where shall I find harbor in this world?
My voice is hurled far on a dark wind.
What has God done to me?
CHORAGOS. Too terrible to think of, or
to see.
OEDIPUS. O cloud of night,
Never to be turned away: night coming
on,
I can not tell how: night like a shroud!
My fair winds brought me here.
                              O God. Again
The pain of the spikes where I had sight,
The flooding pain
Of memory, never to be gouged out.
CHORAGOS. This is not strange.
You suffer it all twice over, remorse
in pain,
Pain in remorse.
OEDIPUS. Ah dear friend
Are you faithful even yet, you alone?
Are you still standing near me, will you
stay here,
Patient, to care for the blind?
                              The blind man!
Yet even blind I know who it is attends
me,
By the voice's tone—
Though my new darkness hide the com-
forter.
CHORAGOS. Oh fearful act!
What god was it drove you to rake black
Night across your eyes?
OEDIPUS. Apollo. Apollo. Dear
Children, the god was Apollo.
He brought my sick, sick fate upon me.
But the blinding hand was my own!
How could I bear to see
When all my sight was horror every-
where?
CHORAGOS. Everywhere; that is true.
OEDIPUS. And now what is left?
Images? Love? A greeting even,
Sweet to the senses? Is there anything?
Ah, no, friends: lead me away.
Lead me away from Thebes.
                              Lead the great wreck

And hell of Oedipus, whom the gods hate.
CHORAGOS. Your fate is clear, you are not
blind to that.
Would God you had never found it out!
OEDIPUS. Death take the man who unbound
My feet on that hillside
And delivered me from death to life!
What life?
If only I had died,
This weight of monstrous doom
Could not have dragged me and my
darlings down.
CHORAGOS. I would have wished the same.
OEDIPUS. Oh never to have come here
With my father's blood upon me! Never
To have been the man they call his
mother's husband!
Oh accurst! Oh child of evil,
To have entered that wretched bed—
                              the selfsame one!
More primal than sin itself, this fell to me.
CHORAGOS. I do not know how I can answer
you.
You were better dead than alive and blind.
OEDIPUS. Do not counsel me any more. This
punishment
That I have laid upon myself is just.
If I had eyes,
I do not know how I could bear the sight
Of my father, when I came to the house
of Death,
Or my mother: for I have sinned against
them both
So vilely that I could not make my peace
By strangling my own life.
                              Or do you think my children,
Born as they were born, would be sweet
to my eyes?
Ah never, never! Nor this town with its
high walls,
Nor the holy images of the gods.
                                        For I,
Thrice miserable!—Oedipus, noblest of
all the line
Of Kadmos, have condemned myself to
enjoy
These things no more, by my own male-
diction
Expelling that man whom the gods
declared

To be a defilement in the house of Laïos.
After exposing the rankness of my own guilt,
How could I look men frankly in the eyes?
No, I swear it,
If I could have stifled my hearing at its source,
I would have done it and made all this body
A tight cell of misery, blank to light and sound:
So I should have been safe in a dark agony
Beyond all recollection.
                          Ah Kithairon!
Why did you shelter me? When I was cast upon you,
Why did I not die? Then I should never
Have shown the world my execrable birth.

Ah Polybos! Corinth, city that I believed
The ancient seat of my ancestors: how fair
I seemed, your child! And all the while this evil
Was cancerous within me!
                          For I am sick
In my daily life, sick in my origin.

O three roads, dark ravine, woodland and way
Where three roads met: you, drinking my father's blood,
My own blood, spilled by my own hand: can you remember
The unspeakable things I did there, and the things
I went on from there to do?
                          O marriage, marriage!
The act that engendered me, and again the act
Performed by the son in the same bed—
                          Ah, the net
Of incest, mingling fathers, brothers, sons,
With brides, wives, mothers: the last evil
That can be known by men: no tongue can say
How evil!

    No. For the love of God, conceal me
Somewhere far from Thebes; or kill me; or hurl me

Into the sea, away from men's eyes for ever.
    Come, lead me. You need not fear to touch me.
Of all men, I alone can bear this guilt.
                    [*Enter* CREON.]
CHORAGOS. We are not the ones to decide; but Creon here
May fitly judge of what you ask. He only
Is left to protect the city in your place.
OEDIPUS. Alas, how can I speak to him? What right have I
To beg his courtesy whom I have deeply wronged?
CREON. I have not come to mock you, Oedipus,
Or to reproach you, either.
[*To* ATTENDANTS.]—You, standing there:
If you have lost all respect for man's dignity,
At least respect the flame of Lord Helios:
Do not allow this pollution to show itself
Openly here, an affront to the earth
And Heaven's rain and the light of day.
    No, take him
Into the house as quickly as you can.
For it is proper
That only the close kindred see his grief.
OEDIPUS. I pray you in God's name, since your courtesy
Ignores my dark expectation, visiting
With mercy this man of all men most execrable:
Give me what I ask—for your good, not for mine.
CREON. And what is it that you would have me do?
OEDIPUS. Drive me out of this country as quickly as may be
To a place where no human voice can ever greet me.
CREON. I should have done that before now—only,
God's will had not been wholly revealed to me.
OEDIPUS. But his command is plain: the parricide
Must be destroyed. I am that evil man.
CREON. That is the sense of it, yes; but as things are,

We had best discover clearly what is to be done.

OEDIPUS. You would learn more about a man like me?

CREON. You are ready now to listen to the god.

OEDIPUS. I will listen. But it is to you
That I must turn for help. I beg you, hear me.
The woman in there—
Give her whatever funeral you think proper:
She is your sister.
          —But let me go, Creon!
Let me purge my father's Thebes of the pollution
Of my living here, and go out to the wild hills,
To Kithairon, that has won such fame with me,
The tomb my mother and father appointed for me,
And let me die there, as they willed I should.
And yet I know
Death will not ever come to me through sickness
Or in any natural way: I have been preserved
For some unthinkable fate. But let that be.
As for my sons, you need not care for them.
They are men, they will find some way to live.
But my poor daughters, who have shared my table,
Who never before have been parted from their father—
Take care of them, Creon; do this for me.
And will you let me touch them with my hands
A last time, and let us weep together?
Be kind, my lord,
Great prince, be kind!
          Could I but touch them,
They would be mine again, as when I had my eyes.

[*Enter* ANTIGONE *and* ISMENE, *attended.*]
Ah, God!
Is it my dearest children I hear weeping?
Has Creon pitied me and sent my daughters?

CREON. Yes, Oedipus: I knew that they were dear to you
In the old days, and know you must love them still.

OEDIPUS. May God bless you for this—and be a friendlier
Guardian to you than he has been to me!
Children, where are you?
Come quickly to my hands: they are your brother's—
Hands that have brought your father's once clear eyes
To this way of seeing—
          Ah dearest ones,
I had neither sight nor knowledge then, your father
By the woman who was the source of his own life!
And I weep for you—having no strength to see you—,
I weep for you when I think of the bitterness
That men will visit upon you all your lives.
What homes, what festivals can you attend
Without being forced to depart again in tears?
And when you come to marriageable age,
Where is the man, my daughters, who would dare
Risk the bane that lies on all my children?
Is there any evil wanting? Your father killed
His father; sowed the womb of her who bore him;
Engendered you at the fount of his own existence!
That is what they will say of you.
          Then, whom
Can you ever marry? There are no bridegrooms for you,
And your lives must wither away in sterile dreaming.
O Creon, son of Menoikeus!
You are the only father my daughters have,

Since we, their parents, are both of us
gone for ever.

They are your own blood: you will not
let them

Fall into beggary and loneliness;

You will keep them from the miseries
that are mine!

Take pity on them; see, they are only
children,

Friendless except for you. Promise me
this,

Great Prince, and give me your hand in
token of it. [CREON *clasps his right
hand.*]

Children:

I could say much, if you could understand me,

But as it is, I have only this prayer for
you:

Live where you can, be as happy as you
can—

Happier, please God, than God has made
your father!

CREON. Enough. You have wept enough.
Now go within.

OEDIPUS. I must; but it is hard.

CREON.   Time eases all things.

OEDIPUS. But you must promise—

CREON.   Say what you desire.

OEDIPUS. Send me from Thebes!

CREON.   God grant that I may!

OEDIPUS. But since God hates me . . .

CREON.   No, he will grant your wish.

OEDIPUS. You promise?

CREON. I can not speak beyond my knowledge.

OEDIPUS. Then lead me in.

CREON. Come now, and leave your children.

OEDIPUS. No! Do not take them from me!

CREON.   Think no longer

That you are in command here, but
rather think

How, when you were, you served your
own destruction.

[*Exeunt into the house all but the* CHORUS;
the CHORAGOS *chants directly to the
audience.*]

CHORAGOS. Men of Thebes: look upon
Oedipus.

This is the king who solved the famous
riddle

And towered up, most powerful of men.

No mortal eyes but looked on him with
envy,

Yet in the end ruin swept over him.

Let every man in mankind's frailty

Consider his last day; and let none

Presume on his good fortune until he find

Life, at his death, a memory without pain.

A cosmic malignity that appears to reinforce the vice and stupidity of human beings posed for men of the English Renaissance much the same question that Sophocles had raised in Athens. Indeed, the tragic question differs little from age to age, from nation to nation. Whatever its form, it always asks, how shall we live, given a world like ours? The world which tragedy presents is usually dark, but few have been so dark as that of King Lear. The tragic dramatist has always been—irrespective of period—acutely sensitive to evil and painfully aware of its omnipresence. He has seen the guilty brought to justice, but he has also seen the innocent struck down with the guilty. This apparent blindness of Fate to any distinction among its victims is a significant clue to the tragic vision: the universe seems wholly indifferent to man's plight. Thus Gloucester, in *King Lear*, will cry out:

> As flies to wanton boys, are we to the gods,
> They kill us for their sport.

Yet Gloucester's statement does not define the tragic vision; if it did, that vision would be, not darkened, but black. His words reveal, chiefly, the limitations of Gloucester's cosmology; and before the end of the play he will be blind in fact, as he has been until then in understanding. But Gloucester is not in any case the tragic hero, and so it is to Lear himself, and the world that Shakespeare created around him, that we must look for comprehension of this drama.

To create the world of *King Lear* (in 1604–1605), Shakespeare took materials from an old play on the same subject, from a political romance, and from recent historical events. Out of these he imaged a world in which a querulous old man first strips himself of worldly power, and then seeks to clothe himself instead with forced pledges of love. Instead of an old age free from the burdens of kingship and warmed with filial affection, Lear pulls down on his head, and upon the heads of those that love him, disasters so great and so out of proportion to his folly that we must agree with him: he is more sinned against than sinning. The world of Lear seems to be a world in which even acts of good faith lead to evil consequences. In that world, not knowledge or power, but only stoic patience, humility, and compassion can help poor, unaccommodated man to survive. But pagan Lear's play suggests not the simple Christian message that can be read in his discovery of sympathy for the humble creatures on the heath—important as that discovery is for Lear—but rather that when good and evil contend, in the souls of men and in their societies, evil can triumph long enough to destroy good men.

KING LEAR*

William Shakespeare

LEAR, KING OF BRITAIN
KING OF FRANCE
DUKE OF BURGUNDY
DUKE OF CORNWALL
DUKE OF ALBANY
EARL OF KENT
EARL OF GLOUCESTER
EDGAR, SON TO GLOUCESTER
EDMUND, BASTARD SON TO GLOUCESTER
CURAN, A COURTIER
OLD MAN, TENANT TO GLOUCESTER
DOCTOR
LEAR'S FOOL

OSWALD, STEWARD TO GONERIL
A CAPTAIN UNDER EDMUND'S COMMAND
GENTLEMEN
A HERALD
SERVANTS TO CORNWALL
GONERIL
REGAN } DAUGHTERS TO LEAR
CORDELIA
KNIGHTS ATTENDING ON LEAR, OFFICERS, MESSENGERS, SOLDIERS, ATTENDANTS

Scene: *Britain*

ACT I

Scene i

Enter Kent, Gloucester, and Edmund.

KENT. I thought the King had more affected the Duke of Albany than Cornwall.

GLOUCESTER. It did always seem so to us; but now, in the division of the kingdom, it appears not which of the dukes he 5 values most, for equalities are so weighed that curiosity in neither can make choice of either's moiety.

KENT. Is not this your son, my lord?

GLOUCESTER. His breeding, sir, hath been 10 at my charge. I have so often blushed to

---

*This text is that of the Pelican Shakespeare, edited by Alfred Harbage. It follows the text of the First Folio of 1623, with additions from the quarto of 1608. The quarto edition was not divided into acts and scenes; the divisions here supplied are those of the Globe edition, which in turn is that of the folio, except that Act II, Scene ii of the latter has been subdivided into Scenes ii, iii, and iv.

The present edition follows the Folio text, although it adds in square brackets the passages appearing only in the quarto of 1608.

I,i,1 *affected:* warmly regarded 2 *Albany:* i.e. Scotland (once ruled by 'Albanacte')

---

6 *equalities ... weighed:* i.e. the portions weigh so equally 7–8 *curiosity ... moiety:* careful analysis by neither can make him prefer the other's portion 10 *breeding:* rearing 12 *brazed:* brazened

acknowledge him that now I am brazed to't.

KENT. I cannot conceive you.

GLOUCESTER. Sir, this young fellow's 15 mother could; whereupon she grew round-wombed, and had indeed, sir, a son for her cradle ere she had a husband for her bed. Do you smell a fault?

KENT. I cannot wish the fault undone, 20 the issue of it being so proper.

GLOUCESTER. But I have a son, sir, by order of law, some year elder than this who yet is no dearer in my account: though this knave came something saucily to the 25 world before he was sent for, yet was his mother fair, there was good sport at his making, and the whoreson must be acknowledged. Do you know this noble gentleman, Edmund? 30

EDMUND. No, my lord.

GLOUCESTER. My Lord of Kent. Remember him hereafter as my honorable friend.

EDMUND. My services to your lordship.

KENT. I must love you, and sue to know 35 you better.

EDMUND. Sir, I shall study deserving.

GLOUCESTER. He hath been out nine years, and away he shall again.   *Sound a sennet.* The King is coming. 40

Enter one bearing a coronet, then King Lear, then the Dukes of Cornwall and Albany, next Goneril, Regan, Cordelia, and Attendants.

LEAR. Attend the lords of France and Burgundy, Gloucester.

GLOUCESTER. I shall, my lord.
                                    Exit with Edmund.
LEAR. Meantime we shall express our darker purpose.

Give me the map there. Know that we have divided 45

In three our kingdom; and 'tis our fast intent

To shake all cares and business from our age,

Conferring them on younger strengths while we

Unburdened crawl toward death. Our son of Cornwall,

And you our no less loving son of Albany, 50

We have this hour a constant will to publish

Our daughters' several dowers, that future strife

May be prevented now. The princes, France and Burgundy,

Great rivals in our youngest daughter's love,

Long in our court have made their amorous sojourn, 55

And here are to be answered. Tell me, my daughters

(Since now we will divest us both of rule,

Interest of territory, cares of state),

Which of you shall we say doth love us most,

That we our largest bounty may extend 60

Where nature doth with merit challenge. Goneril,

Our eldest-born, speak first.

GONERIL. Sir, I love you more than word can wield the matter;

Dearer than eyesight, space, and liberty;

Beyond what can be valuèd, rich or rare; 65

No less than life, with grace, health, beauty, honor;

As much as child e'er loved, or father found;

A love that makes breath poor, and speech unable.

Beyond all manner of so much I love you.

CORDELIA. [*aside*] What shall Cordelia speak? Love, and be silent. 70

---

14 *conceive:* understand (with pun following) 21 *proper:* handsome 24 *account:* estimation 25 *saucily:* (1) impertinently (2) bawdily 28 *whoreson:* (affectionate abuse, but literally applicable, like 'knave' above) 38 *out:* away (for training, or in military service) 39 S.D. *sennet:* trumpet flourish (heralding a procession) 44 *darker purpose:* more secret intention (to require declarations of affection)

---

46 *fast:* firm 51 *constant ... publish:* fixed intention to announce 52 *several:* individual 55 *amorous sojourn:* i.e. visit of courtship 58 *Interest:* legal possession 61 *nature ... challenge:* natural affection matches other merits 63 *wield:* handle 64 *space:* scope (for the exercise of 'liberty') 68 *breath:* voice *unable:* inadequate

LEAR. Of all these bounds, even from this
    line to this,
With shadowy forests and with champains
    riched,
With plenteous rivers and wide-skirted
    meads,
We make thee lady. To thine and Albany's
    issues
Be this perpetual.—What says our second
    daughter,   75
Our dearest Regan, wife of Cornwall?
REGAN. I am made of that self mettle as my
    sister,
And prize me at her worth. In my true
    heart
I find she names my very deed of love;
Only she comes too short, that I pro-
    fess   80
Myself an enemy to all other joys
Which the most precious square of sense
    possesses,
And find I am alone felicitate
In your dear Highness' love.
CORDELIA.   [aside] Then poor Cordelia;
And yet not so, since I am sure my
    love's   85
More ponderous than my tongue.
LEAR. To thee and thine hereditary ever
Remain this ample third of our fair king-
    dom,
No less in space, validity, and pleasure
Than that conferred on Goneril.—Now,
    our joy,   90
Although our last and least; to whose
    young love
The vines of France and milk of Burgundy
Strive to be interest; what can you say to
    draw
A third more opulent than your sisters?
    Speak.
CORDELIA. Nothing, my lord.   95

LEAR. Nothing?
CORDELIA. Nothing.
LEAR. Nothing will come of nothing. Speak
    again.
CORDELIA. Unhappy that I am, I cannot
    heave   100
My heart into my mouth. I love your
    Majesty
According to my bond, no more nor less.
LEAR. How, how, Cordelia? Mend your
    speech a little,
Lest you may mar your fortunes.
CORDELIA.   Good my lord,
You have begot me, bred me, loved
    me. I   105
Return those duties back as are right fit,
Obey you, love you and most honor you.
Why have my sisters husbands if they say
They love you all? Haply, when I shall
    wed,
That lord whose hand must take my plight
    shall carry   110
Half my love with him, half my care and
    duty.
Sure I shall never marry like my sisters,
To love my father all.
LEAR. But goes thy heart with this?
CORDELIA.   Ay, my good lord.
LEAR. So young, and so untender?   115
CORDELIA. So young, my lord, and true.
LEAR. Let it be so, thy truth then be thy
    dower!
For, by the sacred radiance of the sun,
The mysteries of Hecate and the night,
By all the operation of the orbs   120
From whom we do exist and cease to be,
Here I disclaim all my paternal care,
Propinquity and property of blood,
And as a stranger to my heart and me
Hold thee from this for ever. The bar-
    barous Scythian,   125
Or he that makes his generation messes
To gorge his appetite, shall to my bosom

---

72 champains riched: plains enriched 73 wide-
skirted: far-spreading 74 issues: descendants
75 perpetual: in perpetuity 78 prize . . . worth:
value me at her value 79 my very deed of: the
true fact of my 82 Which . . . possesses: which
the most precise measurement by the senses holds
to be most precious 83 felicitate: made happy
96 ponderous: weighty 89 validity: value pleasure:
pleasing qualities 91 least: smallest, youngest
92 vines: vineyards milk: pasture-lands (?) 93
interest: concerned as interested parties

---

102 bond: obligation 106 Return . . . fit: i.e.
am fittingly dutiful in return 110 plight: pledge,
troth-plight 119 Hecate: infernal goddess, pa-
troness of witches 120 operation . . . orbs: astrological influences 123 Propinquity: relationship
property: i.e. common property, something
shared 125 Scythian: (proverbially barbarous)
126 makes. . . messes: makes meals of his offspring

Be as well neighbored, pitied, and relieved,
As thou my sometime daughter.
KENT.   Good my liege—
LEAR. Peace Kent!   130
Come not between the dragon and his
  wrath.
I loved her most, and thought to set my rest
On her kind nursery.—Hence and avoid
  my sight!—
So be my grave my peace as here I give
Her father's heart from her! Call France.
  Who stirs!   135
Call Burgundy. Cornwall and Albany,
With my two daughters' dowers digest the
  third;
Let pride, which she calls plainness, marry
  her.
I do invest you jointly with my power,
Preeminence, and all the large effects   140
That troop with majesty. Ourself, by
  monthly course,
With reservation of an hundred kinghts,
By you to be sustained, shall our abode
Make with you by due turn. Only we shall
  retain
The name, and all th' addition to a king.
  The sway,   145
Revenue, execution of the rest,
Belovèd sons, be yours; which to confirm,
This coronet part between you.
KENT.   Royal Lear,
Whom I have ever honored as my king,
Loved as my father, as my master fol-
  lowed,   150
As my great patron thought on in my
  prayers—
LEAR. The bow is bent and drawn; make from
  the shaft.
KENT. Let it fall rather, though the fork
  invade
The region of my heart. Be Kent unman-
  nerly

When Lear is mad. What wouldst thou
  do, old man?   155
Think'st thou that duty shall have dread
  to speak
When power to flattery bows? To plain-
  ness honor's bound
When majesty falls to folly. Reserve thy
  state,
And in thy best consideration check
This hideous rashness. Answer my life my
  judgment,   160
Thy youngest daughter does not love thee
  least,
Nor are those empty-hearted whose low
  sounds
Reverb no hollowness.
LEAR.   Kent, on thy life, no more!
KENT. My life I never held but as a pawn
To wage against thine enemies; ne'er fear
  to lose it,   165
Thy safety being motive.
LEAR.   Out of my sight!
KENT. See better, Lear, and let me still
  remain
The true blank of thine eye.
LEAR. Now by Apollo—
KENT.   Now by Apollo, King,
Thou swear'st thy gods in vain.
LEAR.   O vassal! Miscreant!   170
                        [*Grasping his sword.*]
ALBANY, CORNWALL. Dear sir, forbear!
KENT. Kill thy physician, and thy fee
  bestow
Upon the foul disease. Revoke thy gift,
Or, whilst I can vent clamor from my
  throat,
I'll tell thee thou dost evil.
LEAR.   Hear me, recreant,   175
On thine allegiance, hear me!
That thou hast sought to make us break
  our vows,

---

129 *sometime:* former 131 *his:* its 132 *set my rest:* (1) risk my stake (a term in the card game primero) (2) rely for my repose 133 *nursery:* nursing, care 134 *So . . . peace as:* let me rest peacefully in my grave only as 140 *effects:* tokens 141 *Ourself:* I (royal plural) 145 *th' addition:* honors and prerogatives 147 *coronet:* (symbol of rule, not necessarily the royal crown) 152 *make:* make away 153 *fall:* strike *fork:* two-pronged head

158 *Reserve thy state:* retain your kingly authority 159 *best consideration:* most careful deliberation 160 *Answer my life:* i.e. I'll stake my life on 163 *Reverb no hollowness:* i.e. do not reverberate (like a drum) as a result of hollowness 164 *pawn:* stake 165 *wage:* wager, pit 166 *motive:* the moving cause 167 *still:* always 168 *blank:* center of the target (to guide your aim truly) 170 *Miscreant* (1) rascal (2) infidel 175 *recreant:* traitor 177 *That:* in that, since

Which we durst never yet, and with
strained pride
To come betwixt our sentence and our
power,
Which nor our nature nor our place can
bear,   180
Our potency made good, take thy reward.
Five days we do allot thee for provision
To shield thee from disasters of the world,
And on the sixth to turn thy hated back
Upon our kingdom. If, on the tenth day
following,   185
Thy banished trunk be found in our do-
minions,
The moment is thy death. Away. By
Jupiter,
This shall not be revoked.
KENT. Fare thee well, King. Sith thus thou
wilt appear,
Freedom lives hence, and banishment is
here.   190
[*To Cordelia*] The gods to their dear
shelter take thee, maid,
That justly think'st and hast most rightly
said.
[*To Regan and Goneril*] And your large
speeches may your deeds approve,
That good effects may spring from words
of love.
Thus Kent, O princes, bids you all
adieu;   195
He'll shape his old course in a country
new.   *Exit.*

*Flourish. Enter Gloucester, with France
and Burgundy; Attendants.*

GLOUCESTER. Here's France and Burgundy,
my noble lord.
LEAR. My Lord of Burgundy,
We first address toward you, who with
this king
Hath rivalled for our daughter. What in
the least   200
Will you require in present dower with her,

Or cease your quest of love?
BURGUNDY.   Most royal Majesty,
I crave no more than hath your Highness
offered,
Nor will you tender less.
LEAR.   Right noble Burgundy,
When she was dear to us, we did hold
her so;   205
But now her price is fallen. Sir, there she
stands.
If aught within that little seeming sub-
stance,
Or all of it, with our displeasure pieced
And nothing more, may fitly like your
Grace,
She's there, and she is yours.
BURGUNDY.   I know no answer.   210
LEAR. Will you, with those infirmities she
owes,
Unfriended, new adopted to our hate,
Dow'red with our curse, and strangered
with our oath,
Take her, or leave her?
BURGUNDY.   Pardon me, royal sir.
Election makes not up on such condi-
tions.   215
LEAR. Then leave her, sir, for by the pow'r
that made me
I tell you all her wealth [*to France*] For
you, great King,
I would not from your love make such a
stray
To match you where I hate; therefore
beseech you
T' avert your liking a more worthier
way   220
Than on a wretch whom nature is ashamed
Almost t' acknowledge hers.
FRANCE.   This is most strange,
That she whom even but now was your
best object,
The argument of your praise, balm of your
age,
The best, the dearest, should in this trice
of time   225

---

178 *strained:* excessive 179 *To come ... power:*
i.e. to oppose my power to sentence 181 *Our
... good:* if my power is to be demonstrated as
real 183 *disasters:* accidents 186 *trunk:* body
189 *Sith:* since 193 *approve:* confirm 194
effects: consequences 196 *shape ... course:* keep
to his customary ways (of honesty)

207 *seeming substance:* i.e. nothing, mere
shell 208 *pieced:* joined 211 *owes:* owns 213
strangered with: made alien by 215 *Election ...
conditions:* no choice is possible on such terms
218 *make ... stray:* stray so far as 220 *avert:*
turn 223 *best:* favorite 224 *argument:* theme

Commit a thing so monstrous to dismantle
So many folds of favor. Sure her offense
Must be of such unnatural degree
That monsters it, or your fore-vouched
  affection
Fall'n into taint; which to believe of
  her   230
Must be a faith that reason without
  miracle
Should never plant in me.
CORDELIA.   I yet beseech your Majesty,
If for I want that glib and oily art
To speak and purpose not since what I
  well intend
I'll do't before I speak, that you make
  known   235
It is no vicious blot, murder, or foulness,
No unchaste action or dishonorèd step,
That hath deprived me of your grace and
  favor;
But even for want of that for which I am
  richer—
A still-soliciting eye, and such a tongue 240
That I am glad I have not, though not to
  have it
Hath lost me in your liking.
LEAR.   Better thou
Hadst not been born than not t' have
  pleased me better.
FRANCE. Is it but this? A tardiness in nature
Which often leaves the history un-
  spoke   245
That it intends to do. My Lord of Bur-
  gundy,
What say you to the lady? Love's not love
When it is mingled with regards that
  stands
Aloof from th' entire point. Will you have
  her?
She is herself a dowry.

BURGUNDY.   Royal King,   250
Give but that portion which yourself pro-
  posed,
And here I take Cordelia by the hand,
Duchess of Burgundy.
LEAR. Nothing. I have sworn. I am firm.
BURGUNDY. I am sorry then you have so lost
a father   255
That you must lose a husband.
CORDELIA.   Peace be with Burgundy.
Since that respects of fortune are his love,
I shall not be his wife.
FRANCE. Fairest Cordelia, that art most rich
  being poor,
Most choice forsaken, and most loved
  despised,   260
Thee and thy virtues here I seize upon.
Be it lawful I take up what's cast away.
Gods, gods! 'Tis strange that from their
  cold'st neglect
My love should kindle to inflamed respect.
Thy dow'rless daughter, King, thrown to
  my chance,   265
Is queen of us, of ours, and our fair
  France.
Not all the dukes of wat'rish Burgundy
Can buy this unprized precious maid of
  me.
Bid them farewell, Cordelia, though un-
  kind.
Thou losest here, a better where to find   270
LEAR. Thou hast her, France; let her be
  thine, for we
Have no such daughter, nor shall ever see
That face of hers again. Therefore be gone
Without our grace, our love, our benison.
Come, noble Burgundy.   275

Flourish. Exeunt Lear, Burgundy, Corn-
wall, Albany, Gloucester, and Attendants.

FRANCE. Bid farewell to your sisters.
CORDELIA. The jewels of our father, with
  washed eyes
Cordelia leaves you. I know you what you
  are;

---

226 *to dismantle:* so to strip off 229 *That*
monsters it: as makes it monstrous (i.e. abnormal,
freakish) *fore-vouched:* previously sworn 230
taint: decay (with the implication that the affection, and the oath attesting it, were tainted in the
first place) 231 *reason . . . miracle:* i.e. rational,
unaided by miraculous, means of persuasion
234 *purpose not:* i.e. without intending to act in
accordance with my words 240 *still-soliciting:*
always-begging 244 *tardiness in nature:* natural
reticence 245 *history unspoke:* actions unan-
nounced 247–248 *mingled . . . point:* i.e. mixed
with irrelevant considerations

257 *respects:* considerations 264 *inflamed re-*
spect: ardent regard 267 *wat'rish:* (1) watery,
weak (2) watered, diluted 268 *unprized:* un-
valued 270 *here:* this place *where:* other place
274 *benison:* blessing 277 *jewels:* i.e. things held
precious (cf. I. 259) *washed:* tear-washed

And, like a sister, am most loath to call
Your faults as they are named. Love well
    our father.   280
To your professèd bosoms I commit him;
But yet, alas, stood I within his grace,
I would prefer him to a better place.
So farewell to you both.
REGAN. Prescribe not us our duty.
GONERIL.   Let your study 285
Be to content your lord, who hath received
    you
At fortune's alms. You have obedience
    scanted,
And well are worth the want that you have
    wanted.
CORDELIA. Time shall unfold what plighted
    cunning hides,
Who covers faults, at last with shame
    derides.   290
Well may you prosper.
FRANCE.   Come, my fair Cordelia.
                    Exit France and Cordelia.
GONERIL. Sister, it is not little I have to say
of what most nearly appertains to us both.
I think our father will hence to-night.
REGAN. That's most certain, and with   295
you; next month with us.

GONERIL. You see how full of changes his
age is. The observation we have made of
it hath not been little. He always loved
our sister most, and with what poor   300
judgment he hath now cast her off appears
too grossly.
REGAN. 'Tis the infirmity of his age; yet he
hath ever but slenderly known himself.
GONERIL. The best and soundest of his   305
time hath been but rash; then must we
look from his age to receive not alone the
imperfections of long-ingraffed condition,
but therewithal the unruly waywardness
that infirm and choleric years bring   310
with them.
REGAN. Such unconstant starts are we like
to have from him as this of Kent's
banishment.
GONERIL. There is further compliment   315
of leave-taking between France and him.
Pray you let us hit together; if our father
carry authority with such disposition as
he bears, this last surrender of his will but
offend us.   320
REGAN. We shall further think of it.
GONERIL. We must do something, and i' th'
heat.   *Exeunt.*

Scene ii

Enter Bastard
[*Edmund, solus, with a letter*].

EDMUND. Thou, Nature, art my goddess; to
    thy law
My services are bound. Wherefore should
    I
Stand in the plague of custom, and permit
The curiosity of nations to deprive me,
For that I am some twelve or fourteen
    moonshines   5

Lag of a brother? Why bastard? Where-
    fore base,
When my dimensions are as well compact,
My mind as generous, and my shape as
    true,
As honest madam's issue? Why brand they
    us
With base? with baseness? Bastardy base?
    Base?   10
Who, in the lusty stealth of nature, take
More composition and fierce quality

279 *like a sister:* i.e. with sisterly loyalty   280
as . . . named: by their true names   281 *professèd:*
i.e. love-professing   283 *prefer:* promote   287
alms: small offerings   288 *worth . . . wanted:* i.e.
deserving no affection since you have shown no
affection   289 *plighted:* pleated, enfolded   290
Who . . . derides: i.e. time at first conceals faults,
then exposes them to shame   302 *grossly:* crudely
conspicuous   304 *known himself:* i.e. been aware
of what he truly is   305 *of his time:* period of
his past life   308 *long-ingraffed:* ingrown, chronic
309 *therewithal:* along with that   312 *unconstant
starts:* impulsive moves   315 *compliment:* for-

mality   317 *hit:* agree   319 *surrender:* i.e. yielding
up of authority   320 *offend:* harm   322–323 *i' th'
heat:* i.e. while the iron is hot

I,ii,1 *Nature:* i.e. the material and mechanistic
as distinct from the spiritual and heaven-ordained
3 *Stand . . . custom:* submit to the affliction of
convention   4 *curiosity:* nice distinctions   5 *For
that:* because   *moonshines:* months   6 *Lag of:*
behind (in age)   7 *compact:* fitted, matched   8
generous: befitting the high-born   9 *honest:* chaste
11 *lusty . . . nature:* secrecy of natural lust   12
composition: completeness of constitution,
robustness   *fierce:* mettlesome, thoroughbred

Than doth, within a dull, stale, tirèd bed,
Go to th' creating a whole tribe of fops
Got 'tween asleep and wake? Well then, 15
Legitimate Edgar, I must have your
land.
Our father's love is to the bastard Ed-
mund
As to th' legitimate. Fine word, 'legiti-
mate.'
Well, my legitimate, if this letter speed,
And my invention thrive, Edmund the
base   20
Shall top th' legitimate. I grow, I prosper.
Now, gods, stand up for bastards.

Enter Gloucester.

GLOUCESTER. Kent banished thus? and
France in choler parted?
And the King gone to-night? prescribed
his pow'r?
Confined to exhibition? All this done 25
Upon the gad? Edmund, how now? What
news?
EDMUND. So please your lordship, none.
GLOUCESTER. Why so earnestly seek you to
put up that letter?
EDMUND. I know no news, my lord.
GLOUCESTER. What paper were you read-
ing?   30
EDMUND. Nothing, my lord.
GLOUCESTER. No? What needed then that
terrible dispatch of it into your pocket?
The quality of nothing hath not such need
to hide itself. Let's see. Come if it be 35
nothing, I shall not need spectacles.
EDMUND. I beseech you, sir, pardon me. It is
a letter from my brother that I have not
all o'er-read; and for so much as I have
perused, I find it not fit for your o'er- 40
looking.
GLOUCESTER. Give me the letter, sir.
EDMUND. I shall offend, either to detain or
give it. The contents, as in part I understand them, are to blame.   45
GLOUCESTER. Let's see, let's see.
EDMUND. I hope, for my brother's justifica-

tion, he wrote this but as an essay or taste
of my virtue.
GLOUCESTER. (*reads*) 'This policy and re- 50
verence of age makes the world bitter to
the best of our times; keeps our fortunes
from us till our oldness cannot relish them.
I begin to find an idle and fond bondage
in the oppression of aged tyranny,   55
who sways, not as it hath power, but as it
is suffered. Come to me, that of this I may
speak more. If our father would sleep till
I waked him, you should enjoy half his
revenue for ever, and live the beloved   60
of your brother,   EDGAR.'
Hum! Conspiracy? 'Sleep till I waked him,
you should enjoy half his revenue.' My
son Edgar! Had he a hand to write this?
A heart and brain to breed it in?   65
When came you to this? Who brought it?
EDMUND. It was not brought me, my lord;
there's the cunning of it. I found it thrown
in at the casement of my closet.
GLOUCESTER. You know the character to   70
be your brother's?
EDMUND. If the matter were good, my lord,
I durst swear it were his; but in respect
of that, I would fain think it were not.
GLOUCESTER. It is his.   75
EDMUND. It is his hand, my lord; but I hope
his heart is not in the contents.
GLOUCESTER. Has he never before sounded
you in this business?
EDMUND. Never, my lord. But I have   80
heard him oft maintain it to be fit that,
sons at perfect age, and fathers declined,
the father should be as ward to the son,
and the son manage his revenue.
GLOUCESTER. O villain, villain! His very 85
opinion in the letter. Abhorred villain,
unnatural, detested, brutish villain; worse
than brutish! Go, sirrah, seek him. I'll

---

14 *fops:* fools 15 *Got:* begotten 20 *invention*
thrive: plot succeed 24 *prescribed:* limited 25
exhibition: an allowance, a pension 26 *gad:* spur
28 *put up:* put away 40–41 *o'erlooking:* examination 45 *to blame:* blameworthy

48 *essay:* trial *taste:* test 50–51 *policy and*
reverence: policy of reverencing 51–52 *the best*
of our times: our best years 54 *idle, fond:* foolish
(synonyms) 55–56 *who sways:* which rules 57
suffered: allowed 60 *revenue:* income 66 *to this:*
upon this 69 *casement:* window *closet:* room
70 *character:* handwriting 72 *matter:* contents
73–74 *in respect of that:* i.e. considering what
those contents are 74 *fain:* prefer to 78–79
sounded you: sounded you out 82 *perfect age:*
prime of life 88 *sirrah:* sir (familiar, or contemptuous, form)

apprehend him. Abominable villain!
Where is he?   90

EDMUND. I do not well know, my lord. If it
shall please you to suspend your indignation against my brother till you can derive
from him better testimony of his intent,
you should run a certain course; where,   95
if you violently proceed against him, mis-
taking his purpose, it would make a great
gap in your own honor and shake in
pieces the heart of his obedience. I dare
pawn down my life for him that he   100
hath writ this to feel my affection to your
honor, and to no other pretense of danger.

GLOUCESTER. Think you so?

EDMUND. If your honor judge it meet, I will
place you where you shall hear us con-   105
fer of this and by an auricular assurance
have your satisfaction, and that without
any further delay than this very evening.

GLOUCESTER. He cannot be such a monster.

EDMUND. Nor is not, sure.   110

GLOUCESTER. To his father, that so tenderly
and entirely loves him. Heaven and earth!
Edmund, seek him out; wind me into him,
I pray you; frame the business after your
own wisdom. I would unstate myself   115
to be in a due resolution.

EDMUND. I will seek him, sir, presently; convey the business as I shall find means, and
acquaint you withal.

GLOUCESTER. These late eclipses in the sun   120
and moon portend no good to us. Though
the wisdom of nature can reason it thus
and thus, yet nature finds itself scourged
by the sequent effects. Love cools, friendship falls off, brothers divide. In cities,   125
mutinies; in countries, discord; in palaces,

treason; and the bond cracked 'twixt son
and father. This villain of mine comes
under the prediction, there's son against
father; the King falls from bias of na-   130
ture, there's father against child. We have
seen the best of our time. Machinations,
hollowness, treachery, and all ruinous disorders follow us disquietly to our graves.
Find out this villain, Edmund, it shall   135
lose thee nothing; do it carefully. And the
noble and true-hearted Kent banished; his
offense, honesty. 'Tis strange.   *Exit.*

EDMUND. This is the excellent foppery of the
world, that when we are sick in for-   140
tune, often the surfeits of our own behavior,
we make guilty of our disasters the sun, the
moon, and stars; as if we were villains on
necessity; fools by heavenly compulsion;
knaves, thieves, and treachers by   145
spherical predominance; drunkards, liars,
and adulterers by an enforced obedience
of planetary influence; and all that we
are evil in, by a divine thrusting on. An
admirable evasion of whoremaster   150
man, to lay his goatish disposition on the
charge of a star. My father compounded
with my mother under the Dragon's Tail,
and my nativity was under Ursa Major,
so that it follows I am rough and   155
lecherous. Fut! I should have been that
I am, had the maidenliest star in the
firmament twinkled on my bastardizing.
Edgar—

Enter Edgar.

and pat he comes, like the catastrophe   160
of the old comedy. My cue is villainous

---

95 *run . . . course:* i.e. know where you are
going   101 *feel:* feel out, test   *affection:* attach-
ment, loyalty   102 *pretense of danger:* dangerous
intention   104 *judge it meet:* consider it fitting
206 *by . . . assurance:* i.e. by the proof of your
own ears   113 *wind me:* worm   114 *frame:* plan
115–116 *unstate . . . resolution:* i.e. give everything
to know for certain   117 *presently:* at once   117–
118 *convey:* conduct   119 *withal:* therewith   120
late: recent   122 *wisdom of nature:* natural lore,
science   122–124 *can . . . effects:* i.e. can supply
explanations, yet punitive upheavals in nature
(such as earthquakes) follow   123 *scourged:*
whipped   124 *sequent:* following   126 *mutinies:*
rebellions

128–129 *comes . . . prediction:* i.e. is included
among these ill-omened things   130–131 *bias of
nature:* natural tendency   135–136 *lose thee nothing:* i.e. you will not lose by it   139 *foppery:*
foolishness   140–141 *we are sick . . . surfeits:*
i.e. our fortunes grow sickly, often from the
excesses   145 *treachers:* traitors   145–146 *spherical
predominance:* i.e. ascendancy, or rule, of a particular sphere   151 *goatish:* lecherous   152 *compounded:* (1) came to terms (2) created   153, 154
Dragon's Tail, Ursa Major: (constellations,
cited because of the suggestiveness of their
names)   153 *nativity:* birthday   160 *catastrophe:*
conclusion

melancholy, with a sigh like Tom o'
Bedlam.—O, these eclipses do portend
these divisions. Fa, sol, la, mi.

EDGAR. How now, brother Edmund; 165
what serious contemplation are you in?

EDMUND. I am thinking, brother, of a prediction I read this other day, what should
follow these eclipses.

EDGAR. Do you busy yourself with that? 170

EDMUND. I promise you, the effects he writes
of succeed unhappily: as of unnaturalness
between the child and the parent; death,
dearth, dissolutions of ancient amities;
divisions in state, menaces and male- 175
dictions against king and nobles; needless
diffidences, banishment of friends, dissipa-
tion of cohorts, nuptial breaches, and I
know not what.

EDGAR. How long have you been a 180
sectary astronomical?

EDMUND. Come, come, when saw you my
father last?

EDGAR. The night gone by.

EDMUND. Spake you with him? 185

EDGAR. Ay, two hours together.

EDMUND. Parted you in good terms? Found
you no displeasure in him by word nor
countenance?

EDGAR. None at all. 190

EDMUND. Bethink yourself wherein you may
have offended him; and at my entreaty
forbear his presence until some little time

hath qualified the heat of his displeasure,
which at this instant so rageth in him 195
that with the mischief of your person it
would scarcely allay.

EDGAR. Some villain hath done me wrong.

EDMUND. That's my fear. I pray you have a
continent forbearance till the speed of 200
his rage goes slower; and as I say, retire
with me to my lodging, from whence I will
fitly bring you to hear my lord speak.
Pray ye, go; there's my key. If you do stir
abroad, go armed. 205

EDGAR. Armed, brother?

EDMUND. Brother, I advise you to the best.
Go armed. I am no honest man if there
be any good meaning toward you. I have
told you what I have seen and heard; 210
but faintly, nothing like the image and
horror of it. Pray you away.

EDGAR. Shall I hear from you anon?

EDMUND. I do serve you in this business.
                                    Exit [Edgar].
A credulous father, and a brother 215
noble,
Whose nature is so far from doing harms
That he suspects none; on whose foolish
honesty
My practices ride easy. I see the business.
Let me, if not by birth, have lands by wit;
All with me's meet that I can fashion 220
fit.   *Exit.*

Scene iii

Enter Goneril and Steward [Oswald].

GONERIL. Did my father strike my gentleman
for chiding of his fool?

OSWALD. Ay, madam.

GONERIL. By day and night, he wrongs me!
Every hour

He flashes into one gross crime or other
That sets us all at odds. I'll not endure
it. 5
His knights grow riotous, and himself
upbraids us
On every trifle. When he returns from
hunting,

161–162 *Tom o' Bedlam:* (a type of beggar,
mad or pretending to be, so named from the
London madhouse, Bethlehem or 'Bedlam'
Hospital) 172 *succeed unhappily:* unluckily
follow *unnaturalness:* unkindness, enmity 177
diffidences: instances of distrust 177–178 *dissipa-
tion of cohorts:* melting away of supporters 181
sectary astronomical: of the astrological sect
189 *countenance:* expression, look 194 *qualified*

moderated 196 *mischief:* injury 197 *allay:* be
appeased 200 *continent forbearance:* cautious
inaccessibility 203 *fitly:* conveniently 211
image and horror: horrible true picture 213
anon: soon 218 *practices:* plots 219 *wit:*
intelligence 220 *meet:* proper, acceptable 220
fashion fit: i.e. rig up, shape to the purpose
    I, iii, 3 *day and night:* (an oath) 4 *crime:*
offense 6 *riotous:* boisterous

I will not speak with him. Say I am sick.
If you come slack of former services,
You shall do well; the fault of it I'll
    answer.   [*Horns within.*]   10
OSWALD. He's coming, madam; I hear him.
GONERIL. Put on what weary negligence you
    please,
You and your fellows. I'd have it come
    to question.
If he distaste it, let him to my sister,
Whose mind and mine I know in that are
    one,   15
Not to be overruled. Idle old man,
That still would manage those authorities
That he hath given away. Now, by my
    life,

Old fools are babes again, and must be
    used .
With checks as flatteries, when they are
    seen abused.   20
Remember what I have said.
OSWALD. Well, madam.
GONERIL. And let his kinghts have colder
    looks among you.
What grows of it, no matter; advise your
    fellows so.
I would breed from hence occasions, and
    I shall,
That I may speak. I'll write straight to
    my sister   25
To hold my course. Prepare for dinner.
                                    Exeunt.

Scene iv

Enter Kent [disguised].

KENT. If but as well I other accents borrow
That can my speech defuse, my good
    intent
May carry through itself to that full issue
For which I razed my likeness. Now,
    banished Kent,
If thou canst serve where thou dost stand
    condemned,   5
So may it come, thy master whom thou
    lov'st
Shall find thee full of labors.

    Horns within Enter Lear, Knight,
                          and Attendants.

LEAR. Let me not stay a jot for dinner; go
get it ready. [*Exit an Attendant.*] How now,
what art thou?   10
KENT. A man, sir.
LEAR. What dost thou profess? What wouldst
thou with us?
KENT. I do profess to be no less than I seem,
to serve him truly that will put me in   15
trust, to love him that is honest, to con-

verse with him that is wise and says little,
to fear judgment, to fight when I cannot
choose, and to eat no fish.
LEAR. What art thou?   20
KENT. A very honest-hearted fellow, and as
poor as the King.
LEAR. If thou be'st as poor for a subject as
he's for a king, thou art poor enough.
What wouldst thou?   25
KENT. Service.
LEAR. Who wouldst thou serve?
KENT. You.
LEAR. Dost thou know me, fellow?
KENT. No, sir, but you have that in your   30
countenance which I would fain call
master.
LEAR. What's that?
KENT. Authority.
LEAR. What services canst thou do?   35
KENT. I can keep honest counsel, ride, run,
mar a curious tale in telling it and deliver
a plain message bluntly. That which ordi-
nary men are fit for I am qualified in, and
the best of me is diligence.   40

9 *come . . . services:* i.e. serve him less well than
formerly   10 *answer:* answer for   13 *question:*
i.e. open issue, a thing discussed   14 *distaste:*
dislike   16 *Idle:* foolish   20 *checks . . . abused:*
restraints in place of cajolery when they (the old
men) are seen to be deceived (about their true
state)   24–25 *breed . . . speak:* i.e. make an issue
of it so that I may speak

I, iv, 2 *defuse:* disorder, disguise   3 *full issue:*

perfect result   4 *razed my likeness:* erased my
natural appearance   10 *stay:* wait   12 *profess:*
do, work at (with pun following)   14 *profess:*
claim   16 *converse:* associate   18 *judgment:* i.e.
God's judgment   19 *eat no fish:* be a Protestant
(anachronism), or avoid unmanly diet (?)   31
fain: like to   36 *keep honest counsel:* keep counsel
honestly, i.e. respect confidences   37 *curious:* elaborate, embroidered (as contrasted with 'plain')

LEAR. How old art thou?

KENT. Not so young, sir, to love a woman for singing, nor so old to dote on her for anything. I have years on my back forty-eight.   45

LEAR. Follow me; thou shalt serve me. If I like thee no worse after dinner, I will not part from thee yet. Dinner, ho, dinner! Where's my knave? my fool? Go you and call my fool hither. *Exit an Attendant.*   50

Enter Steward [Oswald].

You, you, sirrah, where's my daughter?

OSWALD. So please you—   *Exit.*

LEAR. What says the fellow there? Call the clotpoll back. [*Exit Knight.*] Where's my fool? Ho, I think the world's asleep.   55

Enter Knight.

How now? Where's that mongrel?

KNIGHT. He says, my lord, your daughter is not well.

LEAR. Why came not the slave back to me when I called him?   60

KNIGHT. Sir, he answered me in the roundest manner, he would not.

LEAR. He would not?

KNIGHT. My lord, I know not what the matter is; but to my judgment your   65 Highness is not entertained with that ceremonious affection as you were wont. There's a great abatement of kindness appears as well in the general dependants as in the Duke himself also and your   70 daughter.

LEAR. Ha? Say'st thou so?

KNIGHT. I beseech you pardon me, my lord, if I be mistaken; for my duty cannot be silent when I think your Highness   75 wronged.

LEAR. Thou but rememb'rest me of mine own conception. I have perceived a most faint neglect of late, which I have rather blamed as mine own jealous curiosity than as a   80 very pretense and purpose of unkindness.

I will look further into't. But where's my fool? I have not seen him this two days.

KNIGHT. Since my young lady's going into France, sir, the fool hath much pined   85 away.

LEAR. No more of that; I have noted it well. Go you and tell my daughter I would speak with her.   [*Exit Knight.*] Go you, call hither my fool.   90

[*Exit an Attendant.*]

Enter Steward [Oswald].

O, you, sir, you! Come you hither, sir. Who am I, sir?

OSWALD. My lady's father.

LEAR. 'My lady's father'? My lord's knave, you whoreson dog, you slave, you cur!   95

OSWALD. I am none of these, my lord; I beseech your pardon.

LEAR. Do you bandy looks with me, you rascal?   [*Strikes him.*]

OSWALD. I'll not be strucken, my lord.   100

KENT. Nor tripped neither, you base football player.   [*Trips up his heels.*]

LEAR. I thank thee, fellow. Thou serv'st me, and I'll love thee.

KENT. Come, sir, arise, away. I'll teach   105 you differences. Away, away. If you will measure your lubber's length again, tarry; but away. Go to! Have you wisdom? So.

[*Pushes him out.*]

LEAR. Now, my friendly knave, I thank thee. There's earnest of thy service.   110

[*Gives money.*]

Enter Fool.

FOOL. Let me hire him too. Here's my cox-comb.   [*Offers Kent his cap.*]

LEAR. How now, my pretty knave? How dost thou?

FOOL. Sirrah, you were best take my   115 coxcomb.

KENT. Why, fool?

FOOL. Why? For taking one's part that's out

---

49 *knave:* boy 54 *clotpoll* clodpoll, dolt 66 *entertained:* rendered hospitality 77 *rememb'rest:* remind 79–79 *faint neglect:* i.e. the 'weary negligence' of I, iii, 12 80 *jealous curiosity:* i.e. suspicious concern about trifles 81 *very pretense:* true intention

98 *bandy:* volley, exchange 100 *strucken:* struck 101 *football:* (an impromptu street and field game, held in low esteem) 106 *differences:* distinctions in rank 108 *Go to!... wisdom:* i.e. Get along! Do you know what's good for you? 110 *earnest:* part payment cox 111 *coxcomb:* (cap of the professional fool, topped with an imitation comb)

of favor. Nay, an thou canst not smile as
the wind sits, thou'lt catch cold shortly. 120
There, take my coxcomb. Why, this fellow
has banished two on's daughters, and did
the third a blessing against his will. If thou
follow him, thou must needs wear my
coxcomb.—How now, nuncle? Would 125
I had two coxcombs and two daughters.

LEAR. Why, my boy?

FOOL. If I gave them all my living, I'ld keep
my coxcombs myself. There's mine; beg
another of thy daughters.   130

LEAR. Take heed, sirrah—the whip.

FOOL. Truth's a dog must to kennel; he must
be whipped out, when the Lady Brach
may stand by th' fire and stink.

LEAR. A pestilent gall to me.   135

FOOL. Sirrah, I'll teach thee a speech.

LEAR. Do.

FOOL. Mark it nuncle.
  Have more than thou showest,
  Speak less than thou knowest,   140
  Lend less than thou owest,
  Ride more than thou goest,
  Learn more than thou trowest,
  Set less than thou throwest;
  Leave thy drink and thy whore,   145
  And keep in-a-door,
  And thou shalt have more
  Than two tens to a score.

KENT. This is nothing, fool.

FOOL. Then 'tis like the breath of an 150
unfee'd lawyer—you gave me nothing for't.
Can you make no use of nothing, nuncle?

LEAR. Why no, boy. Nothing can be made out
of nothing.

FOOL. [to Kent] Prithee tell him, so much 155
the rent of his land comes to; he will not
believe a fool.

LEAR. A bitter fool.

FOOL. Dost thou know the difference, my
boy, between a bitter fool and a sweet 160
one?

LEAR. No, lad; teach me.

FOOL.
  That lord that counselled thee
    To give away thy land,
  Come place him here by me—   165
    Do thou for him stand.
  The sweet and bitter fool
    Will presently appear;
  The one in motley here,
    The other found out there.   170

LEAR. Dost thou call me fool, boy?

FOOL. All thy other titles thou hast given
away; that thou wast born with.

KENT. This is not altogether fool, my lord.

FOOL. No, faith; lords and great men will 175
not let me. If I had a monopoly out, they
would have part on't. And ladies too, they
will not let me have all the fool to myself;
they'll be snatching. Nuncle, give me an
egg, and I'll give thee two crowns.   180

LEAR. What two crowns shall they be?

FOOL. Why, after I have cut the egg i' th'
middle and eat up the meat, the two
crowns of the egg. When thou clovest thy
crown i' th' middle and gav'st away 185
both parts, thou bor'st thine ass on thy
back o'er the dirt. Thou hadst little wit in
thy bald crown when thou gav'st thy golden
one away. If I speak like myself in this,
let him be whipped that first finds it so. 190
[Sings] Fools had ne'er less grace in a year,
  For wise men are grown foppish,
And know not how their wits to wear,
  Their manners are so apish.

119–120 smile . . . sits: i.e. adapt yourself to
prevailing forces 122 banished: i.e. provided the
means for them to become alien to him 125
nuncle: mine uncle 133 Brach: hound bitch 135
gall: sore, source of irritation 141 owest:
borrow (?) own, keep (?) 142 goest: walk 143
Learn: hear, listen to trowest: believe 144 Set
. . . throwest: stake less than you throw for (i.e.
play for odds) 147–148 have . . . score: i.e. do
better than break even 150 breath: voice, counsel
(reliable only when paid for) 156 rent . . . land:
(nothing, since he has no land)

160 bitter, sweet: satirical, non-satirical 166
Do . . . stand: (the Fool thus identifying Lear as
his own foolish counsellor) 170 found out: revealed (since Lear is the 'born' fool as distinct
from himself, the fool in motley, professionally
satirical) 176 let me: (i.e. be all fool, since they
seek a share of folly) 179 snatching: (like greedy
courtiers seeking shares in royal patents of
monopoly) 186–187 bor'st . . . dirt: (thus foolishly reversing normal behavior) 189 like myself:
i.e. like a fool 190 let . . . so: i.e. let him be
whipped (as a fool) who mistakes this truth as
my typical folly 191 grace . . . year: favor at any
time 192 foppish: foolish 193 their wits to
wear: i.e. to use their intelligence

LEAR. When were you wont to be so full   195
of songs, sirrah?

FOOL. I have used it, nuncle, e'er since thou
mad'st thy daughters thy mothers; for
when thou gav'st them the rod, and put'st
down thine own breeches,   200
[*Sings*] Then they for sudden joy did weep,
        And I for sorrow sung,
        That such a king should play bo-
        peep
        And go the fools among.
Prithee, nuncle, keep a schoolmaster   205
that can teach thy fool to lie. I would fain
learn to lie.

LEAR. An you lie, sirrah, we'll have you
whipped.

FOOL. I marvel what kin thou and thy   210
daughters are. They'll have me whipped for
speaking true; thou'lt have me whipped
for lying; and sometimes I am whipped
for holding my peace. I had rather be any
kind o'thing than a fool, and yet I   215
would not be thee, nuncle: thou hast pared
thy wit o' both sides and left nothing i' th'
middle. Here comes one o' the parings.

Enter Goneril.

LEAR. How now, daughter? What makes that
frontlet on? You are too much of   220
late i' th' frown.

FOOL. Thou wast a pretty fellow when thou
hadst no need to care for her frowning.
Now thou art an O without a figure. I am
better than thou art now: I am a fool,   225
thou art nothing. [*to Goneril*] Yes, forsooth,
I will hold my tongue. So your face bids
me, though you say nothing. Mum, mum,
        He that keeps nor crust nor crum,
        Weary of all, shall want some.—   230
[*Points at Lear.*] That's a shealed peascod.

GONERIL. Not only, sir, this your all-licensed
fool,
But other of your insolent retinue

Do hourly carp and quarrel, breaking forth
In rank and not-to-be-endurèd riots.   235
Sir,
I had thought by making this well known
unto you
To have found a safe redress, but now
grow fearful,
By what yourself too late have spoke and
done,
That you protect this course, and put it on
By your allowance; which if you should,
the fault,   240
Would not 'scape censure, nor the re-
dresses sleep,
Which, in the tender of a wholesome weal,
Might in their working do you that offense,
Which else were shame, that then necessity
Will call discreet proceeding.   245

FOOL. For you know, nuncle,
        The hedge-sparrow fed the cuckoo so
        long
        That it's had it head bit off by it young.
So out went the candle, and we were
left darkling.

LEAR. Are you our daughter?   250

GONERIL. I would you would make use of
your good wisdom
(Whereof I know you are fraught) and put
away
These dispositions which of late transport
you
From what you rightly are.

FOOL. May not an ass know when the cart
draws the horse?   255
Whoop, Jug, I love thee!

LEAR. Does any here know me? This is not
Lear.
Does Lear walk thus? speak thus? Where
are his eyes?

---

234 *carp:* complain   237 *safe:* sure   239 *put
it on:* instigate it   240 *allowance:* approval   241
redresses sleep: correction lie dormant   242 *tender
of:* care for   *weal:* state   243–245 *Might . . .
proceeding:* in their operation might be considered humiliating to you but, under the circumstances, are merely prudent   247 *cuckoo:*
(an image suggesting illegitimacy as well as
voraciousness, since the cuckoo lays its eggs in
the nests of other birds)   248 *it:* its   249 *darkling:* in the dark (like the dead hedge-sparrow and
the threatened Lear)   252 *fraught* freighted, laden
253 *dispositions:* moods   256 *Jug:* Joan (evidently
part of some catch-phrase)

---

197 *used:* practiced   203 *play bo-peep:* i.e. act
like a child   208 *An:* if   216–218 *pared . . .
middle:* i.e. completely disposed of your wits
(indisposing of your power)   220 *frontlet:* band
worn across the brow: hence, frown   224 *O . . .
figure:* cipher without a digit to give it value   229
crum: soft bread within the crust   230 *want:*
need   231 *shealed:* shelled, empty   *peascod:* pea-
pod   232 *all-licensed:* all-privileged

Either his notion weakens, his discernings
Are lethargied—Ha! Waking? 'Tis not
so.   260
Who is it that can tell me who I am?
FOOL. Lear's shadow.
LEAR. I would learn that; for, by the marks
of sovereignty,
Knowledge, and reason, I should be false
persuaded
I had daughters.   265
FOOL. Which they will make an obedient
father.
LEAR. Your name, fair gentlewoman?
GONERIL. This admiration, sir, is much o' th'
savor
Of other your new pranks. I do beseech
you
To understand my purposes aright.   270
As you are old and reverend, should be
wise.
Here do you keep a hundred knights and
squires,
Men so disordered, so deboshed, and bold
That this our court, infected with their
manners,
Shows like a riotous inn. Epicurism and
lust   275
Makes it more like a tavern or a brothel
Than a graced palace. The shame itself
doth speak
For instant remedy. Be then desired
By her that else will take the thing she begs
A little to disquantity your train,   280
And the remainders that shall still depend
To be such men as may besort your age,
Which know themselves, and you.
LEAR.   Darkness and devils!
Saddle my horses; call my train together.
Degenerate bastard, I'll not trouble
thee: 285

---

259 *notion:* understanding 260 *Ha! Waking:*
i.e. so I am really awake (presumably accompanied by the 'business' of pinching himself) 263
marks of sovereignty: evidences that I am King
(and hence the father of the princesses) 268
admiration: air of wonderment 273 *deboshed:*
debauched 275 *Epicurism:* loose living 277
graced: honored *shame:* disgrace 280 *disquantity
your train:* reduce the size of your retinue 281
depend: be attached 282 *besort:* befit 283 *Which
know:* i.e. who are aware of the status of 285
Degenerate: unnatural, fallen away from kind

Yet have I left a daughter.
GONERIL. You strike my people, and your
disordered rabble
Make servants of their betters.

Enter Albany.

LEAR. Woe that too late repents.—O, sir, are
you come?
Is it your will? Speak, sir.—Prepare my
horses.   290
Ingratitude! thou marble-hearted fiend,
More hideous when thou show'st thee in
a child
Than the sea-monster.
ALBANY.   Pray, sir, be patient.
LEAR. Detested kite, thou liest.
My train are men of choice and rarest
parts,   295
That all particulars of duty know
And in the most exact regard support
The worships of their name. O most small
fault,
How ugly didst thou in Cordelia show!
Which, like an engine, wrenched my frame
of nature   300
From the fixed place; drew from my heart
all love
And added to the gall. O Lear, Lear, Lear!
Beat at this gate that let thy folly in
                          [*Strikes his head.*]
And thy dear judgment out. Go, go, my
people.
ALBANY. My lord, I am guiltless, as I am
ignorant   305
Of what hath moved you.
LEAR.   It may be so, my lord.
Hear, Nature, hear; dear goddess, hear:
Suspend thy purpose if thou didst intend
To make this creature fruitful.
Into her womb convey sterility,   310
Dry up in her the organs of increase,
And from her derogate body never spring
A babe to honor her. If she must teem,
Create her child of spleen, that it may live

---

294 *Detested kite:* detestable bird of prey 295
parts: accomplishments 297 *exact regard:* careful attention, punctiliousness 298 *worships:*
honor 300 *engine:* destructive contrivance of
war 300–301 *wrenched . . . place:* set askew my
natural structure, distorted my normal self 302
gall: bitterness 312 *derogate:* degraded 313
teem: increase 314 *spleen:* ill-humor, spitefulness

And be a thwart disnatured torment to
her.   315
Let it stamp wrinkles in her brow of youth,
With cadent tears fret channels in her
cheeks,
Turn all her mother's pains and benefits
To laughter and contempt, that she may
feel
How sharper than a serpent's tooth it is 320
To have a thankless child. Away, away!
                                                    Exit.
ALBANY. Now, gods that we adore, whereof
comes this?
GONERIL. Never afflict yourself to know more
of it,
But let his disposition have that scope
As dotage gives it.   325

                Enter Lear.

LEAR. What, fifty of my followers at a clap?
Within a fortnight?
ALBANY.   What's the matter, sir?
LEAR. I'll tell thee. [*to Goneril*] Life and
death, I am ashamed
That thou hast power to shake my man-
hood thus!
That these hot tears, which break from me
perforce,   330
Should make thee worth them. Blasts and
fogs upon thee!
Th' untented woundings of a father's curse
Pierce every sense about thee! Old fond
eyes,
Beweep this cause again I'll pluck ye out
And cast you, with the waters that you
loose,   335
To temper clay. [Yea, is it come to this?]
Ha! Let is be so. I have another daughter,
Who I am sure is kind and comfortable.
When she shall hear this of thee, with her
nails
She'll flay thy wolvish visage. Thou shalt
find   340

That I'll resume the shape which thou dost
think
I have cast off for ever.
                Exit Lear with Kent and Attendants.
GONERIL.   Do you mark that?
ALBANY. I cannot be so partial, Goneril,
To the great love I bear you—
GONERIL. Pray you, content.—What, Oswald,
ho!   345
[*To Fool*] You, sir, more knave than fool,
after your master!
FOOL. Nuncle Lear, nuncle Lear, tarry. Take
the fool with thee.
      A fox, when one has caught her,
      And such a daughter,
      Should sure to the slaughter,   350
      If my cap would buy a halter.
      So the fool follows after.   *Exit.*
GONERIL. This man hath had good counsel
—a hundred knights!
'Tis politic and safe to let him keep
At point a hundred knights—yes, that on
every dream,   355
Each buzz, each fancy, each complaint,
dislike,
He may enguard his dotage with their
pow'rs
And hold our lives in mercy.—Oswald, I
say!
ALBANY. Well, you may fear too far.
GONERIL.   Safer than trust too far.
Let me still take away the harms I
fear,   360
Not fear still to be taken. I know his heart.
What he hath uttered I have writ my sister.
If she sustain him and his hundred knights,
When I have showed th' unfitness—

                Enter Steward [Oswald].

                                    How now, Oswald?
What, have you writ that letter to my
sister?   365

---

315 *thwart disnatured:* perverse unnatural 316
cadent: falling *fret* wear   318 *pains and benefits* care and offerings 325 *disposition* mood
330 *perforce:* by force, against my will   332 *untented:* untentable, too deep for treatment by a
probe   333 *sense about:* faculty possessed by
fond: foolish 334 *Beweep this cause:* if you weep
over this matter 335 *loose:* let loose 336 *temper:*
soften   338 *comfortable:* ready to comfort

341 *shape:* i.e. rôle of authority 343–344 *partial
. . . To:* made partial . . . by 347 *the fool:* i.e. both
your fool and your folly 350 *slaughter:* hanging
and quartering   351, 352 *halter, after:* (pronounced 'hauter,' 'auter') 353 *good counsel:* i.e.
from such company (ironic) 354 *politic:* prudent
355 *At point:* in arms   356 *buzz:* murmur 358
in mercy: at his mercy 360 *still . . . harms:* always
eliminate the sources of injury   361 *still . . .
taken:* always to be overtaken (by them)

OSWALD. Ay, madam.

GONERIL. Take you some company, and away
to horse.

Inform her full of my particular fear,
And thereto add such reasons of your own
As may compact it more. Get you gone, 370
And hasten your return. [*Exit Oswald.*]
No, no, my lord,
This milky gentleness and course of yours,

Though I condemn not, yet under pardon,
You are much more ataskèd for want of
wisdom
Than praised for harmful mildness.   375

ALBANY. How far your eyes may pierce I
cannot tell;
Striving to better, oft we mar what's well.

GONERIL. Nay then—

ALBANY. Well, well; th' event.   *Exeunt.*

Scene v

Enter Lear, Kent, and Fool.

LEAR. Go you before to Gloucester with these
letters. Acquaint my daughter no further
with anything you know than comes from
her demand out of the letter. If your
diligence be not speedy, I shall be there   5
afore you.

KENT. I will not sleep, my lord, till I have
delivered your letter.   *Exit.*

FOOL. If a man's brains were in's heels, were't
not in danger of kibes?   10

LEAR. Ay, boy.

FOOL. Then I prithee be merry. Thy wit shall
not go slipshod.

LEAR. Ha, ha, ha.

FOOL. Shalt see thy other daughter will   15
use thee kindly; for though she's as like
this as a crab's like an apple, yet I can tell
what I can tell.

LEAR. What canst tell, boy?

FOOL. She will taste as like this as a crab   20
does to a crab. Thou canst tell why one's
nose stands i' th' middle on's face?

LEAR. No.

FOOL. Why, to keep one's eyes of either side's
nose, that what a man cannot smell out   25
he may spy into.

LEAR. I did her wrong.

FOOL. Canst tell how an oyster makes his
shell?

LEAR. No.   30

FOOL. Nor I neither; but I can tell why a
snail has a house.

LEAR. Why?

FOOL. Why, to put 's head in; not to give it
away to his daughters, and leave his   35
horns without a case.

LEAR. I will forget my nature. So kind a
father!—Be my horses ready?

FOOL. Thy asses are gone about 'em. The
reason why the seven stars are no moe   40
than seven is a pretty reason.

LEAR. Because they are not eight.

FOOL. Yes indeed. Thou wouldst make a
good fool.

LEAR. To take 't again perforce—Mon-   45
ster ingratitude!

FOOL. If thou wert my fool, nuncle, I'ld have
thee beaten for being old before thy time.

LEAR. How's that?

FOOL. Thou shouldst not have been old   50
till thou hadst been wise.

LEAR. O, let me not be mad, not mad, sweet
heaven! Keep me in temper; I would not
be mad!

Enter a Gentleman.

---

366 *some company:* an escort 368 *particular
own* 370 *compact it more:* substantiate it
further 372 *milky ... course:* mildly gentle way
374 *ataskèd:* censured, taken to task 375 *harmful
mildness:* mildness that proves harmful 379 *th'
event:* the outcome, i.e. we shall see what happens
I, v, 4 *demand out of:* i.e. questioning provoked
by reading 10 *kibes:* chilblains 12 *wit ...
slipshod:* intelligence (brain) shall not go slip-
pered (because of 'kibes') 15 *Shalt:* thou shalt

16 *kindly* after her kind, i.e. in the same way as
this daughter 17 *crab* crabapple 27 *her:* i.e.
Cordelia (the first of the remarkable intimations
of Lear's inner thoughts in this scene) 35 *horns:*
i.e. snail's horns (with pun on cuckold's horns;
the legitimacy of Goneril and Regan being,
figuratively, suspect throughout) 36 *case:* covering 37 *nature:* i.e. fatherly instincts 40 *moe*
more 44 *perforce:* by force 53 *in temper:* properly balanced

How now, are the horses ready?   55
GENTLEMAN. Ready, my lord.
LEAR. Come boy.
FOOL. She that's a maid now, and laughs at

my departure,
Shall not be a maid long, unless things
be cut shorter.   *Exeunt.*

ACT II

Scene i

Enter Bastard [Edmund] and Curan severally.

EDMUND. Save thee, Curan.

CURAN. And you, sir. I have been with your
father, and given him notice that the Duke
of Cornwall and Regan his Duchess will
be here with him this night.   5

EDMUND. How comes that?

CURAN. Nay, I know not. You have heard
of the news abroad—I mean the whispered
ones, for they are yet but ear-kissing
arguments?   10

EDMUND. Not I. Pray you, what are they?

CURAN. Have you heard of no likely wars
toward, 'twixt the Dukes of Cornwall and
Albany?

EDMUND. Not a word.   15

CURAN. You may do, then, in time. Fare you
well, sir.   *Exit.*

EDMUND. The Duke be here to-night? The
better best!

This weaves itself perforce into my business.

My father hath set guard to take my
brother,

And I have one thing of a queasy question   20

Which I must act. Briefness and fortune,
work!

Brother, a word: descend. Brother, I say!

Enter Edgar.

My father watches. O sir, fly this place.
Intelligence is given where you are hid.

You have now the good advantage of the
night.   25

Have you not spoken 'gainst the Duke of
Cornwall?

He's coming hither; now i' th' night, i'
th' haste,

And Regan with him. Have you nothing
said

Upon his party 'gainst the Duke of Albany?

Advise yourself.

EDGAR.   I am sure on't, not a word. 30

EDMUND. I hear my father coming. Pardon
me:

In cunning I must draw my sword upon
you.

Draw, seem to defend yourself; now quit
you well.—

Yield! Come before my father! Light ho,
here!—

Fly, brother.—Torches, torches!—So farewell.   *Exit Edgar.* 35

Some blood drawn on me would beget
opinion

Of my more fierce endeavor. [*Wounds his
arm.*] I have seen drunkards

Do more than this in sport.—Father,
father!

Stop, stop! No help?

Enter Gloucester, and Servants with torches.

GLOUCESTER. Now, Edmund, where's the
villain?   40

EDMUND. Here stood he in the dark, his
sharp sword out,

59–60 *She . . . shorter:* (an indecent gag addressed to the audience, calculated to embarrass
the maids who joined in the laughter)
II, i, 1 *Save:* God save 9–10 *ear-kissing arguments:* whispered topics 12 *likely:* probable
13 *toward:* impending 17 *better best:* (hyperbole)
18 *perforce:* of necessity (?) of its own accord (?)

20 *of . . . question:* delicately balanced as to outcome, touch-and-go 21 *Briefness and fortune:*
decisive speed and good luck 28 *Upon his party*
'gainst: i.e. reflecting upon his feud against 29
Advise yourself: take thought 30 *on't:* of it 32
In cunning: i.e. as a ruse 33 *quit you:* acquit
yourself

Mumbling of wicked charms, conjuring the moon
To stand auspicious mistress.

GLOUCESTER.   But where is he?

EDMUND. Look, sir, I bleed.

GLOUCESTER.
                    Where is the villain, Edmund?

EDMUND. Fled this way, sir, when by no means he could—   45

GLOUCESTER. Pursue him, ho! Go after. [*Exeunt some Servants.*] By no means what?

EDMUND. Persuade me to the murder of your lordship;
But that I told him the revenging gods
'Gainst parricides did all the thunder bend;
Spoke with how manifold and strong a bond   50
The child was bound to th' father—sir, in fine,
Seeing how loathly opposite I stood
To his unnatural purpose, in fell motion
With his preparèd sword he charges home
My unprovided body, latched mine arm;   55
And when he saw my best alarumed spirits
Bold in the quarrel's right, roused to th' encounter,
Or whether gasted by the noise I made,
Full suddenly he fled.

GLOUCESTER.   Let him fly far.
Not in this land shall he remain uncaught;   60
And found—dispatch. The noble Duke my master,
My worthy arch and patron, comes tonight:
By his authority I will proclaim it
That he which finds him shall deserve our thanks,
Bringing the murderous coward to the stake;   65

He that conceals him, death.

EDMUND. When I dissuaded him from his intent
And found him pight to do it, with curst speech
I threatened to discover him. He replied,
'Thou unpossessing bastard; dost thou think,   70
If I would stand against thee, would the reposal
Of any trust, virtue, or worth in thee
Make thy words faithed? No. What I should deny
(As this I would, ay, though thou didst produce
My very character) I'ld turn it all   75
To thy suggestion, plot, and damnèd practice;
And thou must make a dullard of the world,
If they not thought the profits of my death
Were very pregnant and potential spirits
To make thee seek it.'

GLOUCESTER.
                    O strange and fast'ned villain!   80
Would he deny his letter, said he? I never got him.   *Tucket within.*
Hark, the Duke's trumpets. I know not why he comes.
All ports I'll bar; the villain shall not 'scape;
The Duke must grant me that. Besides, his picture
I will send far and near, that all the kingdom   85
May have due note of him; and of my land,
Loyal and natural boy, I'll work the means
To make thee capable.

---

49 *bend:* aim   51 *in fine:* finally   52 *loathly opposite:* in loathing opposition   53 *fell:* deadly   55 *unprovided:* undefended   *latched:* lanced, pierced   56 *best alarumed:* fully aroused   57 *Bold . . . right:* confident in the justice of the cause   58 *gasted:* struck aghast   61 *dispatch:* (equivalent to 'death' or 'finis')   62 *arch:* superior

68 *pight:* determined, set   *curst:* angry   69 *discover:* expose   70 *unpossessing:* having no claim, landless   71 *reposal:* placing   72 *faithed:* believed   75 *character:* written testimony   76 *suggestion:* instigation   *practice:* devices   77 *make . . . world:* i.e. consider everyone stupid   78 *not thought:* did not think   79 *pregnant . . . spirits:* teeming and powerful spirits, i.e. the devils which 'possess' him   80 *fast'ned:* confirmed   81 *got* begot   S.D. *Tucket:* (personal signature in trumpet notes)   88 *capable:* i.e. legitimate, able to inherit

Enter Cornwall, Regan, and Attendants.

CORNWALL. How now, my noble friend?
Since I came hither (Which I can call but
now) I have heard strange news.   90
REGAN. If it be true, all vengeance comes too
short
Which can pursue th' offender. How dost,
my lord?
GLOUCESTER. O madam, my old heart is
cracked, it's cracked.
REGAN. What, did my father's godson seek
your life?
He whom my father named, your Edgar? 95
GLOUCESTER. O lady, lady, shame would have
it hid.
REGAN. Was he not companion with the
riotous knights
That tended upon my father?
GLOUCESTER. I know not, madam. 'Tis too
bad, too bad.
EDMUND. Yes, madam, he was of that con-
sort.   100
REGAN. No marvel then though he were ill
affected.
'Tis they have put him on the old man's
death,
To have th' expense and waste of his rev-
enues.
I have this present evening from my sister
Been well informed of them, and with such
cautions   105
That, if they come to sojourn at my house,
I'll not be there.
CORNWALL.   Nor I, assure thee, Regan.
Edmund, I hear that you have shown your
father
A childlike office.
EDMUND.   It was my duty, sir.
GLOUCESTER. He did bewray his practice, and
received   110
This hurt you see, striving to apprehend
him.
CORNWALL. Is he pursued?

GLOUCESTER.   Ay, my good lord.
CORNWALL. If he be taken, he shall never
more
Be feared of doing harm. Make your own
purpose,
How in my strength you please. For you,
Edmund,   115
Whose virtue and obedience doth this
instant
So much commend itself, you shall be
ours.
Natures of such deep trust we shall much
need;
You we first seize on.
EDMUND.   I shall serve you, sir,
Truly, however else.
GLOUCESTER.
          For him I thank your Grace.   120
CORNWALL. You know not why we came to
visit you?
REGAN. Thus out of season, threading dark-
eyed night.
Occasions, noble Gloucester, of some
prize,
Wherein we must have use of your advice.
Our father he hath writ, so hath our
sister,   125
Of differences, which I best thought it fit
To answer from our home. The several
messengers
From hence attend dispatch. Our good old
friend,
Lay comforts to your bosom, and bestow
Your needful counsel to our businesses, 130
Which craves the instant use.
GLOUCESTER.   I serve you, madam.
Your Graces are right welcome.
                    Exeunt. Flourish.

---

114 *of doing:* lest he do 114–115 *Make . . .
please:* i.e. accomplish your purpose, making free
use of my powers 116 *virtue and obedience:*
virtuous obedience 123 *prize:* price, importance
126 *differences:* quarrels *which:* (refers, indefi-
nitely, to the whole situation) 127 *answer . . .
home:* cope with away from home (where she
need not receive Lear) 128 *attend dispatch:*
i.e. await settlement of the business 129 *Lay . . .
bosom:* be consoled (about your own trouble)
130 *needful:* needed 131 *craves . . . use* requires
immediate transaction (?) or use of your counsel (?)

---

90 *call:* i.e. say was 100 *consort:* company, set
101 *affected:* disposed 102 *put:* set 103 *expense and waste:* wasteful expenditure 109
childlike: filial 110 *bewray his practice:* expose
his plot

Scene ii

Enter Kent and Steward [Oswald], severally.

OSWALD. Good dawning to thee, friend. Art
of this house?

KENT. Ay.

OSWALD. Where may we set our horses?

KENT. I' th' mire.

OSWALD. Prithee, if thou lov'st me, tell
me.   5

KENT. I love thee not.

OSWALD. Why then, I care not for thee.

KENT. If I had thee in Lipsbury Pinfold, I
would make thee care for me.

OSWALD. Why dost thou use me thus? I   10
know thee not.

KENT. Fellow, I know thee.

OSWALD. What dost thou know me for?

KENT. A knave, a rascal, an eater of broken
meats; a base, proud, shallow, beggarly,   15
three-suited, hundred-pound, filthy worsted-stocking knave; a lily-livered, action-
taking, whoreson, glass-gazing, superserviceable, finical rogue; one-trunk-in-
heriting slave; one that wouldst be a   20
bawd in way of good service, and art nothing but the composition of a knave, beggar, coward, pander, and the son and heir
of a mongrel bitch; one whom I will beat
into clamorous whining if thou deny'st   25
the least syllable of thy addition.

OSWALD. Why, what a monstrous fellow art
thou, thus to rail on one that is neither
known of thee nor knows thee!

KENT. What a brazen-faced varlet art thou   30
to deny thou knowest me! Is it two days

ago since I tripped up thy heels and beat
thee before the King? [*Draws his sword.*]
Draw, you rogue, for though it be night,
yet the moon shines. I'll make a sop o'   35
th' moonshine of you. You whoreson cullionly barbermonger, draw!

OSWALD. Away, I have nothing to do with
thee.

KENT. Draw, you rascal. You come with   40
letters against the King, and take Vanity
the puppet's part against the royalty of
her father. Draw, you rogue, or I'll so
carbonado your shanks. Draw, you rascal.
Come your ways!   45

OSWALD. Help, ho! Murder! Help!

KENT. Strike, you slave! Stand, rogue! Stand,
you neat slave! Strike!   [*Beats him.*]

OSWALD. Help, ho! Murder, murder!

*Enter Bastard [Edmund, with his rapier
drawn], Cornwall, Regan, Gloucester,
Servants.*

EDMUND. How now? What's the matter?   50
Part!

KENT. With you, goodman boy, if you please!
Come, I'll flesh ye; come on, young master.

GLOUCESTER. Weapons? Arms? What's the
matter here?   55

CORNWALL. Keep peace, upon your lives.
He dies that strikes again. What is the
matter?

REGAN. The messengers from our sister and
the King.   60

CORNWALL. What is your difference? Speak.

OSWALD. I am scarce in breath, my lord.

KENT. No marvel, you have so bestirred your
valor. You cowardly rascal, nature disclaims in thee. A tailor made thee.   65

II, ii, 1 *dawning:* (perhaps indicating that it is
too early for 'good morning') *Art . . . house:* i.e.
do you belong to this household   8 *Lipsbury
Pinfold:* i.e. between the teeth (cant term: 'pen in
the region of the lips')   14–15 *broken meats:*
scraps   16 *three-suited:* with three suits (the
wardrobe allowed serving-men)   *hundred-pound:*
(the minimal estate for anyone aspiring to gentility)   16–17 *worsted-stocking:* (serving-men's
attire)   17–18 *action-taking:* i.e. cowardly (re-
sorting to law instead of fighting)   18, 19 *glass-
gazing, superserviceable, finical:* i.e. conceited,
toadying, foppish   19–20 *inheriting:* possessing
20–21 *a bawd . . . service:* i.e. a pander, if pleasing
your employer required it   22 *composition* composite   26 *addition:* titles

---

35–36 *sop o' th' moonshine:* i.e. something that
sops up moonshine through its perforations   36–
37 *cullionly barbermonger:* vile fop (i.e. always
dealing with hairdressers)   41–42 *Vanity the
puppet:* i.e. Goneril (here equated with a stock
figure in morality plays, now dwindled into
puppet shows)   44 *carbonado:* dice (like a steak)
45 *your ways* get along   48 *neat:* primping   52
goodman boy: (doubly contemptuous, since peasants were addressed as 'goodmen')   53 *flesh ye:*
give you your first taste of blood   63 *bestirred:*
exercised   64–65 *disclaims:* claims no part

CORNWALL. Thou art a strange fellow. A tailor make a man?

KENT. A tailor, sir. A stonecutter or a painter could not have made him so ill, though they had been but two years o' th' trade. 70

CORNWALL. Speak yet, how grew your quarrel?

OSWALD. This ancient ruffian, sir, whose life I have spared at suit of his gray bread—

KENT. Thou whoreson zed, thou unneces- 75 sary letter! My lord, if you will give me leave, I will tread this unbolted villain into mortar and daub the wall of a jakes with him. Spare my gray beard? you wagtail.

CORNWALL. Peace, sirrah! 80 You beastly knave, know you no reverence?

KENT. Yes, sir, but anger hath a privilege.

CORNWALL. Why art thou angry?

KENT. That such a slave as this should wear a sword,
Who wears no honesty. Such smiling rogues as these 85
Like rats oft bite the holy cords atwain
Which are too intrinse t' unloose; smooth every passion
That in the natures of their lords rebel,
Being oil to fire, snow to the colder moods;
Renege, affirm, and turn their halcyon beaks 90
With every gale and vary of their masters,
Knowing naught, like dogs, but following.
A plague upon your epileptic visage!
Smile you my speeches, as I were a fool?

Goose, if I had you upon Sarum Plain, 95
I'ld drive ye cackling home to Camelot.

CORNWALL. What, art thou mad, old fellow?

GLOUCESTER. How fell you out? Say that.

KENT. No contraries hold more antipathy
Than I and such a knave. 100

CORNWALL. Why dost thou call him knave? What is his fault?

KENT. His countenance likes me not.

CORNWALL. No more perchance does mine, nor his, nor hers. 105

KENT. Sir, 'tis my occupation to be plain:
I have seen better faces in my time
Than stands on any shoulder that I see
Before me at this instant.

CORNWALL.   This is some fellow
Who, having been praised for bluntness, doth affect 110
A saucy roughness, and constrains the garb
Quite from his nature. He cannot flatter, he;
An honest mind and plain—he must speak truth.
An they will take it, so; if not, he's plain.
These kind of knaves I know which in this plainness 115
Harbor more craft and more corrupter ends
Than twenty silly-ducking observants
That stretch their duties nicely.

KENT. Sir, in good faith, in sincere verity,
Under th' allowance of your great aspect, 120
Whose influence, like the wreath of radiant fire
On flick'ring Phoebus' front—

CORNWALL.   What mean'st by this?

---

68 *stonecutter:* sculptor 74 *At suit of:* on the plea of, moved to mercy by 75 *zed:* z (last and least useful of letters) 77 *unbolted:* unsifted, crude 78 *jakes:* privy 79 *wagtail:* (any of several birds whose tail-feathers wag or bob, suggesting obsequiousness or effeminacy) 81 *beastly:* beast-like, irrational 86 *holy cords:* sacred bonds (between parents and children, husbands and wives, man and God) 87 *intrinse:* intrinsic, inextricable *smooth:* flatter, cater to 88 *rebel:* (i.e. against reason and moral restraint) 89 *Being . . . moods:* (i.e. feeders of intemperance) 90 *Renege:* deny 90 *halcyon beaks:* kingfisher beaks (supposedly servings as weathervanes when the birds were hung up by their necks) 91 *gale and varying:* varying wind 93 *epileptic:* contorted in a grin (?) 94 *Smile you:* smile you at, mock you

95 *Sarum Plain:* Salisbury Plain (said to have been associated with geese, but the allusion remains cryptic) 96 *Camelot:* legendary seat of King Arthur, variously sited at Winchester, near Cadbury, in Wales, etc. 99 *contraries:* opposites 111–112 *constrains . . . nature:* distorts the plain fashion from its true nature, caricatures it 117 *silly-ducking observants:* ludicrously bowing form-serves 118 *nicely:* fussily 120 *allowance:* approval *aspect:* (1) appearance (2) heavenly position 121 *influence:* astrological force 122 *Phoebus' front:* sun's forehead (i.e. face) 123 *go . . . dialect:* depart from my way of speaking

KENT. To go out of my dialect, which you
   discommend so much. I know, sir, I am
   no flatterer. He that beguiled you in a 125
   plain accent was a plain knave, which, for
   my part, I will not be, though I should
   win your displeasure to entreat me to't.

CORNWALL. What was th' offense you gave
   him?

OSWALD. I never gave him any.   130
   It pleased the King his master very late
   To strike at me, upon his misconstruction;
   When he, compact, and flattering his dis-
   pleasure,
   Tripped me behind; being down, insulted,
   railed,
   And put upon him such a deal of man 135
   That worthied him, got praises of the King
   For him attempting who was self-subdued;
   And, in the fleshment of this dread exploit,
   Drew on me here again.

KENT.   None of these rogues and cowards
   But Ajax is their fool.

CORNWALL.   Fetch forth the stocks! 140
   You stubborn ancient knave, you reverent
   braggart,
   We'll teach you.

KENT.   Sir, I am too old to learn.
   Call not your stocks for me, I serve the
   King—
   On whose employment I was sent to you;
   You shall do small respect, show too bold
   malice   145
   Against the grace and person of my
   master,
   Stocking his messenger.

CORNWALL. Fetch forth the stocks. As I have
   life and honor,

There shall he sit till noon.

REGAN. Till noon? Till night, my lord, and
   all night too.   150

KENT. Why, madam, if I were your father's
   dog,
   You should not use me so.

REGAN.   Sir, being his knave, I will.

CORNWALL. This is a fellow of the selfsame
   color
   Our sister speaks of. Come, bring away
   the stocks.   Stocks brought out.

GLOUCESTER. Let me beseech your Grace not
   to do so.   155
   His fault is much, and the good King his
   master
   Will check him for't. Your purposed low
   correction
   Is such as basest and contemnèd'st
   wretches
   For pilf'rings and most common trespasses
   Are punished with.   160
   The King his master needs must take it ill
   That he, so slightly valued in his mes-
   senger,
   Should have him thus restrained.

CORNWALL.   I'll answer that.

REGAN. My sister may receive it much more
   worse,
   To have her gentleman abused, assault-
   ed,   165
   For following her affairs. Put in his legs.
                          [Kent is put in the stocks.]

CORNWALL. Come, my lord, away!
            Exit [with all but Gloucester and Kent.]

GLOUCESTER. I am sorry for thee, friend. 'Tis
   the Duke's pleasure,
   Whose disposition all the world well
   knows
   Will not be rubbed nor stopped. I'll entreat
   for thee.   170

KENT. Pray do not, sir. I have watched and
   travelled hard.
   Some time I shall sleep out, the rest I'll
   whistle.

---

125 *He:* (the type of plain-speaker Cornwall
has condemned) 127–128 *though ... to't:* though
I should persuade your disapproving self to beg
me to do so (? with 'displeasure' sarcastically
substituted for 'grace') 131 *very late:* quite
recently 132 *misconstruction:* misunderstanding
133 *compact:* in league with 135 *And put ...
man:* i.e. affected such excessive manliness 136
worthied: enhanced his worth 137 *For him ...
self-subdued:* for assailing him (Oswald) who
chose not to resist 138 *fleshment of:* blood-
thirstiness induced by 139 *None ... fool:* i.e.
the Ajax type, stupidly belligerent, is the favorite
butt of cowardly rogues like Oswald 141 *Stubborn:* rude *reverent:* aged 145 *malice:* ill will
146 *grace:* royal honor

---

153 *color:* kind 154 *away:* along 157 *check:*
rebuke *purposed:* intended 158 *contemnèd'st:*
most harshly sentenced 162 *slightly valued in:*
i.e. little respected in the person of 163 *answer:*
answer for 169 *disposition:* inclination 170
rubbed: deflected (bowling term) 171 *watched:*
gone sleepless

A good man's fortune may grow out at heels.

Give you good morrow.

GLOUCESTER. The Duke's to blame in this. 175

'Twill be ill taken.   *Exit.*

KENT. Good King, that must approve the common saw,

Thou out of heaven's benediction com'st

To the warm sun.

Approach, thou beacon to this under globe,   180

That by thy comfortable beams I may

Peruse this letter. Nothing almost sees miracles

But misery. I know 'tis from Cordelia,

Who hath most fortunately been informed

Of my obscured course. And shall find time   185

From this enormous state, seeking to give

Losses their remedies.—All weary and o'erwatched,

Take vantage, heavy eyes, not to behold

This shameful lodging. Fortune, good night;

Smile once more, turn thy wheel.   190

[*Sleeps.*]

Scene *iii*

Enter Edgar.

EDGAR. I heard myself proclaimed,

And by the happy hollow of a tree

Escaped the hunt. No port is free, no place

That guard and most unusual vigilance

Does not attend my taking. Whiles I may 'scape,   5

I will preserve myself; and am bethought

To take the basest and most poorest shape

That ever penury, in contempt of man,

Brought near to beast: my face I'll grime with filth,

Blanket my loins, elf all my hairs in knots,   10

And with presented nakedness outface

The winds and persecutions of the sky.

The country gives me proof and precedent

Of Bedlam beggars, who, with roaring voices,

Strike in their numbed and mortified bare arms   15

Pins, wooden pricks, nails, sprigs of rosemary;

And with this horrible object, from low farms,

Poor pelting villages, sheepcotes, and mills,

Sometimes with lunatic bans, sometime with prayers,

Enforce their charity. Poor Turlygod, poor Tom,   20

That's something yet: Edgar I nothing am.   *Exit.*

Scene *iv*

Enter Lear, Fool, and Gentleman.

LEAR. 'Tis strange that they should so depart from home,

And not send back my messenger.

GENTLEMAN.   As I learned,

The night before there was no purpose in them

---

173 *A good . . . heels:* i.e. it is no disgrace to decline in fortune 174 *Give:* God give 176 *taken:* received 177 *approve:* demonstrate the truth of *saw:* saying, proverb 178–179 *Thou . . . sun:* (proverb. meaning from better to worse, i.e. from heavenly shelter to earthly exposure—'the heat of the day') 180 *beacon . . . globe:* i.e. the sun (here viewed as benign) 182 *Nothing . . . misery:* i.e. miraculous aid is seldom seen (or searched for?) except by the miserable 185 *obscurèd:* disguised 185–187 *And . . . remedies* (incoherent: perhaps corrupt, or perhaps snatches read from the letter) 186 *enormous state* monstrous situation 187 *Losses:* reverses 188 *vantage:*

i.e. advantage of sleep 189 *lodging:* (in the stocks) 190 *wheel:* (Fortune's wheel was represented as vertical. Kent is at its bottom.)

II, iii, 2 *happy hollow:* i.e. lucky hiding-place 5 *attend my taking:* contemplate my capture 6 *bethought:* in mind 10 *elf:* tangle (into 'elf-locks') 11 *presented* a show of 13 *proof:* example 14 *Bedlam:* (see I, ii,) 15 *Strike:* stick *mortified:* deadened to pain 16 *pricks:* skewers 17 *object:* picture 18 *pelting:* paltry 19 *bans:* curses 20 *Turlygod:* (unidentified, but evidently another name for a Tom o'Bedlam) 21 *Edgar:* i.e. as Edgar

II, iv, 3 *purpose:* intention

Of this remove.

KENT.   Hail to thee, noble master.

LEAR. Ha!   5

Mak'st thou this shame thy pastime?

KENT.   No, my lord.

FOOL. Ha, ha, he wears cruel garters. Horses
are tied by the heads, dogs and bears by
th' neck, monkeys by th' loins, and men
by th' legs. When a man's over-lusty at   10
legs, then he wears wooden nether-stocks.

LEAR. What's he that hath so much thy place
mistook
To set thee here?

KENT.   It is both he and she,
Your son and daughter.

LEAR. No.   15

KENT. Yes.

LEAR. No, I say.

KENT. I say yea.

LEAR. No, no, they would not.

KENT. Yes, they have.   20

LEAR. By Jupiter, I swear no!

KENT. By Juno, I swear ay!

LEAR.   They durst not do't;
They could not, would not do't. 'Tis worse
than murder
To do upon respect such violent outrage.
Resolve me with all modest haste which
way   25
Thou mightst deserve or they impose this
usage,
Coming from us.

KENT.   My lord, when at their home
I did commend your Highness' letters to
them,
Ere I was risen from the place that showed
My duty kneeling, came there a reeking
post,   30
Stewed in his haste, half breathless, pant-
ing forth
From Goneril his mistress salutations;
Delivered letters, spite of intermission,

Which presently they read; on whose con-
tents
They summoned up their meiny, straight
took horse,   35
Commanded me to follow and attend
The leisure of their answer, gave me cold
looks;
And meeting here the other messenger,
Whose welcome I perceived had poisoned
mine,
Being the very fellow which of late   40
Displayed so saucily against your High-
ness,
Having more man than wit about me,
drew;
He raised the house with loud and coward
cries.
Your son and daughter found this trespass
worth
The shame which here it suffers.   45

FOOL. Winter's not gone yet, if the wild geese
fly that way.
      Fathers that wear rags
         Do make their children blind,
      But fathers that bear bags
         Shall see their children kind.   50
      Fortune, that arrant whore,
         Ne'er turns the key to th' poor.
But for all this, thou shalt have as many
dolors for thy daughters as thou canst
tell in a year.   55

LEAR. O, how this mother swells up toward
my heart!
Hysterica passio, down, thou climbing
sorrow;
Thy element's below. Where is this
daughter?

KENT. With the Earl, sir, here within.

─────────

34 *presently:* immediately *on:* on the strength
of   35 *meiny:* attendants   41 *Displayed:*
showed off   42 *man:* manhood   *wit:* sense   43
raised: aroused   46 *Winter's . . . way:* i.e. the ill
season continues according to these signs (with
Cornwall and Regan equated with 'wild geese,'
proverbially evasive)   47 *blind:* (to their fathers'
needs)   48 *bags:* (of gold)   51 *Fortune . . . whore:*
(because so fickle and callous)   52 *turns the key:*
i.e. opens the door   54 *dolors:* sorrows (with pun
on 'dollars,' continental coins)   55 *tell:* count
56, 57 *mother, Hysterica passio:* hysteria (the
popular and the medical terms)   57 *element:*
proper place

─────────

3 *remove:* removal   7 *cruel:* painful (with pun
on 'crewel,' a yarn used in garters)   10–11 *over-
lusty at legs:* i.e. too much on the go (?) or too
much given to kicking (?)   11 *nether-stocks:*
stockings (as distinct from 'upper-stocks' or
breeches)   24 *To . . . outrage:* i.e. to show such
outrageous disrespect   25 *Resolve:* enlighten
modest: seemly   28 *commend:* entrust   31 *Stewed:*
steaming   33 *spite of intermission:* in disregard
of its being an interruption

LEAR.   Follow me not;
  Stay here.   *Exit.* 60
GENTLEMAN. Made you no more offense but
  what you speak of?
KENT. None.
  How chance the King comes with so small
  a number?
FOOL. An thou hadst been set i' th' stocks for
  that question, thou'dst well deserved it. 65
KENT. Why, fool?
FOOL. We'll set thee to school to an ant, to
  teach thee there's no laboring i' th' winter.
  All that follow their noses are led by their
  eyes but blind men, and there's not a 70
  nose among twenty but can smell him that's
  stinking. Let go thy hold when a great
  wheel runs down a hill, lest it break thy
  neck with following. But the great one that
  goes upward, let him draw thee after. 75
  When a wise man gives thee better counsel,
  give me mine again. I would have none
  but knaves follow it since a fool gives it.
    That sir which serves and seeks for gain,
      And follows but for form,   80
    Will pack when it begins to rain
      And leave thee in the storm.
    But I will tarry; the fool will stay,
      And let the wise man fly.
    The knave turns fool that runs away; 85
      The fool no knave, perdy.
KENT. Where learned you this, fool?
FOOL. Not i' th' stocks, fool.

                Enter Lear and Gloucester.

LEAR. Deny to speak with me? They are sick,
  they are weary,
  They have travelled all the night? Mere
  fetches,   90
  The images of revolt and flying off!
  Fetch me a better answer.

---

69 *no laboring . . . winter:* (Lear, accompanied
by 'so small a number,' is equated with winter
bereft of workers, such as ants.) 69–72 *All . . .
stinking:* i.e. almost anyone can smell out a
person decayed in fortune 77–78 *none but
knaves:* (Here and in what follows the Fool
repudiates his advice to abandon Lear.) 80 *form:*
show 81 *pack:* be off 85 *The knave . . . away:*
i.e. faithlessness is the true folly 86 *perdy:* I
swear (from *par dieu*) 88 *fool:* (persiflage, but
also a term of honor; cf. V,iii, 306) 90 *fetches:*
counterfeit reasons, false likenesses of truth 91
images: true likenesses *flying off:* revolt

GLOUCESTER.   My dear lord,
  You know the fiery quality of the Duke,
  How unremovable and fixed he is
  In his own course.   95
LEAR. Vengeance, plague, death, confu-
  sion!
  Fiery? What quality? Why, Gloucester,
  Gloucester,
  I'd speak with the Duke of Cornwall and
  his wife.
GLOUCESTER. Well, my good lord, I have
  informed them so.
LEAR. Informed them? Dost thou understand
  me, man?   100
GLOUCESTER. Ay, my good lord.
LEAR. The King would speak with Cornwall.
  The dear father
  Would with his daughter speak, com-
  mands—tends—service.
  Are they informed of this? My breath and
  blood!
  Fiery? The fiery Duke, tell the hot Duke
  that—   105
  No, but not yet. Maybe he is not well.
  Infirmity doth still neglect all office
  Whereto our health is bound. We are not
  ourselves
  When nature, being oppressed, commands
  the mind
  To suffer with the body. I'll forbear; 110
  And am fallen out with my more headier
  will
  To take the indisposed and sickly fit
  For the sound man.—Death on my state!
  Wherefore
  Should he sit here? This act persuades me
  That this remotion of the Duke and her 115
  Is practice only. Give me my servant forth.
  Go tell the Duke and's wife I'ld speak with
  them!
  Now, presently! Bid them come forth and
  hear me,
  Or at their chamber door I'll beat the
  drum

---

93 *quality:* disposition 102 *tends:* attends,
awaits (?) or tenders, offers (?) 107 *all office:*
duties 108 *Whereto . . . bound:* to which, in
health, we are bound 111 *headier:* headstrong
114 *he:* i.e. Kent 115 *remotion:* remaining remote, inaccessible 116 *practice:* trickery 118
presently: immediately

Till it cry sleep to death.   120

GLOUCESTER. I would have all well betwixt
you.   *Exit.*

LEAR. O me, my heart, my rising heart! But
down!

FOOL. Cry to it, nuncle, as the cockney did
to the eels when she put 'em i' th' paste
alive. She knapped 'em o' th' coxcombs 125
with a stick and cried, 'Down, wantons,
down!' 'Twas her brother that, in pure
kindness to his horse, buttered his hay.

Enter Cornwall, Regan, Gloucester, Servants.

LEAR. Good morrow to you both.

CORNWALL.   Hail to your Grace.
                    Kent here set at liberty.

REGAN. I am glad to see your Highness. 130

LEAR. Regan, I think you are. I know what
reason
I have to think so. If thou shouldst not be
glad,
I would divorce me from thy mother's
tomb,
Sepulchring an adultress. [*to Kent*] O, are
you free?
Some other time for that.—Beloved Regan,   135
Thy sister's naught. O Regan, she hath
tied
Sharp-toothed unkindness, like a vulture,
here.
I can scarce speak to thee. Thou'lt not
believe
With how depraved a quality—O Regan!

REGAN. I pray you, sir, take patience. I have
hope   140
You less know how to value her desert
Than she to scant her duty.

LEAR.   Say? how is that?

REGAN. I cannot think my sister in the least

Would fail her obligation. If, sir, perchance
She have restrained the riots of your fol-
lowers,   145
'Tis on such ground, and to such whole-
some end,
As clears her from all blame.

LEAR. My curses on her!

REGAN.   O, sir, you are old;
Nature in you stands on the very verge
Of his confine. You should be ruled, and
led   150
By some discretion that discerns your state
Better than you yourself. Therefore I pray
you
That to our sister you do make return;
Say you have wronged her.

LEAR.   Ask her forgiveness?
Do you but mark how this becomes the
house: 155
'Dear daughter, I confess that I am old.
                                    [*Kneels.*]
Age is unnecessary. On my knees I beg
That you'll vouchsafe me raiment, bed,
and food.'

REGAN. Good sir, no more. These are un-
sightly tricks.
Return you to my sister.

LEAR.   [*rises*] Never, Regan.   160
She hath abated me of half my train,
Looked black upon me, struck me with
her tongue
Most serpent-like upon the very heart.
All the stored vengeances of heaven fall
On her ingrateful top! Strike her young
bones,
You taking airs, with lameness.

CORNWALL.   Fie, sir, fie!   165

LEAR. You nimble lightnings, dart your
blinding flames
Into her scornful eyes! Infect her beauty,
You fen-sucked fogs drawn by the pow'rful
sun
To fall and blister.

---

120 *cry:* pursue with noise (like a pack or 'cry'
of hounds) 123 *cockney:* city-dweller 124 *paste:*
pastry pie 125 *knapped* rapped 126 *wantons:*
i.e. frisky things 128 *buttered his hay:* (another
example of rustic humor at the expense of
cockney inexperience) 133–134 *divorce . . . adultress:* i.e. refuse to be buried with your mother
since such a child as you must have been con-
ceived in adultery 139 *how . . . quality:* i.e. what
innate depravity 140 *have hope:* i.e. suspect
142 *scant:* (in effect, a double negative: 'do'
would be more logical though less emphatic)

149–150 *Nature . . . confine:* i.e. your life nears
the limit of its tenure 151 *some discretion . . .
state:* someone discerning enough to recognize
your condition 155 *the house:* household or
family decorum 160 *abated:* curtailed 164
ingrateful top: ungrateful head 165 *taking:*
infectious 168 *fen-sucked:* drawn up from
swamps 169 *fall and blister:* strike and raise
blisters (such as those of smallpox)

REGAN.   O the blest gods!
So will you wish on me when the rash
  mood is on.   170
LEAR. No, Regan, thou shalt never have my
  curse.
Thy tender-hefted nature shall not give
Thee o'er to harshness. Her eyes are fierce,
  but thine
Do comfort, and not burn. 'Tis not in thee
To grudge my pleasures, to cut off my
  train,   175
To bandy hasty words, to scant my sizes,
And, in conclusion, to oppose the bolt
Against my coming in. Thou better
  know'st
The offices of nature, bond of childhood,
Effects of courtesy, dues of gratitude. 180
Thy half o' th' kingdom hast thou not
  forgot,
Wherein I thee endowed.
REGAN.   Good sir, to th' purpose.
                                  Tucket within.
LEAR. Who put my man i' th' stocks?
CORNWALL.   What trumpet's that?
REGAN. I know't—my sister's. This approves
  her letter,
That she would soon be here.

                  Enter Steward [Oswald].

                          Is your lady come? 185
LEAR. This is a slave, whose easy-borrowèd
  pride
Dwells in the fickle grace of her he follows.
Out, varlet, from my sight.
CORNWALL.   What means your Grace?
LEAR. Who stocked my servant? Regan, I
  have good hope
Thou didst not know on't.

                  Enter Goneril.

Who comes here? O heavens! 190
If you do love old men, if your sweet sway
Allow obedience, if you yourselves are old,

Make it your cause. Send down, and take
  my part.
[*To Goneril*] Art not ashamed to look upon
  this beard? ·
O Regan, will you take her by the
  hand?   195
GONERIL. Why not by th' hand, sir? How
  have I offended?
All's not offense that indiscretion finds
And dotage terms so.
LEAR.   O sides, you are too tough!
Will you yet hold? How came my man i'
  th' stocks?
CORNWALL. I set him there, sir; but his own
  disorders   200
Deserved much less advancement
LEAR.   You? Did you?
REGAN. I pray you, father, being weak, seem
  so.
If till the expiration of your month
You will return and sojourn with my sister,
Dismissing half your train, come then to
  me.   205
I am now from home, and out of that
  provision
Which shall be needful for your entertain-
  ment.
LEAR. Return to her, and fifty men dismissed?
No, rather I abjure all roofs, and choose
To wage against the enmity o' th' air, 210
To be a comrade with the wolf and owl,
Necessity's sharp pinch. Return with her?
Why, the hot-blooded France, that dower-
  less took
Our youngest born, I could as well be
  brought
To knee his throne, and, squire-like, pen-
  sion beg   215
To keep base life afoot. Return with her?
Persuade me rather to be slave and
  sumpter
To this detested groom.

---

172 *tender-hefted:* swayed by tenderness, gently disposed   176 *bandy:* volley   *sizes:* allowances 177 *oppose the bolt:* i.e. bar the door   179 *offices of nature:* natural duties   180 *Effects:* actions 182 *purpose:* point   184 *approves:* confirms 185 *easy-borrowèd* acquired on small security   186 *grace:* favor   187 *varlet:* low fellow   192 *Allow:* approve

193 *Make . . . cause:* i.e. make my cause yours 197 *indiscretion finds:* ill judgment detects as such 198 *sides:* breast (which should burst with grief) 200 *less advancement:* i.e. more abasement   201 *seem so:* i.e. act the part   207 *entertainment:* lodging   210 *wage:* fight   212 *Necessity's sharp pinch:* (a summing up of the hardships previously listed)   213 *hotblooded:* choleric (cf. I, ii, 23)   215 *knee:* kneel at   *squire-like:* like an attendant 217 *sumpter:* packhorse   218 *groom:* i.e. Oswald

GONERIL.   At your choice, sir.
LEAR. I prithee, daughter, do not make me
mad.
I will not trouble thee, my child; fare-
well.   220
We'll no more meet, no more see one
another.
But yet thou art my flesh, my blood, my
daughter;
Or rather a disease that's in my flesh,
Which I must needs call mine. Thou art
a boil,
A plague-sore, or embossèd carbuncle 225
In my corrupted blood. But I'll not chide
thee.
Let shame come when it will, I do not call
it.
I do not bid the thunder-bearer shoot,
Nor tell tales of thee to high-judging
Jove.
Mend when thou canst, be better at thy
leisure;   230
I can be patient, I can stay with Regan,
I and my hundred knights.
REGAN.   Not altogether so.
I looked not for you yet, nor am provided
For your fit welcome. Give ear, sir, to my
sister;
For those that mingle reason with your
passion   235
Must be content to think you old, and so—
But she knows what she does.
LEAR.   Is this well spoken?
REGAN. I dare avouch it, sir. What, fifty fol-
lowers?
Is it not well? What should you need of
more?
Yea, or so many, sith that both charge
and danger   240
Speak 'gainst so great a number? How
in one house
Should many people, under two com-
mands,
Hold amity? 'Tis hard, almost impossible.
GONERIL. Why might not you, my lord, re-
ceive attendance

From those that she calls servants, or from
mine?   245
REGAN. Why not, my lord? If then they
chanced to slack ye,
We could control them. If you will come
to me
(For now I spy a danger), I entreat you
To bring but five-and-twenty. To no
more
Will I give place or notice.   250
LEAR. I gave you all.
REGAN.   And in good time you gave it.
LEAR. Made you my guardians, my deposi-
taries,
But kept a reservation to be followèd
With such a number. What, must I come
to you
With five-and-twenty? Regan, said you
so?   255
REGAN. And speak't again, my lord. No more
with me.
LEAR. Those wicked creatures yet do look
well-favored
When others are more wicked; not being
the worst
Stands in some rank of praise. [to Goneril]
I'll go with thee.
Thy fifty yet doth double five-and-
twenty,   260
And thou art twice her love.
GONERIL.   Hear me, my lord.
What need you five-and-twenty? ten? or
five?
To follow in a house where twice so many
Have a command to tend you?
REGAN.   What need one? 265
LEAR. O reason not the need! Our basest
beggars
Are in the poorest thing superfluous.
Allow not nature more than nature needs,
Man's life is cheap as beast's. Thou art
a lady:

---

225 embossèd: risen to a head 228 thunder-
bearer: i.e. Jupiter 229 high-judging: judging
from on high 235 mingle . . . passion: interpret
your passion in the light of reason 238 avouch:
swear by 240 sith that: since charge: expense

246 slack: neglect 250 notice: recognition 252
depositaries: trustees 253 kept . . . to be: stipu-
lated that I be 257 well-favored: comely 259
Stands . . . praise: i.e. is at least relatively praise-
worthy 261 her love: i.e. as loving as she 266
reason: analyze 267 Are . . . superfluous: i.e. have
some poor possession not utterly indispensable
268 than nature needs: i.e. than life needs for
mere survival

If only to go warm were gorgeous, 270
Why, nature needs not what thou gorgeous
  wear'st,
Which scarcely keeps thee warm. But, for
  true need—
You heavens, give me that patience, pa-
  tience I need.
You see me here, you gods, a poor old
  man,
As full of grief as age, wretched in
  both.   275
If it be you that stirs these daughters'
  hearts
Against their father, fool me not so much
To bear it tamely; touch me with noble
  anger,
And let not women's weapons, water
  drops,
Stain my man's cheeks. No, you unnatural
  hags!   280
I will have such revenges on you both
That all the world shall—I will do such
  things—
What they are, yet I know not; but they
  shall be
The terrors of the earth. You think I'll
  weep.
No, I'll not weep. *Storm and tempest.* 285
I have full cause of weeping, but this heart
Shall break into a hundred thousand flaws
Or ere I'll weep. O fool, I shall go mad!
Exeunt Lear, Fool, Kent, and Gloucester.
CORNWALL. Let us withdraw; 'twill be a
  storm.
REGAN. This house is little; the old man and's
  people   290
Cannot be well bestowed.

GONERIL. 'Tis his own blame; hath put him-
  self from rest
And must needs taste his folly.
REGAN. For his particular, I'll receive him
  gladly,
But not one follower.
GONERIL.   So am I purposed. 295
Where is my Lord of Gloucester?
CORNWALL. Followèd the old man forth.

Enter Gloucester.

                          He is returned.
GLOUCESTER. The King is in high rage.
CORNWALL.   Whither is he going?
GLOUCESTER. He calls to horse, but will I
  know not whither.
CORNWALL. 'Tis best to give him way; he
  leads himself.   300
GONERIL. My lord, entreat him by no means
  to stay.
GLOUCESTER. Alack, the night comes on, and
  the high winds
Do sorely ruffle. For many miles about
There's scarce a bush.
REGAN.   O, sir, to willful men
The injuries that they themselves pro-
  cure   305
Must be their schoolmasters. Shut up your
  doors.
He is attended with a desperate train,
And what they may incense him to, being
  apt
To have his ear abused, wisdom bids fear.
CORNWALL. Shut up your doors, my lord;
  'tis a wild night.   310
My Regan counsels well. Come out o' th'
  storm.   *Exeunt.*

ACT III

Scene i

*Storm still. Enter Kent and
a Gentleman severally.*

KENT. Who's there besides foul weather?
GENTLEMAN. One minded like the weather,
  most unquietly.

270–272 *If . . . warm:* i.e. if to be dressed warmly
(i.e. for need) were considered sufficiently gorgeous, you would not need your present attire,
which is gorgeous rather than warm   277 *fool:*
play with, humiliate   287 *flaws:* fragments   288
Or ere: before   292 *hath . . . rest:* i.e. he himself
is responsible for leaving his resting place with

her (?) or, he is self-afflicted (?)   294 *particular:*
own person   295 *purposed:* determined   303
ruffle: rage   308 *apt . . . abused:* i.e. predisposed
to listen to ill counsel

III, i, 2 *minded . . . unquietly:* i.e. in disturbed
mood

KENT. I know you. Where's the King?

GENTLEMAN. Contending with the fretful elements;

Bids the wind blow the earth into the
sea,   5
Or swell the curlèd waters 'bove the main,
That things might change or cease; tears
his white hair,
Which the impetuous blasts, with eyeless
rage,
Catch in their fury and make nothing of;
Strives in his little world of man to out-
scorn   10
The to-and-fro-conflicting wind and rain.
This night, wherein the cub-drawn bear
would couch,
The lion and the belly-pinchèd wolf
Keep their fur dry, unbonneted he runs,
And bids what will take all.

KENT.   But who is with him?   15

GENTLEMAN. None but the fool, who labors
to outjest
His heart-struck injuries.

KENT.   Sir, I do know you,
And dare upon the warrant of my note
Commend a dear thing to you. There is
division,
Although as yet the face of it is cov-
ered   20
With mutual cunning, 'twixt Albany and
Cornwall;
Who have—as who have not, that their
great stars
Throned and set high?—servants, who
seem no less,
Which are to France the spies and specu-
lations
Intelligent of our state. What hath been
seen,   25

Either in snuffs and packings of the Dukes,
Or the hard rein which both of them have
borne
Against the old kind King, or something
deeper,
Whereof, perchance, these are but furnish-
ings—
But, true it is, from France there comes a
power   30
Into this scatterèd kingdom, who already,
Wise in our negligence, have secret feet
In some of our best ports and are at point
To show their open banner. Now to you:
If on my credit you dare build so far   35
To make your speed to Dover, you shall find
Some that will thank you, making just
report
Of how unnatural and bemadding sorrow
The King hath cause to plain.
I am a gentleman of blood and breeding,   40
And from some knowledge and assurance
offer
This office to you.

GENTLEMAN. I will talk further with you.

KENT.   No, do not.
For confirmation that I am much more
Than my out-wall, open this purse and
take   45
What it contains. If you shall see Cordelia,
As fear not but you shall, show her this
ring,
And she will tell you who that fellow is
That yet you do not know. Fie on this
storm!
I will go seek the King.   50

GENTLEMAN. Give me your hand. Have you
no more to say?

KENT. Few words, but, to effect, more than
all yet:
That when we have found the King—in
which your pain
That way, I'll this—he that first lights on
him
Holla the other.   *Exeunt severally*   55

---

4 *Contending:* quarrelling 6 *main:* mainland
7 *change:* revert to chaos (?) or, improve (?)
8 *eyeless:* (1) blind (2) invisible 10 *little world:*
(the 'microcosm,' which is disturbed like the
great world or 'macrocosm') 12 *cub-drawn:*
cubsucked (and hence ravenous) 13 *belly-
pinchèd:* famished 15 *take all:* (the cry of the
desperate gambler in staking his last) 18 *warrant
. . . note:* assurance of my knowledge 19 *Commend . . . thing:* entrust a precious matter 22
that: whom *stars* destinies 23 *Throned:* have
throned *no less:* i.e. truly so 24 *speculations:*
spies 25 *Intelligent:* supplying intelligence

26 *snuffs:* quarrels *packings:* intrigues 27
hard rein . . . borne: i.e. harsh curbs . . . exercised
29 *furnishings:* pretexts 30 *power:* army 31
scatterèd: divided 35 *my credit:* trust in me
build: take constructive action 38 *bemadding sorrow:* maddening grievances 39 *plain:* lament 42
office: service 45 *out-wall:* surface appearance
52 *to effect:* in their import 53 *pain:* pains, care

Scene ii

Storm still. Enter Lear and Fool.

LEAR. Blow, winds, and crack your cheeks.
Rage, blow.
You cataracts and hurricanoes, spout
Till you have drenched our steeples,
drowned the cocks.
You sulph'rous and thought-executing
fires,
Vaunt-couriers to oak-cleaving thunder-
bolts,   5
Singe my white head. And thou, all-
shaking thunder,
Strike flat the thick rotundity o' th' world,
Crack Nature's moulds, all germains spill
at once,
That makes ingrateful man.
FOOL. O nuncle, court holy-water in a dry   10
house is better than this rain water our o'
door. Good nuncle, in; ask thy daughters
blessing. Here's a night pities neither wise
men nor fools.
LEAR. Rumble thy bellyful. Spit, fire. Spout,
rain.   15
Nor rain, wind, thunder, fire are my
daughters.
I tax not you, you elements, with unkindness.
I never gave you kingdom, called you
children;
You owe me no subscription. Then let fall
Your horrible pleasure. Here I stand your
slave,   20
A poor, infirm, weak, and despised old
man.
But yet I call you servile ministers,
That will with two pernicious daughters
join
Your high-engendered battles 'gainst a
head

So old and white as this. O, ho! 'tis
foul.   25
FOOL. He that has a house to put's head in
has a good headpiece.
The codpiece that will house
Before the head has any,
The head and he shall louse:
So beggars marry many.   30
The man that makes his toe
What he his heart should make
Shall of a corn cry woe,
And turn his sleep to wake.
For there was never yet fair woman but   35
she made mouths in a glass.

Enter Kent.

LEAR. No, I will be the pattern of all pati-
ence;
I will say nothing.
KENT. Who's there?
FOOL. Marry, here's grace and a codpiece;
that's a wise man and a fool.   40
KENT. Alas, sir, are you here? Things that
love night
Love not such nights as these. The wrath-
ful skies
Gallow the very wanderers of the dark
And make them keep their caves. Since I
was man,
Such sheets of fire, such bursts of horrid
thunder,   45
Such groans of roaring wind and rain, I
never
Remember to have heard. Man's nature
cannot carry
Th' affliction nor the fear.

III, ii, 2 *hurricanoes:* waterspouts 3 *cocks:* weathercocks 4 *thought-executing fires:* i.e. flashes of lightning swift as thought (?) or, dazing, benumbing the mind (?) 5 *Vauntcouriers:* heralds 8 *moulds:* (in which Nature's creations are formed) *germains:* seeds 10 *court holy-water:* flattery (slang) 17 *tax:* charge 19 *subscription:* deference 20 *pleasure:* will 22 *ministers:* agents 24 *high-engendered battles:* heavenly battalions

27–30 *The codpiece . . . many:* (The moral of the rime is that improvident cohabitation spells penury.) 27 *codpiece:* padded gusset at the crotch of the trunks (slang for 'phallus') 29 *he:* it 30 *many:* (head-lice and body-lice, accompanying poverty) 31–34 *The man . . . wake:* (a parallel instance of misery deriving from reckless impulse: to transpose the tender and precious heart and the tough and base toe is to invite injury; with 'heart' also suggesting Cordelia) 36 *made . . . glass:* i.e. posed before a mirror (irrelevant, except as vanity is a form of folly, the Fool's general theme) 43 *Gallow:* frighten 44 *keep their caves:* i.e. keep under cover 45 *horrid:* horrible 47 *carry:* bear

LEAR.   Let the great gods
That keep this dreadful pudder o'er our
  heads
Find out their enemies now. Tremble,
  thou wretch,   50
That hast within thee undivulgèd crimes
Unwhipped of justice. Hide thee, thou
  bloody hand,
Thou perjured, and thou simular of virtue
That art incestuous. Caitiff, to pieces
  shake,
That under covert and convenient seem-
  ing   55
Has practiced on man's life. Close pent-up
  guilts,
Rive your concealing continents and cry
These dreadful summoners grace. I am a
  man
More sinned against than sinning.

KENT.   Alack, bareheaded?
Gracious my lord, hard by here is a
  hovel;   60
Some friendship will it lend you 'gainst
  the tempest.
Repose you there, while I to this hard
  house
(More harder than the stones whereof 'tis
  raised,
Which even but now, demanding after you,
Denied me to come in) return, and
  force   65
Their scanted courtesy.

LEAR.   My wits begin to turn.
Come on, my boy. How dost, my boy?
  Art cold?
I am cold myself. Where is this straw, my
  fellow?
The art of our necessities is strange,
And can make vile things precious. Come,
  your hovel.   70

Poor fool and knave, I have one part in
  my heart
That's sorry yet for thee.

FOOL. [*sings*]
He that has and a little tiny wit,
    With, heigh-ho, the wind and the rain,
  Must make content with his fortunes
    fit   75
  Though the rain it raineth every day.

LEAR. True, boy. Come, bring us to this
  hovel.   *Exit with Kent.*

FOOL. This is a brave night to cool a cour-
  tesan. I'll speak a prophecy ere I go:
  When priests are more in word than
    matter;   80
  When brewers mar their malt with
    water;
  When nobles are their tailors' tutors,
  No heretics burned, but wenches' sui-
    tors;
  When every case in law is right,
  No squire in debt nor no poor
    knight;   85
  When slanders do not live in tongues,
  Nor cutpurses come not to throngs;
  When usurers tell their gold i' th' field,
  And bawds and whores do churches
    build—
  Then shall the realm of Albion   90
  Come to great confusion.
  Then comes the time, who lives to see't,
  That going shall be used with feet.
  This prophecy Merlin shall make, for I
  live before his time.   *Exit.* 95

---

49 *pudder:* turmoil 50 *Find ... enemies:* i.e.
discover sinners (by their show of fear) 53
simular: counterfeit 55 *seeming:* hypocrisy 56
practiced on: plotted against *Close* secret 57
Rive: split, break through *continents* containers,
covers 57 *summoners:* arresting officers of ec-
clesiastical courts *grace:* mercy 60 *Gracious my
lord:* my gracious lord 62 *house:* household
(both building and occupants) 64 *demanding
after:* inquiring for 66 *scanted:* stinted 69 *art:*
magic skill (as in alchemy)

75 *make ... fit:* i.e. reconcile himself to his
fortunes 78 *brave:* fine 80 *are ... matter:* i.e.
can outshine the gospel message (At present
their ability to speak is quite unworthy of their
theme.) 81 *mar:* i.e. dilute (At present they
dilute water with malt, producing very small
beer.) 82 *are ... tutors:* i.e. are no longer subservient to fashion (Each subsequent line also
reverses the present state of affairs.) 83 *burned:*
(pun on contracting venereal disease) *wenches'
suitors:* i.e. libertines 88 *tell:* count *i' th' field:*
(instead of in secret places) 90 *Albion:* England
91 *confusion:* ruin (ironic: an edifice of abuses is
'ruined' by reform) 93 *going ... feet:* walking
will be done with feet (the humor of anticlimax,
but suggesting a return to normality) 94 *Merlin:*
(a legendary magician associated with King
Arthur, who reigned later than King Lear)

Scene iii

Enter Gloucester and Edmund.

GLOUCESTER. Alack, alack, Edmund, I like
not this unnatural dealing. When I desired
their leave that I might pity him, they took
from me the use of mine own house,
charged me on pain of perpetual dis-   5
pleasure neither to speak of him, entreat
for him, or any way sustain him.

EDMUND. Most savage and unnatural.

GLOUCESTER. Go to; say you nothing. There
is division between the Dukes, and a   10
worse matter than that. I have received
a letter this night—'tis dangerous to be
spoken—I have locked the letter in my
closet. These injuries the King now bears
will be revenged home; there is part   15
of a power already footed; we must incline
to the King. I will look him and privily
relieve him. Go you and maintain talk
with the Duke, that my charity be not of
him perceived. If he ask for me, I am   20
ill and gone to bed. If I die for it, as no
less is threatened me, the King my old
master must be relieved. There is strange
things toward, Edmund; pray you be
careful.   *Exit.* 25

EDMUND. This courtesy forbid thee shall the
    Duke
Instantly know, and of that letter too.
This seems a fair deserving, and must draw
    me
That which my father loses—no less than
    all.
The younger rises when the old doth fall.
                                          Exit. 30

Scene iv

Enter Lear, Kent, and Fool.

KENT. Here is the place, my lord. Good my
    lord, enter.
The tyranny of the open night's too rough
For nature to endure.   *Storm still.*

LEAR.   Let me alone.

KENT. Good my lord, enter here.

LEAR.   Wilt break my heart?

KENT. I had rather break mine own. Good
    my lord, enter.   5

LEAR. Thou think'st 'tis much that this con-
    tentious storm
Invades us to the skin. So 'tis to thee,
But where the greater malady is fixed
The lesser is scarce felt. Thou'dst shun a
    bear;
But if thy flight lay toward the roaring
    sea,   10
Thou'dst meet the bear i' th' mouth.
    When the mind's free,
The body's delicate. The tempest in my
    mind
Doth from my senses take all feeling else
Save what beats there. Filial ingrati-
    tude,   15
Is it not as this mouth should tear this
    hand
For lifting food to't? But I will punish
    home.
No, I will weep no more. In such a night
To shut me out! Pour on; I will endure.
In such a night as this! O Regan,
    Goneril,   20
Your old kind father, whose frank heart
    gave all—
O, that way madness lies; let me shun
    that.
No more of that.

KENT.   Good my lord, enter here

LEAR. Prithee go in thyself; seek thine own
    ease.

III, iii, 3 *pity:* have mercy upon   6 *entreat:*
plead   10 *division:* contention   *worse:* more
serious   13 *closet:* chamber   15 *home:* thoroughly
power: army   16 *footed:* landed   *incline to:* side
with   17 *look:* search for   *privily:* secretly   23
toward: imminent   25 *courtesy:* kind attention
(to Lear)   27 *fair deserving:* i.e. action that
should win favor

III, iv, 1 *Good my lord:* my good lord   4
break my heart: i.e. by removing the dist-
raction of more physical distress   8 *fixed:* lodged
11 *i' th' mouth:* i.e. in the teeth   12 *free:* free
of care   17 *home:* i.e. to the hilt   21 *frank:*
liberal

This tempest will not give me leave to
ponder   25
On things would hurt me more, but I'll
go in.
[*To the Fool*] In, boy; go first. You house-
less poverty—
Nay, get thee in. I'll pray, and then I'll
sleep.   *Exit Fool.*
Poor naked wretches, wheresoe'er you are,
That bide the pelting of this pitiless
storm,   30
How shall your houseless heads and unfed
sides,
Your looped and windowed raggedness,
defend you
From seasons such as these? O, I have
ta'en
Too little care of this! Take physic, pomp;
Expose thyself to feel what wretches
feel,   35
That thou mayst shake the superflux to
them
And show the heavens more just.
EDGAR. [*within*] Fathom and half, fathom and
half! Poor Tom!

Enter Fool.

FOOL. Come not in here, nuncle; here's a
spirit. Help me, help me!   40
KENT. Give me thy hand. Who's there?
FOOL. A spirit, a spirit. He says his name's
poor Tom.
KENT. What art thou that dost grumble there
i' th' straw?   45
Come forth.

Enter Edgar [as Tom o' Bedlam].

EDGAR. Away! the foul fiend follows me.
Through the sharp hawthorn blow the
winds. Humh! go to thy bed, and warm
thee.   50
LEAR. Didst thou give all to thy daughters?
And art thou come to this?
EDGAR. Who gives anything to poor Tom?

27 *houseless:* unsheltered 32 *looped:* loopholed
34 *Take physic, pomp:* i.e. cure yourself, you
vainglorious ones 36 *superflux:* superfluities 38
Fathom and half: (nautical cry in taking sound-
ings, perhaps suggested by the deluge) 48–49
Through . . . winds: (cf. ll 109–110; a line from a
ballad) 49–50 *go . . . thee:* (evidently a popular
retort; cf. *Taming of the Shrew*, Induction, I, 10)

whom the foul fiend hath led through fire
and through flame, through ford and   55
whirlpool, o'er bog and quagmire; that
hath laid knives under his pillow and
halters in his pew, set ratsbane by his
porridge, made him proud of heart, to
ride on a bay trotting horse over four-   60
inched bridges, to course his own shadow
for a traitor. Bless thy five wits, Tom's
acold. O, do, de, do, de, do, de. Bless thee
from whirlwinds, star-blasting, and taking.
Do poor Tom some charity, whom the   65
foul fiend vexes. There could I have him
now—and there—and there again—and
there—   *Storm still.*
LEAR. Has his daughters brought him to this
pass?
Couldst thou save nothing? Wouldst thou
give 'em all?   70
FOOL. Nay, he reserved a blanket, else we
had been all shamed.
LEAR. Now all the plagues that in the pendulous air
Hang fated o'er men's faults light on thy
daughters!
KENT. He hath no daughters, sir.   75
LEAR. Death, traitor; nothing could have
subdued nature
To such a lowness but his unkind daugh-
ters.
Is it the fashion that discarded fathers
Should have thus little mercy on their
flesh?
Judicious punishment—'twas this flesh
begot   80
Those pelican daughters.
EDGAR. Pillicock sat on Pillicock Hill. Alow,
alow, loo, loo!

57–58 *knives, halters, ratsbane:* (temptations
to suicide) 58 *pew:* a gallery or balcony 60–61
ride . . . bridges: i.e. take mad risks 61–62 *course
. . . traitor:* chase his own shadow as an enemy
64 *star-blasting:* i.e. becoming the victim of
malignant stars *taking:* pestilence 69 *pass:* evil
condition 71 *blanket:* (to cover his nakedness)
72–73 *pendulous:* ominously suspended 73 *Hang
. . . faults:* i.e. destined to chastise sins 79 *have
. . . flesh:* i.e. torture themselves 81 *pelican:* i.e.
feeding upon the parent's blood (a supposed
habit of this species of bird) 82 *Pillicock . . .
Hill* (probably from a nursery rime; 'Pillicock' is
a pet-name for a child) *Alow . . . loo:* (hunting
cry?)

FOOL. This cold night will turn us all to fools
and madmen.   85

EDGAR. Take heed o' th' foul fiend; obey thy
parents; keep thy words' justice; swear
not; commit not with man's sworn spouse;
set not thy sweet heart on proud array.
Tom's acold.   90

LEAR. What hast thou been?

EDGAR. A servingman, proud in heart and
mind; that curled my hair, wore gloves in
my cap; served the lust of my mistress'
heart, and did the act of darkness   95
with her; swore as many oaths as I spake
words, and broke them in the sweet face
of heaven. One that slept in the contriving
of lust, and waked to do it. Wine loved I
deeply, dice dearly; and in woman out-   100
paramoured the Turk. False of heart, light
of ear, bloody of hand; hog in sloth, fox
in stealth, wolf in greediness, dog in madness, lion in prey. Let not the creaking of
shoes nor the rustling of silks betray   105
thy poor heart to woman. Keep thy foot
out of brothels, thy hand out of plackets,
thy pen from lenders' books, and defy the
foul fiend. Still through the hawthorn
blows the cold wind; says suum, mun,   110
nonny. Dolphin my boy, boy, sessa! let
him trot by.   *Storm still.*

LEAR. Thou wert better in a grave than to
answer with thy uncovered body this extremity of the skies. Is man no more   115
than this? Consider him well. Thou ow'st
the worm no silk, the beast no hide, the
sheep no wool, the cat no perfume. Ha!
here's three on's are sophisticated. Thou
art the thing itself; unaccommodated   120

man is no more but such a poor, bare,
forked animal as thou art. Off, off, you
lendings! Come, unbutton here.
                        [*Begins to disrobe.*]

FOOL. Prithee, nuncle, be contented; 'tis a
naughty night to swim in. Now a little   125
fire in a wild field were like an old lecher's
heart—a small spark, all the rest on's body
cold. Look, here comes a walking fire.

Enter Gloucester with a torch.

EDGAR. This is the foul Flibbertigibbet. He
begins at curfew, and walks till the   130
first cock. He gives the web and the pin,
squints the eye, and makes the harelip;
mildews the white wheat, and hurts the
poor creature of earth.

Swithold footed thrice the 'old;   135
He met the nightmare, and her nine fold;
    Bid her alight
    And her troth plight,
And aroint thee, witch, aroint thee!

KENT. How fares your Grace?   140

LEAR. What's he?

KENT. Who's there? What is't you seek?

GLOUCESTER. What are you there? Your
names?

EDGAR. Poor Tom, that eats the swimming
frog, the toad, the todpole, the wall-   145
newt and the water; that in the fury of his
heart, when the foul fiend rages, eats cow-
dung for sallets, swallows the old rat and
the ditch-dog, drinks the green mantle of
the standing pool; who is whipped   150
from tithing to tithing, and stock-punished

---

87 *justice:* i.e. dependability   88 *commit not:*
(i.e. adultery)   93–94 *gloves . . . cap:* (a fashion
with Elizabethan gallants)   100–101 *out-para-*
moured the Turk: outdid the Sultan in mistress-
keeping   101–102 *light of ear:* i.e. attentive to
flattery and slander   104, 105 *creaking, rustling:*
(both considered seductively fashionable sounds)
107 *plackets:* slits in skirts   108 *pen . . . books:*
(in signing for loans)   110 *suum . . . nonny:* (the
refrain of the wind?)   111–112 *Dolphin . . . trot*
by: (variously explained as cant phrases or ballad
refrain, equivalent to 'Let it go')   114 *answer:*
bear the brunt of   116 *ow'st* have borrowed from
118 *cat:* civet cat   119 *sophisticated:* altered by
artifice   120 *unaccommodated:* unpampered

122 *forked:* two-legged   123 *lendings:* borrowed
coverings   125 *naughty:* evil   126 *wild:* barren
129 *Flibbertigibbet:* (a dancing devil)   130 *curfew:*
(9 p.m.)   130–131 *first cock:* (midnight)   131
web . . . pin: cataract of the eye   132 *squints:*
crosses   133 *white:* ripening   135 *Swithold:* St.
Withold (Anglo-Saxon exorcist)   *footed:* walked
over   *'old:* wold, uplands   136 *nightmare:* incubus, demon   *fold:* offspring   137 *alight:* i.e.
from the horse she was afflicting   138 *her troth*
plight: plight her troth, pledge her good intentions   139 *aroint thee:* be gone (a direct command, concluding the charm)   145 *todpole:*
tadpole   146 *water:* water-newt   148 *sallets:*
salads   149 *ditch-dog* (carcass)   *mantle:* scum
150 *standing:* stagnant   151 *tithing:* a ten-family
district within a parish   *stock-punished:* placed
in the stocks

and imprisoned; who hath had three suits
to his back, six shirts to his body,
    Horse to ride, and weapon to wear,
    But mice and rats, and such small
      deer,   155
    Have been Tom's food for seven long
      year.
Beware my follower! Peace, Smulkin,
peace, thou fiend!

GLOUCESTER. What, hath your Grace no
better company?

EDGAR. The prince of darkness is a gentleman.
Modo he's called, and Mahu.   160

GLOUCESTER. Our flesh and blood, my lord,
is grown so vile
That it doth hate what gets it.

EDGAR. Poor Tom's acold.

GLOUCESTER. Go in with me. My duty cannot
suffer
T' obey in all your daughters' hard com-
    mands.   165
Though their injunction be to bar my
    doors
And let this tyrannous night take hold
    upon you,
Yet have I ventured to come seek you
    out
And bring you where both fire and food
    is ready.

LEAR. First let me talk with this philoso-
    pher.   170
What is the cause of thunder?

KENT. Good my lord, take his offer; go into
th' house.

LEAR. I'll talk a word with this same learnèd
    Theban.
What is your study?

EDGAR. How to prevent the fiend, and to
kill vermin.   175

LEAR. Let me ask you one word in private.

KENT. Importune him once more to go, my
    lord.
His wits begin t' unsettle.

GLOUCESTER.   Canst thou blame him?
                             Storm still.
His daughters seek his death. Ah, that
good Kent,
He said it would be thus, poor banished
man!   180
Thou say'st the King grows mad—I'll tell
thee, friend,
I am almost mad myself. I had a son,
Now outlawed from my blood; he sought
    my life
But lately, very late. I loved him, friend,
No father his son dearer. True to tell
    thee,   185
The grief hath crazed my wits. What a
night's this!
I do beseech your Grace—

LEAR.   O, cry you mercy, sir.
Noble philosopher, your company.

EDGAR. Tom's acold.

GLOUCESTER. In, fellow, there, into th' hovel;
keep thee warm.   190

LEAR. Come, let's in all.

KENT.   This way, my lord.

LEAR.   With him!
I will keep still with my philosopher.

KENT. Good my lord, soothe him; let him
take the fellow.

GLOUCESTER. Take him you on.

KENT. Sirrah, come on; go along with us.   195

LEAR. Come, good Athenian.

GLOUCESTER. No words, no words! Hush.

EDGAR.
    Child Rowland to the dark tower came;
    His word was still, 'Fie, foh, and fum,
    I smell the blood of a British man.'   200
                                  Exeunt.

---

155 *deer:* game (adapted from lines in the
romance *Bevis of Hampton*) 157, 160 *Smulkin,
Modo, Mahu:* (devils described in Harsnett's
Declaration, 1603) 162 *gets:* begets (a reference
to Edgar, Goneril, and Regan) 164 *suffer:*
permit 173 *Theban:* (an unexplained association
of Thebes with philosophy, i.e. science) 174
study: i.e. scientific specialty 175 *prevent:* thwart

183 *outlawed . . . blood:* proscribed as no child
of mine 187 *cry you mercy:* I beg your pardon
193 *soothe:* humor 194 *you on:* along with you
196 *Athenian:* i e. philosopher 198 *Child:* (i.e. a
candidate for knighthood) *Rowland:* Roland of
the Charlemagne legends (the line perhaps from
a lost ballad) 199 *His word was still:* i.e. his
repeated word, his motto, was always 199–200
Fie . . . man (absurdly heroic)

Scene v

Enter Cornwall and Edmund.

CORNWALL. I will have my revenge ere I depart his house.

EDMUND. How, my lord, I may be censured, that nature thus gives way to loyalty, something fears me to think of.   5

CORNWALL. I now perceive it was not altogether your brother's evil disposition made him seek his death; but a provoking merit, set awork by a reproveable badness in himself.   10

EDMUND. How malicious is my fortune that I must repent to be just! This is the letter which he spoke of, which approves him an intelligent party to the advantages of France. O heavens, that this treason   15
were not! or not I the detector!

CORNWALL. Go with me to the Duchess.

EDMUND. If the matter of this paper be certain, you have mighty business in hand.

CORNWALL. True or false, it hath made   20
thee Earl of Gloucester. Seek out where thy father is, that he may be ready for our apprehension.

EDMUND. [*aside*] If I find him comforting the King, it will stuff his suspicion more   25
fully.—I will persever in my course of loyalty, though the conflict be sore between that and my blood.

CORNWALL. I will lay trust upon thee, and thou shalt find a dearer father in my love.   *Exeunt.*   30

Scene vi

Enter Kent and Gloucester.

GLOUCESTER. Here is better than the open air; take it thankfully. I will piece out the comfort with what addition I can. I will not be long from you.

KENT. All the power of his wits have given   5
way to his impatience. The gods reward your kindness.   *Exit [Gloucester].*

Enter Lear, Edgar, and Fool.

EDGAR. Fraretto calls me, and tells me Nero is an angler in the lake of darkness. Pray, innocent, and beware the foul fiend.   10

FOOL. Prithee, nuncle, tell me whether a madman be a gentleman or a yeoman.

LEAR. A king, a king.
FOOL. No, he's a yeoman that has a gentleman to his son; for he's a mad yeoman   15
that sees his son a gentleman before him.

LEAR. To have a thousand with red burning spits
Come hizzing in upon 'em—

EDGAR. The foul fiend bites my back.

FOOL. He's mad that trusts in the tame-   20
ness of a wolf, a horse's health, a boy's love, or a whore's oath.

LEAR. It shall be done; I will arraign them straight.
[*To Edgar*] Come, sit thou here, most learned justice.
[*To the Fool*] Thou, sapient sir, sit here.
Now, you she-foxes—   25

EDGAR. Look, where he stands and glares. Want'st thou eyes at trial, madam?

III, v, 3 *censured:* judged 5 *something fears me:* frightens me somewhat 8–10 *a provoking . . . himself:* i.e. evil justice incited by evil (a case of poison driving out poison) 13 *approves:* proves 14 *intelligent . . . advantages:* spying partisan on behalf of 24 *comforting:* aiding 26 *persever:* persevere 28 *blood:* natural feelings 29 *lay . . . thee:* trust you (?) reward you with a place of trust (?)

III, vi, 6 *impatience:* rage 8 *Fraretto:* (a devil

mentioned in Harsnett's *Declaration*) 9 *Nero:* (In Rabelais, Trajan was the angler, Nero a fiddler, in Hades.) 10 *innocent:* hapless victim, plaything 12 *yeoman:* a property owner, next in rank to a gentleman (The allusion is to self-penalizing indulgence of one's children.) 16 *sees:* i.e. sees to it 18 *hizzing:* hissing (Lear is musing on vicious military retaliation.) 23 *arraign:* bring to trial 26 *he:* Lear (?) or one of Edgar's 'devil's (?) 27 *eyes:* such eyes (?) or spectators (?)

Come o'er the bourn, Bessy, to me.

FOOL. Her boat hath a leak,

And she must not speak   30

Why she dares not come over to thee.

EDGAR. The foul fiend haunts poor Tom in
the voice of a nightingale. Hoppedance
cries in Tom's belly for two white herring.
Croak not, black angel; I have no food   35
for thee.

KENT. How do you, sir? Stand you not so
amazed.

Will you lie down and rest upon the
cushions?

LEAR. I'll see their trial first. Bring in their
evidence.

[*To Edgar*] Thou, robèd man of justice,
take thy place.   40

[*To the Fool*] And thou, his yokefellow of
equity,

Bench by his side. [*to Kent*] You are o'
th' commission;

Sit you too.

EDGAR. Let us deal justly.

Sleepest or wakest thou, jolly shepherd?   45

Thy sheep be in the corn;

And for one blast of thy minikin mouth

Thy sheep shall take no harm.

Purr, the cat is gray.

LEAR. Arraign her first. 'Tis Goneril, I   50
here take my oath before this honorable
assembly, kicked the poor King her father.

FOOL. Come hither, mistress. Is your name
Goneril?

LEAR. She cannot deny it.   55

FOOL. Cry you mercy, I took you for a
joint-stool.

LEAR. And here's another, whose warped
looks proclaim

What store her heart is made on. Stop
her there!

Arms, arms, sword, fire! Corruption in
the place!

False justicer, why hast thou let her
'scape?   60

EDGAR. Bless thy five wits!

KENT. O pity! Sir, where is the patience now
That you so oft have boasted to retain?

EDGAR. [*aside*] My tears begin to take his
part so much

They mar my counterfeiting.   65

LEAR. The little dogs and all,

Tray, Blanch, and Sweetheart—see, they
bark at me.

EDGAR. Tom will throw his head at them.
Avaunt, you curs.

Be thy mouth or black or white,   70

Tooth that poisons if it bite;

Mastiff, greyhound, mongrel grim,

Hound or spaniel, brach or lym,

Or bobtail tike, or trundle-tail—

Tom will make him weep and wail;   75

For, with throwing thus my head,

Dogs leaped the hatch, and all are fled.

Do, de, de, de. Sessa! Come, march to
wakes and fairs and market towns. Poor
Tom, thy horn is dry.   80

LEAR. Then let them anatomize Regan. See
what breeds about her heart. Is there any
cause in nature that makes these hard
hearts? [*to Edgar*] You, sir, I entertain for
one of my hundred; only I do not like   85
the fashion of your garments. You will say
they are Persian; but let them be changed.

KENT. Now, good my lord, lie here and rest
awhile.

---

28 *bourn:* brook (Edgar's line is from a popular
song; the Fool's are a ribald improvisation.)
33 *nightingale:* i.e. the fool *Hoppedance:* (a devil
mentioned in Harsnett's *Declaration* as 'Hobber-
didance') 34 *white:* unsmoked (in contrast with
'black angel,' i.e. smoked devil) 36 *amazed:* bewildered 42 *commission:* those commissioned as
King's justices 46 *corn:* wheatfield 47 *one . . .
mouth:* one strain on your delicate shepherd's
pipe (?) 49 *gray:* (Gray cats were among the
forms supposedly assumed by devils.)   56 *Cry
. . . joint-stool:* (a cant expression for 'Pardon
me for failing to notice you,' but two joint-
stools—cf. 'warped,' l. 57—were probably the
actual stage objects arraigned as Goneril and
Regan)

59 *Corruption . . . place:* i.e. bribery in the
court 64 *take his part:* i.e. fall on his behalf
65 *counterfeiting:* i.e. simulating madness 73
brach: hound bitch *lym:* blood-hound 74 *Bobtail
. . . trundle-tail:* short-tailed cur or long-tailed
77 *hatch:* lower half of a 'Dutch door' 78 *Sessa:*
(interjection, equivalent to 'Away!') 79 *wakes:*
parish feasts 79–80 *Poor . . . dry:* (Edgar expresses his exhaustion in his rôle, by an allusion
to the horns proffered by Tom o' Bedlams in
begging drink.) 87 *Persian:* (Persian costume
was reputedly gorgeous. Ironically, or in actual
delusion, Lear refers thus to Edgar's rags, as he
refers to bed curtains in l. 89.)

LEAR. Make no noise, make no noise; draw the curtains.
So, so. We'll go to supper i' th' morning.
FOOL. And I'll go to bed at noon.   90

Enter Gloucester.

GLOUCESTER. Come hither, friend. Where is the King my master?
KENT. Here, sir, but trouble him not; his wits are gone.
GLOUCESTER. Good friend, I prithee take him in thy arms.
I have o'erheard a plot of death upon him.
There is a litter ready; lay him in't   95
And drive toward Dover, friend, where thou shalt meet
Both welcome and protection. Take up thy master.
If thou shouldst dally half an hour, his life,
With thine and all that offer to defend him,
Stand in assurèd loss. Take up, take up,   100
And follow me, that will to some provision
Give thee quick conduct.
KENT.   Oppressèd nature sleeps.
This rest might yet have balmed thy broken sinews,

Which, if convenience will not allow,
Stand in hard cure. [*to the Fool*] Come, help to bear thy master.   105
Thou must not stay behind.
GLOUCESTER.   Come, come, away!
                Exeunt [all but Edgar].
EDGAR. When we our betters see bearing our woes,
We scarcely think our miseries our foes.
Who alone suffers suffers most i' th' mind,
Leaving free things and happy shows behind;   110
But then the mind much sufferance doth o'erskip
When grief hath mates, and bearing fellowship.
How light and portable my pain seems now,
When that which makes me bend makes the King bow.
He childed as I fatherèd. Tom, away.   115
Mark the high noises, and thyself bewray
When false opinion, whose wrong thoughts defile thee,
In thy just proof repeals and reconciles thee.
What will hap more to-night, safe 'scape the King!
Lurk, lurk.   [*Exit.*]

Scene vii

Enter Cornwall, Regan, Goneril, Bastard [Edmund], and Servants.

CORNWALL. [*to Goneril*] Post speedily to my lord your husband; show him this letter.
The army of France is landed. [*to Servants*] Seek out the traitor Gloucester.
                Exeunt some Servants.
REGAN. Hang him instantly.   5

GONERIL. Pluck out his eyes.
CORNWALL. Leave him to my displeasure.
Edmund, keep you our sister company.
The revenges we are bound to take upon your traitorous father are not fit for   10
your beholding. Advise the Duke where you are going, to a most festinate preparation. We are bound to the like. Our posts shall be swift and intelligent betwixt us.

---

101 *provision:* supplies 102 *conduct:* guidance 103 *balmed:* healed 103 *sinews* nerves 104 *convenience:* propitious circumstances 105 *Stand ... cure:* will be hard to cure 107 *our woes:* woes like ours 108 *our foes:* i.e. our peculiar foes (They seem rather a part of universal misery.) 110 *free:* carefree *shows:* scenes 111 *sufferance:* suffering 112 *bearing fellowship:* enduring has company 113 *portable:* bearable

116 *Mark ... noises:* i.e. heed the rumors concerning those in power (?) *bewray:* reveal 117 *wrong thoughts:* misconceptions 118 *In ... reconciles thee:* i.e. upon your vindication recalls you and makes peace with you 119 *What ... more:* whatever more happens 120 *Lurk:* i.e. keep covered
III, vii, 9 *bound:* required 12 *festinate:* speedy 14 *intelligent:* informative

Farewell, dear sister; farewell, my Lord   15
of Gloucester.

Enter Steward [Oswald].

How now? Where's the King?
OSWALD. My Lord of Gloucester hath con-
veyed him hence.
Some five or six and thirty of his knights,
Hot questrists after him, met him at
gate;   20
Who, with some other of the lord's depen-
dants,
Are gone with him toward Dover, where
they boast
To have well-armèd friends.
CORNWALL.   Get horses for your mistress.
                                  Exit Oswald.
GONERIL. Farewell, sweet lord, and sister.
CORNWALL. Edmund, farewell.
                    [Exeunt Goneril and Edmund.]
    Go seek the traitor Gloucester,   25
Pinion him like a thief, bring him before
us.   *[Exeunt other Servants.]*
Though well we may not pass upon his life
Without the form of justice, yet our power
Shall do a court'sy to our wrath, which
men
May blame, but not control.

Enter Gloucester and Servants.

                    Who's there, the traitor?   30
REGAN. Ingrateful fox, 'tis he.
CORNWALL. Bind fast his corky arms.
GLOUCESTER. What means your Graces?
Good my friends, consider
You are my guests. Do me no foul play,
friends.
CORNWALL. Bind him, I say.   35
                    [Servants bind him.]
REGAN. Hard, hard! O filthy traitor.
GLOUCESTER. Unmerciful lady as you are, I'm
none.
CORNWALL. To this chair bind him. Villain,
thou shalt find—
                    [Regan plucks his beard.]
GLOUCESTER. By the kind gods, 'tis most
ignobly done

15–16 *Lord of Gloucester:* (as now endowed
with his father's title and estates)   20 *questrists:*
seekers   27 *pass upon:* issue a sentence against
29 *do a court'sy to:* i.e. defer to, act in conformity
with   32 *corky:* (because aged)

To pluck me by the beard.   40
REGAN. So white, and such a traitor?
GLOUCESTER.   Naughty lady,
These hairs which thou dost ravish from
my chin
Will quicken and accuse thee. I am your
host.
With robber's hands my hospitable favors
You should not ruffle thus. What will you
do?   45
CORNWALL. Come, sir, what letters had you
late from France?
REGAN. Be simple-answered, for we know
the truth.
CORNWALL. And what confederacy have you
with the traitors
Late footed in the kingdom?
REGAN. To whose hands you have sent the
lunatic King.   50
Speak.
GLOUCESTER. I have a letter guessingly set
down,
Which came from one that's of a neutral
heart,
And not from one opposed.
CORNWALL.   Cunning.
REGAN.   And false.
CORNWALL. Where hast thou sent the king?
GLOUCESTER. To Dover.   55
REGAN. Wherefore to Dover? Wast thou not
charged at peril—
CORNWALL. Wherefore to Dover? Let him
answer that.
GLOUCESTER. I am tied to th' stake, and I
must stand the course.
REGAN. Wherefore to Dover?
GLOUCESTER. Because I would not see thy
cruel nails   60
Pluck out his poor old eyes; nor thy fierce
sister
In his anointed flesh stick boarish fangs.
The sea, with such a storm as his bare head
In hell-black night endured, would have
buoyed up

---

41 *Naughty:* evil   43 *quicken:* come to life   44
favors: features   45 *ruffle:* tear at   46 *late:* of late
47 *Be simple-answered:* i.e. give plain answers
49 *footed:* landed   52 *guessingly:* i.e. tentatively,
not stated as an assured fact   56 *charged at peril:*
ordered on peril of your life   58 *course:* coursing
(as by a string of dogs baiting a bear or bull tied
in the pit)   62 *anointed:* (as king)   64 *buoyed:*
surged

And quenched the stelled fires. 65
Yet, poor old heart, he holp the heavens
  to rain.
If wolves had at thy gate howled that stern
  time,
Thou shouldst have said, 'Good porter,
  turn the key.'
All cruels else subscribe. But I shall see
The wingèd vengeance overtake such
  children. 70
CORNWALL. See't shalt thou never. Fellows,
  hold the chair.
Upon these eyes of thine I'll set my foot.
GLOUCESTER. He that will think to live till
  he be old,
Give me some help.—O cruel! O ye gods!
REGAN. One side will mock another. Th'
  other too. 75
CORNWALL. If you see vengeance—
1. Servant.   Hold your hand, my lord!
I have served you ever since I was a
  child;
But better service have I never done you
Than now to bid you hold.
REGAN.   How now, you dog?
1. SERVANT. If you did wear a beard upon
  your chin, 80
I'ld shake it on this quarrel. What do you
  mean!
CORNWALL. My villain!   [*Draw and fight.*]
1. SERVANT. Nay, then, come on, and take
  the chance of anger.
REGAN. Give me thy sword. A peasant stand
  up thus?
  [*She takes a sword and runs at him
    behind,*] *kills him.*
1. SERVANT. O, I am slain! My lord, you
  have one eye left 85
To see some mischief on him. O!

---

65 *stellèd:* starry 66 *holp:* helped 68 *turn the
key:* i.e. let them come in to shelter 69 *All . . .
subscribe:* i.e. at such times all other cruel creatures give way, agree to renounce their cruelty (?)
70 *wingèd:* heavenly (?) or swift (?) 73 *will think:*
hopes, expects 75 *mock:* i.e. subject to ridicule
(because of the contrast) 81 *shake it:* (as Regan
has done with Gloucester's—an act of extreme
defiance) *on this quarrel:* in this cause *What . . .
mean:* i.e. how dare you (The words are given to
Regan by most editors, but they are no more
'un-servantlike' than those that precede them.)
82 *My villain:* i.e. my serf (with play on its more
modern meaning) 86 *mischief:* injury

CORNWALL. Lest it see more, prevent it. Out,
  vile jelly.
Where is thy lustre now?
GLOUCESTER. All dark and comfortless.
  Where's my son Edmund?
Edmund, enkindle all the sparks of
  nature 90
To quit this horrid act.
REGAN.   Out, treacherous villain;
Thou call'st on him that hates thee. It was
  he
That made the overture of thy treasons to
  us;
Who is too good to pity thee.
GLOUCESTER. O my follies! Then Edgar was
  abused. 95
Kind gods, forgive me that, and prosper
  him.
REGAN. Go thrust him out at gates, and let
  him smell
His way to Dover.
        Exit one with Gloucester.
      How is't, my lord? How look you?
CORNWALL. I have received a hurt. Follow
  me, lady.
Turn out that eyeless villain. Throw this
  slave 100
Upon the dunghill. Regan, I bleed apace.
Untimely comes this hurt. Give me your
  arm.   *Exeunt.*
2. SERVANT. I'll never care what wickedness
  I do,
If this man come to good.
3. SERVANT.   If she live long,
And in the end meet the old course of
  death, 105
Women will all turn monsters.
2. SERVANT. Let's follow the old Earl, and
  get the bedlam
To lead him where he would. His roguish
  madness
Allows itself to anything.   [*Exit.*]
3. SERVANT. Go thou. I'll fetch some flax and
  whites of eggs 110
To apply to his bleeding face. Now heaven
  help him.   *Exit.*

---

90 *nature:* natural feeling 91 *quit:* requite,
avenge *horrid:* horrible 93 *overture:* disclosure
95 *abused:* wronged 98 *How look you:* i.e. how
looks it with you, what is your condition 105
meet . . . death: i.e. die a natural death 108–109
his roguish . . . anything: i.e. his being an irresponsible wanderer allows him to do anything

ACT IV

Scene i

Enter Edgar.

EDGAR. Yet better thus, and known to be contemned,
Than still contemned and flattered. To be worst,
The lowest and most dejected thing of fortune,
Stands still in esperance, lives not in fear.
The lamentable change is from the best; 5
The worst returns to laughter. Welcome then,
Thou unsubstantial air that I embrace:
The wretch that thou hast blown unto the worst
Owes nothing to thy blasts.

Enter Gloucester and an Old Man.

But who comes here?
My father, poorly led? World, world, O world! 10
But that thy strange mutations make us hate thee,
Life would not yield to age.

OLD MAN.   O my good lord,
I have been your tenant, and your father's tenant,
These fourscore years.

GLOUCESTER. Away, get thee away. Good friend, be gone. 15
Thy comforts can do me no good at all;
Thee they may hurt.

OLD MAN.   You cannot see your way.

GLOUCESTER. I have no way, and therefore want no eyes;
I stumbled when I saw. Full oft 'tis seen

Our means secure us, and our mere defects 20
Prove our commodities. O dear son Edgar,
The food of thy abusèd father's wrath,
Might I but live to see thee in my touch
I'ld say I had eyes again!

OLD MAN.   How now? Who's there?

EDGAR. [*aside*] O gods! Who is't can say 'I am at the worst'? 25
I am worse than e'er I was.

OLD MAN.   'Tis poor mad Tom.

EDGAR. [*aside*] And worse I may be yet. The worst is not
So long as we can say 'This is the worst.'

OLD MAN. Fellow, where goest?

GLOUCESTER.   Is it a beggarman?

OLD MAN. Madman and beggar too. 30

GLOUCESTER. He has some reason, else he could not beg.
I' th' last night's storm I such a fellow saw,
Which made me think a man a worm. My son
Came then into my mind, and yet my mind
Was then scarce friends with him. I have heard more since. 35
As flies to wanton boys are we to th' gods;
They kill us for their sport.

EDGAR.   [*aside*] How should this be?
Bad is the trade that must play fool to sorrow,
Ang'ring itself and others.—Bless thee, master.

GLOUCESTER. Is that the naked fellow?

OLD MAN.   Ay, my lord. 40

GLOUCESTER. Get thee away. If for my sake
Thou wilt o'ertake us hence a mile or twain

IV, i, 1 *contemned:* despised 2 *dejected:* cast down, abased 4 *esperance:* hope 6 *The worst ...laughter:* i.e. the worst extreme is the point of return to happiness 9 *nothing:* i.e. nothing good (and hence he is free of debt) 10 *poorly:* poor-like, i.e. like a blind beggar (?) 11–12 *But ...age:* i.e. were it not for your hateful mutability, we would never be reconciled to old age and death 16 *comforts:* ministrations 17 *hurt:* do injury (since they are forbidden) 18 *want:* need

20–21 *Our means ... commodities:* i.e. prosperity makes us rash, and sheer affliction proves a boon 22 *food:* i.e. the object fed upon *abusèd:* deceived 23 *in:* i.e. by means of 27–28 *The worst ... worst:* (because at the very worst there will be no such comforting thought) 31 *reason:* powers of reason 33–34 *My son ... mind:* (because it was actually he—a natural touch) 36 *wanton:* irresponsibly playful 39 *Ang'ring:* offending

I' th' way toward Dover, do it for ancient
   love;
And bring some covering for this naked
   soul,
Which I'll entreat to lead me.
OLD MAN.   Alack, sir, he is mad.   45
GLOUCESTER. 'Tis the time's plague when
   madmen lead the blind.
Do as I bid thee, or rather do thy pleasure.
Above the rest, be gone.
OLD MAN. I'll bring him the best 'parel that
   I have,
Come on't what will.   Exit.   50
GLOUCESTER. Sirrah naked fellow—
EDGAR. Poor Tom's acold. [aside] I cannot
   daub it further.
GLOUCESTER. Come hither, fellow.
EDGAR. [aside] And yet I must.—Bless thy
   sweet eyes, they bleed.
GLOUCESTER. Know'st thou the way to
   Dover?   55
EDGAR. Both stile and gate, horseway and
   footpath. Poor Tom hath been scared out
   of his good wits. Bless thee, good man's
   son, from the foul fiend. Five fiends have
   been in poor Tom at once: of lust, as   60
   Obidicut; Hobbididence, prince of dumbness; Mahu, of stealing; Modo, of
   murder; Flibbertigibbet, of mopping and

mowing, who since possesses chamber-
   maids and waiting women. So, bless   65
   thee, master.
GLOUCESTER. Here, take this purse, thou
   whom the heavens' plagues
Have humbled to all strokes. That I am
   wretched
Makes thee the happier. Heavens, deal so
   still!
Let the superfluous and lust-dieted
   man,   70
That slaves your ordinance, that will not
   see
Because he does not feel, feel your pow'r
   quickly;
So distribution should undo excess,
And each man have enough. Dost thou
   know Dover?
EDGAR. Ay, master.   75
GLOUCESTER. There is a cliff, whose high and
   bending head
Looks fearfully in the confinèd deep.
Bring me but to the very brim of it,
And I'll repair the misery thou dost bear
With something rich about me. From that
   place   80
I shall no leading need.
EDGAR.   Give me thy arm.
Poor Tom shall lead thee.   Exeunt.

Scene ii

*Enter Goneril, Bastard [Edmund], and
   Steward [Oswald].*

GONERIL. Welcome, my lord. I marvel our
   mild husband
Not met us on the way. [to Oswald] Now,
   where's your master?
OSWALD. Madam, within, but never man so
   changed.
I told him of the army that was landed:

He smiled at it. I told him you were com-
   ing: 5
His answer was, 'The worse.' Of Glouces-
   ter's treachery
And of the loyal service of his son
When I informed him, then he called me sot
And told me I had turned the wrong side
   out.
What most he should dislike seems pleas-
   ant to him;   10

43 *ancient love:* i.e. such love as formerly
bound master and man (nostalgic) 46 *time's
plague:* i.e. malady characteristic of these times
47 *thy pleasure:* as you please 49 *'parel:*
apparel 52 *daub it:* lay it on, act the part
61 *Obidicut:* Hoberdicut (a devil mentioned in
Harsnett's *Declaration,* as are the four following) 61–62 *dumbness:* muteness (Shakespeare
identifies each devil with some form of posses-

sion.) 63–64 *mopping and mowing:* grimaces,
affected facial expressions 68 *humbled to:* reduced to bearing humbly 69 *happier:* i.e. less
wretched 70 *superfluous:* possessed of superfluities *lust-dieted:* i.e. whose desires are feasted
71 *slaves your ordinance:* subordinates your injunction (to share) 76 *bending:* overhanging 77
in . . . deep: i.e. to the sea hemmed in below
   IV, ii, 2 *Not met:* has not met 8 *sot:* fool

What like, offensive.

GONERIL. [*to Edmund*] Then shall you go no
   further.
It is the cowish terror of his spirit,
That dares not undertake. He'll not feel
   wrongs
Which tie him to an answer. Our wishes on
   the way
May prove effects. Back, Edmund, to my
   brother.   15
Hasten his musters and conduct his pow'rs.
I must change names at home, and give
   the distaff
Into my husband's hands. This trusty
   servant
Shall pass between us. Ere long you are
   like to hear
(If you dare venture in your own behalf) 20
A mistress's command. Wear this. Spare
   speech.   [*Gives a favor.*]
Decline your head. This kiss, if it durst
   speak,
Would stretch thy spirits up into the air.
Conceive, and fare thee well.
EDMUND. Yours in the ranks of death.   *Exit.*
GONERIL.   My most dear Gloucester.   25
O, the difference of man and man:
To thee a woman's services are due;
My fool usurps my body.
OSWALD.
       Madam, here comes my lord. [*Exit.*]

Enter Albany.

GONERIL. I have been worth the whistle.
ALBANY.   O Goneril,
You are not worth the dust which the rude
   wind   30

---

11 *What like:* what he should like 12 *cowish:*
cowardly 13 *undertake:* engage 14 *an answer:*
retaliation 14–15 *Our wishes ... effects:* i.e. our
wishes, that you might supplant Albany, may
materialize 16 *musters:* enlistments *conduct his
pow'rs:* lead his army 17 *change names:* i.e.
exchange the name of 'mistress' for 'master'
distaff: spinning-staff (symbol of the housewife)
21 *mistress's:* (At present she plays the rôle of
master, but, mated with Edmund, she would
again 'change names.') 24 *Conceive:* (1) understand (2) quicken (with the seed I have planted
in you) 28 *usurps:* wrongfully occupies 29
worth the whistle: i.e. valued enough to be welcomed home ('not worth the whistle' applying
proverbially to a 'poor dog')

Blows in your face. [I fear your disposi-
   tion:
That nature which contemns its origin
Cannot be borderèd certain in itself.
She that herself will sliver and disbranch
From her material sap, perforce must
   wither   35
And come to deadly use.
GONERIL. No more; the text is foolish.
ALBANY. Wisdom and goodness to the vile
   seem vile;
Filths savor but themselves. What have
   you done?
Tigers not daughters, what have you per-
   formed?   40
A father, and a gracious agèd man,
Whose reverence even the head-lugged
   bear would lick,
Most barbarous, most degenerate, have
   you madded.
Could my good brother suffer you to do
   it?
A man, a prince, by him so benefited!   45
If that the heavens do not their visible
   spirits
Send quickly down to tame these vile
   offenses,
It will come,
Humanity must perforce prey on itself,
Like monsters of the deep.]
GONERIL.   Milk-livered man,   50
That bear'st a cheek for blows, a head for
   wrongs;
Who hast not in thy brows an eye dis-
   cerning
Thine honor from thy suffering; [that not
   know'st
Fools do those villains pity who are
   punished

---

31 *fear your disposition:* distrust your nature
33 *borderèd certain:* safely contained (It will be
unpredictably licentious.) 34 *sliver, disbranch:*
cut off 35 *material sap:* sustaining stock, nour-
ishing trunk 39 *savor:* relish 42 *head-lugged:*
dragged with a head-chain (hence, surly) *lick:*
i.e. treat with affection 43 *degenerate:* unnatural
madded: maddened 46 *visible:* made visible,
material 48 *It:* i.e. chaos 50 *Milk-livered:* i.e.
spiritless 52–53 *discerning ... suffering:* dis-
tinguishing between dishonor and tolerance 54
Fools: i.e. only fools

Ere they have done their mischief. Where's
  thy drum?   55
France spreads his banners in our noise-
  less land,
With plumèd helm thy state begins to
  threat,
Whilst thou, a moral fool, sits still and
  cries
'Alack, why does he so?']
ALBANY.   See thyself, devil:
  Proper deformity seems not in the fiend   60
  So horrid as in woman.
GONERIL.   O vain fool!
ALBANY. Thou changèd and self-covered
  thing, for shame
  Bemonster not thy feature. Were't my
  fitness
  To let these hands obey my blood,
  They are apt enough to dislocate and
  tear   65
  Thy flesh and bones. Howe'er thou art a
  fiend,
  A woman's shape doth shield thee.
GONERIL. Marry, your manhood—mew!

            Enter a Messenger.

ALBANY. What news?
MESSENGER. O, my good lord, the Duke of
  Cornwall's dead,   70
  Slain by his servant, going to put out
  The other eye of Gloucester.
ALBANY.   Gloucester's eyes?
MESSENGER. A servant that he bred, thrilled
  with remorse,
  Opposed against the act, bending his
  sword
  To his great master; who, thereat en-
  raged,   75

Flew on him, and amongst them felled
  him dead;
But not without that harmful stroke which
  since
Hath plucked him after.
ALBANY.   This shows you are above,
  You justicers, that these our nether
  crimes
  So speedily can venge. But, O poor
  Gloucester,   80
  Lost he his other eye?
MESSENGER.   Both, both, my lord.
  This letter, madam, craves a speedy
  answer.
  'Tis from your sister.
GONERIL.   [*aside*] One way I like this well;
  But being widow, and my Gloucester with
  her,
  May all the building in my fancy pluck 85
  Upon my hateful life. Another way
  The news is not so tart.—I'll read, and
  answer.   [*Exit.*]
ALBANY. Where was his son when they did
  take his eyes?
MESSENGER. Come with my lady hither.
ALBANY.   He is not here.
MESSENGER. No, my good lord; I met him
  back again.   90
ALBANY. Knows he the wickedness?
MESSENGER. Ay, my good lord. 'Twas he in-
  formed against him,
  And quit the house on purpose, that their
  punishment
  Might have the freer course.
ALBANY.   Gloucester, I live
  To thank thee for the love thou showed'st
  the King,   95
  And to revenge thine eyes. Come hither,
  friend.
  Tell me what more thou know'st.

                              Exeunt.

---

55 *drum:* i.e. military preparation 56 *noiseless:*
i.e. unaroused 57 *helm:* war-helmet 58 *moral:*
moralizing   60 *Proper:* i.e. fair-surfaced   62
changèd: transformed (diabolically, as in witch-
craft) *self-covered:* i.e. your natural self overwhelmed by evil (?) or devil disguised as
woman (?) 63 *Bemonster . . . feature:* i.e. do not
exchange your human features for a monster's
my fitness: fit for me 64 *blood:* passion 68
Marry: (oath, derived from 'By Mary') *your
manhood—mew:* i.e. 'What a man!' followed by
a contemptuous interjection (?) or mew up
(contain) this display of manliness 71 *going to:*
about to 73 *bred:* reared *thrilled with remorse:*
in the throes of pity

---

76 *amongst them:* i.e. aided by the others 78
plucked him after: drawn him along (to death)
79 *justicers:* dispensers of justice *nether crimes:*
sins committed here below 80 *venge:* avenge
82 *craves:* requires 85–86 *May . . . life:* i.e. may
make my life hateful by destroying my dream-
castles *Another way:* the other way (alluded to
in l. 83, probably the removal of Cornwall as an
obstacle to sole reign with Edmund) 86 *tart:*
distasteful 90 *back:* going back

Scene iii

Enter Kent and a Gentleman.

KENT. Why the King of France is so suddenly gone back know you no reason?

GENTLEMAN. Something he left imperfect in the state, which since his coming forth is thought of, which imports to the king- 5
dom so much fear and danger that his personal return was most required and necessary.

KENT. Who hath he left behind him general?

GENTLEMAN. The Marshal of France, Monsieur La Far.   10

KENT. Did your letters pierce the Queen to any demonstration of grief?

GENTLEMAN. Ay, sir. She took them, read them in my presence,
And now and then an ample tear trilled down
Her delicate cheek. It seemed she was a queen   15
Over her passion, who, most rebel-like,
Sought to be king o'er her.

KENT.   , O, then it movèd her?

GENTLEMAN. Not to a rage. Patience and sorrow strove
Who should express her goodliest. You have seen
Sunshine and rain at once—her smiles and tears   20
Were like, a better way: those happy smilets
That played on her ripe lip seem not to know
What guests were in her eyes, which parted thence
As pearls from diamonds dropped. In brief,
Sorrow would be a rarity most belovèd, 25
If all could so become it.

KENT.   Made she no verbal question?

GENTLEMAN. Faith, once or twice she heaved the name of father
Pantingly forth, as if it pressed her heart;
Cried 'Sisters, sisters, shame of ladies, sisters!
Kent, father, sisters? What, i' th' storm i' th' night?   30
Let pity not be believed!' There she shook
The holy water from her heavenly eyes,
And clamor moistened; then away she started
To deal with grief alone.

KENT.   It is the stars,
The stars above us govern our conditions;   35
Else one self mate and make could not beget
Such different issues. You spoke not with her since?

GENTLEMAN. No.

KENT. Was this before the King returned?

GENTLEMAN.   No, since.

KENT. Well, sir, the poor distressèd Lear's i' th' town;   40
Who sometime, in his better tune, remembers
What we are come about, and by no means
Will yield to see his daughter.

GENTLEMAN.   Why, good sir?

KENT. A sovereign shame so elbows him; his own unkindness,
That stripped her from his benediction, turned her   45
To foreign casualties, gave her dear rights
To his dog-hearted daughters—these things sting
His mind so venomously that burning shame
Detains him from Cordelia.

GENTLEMAN.   Alack, poor gentleman.

27–28 *heaved . . . forth:* uttered . . . chokingly
31 *Let pity:* let it for pity (?) 33 *clamor moistened:* i.e. mixed, and thus muted, lamentation with tears 35 *govern our conditions:* determine our characters 36 *Else . . . make:* otherwise the same husband and wife 37 *issues:* children 41 *better tune:* i.e. more rational state, less jangled 44 *sovereign:* overruling *elbows:* jogs 45 *stripped:* cut off (cf. 'disbranch,' IV, ii, 34) *benediction:* blessing 46 *casualties:* chances

IV, iii, 3–4 *imperfect . . . state:* i.e. rift in affairs of state 5 *imports:* means 6 *fear:* uneasiness 7 *most:* most urgently 11 *pierce:* goad 14 *trilled:* trickled 16 *who:* which 19 *goodliest:* i.e. most becomingly 21 *Were . . . way:* i.e. improved upon that spectacle 25 *rarity:* gem

KENT. Of Albany's and Cornwall's powers
   you heard not?   50
GENTLEMAN. 'Tis so; they are afoot.
KENT. Well, sir, I'll bring you to our master
   Lear
   And leave you to attend him. Some dear
   cause

Will in concealment wrap me up awhile.
When I am known aright, you shall not
   grieve   55
Lending me this acquaintance. I pray you
   go
Along with me.   *Exeunt.*

Scene iv

Enter, with Drum and Colors, Cordelia,
Gentleman [Doctor], and Soldiers.

CORDELIA. Alack, 'tis he! Why, he was met
   even now
As mad as the vexed sea, singing aloud,
Crowned with rank fumiter and furrow
   weeds,
With hardocks, hemlock, nettles, cuckoo
   flow'rs,
Darnel, and all the idle weeds that grow   5
In our sustaining corn. A century send
   forth!
Search every acre in the high-grown field
And bring him to our eye. [*Exit an Officer.*]
   What can man's wisdom
In the restoring his bereavèd sense?
He that helps him take all my outward
   worth.   10
DOCTOR. There is means, madam.
   Our foster nurse of nature is repose,
   The which he lacks. That to provoke in
   him
   Are many simples operative, whose power
   Will close the eye of anguish.

CORDELIA.   All blest secrets,   15
All you unpublished virtues of the earth,
Spring with my tears; be aidant and re-
   mediate
In the good man's distress. Seek, seek for
   him,
Lest his ungoverned rage dissolve the life
That wants the means to lead it.

Enter Messenger.

MESSENGER.   News, madam.   20
The British pow'rs are marching hither-
   ward.
CORDELIA. 'Tis known before. Our prepara-
   tion stands
In expectation of them. O dear father,
It is thy business that I go about.
Therefore great France   25
My mourning, and importuned tears hath
   pitied.
No blown ambition doth our arms incite,
But love, dear love, and our aged father's
   right.
Soon may I hear and see him!   *Exeunt.*

Scene v

Enter Regan and Steward [Oswald.]

REGAN. But are my brother's pow'rs set
   forth?

OSWALD.   Ay, madam.
REGAN. Himself in person there?
OSWALD.   Madam, with much ado.
   Your sister is the better soldier.

---

51 *'Tis so:* i.e. I have to this extent   53 *dear*
cause: important purpose

IV, iv, 3 *fumiter:* fumitory *furrow weeds:* (those
that appear after ploughing?)   4 *hardocks* (variously identified as burdock, 'hoar dock,' 'har-
lock,' etc.)   5 *Darnel:* tares   *idle:* useless   6
sustaining corn: life-giving wheat   *century:* troop
of a hundred men   8 *can:* i.e. can accomplish
9 *bereaved:* bereft   10 *outward worth:* material

possessions   12 *foster:* fostering   13 *provoke:*
induce   14 *simples operative:* medicinal herbs,
sedative   16 *unpublished virtues:* i.e. little-known
benign herbs   17 *Spring:* grow   *remediate* re-
medial   20 *wants:* lacks   *means:* i.e. power of
reason   *lead it:* govern it (the rage)   25 *There-*
fore: therefore, because of that   26 *importuned:*
importunate   27 *blown:* swollen

IV, v, 2 *much ado:* great bother

REGAN. Lord Edmund spake not with your
  lord at home?
OSWALD. No, madam.   5
REGAN. What might import my sister's letter
  to him?
OSWALD. I know not, lady.
REGAN. Faith, he is posted hence on serious
  matter.
  It was great ignorance, Gloucester's eyes
    being out,
  To let him live. Where he arrives he
    moves   10
  All hearts against us. Edmund, I think, is
    gone,
  In pity of his misery, to dispatch
  His nighted life; moreover, to descry
  The strength o' th' enemy.
OSWALD. I must needs after him, madam,
  with my letter.   15
REGAN. Our troops set forth to-morrow. Stay
  with us.
  The ways are dangerous.
OSWALD.   I may not, madam.
  My lady charged my duty in this business.
REGAN. Why should she write to Edmund?
  Might not you
  Transport her purposes by word?
    Belike,   20
  Some things—I know not what. I'll love
    thee much,

Let me unseal the letter.
OSWALD.   Madam, I had rather—
REGAN. I know your lady does not love her
  husband,
  I am sure of that; and at her late being here
  She gave strange eliads and most speaking
    looks   25
  To noble Edmund. I know you are of her
    bosom.
OSWALD. I, madam?
REGAN. I speak in understanding—y'are, I
  know't—
  Therefore I do advise you take this note:
  My lord is dead; Edmund and I have
    talked,   30
  And more convenient is he for my hand
  Than for your lady's. You may gather
    more.
  If you do find him, pray you give him this;
  And when your mistress hears thus much
    from you,
  I pray desire her call her wisdom to her.   35
  So fare you well.
  If you do chance to hear of that blind
    traitor,
  Preferment falls on him that cuts him off.
OSWALD. Would I could meet him, madam! I
  should show
  What party I do follow.
REGAN.   Fare thee well.   *Exeunt.*   40

Scene vi

Enter Gloucester and Edgar.

GLOUCESTER. When shall I come to th' top
  of that same hill?
EDGAR. You do climb up it now. Look how
  we labor.
GLOUCESTER. Methinks the ground is even.
EDGAR.   Horrible steep.
  Hark, do you hear the sea?
GLOUCESTER.   No, truly.
EDGAR. Why, then, your other senses grow
  imperfect   5

By your eyes' anguish.
GLOUCESTER.   So may it be indeed.
  Methinks thy voice is altered, and thou
    speak'st
  In better phrase and matter than thou
    didst.
EDGAR. Y'are much deceived. In nothing am
  I changed
  But in my garments.   10
GLOUCESTER. Methinks y'are better spoken.
EDGAR. Come on, sir; here's the place. Stand
  still. How fearful

---

6 *import:* bear as its message   7 *is posted:* has
sped   8 *ignorance:* error   13 *nighted:* benighted,
blinded   18 *charged:* strictly ordered   20 *Transport her purposes:* convey her intentions   *Be-
like:* probably   24 *late:* recently   25 *eliads:*
amorous glances   26 *of her bosom:* in her con-

fidence   29 *take this note:* note this   31 *convenient:* appropriate   32 *gather more:* i.e. draw
your own conclusions   33 *this:* this word, this
reminder   35 *call:* recall   38 *Preferment:* advancement
  IV, vi, 6 *anguish:* affliction

And dizzy 'tis to cast one's eyes so low!
The crows and choughs that wing the
  midway air
Show scarce so gross as beetles. Halfway
  down   15
Hangs one that gathers sampire—dreadful
  trade;
Methinks he seems no bigger than his
  head.
The fishermen that walk upon the beach
Appear like mice; and yond tall anchoring
  bark,
Diminished to her cock; her cock, a
  buoy   20
Almost too small for sight. The murmur-
  ing surge
That on th' unnumb'red idle pebble chafes
Cannot be heard so high. I'll look no more,
Lest my brain turn, and the deficient sight
Topple down headlong.
GLOUCESTER.   Set me where you stand.   25
EDGAR. Give me your hand. You are now
  within a foot
Of th' extreme verge. For all beneath the
  moon
Would I not leap upright.
GLOUCESTER.   Let go my hand.
Here, friend, 's another purse; in it a jewel
Well worth a poor man's taking. Fairies
  and gods   30
Prosper it with thee. Go thou further off;
Bid me farewell, and let me hear thee
  going.
EDGAR. Now fare ye well, good sir.
GLOUCESTER.   With all my heart.
EDGAR. [aside] Why I do trifle thus with his
  despair
Is done to cure it.
GLOUCESTER.   O you mighty gods!   35
                        [He kneels.]

This world I do renounce, and in your
  sights
Shake patiently my great affliction off.
If I could bear it longer and not fall
To quarrel with your great opposeless
  wills,
My snuff and loathèd part of nature
  should   40
Burn itself out. If Edgar live, O bless him!
Now, fellow, fare thee well. [He falls for-
  ward and swoons.]
EDGAR.   Gone, sir—farewell.
And yet I know not how conceit may rob
The treasury of life when life itself
Yields to the theft. Had he been where he
  thought,   45
By this had thought been past. Alive or
  dead?
Ho you, sir! Friend! Hear you, sir? Speak!
Thus might he pass indeed. Yet he revives.
What are you, sir?
GLOUCESTER.   Away, and let me die.
EDGAR. Hadst thou been aught but gossamer,
  feathers, air,   50
So many fathom down precipitating,
Thou'dst shivered like an egg; but thou
  dost breathe,
Hast heavy substance, bleed'st not,
  speak'st, art sound.
Ten masts at each make not the altitude
Which thou hast perpendicularly fell.   55
Thy life 's a miracle. Speak yet again.
GLOUCESTER. But have I fall'n, or no?
EDGAR. From the dread summit of this
  chalky bourn.
Look up a-height. The shrill-gorged lark
  so far
Cannot be seen or heard. Do but look
  up.   60
GLOUCESTER. Alack, I have no eyes.
Is wretchedness deprived that benefit
To end itself by death? 'Twas yet some
  comfort

---

14 *choughs:* jackdaws *midway:* i.e. halfway
down   15 *gross:* large   16 *sampire:* samphire
(aromatic herb used in relishes)   19 *anchoring:*
anchored   20 *Diminished . . . cock:* reduced to
the size of her cockboat   22 *unnumb'red idle
pebble:* i.e. barren reach of countless pebbles
24 *the deficient sight:* i.e. my dizziness   25 *Topple:*
topple me   28 *upright:* i.e. even upright, let alone
forward   30 *Fairies:* (the usual wardens of
treasure)   34 *Why . . . trifle:* i.e. the reason I toy
with ('done' in l. 35 being redundant)

38–39 *fall . . . with:* i.e. rebel against (irreligi-
ously)   39 *opposeless:* not to be opposed   40
My snuff . . . nature: i.e. the guttering and hateful
tag end of my life   43 *conceit:* imagination   45
Yields to: i.e. welcomes   51 *precipitating:* falling
54 *at each:* end to end   56 *life:* survival   58
bourn: boundary, headland   59 *a-height:* on high
gorged: throated

When misery could beguile the tyrant's
rage
And frustrate his proud will.

EDGAR.   Give me your arm.   65
Up—so. How is't? Feel you your legs?
You stand.

GLOUCESTER. Too well, too well.

EDGAR.   This is above all strangeness.
Upon the crown o' th' cliff what thing was
that
Which parted from you?

GLOUCESTER.   A poor unfortunate beggar.

EDGAR. As I stood here below, methought his
eyes   70
Were two full moons; he had a thousand
noses,
Horns whelked and waved like the enridgèd sea.
It was some fiend. Therefore, thou happy
father,
Think that the clearest gods, who make
them honors
Of men's impossibilities, have preservèd
thee.   75

GLOUCESTER. I do remember now. Hence-
forth I'll bear
Affliction till it do cry out itself
'Enough, enough, and die.' That thing
you speak of,
I took it for a man. Often 'twould say
'The fiend, the fiend'—he led me to that
place.   80

EDGAR. Bear free and patient thoughts.

Enter Lear [mad, bedecked with weeds].

                             But who comes here?
The safer sense will ne'er accommodate
His master thus.

LEAR. No, they cannot touch me for
coining;
I am the King himself.   85

EDGAR. O thou side-piercing sight!

---

64 *beguile:* outwit   66 *Feel:* test   72 *whelked:*
corrugated   *enridgèd:* blown into ridges   73
happy father: lucky old man   74 *clearest:* purest
74–75 *who ... impossibilities:* i.e. whose glory it
is to do for man what he cannot do for himself
81 *free:* (of despair)   82 *safer:* saner   *accommodate:* accoutre   83 *His:* its   84 *touch:* i.e. interfere with   *coining:* minting coins (a royal pre-
rogative)

LEAR. Nature's above art in that respect.
There's your press money. That fellow
handles his bow like a crow-keeper. Draw
me a clothier's yard. Look, look, a   90
mouse! Peace, peace; this piece of toasted
cheese will do't. There's my gauntlet; I'll
prove it on a giant. Bring up the brown
bills. O, well flown, bird. I' th' clout,
i' th' clout—hewgh!   95
Give the word.

EDGAR. Sweet marjoram.

LEAR. Pass.

GLOUCESTER. I know that voice.

LEAR. Ha! Goneril with a white beard?   100
They flattered me like a dog, and told me
I had the white hairs in my beard ere the
black ones were there. To say 'ay' and 'no'
to everything that I said! 'Ay' and 'no'
too was no good divinity. When the   105
rain came to wet me once, and the wind to
make me chatter; when the thunder would
not peace at my bidding; there I found
'em, there I smelt 'em out. Go to, they are
not men o' their words. They told   110
me I was everything. 'Tis a lie—I am not
ague-proof.

GLOUCESTER. The trick of that voice I do well
remember.
Is't not the King?

LEAR.   Ay, every inch a king.

---

87 *Nature ... respect:* i.e. a born king is above
a made king in legal immunity (cf. the coeval
debate on the relative merits of poets of nature,
i.e. born, and poets of art, i.e. made by self-
effort)   88 *press money:* i.e. the 'king's shilling'
(token payment on military impressment or
enlistment)   89 *crow-keeper:* i.e. farmhand ward-
ing off crows   90 *clothier's yard:* i.e. arrow
(normally a yard long)   92 *gauntlet:* armored
glove (hurled as challenge)   93 *prove it on:*
maintain it against   93–94 *brown bills:* varnished
halberds   94 *well flown:* (hawking cry)   *clout:*
bull's-eye (archery term)   95 *word:* password
96 *Sweet marjoram:* (herb, associated with treating madness?)   100 *like a dog:* i.e. fawningly
102 *I ... beard:* i.e. I was wise   103 *To say ...
'no':* i.e. to agree   105 *no good divinity:* i.e. bad
theology (For 'good divinity' cf. 2 Corinthians
1:18: 'But as God is true, our word to you was
not yea and nay'; also Matthew 5:36–37, James
5:12.)   112 *ague-proof:* proof against chills and
fever   113 *trick:* peculiarity

When I do stare, see how the subject
quakes.
I pardon that man's life. What was thy
cause?   115
Adultery?
Thou shalt not die. Die for adultery? No.
The wren goes to't, and the small gilded
fly
Does lecher in my sight.
Let copulation thrive; for Gloucester's
bastard son   120
Was kinder to his father than my daughters
Got 'tween the lawful sheets.
To't, luxury, pell-mell, for I lack soldiers.
Behold yond simp'ring dame,
Whose face between her forks presages
snow,   125
That minces virtue, and does shake the
head
To hear of pleasure's name.
The fitchew nor the soilèd horse goes to't
With a more riotous appetite.
Down from the waist they are Centaurs,
Though women all above.   130
But to the girdle do the gods inherit,
Beneath is all the fiend's.
There's hell, there's darkness, there is
the sulphurous pit; burning, scalding,
stench, consumption. Fie, fie, fie! pah,   135
pah! Give me an ounce of civet; good
apothecary, sweeten my imagination!
There's money for thee.
GLOUCESTER. O, let me kiss that hand.
LEAR. Let me wipe it first; it smells of
mortality.   140
GLOUCESTER. O ruined piece of nature; this
great world
Shall so wear out to naught. Dost thou
know me?

LEAR. I remember thine eyes well enough.
Dost thou squiny at me? No, do thy
worst, blind Cupid; I'll not love. Read 145
thou this challenge; mark but the penning
of it.
GLOUCESTER. Were all thy letters suns, I
could not see.
EDGAR. [aside] I would not take this from
report—it is,   150
And my heart breaks at it.
LEAR. Read.
GLOUCESTER. What, with the case of eyes?
LEAR. O, ho, are you there with me? No 155
eyes in your head, nor no money in your
purse? Your eyes are in a heavy case,
your purse in a light; yet you see how this
world goes.
GLOUCESTER. I see it feelingly.   160
LEAR. What, art mad? A man may see how this
world goes with no eyes. Look with thine
ears. See how yond justice rails upon yond
simple thief. Hark in thine ear. Change
places and, handy-dandy, which is 165
the justice, which is the thief? Thou hast
seen a farmer's dog bark at a beggar?
GLOUCESTER. Ay, sir.
LEAR. And the creature run from the cur.
There thou mightst behold the great 170
image of authority—a dog's obeyed in
office.
Thou rascal beadle, hold thy bloody hand!
Why dost thou lash that whore? Strip thy
own back.
Thou hotly lusts to use her in that kind
For which thou whip'st her. The usurer
hangs the cozener.   175
Through tattered clothes small vices do
appear;
Robes and furred gowns hide all. Plate
sin with gold,

---

115 *cause:* case 119 *lecher:* copulate 122 *Got:* begotten 123 *luxury:* lechery *for . . . soldiers:* (and therefore a higher birth rate) 125 *whose . . . snow:* i.e. who presents the signs of being sexually cold (*between her forks,* i.e. legs, modifies *snow*) 126 *minces:* mincingly affects 127 *pleasure's name:* i.e. the very name of sexual indulgence 128 *fitchew:* polecat, prostitute *soilèd:* pastured 129 *Centaurs:* (lustful creatures of mythology, half-human and half-beast) 131 *girdle:* waist *inherit:* possess 136 *civet:* musk perfume 140 *mortality:* death 141–142 *this . . . naught:* i.e. the universe (macrocosm) will decay like this man (microcosm; cf. III, i, 10)

149 *take:* accept 154 *case:* sockets 155 *are . . . me:* is that the situation 157 *case:* plight (pun) 160 *feelingly:* (1) only by touch (2) by feeling pain 164 *simple:* mere 165 *handy-dandy:* (old formula used in the child's game of choosing which hand) 170 *great image:* universal symbol 171–172 *a dog's . . . office:* i.e. man bows to authority regardless of who exercises it 173 *beadle:* parish constable 174 *lusts:* wish (suggestive form of 'lists') *kind:* i.e. same act 175 *The usurer . . . cozener:* i.e. the great cheat, some money-lending judge, sentences to death the little cheat 176 *appear:* show plainly

And the strong lance of justice hurtless
   breaks;
Arm it in rags, a pygmy's straw does
   pierce it.
None does offend, none—I say none! I'll
   able 'em.   180
Take that of me, my friend, who have the
   power
To seal th' accuser's lips. Get thee glass
   eyes
And, like a scurvy politician, seem
To see the things thou dost not. Now, now,
   now, now!
Pull off my boots. Harder, harder! So. 185
EDGAR. O, matter and impertinency mixed;
   Reason in madness.
LEAR. If thou wilt weep my fortunes, take
   my eyes.
I know thee well enough; thy name is
   Gloucester.
Thou must be patient. We came crying
   hither;   190
Thou know'st, the first time that we smell
   the air
We wawl and cry. I will preach to thee.
   Mark.
GLOUCESTER. Alack, alack the day.
LEAR. When we are born, we cry that we
   are come
To this great stage of fools.—This' a good
   block.   195
It were a delicate stratagem to shoe
A troop of horse with felt. I'll put't in
   proof,
And when I have stol'n upon these son-
   in-laws,
Then kill, kill, kill, kill, kill, kill!

Enter a Gentleman with Attendants.

GENTLEMAN. O, here he is! Lay hand upon
   him.—Sir,   200
Your most dear daughter—
LEAR. No rescue? What, a prisoner? I am
   even

The natural fool of fortune. Use me well;
You shall have ransom. Let me have
   surgeons;
I am cut to th' brains.
GENTLEMAN.   You shall have anything. 205
LEAR. No seconds? All myself?
Why, this would make a man a man of salt,
To use his eyes for garden waterpots,
Ay, and laying autumn's dust. I will die
   bravely,
Like a smug bridegroom. What, I will be
   jovial!   210
Come, come, I am a king; masters, know
   you that?
GENTLEMAN. You are a royal one, and we
   obey you.
LEAR. Then there's life in't. Come, an you
   get it, you shall get it by running. Sa, sa,
   sa, sa!   215
   Exit [running, followed by Attendants].
GENTLEMAN. A sight most pitiful in the
   meanest wretch,
Past speaking of in a king. Thou hast one
   daughter
Who redeems nature from the general
   curse
Which twain have brought her to.
EDGAR. Hail, gentle sir.
GENTLEMAN.
   Sir, speed you. What's your will? 220
EDGAR. Do you hear aught, sir, of a battle
   toward?
GENTLEMAN. Most sure and vulgar. Every
   one hears that
Which can distinguish sound.
EDGAR.   But, by your favor,
How near's the other army?
GENTLEMAN. Near and on speedy foot. The
   main descry   225
Stands on the hourly thought.

---

178 *hurtless:* without hurting 179 *Arm . . .
rags:* i.e. armored (cf. 'Plate,' l. 177) only in rags
180 *able:* authorize 181 *that:* (i.e. the assurance
of immunity) 183 *scurvy politician:* vile oppor-
tunist 186 *matter and impertinency:* sense and
nonsense 195 *block:* felt hat (?) 196 *delicate:*
subtle 197 *in proof:* to the test

203 *natural fool:* born plaything 204 *cut:*
wounded 206 *salt:* i.e. all tears 210 *smug
bridegroom:* spruce bridegroom (the image suggested by the secondary meaning of 'bravely,' i.e.
handsomely, and the sexual suggestion of 'will
die') 214 *life:* (and therefore 'hope') 215 *Sa . . .
sa:* (hunting and rallying cry) 218 *general curse:*
universal condemnation 219 *twain:* i.e. the other
two 220 *speed:* God speed 221 *toward:* impending 222 *sure and vulgar:* commonly known
certainty 225 *on speedy foot:* rapidly marching
225–226 *main . . . thought:* sight of the main
body is expected hourly

EDGAR.　　　　　I thank you, sir. That's all.

GENTLEMAN. Though that the Queen on
　special cause is here,

　Her army is moved on.

EDGAR.　　　I thank you, sir. *Exit Gentleman.*

GLOUCESTER. You ever-gentle gods, take my
　breath from me;

　Let not my worser spirit tempt me
　again　　　　　　　　　　　　　　　230

　To die before you please.

EDGAR.　　　　　　　Well pray you, father.

GLOUCESTER. Now, good sir, what are you?

EDGAR. A most poor man, made tame to
　fortune's blows,

　Who, by the art of known and feeling
　sorrows,

　Am pregnant to good pity. Give me your
　hand;　　　　　　　　　　　　　235

　I'll lead you to some biding.

GLOUCESTER.　　　　　　　Hearty thanks.

　The bounty and the benison of heaven

　To boot, and boot.

　　　　　Enter Steward [Oswald].

OSWALD.

　　　　A proclaimed prize! Most happy;

　That eyeless head of thine was first framed
　flesh

　To raise my fortunes. Thou old unhappy
　traitor,　　　　　　　　　　　240

　Briefly thyself remember. The sword is out

　That must destroy thee.

GLOUCESTER.　　　Now let thy friendly hand

　Put strength enough to't.

　　　　　　　　　　[Edgar interposes.]

OSWALD.　　　　Wherefore, bold peasant,

　Dar'st thou support a published traitor?
　Hence,

　Lest that th' infection of his fortune
　take　　　　　　　　　　　　　245

　Like hold on thee. Let go his arm.

EDGAR. Chill not let go, zir, without vurther
　'casion.

OSWALD. Let go, slave, or thou diest.

EDGAR. Good gentleman, go your gait, and
　let poor voke pass. An chud ha' bin 250
　zwaggered out of my life, 'twould not ha'
　bin zo long as 'tis by a vortnight. Nay,
　come not near th' old man. Keep out, che
　vore ye, or Ise try whether your costard
　or my ballow be the harder. Chill be 255
　plain with you.

OSWALD. Out, dunghill!　　　　　*[They fight.]*

EDGAR. Chill pick your teeth, zir. Come. No
　matter vor your foins.　　　*[Oswald falls.]*

OSWALD. Slave, thou hast slain me. Villain,
　take my purse.　　　　　　　　　260

　If ever thou wilt thrive, bury my body,

　And give the letters which thou find'st
　about me

　To Edmund Earl of Gloucester. Seek him
　out

　Upon the English party. O, untimely
　death!

　Death!　　　　　　　　*[He dies.]* 265

EDGAR. I know thee well. A serviceable vil-
　lain,

　As duteous to the vices of thy mistress

　As badness would desire.

GLOUCESTER.　　　　　What, is he dead?

EDGAR. Sit you down, father; rest you.

　Let's see these pockets; the letters that he
　speaks of　　　　　　　　　270

　May be my friends. He's dead; I am only
　sorry

　He had no other deathsman. Let us see.

　Leave, gentle wax; and, manners, blame
　us not

　To know our enemies' minds. We rip
　their hearts;

---

230 *worser spirit:* i.e. bad angel　233 *tame:*
submissive　234 *art . . . sorrows:* i.e. lesson of
sorrows painfully experienced　235 *pregnant:*
prone　236 *biding:* biding place　237 *benison:*
blessing　238 *proclaimed prize:* i.e. one with a
price on his head　*happy:* lucky　239 *framed
flesh:* born, created　241 *thyself remember:* i.e.
pray, think of your soul　242 *friendly:* i.e. unconsciously befriending　244 *published:* proclaimed

247 *Chill:* I'll (rustic dialect)　*vurther 'casion:*
further occasion　249 *gait:* way　250 *voke:* folk
An chud: if I could　251 *zwaggered:* swaggered,
bluffed　253–254 *che vore:* I warrant, assure
254 *Ise:* I shall　*costard:* head　255 *ballow:*
cudgel　258 *Chill pick:* i.e. I'll knock out　259
foins: thrusts　260 *Villain:* serf　262 *letters:*
letter　*about:* upon　264 *party:* side　266 *serviceable:* usable　267 *duteous:* ready to serve　272
deathsman: executioner　273 *Leave, gentle wax:*
by your leave, kind seal (formula used in opening
sealed documents)　274 *To know:* i.e. for growing
intimate with

Their papers is more lawful.   275
                        Reads the letter.
'Let our reciprocal vows be remembered.
You have many opportunities to cut him
off. If your will want not, time and place
will be fruitfully offered. There is nothing
done, if he return the conqueror. Then   280
am I the prisoner, and his bed my gaol;
from loathed warmth whereof deliver me,
and supply the place for your labor.
    'Your (wife, so I would say) affectionate
        servant,   'GONERIL.'
O   indistinguished space of woman's
    will—   285
A plot upon her virtuous husband's life,
And the exchange my brother! Here in
    the sands
Thee I'll rake up, the post unsanctified
Of murderous lechers; and in the mature
    time

With this ungracious paper strike the
    sight   290
Of the death-practiced Duke. For him 'tis
    well
That of thy death and business I can tell.
GLOUCESTER. The King is mad. How stiff is
    my vile sense,
That I stand up, and have ingenious feel-
    ing
Of my huge sorrows! Better I were dis-
    tract;   295
So should my thoughts be severed from my
    griefs,
And woes by wrong imaginations lose
The knowledge of themselves.
                        Drum afar off.
EDGAR.   Give me your hand.
Far off methinks I hear the beaten drum.
Come, father, I'll bestow you with a
    friend.   *Exeunt.* 300

Scene vii

*Enter Cordelia, Kent, [Doctor,] and Gentle-
man.*

CORDELIA. O thou good Kent, how shall I
    live and work
To match thy goodness? My life will be
    too short
And every measure fail me.
KENT. To be acknowledged, madam, is
    o'erpaid.
All my reports go with the modest
    truth;   5
Nor more nor clipped, but so.
CORDELIA.   Be better suited.
These weeds are memories of those worser
    hours.
I prithee put them off.
KENT.   Pardon, dear madam.

Yet to be known shortens my made intent.
My boon I make it that you know me
    not   10
Till time and I think meet.
CORDELIA. Then be't so, my good lord. [*to
    the Doctor*] How does the King?
DOCTOR. Madam, sleeps still.
CORDELIA. O you kind gods,   15
Cure this great breach in his abusèd
    nature!
Th' untuned and jarring senses, O, wind
    up
Of this child-changèd father!
DOCTOR. So please your Majesty
That we may wake the King? He hath
    slept long.   20
CORDELIA. Be governed by your knowledge,
    and proceed

---

275 *Their papers:* i.e. to rip their papers 278
want not: is not lacking 281 *gaol:* jail 284 *would:*
wish to   285 *indistinguished:* unlimited *will:*
desire 287 *exchange:* substitute 288 *rake up:*
cover, bury 289 *in the mature:* at the ripe 290
strike: blast 291 *deathpracticed:* whose death is
plotted 293 *stiff:* obstinate *vile sense:* i.e. hateful
consciousness 294 *ingenious feeling:* i.e. awareness 295 *distract:* distracted 297 *wrong imaginations:* i.e. delusions 300 *bestow:* lodge

IV, vii, 5 *go:* conform   6 *clipped:* i.e. less
(curtailed) *suited:* attired 7 *weeds:* clothes
memories: reminders 9 *Yet . . . intent:* i.e. to
reveal myself just yet would mar my plan 10
My boon . . . it: the reward I ask is 11 *meet:*
proper 16 *abusèd:* confused, disturbed 17 *jarring:*
discordant *wind up:* tune 18 *child-changèd* (1)
changed to a child (2) changed by his children
(suggesting 'changeling,' wherein mental defect
is associated with the malignance of witches)

I' th' sway of your own will. Is he arrayed?

Enter Lear in a chair carried by Servants.

GENTLEMAN. Ay, madam. In the heaviness of
  sleep
We put fresh garments on him.
DOCTOR. Be by, good madam, when we do
  awake him.   25
I doubt not of his temperance.
CORDELIA.   Very well. [*Music.*]
DOCTOR. Please you draw near. Louder the
  music there.
CORDELIA. O my dear father, restoration hang
Thy medicine on my lips, and let this
  kiss   30
Repair those violent harms that my two
  sisters
Have in thy reverence made.
KENT.   Kind and dear princess.
CORDELIA. Had you not been their father,
  these white flakes
Did challenge pity of them. Was this a
  face
To be opposed against the jarring
  winds?   35
To stand against the deep dread-bolted
  thunder?
In the most terrible and nimble stroke
Of quick cross lightning to watch, poor
  perdu,
With this thin helm? Mine enemy's dog,
Though he had bit me, should have stood
  that night   40
Against my fire; and wast thou fain, poor
  father,
To hovel thee with swine and rogues for-
  lorn
In short and musty straw? Alack, alack,
'Tis wonder that thy life and wits at once
Had not concluded all.—He wakes. Speak
  to him.   45
DOCTOR. Madam, do you; 'tis fittest.

---

22 *I' th' sway of:* according to 31 *harms:*
wounds 32 *reverence:* reverend person 33 *flakes:*
strands of hair 34 *challenge:* demand 36 *deep
dread-bolted:* deep-voiced and full of dreadful
bolts 38 *perdu:* (1) expendable outpost (military
term) (2) lost one 39 *helm:* military helmet;
here, thin hair 41 *fain:* glad 43 *short:* scanty
(?) tramped to fragments (?)

CORDELIA. How does my royal lord? How
  fares your Majesty?
LEAR. You do me wrong to take me out o'
  th' grave.
Thou art a soul in bliss; but I am bound
Upon a wheel of fire, that mine own
  tears   50
Do scald like molten lead.
CORDELIA.   Sir, do you know me?
LEAR. You are a spirit, I know. Where did
  you die?
CORDELIA. Still, still, far wide!
DOCTOR. He's scarce awake. Let him alone
  awhile.
LEAR. Where have I been? Where am I? Fair
  daylight?   55
I am mightily abused. I should e'en die
  with pity
To see another thus. I know not what to
  say.
I will not swear these are my hands. Let's
  see—
I feel this pin prick. Would I were assured
Of my condition.
CORDELIA.   O look upon me, sir, 60
And hold your hand in benediction o'er
  me.
You must not kneel.
LEAR.   Pray, do not mock me.
I am a very foolish fond old man,
Fourscore and upward, not an hour more
  nor less;
And, to deal plainly,   65
I fear I am not in my perfect mind.
Methinks I should know you, and know
  this man;
Yet I am doubtful, for I am mainly
  ignorant
What place this is; and all the skill I have
Remembers not these garments; nor I
  know not   70
Where I did lodge last night. Do not laugh
  at me;
For, as I am a man, I think this lady
To be my child Cordelia.
CORDELIA.   And so I am! I am!

---

50 *wheel of fire:* (implement combining the
tortures of breaking and burning, figuring in
medieval visions of hell) 53 *wide:* off the mark
55 *abused:* confused

LEAR. Be your tears wet? Yes, faith. I pray
weep not.
If you have poison for me, I will drink
it.   75
I know you do not love me; for your
sisters
Have, as I do remember, done me wrong.
You have some cause, they have not.
CORDELIA.   No cause, no cause.
LEAR. Am I in France?
KENT.   In your own kingdom, sir.
LEAR. Do not abuse me.   80
DOCTOR. Be comforted, good madam. The
great rage
You see is killed in him; [and yet it is
danger
To make him even o'er the time he has
lost.]
Desire him to go in. Trouble him no more
Till further settling.   85
CORDELIA. Will't please your Highness walk?
LEAR.   You must bear with me.

Pray you now, forget and forgive. I am
old and foolish.
    Exeunt. Manent Kent and Gentleman.
GENTLEMAN. Holds it true, sir, that the Duke
of Cornwall was so slain?
KENT. Most certain, sir.
GENTLEMAN. Who is conductor of his peo-
ple?   90
KENT. As 'tis said, the bastard son of
Gloucester.
GENTLEMAN. They say Edgar, his banished
son, is with the Earl of Kent in Germany.
KENT. Report is changeable. 'Tis time to 95
look about; the powers of the kingdom
approach apace.
GENTLEMAN. The arbitrement is like to be
bloody. Fare you well, sir.   *Exit.*
KENT. My point and period will be throughly
wrought,   100
Or well or ill, as this day's battle's fought.
                                          Exit.

ACT V

Scene i

*Enter, with Drum and Colors, Edmund,
Regan, Gentleman, and Soldiers.*

EDMUND. Know of the Duke if his last pur-
pose hold,
Or whether since he is advised by aught
To change the course. He's full of altera-
tion
And self-reproving. Bring his constant
pleasure.   [*Exit an Officer.*]
REGAN. Our sister's man is certainly mis-
carried.   5
EDMUND. 'Tis to be doubted, madam.
REGAN.   Now, sweet lord,
You know the goodness I intend upon you.

Tell me, but truly—but then speak the
truth—
Do you not love my sister?
EDMUND.   In honored love.
REGAN. But have you never found my
brother's way   10
To the forfended place?
EDMUND.   That thought abuses you.
REGAN. I am doubtful that you have been
conjunct
And bosomed with her, as far as we call
hers.
EDMUND. No, by mine honor, madam.
REGAN. I never shall endure her. Dear my
lord,   15

---

80 *abuse:* deceive 83 *even o'er:* fill in 85
settling: calming 96 *powers:* armies 97 *arbitrement:* decisive action 100 *My point ... wrought:*
i.e. my destiny will be completely worked out
101 *Or:* either
    V, i, S.D. *Drum and Colors:* drummer and
standard-bearers 1 *Know:* learn *last purpose
hold:* most recent intention (i.e. to fight) holds

good 2 *advised:* induced 4 *constant pleasure:*
firm decision 5 *miscarried:* met with mishap
6 *doubted:* feared 7 *goodness I intend:* boon
I plan to confer 9 *honored:* honorable 11 *forfended:* forbidden 11 *abuses* deceives 12–13
doubtful ... hers: i.e. fearful you have been
intimately linked with her both in mind and
body

Be not familiar with her.
EDMUND.   Fear me not.
She and the Duke her husband!

*Enter, with Drum and Colors, Albany,
Goneril, Soldiers.*

GONERIL. [*aside*] I had rather lose the battle
than that sister
Should loosen him and me.
ALBANY. Our very loving sister, well
bemet.   20
Sir, this I heard: the King is come to his
daughter,
With others whom the rigor of our state
Forced to cry out. Where I could not be
honest,
I never yet was valiant. For this business,
It touches us as France invades our
land,   25
Not bolds the King with others, whom I
fear
Most just and heavy causes make oppose.
EDMUND. Sir, you speak nobly.
REGAN.   Why is this reasoned?
GONERIL. Combine together 'gainst the ene-
my;
For these domestic and particular broils 30
Are not the question here.
ALBANY.   Let's then determine
With th' ancient of war on our proceed-
ing.
EDMUND. I shall attend you presently at your
tent.
REGAN. Sister, you'll go with us?
GONERIL. No.   35
REGAN. 'Tis most convenient. Pray go with
us.
GONERIL. O ho, I know the riddle.—I will go.
                    Exeunt both the Armies.

---

19 *loosen:* separate 20 *bemet:* met 22 *rigor:*
tyranny 23 *honest:* honorable 25 *touches us as:*
concerns me because 26–27 *Not bolds . . . oppose:*
i.e. but not because he supports the King and
others whose truly great grievances arouse them
to arms 28 *reasoned:* argued 30 *particular
broils:* private quarrels 31 *question:* issue 32
th' ancient of war: i.e. seasoned officers 33 *presently:* immediately 35 *convenient:* fitting *with
us:* (i.e. with her rather than Edmund as each
leads an 'army' from the stage) 37 *riddle:* (i.e.
the reason for Regan's strange demand)

Enter Edgar.

EDGAR. [*to Albany*] If e'er your Grace had
speech with man so poor,
Hear me one word.
ALBANY. [*to those departing*] I'll overtake
you. [*to Edgar*] Speak.
EDGAR. Before you fight the battle, ope this
letter.   40
If you have victory, let the trumpet sound
For him that brought it. Wretched though
I seem,
I can produce a champion that will prove
What is avouchèd there. If you miscarry,
Your business of the world hath so an
end,   45
And machination ceases. Fortune love you.
ALBANY. Stay till I have read the letter.
EDGAR.   I was forbid it.
When time shall serve, let but the herald
cry,
And I'll appear again.
ALBANY. Why, fare thee well. I will o'erlook
thy paper.   50
                              Exit Edgar.

Enter Edmund.

EDMUND. The enemy's in view; draw up your
powers.
Here is the guess of their true strength
and forces
By diligent discovery; but your haste
Is now urged on you.
ALBANY.   We will greet the time. *Exit.*
EDMUND. To both these sisters have I sworn
my love;   55
Each jealous of the other, as the stung
Are of the adder. Which of them shall I
take?
Both? One? Or neither? Neither can be
enjoyed,
If both remain alive. To take the widow

---

38 *had speech:* i.e. has condescended to speak
41 *sound:* sound a summons 43 *prove:* (in trial
by combat) 44 *avouchèd:* charged 46 *machination:* i.e. all plots and counterplots 50 *o'erlook:*
look over 51 *powers:* troops 52 *guess:* estimate
53 *discovery:* reconnoitering 54 *greet:* i.e. meet
the demands of 56 *jealous:* suspicious

Exasperates, makes mad her sister Gon-
eril;   60
And hardly shall I carry out my side,
Her husband being alive. Now then, we'll
use
His countenance for the battle, which
being done,
Let her who would be rid of him devise

His speedy taking off. As for the mercy   65
Which he intends to Lear and to Cordelia—
The battle done, and they within our
power,
Shall never see his pardon; for my state
Stands on me to defend, not to debate.
                                                    Exit.

Scene ii

*Alarum within. Enter, with Drum and
Colors, Lear held by the hand by Cordelia; and Soldiers [of France], over the
stage and exeunt.*

Enter Edgar and Gloucester.

EDGAR. Here, father, take the shadow of this
tree
For your good host. Pray that the right
may thrive.
If ever I return to you again,
I'll bring you comfort.
GLOUCESTER.   Grace go with you, sir.
                                            Exit Edgar.

Alarum and retreat within. Enter Edgar.

EDGAR. Away, old man! Give me thy hand.
Away!   5
King Lear hath lost, he and his daughter
ta'en.
Give me thy hand. Come on.
GLOUCESTER. No further, sir. A man may rot
even here.
EDGAR. What, in ill thoughts again? Men
must endure
Their going hence, even as their coming
hither;   10
Ripeness is all. Come on.
GLOUCESTER. And that's true too.   *Exeunt.*

Scene iii

*Enter, in conquest, with Drum and Colors,
Edmund; Lear and Cordelia as prisoners;
Soldiers, Captain.*

EDMUND. Some officers take them away.
Good guard
Until their greater pleasures first be known
That are to censure them.
CORDELIA.   We are not the first
Who with best meaning have incurred the
worst.
For thee, oppressèd king, I am cast
down;   5
Myself could else outfrown false Fortune's
frown.

Shall we not see these daughters and these
sisters?
LEAR. No, no, no, no! Come, let's away to
prison.
We two alone will sing like birds i' th'
cage.
When thou dost ask me blessing, I'll kneel
down   10
And ask of thee forgiveness. So we'll
live,
And pray, and sing, and tell old tales, and
laugh
At gilded butterflies, and hear poor rogues
Talk of court news; and we'll talk with
them too—

61 *hardly . . . side:* with difficulty shall I play
my part (as Goneril's lover, or as a great power
in England?) 63 *countenance:* backing 68–69
my state . . . debate: i.e. my status depends upon
my strength, not my arguments
V, ii, S.D. *Alarum and retreat:* (trumpet
sounds, signalling the beginning and the ending of a battle) 6 *ta'en:* captured 8 *rot:*
i.e. die   9 *ill:* i.e. suicidal   *endure:* put up with,

suffer through   11 *Ripeness:* i.e. the time
decreed by the gods for the fruit to fall from
the branch
V, iii, 2 *greater pleasures:* i.e. the desires of
those in higher command   3 *censure:* judge   4
meaning: intentions 10–11 *When . . . forgiveness:*
(cf. IV, vii, 60–62) 12–14 *laugh . . . news:* view
with amusement bright ephemera, such as gallants preoccupied with court gossip

Who loses and who wins; who's in, who's
   out—   15
And take upon 's the mystery of things
As if we were God's spies; and we'll wear
   out,
In a walled prison, packs and sects of
   great ones
That ebb and flow by th' moon.

EDMUND.   Take them away.

LEAR. Upon such sacrifices, my Cordelia,   20
   The gods themselves throw incense. Have
     I caught thee?
He that parts us shall bring a brand from
   heaven
And fire us hence like foxes. Wipe thine
   eyes.
The goodyears shall devour them, flesh
   and fell,
Ere they shall make us weep! We'll see
   'em starved first.   25
Come.

       Exeunt Lear and Cordelia, guarded.

EDMUND. Come hither, captain; hark.
   Take thou this note. [*Gives a paper.*] Go
   follow them to prison.
One step I have advanced thee. If thou
   dost
As this instructs thee, thou dost make thy
   way   30
To noble fortunes. Know thou this, that
   men
Are as the time is. To be tender-minded
Does not become a sword. Thy great
   employment
Will not bear question. Either say thou'lt
   do't,
Or thrive by other means.

CAPTAIN.   I'll do't, my lord.   35

16–17 *take . . . spies:* i.e. contemplate the
wonder of existence as if with divine insight,
seek eternal rather than temporal truths 17 *wear
out:* outlast 18–19 *packs . . . moon:* i.e. partisan
and intriguing clusters of 'great ones' who gain
and lose power monthly 20–21 *Upon . . . incense:*
i.e. the gods themselves are the celebrants at
such sacrificial offerings to love as we are 22–
23 *He . . . foxes:* i.e. to separate us, as foxes are
smoked out and scattered, would require not a
human but a heavenly torch 24 *goodyears:* (un-
defined forces of evil) *fell:* hide 32 *as the time
is:* (i.e. ruthless in war) 33 *become:* befit 34
bear question: admit discussion

EDMUND. About it; and write happy when
   th' hast done.
Mark, I say instantly, and carry it so
As I have set it down.

CAPTAIN. I cannot draw a cart, nor eat dried
   oats—
If it be man's work, I'll do't.   *Exit.*   40

*Flourish. Enter Albany, Goneril, Regan,
Soldiers.*

ALBANY. Sir, you have showed to-day your
   valiant strain,
And fortune led you well. You have the
   captives
Who were the opposites of this day's strife.
I do require them of you, so to use them
As we shall find their merits and our
   safety   45
May equally determine.

EDMUND.   Sir, I thought it fit
To send the old and miserable King
To some retention⌈and appointed guard;⌉
Whose age had charms in it, whose title
   more,
To pluck the common bosom on his
   side   50
And turn our impressed lances in our eyes
Which do command them. With him I
   sent the Queen,
My reason all the same; and they are
   ready
To-morrow, or at further space, t' appear
Where you shall hold your session. At this
   time   55
We sweat and bleed, the friend hath lost
   his friend,
And the best quarrels, in the heat, are
   cursed
By those that feel their sharpness.
The question of Cordelia and her father
Requires a fitter place.

ALBANY.   Sir, by your patience,   60
I hold you but a subject of this war,

---

36 *write happy:* consider yourself fortunate
43 *opposites of:* enemies in   45 *merits:* deserts
48 *some . . . guard:* detention under duly appointed guards 50 *pluck . . . bosom:* draw popular
sympathy 53 *turn . . . eyes:* i.e. make our con-
scripted lancers turn on us   54 *space:* interval
55 *session:* trials 57 *best quarrels:* worthiest
causes 58 *sharpness:* i.e. painful effects   61
subject of: subordinate in

Not as a brother.

REGAN. That's as we list to grace him.
Methinks our pleasure might have been demanded
Ere you had spoke so far. He led our powers,   65
Bore the commission of my place and person,
The which immediacy may well stand up
And call itself your brother.

GONERIL.   Not so hot!
In his own grace he doth exalt himself
More than in your addition.

REGAN.   In my rights 70
By me invested, he compeers the best.

ALBANY. That were the most if he should husband you.

REGAN. Jesters do oft prove prophets.

GONERIL.   Holla, holla!
That eye that told you so looked but asquint.

REGAN. Lady, I am not well; else I should answer   75
From a full-flowing stomach. General,
Take thou my soldiers, prisoners, patrimony;
Dispose of them, of me; the walls is thine.
Witness the world that I create thee here
My lord and master.

GONERIL.   Mean you to enjoy him? 80

ALBANY. The let-alone lies not in your good will.

EDMUND. Nor in thine, lord.

ALBANY.   Half-blooded fellow, yes.

REGAN. [to Edmund] Let the drum strike, and prove my title thine.

ALBANY. Stay yet; hear reason. Edmund, I arrest thee
On capital treason; and, in thy attaint, 85

---

63 *list to grace:* please to honor 67 *immediacy:* i.e. present status (as my deputy) 70 *your addition:* honors conferred by you 71 *compeers:* equals 72 *most:* i.e. most complete investiture in your rights *husband:* wed 74 *asquint:* cross-eyed, crookedly 76 *stomach:* anger 77 *patrimony:* inheritance 78 *walls is thine:* i.e. you have stormed the citadel (myself) 81 *let-alone:* permission 82 *Half-blooded:* i.e. by birth only half noble 83 *Let . . . thine:* i.e. fight and win for yourself my rights in the kingdom 85 *in thy attaint:* i.e. as party to your corruption (cf. the 'serpent' of Eden)

This gilded serpent. [*Points to Goneril.*]
For your claim, fair sister,
I bar it in the interest of my wife.
'Tis she is subcontracted to this lord,
And I, her husband, contradict your banes.
If you will marry, make your loves to me;   90
My lady is bespoke,

GONERIL.   An interlude!

ALBANY. Thou art armed, Gloucester. Let the trumpet sound.
If none appear to prove upon thy person
Thy heinous, manifest, and many treasons,
There is my pledge. [*Throws down a glove.*]
I'll make it on thy heart,   95
Ere I taste bread, thou art in nothing less
Than I have here proclaimed thee.

REGAN.   Sick, O, sick!

GONERIL. [*aside*] If not, I'll ne'er trust medicine.

EDMUND. There's my exchange. [*Throws down a glove.*]
What in the world he is
That names me traitor, villain-like he lies.   100
Call by the trumpet. He that dares approach,
On him, on you, who not? I will maintain
My truth and honor firmly.

ALBANY. A herald, ho!

EDMUND.   A herald, ho, a herald!

ALBANY. Trust to thy single virtue; for thy soldiers,   105
All levied in my name, have in my name
Took their discharge.

REGAN.   My sickness grows upon me.

ALBANY. She is not well. Convey her to my tent.   *Exit Regan, attended.*

Enter a Herald.

Come hither, herald. Let the trumpet sound,

---

88 *subcontracted:* i.e. engaged, though previously married (sarcastic play on 'precontracted,' a legal term applied to one facing an impediment to marriage because previously engaged to another) 89 *contradict your banes:* forbid your banns, i.e. declare an impediment 90 *loves:* love-suits 91 *An interlude:* a quaint playlet (equivalent to saying 'How dramatic!' or 'How comical!') 95 *make:* prove 96 *nothing less:* i.e. no respect less guilty 98 *medicine:* i.e. poison 101 *trumpet:* trumpeter 105 *single virtue:* unaided prowess

And read out this.   110
CAPTAIN. Sound, trumpet!

A trumpet sounds.

HERALD. (*reads*) 'If any man of quality or
degree within the lists of the army will
maintain upon Edmund, supposed Earl
of Gloucester, that he is a manifold 115
traitor, let him appear by the third sound
of the trumpet. He is bold in his defense.'
EDMUND. Sound!   *First trumpet.*
HERALD. Again!   *Second trumpet.*
     Again!   *Third trumpet.* 120

Trumpet answers within.

*Enter Edgar, armed, at the third sound, a
Trumpet before him.*

ALBANY. Ask him his purposes, why he
     appears
Upon this call o' th' trumpet.
HERALD.   What are you?
     Your name, your quality, and why you
     answer
This present summons?
EDGAR.   Know my name is lost,
     By treason's tooth bare-gnawn and
     canker-bit;   125
Yet am I noble as the adversary
I come to cope.
ALBANY.   Which is that adversary?
EDGAR. What's he that speaks for Edmund
     Earl of Gloucester?
EDMUND. Himself. What say'st thou to
     him?
EDGAR.   Draw thy sword.
     That, if my speech offend a noble
     heart,   130
Thy arm may do thee justice. Here is
     mine.
Behold it is my privilege,
The privilege of mine honors,
My oath, and my profession. I protest—
Maugre thy strength, place, youth, and
     eminence,   135
Despite thy victor sword and fire-new
     fortune,

Thy valor and thy heart—thou art a
     traitor,
False to thy gods, thy brother, and thy
     father,
Conspirant 'gainst this high illustrious
     prince,
And from th' extremest upward of thy
     head   140
To the descent and dust below thy foot
A most toad-spotted traitor. Say thou
     'no,'
This sword, this arm, and my best spirits
     are bent
To prove upon thy heart, whereto I speak,
Thou liest.   145
EDMUND. In wisdom I should ask thy name,
     But since thy outside looks so fair and
     warlike,
And that thy tongue some say of breeding
     breathes,
What safe and nicely I might well delay
By rule of knighthood I disdain and
     spurn.   150
Back do I toss these treasons to thy head,
With the hell-hated lie o'erwhelm thy
     heart,
Which—for they yet glance by and
     scarcely bruise—
This sword of mine shall give them instant
     way
Where they shall rest for ever. Trumpets,
     speak!   155

Alarums. Fight. Edmund falls.

ALBANY. Save him, save him.
GONERIL.   This is practice, Gloucester.
     By th' law of war thou wast not bound to
     answer

---

113 *degree:* rank *lists:* muster 125 *canker-bit:*
eaten, as by the rose-caterpillar 132–134 *it . . .
profession:* i.e. wielding this sword is the privilege
of my knightly honor, oath, and function
135 *Maugre:* in spite of 136 *fire-new:* brand-new

137 *heart:* courage 139 *Conspirant:* in conspiracy 140 *extremest upward:* uppermost
extreme 141 *descent and dust:* i.e. all that
intervenes from the head to the dust 142
toad-spotted: i.e. exuding venom like a toad
143 *bent:* directed 146 *wisdom:* prudence 148
some say: some assay, i.e. proof (?) or, one might
say (?) 149 *safe and nicely:* cautiously and
punctiliously 151 *treasons:* accusations of treason 152 *hell-hated:* hateful as hell 153–155
Which . . . ever: i.e. the accusations of treason,
now flying about harmlessly, will be routed into
you with my sword-thrust and lodge there permanently 156 *Save him:* spare him (cf. l. 160)
practice: trickery

An unknown opposite. Thou art not van-
quished,
But cozened and beguiled.
ALBANY.   Shut your mouth, dame,
Or with this paper shall I stop it.—Hold,
sir.—   160
[*To Goneril*] Thou worse than any name,
read thine own evil.
No tearing, lady! I perceive you know it.
GONERIL. Say if I do—the laws are mine, not
thine.
Who can arraign me for't?
ALBANY.   Most monstrous! O,
Know'st thou this paper?   165
GONERIL.   Ask me not what I know. *Exit.*
ALBANY. Go after her. She's desperate;
govern her.   [*Exit an Officer.*]
EDMUND. What you have charged me with,
that have I done,
And more, much more. The time will
bring it out.
'Tis past, and so am I.—But what art
thou   170
That hast this fortune on me? If thou'rt
noble,
I do forgive thee.
EDGAR.   Let's exchange charity.
I am no less in blood than thou art,
Edmund;
If more, the more th' hast wronged me.
My name is Edgar and thy father's son. 175
The gods are just, and of our pleasant
vices
Make instruments to plague us.
The dark and vicious place where thee he
got
Cost him his eyes.
EDMUND.   Th' hast spoken right; 'tis true.
The wheel is come full circle; I am here. 180
ALBANY. Methought thy very gait did pro-
phesy

---

159 *cozened:* cheated 160 *Hold:* wait (If
addressed to Edmund, this suggests a motive for
the 'Save him' of l. 156: i.e. Albany hopes to
obtain a confession.) 163 *mine:* (i.e. as ruler)
167 *govern:* control 180 *fortune on:* i.e. victory
over 172 *charity:* forgiveness and love 174
If more: if greater (since legitimate) 176 *of our
pleasant:* out of our pleasurable 178 *place:* i.e.
the bed of adultery *got:* begot 180 *wheel:* (of
fortune) *here* (at its bottom) 181 *prophesy:*
promise

A royal nobleness. I must embrace thee.
Let sorrow split my heart if ever I
Did hate thee, or thy father.
EDGAR.   Worthy prince, I know't.
ALBANY. Where have you hid yourself? 185
How have you known the miseries of your
father?
EDGAR. By nursing them, my lord. List a
brief tale;
And when 'tis told, O that my heart would
burst!
The bloody proclamation to escape
That followed me so near (O, our lives'
sweetness!   190
That we the pain of death would hourly die
Rather than die at once) taught me to shift
Into a madman's rags, t' assume a sem-
blance
That very dogs disdained; and in this
habit
Met I my father with his bleeding
rings,   195
Their precious stones new lost; became his
guide,
Led him, begged for him, saved him from
despair;
Never—O fault!—revealed myself unto
him
Until some half hour past, when I was
armed,
Not sure, though hoping of this good
success,   200
I asked his blessing, and from first to
last
Told him our pilgrimage. But his flawed
heart—
Alack, too weak the conflict to support—
'Twixt two extremes of passion, joy and
grief,
Burst smilingly.   205
EDMUND. This speech of yours hath moved
me,
And shall perchance do good; but speak
you on—
You look as you had something more to
say.

190–191 *O . . . die:* i.e. how sweet is life that
we would prefer to suffer death-pangs hourly
194 *habit:* attire 195 *rings:* sockets 199 *armed:*
in armor 202 *our pilgrimage:* of our journey
flawed: cracked

ALBANY. If there be more, more woeful, hold
  it in,
  For I am almost ready to dissolve,   210
  Hearing of this.
EDGAR. This would have seemed a period
  To such as love not sorrow; but another,
  To amplify too much, would make much
    more,
  And top extremity.
  Whilst I was big in clamor, came there in
    a man,   215
  Who, having seen me in my worst estate,
  Shunned my abhorred society; but then,
    finding
  Who 'twas that so endured, with his strong
    arms
  He fastenèd on my neck, and bellowèd out
  As he'd burst heaven, threw him on my
    father,   220
  Told the most piteous tale of Lear and
    him
  That ever ear received; which in recount-
    ing
  His grief grew puissant, and the strings of
    life
  Began to crack. Twice then the trumpets
    sounded,
  And there I left him tranced.
ALBANY.   But who was this? 225
EDGAR. Kent, sir, the banished Kent; who
    in disguise
  Followèd his enemy king and did him
    service
  Improper for a slave.

Enter a Gentleman [with a bloody knife].

GENTLEMAN. Help, help! O, help!
EDGAR.   What kind of help?
ALBANY.   Speak, man.
EDGAR. What means this bloody knife?
GENTLEMAN.   'Tis hot, it smokes. 230
  It came even from the heart of—O, she's
    dead.
ALBANY. Who dead? Speak, man.

GENTLEMAN. Your lady, sir, your lady; and
    her sister
  By her is poisonèd; she confesses it.
EDMUND. I was contracted to them both. All
    three   235
  Now marry in an instant.
EDGAR.   Here comes Kent.

Enter Kent.

ALBANY. Produce the bodies, be they alive
    or dead.   [*Exit Gentleman.*]
  This judgment of the heavens, that makes
    us tremble,
  Touches us not with pity.—O, is this he?
  The time will not allow the compli-
    ment   240
  Which very manners urges.
KENT.   I am come
  To bid my king and master aye good
    night.
  Is he not here?
ALBANY.   Great thing of us forgot!
  Speak, Edmund, where's the King? and
    where's Cordelia?
  Goneril and Regan's bodies brought out.
  Seest thou this object, Kent?   245
KENT. Alack, why thus?
EDMUND.   Yet Edmund was beloved.
  The one the other poisoned for my sake,
  And after slew herself.
ALBANY. Even so. Cover their faces.
EDMUND. I pant for life. Some good I mean
    to do,   250
  Despite of mine own nature. Quickly
    send—
  Be brief in it—to the castle, for my writ
  Is on the life of Lear and on Cordelia.
  Nay, send in time.
ALBANY.   Run, run, O, run!
EDGAR. To who, my lord? Who has the
    office? Send   255
  Thy token of reprieve.
EDMUND. Well thought on. Take my sword;
  Give it the captain.

EDGAR.   Haste thee for thy life.

[*Exit Officer.*]

EDMUND. He hath commission from thy wife
and me   260
To hang Cordelia in the prison and
To lay the blame upon her own despair
That she fordid herself.

ALBANY. The gods defend her! Bear him
hence awhile.   [*Edmund is borne off.*]

*Enter Lear, with Cordelia in his arms,
Gentleman, and others following.*

LEAR. Howl, howl, howl! O, you are men of
stones.   265
Had I your tongues and eyes, I'ld use them
so
That heaven's vault should crack. She's
gone for ever.
I know when one is dead, and when one
lives.
She's dead as earth. Lend me a looking
glass.
If that her breath will mist or stain the
stone,   270
Why then she lives.

KENT.   Is this the promised end?

EDGAR. Or image of that horror?

ALBANY.   Fall and cease.

LEAR. This feather stirs; she lives! If it be so,
It is a chance which does redeem all sor-
rows
That ever I have felt.

KENT.   O my good master.   275

LEAR. Prithee away.

EDGAR.   'Tis noble Kent, your friend.

LEAR. A plague upon you murderers, traitors
all;
I might have saved her; now she's gone
for ever.
Cordelia, Cordelia, stay a little. Ha,
What is't thou say'st? Her voice was ever
soft,   280
Gentle, and low—an excellent thing in
woman.
I killed the slave that was a-hanging thee.

GENTLEMAN. 'Tis true, my lords, he did.

---

263 *fordid:* destroyed   270 *stone:* i.e. glass
271 *promised end:* i.e. doomsday   272 *image:*
duplicate *Fall and cease:* i.e. strike once and for
all, make an end of things   274 *redeem:* atone
for

LEAR.   Did I not, fellow?
I have seen the day, with my good biting
falchion
I would have made them skip. I am old
now,   285
And these same crosses spoil me. Who are
you?
Mine eyes are not o'th' best. I'll tell you
straight.

KENT. If fortune brag of two she loved and
hated,
One of them we behold.

LEAR. This is a dull sight. Are you not Kent?

KENT.   The same: 290
Your servant Kent; where is your servant
Caius?

LEAR. He's a good fellow, I can tell you that.
He'll strike, and quickly too. He's dead
and rotten.

KENT. No, my good lord; I am the very man.

LEAR. I'll see that straight.   295

KENT. That from your first of difference and
decay
Have followed your sad steps.

LEAR.   You are welcome hither.

KENT. Nor no man else. All's cheerless, dark,
and deadly.
Your eldest daughters have fordone themselves,
And desperately are dead.

LEAR.   Ay, so I think.   300

ALBANY. He knows not what he says; and
vain is it
That we present us to him.

EDGAR.   Very bootless.

Enter a Messenger.

MESSENGER. Edmund is dead, my lord.

---

284 *falchion:* small sword slightly hooked
286 *crosses:* adversities   *spoil me:* i.e. sap my
strength   287 *tell you straight:* i.e. recognize
you in a moment   288 *two:* (i.e. Lear, and a
hypothetical second extreme example of Fortune's cruelty with whom he may be equated)
loved and hated: i.e. favored, then victimized
290 *sight:* eyesight (Instinctively Lear shuns the
admission that he is dazed and weeping.)   291
Caius: (Kent's alias)   295 *see that straight:*
understand that in a moment   296 *difference and
decay:* change and decline in fortune   298 *Nor
no man else:* i.e. no, nor anyone else   299 *fordone:*
destroyed   300 *desperately:* in a state of despair
302 *bootless:* useless

ALBANY. That's but a trifle here.
You lords and noble friends, know our
intent.
What comfort to this great decay may
come 305
Shall be applied. For us, we will resign,
During the life of this old Majesty,
To him our absolute power; [*to Edgar and
Kent*] you to your rights,
With boot and such addition as your
honors
Have more than merited. All friends shall
taste 310
The wages of their virtue, and all foes
The cup of their deservings.—O, see, see!
LEAR. And my poor fool is hanged: no, no,
no life?
Why should a dog, a horse, a rat, have life,
And thou no breath at all? Thou'lt come
no more, 315
Never, never, never, never, never.
Pray you undo this button. Thank you, sir.
Do you see this? Look on her! Look her
lips,
Look there, look there— *He dies.*
EDGAR. He faints. My lord, my lord—
KENT. Break, heart, I prithee break!

EDGAR. Look up, my lord. 320
KENT. Vex not his ghost. O, let him pass!
He hates him
That would upon the rack of this tough
world
Stretch him out longer.
EDGAR. He is gone indeed.
KENT. The wonder is, he hath endured so
long.
He but usurped his life. 325
ALBANY. Bear them from hence. Our present
business
Is general woe. [*to Kent and Edgar*]
Friends of my soul, you twain
Rule in this realm, and the gored state
sustain.
KENT. I have a journey, sir, shortly to go. 330
My master calls me; I must not say no.
EDGAR. The weight of this sad time we must
obey,
Speak what we feel, not what we ought to
say.
The oldest hath borne most; we that are
young
Shall never see so much, nor live so
long. 335
Exeunt with a dead march.

---

305 *What . . . come:* i.e. whatever means of aiding this ruined great one presents itself 309 *boot:* good measure *addition:* titles, advancement in rank 313 *fool:* i.e. Cordelia ('Fool' was often a term of affection, and sometimes, as in Erasmus and elsewhere in Shakespeare, of praise —as ironic commentary upon self-seeking 'worldly wisdom.') 321 *Vex . . . ghost:* do not trouble his departing spirit 322 *rack:* instrument of torture 325 *usurped:* possessed contrary to (natural) law *obey:* i.e. accept

One of the recurring questions in the discussion of tragedy is the extent to which it is necessary for the tragic hero to be aware of his fate. The pattern of classic tragedy suggested that the hero must perceive his own downfall, be aware of its causes and suffer its consequences, in order for genuine tragedy to take place. Without his self-awareness, there could be, it was thought, none of the illumination, the insight, the growth through suffering, that tragedy was alleged to produce. Allied with this view was the concept that only a great man could be a tragic hero, a man great of soul and feeling as well as highly placed in worldly affairs.

In modern times, under the impetus of the democratic revolutions of the last two centuries with their increased emphasis on the rights and status of the individual, this traditional view has been challenged and modified. Some recent dramatists have written plays using everyday, middle-class characters of no particular perception, plays which challenge this older view of tragedy and test its validity for the twentieth century. One such challenge was offered by Eugene O'Neill's *The Iceman Cometh* in 1946, which evoked a famous *Life* editorial titled "Untragic America." *Life* commented that the play substituted misery for tragedy, and went on to generalize that man in the modern world has lost his tragic sense, and consequently his ability to regard himself with awe, because he no longer sees himself as the center of a battle of cosmic importance or regards his choices as having much consequence.

The very problem on which the *Life* editorial focussed—the question of whether man can hold his destiny in his own hands—is central to Luigi Pirandello's *Henry IV*. Dealing directly with the problem of man's willingness or ability to assume the consequences of deeds knowingly done, it confronts a character of stature with a dilemma in which he must make a difficult choice. Before the start of the play, he has been driven mad as the result of an accident; he has later regained his sanity but has kept his recovery concealed; he has chosen to live in a make-believe world in which his pretended madness is a protective covering. During the course of the play he decides to strip off his illusion and return to normal life; but now an event occurs that makes it necessary for him once more to pretend to be insane, not out of choice this time but to escape the consequences of a killing. Within this situation, the dramatist explores many aspects of the problem of man's will, the extent to which he is or need be responsible for his own fate, the degree to which his tragedy depends on his awareness of his own part in initiating the events that lead to his punishment.

Not only in its concern with the problem of will asserting itself in action, but also in its portrayal of the confusing and shifting borders between appearance and reality, *Henry IV*, written in 1922, is typical of the recurring themes of Pirandello's plays. In the world reflected by this dramatist, one often does not know what is illusion and what is reality—if there is such a thing, or if there is any difference. Is "truth" whatever one thinks it is? If so, then what becomes of intelligence, of will, of the ability to penetrate deception, of the necessity to make choices? Most important of all, what happens in such a fluid world to human identity under conditions of stress? These are typical Pirandellian questions.

Sometimes regarded as too cerebral, as an author of plays designed to trick and puzzle his audiences rather than to move and enlighten them, Pirandello has suffered a decline in reputation. In recent years, however, his affinity with many modern movements of thought—in psychology as well as in drama—has awakened new interest in him. He has, in fact, exerted considerable influence on many developments in avant-garde drama and the new "theater of the absurd." The themes that preoccupied him, and the characters he invented to embody them, have helped to keep alive the question of tragedy in our age; they also relate him to new departures in the drama.

HENRY IV

Luigi Pirandello

translated by
Edward Storer

HENRY IV
THE MARCHIONESS MATILDA SPINA
FRIDA, *her daughter*
CHARLES DI NOLLI, *the young Marquis*
BARON TITO BELCREDI
DOCTOR DIONYSIUS GENONI
HAROLD
  (FRANK)
LANDOLPH
  (LOLO)
ORDULPH
  (MOMO)
BERTHOLD
  (FINO)
The four private counsellors (The names in parentheses are nicknames)

JOHN, *the old waiter*
THE TWO VALETS IN COSTUME

A Solitary Villa in Italy in Our Own Time

ACT ONE

Salon in the villa, furnished and decorated so as to look exactly like the throne room of Henry IV in the royal residence at Goslar. Among the antique decorations there are two modern life-size portraits in oil painting. They are placed against the back wall, and mounted in a wooden stand that runs the whole length of the wall. (It is wide and protrudes, so that it is like a large bench.) One of the paintings is on the right; the other on the left of the throne, which is in the middle of the wall and divides the stand.

The Imperial chair and Baldachin.

The two portraits represent a lady and gentleman, both young, dressed up in carni-

val costumes: one as "Henry IV," the other as the "Marchioness Matilda of Tuscany." Exits to right and left.

When the curtain goes up, the two valets jump down, as if surprised, from the stand on which they have been lying, and go and take their positions, as rigid as statues, on either side below the throne with their halberds in their hands. Soon after, from the second exit, right, enter HAROLD, LANDOLPH, ORDULPH *and* BERTHOLD, *young men employed by the* MARQUIS CHARLES DI NOLLI *to play the part of "Secret Counsellors" at the court of "Henry IV." They are, therefore, dressed like German knights of the eleventh century.* BERTHOLD, *nicknamed. Fino, is just entering on his duties for the first time. His companions are telling him what he has to do and amusing themselves at his expense. The scene is to be played rapidly and vivaciously.*

LANDOLPH (*To* BERTHOLD *as if explaining*) And this is the throne room.

HAROLD At Goslar.

ORDULPH Or at the castle in the Hartz, if you prefer.

HAROLD Or at Worms.

LANDOLPH According as to what's doing, it jumps about with us, now here, now there.

ORDULPH In Saxony.

HAROLD In Lombardy.

LANDOLPH On the Rhine.

ONE OF THE VALETS (*Without moving, just opening his lips*) I say . . .

HAROLD (*Turning round*) What is it?

FIRST VALET (*Like a statue*) Is he coming in or not? (*He alludes to* HENRY IV)

ORDULPH No, no, he's asleep. You needn't worry.

SECOND VALET (*Releasing his pose, taking a long breath and going to lie down again on the stand*) You might have told us at once.

FIRST VALET (*Going over to* HAROLD) Have you got a match, please?

LANDOLPH What? You can't smoke a pipe here, you know.

FIRST VALET (*While* HAROLD *offers him a light*) No; a cigarette. (*Lights his cigarette and lies down again on the stand*)

BERTHOLD (*Who has been looking on in amazement, walking round the room, regarding the costumes of the others*) I say . . . this room . . . these costumes . . . Which Henry IV is it? I don't quite get it. Is he Henry IV of France or not? (*At this* LANDOLPH, HAROLD, *and* ORDULPH, *burst out laughing*)

LANDOLPH (*Still laughing; and pointing to* BERTHOLD *as if inviting the others to make fun of him*) Henry of France he says: ha! ha!

ORDULPH He thought it was the king of France!

HAROLD Henry IV of Germany, my boy: the Salian dynasty!

ORDULPH The great and tragic Emperor!

LANDOLPH He of Canossa. Every day we carry on here the terrible war between Church and State, by Jove.

ORDULPH The Empire against the Papacy!

HAROLD Antipopes against the Pope!

LANDOLPH Kings against anti-kings!

ORDULPH War on the Saxons!

HAROLD And all the rebels Princes!

LANDOLPH Against the Emperor's own sons!

BERTHOLD (*Covering his head with his hands to protect himself against this avalanche of information*) I understand! I understand! Naturally, I didn't get the idea at first. I'm right then: these aren't costumes of the sixteenth century?

HAROLD Sixteenth century be hanged!

ORDULPH We're somewhere between a thousand and eleven hundred.

LANDOLPH Work it out for yourself: if we are before Canossa on the 25th January, 1071 . . .

BERTHOLD (*More confused than ever*) Oh my God! What a mess I've made of it!

ORDULPH Well, just slightly, if you supposed you were at the French court.

BERTHOLD All that historical stuff I've worked up!

LANDOLPH My dear boy, it's four hundred years earlier.

BERTHOLD (*Getting angry*) Good Heavens! You ought to have told me it was Germany and not France. I can't tell you how many books I've read in the last fifteen days.

HAROLD But I say, surely you knew that poor

Tito was Adalbert of Bremen, here?

BERTHOLD Not a damned bit!

LANDOLPH Well, don't you see how it is? When Tito died, the Marquis Di Nolli . . .

BERTHOLD Oh, it was he, was it? He might have told me.

HAROLD Perhaps he thought you knew.

LANDOLPH He didn't want to engage anyone else in substitution. He thought the remaining three of us would do. But *he* began to cry out: "With Adalbert driven away . . ." because, you see, he didn't imagine poor Tito was dead; but that, as Bishop Adalbert, the rival bishops of Cologne and Mayence had driven him off . . .

BERTHOLD (*Taking his head in his hand*) But I don't know a word of what you're talking about.

ORDULPH So much the worse for you, my boy!

HAROLD But the trouble is that not even we know who you are.

BERTHOLD What? Not even you? You don't know who I'm supposed to be?

ORDULPH Hum! "Berthold."

BERTHOLD But which Berthold? And why Berthold?

LANDOLPH (*Solemnly imitating* HENRY IV) "They've driven Adalbert away from me. Well then, I want Berthold! I want Berthold!" That's what he said.

HAROLD We three looked one another in the eyes: who's got to be Berthold?

ORDULPH And so here you are, "Berthold," my dear fellow!

LANDOLPH I'm afraid you will make a bit of a mess of it.

BERTHOLD (*Indignant, getting ready to go*) Ah, no! Thanks very much, but I'm off! I'm out of this!

HAROLD (*Restraining him with the other two, amid laughter*) Steady now! Don't get excited!

LANDOLPH Cheer up, my dear fellow! We don't any of us know who we are really. He's Harold; he's Ordulph; I'm Landolph! That's the way he calls us. We've got used to it. But who are we? Names of the period! Yours, too, is a name of the period: Berthold! Only one of us, poor

Tito, had got a really decent part, as you can read in history: that of the Bishop of Bremen. He was just like a real bishop. Tito did it awfully well, poor chap!

HAROLD Look at the study he put into it!

LANDOLPH Why, he even ordered his Majesty about, opposed his views, guided and counselled him. We're "secret counsellors" —in a manner of speaking only; because it is written in history that Henry IV was hated by the upper aristocracy for surrounding himself at court with young men of the lower classes.

ORDULPH Us, that is.

LANDOLPH Yes, small devoted vassals, a bit dissolute and very gay . . .

BERTHOLD So I've got to be gay as well?

HAROLD I should say so! Same as we are!

ORDULPH And it isn't too easy, you know.

LANDOLPH It's a pity; because the way we're got up, we could do a fine historical reconstruction. There's any amount of material in the story of Henry IV. But, as a matter of fact, we do nothing. We have the form without the content. We're worse than the real secret counsellors of Henry IV; because certainly no one had given them a part to play—at any rate, they didn't feel they had a part to play. It was their life. They looked after their own interests at the expense of others, sold investitures and—what not! We stop here in this magnificent court—for what?—Just doing nothing. We're like so many puppets hung on the wall, waiting for someone to come and move us or make us talk.

HAROLD Ah, no, old sport, not quite that! We've got to give the proper answer, you know. There's trouble if he asks you something and you don't chip in with the cue.

LANDOLPH Yes, that's true.

BERTHOLD Don't rub it in too hard! How the devil am I to give him the proper answer, if I've worked up Henry IV of France, and now he turns out to be Henry IV of Germany? (*The other three laugh*)

HAROLD You'd better start and prepare yourself at once.

ORDULPH We'll help you out.

HAROLD We've got any amount of books on

the subject. A brief run through the main points will do to begin with.

ORDULPH At any rate, you must have got some sort of general idea.

HAROLD Look here! (*Turns him around and shows him the portrait of the Marchioness Matilda on the wall*) Who's that?

BERTHOLD (*Looking at it*) That? Well, the thing seems to me somewhat out of place, anyway: two modern paintings in the midst of all this respectable antiquity!

HAROLD You're right! They weren't there in the beginning. There are two niches there behind the pictures. They were going to put up two statues in the style of the period. Then the places were covered with those canvases there.

LANDOLPH (*Interrupting and continuing*) They would certainly be out of place if they really were paintings!

BERTHOLD What are they, if they aren't paintings?

LANDOLPH Go and touch them! Pictures all right. . . but for him! (*Makes a mysterious gesture to the right, alluding to* HENRY IV) . . . who never touches them! . . .

BERTHOLD No? What are they for him?

LANDOLPH Well, I'm only supposing, you know; but I imagine I'm about right. They're images such as . . . well—such as a mirror might throw back. Do you understand? That one there represents himself, as he is in this throne room, which is all in the style of the period. What's there to marvel at? If we put you before a mirror, won't you see yourself, alive, but dressed up in ancient costume? Well, it's as if there were two mirrors there, which cast back living images in the midst of a world which, as you will see, when you have lived with us, comes to life too.

BERTHOLD I say, look here . . . I've no particular desire to go mad here.

HAROLD Go mad, be hanged! You'll have a fine time!

BERTHOLD Tell me this: how have you all managed to become so learned?

LANDOLPH My dear fellow, you can't go back over eight hundred years of history without picking up a bit of experience.

HAROLD Come on! Come on! You'll see how quickly you get into it!

ORDULPH You'll learn wisdom, too, at this school.

BERTHOLD Well, for Heaven's sake, help me a bit! Give me the main lines, anyway.

HAROLD Leave it to us. We'll do it all between us.

LANDOLPH We'll put your wires on you and fix you up like a first-class marionette. Come along! (*They take him by the arm to lead him away*)

BERTHOLD (*Stopping and looking at the portrait on the wall*) Wait a minute! You haven't told me who that is. The Emperor's wife?

HAROLD No! The Emperor's wife is Bertha of Susa, the sister of Amadeus II of Savoy.

ORDULPH And the Emperor, who wants to be young with us, can't stand her, and wants to put her away.

LANDOLPH That is his most ferocious enemy: Matilda, Marchioness of Tuscany.

BERTHOLD Ah, I've got it: the one who gave hospitality to the Pope!

LANDOLPH Exactly: at Canossa!

ORDULPH Pope Gregory VII!

HAROLD Our *bète noir!* Come on! come on! (*All four move toward the right to go out, when, from the left, the old servant* JOHN *enters in evening dress*)

JOHN (*Quickly, anxiously*) Hss! Hss! Frank! Lolo!

HAROLD (*Turning round*) What is it?

BERTHOLD (*Marveling at seeing a man in modern clothes enter the throne room*) Oh! I say, this is a bit too much, this chap here!

LANDOLPH A man of the twentieth century, here! Oh, go away! (*They run over to him, pretending to menace him and throw him out*)

ORDULPH (*Heroically*) Messenger of Gregory VII, away!

HAROLD Away! Away!

JOHN (*Annoyed, defending himself*) Oh, stop it! Stop it, I tell you!

ORDULPH No, you can't set foot here!

HAROLD Out with him!

LANDOLPH (*To* BERTHOLD) Magic, you know!

He's a demon conjured up by the Wizard of Rome! Out with your swords! (*Makes as if to draw a sword*)

JOHN (*Shouting*) Stop it, will you? Don't play the fool with me! The Marquis has arrived with some friends . . .

LANDOLPH Good! Good! Are there ladies too?

ORDULPH Old or young?

JOHN There are two gentlemen.

HAROLD But the ladies, the ladies, who are they?

JOHN The Marchioness and her daughter.

LANDOLPH (*Surprised*) What do you say?

ORDULPH The Marchioness?

JOHN The Marchioness! The Marchioness!

HAROLD Who are the gentlemen?

JOHN I don't know.

HAROLD (*To* BERTHOLD) They're coming to bring us a message from the Pope, do you see?

ORDULPH All messengers of Gregory VII! What fun!

JOHN Will you let me speak, or not?

HAROLD Go on, then!

JOHN One of the two gentlemen is a doctor, I fancy.

LANDOLPH Oh, I see, one of the usual doctors.

HAROLD Bravo Berthold, you'll bring us luck!

LANDOLPH You wait and see how we'll manage this doctor!

BERTHOLD It looks as if I were going to get into a nice mess right away.

JOHN If the gentlemen would allow me to speak . . . they want to come here into the throne room.

LANDOLPH (*Surprised*) What? She? The Marchioness here?

HAROLD Then this is something quite different! No play-acting this time!

LANDOLPH We'll have a real tragedy: that's what!

BERTHOLD (*Curious*) Why? Why?

ORDULPH (*Pointing to the portrait*) She is that person there, don't you understand?

LANDOLPH The daughter is the fiancée of the Marquis. But what have they come for, I should like to know?

ORDULPH If he sees her, there'll be trouble.

LANDOLPH Perhaps he won't recognize her any more.

JOHN You must keep him there, if he should wake up . . .

ORDULPH Easier said than done, by Jove!

HAROLD You know what he's like!

JOHN —even by force, if necessary! Those are my orders. Go on! Go on!

HAROLD Yes, because who knows if he hasn't already wakened up?

ORDULPH Come on then!

LANDOLPH (*Going toward* JOHN *with the others*) You'll tell us later what it all means.

JOHN (*Shouting after them*) Close the door there, and hide the key! That other door too. (*Pointing to the other door on right*)

JOHN (*To the* TWO VALETS) Be off, you two! There! (*Pointing to exit right*) Close the door after you, and hide the key!

(*The* TWO VALETS *go out by the first door on right.* JOHN *moves over to the left to show in:* DONNA MATILDA SPINA, *the young* MARCHIONESS FRIDA, DR. DIONYSIUS GENONI, *the* BARON TITO BELCREDI *and the young* MARQUIS CHARLES DI NOLLI, *who, as master of the house, enters last.*

DONNA MATILDA SPINA *is about forty-five, still handsome, although there are too patent signs of her attempts to remedy the ravages of time with make-up. Her head is thus rather like a Valkyrie. This facial make-up contrasts with her beautiful sad mouth. A widow for many years, she now has as her friend the* BARON TITO BELCREDI, *whom neither she nor anyone else takes seriously —at least so it would appear.*

What TITO BELCREDI *really is for her at bottom he alone knows; and he is, therefore, entitled to laugh, if his friend feels the need of pretending not to know. He can always laugh at the jests which the beautiful Marchioness makes with the others at his expense. He is slim, prematurely gray, and younger than she is. His head is bird-like in shape. He would be a very vivacious person, if his ductile agility (which among other things makes him a redoubtable swordsman) were not enclosed in a sheath of Arab-like laziness, which is revealed in his strange, nasal drawn-out voice.*

FRIDA, *the daughter of the Marchioness is nineteen. She is sad; because her imperious and too beautiful mother puts her in the shade, and provokes facile gossip against her daughter as well as against herself. Fortunately for her, she is engaged to the* MARQUIS CHARLES DI NOLLI.

CHARLES DI NOLLI *is a stiff young man, very indulgent toward others, but sure of himself for what he amounts to in the world. He is worried about all the responsibilities which he believes weigh on him. He is dressed in deep mourning for the recent death of his mother.*

DR. DIONYSIUS GENONI *has a bold rubicund Satyr-like face, prominent eyes, a pointed beard (which is silvery and shiny) and elegant manners. He is nearly bald. All enter in a state of perturbation, almost as if afraid, and all (except DI NOLLI) looking curiously about the room. At first, they speak sotto voce)*

DI NOLLI (*To* JOHN) Have you given the orders properly?

JOHN Yes, my Lord; don't be anxious about that.

BELCREDI Ah, magnificent! magnificent!

DOCTOR How extremely interesting! Even in the surroundings his raving madness—is perfectly taken into account!

DONNA MATILDA (*Glancing round for her portrait, discovers it, and goes up close to it*) Ah! Here it is! (*Going back to admire it, while mixed emotions stir within her*) Yes . . . Yes . . . (*Calls her daughter* FRIDA)

FRIDA Ah, your portrait!

DONNA MATILDA No, no . . . look again; it's you, not I, there!

DI NOLLI Yes, it's quite true. I told you so, I . . .

DONNA MATILDA But I would never have believed it! (*Shaking as if with a chill*) What a strange feeling it gives one! (*Then looking at her daughter*) Frida, what's the matter? (*She pulls her to her side, and slips*

an arm round her waist) Come: don't you see yourself in me there?

FRIDA Well, I really . . .

DONNA MATILDA Don't you think so? Don't you, really? (*Turning to* BELCREDI) Look at it, Tito! Speak up, man!

BELCREDI (*Without looking*) Ah, no! I shan't look at it. For me, *a priori*, certainly not!

DONNA MATILDA Stupid! You think you are paying me a compliment! (*Turning to* DOCTOR GENONI) What do you say, Doctor? Do say something, please!

(DOCTOR *makes a movement to go near to the picture*)

BELCREDI (*With his back turned, pretending to attract his attention secretly*) —Hss! No, Doctor! For the love of Heaven, have nothing to do with it!

DOCTOR (*Getting bewildered and smiling*) And why shouldn't I?

DONNA MATILDA Don't listen to him! Come here! He's insufferable!

FRIDA He acts the fool by profession, didn't you know that?

BELCREDI (*To the* DOCTOR, *seeing him go over*) Look at your feet, Doctor! Mind where you're going!

DOCTOR Why?

BELCREDI Be careful you don't put your foot in it!

DOCTOR (*Laughing feebly*) No, no. After all, it seems to me there's no reason to be astonished at the fact that a daughter should resemble her mother!

BELCREDI Oh oh! He's done it now; he's said it.

DONNA MATILDA (*With exaggerated anger, advancing toward* BELCREDI) What's the matter? What has he said? What has he done?

DOCTOR (*Candidly*) Well, isn't it so?

BELCREDI (*Answering the* MARCHIONESS) I said there was nothing to be astounded at— and you are astounded! And why so, then, if the thing is so simple and natural for you now?

DONNA MATILDA (*Still more angry*) Fool! fool! It's just because it is so natural! Just because it isn't my daughter who is there. (*Pointing to the canvas*) That is my portrait; and to find my daughter there instead of me fills me with astonishment, an astonishment which, I beg you to believe, is sincere. I forbid you to cast doubts on it.

FRIDA (*Slowly and wearily*) My God! It's always like this . . . quarrels over nothing . . .

BELCREDI (*Also slowly, looking dejected, in accents of apology*) I cast no doubt on anything! I noticed from the beginning that you haven't shared your mother's astonishment; or, if something did astonish you, it was because the likeness between you and the portrait seemed so strong.

DONNA MATILDA Naturally! She cannot recognize herself in me as I was at her age; while I, there, can very well recognize myself in her as she is now!

DOCTOR Quite right! Because a portrait is always there, fixed in the twinkling of an eye: for the young lady something far away and without memories, while, for the Marchioness, it can bring back everything: movements, gestures, looks, smiles, so many things . . .

DONNA MATILDA Exactly!

DOCTOR (*Continuing, turning toward her*) Naturally enough, you can live all these old sensations again in your daughter.

DONNA MATILDA He always spoils every innocent pleasure for me, every touch I have of spontaneous sentiment! He does it merely to annoy me.

DOCTOR (*Frightened at the disturbance he has caused, adopts a professorial tone*) Likeness, dear Baron, is often the result of imponderable things. So one explains that . . .

BELCREDI (*Interrupting the discourse*) Somebody will soon be finding a likeness between you and me, my dear Professor!

DI NOLLI Oh! let's finish with this, please! (*Points to the two doors on the right, as a warning that there is someone there who may be listening*) We've wasted too much time as it is!

FRIDA As one might expect when *he's* present. (*Alludes to* BELCREDI)

DI NOLLI Enough! The Doctor is here; and we have come for a very serious purpose which you all know is important for me.

DOCTOR Yes, that is so! But now, first of all, let's try to get some points down exactly. Excuse me, Marchioness, will you tell me why your portrait is here? Did you present it to him then?

DONNA MATILDA No, not at all. How could I have given it to him? I was just like Frida then—and not even engaged. I gave it to him three or four years after the accident. I gave it to him because his mother wished it so much . . . (*Points to* DI NOLLI)

DOCTOR She was his sister? (*Alludes to* HENRY IV)

DI NOLLI Yes, Doctor; and our coming here is a debt we pay to my mother who has been dead for more than a month. Instead of being here, she and I (*Indicating* FRIDA) ought to be traveling together . . .

DOCTOR . . . taking a cure of quite a different kind!

DI NOLLI —Hum! Mother died in the firm conviction that her adored brother was just about to be cured.

DOCTOR And can't you tell me, if you please, how she inferred this?

DI NOLLI The conviction would appear to have derived from certain strange remarks which he made, a little before mother died.

DOCTOR Oh, remarks! . . . Ah! . . . It would be extremely useful for me to have those remarks, word for word, if possible.

DI NOLLI I can't remember them. I know that mother returned awfully upset from her last visit with him. On her death-bed, she made me promise that I would never neglect him, that I would have doctors see him, and examine him.

DOCTOR Um! Um! Let me see! let me see! Sometimes very small reasons determine . . . and this portrait here then? . . .

DONNA MATILDA For Heaven's sake, Doctor, don't attach excessive importance to this. It made an impression on me because I had not seen it for so many years!

DOCTOR If you please, quietly, quietly . . .

DI NOLLI —Well, yes, it must be about fifteen years ago.

DONNA MATILDA More, more: eighteen!

DOCTOR Forgive me, but you don't quite know what I'm trying to get at. I attach a very great importance to these two portraits. . . . They were painted, naturally, prior to the famous—and most regrettable pageant, weren't they?

DONNA MATILDA Of course!

DOCTOR That is . . . when he was quite in his right mind—that's what I've been trying to say. Was it his suggestion that they should be painted?

DONNA MATILDA Lots of the people who took part in the pageant had theirs done as a souvenir. . .

BELCREDI I had mine done—as "Charles of Anjou!"

DONNA MATILDA . . . as soon as the costumes were ready.

BELCREDI As a matter of fact, it was proposed that the whole lot of us should be hung together in a gallery of the villa where the pageant took place. But in the end, everybody wanted to keep his own portrait.

DONNA MATILDA And I gave him this portrait of me without very much regret . . . since his mother . . . (*Indicates* DI NOLLI)

DOCTOR You don't remember if it was he who asked for it?

DONNA MATILDA Ah, that I don't remember. . . . Maybe it was his sister, wanting to help out. . . .

DOCTOR One other thing: was it his idea, this pageant?

BELCREDI (*At once*) No, no, it was mine!

DOCTOR If you please . . .

DONNA MATILDA Don't listen to him! It was poor Belassi's idea.

BELCREDI Belassi! What had he got to do with it?

DONNA MATILDA Count Belassi, who died, poor fellow, two or three months after . . .

BELCREDI But if Belassi wasn't there when . . .

DI NOLLI Excuse me, Doctor; but is it really necessary to establish whose the original idea was?

DOCTOR It would help me, certainly!

BELCREDI I tell you the idea was mine! There's nothing to be proud of in it, seeing what the result's been. Look here, Doctor, it was like this. One evening, in the first days of November, I was looking at an illustrated German review in the club. I was merely glancing at the pictures, be-cause I can't read German. There was a picture of the Kaiser, at some University town where he had been a student . . . I don't remember which.

DOCTOR Bonn, Bonn!

BELCREDI —You are right: Bonn! He was on horseback, dressed up in one of those ancient German student guild-costumes, followed by a procession of noble students, also in costume. The picture gave me the idea. Already someone at the club had spoken of a pageant for the forthcoming carnival. So I had the notion that each of us should choose for this Tower of Babel pageant to represent some character: a king, an emperor, a prince, with his queen, empress, or lady, alongside of him—and all on horseback. The suggestion was at once accepted.

DONNA MATILDA I had my invitation from Belassi.

BELCREDI Well, he wasn't speaking the truth! That's all I can say, if he told you the idea was his. He wasn't even at the club the evening I made the suggestion, just as he (*Meaning* HENRY IV) wasn't there either.

DOCTOR So he chose the character of Henry IV?

DONNA MATILDA Because I . . . thinking of my name, and not giving the choice any importance, said I would be the Marchioness Matilda of Tuscany.

DOCTOR I . . . don't understand the relation between the two.

DONNA MATILDA —Neither did I, to begin with, when he said that in that case he would be at my feet like Henry IV at Canossa. I had heard of Canossa of course; but to tell the truth, I'd forgotten most of the story; and I remember I received a curious impression when I had to get up my part, and found that I was the faithful and zealous friend of Pope Gregory VII in deadly enmity with the Emperor of Germany. Then I understood why, since I had chosen to represent his implacable enemy, he wanted to be near me in the pageant as Henry IV.

DOCTOR Ah, perhaps because . . .

BELCREDI —Good Heavens, Doctor, because he was then paying furious court to her! (*Indicates the* MARCHIONESS) And she, naturally . . .

DONNA MATILDA Naturally? Not naturally at all . . .

BELCREDI (*Pointing to her*) She couldn't stand him . . .

DONNA MATILDA —No, that isn't true! I didn't dislike him. Not at all! But for me, when a man begins to want to be taken seriously, well . . .

BELCREDI (*Continuing for her*) He gives you the clearest proof of his stupidity.

DONNA MATILDA No, dear; not in this case; because he was never a fool like you.

BELCREDI Anyway, I've never asked you to take me seriously.

DONNA MATILDA Yes, I know. But with him one couldn't joke. (*Changing her tone and speaking to the* DOCTOR) One of the many misfortunes which happen to us women, Doctor, is to see before us every now and again a pair of eyes glaring at us with a contained intense promise of eternal devotion. (*Bursts out laughing*) There is nothing quite so funny. If men could only see themselves with that eternal look of fidelity in their faces! I've always thought it comic; then more even than now. But I want to make a confession—I can do so after twenty years or more. When I laughed at him then, it was partly out of fear. One might have almost believed a promise from those eyes of his. But it would have been very dangerous.

DOCTOR (*With lively interest*) Ah! ah! This is most interesting! Very dangerous, you say?

DONNA MATILDA Yes, because he was very different from the others. And then, I am . . . well . . . what shall I say? . . . a little impatient of all that is pondered, or tedious. But I was too young then, and a woman. I had the bit between my teeth. It would have required more courage than I felt I possessed. So I laughed at him too —with remorse, to spite myself, indeed; since I saw that my own laugh mingled with those of all the others—the other fools—who made fun of him.

BELCREDI My own case, more or less!

DONNA MATILDA You make people laugh at you, my dear, with your trick of always humiliating yourself. It was quite a different affair with him. There's a vast difference. And you—you know—people laugh in your face!

BELCREDI Well, that's better than behind one's back!

DOCTOR Let's get to the facts. He was then already somewhat exalted, if I understand rightly.

BELCREDI Yes, but in a curious fashion, Doctor.

DOCTOR How?

BELCREDI Well, cold-bloodedly so to speak.

DONNA MATILDA Not at all! It was like this, Doctor! He was a bit strange, certainly; but only because he was fond of life: eccentric, there!

BELCREDI I don't say he simulated exaltation. On the contrary, he was often genuinely exalted. But I could swear, Doctor, that he saw himself at once in his own exaltation. Moreover, I'm certain it made him suffer. Sometimes he had the most comical fits of rage against himself.

DOCTOR Yes?

DONNA MATILDA That is true.

BELCREDI (*To* DONNA MATILDA) And why? (*To the* DOCTOR) Evidently, because that immediate lucidity that comes from acting, assuming a part, at once put him out of key with his own feelings, which seemed to him not exactly false, but like something he was obliged to give the value there and then of—what shall I say—of an act of intelligence, to make up for that sincere cordial warmth he felt lacking. So he improvised, exaggerated, let himself go, so as to distract and forget himself. He appeared inconstant, fatuous, and— yes—even ridiculous, sometimes.

DOCTOR And may we say unsociable?

BELCREDI No, not at all. He was famous for getting up things: *tableaux vivants*, dances, theatrical performances for charity: all for the fun of the thing, of course. He was a jolly good actor, you know!

DI NOLLI Madness has made a superb actor of him.

BELCREDI —Why, so he was even in the old days. When the accident happened, after the horse fell . . .

DOCTOR Hit the back of his head, didn't he?

DONNA MATILDA Oh, it was horrible! He was beside me! I saw him between the horse's hoofs! It was rearing!

BELCREDI None of us thought it was anything serious at first. There was a stop in the pageant, a bit of disorder. People wanted to know what had happened. But they'd already taken him off to the villa.

DONNA MATILDA There wasn't the least sign of a wound, not a drop of blood.

BELCREDI We thought he had merely fainted.

DONNA MATILDA But two hours afterward . . .

BELCREDI He reappeared in the drawing-room of the villa . . . that is what I wanted to say . . .

DONNA MATILDA My God! What a face he had. I saw the whole thing at once!

BELCREDI No, no! that isn't true. Nobody saw it, Doctor, believe me!

DONNA MATILDA Doubtless, because you were all like mad men.

BELCREDI Everybody was pretending to act his part for a joke. It was a regular Babel.

DONNA MATILDA And you can imagine, Doctor, what terror struck into us when we understood that he, on the contrary, was playing his part in deadly earnest . . .

DOCTOR Oh, he was there too, was he?

BELCREDI Of course! He came straight into the midst of us. We thought he'd quite recovered, and was pretending, fooling, like all the rest of us . . . only doing it rather better; because, as I say, he knew how to act.

DONNA MATILDA Some of them began to hit him with their whips and fans and sticks.

BELCREDI And then—as a king, he was armed, of course—he drew out his sword and menaced two or three of us. . . . It was a terrible moment, I can assure you!

DONNA MATILDA I shall never forget that scene—all our masked faces hideous and terrified gazing at him, at that terrible mask of his face, which was no longer a mask, but madness personified.

BELCREDI He was Henry IV, Henry IV in person, in a moment of fury.

DONNA MATILDA He'd got into it all the detail and minute preparation of a month's careful study. And it all burned and blazed there in the terrible obsession which lit his face.

DOCTOR Yes, that is quite natural, of course. The momentary obsession of a dilettante became fixed, owing to the fall and the damage to the brain.

BELCREDI (To FRIDA and DI NOLLI) You see the kind of jokes life can play on us. (To DI NOLLI) You were four or five years old. (To FRIDA) Your mother imagines you've taken her place there in that portrait; when, at the time, she had not the remotest idea that she would bring you into the world. My hair is already gray; and he—look at him—(Points to portrait)—ha! A smack on the head, and he never moves again: Henry IV forever!

DOCTOR (Seeking to draw the attention of the others, looking learned and imposing) —Well, well, then it comes, we may say, to this. . . .

(Suddenly the first exit to right, the one nearest footlights, opens, and BERTHOLD enters all excited)

BERTHOLD (Rushing in) I say! I say! (Stops for a moment, arrested by the astonishment which his appearance has caused in the others)

FRIDA (Running away terrified) Oh dear! oh dear! it's he, it's . . .

DONNA MATILDA (Covering her face with her hands so as not to see) Is it, is it he?

DI NOLLI No, no, what are you talking about? Be calm!

DOCTOR Who is it then?

BELCREDI One of our masqueraders.

DI NOLLI He is one of the four youths we keep here to help him out in his madness. . . .

BERTHOLD I beg your pardon, Marquis. . . .

DI NOLLI Pardon be damned! I gave orders that the doors were to be closed, and that nobody should be allowed to enter.

BERTHOLD Yes, sir, but I can't stand it any longer, and I ask you to let me go away this very minute.

DI NOLLI Oh, you're the new valet, are you? You were supposed to begin this morning, weren't you?

BERTHOLD Yes, sir, and I can't stand it, I can't bear it.

DONNA MATILDA (*To* DI NOLLI *excitedly*) What? Then he's not so calm as you said?

BERTHOLD (*Quickly*) —No, no, my lady, it isn't he; it's my companions. You say "help him out with his madness," Marquis; but they don't do anything of the kind. They're the real madmen. I come here for the first time, and instead of helping me . . .

(LANDOLPH *and* HAROLD *come in from the same door, but hesitate on the threshold*)

LANDOLPH Excuse me?

HAROLD May I come in, my Lord?

DI NOLLI Come in! What's the matter? What are you all doing?

FRIDA Oh God! I'm frightened! I'm going to run away. (*Makes toward exit at left*)

DI NOLLI (*Restraining her at once*) No, no, Frida!

LANDOLPH My Lord, this fool here . . . (*Indicates* BERTHOLD)

BERTHOLD (*Protesting*) Ah, no thanks, my friends, no thanks! I'm not stopping here! I'm off!

LANDOLPH What do you mean—you're not stopping here?

HAROLD He's ruined everything, my Lord, running away in here!

LANDOLPH He's made him quite mad. We can't keep him in there any longer. He's given orders that he's to be arrested; and he wants to "judge" him at once from the throne: What is to be done?

DI NOLLI Shut the door, man! Shut the door! Go and close that door! (LANDOLPH *goes over to close it*)

HAROLD Ordulph, alone, won't be able to keep him there.

LANDOLPH —My Lord, perhaps if we could announce the visitors at once, it would turn his thoughts. Have the gentlemen thought under what pretext they will present themselves to him?

DI NOLLI —It's all been arranged! (*To the* DOCTOR) If you, Doctor, think it well to see him at once. . . .

FRIDA I'm not coming! I'm not coming! I'll keep out of this. You too, Mother, for Heaven's sake, come away with me!

DOCTOR —I say . . . I suppose he's not armed, is he?

DI NOLLI —Nonsense! Of course not. (*To* FRIDA) Frida, you know this is childish of you. You wanted to come!

FRIDA I didn't at all. It was mother's idea.

DONNA MATILDA And I'm quite ready to see him. What are we going to do?

BELCREDI Must we absolutely dress up in some fashion or other?

LANDOLPH —Absolutely essential, indispensable, sir. Alas! as you see . . . (*Shows his costume*), there'd be awful trouble if he saw you gentlemen in modern dress.

HAROLD He would think it was some diabolical masquerade.

DI NOLLI As these men seem to be in costume to you, so we appear to be in costume to him, in these modern clothes of ours.

LANDOLPH It wouldn't matter so much if he wouldn't suppose it to be the work of his mortal enemy.

BELCREDI Pope Gregory VII?

LANDOLPH Precisely. He calls him "a pagan."

BELCREDI The Pope a pagan? That's not bad!

LANDOLPH —Yes, sir . . . and a man who calls up the dead! He accuses him of all the diabolical arts. He's terribly afraid of him.

DOCTOR Persecution mania!

HAROLD He'd be simply furious.

DI NOLLI (*To* BELCREDI) But there's no need for you to be there, you know. It's sufficient for the Doctor to see him.

DOCTOR —What do you mean? . . . I? Alone?

DI NOLLI —But they are there. (*Indicates the three young men*)

DOCTOR I don't mean that. . . . I mean if the Marchioness . . .

DONNA MATILDA Of course. I mean to see him too, naturally. I want to see him again.

FRIDA Oh, why, Mother, why? Do come away with me, I implore you!

DONNA MATILDA (*Imperiously*) Let me do as I wish! I came here for this purpose! (*To* LANDOLPH) I shall be "Adelaide," the mother.

LANDOLPH Excellent! The mother of the Empress Bertha. Good! It will be enough if her Ladyship wears the ducal crown and puts on a mantle that will hide her other clothes entirely. (*To* HAROLD) Off you go, Harold!

HAROLD Wait a moment! And this gentleman here? . . . (*Alludes to the* DOCTOR)

DOCTOR —Ah yes . . . we decided I was to be . . . the Bishop of Cluny, Hugh of Cluny!

HAROLD The gentleman means the Abbot. Very good! Hugh of Cluny.

LANDOLPH —He's often been here before!

DOCTOR (*Amazed*) —What? Been here before?

LANDOLPH —Don't be alarmed! I mean that it's an easily prepared disguise. . . .

HAROLD We've made use of it on other occasions, you see!

DOCTOR But . . .

LANDOLPH Oh, no, there's no risk of his remembering. He pays more attention to the dress than to the person.

DONNA MATILDA That's fortunate for me too then.

DI NOLLI Frida, you and I'll get along. Come on, Tito!

BELCREDI Ah no. If she (*Indicates the* MARCHIONESS) stops here, so do I!

DONNA MATILDA But I don't need you at all.

BELCREDI You may not need me, but I should like to see him again myself. Mayn't I?

LANDOLPH Well, perhaps it would be better if there were three.

HAROLD How is the gentleman to be dressed then?

BELCREDI Oh, try and find some easy costume for me.

LANDOLPH (*To* HAROLD) Hum! Yes . . . he'd better be from Cluny too.

BELCREDI What do you mean—from Cluny?

LANDOLPH A Benedictine's habit of the Abbey of Cluny. He can be in attendance on Monsignor. (*To* HAROLD) Off you go! (*To* BERTHOLD) And you too get away and keep out of sight all today. No, wait a moment. (*To* BERTHOLD) You bring here the costumes he will give you. (*To* HAROLD) You go at once and announce the visit of the "Duchess Adelaide" and "Monsignor Hugh of Cluny." Do you understand? (HAROLD *and* BERTHOLD *go off by the first door on the right*)

DI NOLLI We'll retire now. (*Goes off with* FRIDA, *left*)

DOCTOR Shall I be a *persona grata* to him, as Hugh of Cluny?

LANDOLPH Oh, rather! Don't worry about that! Monsignor has always been received here with great respect. You too, my Lady, he will be glad to see. He never forgets that it was owing to the intercession of you two that he was admitted to the Castle of Canossa and the presence of Gregory VII, who didn't want to receive him.

BELCREDI And what do I do?

LANDOLPH You stand a little apart, respectfully: that's all.

DONNA MATILDA (*Irritated, nervous*) You would do well to go away, you know.

BELCREDI (*Slowly, spitefully*) How upset you seem! . . .

DONNA MATILDA (*Proudly*) I am as I am. Leave me alone!

(BERTHOLD *comes in with the costumes*)

LANDOLPH (*Seeing him enter*) Ah, the costumes: here they are. This mantle is for the Marchioness . . .

DONNA MATILDA Wait a minute! I'll take off my hat. (*Does so and gives it to* BERTHOLD)

LANDOLPH Put it down there! (*Then to the* MARCHIONESS, *while he offers to put the ducal crown on her head*) Allow me!

DONNA MATILDA Dear, dear! Isn't there a mirror here?

LANDOLPH Yes, there's one there. (*Points to the door on the left*) If the Marchioness would rather put it on herself . . .

DONNA MATILDA Yes, yes, that will be better. Give it to me! (*Takes up her hat and goes off with* BERTHOLD, *who carries the cloak and the crown*)

BELCREDI Well, I must say, I never thought I should be a Benedictine monk! By the way, this business must cost an awful lot of money.

DOCTOR Like any other fantasy, naturally!

BELCREDI Well, there's a fortune to go upon.

LANDOLPH We have got there a whole wardrobe of costumes of the period, copied to perfection from old models. This is my special job. I get them from the best theatrical costumers. They cost lots of money. (DONNA MATILDA *re-enters, wearing mantle and crown*)

BELCREDI (*At once, in admiration*) Oh magnificent! Truly regal!

DONNA MATILDA (*Looking at* BELCREDI *and bursting out into laughter*) Oh no, no! Take it off! You're impossible. You look like an ostrich dressed up as a monk.

BELCREDI Well, how about the Doctor?

DOCTOR I don't think I look so bad, do I?

DONNA MATILDA No; the Doctor's all right, . . . but you are too funny for words.

DOCTOR Do you have many receptions here then?

LANDOLPH It depends. He often gives orders that such and such a person appear before him. Then we have to find someone who will take the part. Women too. . . .

DONNA MATILDA (*Hurt, but trying to hide the fact*) Ah, women too?

LANDOLPH Oh, yes; many at first.

BELCREDI (*Laughing*) Oh, that's great! In costume, like the Marchioness?

LANDOLPH Oh well, you know, women of the kind that lend themselves to . . .

BELCREDI Ah, I see! (*Perfidiously to the* MARCHIONESS) Look out, you know he's becoming dangerous for you.

(*The second door on the right opens, and* HAROLD *appears making first of all a discreet sign that all conversation should cease*)

HAROLD His Majesty, the Emperor!

(*The* TWO VALETS *enter first, and go and stand on either side of the throne. Then* HENRY IV *comes in between* ORDULPH *and* HAROLD, *who keep a little in the rear respectfully.*

HENRY IV *is about fifty and very pale. The hair on the back of his head is already gray; over the temples and forehead it appears blond, owing to its having been tinted in an evident and puerile fashion. On his cheekbones he has two small, doll-like dabs of color, that stand out prominently against the rest of his tragic pallor. He is wearing*

a penitent's sack over his regal habit, as at Canossa. His eyes have a fixed look which is dreadful to see, and this expression is in strained contrast with the sackcloth. ORDULPH *carries the Imperial crown;* HAROLD, *the sceptre with eagle, and the globe with the cross*)

HENRY IV (*Bowing first to* DONNA MATILDA *and afterward to the* DOCTOR) My lady . . . Monsignor . . . (*Then he looks at* BELCREDI *and seems about to greet him too; when, suddenly, he turns to* LANDOLPH, *who has approached him, and asks him sotto voce and with diffidence*) Is that Peter Damiani?

LANDOLPH No, Sire. He is a monk from Cluny who is accompanying the Abbot.

HENRY IV (*Looks again at* BELCREDI *with increasing mistrust, and then noticing that he appears embarrassed and keeps glancing at* DONNA MATILDA *and the* DOCTOR, *stands upright and cries out*) No, it's Peter Damiani! It's no use, father, your looking at the Duchess. (*Then turning quickly to* DONNA MATILDA *and the* DOCTOR *as though to ward off a danger*) I swear it! I swear that my heart is changed toward your daughter. I confess that if he (*Indicates* BELCREDI) hadn't come to forbid it in the name of Pope Alexander, I'd have repudiated her. Yes, yes, there were people ready to favor the repudiation: the Bishop of Mayence would have done it for a matter of one hundred and twenty farms. (*Looks at* LANDOLPH *a little perplexed and adds*) But I mustn't speak ill of the bishops at this moment! (*More humbly to* BELCREDI) I am grateful to you, believe me, I am grateful to you for the hindrance you put in my way!—God knows, my life's been all made of humiliations: my mother, Adalbert, Tribur, Goslar! And now this sackcloth you see me wearing! (*Changes tone suddenly and speaks like one who goes over his part in a parenthesis of astuteness*) It doesn't matter: clarity of ideas, perspicacity, firmness, and patience under adversity, that's the thing. (*Then turning to all and speaking solemnly*) I know how to make amends for the mistakes I have made; and I can humiliate myself even before you, Peter Damiani. (*Bows profoundly to him and remains curved. Then a suspicion is born in him which he is obliged to utter in menacing tones, almost against his will*) Was it not perhaps you who started that obscene rumor that my holy mother had illicit relations with the Bishop of Augusta?

BELCREDI (*Since* HENRY IV *has his finger pointed at him*) No, no, it wasn't I. . . .

HENRY IV (*Straightening up*) Not true, not true? Infamy! (*Looks at him and then adds*) I didn't think you capable of it! (*Goes to the* DOCTOR *and plucks his sleeve, while winking at him knowingly*) Always the same, Monsignor, those bishops, always the same!

HAROLD (*Softly, whispering as if to help out the doctor*) Yes, yes, the rapacious bishops!

DOCTOR (*To* HAROLD, *trying to keep it up*) Ah, yes, those fellows . . . ah yes . . .

HENRY IV Nothing satisfies them! I was a little boy, Monsignor . . . One passes the time, playing even, when, without knowing it, one is a king. I was six years old; and they tore me away from my mother, and made use of me against her without my knowing anything about it . . . always profaning, always stealing, stealing! . . . One greedier than the other. . . . Hanno worse than Stephen! Stephen worse than Hanno!

LANDOLPH (*Sotto voce, persuasively, to call his attention*) Majesty!

HENRY IV (*Turning round quickly*) Ah yes . . . this isn't the moment to speak ill of the bishops. But this infamy against my mother, Monsignor, is too much. (*Looks at the* MARCHIONESS *and grows tender*) And I can't even weep for her, Lady. . . . I appeal to you who have a mother's heart! She came here to see me from her convent a month ago. . . . They had told me she was dead! (*Sustained pause full of feeling. Then smiling sadly*) I can't weep for her; because if you are here now, and I am like this (*Shows the sackcloth he is wearing*) it means I am twenty-six years old!

HAROLD And that she is therefore alive, Majesty! . . .

ORDULPH Still in her convent!

HENRY IV (*Looking at them*) Ah yes! And I can postpone my grief to another time. (*Shows the* MARCHIONESS *almost with coquetry the tint he has given to his hair*) Look! I am still fair. . . . (*Then slowly as if in confidence*) For you . . . there's no need! But little exterior details do help! A matter of time, Monsignor, do you understand me? (*Turns to the* MARCHIONESS *and notices her hair*) Ah, but I see that you too, Duchess . . . Italian, eh? (*As much as to say "false"; but without any indignation indeed rather with malicious admiration*) Heaven forbid that I should show disgust or surprise! Nobody cares to recognize that obscure and fatal power which sets limits to our will. But I say, if one is born and one dies . . . Did you want to be born, Monsignor? I didn't! And in both cases, independently of our wills, so many things happen we would wish didn't happen, and to which we resign ourselves as best we can! . . .

DOCTOR (*Merely to make a remark, while studying* HENRY IV *carefully*) Alas! Yes, alas!

HENRY IV It's like this: When we are not resigned, out come our desires. A woman wants to be a man . . . an old man would be young again. Desires, ridiculous fixed ideas of course— But reflect! Monsignor, those other desires are not less ridiculous: I mean, those desires where the will is kept within the limits of the possible. Not one of us can lie or pretend. We're all fixed in good faith in a certain concept of ourselves. However, Monsignor, while you keep yourself in order, holding on with both your hands to your holy habit, there slips down from your sleeves, there peels off from you like . . . like a serpent . . . something you don't notice: life, Monsignor! (*Turns to the* MARCHIONESS) Has it never happened to you, my Lady, to find a different self in yourself? Have you always been the same? My God! One day . . . how was it, how was it you were able to commit this or that action? (*Fixes her so intently in the eyes as almost to make her blanch*) Yes, that particular action, that very one: we understand each other!

But don't be afraid: I shall reveal it to none. And you, Peter Damiani, how could you be a friend of that man? . . .

LANDOLPH Majesty!

HENRY IV (*At once*) No, I won't name him! (*Turning to* BELCREDI) What did you think of him? But we all of us cling tight to our conceptions of ourselves, just as he who is growing old dyes his hair. What does it matter that this dyed hair of mine isn't a reality for you, if it *is*, to some extent, for me?—you, you, my Lady, certainly don't dye your hair to deceive the others, nor even yourself; but only to cheat your own image a little before the looking-glass. I do it for a joke! You do it seriously! But I assure you that you too, Madam, are in masquerade, though it be in all seriousness; and I am not speaking of the venerable crown on your brows or the ducal mantle. I am speaking only of the memory you wish to fix in yourself of your fair complexion one day when it pleased you— or of your dark complexion, if you were dark: the fading image of your youth! For you, Peter Damiani, on the contrary, the memory of what you have been, of what you have done, seems to you a recognition of past realities that remain within you like a dream. I'm in the same case too: with so many inexplicable memories—like dreams! Ah! . . . There's nothing to marvel at in it, Peter Damiani! Tomorrow it will be the same thing with our life of today! (*Suddenly getting excited and taking hold of his sackcloth*) This sackcloth here . . . (*Beginning to take it off with a gesture of almost ferocious joy while the* THREE VALETS *run over to him, frightened, as if to prevent his doing so*) Ah, my God! (*Draws back and throws off sackcloth*) Tomorrow, at Bressanone, twenty-seven German and Lombard bishops will sign with me the act of deposition of Gregory VII! No Pope at all! Just a false monk!

ORDULPH (*With the other three*) Majesty! Majesty! In God's name! . . .

HAROLD (*Inviting him to put on the sackcloth again*) Listen to what he says, Majesty!

LANDOLPH Monsignor is here with the Duchess to intercede in your favor.

(*Makes secret signs to the* DOCTOR *to say something at once*)

DOCTOR (*Foolishly*) Ah yes . . . yes . . . we are here to intercede . . .

HENRY IV (*Repenting at once, almost terrified, allowing the three to put on the sackcloth again, and pulling it down over him with his own hands*) Pardon . . . yes . . . yes . . . pardon, Monsignor: forgive me, my Lady. . . . I swear to you I feel the whole weight of the anathema. (*Bends himself, takes his face between his hands, as though waiting for something to crush him. Then changing tone, but without moving, says softly to* LANDOLPH, HAROLD, *and* ORDULPH) But I don't know why I cannot be humble before that man there! (*Indicates* BELCREDI)

LANDOLPH (*Sotto voce*) But why, Majesty, do you insist on believing he is Peter Damiani, when he isn't, at all?

HENRY IV (*Looking at him timorously*) He isn't Peter Damiani?

HAROLD No, no, he is a poor monk, Majesty.

HENRY IV (*Sadly with a touch of exasperation*) Ah! None of us can estimate what we do when we do it from instinct. . . . You perhaps, Madam, can understand me better than the others, since you are a woman and a Duchess. This is a solemn and decisive moment. I could, you know, accept the assistance of the Lombard bishops, arrest the Pope, lock him up here in the castle, run to Rome and elect an anti-Pope; offer alliance to Robert Guiscard —and Gregory VII would be lost! I resist the temptation; and, believe me, I am wise in doing so. I feel the atmosphere of our times and the majesty of one who knows how to be what he ought to be! a Pope! Do you feel inclined to laugh at me, seeing me like this? You would be foolish to do so; for you don't understand the political wisdom which makes this penitent's sack advisable. The parts may be changed tomorrow. What would you do then? Would you laugh to see the Pope a prisoner? No! It would come to the same thing: I dressed as a penitent, today; he, as prisoner tomorrow! But woe to him who doesn't know how to wear his mask, be he king or Pope!—Perhaps he is a bit too cruel! No! Yes, yes, maybe!—You remember, my Lady, how your daughter Bertha, for whom, I repeat, my feelings have changed (*Turns to* BELCREDI *and shouts to his face as if he were being contradicted by him*)—yes, changed on account of the affection and devotion she showed me in that terrible moment . . . (*Then once again to the* MARCHIONESS) . . . you remember how she came with me, my Lady, followed me like a beggar and passed two nights out in the open, in the snow? You are her mother! Doesn't this touch your mother's heart? Doesn't this urge you to pity, so that you will beg His Holiness for pardon, beg him to receive us?

DONNA MATILDA (*Trembling, with feeble voice*) Yes, yes, at once. . . .

DOCTOR It shall be done!

HENRY IV And one thing more! (*Draws them in to listen to him*) It isn't enough that he should receive me! You know he can do *everything—everything* I tell you! He can even call up the dead. (*Touches his chest*) Behold me! Do you see me? There is no magic art unknown to him. Well, Monsignor, my Lady, my torment is really this: that whether here or there (*Pointing to his portrait almost in fear*) I can't free myself from this magic. I am a penitent now, you see; and I swear to you I shall remain so until he receives me. But you two, when the excommunication is taken off, must ask the Pope to do this thing he can so easily do: to take me away from that; (*Indicating the portrait again*) and let me live wholly and freely my miserable life. A man can't always be twenty-six, my Lady. I ask this of you for your daughter's sake too; that I may love her as she deserves to be loved, well disposed as I am now, all tender toward her for her pity. There: it's all there! I am in your hands! (*Bows*) My Lady! Monsignor!

(*He goes off, bowing grandly, through the door by which he entered, leaving everyone stupefied, and the* MARCHIONESS *so profoundly touched, that no sooner has he gone than she breaks out into sobs and sits down almost fainting*)

ACT TWO

Another room of the villa, adjoining the throne room. Its furniture is antique and severe. Principal exit at rear in the background. To the left, two windows looking on the garden. To the right, a door opening into the throne room.

Late afternoon of the same day.

DONNA MATILDA, *the* DOCTOR *and* BELCREDI *are on the stage engaged in conversation; but* DONNA MATILDA *stands to one side, evidently annoyed at what the other two are saying; although she cannot help listening, because, in her agitated state, everything interests her in spite of herself. The talk of the other two attracts her attention, because she instinctively feels the need for calm at the moment.*

BELCREDI It may be as you say, Doctor, but that was my impression.

DOCTOR I won't contradict you; but, believe me, it is only . . . an impression.

BELCREDI Pardon me, but he even said so, and quite clearly. (*Turning to the* MARCHIONESS) Didn't he, Marchioness?

DONNA MATILDA (*Turning round*) What did he say? . . . (*Then not agreeing*) Oh yes . . . but not for the reason you think!

DOCTOR He was alluding to the costumes we had slipped on. . . . Your cloak (*Indicating the* MARCHIONESS) our Benedictine habits. . . . But all this is childish!

DONNA MATILDA (*Turning quickly, indignant*) Childish? What do you mean, Doctor?

DOCTOR From one point of view, it is—I beg you to let me say so, Marchioness! Yet, on the other hand, it is much more complicated than you can imagine.

DONNA MATILDA To me, on the contrary, it is perfectly clear!

DOCTOR (*With a smile of pity of the competent person toward those who do not understand*) We must take into account the peculiar psychology of madmen; which, you must know, enables us to be certain that they observe things and can, for instance, easily detect people who are disguised; can in fact recognize the disguise and yet believe in it; just as children do, for whom disguise is both play and reality. That is why I used the word childish. But the thing is extremely complicated, inasmuch as he must be perfectly aware of being an image to himself and for himself —that image there, in fact! (*Alluding to the portrait in the throne room, and pointing to the left*)

BELCREDI That's what he said!

DOCTOR Very well then— An image before which other images, ours, have appeared: understand? Now he, in his acute and perfectly lucid delirium, was able to detect at once a difference between his image and ours: that is, he saw that ours were make-believes. So he suspected us; because all madmen are armed with a special diffidence. But that's all there is to it! Our make-believe, built up all round his, did not seem pitiful to him. While his seemed all the more tragic to us, in that he, as if in defiance—understand?—and induced by his suspicion, wanted to show us up merely as a joke. That was also partly the case with him, in coming before us with painted cheeks and hair, and saying he had done it on purpose for a jest.

DONNA MATILDA (*Impatiently*) No, it's not that, Doctor. It's not like that! It's not like that!

DOCTOR Why isn't it, may I ask?

DONNA MATILDA (*With decision but trembling*) I am perfectly certain he recognized me!

DOCTOR It's not possible . . . it's not possible!

BELCREDI (*At the same time*) Of course not!

DONNA MATILDA (*More than ever determined, almost convulsively*) I tell you, he recognized me! When he came close up to speak to me—looking in my eyes, right into my eyes—he recognized me!

BELCREDI But he was talking of your daughter!

DONNA MATILDA That's not true! He was talking of me! Of me!

BELCREDI Yes, perhaps, when he said . . .

DONNA MATILDA (*Letting herself go*) About my dyed hair! But didn't you notice that he added at once: "or the memory of your dark hair, if you were dark"? He remembered perfectly well that I was dark—then!

BELCREDI Nonsense! nonsense!

DONNA MATILDA (*Not listening to him, turning to the* DOCTOR) My hair, Doctor, is really dark—like my daughter's! That's why he spoke of her.

BELCREDI But he doesn't even know your daughter! He's never seen her!

DONNA MATILDA Exactly! Oh, you never understand anything! By my daughter, stupid, he meant me—as I was then!

BELCREDI Oh, this is catching! This is catching, this madness!

DONNA MATILDA (*Softly, with contempt*) Fool!

BELCREDI Excuse me, were you ever his wife? Your daughter is his wife—in his delirium: Bertha of Susa.

DONNA MATILDA Exactly! Because I, no longer dark—as he remembered me—but *fair*, introduced myself as "Adelaide," the mother. My daughter doesn't exist for him: he's never seen her—you said so yourself! So how can he know whether she's fair or dark?

BELCREDI But he said dark, speaking generally, just as anyone who wants to recall, whether fair or dark, a memory of youth in the color of the hair! And you, as usual, begin to imagine things! Doctor, you said I ought not to have come! It's she who ought not to have come!

DONNA MATILDA (*Upset for a moment by* BELCREDI'S *remark, recovers herself. Then with a touch of anger, because doubtful*) No, no . . . he spoke of me. . . . He spoke all the time to me, with me, of me. . . .

BELCREDI That's not bad! He didn't leave me a moment's breathing space; and you say he was talking all the time to you? Unless you think he was alluding to you too, when he was talking to Peter Damiani!

DONNA MATILDA (*Defiantly, almost exceeding the limits of courteous discussion*) Who knows? Can you tell me why, from the outset, he showed a strong dislike for you, for you alone? (*From the tone of the question, the expected answer must almost explicitly be: "because he understands you are my lover."*

BELCREDI *feels this so well that he remains silent and can say nothing*)

DOCTOR The reason may also be found in the fact that only the visit of the Duchess Adelaide and the Abbot of Cluny was announced to him. Finding a third person present, who had not been announced, at once his suspicions . . .

BELCREDI Yes, exactly! His suspicion made him see an enemy in me: Peter Damiani! But she's got it into her head, that he recognized her . . .

DONNA MATILDA There's no doubt about it! I could see it from his eyes, doctor. You know, there's a way of looking that leaves no doubt whatever. . . . Perhaps it was only for an instant, but I am sure!

DOCTOR It is not impossible: a lucid moment . . .

DONNA MATILDA Yes, perhaps. . . . And then his speech seemed to me full of regret for his and my youth—for the horrible thing that happened to him, that has held him in that disguise from which he has never been able to free himself, and from which he longs to be free—he said so himself!

BELCREDI Yes, so as to be able to make love to your daughter, or you, as you believe—having been touched by your pity.

DONNA MATILDA Which is very great, I would ask you to believe.

BELCREDI As one can see, Marchioness; so much so that a miracle-worker might expect a miracle from it!

DOCTOR Will you let me speak? I don't work miracles, because I am a doctor and not a miracle-worker. I listened very intently to all he said; and I repeat that a certain analogical elasticity, common in all systematized delirium, is evidently with him much—what shall I say?—much relaxed! The elements, that is, of his delirium no longer hold together. It seems to me he has lost the equilibrium of his second personality and sudden recollections drag him—and this is very comforting—not

from a state of incipient apathy, but rather from a morbid inclination to reflective melancholy, which shows a . . . a very considerable cerebral activity. Very comforting, I repeat! Now if, by this violent trick we've planned . . .

DONNA MATILDA (*Turning to the window, in the tone of a sick person complaining*) But how is it that the car has not returned? It's three hours and a half since . . .

DOCTOR What do you say?

DONNA MATILDA The car, Doctor! It's more than three hours and a half . . .

DOCTOR (*Taking out his watch and looking at it*) Yes, more than four hours, by this!

DONNA MATILDA It could have reached here an hour ago at least! But, as usual . . .

BELCREDI Perhaps they can't find the dress . . .

DONNA MATILDA But I explained exactly where it was! (*Impatiently*) And Frida . . . where is Frida?

BELCREDI (*Looking out of the window*) Perhaps she is in the garden with Charles . . .

DOCTOR He'll talk her out of her fright.

BELCREDI She's not afraid, Doctor; don't you believe it: the thing bores her rather . . .

DONNA MATILDA Just don't ask anything of her! I know what she's like.

DOCTOR Let's wait patiently. Anyhow, it will soon be over, and it has to be in the evening . . . It will only be the matter of a moment! If we can succeed in rousing him, as I was saying, and in breaking at one go the threads—already slack—which still bind him to this fiction of his, giving him back what he himself asks for—you remember, he said: "one cannot always be twenty-six years old, madam!"—if we can give him freedom from this torment, which even *he* feels is a torment, then if he is able to recover at one bound the sensation of the distance of time . . .

BELCREDI (*Quickly*) He'll be cured! (*Then emphatically with irony*) We'll pull him out of it all!

DOCTOR Yes, we may hope to set him going again, like a watch which has stopped at a certain hour . . . just as if we had our watches in our hands and were waiting for that other watch to go again. A shake—

so—and let's hope it'll tell the time again after its long stop. (*At this point the* MARQUIS CHARLES DI NOLLI *enters from the principal entrance*)

DONNA MATILDA Oh, Charles! . . . And Frida? Where is she?

DI NOLLI She'll be here in a moment.

DOCTOR Has the car arrived?

DI NOLLI Yes.

DONNA MATILDA Yes? Has the dress come?

DI NOLLI It's been here some time.

DOCTOR Good! Good!

DONNA MATILDA (*Trembling*) Where is she? Where's Frida?

DI NOLLI (*Shrugging his shoulders and smiling sadly, like one lending himself unwillingly to an untimely joke*) You'll see, you'll see! . . . (*Pointing toward the hall*) Here she is! . . . (BERTHOLD *appears at the threshold of the hall, and announces with solemnity*)

BERTHOLD Her Highness the Countess Matilda of Canossa! (FRIDA *enters, magnificent and beautiful, arrayed in the robes of her mother as "Countess Matilda of Tuscany," so that she is a living copy of the portrait in the throne room*)

FRIDA (*Passing* BERTHOLD, *who is bowing, says to him with disdain*) Of Tuscany, of Tuscany! Canossa is just one of my castles!

BELCREDI (*In admiration*) Look! Look! She seems another person. . . .

DONNA MATILDA One would say it were I! Look! Why, Frida, look! She's exactly my portrait, alive!

DOCTOR Yes, yes . . . Perfect! Perfect! The portrait, to the life.

BELCREDI Yes, there's no question about it. She *is* the portrait! Magnificent!

FRIDA Don't make me laugh, or I shall burst! I say, Mother, what a tiny waist you had! I had to squeeze so to get into this!

DONNA MATILDA (*Arranging her dress a little*) Wait! . . . Keep still! . . . These pleats . . . is it really so tight?

FRIDA I'm suffocating! I implore you, be quick! . . .

DOCTOR But we must wait till it's evening!

FRIDA No, no, I can't hold out till evening!

DONNA MATILDA Why did you put it on so soon?

FRIDA The moment I saw it, the temptation was irresistible. . . .

DONNA MATILDA At least you could have called me, or have had someone help you! It's still all crumpled.

FRIDA So I saw, Mother; but they are old creases; they won't come out.

DOCTOR It doesn't matter, Marchioness! The illusion is perfect. (*Then coming nearer and asking her to come in front of her daughter, without hiding her*) If you please, stay there . . . at a certain distance . . . now a little more forward. . . .

BELCREDI For the feeling of the distance of time. . . .

DONNA MATILDA (*Slightly turning to him*) Twenty years after! A disaster! A tragedy!

BELCREDI Now don't let's exaggerate!

DOCTOR (*Embarrassed, trying to save the situation*) No, no! I meant the dress . . . so as to see . . . You know . . .
(*Pointing first to* FRIDA *and then to the* MARCHIONESS)

BELCREDI (*Laughing*) Oh, as for the dress, Doctor, it isn't a matter of twenty years! It's eight hundred! An abyss! Do you really want to shove him across it from there to here? But you'll have to pick him up in pieces with a basket! Just think now: for us it is a matter of twenty years, a couple of dresses, and a masquerade. But, if, as you say, Doctor, time has stopped for and around him: if he lives there (*Pointing to* FRIDA) with her, eight hundred years ago . . . I repeat: the giddiness of the jump will be such, that finding himself suddenly among us . . . (*The* DOCTOR *shakes his head in dissent*) You don't think so?

DOCTOR No, because life, my dear baron, can take up its rhythms. This—our life—will at once become real also to him; and will pull him up directly, wresting from him suddenly the illusion, and showing him that the eight hundred years, as you say, are only twenty! It will be like one of those tricks, such as the leap into space, for instance, of the Masonic rite, which appears to be heaven knows how far, and is only a step down the stairs.

BELCREDI Ah! An idea! Yes! Look at Frida

and the Marchioness, doctor! Which is more advanced in time? We old people, Doctor! The young ones think they are more ahead; but it isn't true: we are more ahead, because time belongs to us more than to them.

DOCTOR If the past didn't alienate us. . . .

BELCREDI It doesn't matter at all! How does it alienate us? They (*Pointing to* FRIDA *and* DI NOLLI) have still to do what we have accomplished, Doctor: to grow old, doing the same foolish things, more or less, as we did. . . . This is the illusion: that one comes forward through a door to life. It isn't so! As soon as one is born, one starts dying; therefore, he who started first is the most advanced of all. The youngest of us is father Adam! Look there: (*Pointing to* FRIDA) eight hundred years younger than all of us—the Countess Matilda of Tuscany. (*He makes her a deep bow*)

DI NOLLI I say, Tito, don't start joking.

BELCREDI Oh, you think I am joking? . . .

DI NOLLI Of course, of course . . . all the time.

BELCREDI Impossible! I've even dressed up as a Benedictine. . . .

DI NOLLI Yes, but for a serious purpose.

BELCREDI Well, exactly. If it has been serious for the others . . . for Frida, now, for instance. (*Then turning to the* DOCTOR) I swear, Doctor, I don't yet understand what you want to do.

DOCTOR (*Annoyed*) You'll see! Let me do as I wish. . . . At present you see the Marchioness still dressed as . . . .

BELCREDI Oh, she also . . . has to masquerade?

DOCTOR Of course! of course! In another dress that's in there ready to be used when it comes into his head he sees the Countess Matilda of Canossa before him.

FRIDA (*While talking quietly to* DI NOLLI *notices the doctor's mistake*) Of Tuscany, of Tuscany!

DOCTOR It's all the same!

BELCREDI Oh, I see; He'll be faced by two of them. . . .

DOCTOR Two, precisely! And then . . .

FRIDA (*Calling him aside*) Come here, doctor! Listen!

DOCTOR Here I am! (*Goes near the two young people and pretends to give some explanations to them*)

BELCREDI (*Softly to* DONNA MATILDA) I say, this is getting rather strong, you know!

DONNA MATILDA (*Looking him firmly in the face*) What?

BELCREDI Does it really interest you as much as all that—to make you willing to take part in . . . ? For a woman this is simply enormous! . . .

DONNA MATILDA Yes, for an ordinary woman.

BELCREDI Oh, no, my dear, for all women— in a question like this! It's an abnegation.

DONNA MATILDA I owe it to him.

BELCREDI Don't lie! You know well enough it's not hurting you!

DONNA MATILDA Well, then where does the abnegation come in?

BELCREDI Just enough to prevent you losing caste in other people's eyes—and just enough to offend me! . . .

DONNA MATILDA But who is worrying about you now?

DI NOLLI (*Coming forward*) It's all right. It's all right. That's what we'll do! (*Turning toward* BERTHOLD) Here you, go and call one of those fellows!

BERTHOLD At once! (*Exit*)

DONNA MATILDA But first of all we've got to pretend that we are going away.

DI NOLLI Exactly! I'll see to that. . . . (*To* BELCREDI) You don't mind staying here?

BELCREDI (*Ironically*) Oh, no, I don't mind, I don't mind! . . .

DI NOLLI We must look out not to make him suspicious again, you know.

BELCREDI Oh, Lord! *He* doesn't amount to anything!

DOCTOR He must believe absolutely that we've gone away. (LANDOLPH *followed by* BERTHOLD *enters from the right*)

LANDOLPH May I come in?

DI NOLLI Come in! Come in! I say—your name's Lolo, isn't it?

LANDOLPH Lolo, or Landolph, just as you like!

DI NOLLI Well, look here: the Doctor and the Marchioness are leaving, at once.

LANDOLPH Very well. All we've got to say is that they have been able to obtain the permission for the reception from His Holiness. He's in there in his own apartments repenting of all he said—and in an awful state to have the pardon! Would you mind coming a minute? . . . If you would, just for a minute . . . put on the dress again. . . .

DOCTOR Why, of course, with pleasure. . . .

LANDOLPH Might I be allowed to make a suggestion? Why not add that the Marchioness of Tuscany has interceded with the Pope that he should be received?

DONNA MATILDA You see, he has recognized me!

LANDOLPH Forgive me . . . I don't know my history very well. I am sure you gentlemen know it much better! But I thought it was believed that Henry IV had a secret passion for the Marchioness of Tuscany.

DONNA MATILDA (*At once*) Nothing of the kind! Nothing of the kind!

LANDOLPH That's what I thought! But he says he's loved her . . . he's always saying it. . . . And now he fears that her indignation for this secret love of his will work him harm with the Pope.

BELCREDI We must let him understand that this aversion no longer exists.

LANDOLPH Exactly! Of course!

DONNA MATILDA (*To* BELCREDI) History says —I don't know whether you know it or not—that the Pope gave way to the supplications of the Marchioness Matilda and the Abbot of Cluny. And I may say, my dear Belcredi, that I intended to take advantage of this fact—at the time of the pageant—to show him my feelings were not so hostile to him as he supposed.

BELCREDI You are most faithful to history, Marchioness. . . .

LANDOLPH Well then, the Marchioness could spare herself a double disguise and present herself with Monsignor (*Indicating the* DOCTOR) as the Marchioness of Tuscany.

DOCTOR (*Quickly, energetically*) No, no! That won't do at all. It would ruin everything. The impression from the confrontation must be a sudden one, give a shock! No, no, Marchioness, you will appear again as the Duchess Adelaide, the mother of the Empress. And then we'll go away. This

is most necessary: that he should know we've gone away. Come on! Don't let's waste any more time! There's a lot to prepare.

(*Exeunt the* DOCTOR, DONNA MATILDA, *and* LANDOLPH, *right*)

FRIDA I am beginning to feel afraid again.

DI NOLLI Again, Frida?

FRIDA It would have been better if I had seen him before.

DI NOLLI There's nothing to be frightened of, really.

FRIDA He isn't furious, is he?

DI NOLLI Of course not! he's quite calm.

BELCREDI (*With ironic sentimental affectation*) Melancholy! Didn't you hear that he loves you?

FRIDA Thanks! That's just why I am afraid.

BELCREDI He won't do you any harm.

DI NOLLI It'll only last a minute.

FRIDA Yes, but there in the dark with him. . . .

DI NOLLI Only for a moment; and I will be near you, and all the others behind the door ready to run in. As soon as you see your mother, your part will be finished.

BELCREDI I'm afraid of a different thing: that we're wasting our time. . . .

DI NOLLI Don't begin again! The remedy seems a sound one to me.

FRIDA I think so too! I feel it! I'm all trembling!

BELCREDI But, mad people, my dear friends —though they don't know it, alas—have this felicity which we don't take into account. . . .

DI NOLLI (*Interrupting, annoyed*) What felicity? Nonsense!

BELCREDI (*Forcefully*) They don't reason!

DI NOLLI What's reasoning got to do with it, anyway?

BELCREDI Don't you call it reasoning that he will have to do—according to us—when he sees her (*Indicates* FRIDA) and her mother? We've reasoned it all out, surely!

DI NOLLI Nothing of the kind: no reasoning at all! We put before him a double image of his own fantasy, or fiction, as the doctor says.

BELCREDI (*Suddenly*) I say, I've never understood why they take degrees in medicine.

DI NOLLI (*Amazed*) Who?

BELCREDI The psychiatrists.

DI NOLLI What ought they to take degrees in, then?

FRIDA If they are psychiatrists, in what else should they take degrees?

BELCREDI In law, of course! All a matter of talk! The more they talk, the more highly they are considered. "Analogous elasticity," "the sensation of distance in time!" And the first thing they tell you is that they don't work miracles—when a miracle's just what is wanted! But they know that the more they say they are not miracle-workers, the more people believe in their seriousness!

BERTHOLD (*Who has been looking through the keyhole of the door on right*) There they are! There they are! They're coming in here.

DI NOLLI Are they?

BERTHOLD He wants to come with them. . . . Yes! . . . He's coming too!

DI NOLLI Let's get away, then! Let's get away, at once! (*To* BERTHOLD) You stop here!

BERTHOLD Must I?

(*Without answering him,* DI NOLLI, FRIDA, *and* BELCREDI *go out by the main exit, leaving* BERTHOLD *surprised. The door on the right opens, and* LANDOLPH *enters first, bowing. Then* DONNA MATILDA *comes in, with mantle and ducal crown as in the first act; also the* DOCTOR *as the* ABBOT OF CLUNY. HENRY IV *is among them in royal dress.* ORDULPH *and* HAROLD *enter last of all*)

HENRY IV (*Following up what he has been saying in the other room*) And now I will ask you a question: how can I be astute, if you think me obstinate?

DOCTOR No, no, not obstinate!

HENRY IV (*Smiling, pleased*) Then you think me really astute?

DOCTOR No, no, neither obstinate, nor astute.

HENRY IV (*With benevolent irony*) Monsignor, if obstinacy is not a vice which can go with astuteness, I hoped that in denying me the former, you would at least allow me a little of the latter. I can assure you I have great need of it. But if you want to keep it all for yourself . . .

DOCTOR I? I? Do I seem astute to you?

HENRY IV No. Monsignor! What do you say? Not in the least! Perhaps in this case, I may seem a little obstinate to you. . . . (*Cutting short to speak to* DONNA MATILDA) With your permission: a word in confidence to the Duchess. (*Leads her aside and asks her very earnestly*) Is your daughter really dear to you?

DONNA MATILDA (*Dismayed*) Why, yes, certainly. . . .

HENRY IV Do you wish me to compensate her with all my love, with all my devotion, for the grave wrongs I have done her—though you must not believe all the stories my enemies tell about my dissoluteness!

DONNA MATILDA No, no, I don't believe them. I never have believed such stories.

HENRY IV Well, then are you willing?

DONNA MATILDA (*Confused*) What?

HENRY IV That I return to love your daughter again? (*Looks at her and adds, in a mysterious tone of warning*) You mustn't be a friend of the Marchioness of Tuscany!

DONNA MATILDA I tell you again that she has begged and tried not less than ourselves to obtain your pardon. . . .

HENRY IV (*Softly, but excitedly*) Don't tell me that! Don't say that to me! Don't you see the effect it has on me, my Lady?

DONNA MATILDA (*Looks at him; then very softly as if in confidence*) You love her still?

HENRY IV (*Puzzled*) Still? Still, you say? You know, then? But nobody knows! Nobody must know!

DONNA MATILDA But perhaps she knows, if she has begged so hard for you!

HENRY IV (*Looks at her and says*) And you love your daughter? (*Brief pause. He turns to the* DOCTOR *with laughing accents*) Ah, Monsignor, it's strange how little I think of my wife! It may be a sin, but I swear to you that I hardly feel her at all in my heart. What is stranger is that her own mother scarcely feels her in her heart. Confess, my Lady, that she amounts to very little for you. (*Turning to* DOCTOR) She talks to me of that other woman, insistently, insistently, I don't know why! . . .

LANDOLPH (*Humbly*) Maybe, Majesty, it is to

disabuse you of some ideas you have had about the Marchioness of Tuscany. (*Then, dismayed at having allowed himself this observation, adds*) I mean just now, of course. . . .

HENRY IV You too maintain that she has been friendly to me?

LANDOLPH Yes, at the moment, Majesty.

DONNA MATILDA Exactly! Exactly! . . .

HENRY IV I understand. That is to say, you don't believe I love her. I see! I see! Nobody's ever believed it, nobody's ever thought it. Better so, then! But enough, enough! (*Turns to the DOCTOR with changed expression*) Monsignor, you see? The reasons the Pope has had for revoking the excommunication have nothing at all to do with the reasons for which he excommunicated me originally. Tell Pope Gregory we shall meet again at Bressanone. And you, Madame, should you chance to meet your daughter in the courtyard of the castle of your friend the Marchioness, ask her to visit me. We shall see if I succeed in keeping her close beside me as wife and Empress. Many women have presented themselves here already assuring me that they were she. And I thought to have her—yes, I tried sometimes—there's no shame in it, with one's wife!—But when they said they were Bertha, and they were from Susa, all of them—I can't think why—started laughing! (*Confidentially*) Understand?—In bed—I undressed—so did she—yes, by God, undressed—a man and a woman—it's natural after all! Like that, we don't bother much about who we are. And one's dress is like a phantom that hovers always near one. Oh, Monsignor, phantoms in general are nothing more than trifling disorders of the spirit: images we cannot contain within the bounds of sleep. They reveal themselves even when we are awake, and they frighten us. I . . . ah . . . I am always afraid when, at night-time, I see disordered images before me. Sometimes I am even afraid of my own blood pulsing loudly in my arteries in the silence of night, like the sound of a distant step in a lonely corridor! . . . But, forgive me! I have kept you standing too long already. I thank you, my Lady, I thank you, Monsignor. (DONNA MATILDA *and the* DOCTOR *go off bowing. As soon as they have gone,* HENRY IV *suddenly changes his tone*) Buffoons, buffoons! One can play any tune on them! And that other fellow . . . Pietro Damiani! . . Caught him out perfectly! He's afraid to appear before me again. (*Moves up and down excitedly while saying this; then sees* BERTHOLD, *and points him out to the other three valets*) Oh, look at this imbecile watching me with his mouth wide open! (*Shakes him*) Don't you understand? Don't you see, idiot, how I treat them, how I play the fool with them, make them appear before me just as I wish? Miserable, frightened clowns that they are! And you (*Addressing the* VALETS) are amazed that I tear off their ridiculous masks now, just as if it wasn't I who had made them mask themselves to satisfy this taste of mine for playing the madman!

LANDOLPH—HAROLD—ORDULPH (*Bewildered, looking at one another*) What? What does he say? What?

HENRY IV (*Answers them imperiously*) Enough! enough! Let's stop it. I'm tired of it. (*Then as if the thought left him no peace*) By God! The impudence! To come here along with her lover! . . . And pretending to do it out of pity! So as not to infuriate a poor devil already out of the world, out of time, out of life! If it weren't supposed to be done out of pity, one can well imagine that fellow wouldn't have allowed it. Those people expect others to behave as they wish all the time. And, of course, there's nothing arrogant in that! Oh, no! Oh, no! It's merely their way of thinking, of feeling, of seeing. Everybody has his own way of thinking; you fellows, too. Yours is that of a flock of sheep—miserable, feeble, uncertain. . . . But those others take advantage of this and make you accept their way of thinking; or, at least, they suppose they do; because, after all, what do they succeed in imposing on you? Words, words which anyone can interpret in his own manner! That's the way public opinion is formed! And it's a bad outlook for a man who finds himself labeled one day with one of these words which everyone repeats; for example "madman," or "imbecile." Don't you think it is rather hard for a man to keep quiet, when he knows that there is a fellow going about trying to persuade everybody that he is as he sees him, trying to fix him in other people's opinion as a "madman" —according to him? Now I am talking seriously! Before I hurt my head, falling from my horse . . . (*Stops suddenly, noticing the dismay of the four young men*) What's the matter with you? (*Imitates their amazed looks*) What? Am I, or am I not, mad? Oh, yes! I'm mad all right! (*He becomes terrible*) Well, then, by God, down on your knees, down on your knees! (*Makes them go down on their knees one by one*) I order you to go down on your knees before me! And touch the ground three times with your foreheads! Down, down! Thet's the way you've got to be before madmen! (*Then annoyed with their facile humiliation*) Get up, sheep! You obeyed me, didn't you? You might have put the strait jacket on me! . . . Crush a man with the weight of a word—it's nothing—a fly! All our life is crushed by the weight of words: the weight of the dead. Look at me here: can you really suppose that Henry IV is still alive? All the same, I speak, and order you live men about! Do you think it's a joke that the dead continue to live?—Yes, *here* it's a joke! But get out into the live world!—Ah, you say: what a beautiful sunrise—for us! All time is before us!—Dawn! We will do what we like with this day. . . . Ah, yes! To Hell with tradition, the old conventions! Well, go on! You will do nothing but repeat the old, old words, while you imagine you are living! (*Goes up to* BERTHOLD *who has now become quite stupid*) You don't understand a word of this, do you? What's your name?

BERTHOLD I? . . . What? . . . Berthold . . .

HENRY IV Poor Berthold! What's your name here?

BERTHOLD I. . . I . . . my name is Fino.

HENRY IV (*Feeling the warning and critical glances of the others, turns to them to reduce them to silence*) Fino?

BERTHOLD Fino Pagliuca, sire.

HENRY IV (*Turning to* LANDOLPH) I've heard you call each other by your nicknames often enough! Your name is Lolo, isn't it?

LANDOLPH Yes, sire . . . (*Then with a sense of immense joy*) Oh Lord! Oh Lord! Then he is not mad. . . .

HENRY IV (*Brusquely*) What?

LANDOLPH (*Hesitating*) No . . . I said . . .

HENRY IV Not mad, any more. No. Don't you see? We're having a joke on those that think I am mad! (*To* HAROLD) I say, boy, your name's Franco. . . . (*To* ORDULPH) And yours . . .

ORDULPH Momo.

HENRY IV Momo, Momo . . . A nice name that!

LANDOLPH So he isn't . . .

HENRY IV What are you talking about? Of course not! Let's have a jolly, good laugh! . . . (*Laughs*) Ah! . . . Ah! . . . Ah! . . .

LANDOLPH—HAROLD—ORDULPH (*Looking at each other half happy and half dismayed*) Then he's cured! . . he's all right! . . .

HENRY IV Silence! Silence! . . . (*To* BERTHOLD) Why don't you laugh? Are you offended? I didn't mean it especially for you. It's convenient for everybody to insist that certain people are mad, so they can be shut up. Do you know why? Because it's impossible to hear them speak! What shall I say of these people who've just gone away? That one is a whore, another a libertine, another a swindler. . . . Don't you think so? You can't believe a word he says. . . . Don't you think so? By the way, they all listen to me terrified. And why are they terrified, if what I say isn't true? Of course, you can't believe what madmen say—yet, at the same time, they stand there with their eyes wide open with terror!—Why? Tell me, tell me, why?— You see I'm quite calm now!

BERTHOLD But, perhaps, they think that . . .

HENRY IV No, no, my dear fellow! Look me well in the eyes! . . . I don't say that it's true—nothing is true, Berthold! But . . . look me in the eyes!

BERTHOLD Well . . .

HENRY IV You see? You see? . . . You have terror in your own eyes now because I seem mad to you! There's the proof of it! (*Laughs*)

LANDOLPH (*Coming forward in the name of the others, exasperated*) What proof?

HENRY IV Your being so dismayed because now I seem again mad to you. You have thought me mad up to now, haven't you? You feel that this dismay of yours can become terror too—something to dash away the ground from under your feet and deprive you of the air you breathe! Do you know what it means to find yourselves face to face with a madman—with one who shakes the foundations of all you have built up in yourselves, your logic, the logic of all your constructions? Madmen, lucky folk, construct without logic, or rather with a logic that flies like a feather. Voluble! Voluble! Today like this and tomorrow—who knows? You say: "This cannot be"; but for them everything can be. You say: "This isn't true!" And why? Because it doesn't seem true to you, or you, or you. . . . (*Indicates the three of them in succession*) . . . and to a hundred thousand others! One must see what seems true to these hundred thousand others who are not supposed to be mad! What a magnificent spectacle they afford, when they reason! What flowers of logic they scatter! I know that when I was a child, I thought the moon in the pond was real. How many things I thought real! I believed everything I was told—and I was happy! Because it's a terrible thing if you don't hold on to that which seems true to you today—to that which will seem true to you tomorrow, even if it is the opposite of that which seemed true to you yesterday. I would never wish you to think, as I have done, on this horrible thing which really drives one mad: that if you were beside another and looking into his eyes—as I one day looked into somebody's eyes—you might as well be a beggar before a door never to be opened to you; for

he who does enter there will never be you, but someone unknown to you with his own different and impenetrable world. . . . (*Long pause. Darkness gathers in the room, increasing the sense of strangeness and consternation in which the four young men are involved.* HENRY IV *remains aloof, pondering on the misery which is not only his, but everybody's. Then he pulls himself up, and says in an ordinary tone*) It's getting dark here. . . .

ORDULPH Shall I go for a lamp?

HENRY IV (*Ironically*) The lamp, yes the lamp! . . . Do you suppose I don't know that as soon as I turn my back with my oil lamp to go to bed, you turn on the electric light for yourselves, here, and even there, in the throne room? I pretend not to see it!

ORDULPH Well, then, shall I turn it on now?

HENRY IV No, it would blind me! I want my lamp!

ORDULPH It's ready here behind the door. (*Goes to the main exit, opens the door, goes out for a moment, and returns with an ancient lamp which is held by a ring at the top*)

HENRY IV Ah, a little light! Sit there around the table, no, not like that; in an elegant, easy, manner! . . . (*To* HAROLD) Yes, you, like that! (*Poses him*) (*Then to* BERTHOLD) You so! . . . and I, here! (*Sits opposite them*) We could do with a little decorative moonlight. It's very useful for us, the moonlight. I feel a real necessity for it, and pass a lot of time looking up at the moon from my window. Who would think, to look at her that she knows that eight hundred years have passed, and that I, seated at the window, cannot really be Henry IV gazing at the moon like any poor devil? But, look, look! See what a magnificent night scene we have here: the emperor surrounded by his faithful counselors! . . . How do you like it?

LANDOLPH (*Softly to* HAROLD, *so as not to break the enchantment*) And to think it wasn't true! . . .

HENRY IV True? What wasn't true?

LANDOLPH (*Timidly as if to excuse himself*) No . . . I mean . . . I was saying this morning to him (*Indicates* BERTHOLD)—he has just started working here—I was saying: what a pity that dressed like this and with so many beautiful costumes in the wardrobe . . . and with a room like that . . . (*Indicates the throne room*)

HENRY IV Well? what's the pity?

LANDOLPH Well . . . that we didn't know . . .

HENRY IV That it was all done in jest, this comedy?

LANDOLPH Because we thought that . . .

HAROLD (*Coming to his assistance*) Yes . . . that it was done seriously!

HENRY IV What do you say? Doesn't it seem serious to you?

LANDOLPH But if you say that . . .

HENRY IV I say that—you are fools! You ought to have known how to create a fantasy for yourselves, not to act it for me, or anyone coming to see me; but naturally, simply, day by day, before nobody, feeling yourselves alive in the history of the eleventh century, here at the court of your emperor, Henry IV! You, Ordulph (*Taking him by the arm*), alive in the castle of Goslar, waking up in the morning, getting out of bed, and entering straight into the dream, clothing yourself in the dream that would be no more a dream, because you would have lived it, felt it all alive in you. You would have drunk it in with the air you breathed; yet knowing all the time that it was a dream, so you could better enjoy the privilege afforded you of having to do nothing else but live this dream, this far off and yet actual dream! And to think that at a distance of eight centuries from this remote age of ours, so colored and so sepulchral, the men of the twentieth century are torturing themselves in ceaseless anxiety to know how their fates and fortunes will work out! Whereas you are already in history with me. . . .

LANDOLPH Yes, yes, very good!

HENRY IV . . . Everything determined, everything settled!

ORDULPH Yes, yes!

HENRY IV And sad as is my lot, hideous as some of the events are, bitter the struggles, and troubled the time—still all his-

tory! All history that cannot change, understand? All fixed for ever! And you could have admired at your ease how every effect followed obediently its cause with perfect logic, how every event took place precisely and coherently in each minute particular! The pleasure, the pleasure of history, in fact, which is so great, was yours.

LANDOLPH Beautiful, beautiful!

HENRY IV Beautiful, but it's finished! Now that you know, I could not do it any more! (*Takes his lamp to go to bed*) Neither could you, if up to now you haven't understood the reason of it! I am sick of it now. (*Almost to himself with violent contained rage*) By God, I'll make her sorry she came here! Dressed herself up as a mother-in-law for me! . . . And he as an abbot! . . . And they bring a doctor with them to study me! . . . Who knows if they don't hope to cure me? . . . Clowns! . . I'd like to smack one of them at least in the face: yes, that one—a famous swordsman, they say! . . . He'll kill me . . . Well, we'll see, we'll see! . . . (*A knock at the door*) Who is it?

THE VOICE OF JOHN Deo Gratias!

HAROLD (*Very pleased at the chance for another joke*) Oh, it's John, it's old John, who comes every night to play the monk.

ORDULPH (*Rubbing his hands*) Yes, yes! Let's make him do it!

HENRY IV (*At once, severely*) Fool, why? Just to play a joke on a poor old man who does it for love of me?

LANDOLPH (*To* ORDULPH) It has to be as if it were true.

HENRY IV Exactly, as if true! Because, only so, truth is not a jest. (*Opens the door and admits* JOHN *dressed as a humble friar with a roll of parchment under his arm*) Come in, come in, Father! (*Then assuming a tone of tragic gravity and deep resentment*) All the documents of my life and reign favorable to me were destroyed deliberately by my enemies. One only has escaped destruction, this, my life, written by a humble monk who is devoted to me. And you would laugh at him! (*Turns affectionately to* JOHN, *and invites him to sit down at the table*) Sit down, Father, sit down! Have the lamp near you! (*Puts the lamp near him*) Write! Write!

JOHN (*Opens the parchment and prepares to write from dictation*) I am ready, your Majesty!

HENRY IV (*Dictating*) "The decree of peace proclaimed at Mayence helped the poor and the good, while it damaged the powerful and the bad. (*Curtain begins to fall*) It brought wealth to the former, hunger and misery to the latter. . . ."

Curtain

ACT THREE

The throne room is so dark that the wall at the bottom is hardly seen. The canvases of the two portraits have been taken away; and, within their frames, FRIDA, *dressed as the "Marchioness of Tuscany," and* CHARLES DI NOLLI, *as "Henry IV," have taken the exact positions of the portraits.*

For a moment, after the raising of the curtain, the stage is empty. Then the door on the left opens; and HENRY IV, *holding the lamp by the ring on top of it, enters. He looks back to speak to the four young men, who, with* JOHN, *are presumedly in the adjoining hall, as at the end of the second act.*

HENRY VI No, stay where you are, stay where you are. I shall manage all right by myself. Good night! (*Closes the door and walks, very sad and tired, across the hall toward the second door on the right, which leads into his apartments*)

FRIDA (*As soon as she sees that he has just passed the throne, whispers from the niche like one who is on the point of fainting away with fright*) Henry . . .

HENRY IV (*Stopping at the voice, as if someone had stabbed him traitorously in the back, turns a terrorstricken face toward the wall at the bottom of the room; raising an arm instinctively, as if to defend himself and ward off a blow*) Who is calling me? (*It is not a question, but an exclamation vibrating with terror, which does not expect a reply from the darkness and the terrible silence of the hall, which suddenly fills him with the suspicion that he is really mad*)

FRIDA (*At his shudder of terror, is herself not less frightened at the part she is playing, and repeats a little more loudly*) Henry! . . . (*But, although she wishes to act the part as they have given it to her, she stretches her head a little out of the frame toward the other frame*)

HENRY IV (*Gives a dreadful cry; lets the lamp fall from his hands to cover his head with his arms, and makes a movement as if to run away*)

FRIDA (*Jumping from frame on to the stand and shouting like a mad woman*) Henry! . . . Henry! . . . I'm afraid! . . . I'm terrified! . . .

(*And while* DI NOLLI *jumps in turn on to the stand and thence to the floor and runs to* FRIDA *who, on the verge of fainting, continues to cry out, the* DOCTOR, DONNA MATILDA, *also dressed as "Matilda of Tuscany,"* TITO BELCREDI, LANDOLPH, BERTHOLD *and* JOHN *enter the hall from the doors on the right and on the left. One of them turns on the light: a strange light coming from lamps hidden in the ceiling so that only the upper part of the stage is well lighted. The others without taking notice of* HENRY IV, *who looks on astonished by the unexpected inrush, after the moment of terror which still causes him to tremble, run anxiously to support and comfort the still shaking* FRIDA, *who is moaning in the arms of her fiancé. All are speaking at the same time*)

DI NOLLI No, no, Frida . . . Here I am . . . I am beside you!

DOCTOR (*Coming with the others*) Enough! Enough! There's nothing more to be done! . . .

DONNA MATILDA He is cured, Frida. Look! He is cured! Don't you see?

DI NOLLI (*Astonished*) Cured?

BELCREDI It was only for fun! Be calm!

FRIDA No! I am afraid! I am afraid!

DONNA MATILDA Afraid of what? Look at him! He was never mad at all! . . .

DI NOLLI That isn't true! What are you saying? Cured?

DOCTOR It appears so. I should say so . . .

BELCREDI Yes, yes! They have told us so. (*Pointing to the four young men*)

DONNA MATILDA Yes, for a long time! He has confided in them, told them the truth!

DI NOLLI (*Now more indignant than astonished*) But what does it mean? If, up to a short time ago . . . ?

BELCREDI Hum! He was acting, to take you in and also us, who in good faith . . .

DI NOLLI Is it possible? To deceive his sister too, right up to the time of her death?

HENRY IV (*Remains apart, peering at one and now at the other under the accusation and the mockery of what all believe to be a cruel joke of his, which is now revealed. He has shown by the flashing of his eyes that he is meditating a revenge, which his violent contempt prevents him from defining clearly, as yet. Stung to the quick and with a clear idea of accepting the fiction they have insidiously worked up as true, he bursts forth at this point*) Go on, I say! Go on!

DI NOLLI (*Astonished at the cry*) Go on! What do you mean?

HENRY IV It isn't *your* sister only that is dead!

DI NOLLI My sister? Yours, I say, whom you compelled up to the last moment, to present herself here as your mother, Agnes!

HENRY IV And was she not *your* mother?

DI NOLLI My mother? Certainly my mother!

HENRY IV But your mother is dead for me, *old and far away!* You have just got down now from there. (*Pointing to the frame from which he jumped down*) And how do you know whether I have not wept her long in secret, dressed even as I am?

DONNA MATILDA (*Dismayed, looking at the others*) What does he say?

DOCTOR (*Much impressed, observing him*) Quietly! quietly, for Heaven's sake!

HENRY IV What do I say? I ask all of you if Agnes was not the mother of Henry IV? (*Turns to* FRIDA *as if she were really*

the "*Marchioness of Tuscany*") You, Marchioness, it seems to me, ought to know.

FRIDA (*Still frightened, draws closer to* DI NOLLI) No, no, I don't know. Not I!

DOCTOR It's the madness returning. . . . Quiet now, everybody!

BELCREDI (*Indignant*) Madness indeed, Doctor! He's acting again! . . .

HENRY IV (*Suddenly*) I? You have emptied those two frames over there, and he stands before my eyes as Henry IV. . . .

BELCREDI We've had enough of this joke now.

HENRY IV Who said joke?

DOCTOR (*Loudly to* BELCREDI) Don't excite him, for the love of God!

BELCREDI (*Without lending an ear to him, but speaking louder*) But they have said so (*Pointing again to the four young men*), they, they!

HENRY IV (*Turning round and looking at them*) You? Did you say it was all a joke?

LANDOLPH (*Timid and embarrassed*) No . . . really we said that you were cured.

BELCREDI Look here! Enough of this! (*To* DONNA MATILDA) Doesn't it seem to you that the sight of him (*Pointing to* DI NOLLI), Marchioness, and that of your daughter dressed so, is becoming intolerably childish?

DONNA MATILDA Oh, be quiet! What does the dress matter, if he is cured?

HENRY IV Cured, yes! I am cured! (*To* BELCREDI) Ah, but not to let it end this way all at once, as you suppose! (*Attacks him*) Do you know that for twenty years nobody has ever dared to appear before me here like you and that gentleman? (*Pointing to the* DOCTOR)

BELCREDI Of course I know it. As a matter of fact, I too appeared before you this morning dressed . . .

HENRY IV As a monk, yes!

BELCREDI And you took me for Peter Damiani! And I didn't even laugh, believing, in fact, that . . .

HENRY IV That I was mad! Does it make you laugh seeing her like that, now that I am cured? And yet you might have remembered that in my eyes her appearance now . . . (*Interrupts himself with a gesture of contempt*) Ah! (*Suddenly turns to the* DOCTOR) You are a doctor, aren't you?

DOCTOR Yes.

HENRY IV And you also took part in dressing her up as the Marchioness of Tuscany? To prepare a counter-joke for me here, eh?

DONNA MATILDA (*Impetuously*) No, no! What do you say? It was done for you! I did it for your sake.

DOCTOR (*Quickly*) To attempt, to try, not knowing . . .

HENRY IV (*Cutting him short*) I understand. I say counter-joke, in his case (*Indicates* BELCREDI) because he believes that I have been carrying on a jest. . . .

BELCREDI But excuse me, what do you mean? You say yourself you are cured.

HENRY IV Let me speak! (*To the* DOCTOR) Do you know, Doctor, that for a moment you ran the risk of making me mad again? By God, to make the portraits speak; to make them jump alive out of their frames . . .

DOCTOR But you saw that all of us ran in at once, as soon as they told us . . .

HENRY IV Certainly! (*Contemplates* FRIDA *and* DI NOLLI, *and then looks at the* MARCHION-ESS, *and finally at his own costume*) The combination is very beautiful. . . . Two couples. . . . Very good, very good, Doctor! For a madman, not bad! . . . (*With a slight wave of his hand to* BELCREDI) It seems to him now to be a carnival out of season, eh? (*Turns to look at him*) We'll get rid now of this masquerade costume of mine, so that I may come away with you. What do you say?

BELCREDI With me? With us!

HENRY IV Where shall we go? To the Club? In dress coats and with white ties? Or shall both of us go to the Marchioness' house?

BELCREDI Wherever you like! Do you want to remain here still, to continue—alone—what was nothing but the unfortunate joke of a day of carnival? It is really incredible, incredible how you have been able to do all this, freed from the disaster that befell you!

HENRY IV Yes, you see how it was! The fact is that falling from my horse and striking my head as I did, I was really mad for I know not how long. . . .

DOCTOR Ah! Did it last long?

HENRY IV (*Very quickly to the* DOCTOR) Yes, Doctor, a long time! I think it must have been about twelve years. (*Then suddenly turning to speak to* BELCREDI) Thus I saw nothing, my dear fellow, of all that, after that day of carnival, happened for you but not for me: how things changed, how my friends deceived me, how my place was taken by another, and all the rest of it! And suppose my place had been taken in the heart of the woman I loved? . . . And how should I know who was dead or who had disappeared? . . . All this, you know, wasn't exactly a joke for me, as it seems to you. . . .

BELCREDI No, no! I don't mean that! I mean after . . .

HENRY IV Ah, yes? After? One day—(*Stops and addresses the* DOCTOR) A most interesting case, Doctor! Study me well! Study me carefully! (*Trembles while speaking*) All by itself, who knows how, one day the trouble here (*Touches his forehead*) mended. Little by little, I open my eyes, and at first I don't know whether I am asleep or awake. Then I know I am awake. I touch this thing and that; I see clearly again. . . . Ah!—then, as *he* says (*Alludes to* BELCREDI) away, away with this masquerade, this incubus! Let's open the windows, breathe life once again! Away! Away! Let's run out! (*Suddenly pulling himself up*) But where? And to do what? To show myself to all, secretly, as Henry IV, not like this, but arm in arm with you, among my dear friends?

BELCREDI What are you saying?

DONNA MATILDA Who could think it? It's not to be imagined. It was an accident.

HENRY IV They all said I was mad before. (*To* BELCREDI) And you know it! You were more ferocious than anyone against those who tried to defend me.

BELCREDI Oh, that was only a joke!

HENRY IV Look at my hair! (*Shows him the hair on the nape of his neck*)

BELCREDI But mine is gray too!

HENRY IV Yes, with this difference: that mine went gray here, as Henry IV, do you understand? And I never knew it! I perceived it all of a sudden, one day, when I opened my eyes; and I was terrified because I understood at once that not only had my hair gone gray, but that I was all gray, inside; that everything had fallen to pieces, that everything was finished; and I was going to arrive, hungry as a wolf, at a banquet which had already been cleared away. . . .

BELCREDI Yes, but, what about the others? .

HENRY IV (*Quickly*) Ah, yes, I know! They couldn't wait until I was cured, not even those, who, behind my back, pricked my saddled horse till it bled. . . .

DI NOLLI (*Agitated*) What, what?

HENRY IV Yes, treacherously, to make it rear and cause me to fall.

DONNA MATILDA (*Quickly, in horror*) This is the first time I knew that.

HENRY IV That was also a joke, probably!

DONNA MATILDA But who did it? Who was behind us, then?

HENRY IV It doesn't matter who it was. All those that went on feasting and were ready to leave me their scrapings, Marchioness, of miserable pity, or some dirty remnant of remorse in the filthy plate! Thanks! (*Turning quickly to the* DOCTOR) Now, Doctor, the case must be absolutely new in the history of madness; I preferred to remain mad—since I found everything ready and at my disposal for this new exquisite fantasy. I would live it—this madness of mine—with the most lucid consciousness; and thus revenge myself on the brutality of a stone which had dented my head. The solitude—this solitude—squalid and empty as it appeared to me when I opened my eyes again—I determined to deck it out with all the colors and splendors of that far off day of carnival, when you (*Looks at* DONNA MATILDA *and points* FRIDA *out to her*)— when you, Marchioness, triumphed. So I would oblige all those who were around me to follow, by God, at my orders that famous pageant which had been—for you

and not for me—the jest of a day. I would make it become—forever—no more a joke but a reality, the reality of a real madness: here, all in masquerade, with throne room, and these my four secret counselors: secret and, of course, traitors. (*He turns quickly toward them*) I should like to know what you have gained by revealing the fact that I was cured! If I am cured, there's no longer any need of you, and you will be discharged! To give anyone one's confidence . . . that is really the act of a madman. But now I accuse you in my turn. (*Turning to the others*) Do you know? They thought (*Alludes to the others*) they could make fun of me too with you. (*Bursts out laughing. The others laugh, but shamefacedly, except* DONNA MATILDA)

BELCREDI (*To* DI NOLLI) Well, imagine that. . . . That's not bad. . . .

DI NOLLI (*To the four young men*) You?

HENRY IV We must pardon them. This dress (*Plucking his dress*) which is for me the evident, voluntary caricature of that other continuous, everlasting masquerade, of which we are the involuntary puppets (*Indicates* BELCREDI), when without knowing it, we mask ourselves with that which we appear to be . . . ah, that dress of theirs, this masquerade of theirs, of course, we must forgive it them, since they do not yet see it is identical with themselves. . . . (*Turning again to* BELCREDI) You know, it is quite easy to get accustomed to it. One walks about as a tragic character, just as if it were nothing . . . (*Imitates the tragic manner*) in a room like this. . . . Look here, Doctor! I remember a priest, certainly Irish, a nice-looking priest, who was sleeping in the sun one November day, with his arm on the corner of the bench of a public garden. He was lost in the golden delight of the mild sunny air which must have seemed for him almost summery. One may be sure that in that moment he did not know any more that he was a priest, or even where he was. He was dreaming. . . . A little boy passed with a flower in his hand. He touched the priest with it here on the neck. I saw him open his laughing eyes, while all his mouth smiled with the beauty of his dream. He was forgetful of everything. . . . But all at once, he pulled himself together, and stretched out his priest's cassock; and there came back to his eyes the same seriousness which you have seen in mine; because the Irish priests defend the seriousness of their Catholic faith with the same zeal with which I defend the sacred rights of hereditary monarchy! I am cured, gentlemen: because I can act the madman to perfection, here; and I do it very quietly. I'm only sorry for you that have to live your madness so agitatedly, without knowing it or seeing it.

BELCREDI It comes to this, then, that it is we who are mad. That's what it is!

HENRY IV (*Containing his irritation*) But if you weren't mad, both you and she (*Indicating the* MARCHIONESS), would you have come here to see me?

BELCREDI To tell the truth, I came here believing that you were the madman.

HENRY IV (*Suddenly indicating the* MARCHIONESS) And she?

BELCREDI Ah, as for her . . . I can't say. I see she is fascinated by your words, by this *conscious* madness of yours. (*Turns to her*) Dressed as you are (*Speaking to her*), you could even remain here to live it out, Marchioness.

DONNA MATILDA You are insolent!

HENRY IV (*Conciliatingly*) No, Marchioness, what he means to say is that the miracle would be complete, according to him, with you here, who—as the Marchioness of Tuscany, you well know—could not be my friend, save, as at Canossa, to give me a little pity. . . .

BELCREDI Or even more than a little! She said so herself!

HENRY IV (*To the* MARCHIONESS, *continuing*) And even, shall we say, a little remorse! . . .

BELCREDI Yes, that too she has admitted.

DONNA MATILDA (*Angry*) Now look here . . .

HENRY IV (*Quickly, to placate her*) Don't bother about him! Don't mind him! Let him go on infuriating me—though the

Doctor's told him not to. (*Turns to* BELCREDI) But do you suppose I am going to trouble myself any more about what happened between us—the share you had in my misfortune with her (*Indicates the* MARCHIONESS *to him and pointing* BELCREDI *out to her*), the part he has now in your life? This is my life! Quite a different thing from your life! Your life, the life in which you have grown old—I have not lived that life. (*To* DONNA MATILDA) Was this what you wanted to show me with this sacrifice of yours, dressing yourself up like this, according to the Doctor's idea? Excellently done, Doctor! Oh, an excellent idea: "As we were then, eh? and as we are now?" But I am not a madman according to your way of thinking, Doctor. I know very well that that man there (*Indicates* DI NOLLI) cannot be me; because I am Henry IV, and have been, these twenty years, cast in this eternal masquerade. She has lived these years! (*Indicates the* MARCHIONESS) She has enjoyed them and has become—look at her!—a woman I can no longer recognize. It is so that I knew her! (*Points to* FRIDA *and draws near her*) This is the Marchioness I know, always this one! . . . You seem a lot of children to be so easily frightened by me. . . . (*To* FRIDA) And you're frightened too, little girl, aren't you, by the jest that they made you take part in—though they didn't understand it wouldn't be the jest they meant it to be, for me? Oh miracle of miracles! Prodigy of prodigies! The dream alive in you! More than ever, alive in you! It was an image that wavered there and they've made you come to life! Oh, mine! You're mine, mine, mine in my own right! (*He holds her in his arms, laughing like a madman, while all stand still terrified. Then as they advance to tear* FRIDA *from his arms, he becomes furious, terrible, and cries imperiously to his* VALETS) Hold them! Hold them! I order you to hold them!

(*The four young men amazed, yet fascinated, move to execute his orders, automatically, and seize* DI NOLLI, *the* DOCTOR, *and* BELCREDI)

BELCREDI (*Freeing himself*) Leave her alone! Leave her alone! You're no madman!

HENRY IV (*In a flash, draws the sword from the side of* LANDOLPH, *who is close to him*) I'm not mad, eh! Take that, you! . . . (*Drives sword into him. A cry of horror follows. All rush over to assist* BELCREDI, *crying out together*)

DI NOLLI Has he wounded you?

BERTHOLD Yes, yes, seriously!

DOCTOR I told you so!

FRIDA Oh God, oh God!

DI NOLLI Frida, come here!

DONNA MATILDA He's mad, mad!

DI NOLLI Hold him!

BELCREDI (*While they take him away by the left exit, he protests as he is borne out*) No, no, you're not mad! You're not mad. He's not mad!

(*They go out by the left amid cries and excitement. After a moment, one hears a still sharper, more piercing cry from* DONNA MATILDA, *and then, silence*)

HENRY IV (*Who has remained on the stage between* LANDOLPH, HAROLD, *and* ORDULPH, *with his eyes almost starting out of his head, terrified by the life of his own masquerade which has driven him to crime*) Now, yes . . . we'll have to . . . (*Calls his* VALETS *around him as if to protect him*) Here we are . . . together . . . forever!

Curtain

Part Four

NEW DEPARTURES

Everyone, we have said, knows what a comedy is; it can also be claimed that everyone has at least a general feeling of how a tragedy differs from a comedy. The road signs appear early in each mode to indicate which destination we are headed for, success or catastrophe; and the road signs have been appearing thus early for twenty-five hundred years. We have learned, as a result, to read them so well, and with such confidence, that even when a dramatist like Shakespeare deliberately detours from a tragic destination into a passing comic episode, we do not lose our way. Tragicomedy presents no serious problems of response.

Of course, comedy and tragedy and tragicomedy do not exhaust the possibilities of dramatic types. In fact, because plays like Ibsen's *A Doll's House* (1879) seemed to be neither comedy nor tragedy (nor tragicomedy), his contemporaries, seeking the reassurance of categories, created a new one—the "problem play"—with which to contain them. That phrase has remained current, and the "problem play" has almost gained the status of a fourth mode. However inadequate that phrase is as a description of a particular kind of drama (is *Lysistrata* a play *without* a problem, or is *Lear*?), the kind of play it designates presents no more obstacles to immediate response than does tragicomedy. That is, if on the one hand tragicomedy has always been recognized as a mixed mode, still the elements in the mixture remained always clearly separable; one still distinguished in general the comic element from the tragic. And if, on the other, the problem play was felt to be, in ways not very clearly defined, different from both comedy and tragedy, still it dealt with a world evidently coherent, and it compelled responses similar to those accorded the "purer" modes; the audience still differentiated the serious from the comic. And despite the achievements of Shakespeare and Ibsen and their followers, playwrights and critics have long continued to assume that comedies and tragedies were separate and equally viable kinds of plays.

For the avant-garde of our century, however, the making of these basic distinctions no longer seems valuable, or even, perhaps, possible, and the plays they have written and are now writing reveal ambiguities far more critical than those that troubled Ibsen's age or Shakespeare's. Between the two world wars, the plays of Pirandello and Bertolt Brecht, among others, exploited dramatic situations which even to Ibsen would have appeared tragic or at least obviously painful. But as these later men handled such situations, the pain is often shot so full of laughter that any clear distinction between categories is difficult to make. The question is no longer merely that of tragic tension relieved by comic detonation (nor of tragic effect heightened by comic offset), nor even that of a hybrid type of play that in a measure turns its back on both "pure" modes in favor of exploring social problems. For the avant-garde proclaim (and there is much evidence to support them) that they have brought off a revolution: they are less concerned with further modifications of existing modes than with the considered creation of new ones—new ones that will be commensurate with man's altered view of himself at midcentury. For the midcentury audience in the theater, this revolution produces frequent bewilderment, because what chiefly characterizes this new drama is an interpenetration of the tragic by the comic, of the comic by the tragic, so radical that the familiar features of both have been altered almost beyond recognition.

The essays that follow seek to explain in some detail what has happened. Briefly put, this is that moderns like Pirandello and Brecht, together with such contemporaries of ours as Samuel Beckett, Eugène Ionesco, and Edward Albee, have come up against one of the recurring dilemmas of cultural history: new wine cannot in fact be poured into old bottles. Brecht's and Ionesco's wine is new indeed, and so explosive that it would shatter the literary vessels that might otherwise have contained it: comedy and tragedy. The older modes, to change the metaphor, have been stood on their heads; or, more drastically still, they have been—as the title of the essay by Ellen Douglass Leyburn indicates—transposed and thoroughly confused. Hence Ionesco calls *The Chairs* "a tragic farce." Hence we are asked to laugh at plays which on reflection strike us as more terrible than tragedy, and to weep at plays (like those of Tennessee Williams or Arthur Miller) whose central characters and situations have been the stock in trade for generations of comic writers.

Professor Morse Peckham, in the excerpt from his book *Beyond the Tragic Vision*, takes a further step: he contends that we have outgrown, or at least outlived, comedy and tragedy, which belong to a Western tradition that ends conclusively with the nineteenth century. It is true that the cultural crisis of our time has a long history (Shakespeare and Donne, one may guess, would have understood it). But in our own day, according to Professor Peckham's analysis, the sense of crisis has been sharpened by a focussing on basic cosmological issues; at the same time, because of two world wars and an experiment in genocide, because of the cold war and the emergence of the hot line, it has spread its pall over a growing number of people. God is dead, as Nietzsche wrote in *The Gay Science*, and the news is beginning to filter down to man; as soon as it has done so, man will see the world as without plan or purpose or meaning; he will then see himself and his world as absurd. It is not inconceivable that this recognition may provide a new starting-point for the creation of values.

The assumption of the absurdity of man's midcentury posture has produced what Martin Esslin calls the Theater of the Absurd, and at present Eugène Ionesco is its foremost exponent. His plays project an empty world that is terrifying in its meaninglessness; yet it is also an absurd world in the old commonly accepted meaning of the term: *preposterous, ludicrous, silly.* And being absurd, it compels our immediate laughter—until, that is, we recognize ourselves, as all comedy asks that we do, in the drama's characters. Then we suddenly discover that we inhabit a world that is also tragic but that has somehow gone beyond tragedy.

COMEDY AND TRAGEDY TRANSPOSED

Ellen Douglass Leyburn

The remark of Socrates at the end of the *Symposium* that the genius of tragedy and comedy are the same has usually been taken as a joking paradox meant to round off gaily a night of talking and drinking. Yet its measure of truth has haunted responses to the supreme achievements in drama. The heightening of the tragedy of Lear by the Fool, "who labours to outjest his heart-struck injuries," on the one hand, and the deepening of the comedy of *Le Misanthrope* through the suffering of Alceste, on the other, are enough to make us pause before dismissing the remark of Socrates. Plato's jest, if indeed it be jest, seems nearer to the truth of what we find in postclassical drama than does Aristotle's strict separation of tragedy and comedy.

Nevertheless, we have had the feeling until recently that when we used the terms, we knew at least vaguely what they meant and could be understood by others when we used them to distinguish kinds of drama which were distinct even when they appeared in the same play. The assumption that tragedy is one dramatic mode and comedy another has been the foundation of all the varied and elaborate structures of definition of both genres. And the same assumption persists in the proliferation of analyses of the death of tragedy which have followed Joseph Wood Krutch's lament over the paralysis of tragic power in modern man in his much-quoted chapter called "The Tragic Fallacy," which appeared as long ago as the Twenties and fits the whole thesis of his book *The Modern Temper*. The very force of Krutch's indictment grows from his knowing so clearly what he thinks the demands of tragedy are and wherein modern drama is deficient. This clarity of conviction about the nature of tragedy is equally marked in more recent treatments of the same theme, such as William Van O'Connor's *Climates of Tragedy*, which appeared during the Second World War, and George Steiner's *The Death of Tragedy*, which has appeared still more recently. The same assurance marks criticism of comedy. However varied their definitions, the critics resemble each other in seeming to know what it is they are defining.

What I should like to suggest is that in modern drama comedy has so far invaded tragedy—and tragedy, comedy—that the terms have lost their old distinctness. Whereas comedy has for centuries displayed man's weakness, this now seems to be the function of tragedy—or of drama which is intended to arouse the emotions commonly called tragic, whatever new name we try to find for the plays of Tennessee Williams or Arthur Miller or John Osborne. Whereas tragedy has in earlier eras looked at man in "boundary situations," it is now the comedies of Beckett and Ionesco which show man in extremity; and the equally terrifying plays of Pinter and Duerrenmatt make use of grotesque comedy to reveal the precariousness of life and the condition of man confronted with pervasive evil. Duerrenmatt's note on *The Visit* ends: "*The Visit of the Old Lady* is a wicked play, yet for this very reason it must not be presented wickedly, but most humanely, with sadness, not with anger, but also with humor, for nothing harms this comedy—which ends tragically—more than brutal seriousness." Tragedy and comedy seem to have shifted not only in perspective and in substance, but also in effect. Our responses are almost the reverse of what used to be the conventional attitudes to tragedy and comedy. We resist tragic identification with the miserable characters of most of our serious drama and look at them with the detachment which has hitherto seemed appropriate to critical comedy. Conversely, the comedies that end tragically compel us into a strange and unwilling empathy rather than into comic judgment: in the seemingly odd characters we recognize our most familiar selves, and in their fantastic plights, the very situations in which we are involved.

The dramatists of the absurd are clearly conscious of this interpenetration of tragedy and comedy and deliberately exploit its disturbing imaginative effect. Ionesco makes the illuminating statement: "Personally, I have never understood the distinctions that are made between the comic and the tragic. Since the comic is the intuition of the absurd, it seems to me more hopeless than the tragic. . . . The comic offers no escape . . . the comical is tragic, and the tragedy of man, derisory." Ionesco's assertion is highly characteristic not just of his own attitude, repeatedly expressed in comments on his plays and manifested in the plays themselves, but also of the mood of much of the drama of the absurd besides his own. The writers of serious plays, on the contrary, seem unaware of the intrusion of comic elements into their pathetic worlds. They solemnly present their small characters and seem to demand for them the large emotional response aroused by tragedy. This unawareness confuses the artistic effect of their plays; but it is in itself an impressive demonstration of the pervasiveness of the interpenetration of tragedy and comedy which marks the drama of our time. The shifts in the nature of both tragedy and comedy reflect the convulsion of society and of man's sense of himself which characterizes the world which the dramatists inhabit.

Arthur Miller and Tennessee Williams are perhaps the most striking examples of contemporary dramatists who consider themselves writers of tragedies and yet have produced plays in which the themes and characters resemble those of earlier critical comedy. There are almost as many contradictions as theories among definitions of tragedy; but two criteria which are consistently used by critics with otherwise extremely diverse theories are that tragedy should have a hero with stature enough to make his suffering significant and that its course of action should produce enlightenment. Neither of these criteria is fulfilled, I think, by the plays of Williams and Miller. The protagonists arouse pity, but little admiration and little of the identification necessary for tragic terror; and in the rhythm of the plays the emphasis is largely on passion rather than on purpose and perception. On the other hand, both dramatists focus their plays on the very kind of human weakness which has hitherto been the subject of critical or realistic comedy. The self-deception of their leading characters is of the sort which earlier dramatists have held up to ridicule. It is the anomaly of a pathetic view of characters formerly seen as objects of satire which makes the difficulty for the traditionalist in responding to such plays according to the authors' intentions. The contradictory feelings which the characters evoke seem to me more important than their sheer inadequacy as tragic heroes so much stressed by Krutch and his followers. The discrepancy between expectation and event for such characters lacks the kind of irony which has been thought of as tragic; and of enlightenment there is little or none.

Death of a Salesman and *A Streetcar Named Desire*, each the most successful play of its author, well illustrate all of these points.

It was in answer to the criticism of Willy Loman as a tragic hero that Miller wrote "Tragedy and the Common Man" to serve as introduction to a Viking Press edition of *Death of a Salesman*. His contention is that "the common man is as apt a subject for tragedy in its highest sense as kings were," a judgment with which in our day few would quarrel. It is not Willy's low station, but his low intelligence (or if intelligence seems too narrow a word, his lack of sheer force of being) which keeps his woes from affecting us as do those of Orestes, Hamlet, Medea, and Macbeth—the tragic figures of the past whom Miller cites. "Ineffectual" is the word which seems to characterize Willy both as salesman and as father. His constant need of bolstering from both Linda and Charley and his pitiful efforts to win the respect of Biff in order to feed his own self-esteem make it strange for Miller to say in reference to him that "the tragic hero is intent upon claiming his whole due as a personality," though Willy's personality is so small that the comment has a kind of unintentional irony. Even apart from the hallucinated scenes with Ben and the suggestions of actual insanity, Willy's characteristic state is bewilderment. He enters the play puzzled by his fruitless effort to reach his territory, and he leaves it persuading himself that Biff will be "magnificent . . . with twenty thousand dollars in his pocket." The lack of integrity which has made him teach Biff to steal seems to be the result of inability to distinguish truth from falsehood rather than of deliberate dishonesty. Biff, who for all his limitations comes much nearer to self-realization than his father does, tries to open Willy's eyes: "The man don't know who we are! The man is gonna know! (*To Willy*) We never told the truth for ten minutes in this house! . . . Pop! I'm a dime a dozen, and so are you!" But Biff's tears simply send Willy into a new "phony dream"; and the son's comment at his father's grave is: "Charley, the man didn't know who he was." This hardly fits Miller's conception of tragedy as

"a man's total compulsion to evaluate himself justly." Rather, Willy's self-deception, although Miller treats it so as to win compassion, is of exactly the sort which has regularly marked the comic figure. Even his physical defects of fatness and flabbiness which make the salesman laugh at him and call him "walrus" and his loudmouthed over-heartiness of manner identify him with a long line of aging comic butts who have tried to convince an unbelieving world and themselves that they are "well liked." It is worth notice in passing that *A View from the Bridge* again depicts a man past middle age who has no power to "evaluate himself justly" and that in the later play sexual jealousy over a young girl brings the pathetic protagonist even nearer to one of the stereotypes of comedy.

The counterpart to the amorous old fool in traditional comedy has been the woman who tries to trade upon fading sexual attractiveness; and it is this formula which Williams transmutes into the heartrending character of Blanche DuBois. Like Willy, she seeks and is given bolstering from the other characters; and Stella, like Linda in *Salesman*, not only gives the needed compliments but urges the other characters to tell Blanche how pretty her finery is and how fresh and attractive she looks. But Williams is more willing than Miller is to let harsh judgment of his weakling have expression in the play. Willy hears the voice of reality largely through the kindly tones of Charley, who does tell him to grow up, but endures his insults and gives him money under the fiction of weekly loans, whereas Blanche has to listen to the taunts of Stella's husband, whom she regards as "subhuman." Miller depends primarily on Willy's own self-revelation to show the audience the discrepancies between Willy as he is and Willy as he thinks he is. Williams, in contrast, uses the harsh judgment of Stanley not only to add to Blanche's misery, but also to enlighten the audience about her "lies and conceit and tricks." The conflict between the dream and the grim reality is thus accentuated through the hostility of the character who reveals the ugly truth. By giving Blanche a personal antagonist when she is already incapable of coping with her inner plight and has "run for protection . . . from under one leaky roof to another leaky roof—because it was storm—all storm, and [she] was—caught in the center," Williams intensifies her woe and provides the bitter irony of her seeking shelter under the roof of her sharpest critic. At the same time, the audience is made to see her partly through Stanley's eyes. He becomes a kind of satiric chorus within the play, which heightens the anomaly of our being asked to respond with tragic emotions to so wretched a figure as Blanche. But Stanley is far more than simply an interpreter. It is he who, through his cruel disillusioning of Mitch, makes Blanche lose what tenuous hold on reality she has had and brings about her final desolate departure to the mental hospital, still trying to enact the part of the gracious lady, depending on "the kindness of strangers."

Both of these plays are full of irony, even of the irony of fate; but we miss the grandeur which pits the tragic hero against his fate and leads to tragic irony. There is a strong element of the ludicrous which makes the plights of both Willy and Blanche more painful. Fate, in the form of the social order, does seem to have played a cruel joke on the simple-minded and well-meaning Willy Loman in giving him the false goals of success through personality and of getting away with whatever can be filched. In his refusal to be enlightened by Biff, he does seem to go off to his useless suicide as the dupe of a power he cannot combat. Blanche is equally the victim of a hideous practical joke. She is ridiculous in her effort to charm the naïve Mitch with her pretense of innocence. And in her case, the fate which finally tricks her takes the very palpable form of Stanley, though the state to which she has been reduced before the play begins can be called a joke played on her by fate in the form of the social order, just as society has largely represented fate for Willy. But both are too weak to achieve a tragic protest. Since they are simply victims, the irony leaves us uncomfortable at the advantage

taken of weakness rather than filled with awe at heroic man confronting mysterious forces within him and without. The ambivalence of the response to both plays comes from the fact that the protagonists are self-deluded enough to seem appropriate objects of mockery; but they are too miserable and too sympathetically viewed by their creators to allow the audience to feel as comic the irony in what happens to them. Consequently, the plays present a seemingly double vision on the part of the playwrights and have a disconcertingly mixed effect.

This kind of apparently unintentional doubleness marks a great number of contemporary plays. It would be easy to link many other soberly treated characters, such as the disagreeable ones of John Osborne or the sentimentalized ones of William Inge, with the traditional figures of critical comedy. The plays of Williams and Miller seem more impressive demonstrations of the penetration of serious drama by comic types only because Williams and Miller seem to make larger tragic claims.

Since the writers of absurd comedy are highly conscious of the doubleness of their plays and use it with full artistic awareness and often with great artistic skill, their plays are much more profoundly disturbing than are those of the humorless writers of serious plays with weak heroes. The contradictions of pain and amusement in the best comedies of the absurd are evoked with clear intention and the most deliberate finesse. Ionesco is the playwright who has been most explicit about his conception of the theatre as the mirror of the contradictions of life: "I try to project on the stage my inner conflict (incomprehensible to myself) telling myself always that, the microcosm being the image of the macrocosm, it can be that this interior world, broken, disarticulated, is in some way the mirror or the symbol of universal contradictions." It is the absurdity, the tragic comedy, of life itself of which these dramatists seek to make their plays the image. The surface effect of most of their plays is comic; but the vision which informs it is largely tragic. Martin Esslin in *The Theatre of the Absurd* quotes Pinter's comment: "The point about tragedy is that it is *no longer* funny." The writers of the "funny" plays of our time are concerned with the same ultimate questions about man's identity and his destiny which in earlier periods have led to the writing of tragedy. One after another of the plays of Beckett and Ionesco, of Pinter and Duerrenmatt, show man in extremity and posing ultimate questions about his very existence: who he is, why he lives, and why he suffers. Yet these plays which reach no comic resolution and raise ultimate rather than temporal questions are clearly comic in the sense of being outrageously funny. The farcical element in the dramaturgy, with its dependence on mime and music-hall slapstick devices, has been much discussed. My concern here is not with the arts the playwrights use to evoke laughter; but with the fact that the plays do evoke it and use it exactly to sharpen the terror. Comedy is an essential part of the situations presented and makes their desperateness more real. The seemingly meaningless repetitions of the dialogue—as skilful a use of language as the most florid passages in heroic drama, the clowning and dependence on farcical gesture, the monopolizing of the stage by objects, bear an organic relation to the absurd situations and are the very means by which the dramatists produce the feeling (to quote Ionesco again) that "in a space without space, all seems to be volatilized, all is *menaced* [my italics] . . . by an imminent, silent engulfment, in I know not what abyss, beyond day and beyond night." The plays as wholes present comic incongruity raised to tragic proportions and effecting in the audience tragic involvement and the tragic feelings of pity and terror. Because of the intense reality of these dramas and because they do raise more fundamental questions, the mixture of feelings they produce is nearer to the old tragic emotion than that of contemporary plays of solely tragic intention. Again, two very familiar plays offer proof of all the points suggested. *Waiting for Godot* and *The Chairs* are both funny and terrible.

The two tramps in Beckett's play are preoccupied with the question which confronts all men and has lately been asked more insistently perhaps than ever before: why live at all? Indeed, their recurrent attempts at suicide make one of the unifying repetitions in the circular motion of the play, if their painfully funny frustrations of action can be called motion. They debate the question of *The Myth of Sisyphus* and seem to stumble upon a measure of Camus's answer. For if they do not decide to live and protest, their very persistence in waiting constitutes a kind of protest. They differ from Camus, of course, in not being sure that Godot will *not* come in spite of their continually baffled hopes. This refusal quite to accept the logic of their own experience is part of what makes us enter into their situation with the kind of identification we accord to tragic characters. It does not require the constant reminders Beckett puts into their mouths that "We are all humanity," to make us recognize ourselves in their already battered state and in the beatings and subjection to physical infirmity within the play. We are drawn to them not just by their clowning and by our amusement at the brisk turns of stichomythia with which they try to amuse themselves. They are irresistibly appealing in their uneasy need of each other, in their very endurance of what we must endure. And we give them the kind of empathy which we withhold from Willy Loman and Blanche DuBois.

The old couple in *The Chairs* ask the still more elementary question of who we are. They show man not just at the limits of his being as man, but beyond identity; and yet in their need to affirm their identity, to leave some message, they too compel us to ally ourselves with them. The frenzy of their attempts to establish connection with the "real" invisible characters and their being crowded apart even from each other by the oppressive multiplication of chairs make vivid their inability to exist even before their suicide in the dank waters that surround their island. Their own progressive loss of the power of articulate speech and the inane babblings of the dumb orator whom they leave as their surrogate are the audible counterpart of the visual image. The laughter which Ionesco evokes by the farcical movement and by the ridiculous echoing "orphan-dworfan" speech, which finally becomes the "Arf . . . arf . . . arf" of helpless barking, makes the tragic effect much deeper than could a direct appeal to the pity and terror in which the search for identity involves us.

The shifting of ground in the realms of tragedy and comedy poses for contemporary critics an awkward problem of terminology. The old phrases like "mixed drama" and "tragicomedy," which sufficed to describe the combination in one play of known and recognizable modes, have little relevance to the strange new genres which seem to be evolving. Furthermore, while the serious plays with weak characters and the comic plays which move us tragically seem to be opposite and complementary parts of the same phenomenon, the dramatic rendering of the dislocation of our times, they are so different in substance and in effect that no one term could conceivably embrace both.

The rather cumbersome phrase "Theatre of the Absurd," to which Esslin's book with that title has given wider currency, is useful for the funny plays of tragic import; *The Dark Comedy*, the title of the valuable study by J. L. Styan, which has appeared since this essay was first written, supplies another usable designation; but no new term seems to have been invented for the corresponding and opposite kind of plays which treat ridiculous characters pathetically. As we grope toward nomenclature and definition (a groping perhaps not unrelated to the struggles of Ionesco's characters with language) we come back broodingly to Plato's joke at the end of the *Symposium:* "the chief thing which he remembered was Socrates compelling the other two to acknowledge that the genius of comedy was the same with that of tragedy, and that the true artist in tragedy was an artist in comedy also. To this they were constrained to assent, being drowsy, and not quite following the argument."

BEYOND TRAGEDY

Morse Peckham

O Mensch! Gib acht!
Was spricht die tiefe Mitternacht?
"Ich schlief, ich schlief—,
Aus tiefem Traum bin ich erwacht:—
Die Welt ist tief,
Und tiefer als der Tag gedacht.
Tief ist ihr Weh—,
Lust—tiefer noch als Herzeleid;
Weh spricht: Vergeh!
Doch alle Lust will Ewigkeit—,
—will tiefe, tiefe Ewigkeit!"

O man! Listen! What does the deep Midnight
urge? "I slept, I slept—, from deep dreaming
I am awakened:—the world is deep, and
deeper than the day has thought. Deep is
the world's woe—, joy—deeper still than
agony; woe urges: Perish! Yet all of joy
wants eternal being, wants deep, deep eternal
being!"

This is the climactic Song of the Midnight
Bell in Part III of *Thus Spoke Zarathustra*,
which Friedrich Nietzsche wrote in his
fortieth year (he was born in 1844). It was
in January, 1884, and Part III was published
later that same year, Parts I and II having
been published at different times in 1883.
The midnight is the voice of the deepest
forces in man, powers below the unconscious mind, below Schopenhauer's will,
even, powers that unite man to the biologi-
cal world, and beyond that to the forces
of the universe.

The midnight, as Nietzsche came to
realize, is the source of the human will to
power, man's drive to dominate, control,
and master his environment, not to adjust
to it, for man cannot adjust to his environment. The effort to adjust is a will to submission, which leads to asceticism, to self-
denial, to the desire to perish. The effort to
adjust must always fail, for between man
and his environment is an eternal disparity;
man's mind is but an instrument of the
midnight powers, and an instrument is
necessarily other than the object it mani-
pulates. Now the midnight is awakened
from the profound slumber into which the
will to submissive adjustment (what in this
book is called the gratification of the
orientative drive) had, throughout human
history, cast it by its magic illusions.

The day, those human powers which make
life fair and beautiful, had known that the
world is deep, and that deep is the world's
sorrow; that is why the day, the beneficent
powers of Apollo, the god of the sun, had
come to man's rescue. But the day had not
known that the world's joy is deeper than
its agony. Man's suffering says to him:
Surrender, submit, give up, die, perish,
vanish. But joy wants eternal being. If there
were such a word, "*Ewigkeit*" would best
be translated "foreverness." "Eternity,"
which is sometimes the word translators use,

is wrong, for in the tradition of the English language it implies, as we have so often seen, something outside of the sensory world we know, something that transcends the reality before us. But by *"Ewigkeit"* Nietzsche means the power to reject the past and ignore the future—both are unrealities—and to live only in the eternal present, satisfying to its profoundest depths the drive toward reality. "Joy is deeper than sorrow"; it is what Mallarmé, Cézanne, and Gauguin were discovering in these same years. Like these artists, Nietzsche too found embodiment or incarnation of value in style, in art, and like them he found identity deeper than the level of personality, for personality is the realm of sorrow; it is also the realm of good and evil, of morality. Nietzsche, like his fellows, had to go beyond good and evil to discover moral responsibility.

Gauguin, in the passage I have quoted from, after he says that one must insult the official, the impressionists, the neo-impressionists, the old public and the new, adds that one must also "no longer have a wife and children who disown you. Of what importance is insult? Of what importance is misery? So much for human conduct . . ." that is, morality as the Philistine knows it. And Gauguin had so perfectly expressed the heart of Nietzsche's thinking when he said that philosophy is not a reality but a weapon, that it seems almost impossible that he had not read the works of the German, who in 1888 could wish that he were writing in French, for cultural vitality, he was convinced, had left Germany—and England too—and was to be found only in France. Yet whether Gauguin had really read Nietzsche or not is of no importance; both men, born only four years apart, were the product of the same cultural forces; but Nietzsche went beyond the point the Frenchman had reached. The mind, Nietzsche realized, can only create weapons, instrumental constructs with which to come to grips with reality. His first transvaluation of all values—the evaluation of everything on a new principle—lay in precisely this realization, that "truths" are but "instruments," including "moral truths." As I suggested

earlier, this is very much the position that Robert Browning was working out in the 1870's and 1880's. But then Nietzsche went beyond that position, and thus he went beyond the Frenchmen. To understand this it is useful to quote a passage near the end of Part IV of *Zarathustra*, which he wrote in 1885. It comes immediately after he has repeated the Song of the Midnight Bell.

> For all joy wants eternal being for all things; it wants honey, the dregs of wine, midnight, graves, the consolation of tears at the graveside, the gilded red of evening. What does joy not want! joy is thirstier, heartier, hungrier, more terrible, more secret than all woe, . . . joy wants love, hate; infinitely rich, joy gives, throws away, begs that someone take, thanks the taker, would like to be hated; so rich is joy that it thirsts for sorrow, for hell, for hate, for shame, for the crippled, for the *world*—and this world! oh, joy knows it well! . . . For joy wants itself; therefore it wants heart's agony. Oh happiness! Oh sorrow! Oh break, heart.

This is the reality which releases the joy that is deeper than sorrow, the world of contradictions that forces the human mind to create an instrumental construct to deal with it. The Frenchmen had seen that value arises when identity creates itself by symbolizing itself in aesthetic structure. But they remained turned away from the world of personality, society, and nature, for there lay the horror. Nietzsche, however, turned back toward the horror, for to him it was neither horror nor beauty. Since it was both hell and heaven, it was neither; it was simply there to be dealt with. And man deals with it not by one transvaluation of all values, but by a continuous transvaluation. A transvaluation creates new values, but these new values must themselves, since they are but instruments, be continually restructured. Hence, when in the 1890's and the first decade of this century, Nietzsche began to be recognized and read, he had a tremendous impact on art. For the artists, Matisse and Picasso, Schönberg and Joyce, the men of the new century, solved a problem the generation of Mallarmé and Gauguin and Debussy had bequeathed. Once the artist has created a style which symbolizes his identity, what does he do with it? It threatens to degenerate into a mannerism; it keeps the artist active, busy, but his identity begins to fade. That happened to Gauguin and to Debussy, and would have happened to Cézanne had not his gigantic mind created an inexhaustible and almost unsolvable problem of aesthetic structure. The new artists, learning from Nietzsche, entered upon careers of continuously transforming their style, and this continuous transformation meant a continuous renewal of identity. It was an endless and ever joyful—witness Matisse in his half-crippled old age, still joyously creating —transvaluation of aesthetic values, for it was a continuously renewed encounter of the structuring mind with reality, the reality of style and the reality of sensory phenomena, (not, once a style has been created, that there is a difference). Abstract art arose to symbolize that inexhaustible, ever-renewing encounter.

Nietzsche discovered that the true dialogue of the mind is not, as Hegel had thought, a dialogue of the mind with itself, the process called the dialectic, but that the true dialectic lies in the eternally transvaluating encounter between the mind's instrumental constructs and reality in, ... a continuous restructuring of orientations. Further, in that dialectic process between reality and the mind's instruments lie identity, order, meaning, and therefore value, constantly being lost as the instruments dull and break on reality's contradictions, and constantly being renewed as the mind forges new instruments—Gauguin's weapons of savages—to renew the struggle to master the world. The world is nothingness; the midnight bell wakes us from that nothingness to struggle with nothingness, and in that struggle we forge, and continuously reforge, our identities. We cannot succeed in that struggle; nor, once the bell has sounded, can we fail. That struggle is a struggle of joy and sorrow, but the joy is deeper than the sorrow; for being, which is the result of that struggle, is, since we are human beings, better than nothingness.

Therefore, the man who has experienced

the development of nineteenth-century culture—and there are very few who yet have —and has emerged where Nietzsche emerged can no longer entertain himself and the public with the tragic vision. He has gone beyond tragedy. Nietzsche found a resolution to the problem of keeping the antinomies, the contraries, the irreconcilable opposites of life, forever apart. Joy wants those opposites. To resolve them is to submit. Hence, Nietzsche created a new concept of tragedy.

> Saying Yes to life even in its strangest and hardest problems, the will to life rejoicing over its own inexhaustibility even in the very sacrifice of its highest types—that is what I call Dionysian [of the midnight] that is what I guessed to be the bridge to the psychology of the *tragic poet*. Not in order to be liberated from terror and pity, not in order to purge oneself of a dangerous affect by its vehement discharge—Aristotle understood it that way—but in order to be *oneself* the eternal joy of becoming, beyond all terror and pity—that joy which includes even joy in destroying.

But this is to use the word "tragic" in such a profoundly new way that no connection between the old meaning and the new survives. We are aware of this when we see our critics fumble with the best of modern drama, Shaw's *Heartbreak House*, for example, Samuel Beckett, or Ionesco. In truth, no truly twentieth-century man can write a tragedy. For twentieth-century man is but a continuation of nineteenth-century man, and Nietzsche's vision has been but sharpened and refined by the existentialists, the logical positivists, and the instrumentalists and operationalists, among whom is P. W. Bridgman, whose recent *The Way Things Are* is a most brilliant, scientific, and satisfying example of the stage of thinking Nietzsche reached. Nor can a truly twentieth-century man write a comedy, either.

Tragedy is supposed to be a profounder vision of human life than comedy, but from the Nietzschean point of view, they are both sentimentalities which man has outgrown. It has been said that tragedy reconciles us to life. Perfectly true. Tragedy is a dramatization of the orientation that man is inadequate to the conditions that life imposes upon us; it shows a great man failing, whether from the ill-will of the gods or from some internal weakness of which he is unaware and for which he cannot, therefore, be held responsible. And therefore tragedy says to us, "If even an Oedipus can fail, if even a Lear can fail, you can forgive yourselves if you fail. Relax!" Hence the discharge of emotional tension which Aristotle so indelicately called "catharsis." In short, tragedy reconciles us to life by persuading us to submit to it. Tragedy encourages what Nietzsche calls the slave-morality of the Philistine. It was by origin, as Nietzsche was one of the first to realize, a religious ritual, and it remains a religious ritual. It consoles us by reinforcing our orientations. Hence, after seeing a tragedy, after seeing murder and incest and the most brutal violations of personality and feeling, we leave the theater with an extraordinary sense of comfort, convinced that all is well with the world. And to tragedy, comedy is complementary. For comedy is a dramatization of the orientation that man is *adequate* to the conditions of experience, that, if he uses his wits, he can triumph over them. Thus the hero of the comedy is not a great man but a very ordinary man, a man like us. Comedy says, "Be consoled. If this very ordinary person can succeed, you can." Both comedy and tragedy reconcile the antinomies, resolve the contradictions, expunge the contraries and the opposites of human experience, the one by saying that they do not exist, the other by saying that it is good and right and just that they should exist.

But Nietzsche, in arriving at the third and, it would seem, the last stage of stylism, at least so far, the continuous renewal of identity by continuous transformation and transvaluation of style in art, in thought, and in individuality, realized that man is neither adequate nor inadequate, that he has grown beyond the old tragic vision, and the old comic vision, that to gratify the orientative drive, man must neither reject the world in the ancient fashion, nor accept it in the Enlightenment fashion. It is neither a world which once held value nor a world which holds value now. From the human point of view, which is all that matters to man, it is without value; nor is there another, transcendental world—Nietzsche was the first to assert roundly that God is dead—from which we descend, or to which we can ascend, or which is the ground of being. The world is without order, without meaning, without value. Human identity has no ground. The world is nothing, but in emerging from that nothingness and in encountering it, we create being. The profoundest satisfaction of the human mind, Nietzsche concluded, is the creation of the world—out of nothingness. From that act of creation emerges the sense of value; and the sense of order, the sense of meaning, and the sense of identity are but our instruments for that act. Joy is deeper than sorrow.

THE ABSURDITY OF THE ABSURD

Martin Esslin

On November 19, 1957, a group of worried actors were preparing to face their audience. The actors were members of the company of the San Francisco Actors' Workshop. The audience consisted of fourteen hundred convicts at the San Quentin penitentiary. No live play had been performed at San Quentin since Sarah Bernhardt appeared there in 1913. Now, forty-four years later, the play that had been chosen, largely because no woman appeared in it, was Samuel Beckett's *Waiting for Godot*.

No wonder the actors and Herbert Blau, the director, were apprehensive. How were they to face one of the toughest audiences in the world with a highly obscure, intellectual play that had produced near riots among a good many highly sophisticated audiences in Western Europe? Herbert Blau decided to prepare the San Quentin audience for what was to come. He stepped onto the stage and addressed the packed, darkened North Dining Hall—a sea of flickering matches that the convicts tossed over their shoulders after lighting their cigarettes. Blau compared the play to a piece of jazz music "to which one must listen for whatever one may find in it." In the same way, he hoped, there would be some meaning, some personal significance for each member of the audience in *Waiting for Godot*.

The curtain parted. The play began. And

what had bewildered the sophisticated audiences of Paris, London, and New York was immediately grasped by an audience of convicts. As the writer of "Memos of a First-Nighter" put it in the columns of the prison paper, the *San Quentin News:*

> The trio of muscle-men, biceps overflowing, who parked all 642 lbs on the aisle and waited for the girls and funny stuff. When this didn't appear they audibly fumed and audibly decided to wait until the house lights dimmed before escaping. They made one error. They listened and looked two minutes too long—and stayed. Left at the end. All shook ...

Or as the writer of the lead story of the same paper reported, under the headline, "San Francisco Group Leaves S.Q. Audience Waiting for Godot":

> From the moment Robin Wagner's thoughtful and limbolike set was dressed with light, until the last futile and expectant handclasp was hesitantly activated between the two searching vagrants, the San Francisco company had its audience of captives in its collective hand. ... Those that had felt a less controversial vehicle should be attempted as a first play here had their fears allayed a short five minutes after the Samuel Beckett piece began to unfold.

A reporter from the San Francisco *Chronicle* who was present noted that the convicts did not find it difficult to understand the play. One prisoner told him, "Godot is society." Said another: "He's the outside." A teacher at the prison was quoted as saying, "They know what is meant by waiting . . . and they knew if Godot finally came, he would only be a disappointment." The leading article of the prison paper showed how clearly the writer had understood the meaning of the play:

> It was an expression, symbolic in order to avoid all personal error, by an author who expected each member of his audience to draw his own conclusions, make his own errors. It asked nothing in point, it forced no dramatized moral on the viewer, it held out no specific hope. . . . We're still waiting for Godot, and shall continue to wait. When the scenery gets too drab and the action too slow, we'll call each other names and swear to part forever—but then, there's no place to go!

It is said that Godot himself, as well as turns of phrase and characters from the play, have since become a permanent part of the private language, the institutional mythology of San Quentin.

Why did a play of the supposedly esoteric avant-garde make so immediate and so deep an impact on an audience of convicts? Because it confronted them with a situation in some ways analogous to their own? Perhaps. Or perhaps because they were unsophisticated enough to come to the theater without any preconceived notions and ready-made expectations, so that they avoided the mistake that trapped so many established critics who condemned the play for its lack of plot, development, characterization, suspense, or plain common sense. Certainly the prisoners of San Quentin could not be suspected of the sin of intellectual snobbery, for which a sizable proportion of the audiences of *Waiting for Godot* have often been reproached; of pretending to like a play they did not even begin to understand, just to appear in the know.

The reception of *Waiting for Godot* at San Quentin, and the wide acclaim plays by Ionesco, Adamov, Pinter, and others have received, testify that these plays, which are so often superciliously dismissed as nonsense or mystification, *have* something to say and *can* be understood. Most of the incomprehension with which plays of this type are still being received by critics and theatrical reviewers, most of the bewilderment they have caused and to which they still give rise, come from the fact that they are part of a new, and still developing, stage convention that has not yet been generally understood and has hardly ever been defined. Inevitably, plays written in this new convention will, when judged by the standards and criteria of another, be regarded as impertinent and outrageous impostures. If a good play must have a cleverly constructed story, these have no story or plot to speak of; if a good play is judged by subtlety of characterization and motivation, these are often without recognizable characters and present the audience with almost mechanical puppets; if a good play has to have a fully explained theme, which is neatly exposed and finally solved, these often have neither a beginning nor an end; if a good play is to hold the mirror up to nature and portray the manners and mannerisms of the age in finely observed sketches, these seem often to be reflections of dreams and nightmares; if a good play relies on witty repartee and pointed dialogue, these often consist of incoherent babblings.

But the plays we are concerned with here pursue ends quite different from those of the conventional play and therefore use quite different methods. They can be judged only by the standards of the theater of the absurd, which it is the purpose of this book to define and clarify.

It must be stressed, however, that the dramatists whose work is here presented and discussed under the generic heading of the theater of the absurd do not form part of any self-proclaimed or self-conscious school or movement. On the contrary, each of the writers in question is an individual who regards himself as a lone outsider, cut off and isolated in his private world. Each has his own personal approach to both subject matter and form; his own roots, sources, and background. If they also, very clearly and in spite of themselves, have a good deal in common, it is because their work most sensitively mirrors and reflects the preoccupations and anxieties, the emotions and thinking of an important segment of their contemporaries in the Western world.

This is not to say that their works are representative of mass attitudes. It is an oversimplification to assume that any age presents a homogeneous pattern. Ours being, more than most others, an age of transition, it displays a bewilderingly stratified picture: medieval beliefs still held and overlaid by eighteenth-century rationalism and mid-nineteenth-century Marxism, rocked by sudden volcanic eruptions of prehistoric fanaticisms and primitive tribal cults. Each of these components of the cultural pattern of the age finds its characteristic artistic expression. The theater of the absurd, however, can be seen as the reflection of what seems the attitude most genuinely representative of our own time's contribution.

The hallmark of this attitude is its sense that the certitudes and unshakable basic assumptions of former ages have been swept away, that they have been tested and found wanting, that they have been discredited as cheap and somewhat childish illusions. The decline of religious faith was masked until the end of World War II by the substitute religions of faith in progress, nationalism, and various totalitarian fallacies. All this was shattered by the war. By 1942, Albert Camus was calmly putting the question why, since life had lost all meaning, man should not seek escape in suicide. In one of the great, seminal heart-searchings of our time, *The Myth of Sisyphus*, Camus tried to diagnose the human situation in a world of shattered beliefs:

> A world that can be explained by reasoning, however faulty, is a familiar world. But in a universe that is suddenly deprived of illusions and of light, man feels a stranger. His is an irremediable exile, because he is deprived of memories of a lost homeland as much as he lacks the hope of a promised land to come. This divorce between man and his life, the actor and his setting, truly constitutes the feeling of Absurdity.

"Absurd" originally means "out of harmony," in a musical context. Hence its dictionary definition: "out of harmony with reason or propriety; incongruous, unreasonable, illogical." In common usage in the English-speaking world, "absurd" may simply mean "ridiculous." But this is not the sense in which Camus uses the word, and in which it is used when we speak of the theater of the absurd. In an essay on Kafka, Ionesco defined his understanding of the term as follows: "Absurd is that which is devoid of purpose.... Cut off from his religious, metaphysical, and transcendental roots, man is lost; all his actions become senseless, absurd, useless."

This sense of metaphysical anguish at the absurdity of the human condition is, broadly speaking, the theme of the plays of Beckett, Adamov, Ionesco, Genet, and the other writers [of theater of the absurd]. But it is not merely the subject matter that defines what is here called the theater of the absurd. A similar sense of the senselessness of life, of the inevitable devaluation of ideals, purity, and purpose, is also the theme of much of the work of dramatists like Giraudoux, Anouilh, Salacrou, Sartre, and Camus himself. Yet these writers differ from the dramatists of the absurd in an important respect: They present their sense of the irrationality of the human condition in the form of highly lucid and logically constructed reasoning, while the theater of the absurd strives to express its sense of the senselessness of the human condition and the inadequacy of the rational approach by the open abandonment of rational devices and discursive thought. While Sartre or Camus express the new content in the old convention, the theater of the absurd goes a step further in trying to achieve a unity between its basic assumptions and the form in which these are expressed. In some senses, the *theater* of Sartre and Camus is less adequate as an expression of the *philosophy* of Sartre and Camus—in artistic, as distinct from philosophic, terms—than the theater of the absurd.

If Camus argues that in our disillusioned age the world has ceased to make sense, he does so in the elegantly rationalistic and discursive style of an eighteenth-century moralist, in well-constructed and polished plays. If Sartre argues that existence comes before essence and that human personality can be reduced to pure potentiality and the freedom to choose itself anew at any moment, he presents his ideas in plays based on brilliantly drawn characters who remain wholly consistent and thus reflect the old convention that each human being has a core of immutable, unchanging essence—in fact, an immortal soul. And the beautiful phrasing and argumentative brilliance of both Sartre and Camus in their relentless probing still, by implication, proclaim a tacit conviction that logical discourse can offer valid solutions, that the analysis of language will lead to the uncovering of basic concepts—Platonic ideas.

This is an inner contradiction that the dramatists of the absurd are trying, by instinct and intuition rather than by conscious effort, to overcome and resolve. The theater of the absurd has renounced arguing *about* the absurdity of the human condition; it merely *presents* it in being—that is, in terms of concrete stage images of the absurdity of existence. This is the difference between the approach of the philosopher and that of the poet; the difference, to take an example from another sphere, between the *idea* of God in the works of Thomas Aquinas or Spinoza and the *intuition* of God in those of St. John of the Cross or Meister Eckhart—the difference between theory and experience.

It is this striving for an integration between the subject matter and the form in which it is expressed that separates the theater of the absurd from the existentialist theater.

The theater of the absurd must also be distinguished from another important, and parallel, trend in the contemporary French theater, which is equally preoccupied with the absurdity and uncertainty of the human condition: the "poetic avant-garde" theater of dramatists like Michel de Ghelderode, Jacques Audiberti, Georges Neveux, and, in the younger generation, Georges Schehadé,

Henri Pichette, and Jean Vauthier, to name only some of its most important exponents. This is an even more difficult dividing line to draw, for the two approaches overlap a good deal. The "poetic avant-garde" relies on fantasy and dream reality as much as the theater of the absurd does; it also disregards such traditional axioms as that of the basic unity and consistency of each character or the need for a plot. Yet basically the "poetic avant-garde" represents a different mood; it is more lyrical, and far less violent and grotesque. Even more important is its different attitude toward language: the "poetic avant-garde" relies to a far greater extent on consciously "poetic" speech; it aspires to plays that are in effect poems, images composed of a rich web of verbal associations.

The theater of the absurd, on the other hand, tends toward a radical devaluation of language, toward a poetry that is to emerge from the concrete and objectified images of the stage itself. The element of language still plays an important, yet subordinate, part in this conception, but what *happens* on the stage transcends, and often contradicts, the *words* spoken by the characters. In Ionesco's *The Chairs*, for example, the poetic content of a powerfully poetic play does not lie in the banal words that are uttered but in the fact that they are spoken to an ever-growing number of empty chairs.

The theater of the absurd is thus part of the "antiliterary" movement of our time, which has found its expression in abstract painting, with its rejection of "literary" elements in pictures; or in the "new novel" in France, with its reliance on the description of objects and its rejection of empathy and anthropomorphism. It is no coincidence that, like all these movements and so many of the efforts to create new forms of expression in all the arts, the theater of the absurd should be centered in Paris.

This does not mean that the theater of the absurd is essentially French. It is broadly based on ancient strands of the Western tradition and has its exponents in Britain, Spain, Italy, Germany, Switzerland, and the United States as well as in France.

Moreover, its leading practitioners who live in Paris and write in French are not themselves Frenchmen.

As a powerhouse of the modern movement, Paris is an international rather than a merely French center: it acts as a magnet attracting artists of all nationalities who are in search of freedom to work and to live nonconformist lives unhampered by the need to look over their shoulder to see, whether their neighbors are shocked. That is the secret of Paris as the capital of the world's individualists: Here, in a world of cafés and small hotels, it is possible to live easily and unmolested.

That is why a cosmopolitan of uncertain origin like Apollinaire; Spaniards like Picasso or Juan Gris; Russians like Kandinsky and Chagall; Rumanians like Tzara and Brancusi; Americans like Gertrude Stein, Hemingway, and E. E. Cummings; an Irishman like Joyce; and many others from the four corners of the world could come together in Paris and shape the modern movement in the arts and literature. The theater of the absurd springs from the same tradition and is nourished from the same roots: An Irishman, Samuel Beckett; a Rumanian, Eugène Ionesco; a Russian of Armenian origin, Arthur Adamov, not only found in Paris the atmosphere that allowed them to experiment in freedom, they also found there the opportunities to get their work produced in theaters.

The standards of staging and production in the smaller theaters of Paris are often criticized as slapdash and perfunctory; that may indeed sometimes be the case; yet the fact remains that there is no other place in the world where so many first-rate men of the theater can be found who are adventurous and intelligent enough to champion the experimental work of new playwrights and to help them acquire a mastery of stage technique—from Lugné-Poë, Copeau, and Dullin to Jean-Louis Barrault, Jean Vilar, Roger Blin, Nicolas Bataille, Jacques Mauclair, Sylvain Dhomme, Jean-Marie Serreau, and a host of others whose names are indissolubly linked with the rise of much that is best in the contemporary theater.

Equally important, Paris also has a highly intelligent theatergoing public, which is receptive, thoughtful, and as able as it is eager to absorb new ideas. Which does not mean that the first productions of some of the more startling manifestations of the theater of the absurd did not provoke hostile demonstrations or, at first, play to empty houses. What matters is that these scandals were the expression of passionate concern and interest, and that even the emptiest houses contained enthusiasts articulate enough to proclaim loudly and effectively the merits of the original experiments they had witnessed.

Yet in spite of these favorable circumstances, inherent in the fertile cultural climate of Paris, the success of the theater of the absurd, achieved within a short span of time, remains one of the most astonishing aspects of this astonishing phenomenon of our age. That plays so strange and puzzling, so clearly devoid of the traditional attractions of the well-made drama, should within less than a decade have reached the stages of the world from Finland to Japan, from Norway to the Argentine, and that they should have stimulated a large body of work in a similar convention, are in themselves powerful and entirely empirical tests of the importance of the theater of the absurd.

The study of this phenomenon as literature, as stage technique, and as a manifestation of the thinking of its age must proceed from the examination of the works themselves. Only then can they be seen as part of an old tradition that may at times have been submerged but one that can be traced back to antiquity, and only after the movement of today has been placed within its historical context can an attempt be made to assess its significance and to establish its importance and the part it has to play within the pattern of contemporary thought.

A public conditioned to an accepted convention tends to receive the impact of artistic experiences through a filter of critical standards, of predetermined expectations and terms of reference, which is the natural result of the schooling of its taste and faculty of perception. This framework of values, admirably efficient in itself, produces only bewildering results when it is faced with a completely new and revolutionary convention—a tug of war ensues between impressions that have undoubtedly been received and critical preconceptions that clearly exclude the possibility that any such impressions could have been felt. Hence the storms of frustration and indignation always caused by works in a new convention.

Questions of biography ought to be irrelevant to the consideration of a work of art; all great works, as E. M. Forster has written, tend toward a state of anonymity. But Bertolt Brecht was an artist who cannot be understood without mention of at least four aspects of his remarkable career. To begin with, he was sixteen when World War I broke out; two years later, while he was studying medicine in Munich, he was called up, and being a medical student he was assigned duties as an orderly in a military hospital. Brecht was already an ardent pacifist, and the effect of his war experience can be described only as traumatic. He was eighteen, and a medical *student*, not a doctor, and yet,

> If the doctor ordered me: "Amputate a leg, Brecht!" I would answer: "Yes, Your Excellency!" and cut off the leg. If I was told: "Make a trepanning!" I opened the man's skull and tinkered with his brains. I saw how they patched people up in order to ship them back to the front as soon as possible.[1]

They in the last sentence refers presumably to his medical superiors, but by extension to all the manipulators who arranged to send patched bodies back into combat. His revulsion to this practice is the subject of an early poem, "The Ballad of the Dead Soldier," in which a corpse is pronounced fit for service, doused with perfume to mask the odor of corruption, and dispatched, goose-stepping, to the front. Brecht was a rebel from childhood on, and in the decade of the twenties, while he worked as drama critic for an Augsburg newspaper, his rebellion was fed by postwar conditions in Germany. It is not surprising that, like many men of his generation (on both sides of the Atlantic), Brecht should have believed that Communism provided a viable answer; and this belief is a second aspect that cannot be avoided. Whether or not he was ever a member of the Party, Brecht was a Marxist, and he dedicated his talent as poet and dramatist to the cause of Communism. Outwardly he never wavered in that allegiance.

But a further aspect of this complex writer is that he was not only a Communist but also an artist, and this dual commitment troubled him throughout his creative life. The nature of the conflict is seen most clearly in the very play (a Lehrstück, or teaching play) with which he had hoped to prescribe the loyalties demanded of the Marxist. It is called *The Measures Taken*, and in writing it the artist characteristically betrayed the Communist; for Brecht as a dramatist could write plays only about people who commanded his interest and sympathy. And *The Measures Taken*, which was intended to teach loyalty to Party above all else, actually begs its own question by asking where the highest loyalty belongs: to a large, nonhuman organization called The Party, or to humanity? The play does not therefore end for all time the question of Party loyalty; instead, it defines the moral dilemma of all Communists. It has been condemned by the Communists themselves. In the greatest of his plays—*Mother Courage*, for example—

---

[1] Quoted in Martin Esslin, *Brecht, The Man and His Work* (Garden City, N. Y.: Doubleday & Company, Inc., 1960), p. 7.

whenever this conflict between artist and propagandist occurs, it is resolved in favor of the artist.

Finally, Brecht's move to Berlin in 1924 brought him into contact with another imaginative rebel in the theater, the producer Erwin Piscator, who was attempting to break the molds of conventional realistic drama by creating an *epic* theater. His aim was to turn to account every theatrical means available—songs, film strips, dance routines, vaudeville sketches, even billboards placed in front of the proscenium on which blatant "messages" could be shown—to impose a left-wing ideology on his audience. His productions were animated lectures; constituting a deliberate break with dramatic realism, they also aimed to destroy the established proclivity of the viewer to identify with what he watches on the stage, by reminding him that he is and should remain *only a critical viewer*. Though Brecht and Piscator differed on fundamental issues, the dramatist nevertheless learned from the producer a flexibility and a variety of dramatic means on which he drew for the rest of his career.

Beyond question the central biographical fact of Brecht's life was the ambivalence of his posture as both Communist and artist: his double commitment is evident in the history of every one of his mature plays. *Mother Courage* (1939) is based on a seventeenth-century picaresque novel by Grimmelshausen, and its setting is the Thirty Years' War (1618–1648) between Catholics and Protestants in northern Europe. Into this setting Brecht introduces his cynical camp-follower, Mother Courage, her daughter Kattrin, and her two sons, Eilif and Swiss Cheese. Mother Courage pursues the troops in her covered wagon, indifferently presiding over her brood of children, and selling the soldiers such necessities of war as shoes and brandy. Brecht intended his title to be taken ironically, and his protagonist to be viewed with disgust as a parasite who survives by war-profiteering. He was therefore angered by the response of the first audience (Zurich, 1941), which insisted, against all Brechtian principle, on identifying with the "heroine," on admiring her courage and resilience in the face of her sufferings and the loss of her three children. Brecht felt that the audience had been carried away by emotion—to him a bourgeois weakness—and had failed to see the real message of the play: that those who profit from war must be made to pay its price. Once again, the dogmatist had been betrayed by the artist; once again, a traditional response had proved too strong for a dramatic theory which takes human nature too little into account. As a dramatic theory, *alienation* possesses inherent interest; but unhappily for the theorist, not even a left-wing audience is willing, apparently, to relinquish the pleasure of identifying with the life on the stage: Brecht's audiences refused to be merely critical. The dramatist was angered but not defeated; he rewrote portions of *Mother Courage* with the aim of hardening the protagonist's character, of placing her at a sufficient distance from the audience to guarantee an "anesthesia of the heart." But following the subsequent Berlin performance of the play, the leading *Communist* critic, Max Schroeder, described Mother Courage as "a humanist saint from the tribe of Niobe and the *mater dolorosa*, who defends the life to which she has given birth with her bared teeth and claws . . ."[2]

Yet despite the failure of the play to deliver its doctrinaire message,

---

[2] Quoted in Esslin, *op. cit.*, p. 230.

Brecht rejected the request of the East Berlin authorities that he make the ending of the play more explicit by giving Mother Courage a "curtain speech" which would clarify the lesson about capitalist aggression and inhuman war-profiteering. Once more the instinct of artistic necessity was both more trustworthy and more powerful than the Marxist commitment; and so the character remains, even with her alterations, spokesman for no group. Instead, she lives, in a rather special sense, an autonomous life of her own. A mass of contradictions, a mixture of the petty, the greedy, and the noble, she transcends the uses Brecht would have made of her.

MOTHER COURAGE

Bertolt Brecht

Translated by
Eric Bentley

MOTHER COURAGE	FIRST SOLDIER
EILIF ⎫	PEASANT
SWISS CHEESE ⎬ *her sons*	SECOND SOLDIER
KATTRIN, *her daughter*	PEASANT WOMAN
RECRUITING OFFICER	SOLDIER, *singing*
SERGEANT	OLD WOMAN
COOK	YOUNG MAN
COMMANDER	SOLDIER
CHAPLAIN	LIEUTENANT
ORDNANCE OFFICER	OLD PEASANT
SERGEANT	FIRST SOLDIER
YVETTE POTTIER	PEASANT WOMAN
ONE EYE	SECOND SOLDIER
SOLDIER	YOUNG PEASANT
COLONEL	
CLERK	
OLDER SOLDIER	THE TIME: 1624–1636
YOUNGER SOLDIER	THE PLACE: *Sweden, Poland, Germany*

PROLOGUE: THE SONG OF MOTHER COURAGE

The wagon of a vivandière.

MOTHER COURAGE *sits on the wagon with her daughter* KATTRIN. *Her sons,* EILIF *and* SWISS CHEESE, *pull the wagon and join in the refrains of the song.* KATTRIN *plays a harmonica.*

Here's Mother Courage and her wagon!
　　Hey, Captain, let them come and buy!
Beer by the keg! Wine by the flagon!
　　Let your men drink before they die!
Sabers and swords are hard to swallow:
　　First you must give them beer to drink.
Then they can face what is to follow—

But let'em swim before they sink!
  Christians, awake! The winter's gone!
  The snows depart, the dead sleep on.
  And though you may not long survive,
  Get out of bed and look alive!
Your men will march till they are dead, sir,
  But cannot fight unless they eat.
The blood they spill for you is red, sir,
  What fires that blood is my red meat.

For meat and soup and jam and jelly
  In this old cart of mine are found:
So fill the hole up in your belly
  Before you fill one underground.
      Christians, awake! The winter's gone!
      The snows depart, the dead sleep on.
      And though you may not long survive,
      Get out of bed and look alive!

I

SPRING, 1624. IN DALARNA, THE SWEDISH KING GUSTAVUS IS RECRUITING FOR
THE CAMPAIGN IN POLAND. THE CANTEEN WOMAN ANNA FIERLING,
COMMONLY KNOWN AS MOTHER COURAGE, LOSES A SON.

Highway outside a town. A TOP SERGEANT *and a* RECRUITING OFFICER *stand shivering.*

RECRUITING OFFICER: How the hell can you line up a squadron in *this* place? You know what I keep thinking about, Sergeant? Suicide. I'm supposed to slap four platoons together by the twelfth—four platoons the Chief's asking for! And they're so friendly around here, I'm scared to sleep nights. Suppose I do get my hands on some character and squint at him so I don't notice he's chicken-breasted and has varicose veins. I get him drunk and relaxed, he signs on the dotted line. I pay for the drinks, he steps outside for a minute. I get a hunch I should follow him to the door, and am I right! Off he's shot like a louse from a scratch. You can't take a man's word any more, Sergeant. There's no loyalty left in the world, no trust, no faith, no sense of honor. I'm losing my confidence in mankind, Sergeant.

SERGEANT: What they could use around here is a good war. What else can you expect with peace running wild all over the place? You know what the trouble with peace is? No organization. And when do you get organization? In a war. Peace is one big waste of equipment. Anything goes, no one gives a damn. See the way they eat? Cheese on rye, bacon on the cheese? Disgusting! How many horses they got in this town? How many young men? Nobody knows! They haven't bothered to count'em! That's peace for you!!! I been places where they haven't had a war in seventy years and you know what? The people can't remember their own names! They don't know who they are! It takes a war to fix that. In a war, everyone registers, everyone's name's on a list. Their shoes are stacked, their corn's in the bag, you count it all up— cattle, men, *et cetera*—and you take it away! That's the story: no organization, no war!

RECRUITING OFFICER: It's the God's truth.

SERGEANT: Course, a war's like every real good deal: hard to get going. But when it's on the road, it's a pisser—everybody's scared off peace—like a crap-shooter that keeps fading to cover his loss. Course, *until* it gets going, they're just as scared off war—afraid to try anything new.

RECRUITING OFFICER: Look, a wagon! Two women and a couple of young punks. Stop 'em, Sergeant. And if there's nothing doing this time, you won't catch *me* freezing my ass in the April wind.

MOTHER COURAGE *enters on her wagon and with her children as in the prologue.*

MOTHER COURAGE: Good day to you, Sergeant.

SERGEANT (*barring the way*): Good day! Who d'you think you are?

MOTHER COURAGE: Tradespeople.

(*She prepares to go.*)

SERGEANT: Halt! Where are you from, riffraff?

EILIF: Second Protestant Regiment!

SERGEANT: Where are your papers?

MOTHER COURAGE: Papers?

SWISS CHEESE: But this is Mother Courage!

SERGEANT: Never heard of her. Where'd she get a name like that?

MOTHER COURAGE: In Riga.

EILIF AND SWISS CHEESE (*reciting together*): They call her Mother Courage because she drove through the bombardment of Riga with fifty loaves of bread in her wagon!

MOTHER COURAGE: They were going moldy, I couldn't help myself.

SERGEANT: No funny business! Where are your papers?

MOTHER COURAGE *rummages among papers in a tin box and clambers down from her wagon.*

MOTHER COURAGE: Here, Sergeant! Here's a whole Bible—I got it in Altötting to wrap my cucumbers in. Here's a map of Moravia—God knows if I'll ever get there. And here's a document saying my horse hasn't got hoof and mouth disease —too bad he died on us, he cost fifteen guilders, thank God I didn't pay it. Is that enough paper?

SERGEANT: Are you making a pass at me? Well, you got another guess coming. You must have a license and you know it.

MOTHER COURAGE: Show a little respect for a lady and don't go telling these grown children of mine I'm making a pass at you. What would I want with you? My license in the Second Protestant Regiment is an honest face—even if *you* wouldn't know how to read it.

RECRUITING OFFICER: Sergeant, we have a case of insubordination on our hands. (*To her:*) Do you know what we need in the army? (MOTHER COURAGE *starts to answer.*) Discipline!

MOTHER COURAGE: I was going to say sausages.

SERGEANT: Name?

MOTHER COURAGE: Anna Fierling.

SERGEANT: So you're all Fierlings.

MOTHER COURAGE: I was talking about me.

SERGEANT: And I was talking about your children.

MOTHER COURAGE: Must they all have the same name? This boy, for instance, I call him Eilif Noyocki—he got the name from his father who told me he was called Koyocki. Or was it Moyocki? Anyhow, the lad remembers him to this day. Only the man he remembers is someone else, a Frenchman with a pointed beard. But he certainly has his father's brains—that man could whip the pants off a farmer's behind before he could turn around. So we all have our own names.

SERGEANT: You're all called something different?

MOTHER COURAGE: Are you pretending you don't get it?

SERGEANT (*pointing at* SWISS CHEESE): He's a Chinese, I suppose.

MOTHER COURAGE: Wrong again. A Swiss.

SERGEANT: After the Frenchman?

MOTHER COURAGE: Frenchman? What Frenchman? Don't confuse the issue, Sergeant, or we'll be here all day. He's a Swiss, but he happens to be called Feyos, a name that has nothing to do with his father, who was called something else—a military engineer, if you please, and a drunkard.

SWISS CHEESE *nods, beaming; even* KATTRIN *smiles.*

SERGEANT: Then how come his name's Feyos?

MOTHER COURAGE: Oh, Sergeant, you have no imagination. *Of course* he's called Feyos: When he came, I was with a Hungarian. He didn't mind. He had a floating kidney, though he never touched a drop. He was a very *honest* man. The boy takes after him.

SERGEANT: But that wasn't his father!

MOTHER COURAGE: I said: he took after him. I call him Swiss Cheese. And that is my daughter Kattrin Haupt, she's half German.

SERGEANT: A nice family, I must say!

MOTHER COURAGE: And we've seen the whole wide world together—this wagon-load and me.

SERGEANT (*writing*): We'll need all that in writing.

RECRUITING OFFICER (*to* EILIF): So you two are the oxen for the wagon? Do they ever let you out of harness?

EILIF: Mother! May I smack him in the puss?

MOTHER COURAGE: You stay where you are. And now, gentlemen, how about a pair of pistols? Or a belt? Sergeant? Yours is worn clean through.

SERGEANT: It's something else *I'm* looking for. These lads of yours are straight as birch-trees. What are such fine specimens doing out of the army?

MOTHER COURAGE (*quickly*): The soldier's life is not for sons of mine!

RECRUITING OFFICER: Why not? It means money. It means fame. Peddling shoes is woman's work. (*To* EILIF:) Step this way and let's see if that's muscle or chicken fat.

MOTHER COURAGE: It's chicken fat. Give him a good hard look, and he'll fall right over.

RECRUITING OFFICER: Well, I hope he doesn't fall on me, that's all. (*He tries to hustle* EILIF *away*.)

MOTHER COURAGE: Let him alone! He's not for you!

RECRUITING OFFICER: He called my face a puss. That is an insult. The two of us will now go settle the affair on the field of honor.

EILIF: Don't worry, Mother, I can handle him.

MOTHER COURAGE: Stay here. You're never happy till you're in a fight. (*To the* OF-FICER:) He has a knife in his boot and he knows how to use it.

RECRUITING OFFICER: I'll draw it out of him like a milk tooth. (*To* EILIF:) Come on, young fellow!

MOTHER COURAGE: Officer, I'll report you to the Colonel, and he'll throw you in jail. His lieutenant is courting my daughter.

SERGEANT (*to* OFFICER): Go easy. (*To* MOTHER COURAGE:) What have you got against the service, wasn't his own father a soldier? Didn't you say he died a soldier's death?

MOTHER COURAGE: He's dead all right. But this one's just a baby. You'll lead him like a lamb to the slaughter. I know you. You'll get five guilders for him.

RECRUITING OFFICER (*to* EILIF): First thing you know, you'll have a new cap and high boots, how about it?

EILIF: Not from you, thanks.

MOTHER COURAGE: "Let's you and me go fishing," said the angler to the worm. (*To* SWISS CHEESE:) Run and tell everybody they're trying to steal your brother! (*She draws a knife.*) Yes, just you try, and I'll cut you down like dogs! We sell cloth, we sell ham, we are peaceful people!

SERGEANT: You're peaceful all right: your knife proves that. Now tell me, how can we have a war without soldiers?

MOTHER COURAGE: Do they have to be mine?

SERGEANT: So that's the trouble! The war should swallow the pits and spit out the peach, huh? Tsk, tsk, tsk: call yourself Mother Courage and then get scared of the war, your breadwinner? Your sons aren't scared, I know that much.

EILIF: No war can scare me.

SERGEANT: Of course not! Take me. The soldier's life hasn't done *me* any harm, has it? I enlisted at seventeen.

MOTHER COURAGE: You haven't reached seventy.

SERGEANT: I will, though.

MOTHER COURAGE: Above ground?

SERGEANT: Are you trying to rile me, telling me I'll die?

MOTHER COURAGE: Suppose it's the truth? Suppose I see it's your fate? Suppose I *know* you're just a corpse on furlough?

SWISS CHEESE: She can look into the future. Everyone says so.

RECRUITING OFFICER: Then by all means look into the Sergeant's future. It might amuse him.

SERGEANT: I don't believe in that stuff.

MOTHER COURAGE (*obeying the* OFFICER): Helmet! (SERGEANT *gives her his helmet.*)

SERGEANT: Anything for a laugh.

MOTHER COURAGE *takes a sheet of parchment and tears it in two.*

MOTHER COURAGE: Eilif, Swiss Cheese, Kattrin! So shall we all be torn asunder if we let ourselves get too deep into this war! (*To the* SERGEANT:) I'll give you the bargain rate, and do it for free. Watch! Death is black, so I draw a black cross.

SWISS CHEESE (*pointing to the second piece of parchment*): And the other she leaves blank, see?

MOTHER COURAGE: I fold them, put them in the helmet, and mix 'em up, the way we're all mixed up from our mother's womb on. Now draw!

RECRUITING OFFICER (*to* EILIF): I don't take just anybody. I'm choosy. And you've got guts, I like that.

SERGEANT (*after hesitating, fishes around in the helmet*): It's a lot of crap!

SWISS CHEESE (*watching over his shoulder*): The black cross! Oh, his number's up!

SERGEANT (*hoarsely*): You cheated me!

MOTHER COURAGE: You cheated yourself the day you enlisted. And now we must drive on. There isn't a war every day in the week.

SERGEANT: Hell, you're not getting away with this! We're taking that bastard of yours with *us*!

EILIF: I'd like that, mother.

MOTHER COURAGE: Quiet—you Finnish devil, you!

EILIF: And Swiss Cheese wants to be a soldier, too.

MOTHER COURAGE: That's news to me. I see I'll have to draw lots for all three of you. (*She goes to one side to do this.*)

RECRUITING OFFICER (*to* EILIF): People've been saying the Swedish soldier is religious. That kind of loose talk has hurt us a lot. One verse of a hymn every Sunday —and then only if you have a voice . . .

MOTHER COURAGE *returns with the slips and puts them in the* SERGEANT'S *helmet.*

MOTHER COURAGE: So they'd desert their old mother, would they, the rascals? They take to war like a cat to cream! Well, there's yours, Eilif, my boy! (*As* EILIF *takes the slip, she snatches it and holds it up.*) See? A cross!

RECRUITING OFFICER (*to* EILIF): If you're going to wet your pants, I'll try your kid brother.

MOTHER COURAGE: Take yours, Swiss Cheese. You should be a better bet—you're my *good* boy. (SWISS CHEESE *draws.*) Don't tell me it's a cross? Is there no saving you either? Just look, Sergeant—a black cross!

SERGEANT: What I don't see is why *I* got one: I always stay well in the rear. (*To the* OFFICER:) It can't be a trick: it gets her own children.

MOTHER COURAGE (*to* KATTRIN): Now all I have left is you. You're a cross in yourself but you have a kind heart. (*She holds the helmet up but takes slip herself.*) Oh dear, there must be some mistake! Don't be too kind, Kattrin, don't be too kind— there's a black cross in your path! So now you all know: be careful! Be very careful! (MOTHER COURAGE *climbs on her wagon, preparing to leave.*)

RECRUITING OFFICER (*to* SERGEANT): Do something!

SERGEANT: I don't feel too good.

RECRUITING OFFICER: Try doing business with her! (*In a loud voice:*) That belt, Sergeant, you could at least take a look at it! Hey, you, the Sergeant will take the belt!

MOTHER COURAGE: Half a guilder. Worth four times the price.

SERGEANT: It's not even a new one. But there's too much wind here. I'll go look at it behind the wagon.

MOTHER COURAGE: It doesn't seem windy to me.

SERGEANT: Maybe it's worth a half guilder at that. There's silver on it.

MOTHER COURAGE (*now following him eagerly behind the wagon*): A solid six ounces worth!

RECRUITING OFFICER (*to* EILIF): I can let you have some cash in advance, how about it? EILIF *hesitates.* MOTHER COURAGE *is behind the wagon.*

MOTHER COURAGE: Half a guilder then. Quick.

SERGEANT: I still don't see why *I* had to draw a cross. As I told you, I always stay in the rear—it's the only place that's safe. You've ruined my afternoon, Mother Courage.

MOTHER COURAGE: You mustn't take on so. Here. Take a shot of brandy. (*He does.*) And go right on staying in the rear. Half a guilder.

The RECRUITING OFFICER *has taken* EILIF *by the arm and drawn him away.*

RECRUITING OFFICER: Ten guilders in advance, and you're a soldier of the king! The women'll be crazy about you, and you can smack me in the puss because I insulted you!

They leave. KATTRIN *makes harsh noises.*

MOTHER COURAGE: Coming, Kattrin, coming! The Sergeant's just paying his bill. (*She bites the half guilder.*) All money is suspect, Sergeant, but your half guilder is good. Let's go. Where's Eilif?

SWISS CHEESE: Gone with the recruiting officer.

Pause.

MOTHER COURAGE: Oh, you simpleton! (*To* KATTRIN:) You can't speak. You *couldn't* tell me.

SERGEANT: That's life, Mother Courage. Take a shot yourself.

MOTHER COURAGE: You must help your brother now, Kattrin.

Brother and sister get into harness together and pull the wagon. They all move off.

SERGEANT (*looking after them*):

When a war gives you all you earn
One day it may claim something in return!

II

IN THE YEARS 1625 AND 1626 MOTHER COURAGE JOURNEYS THROUGH POLAND IN THE BAGGAGE TRAIN OF THE SWEDISH ARMY. SHE MEETS HER BRAVE SON AGAIN BEFORE WALLHOF CASTEL. OF THE SUCCESSFUL SALE OF A CAPON AND GREAT DAYS FOR THE BRAVE SON.

The tent of the Swedish Commander, and the kitchen next to it. Sound of cannon. In the kitchen: MOTHER COURAGE *and the* COOK. *The* COOK *has a Dutch accent.*

COOK: Sixty hellers—for that paltry piece of poultry?

MOTHER COURAGE: Paltry poultry? He's the fattest fowl you ever saw. I could get sixty hellers for him—this Commander can *eat!*

COOK: They're ten hellers a dozen on every street corner.

MOTHER COURAGE: A capon like that on every street corner? With a siege going on and people all skin and bones? Maybe you can find a field rat some place. I said maybe, because we're all out of them too. All right, then, in a siege, my price for this giant capon is fifty hellers.

COOK: *We're* doing the besieging, it's the other side that's "in a siege"!

MOTHER COURAGE: A fat lot of difference that makes—we don't have a thing to eat either. Look at the farmers round here. They haven't a thing.

COOK: Sure they have. They hide it.

MOTHER COURAGE: They haven't a thing! They're ruined. They're so hungry they dig up roots to eat. I could boil that

leather belt of yours and make their mouths water with it. And I'm supposed to let a capon go for forty hellers?

COOK: Thirty. I said thirty hellers.

MOTHER COURAGE: I know *your* problem. If you don't find something to eat and quick, the Commander will cut your fat head off!

COOK: Look! Here's a piece of beef. I am about to roast it. I give you one more chance.

MOTHER COURAGE: Roast it. Go ahead. It's only twelve months old.

COOK: Twelve hours old! Why, only yesterday it was a cow—I saw it running around!

MOTHER COURAGE: Then it must have started stinking before it died.

COOK: I'll cook it five hours if I have to.

MOTHER COURAGE: Put plenty of pepper in.

THE SWEDISH COMMANDER, THE CHAPLAIN, *and* EILIF *enter the tent. The* COMMANDER *claps* EILIF *on the shoulder.*

COMMANDER: In your Commander's tent you go, Eilif, my son, sit at my right hand! Well done, good and faithful servant—you've played the hero in God's own war and you'll get a gold bracelet out of it yet if I have any say in the matter! We come to save their souls and what do they do, the filthy, irreligious sons of bitches? Try to hide their cattle from us—meanwhile stuffing beef into their priests at both ends! But you showed 'em—so here's a can of red wine for you. We'll drink together. (*They do so.*) The chaplain gets the dregs, he's so pious. And now, my hearty, what would you like for dinner?

EILIF: How about a slice of meat?

COOK: Nothing to eat—so he brings company to eat it.

MOTHER COURAGE: Sh!

COMMANDER: Cook! Meat!!

EILIF: Tires you out, skinning peasants. Gives you an appetite.

MOTHER COURAGE: Dear God, it's my Eilif!

COOK: Who?

MOTHER COURAGE: My eldest. It's two years since I saw him. He must be *high* in favor—the Commander inviting him to dinner! And what do you have to eat? Nothing. The Commander's guest wants meat! Take my advice: buy the capon. The price is one hundred hellers.

The COMMANDER *has sat down with* EILIF *and the* CHAPLAIN.

COMMANDER (*roaring*): Dinner, you pig! Or I'll have your head!

COOK: This is blackmail. Give me the damn thing!

MOTHER COURAGE: A paltry piece of poultry like this?

COOK: You were right. Give it here. It's highway robbery, fifty hellers.

MOTHER COURAGE: One hundred hellers. No price is too high for the Commander's guest of honor.

COOK: Well, you might at least pluck the wretched thing till I have a fire going.

MOTHER COURAGE *sits down to pluck the capon.*

MOTHER COURAGE: I can't wait to see his face when he sees me.

COMMANDER: Another glass, my son! It's my favorite Falernian. There's only one keg left but it's worth it to meet a soldier that still believes in God! Our chaplain here only preaches. He hasn't a clue how things get done. So now, Eilif my boy,

tell us how you fixed the peasants and grabbed the twenty bullocks.

EILIF: It was like this. I found out the peasants had hidden the oxen in a certain wood. The people from the town were to pick them up there. So I let them go for their oxen in peace—they should know better than me where they are, I said to myself. Meanwhile I made my men crazy for meat. Their rations were short already. I made sure they got shorter. Finally, their mouths would water at the sound of *any* word beginning with M—like mother.

COMMANDER: Smart kid!

EILIF: Not bad. The rest was a snap. Only the peasants had clubs—and outnumbered us three to one. They made a murderous attack on us. Four of them drove me into a clump of trees, knocked my sword from my hand, and screamed: Surrender! What now? I said to myself, they'll make mincemeat of me.

COMMANDER: So what did you do?

EILIF: I laughed.

COMMANDER: You what?

EILIF: I laughed. And so we got to talking. I came right down to business and said: "Twenty guilders an ox is too much, I bid fifteen." Like I wanted to buy. That foxed 'em. So while they were scratching their heads, I reached for my good sword and cut 'em to ribbons. Necessity knows no law, huh?

COMMANDER: What do *you* say, keeper of souls?

CHAPLAIN: Strictly speaking, that saying is not in the Bible. Our Lord made five hundred loaves out of five so that no necessity should arise. So when he told men to love their neighbors, their bellies were full. Things have changed since his day.

COMMANDER (*laughing*): Things have changed! Some wine for those wise words, you old Pharisee! Eilif my boy, you cut them to ribbons in a great cause! As for our fellows, "they were hungry and you gave them to eat!" You don't know how I value a brave soldier like you. (*He points to the map.*) Let's take a look at our position. It isn't all it might be, is it?

MOTHER COURAGE: He must be a very bad commander, this fellow.

COOK: Just a greedy one. Why bad?

MOTHER COURAGE: He says he needs *brave* soldiers. If his plan of campaign was any good, wouldn't plain ordinary soldiers do? Bravery! In a good country, such virtues wouldn't be needed. We could all be cowards and relax.

COMMANDER: I bet your father was a soldier.

EILIF: A very great soldier. My mother warned me about it. In a little song.

COMMANDER: Sing it! (*Roaring:*) Bring that meat!

EILIF: It's called The Fishwife and the Soldier.

THE FISHWIFE AND THE SOLDIER

To a soldier lad comes an old fishwife
    And this old fishwife, says she:
A gun will shoot, a knife will knife,
    You will drown if you fall in the sea.
Keep away from the ice if you want my
    advice,
    Says the old fishwife, says she.
The soldier laughs and loads his gun
Then grabs his knife and starts to run:
    It's the life of a hero for me!
From the north to the south I shall
    march through the land
With a knife at my side and a gun in my
    hand!
    Says the soldier lad, says he.

When the lad defies the fishwife's cries
    The old fishwife, says she:
The young are young, the old are wise,
    You will drown if you fall in the sea.
Don't ignore what I say or you'll rue it
    one day!
    Says the old fishwife, says she.
But gun in hand and knife at side
The soldier steps into the tide:
    It's the life of a hero for me!
When the new moon is shining on shingle
    roofs white
We are all coming back, go and pray for
    that night!

Says the soldier lad, says he.

And the fishwife old does what she's told:
    Down upon her knees drops she.
When the smoke is gone, the air is cold,
    Your heroic deeds won't warm me!
See the smoke, how it goes! May God
    scatter his foes!
    Down upon her knees drops she.
But gun in hand and knife at side
The lad is swept out by the tide:
    He floats with the ice to the sea.
And the new moon is shining on shingle
    roofs white.
But the lad and his laughter are lost in
    the night:
    He floats with the ice to the sea.

The third stanza has been sung by MOTHER
COURAGE, *somewhat to the* COMMANDER'S
surprise.

COMMANDER: What goes on in my kitchen? The liberties they take nowadays!

EILIF *has now left the tent for the kitchen. He embraces his mother.*

EILIF: You! Mother! Where are the others?

MOTHER COURAGE (*still in his arms*): Happy as ducks in a pond. Swiss Cheese is paymaster with the Second Protestant Regiment.

EILIF: Paymaster, eh?

MOTHER COURAGE: At least he isn't in the fighting.

EILIF: Your feet holding up?

MOTHER COURAGE: I have a bit of trouble getting my shoes on in the morning.

COMMANDER (*also in the kitchen by now*): So! You're his mother? I hope you have more sons for me like this young fellow?

EILIF: If I'm not the lucky one! To be the Commander's guest—while you sit listening in the kitchen!

MOTHER COURAGE: I heard you all right. (*She gives him a clout on the ear.*)

EILIF (*grinning*): Because I took the oxen?

MOTHER COURAGE: No. Because you didn't surrender when the four peasants tried to make mincemeat of you! Didn't I teach you to take care of yourself, you Finnish devil, you?

III

THREE YEARS PASS, AND MOTHER COURAGE, WITH PARTS OF A FINNISH
REGIMENT, IS TAKEN PRISONER. HER DAUGHTER IS SAVED, HER
WAGON LIKEWISE, BUT HER HONEST SON DIES.

A camp. The regimental flag is flying from a pole. Afternoon. MOTHER COURAGE'S *clothes-line is tied to the wagon at one end, to a cannon at the other. She and* KATTRIN *are folding the wash on the cannon. At the same time she is bargaining with an* ORDNANCE OFFICER *over a bag of bullets.* SWISS CHEESE, *wearing his Paymaster's uniform, looks on.* YVETTE POTTIER, *a very good-looking young person, is sewing at a colored hat, a glass of brandy before her. Her red boots are nearby; she is in stocking feet.*

ORDNANCE OFFICER: I'm letting you have the bullets for two guilders. Dirt cheap. 'Cause I need the money. The Colonel's been drinking for three days and we're out of liquor.

MOTHER COURAGE: They're army property. If they find them here, I'll be court-martialled. You sell your bullets, you bastards, and send your men out to fight with nothing to shoot with.

ORDNANCE OFFICER: If you scratch my back, I'll scratch yours.

MOTHER COURAGE: I won't touch army stuff. Not at that price.

ORDNANCE OFFICER: You can resell 'em for five guilders, maybe eight—to the Ordnance officer of the 4th Regiment. All you have to do is give him a receipt for twelve. He hasn't a bullet left.

MOTHER COURAGE: Why don't you do it yourself?

ORDNANCE OFFICER: I don't trust him: we're friends.

MOTHER COURAGE (*taking the bag, to* KAT-TRIN): Take it round the back and pay him a guilder and a half. (*As the* OFFICER *starts to protest:*) A guilder and a half! (KATTRIN *drags the bag away, the* OFFICER *follows. To* SWISS CHEESE:) Here's your underwear. Take care of it. It's October, autumn may come at any time. I don't say it must, but it may. Nothing *must* come, not even the seasons. Only your books *must* balance. Do your books balance, Mr. Paymaster?

SWISS CHEESE: Yes, Mother.

MOTHER COURAGE: Don't forget they made you paymaster because you're honest and so simple you'd never think of running off with the cash. Don't lose that under-wear.

SWISS CHEESE: No, Mother. I'll put it under the mattress.

ORDNANCE OFFICER: I'll go with you, Pay-master.

MOTHER COURAGE: Don't teach him any finagling.

THE ORDNANCE OFFICER *and* SWISS CHEESE *leave.*

YVETTE (*waving to the* OFFICER): You might at least say good-bye!

MOTHER COURAGE (*to* YVETTE): I don't like that: he's no company for my Swiss Cheese. But the war's not making a bad start: if I look ahead and make no mistakes, business will be good. (*Noticing the brandy:*) Don't you know you shouldn't drink in the morning—with your sickness and all?

YVETTE: Who says I'm sick? That's a libel!

MOTHER COURAGE: They all say so.

YVETTE: Then they're all liars! I'm desperate, Mother Courage. They avoid me like a stinking fish. Because of those lies! So what am I fixing this hat for? (*She throws it down.*) That's why I drink in the morn-ing. It gives you crow's feet, so what? The whole regiment knows me. I should have stayed home when my first was unfaithful. But pride isn't for the likes of us. You eat dirt or down you go.

MOTHER COURAGE: Don't start in again about your friend Peter Piper and How It All Happened—in front of my innocent daughter.

YVETTE: She's the one that *should* hear it. So she'll get hardened against love.

MOTHER COURAGE: That's something no one ever gets hardened against.

YVETTE: He was an army cook, blond, Dutch, and thin. Kattrin, beware of thin men! I didn't. I didn't even know he'd had another girl before me and she called him Peter Piper because he never took his pipe out of his mouth even in bed—it meant so little to him. (*She sings:*)

THE CAMP FOLLOWER'S SONG

Scarce seventeen was I when
  The foe came to our land
And laid aside his saber
  And took me by the hand.
    And we performed by day
    The sacred rite of May
    And we performed by night
    Another sacred rite.
    The regiment, well exercised,
    Presented arms, then stood at ease,
    Then took us off behind the trees
    Where we fraternized.

Each of us had her foe and
  A cook fell to my lot.
I hated him by daylight
  But in the dark did not.
    So we perform by day
    The sacred rite of May
    And we perform by night
    That other sacred rite.
    The regiment, well exercised,
    Presents its arms, then stands at ease,
    Then takes us off behind the trees
    Where we fraternize.
Ecstasy filled my heart, O
  My love seemed heaven-born!
Yet why were people saying
  It was not love but scorn?
    The springtime's soft amour
    Through summer may endure
    But swiftly comes the fall
    And winter ends it all.
    December came. All of the men
    Filed past the trees where once we hid
    Then quickly marched away and did
    Not come back again.

YVETTE: I made the mistake of running after him. I never found him. It's ten years ago now. (YVETTE *goes behind the wagon.*)

MOTHER COURAGE: You're leaving your hat.

YVETTE: For the birds.

MOTHER COURAGE: Let that be a lesson to you, Kattrin: never start anything with a soldier. Love does seem heaven-born, so watch out: they tell you they worship the ground under your feet—did you wash 'em yesterday, while we're on the subject?—then, if you don't look out, you're their slave for life.

THE CHAPLAIN *comes in with the* COOK.

CHAPLAIN: Mother Courage, I bring a message from your son Eilif. The cook came with me—you've made an impression on him.

COOK: Oh, I thought I'd get a little whiff of the breeze.

MOTHER COURAGE: You're welcome to it, but what does Eilif want? I don't have any money!

CHAPLAIN: My message is for his brother, the paymaster.

MOTHER COURAGE: He's not here. He's not anywhere. Look, he is not his brother's paymaster: I won't have him led into temptation! (*She takes money from a purse.*) Give him this. But it's a sin—he's speculating in mother love.

COOK: Maybe not for long. How d'you know he'll come back alive? You're hard, you women. A glass of brandy wouldn't cost you much. But no, you say, no—and six feet under goes your man.

CHAPLAIN: My dear Cook, you talk as if dying for one's beliefs were a misfortune —it is the highest privilege! This is not just any war, remember it is a religious war, and therefore pleasing unto God.

COOK: I see that. In one sense it's a war because of all the cheating, plunder, rape, and so forth, but it's different from all other wars because it's a religious war and therefore pleasing unto God. At that it does make you thirsty.

CHAPLAIN (*to* MOTHER COURAGE): He says you've betwitched him. He says he dreams about you.

COOK (*lighting his pipe*): Innocent dreams!

I dream of a fair lady dispensing brandy! Stop embarrassing me! The stories you were telling on the way over still have me blushing.

MOTHER COURAGE: I must get you two something to drink, or you'll be making improper advances out of sheer boredom.

CHAPLAIN: That is indeed a temptation— said the Court Chaplain, as he gave way to it. And who is this captivating young person?

MOTHER COURAGE (*looking at Kattrin*): That is not a captivating young person. That is a respectable young person. (*And she goes with* COOK *and* CHAPLAIN *behind the wagon.*)

MOTHER COURAGE: The trouble with Poland is the Poles. It's true our Swedish king moved in on them with his army—but instead of maintaining the peace the Poles would keep interfering. So their blood is on their own heads, *I* say.

CHAPLAIN: Anyway, since the German Kaiser had enslaved them, King Gustavus had no alternative but to liberate them!

COOK: Just what *I* always say. Your health, Mother Courage, your brandy is first-rate, I'm never mistaken in a face. This war is a religious war.

KATTRIN *watches them go behind the wagon, leaves the washing, picks up the hat, sits, takes up the red boots. The* COOK *sings:*

LUTHER'S HYMN

A mighty fortress is our God
A bulwark never failing.
Our helper He, amid the flood
Of mortal ills prevailing.
For still our ancient Foe
Doth seek to work us woe.
His craft and power are great
And armed with cruel hate
On earth is not his equal.

COOK: And King Gustavus liberated Poland from the Germans. Who could deny it? Then his appetite grew with eating, and he liberated *Germany* from the Germans. Made quite a profit on the deal, I'm told.

CHAPLAIN: That is a calumny! The Swedish king puts religion first!

MOTHER COURAGE: What's more, you eat his bread.

COOK: I don't eat his bread: I bake his bread.

MOTHER COURAGE: He'll never be conquered, that man, and you know why? We all back him up—the little fellows like you and me. Oh yes, to hear the big fellows talk, they're fighting for their beliefs and so on, but if you look into it, you find they're not that silly: they do want to make a profit on the deal. So you and I back them up!

COOK: Surely.

CHAPLAIN (*pointing to flag, to* COOK): And as a Dutchman you'd do well to look which flag is flying here!

MOTHER COURAGE: To our Protestant flag!

COOK: A toast!

And now KATTRIN *has begun to strut about with hat and boots on. Suddenly: cannon and shots. Drums.* MOTHER COURAGE, THE COOK, *and* THE CHAPLAIN *rush round to the front of the wagon, the two last with glasses in their hands. The* ORDNANCE OFFICER *and a* SOLDIER *come running for the cannon. They try to push it.*

MOTHER COURAGE: Hey, let me get my wash off that gun!

ORDNANCE OFFICER: Surprise attack! The Catholics! We don't know if we can get away! (*To the* SOLDIER:) Bring that gun! (*He runs off.*)

COOK: Good God! I must go to the commander. Mother Courage, I'll be back soon—for a short conversation. (*He rushes off.*)

MOTHER COURAGE: Hey, you're leaving your pipe!

COOK (*off*): Keep it for me, I'll need it!

MOTHER COURAGE: This *would* happen just when we were making money.

CHAPLAIN: "Blessed are the peacemakers!" A good slogan for wartime. Well, I must be going too. Yes, if the enemy's so close, it can be dangerous. I wish I had a cloak.

MOTHER COURAGE: I'm lending no cloaks. Not even to save a life. I've had experience in that line.

CHAPLAIN: But I'm in special danger— because of my religion!

MOTHER COURAGE (*bringing him a cloak*): It's against my better judgment. Now run!

CHAPLAIN: Thank you, you're very generous, but on second thought I better stay put. If I run, I might attract attention.

THE SOLDIER *is still struggling with the cannon.*

MOTHER COURAGE: Let it alone, you idiot, who's going to pay you for this? *You'll* pay—with your life. Let me keep it for you.

SOLDIER (*running off*): You're my witness: I tried!

MOTHER COURAGE: I'll swear to that. (*And now she sees* KATTRIN *with the hat and boots.*) Yvette's hat! Take it off this minute! Are you crazy—with the enemy coming? (*She tears it off her head.*) They'll make a whore of you when they see it! And she has the boots on, too, straight from Babylon, I'll soon fix that. (*She pulls at the boots.*) Chaplain, help me with these boots, I'll be right back. (*She runs to the wagon.*)

YVETTE *enters, powdering her face.*

YVETTE: What's this—the Catholics are coming? Where's my hat? Who's been trampling on it? I can't run around in that, what will they think of me? And I've no mirror. (*Coming very close to the* CHAPLAIN:) How do I look? Too much powder?

CHAPLAIN: No—er—just right.

YVETTE: And where are my red boots? (KATTRIN *is hiding her feet under her skirt.*) I left them here! Must I go barefoot? It's a scandal.

Exit YVETTE. SWISS CHEESE *comes running on with a cash-box. Enter* MOTHER COURAGE, *her hands smeared with ashes.*

MOTHER COURAGE (*to* SWISS CHEESE): What have you got there?

SWISS CHEESE: The regimental cash-box.

MOTHER COURAGE: Throw it away! Your paymastering days are over!

SWISS CHEESE: But they trusted me with it! (*He goes to one side.*)

MOTHER COURAGE (*to the* CHAPLAIN): Take your pastor's coat off, or they'll recognize you, cloak or no cloak. (*She is rubbing ashes into* KATTRIN'S *face.*) Keep still!

A little dirt, and you're safe. When a soldier sees a clean face, there's one more whore in the world. That does it. Now stop trembling. Nothing can happen now. (*To* SWISS CHEESE:) Where've you put that cash-box?

SWISS CHEESE: I thought I'd just leave it in the wagon.

MOTHER COURAGE: In my wagon?! Why, they'll hang all three of us!

SWISS CHEESE: Somewhere else then. Maybe I'll run away some place.

MOTHER COURAGE: It's too late for that.

CHAPLAIN (*still changing his clothes*): For Heaven's sake, that Protestant flag!

MOTHER COURAGE (*taking the flag down*): I've had it twenty-five years. I don't notice it any more.

The sound of cannon grows. Blackout. Three days later. Morning. The cannon is gone. MOTHER COURAGE, KATTRIN, THE CHAPLAIN, *and* SWISS CHEESE *sit eating anxiously.*

SWISS CHEESE: This is the third day I've sat doing nothing. The sergeant has always been patient with me, but by this time he must be asking himself: Now where is Swiss Cheese with that cash-box?

MOTHER COURAGE: Be glad they're not on the trail.

CHAPLAIN: What about me? I can't even hold service here. It is written: "Out of the abundance of the heart the tongue speaketh"—but woe is me if *my* tongue speaketh!

MOTHER COURAGE: So here you sit—one with his religion, the other with his cash-box! I don't know which is more dangerous.

CHAPLAIN: We're in God's hands now.

MOTHER COURAGE: Oh, I hope we're not as desperate as *that*! But it *is* hard to sleep at night. It'd be easier if you weren't here, Swiss Cheese. All the same I've not done badly.

CHAPLAIN: The milk is good. As for the quantity, we may have to reduce our Swedish appetites somewhat. We are defeated.

MOTHER COURAGE: Who's defeated? There've been cases where a defeat is a victory for the little fellows, it's only their honor that's lost, nothing serious. At that, either victory or defeat can be a costly business. The best thing, *I* say, is for politics to kind of get stuck in the mud. (*To* SWISS CHEESE:) Eat!

SWISS CHEESE: I don't like it. How will the sergeant pay the men?

MOTHER COURAGE: Soldiers in flight don't get paid.

SWISS CHEESE: Then they should refuse to flee! No pay, no flight!

MOTHER COURAGE: Swiss Cheese, I've brought you up honest because you're not very bright, but don't overdo it! And now I'm going with the Chaplain to buy a Catholic flag and some meat. (*She disappears into the wagon.*)

CHAPLAIN: She's worried about the cash-box.

SWISS CHEESE: I can get rid of it.

CHAPLAIN: You may be seen. They have spies everywhere. Yesterday one jumped out of the very hole I was relieving myself in. I was so scared I almost broke into a prayer—think how *that* would have given me away! He was a little brute with a patch over one eye.

MOTHER COURAGE *clambers out of the wagon with a basket.*

MOTHER COURAGE (*to* KATTRIN, *holding up the red boots*): You shameless little hussy! She went and switched them—because you called her a captivating young person. (*She puts them in the basket. To* KATTRIN:) Stealing Yvette's boots! She at least gets paid for it, you just *enjoy* strutting like a peacock! Save your proud ways for peacetime!

CHAPLAIN: I don't find her proud.

MOTHER COURAGE: I like her when people say, I never even noticed her. I like her when she's a stone in Dalarna, where there's nothing but stones. (*To* SWISS CHEEESE:) Leave the cash-box where it is, and look after your sister, she needs it. You two are more trouble than a bag of fleas.

MOTHER COURAGE *and* THE CHAPLAIN *leave.*
KATTRIN *clears the dishes away.*

SWISS CHEESE: Not many days more when you can sit in the sun in your shirtsleeves. (KATTRIN *points to a tree.*) Yes, the leaves are yellow already. (*With gestures,* KATTRIN *asks if he wants a drink.*) No, I'm not drinking, I'm thinking. (*Pause.*) Mother says she can't sleep, so I *should* take the cash-box away. I have a place for it: the mole-hole by the river. I can pick it up there—late tonight maybe—and take it to the sergeant. How far can they have fled in three days? The sergeant's eyes'll pop! "You've disappointed me most pleasantly, Swiss Cheese," he'll say, "I trust you with the cash-box, and *you* bring it back!" Yes, Kattrin, I *will* have a glass now.

When KATTRIN *gets behind the wagon, two men confront her. One is a* SERGEANT; *the other doffs his hat and flourishes it in a showy greeting, he has a patch over one eye.*

ONE EYE: Morning, young lady! Have you seen a staff officer from the Second Protestant Regiment?

KATTRIN *is terrified and runs away, spilling her brandy. The two men look at each other, see* SWISS CHEESE, *and withdraw.*

SWISS CHEESE (*starting up*): You're spilling it, can't you see where you're going? I don't understand you. Anyway, I must be leaving. That's what I've decided on. (*He stands up. She tries to make him understand the danger he is in. He pushes her away.*) I know you mean well, poor thing, you just can't get it out. And don't worry about the brandy. I'll live to drink so much brandy—what's one glass? (*He takes the cash-box out of the wagon and puts it under his coat.*) I'll be right back, but don't hold me up, or I'll have to scold you. Yes, I know you're trying to help!

He kisses her as she tries to hold him back, and pulls himself free. Exit SWISS CHEESE. KATTRIN *is now desperate. She runs up and down, making little sounds.* MOTHER COURAGE *and* THE CHAPLAIN *return.* KATTRIN *rushes at her mother.*

MOTHER COURAGE: What is it, what is it, control yourself! Have they done something to you? Where's Swiss Cheese?

(*To the* CHAPLAIN:) And don't you stand around—get that Catholic flag up!

She takes the flag from her basket. THE CHAPLAIN *runs it up the pole.*

CHAPLAIN: God bless our Catholic flag!

MOTHER COURAGE: Now calm down, Kattrin, and tell me all about it. What? That little rascal has taken the cash-box away? Oh, he's going to get a good whipping? Now take your time, don't try to talk, use your hands. I don't like that howling—what will the Chaplain think? A man with one eye? Here?

CHAPLAIN: That fellow is an informer. They've captured Swiss Cheese?

KATTRIN *shakes her head, then shrugs her shoulders. Voices off.* ONE EYE *and the same* SERGEANT *bring in* SWISS CHEESE.

SWISS CHEESE: Let me go! I've nothing on me. You're breaking my shoulder. I am innocent!

SERGEANT: This is where he comes from. These are his friends.

MOTHER COURAGE: Us? Since when?

SWISS CHEESE: I was just getting my lunch here. I paid ten hellers for it. Maybe you saw me on that bench. The food was too salty.

MOTHER COURAGE: That's true. He got his lunch here. And it was too salty.

SERGEANT: Are you pretending you don't know him?

MOTHER COURAGE: I can't know all of them.

CHAPLAIN: He sat there like a law-abiding citizen and never opened his mouth except to eat. Which is necessary.

SERGEANT: Who d'you think you are?

MOTHER COURAGE: He's my bartender. And you must be thirsty. I'll bring you some brandy.

SERGEANT: No liquor while on duty. (*To* SWISS CHEESE:) You were carrying something. You must have hidden it. We saw the bulge in your shirt.

MOTHER COURAGE: Are you sure it was him?

SWISS CHEESE: I think you mean another fellow. There *was* a fellow with something under his shirt. I saw him.

MOTHER COURAGE: I think so too. It's a misunderstanding. Could happen to anyone. Oh, I know what people are like.

I'm Mother Courage and I can tell you this: he looks honest.

SERGEANT: We want the regimental cash-box. And we know the looks of the fellow that's been taking care of it. It's you!

SWISS CHEESE: No! No, it's not!

SERGEANT: If you don't shell out, you're dead, see!

MOTHER COURAGE: Oh, he'd give it to you to save his life, he's not that stupid! Speak up, my boy, the sergeant's giving you one last chance!

SWISS CHEESE: What if I don't have it?

SERGEANT: We'll get it out of you.

ONE EYE *and the* SERGEANT *lead him off.*

MOTHER COURAGE (*shouting after them*): He'll tell you! He's not *that* stupid! And don't you break his shoulder!

She runs a little way after them. Blackout. The same evening. The CHAPLAIN *and* KATTRIN *are waiting.*

MOTHER COURAGE (*entering*): It's a matter of life and death. But the sergeant will still listen to us. Only he mustn't know it's our Swiss Cheese—or they'll say we helped him. It's just a matter of money. But where can *we* get money? Wasn't Yvette here? I just talked with her. She's picked up a Colonel, and she says he might buy her a canteen business.

CHAPLAIN: You'd sell the wagon, everything?

MOTHER COURAGE: Where else would I get the money for the sergeant?

CHAPLAIN: What are you going to live off?

MOTHER COURAGE: That's just it.

Enter YVETTE *with a hoary old* COLONEL. *She embraces* MOTHER COURAGE.

YVETTE: Dear Mrs. Fierling, we meet again! (*Whispering:*) He didn't say no. (*Loud:*) This is my friend, my . . . business adviser. I heard you might want to sell your wagon.

MOTHER COURAGE: I want to pawn it, not sell it. And nothing hasty. You don't find another wagon like this in a hurry.

YVETTE: In that case, I'm not sure I'd be interested. What do *you* think, my dear?

COLONEL: I agree with you, honey bun.

MOTHER COURAGE: It's only for pawn.

YVETTE: But I thought you *had* to have the money?

MOTHER COURAGE: I do have to. But I'd rather run my feet off looking for another offer than just sell. We live off that wagon.

COLONEL: Take it! Take it!

YVETTE: My friend thinks I might take it. (*Turning to him:*) But you think we should buy it outright, don't you?

COLONEL: Oh, I do, bunny, I do!

MOTHER COURAGE: Then you must find one that's for sale.

YVETTE: Yes! We can travel around looking for one! I love going around looking. Especially with you, Poldy!

COLONEL: Really? Do you?

YVETTE: Oh, I love it. I could take weeks of it!

COLONEL: Really? Could you?

YVETTE: If you get the money, when would you pay it back?

MOTHER COURAGE: In two weeks. Maybe one.

YVETTE: I can't make up my mind. Poldy, chéri, advise me! (*Aside to him:*) She'll have to sell, don't worry. That lieutenant —the blond one—remember?—he'll lend me the money. He's crazy about me. He says I remind him of someone. What do you advise?

COLONEL: Oh, I have to warn you against *him*: he's no good, he'll only exploit the situation. I told you, bunny, I told you I'd buy you something? Didn't I tell you that?

YVETTE: I can't let you.

COLONEL: Oh, please, please!

YVETTE: Well, if you think the lieutenant might exploit the situation?

COLONEL: I do think so.

YVETTE: So you advise me to go ahead?

COLONEL: I do, bunny, I do!

YVETTE (*returning to* MOTHER COURAGE): My friend says all right: two hundred guilders. And I need a receipt saying the wagon would be mine in two weeks. With everything in it. I'll look it all over right now. The two hundred can wait. (*To the* COLONEL:) You go on ahead to the camp. I'll follow.

COLONEL (*helping her up the steps of the wagon*): I'll help you up. Come soon, honey bun. (*Exit* COLONEL.)

MOTHER COURAGE: Yvette, Yvette!

YVETTE: There aren't many shoes left.

MOTHER COURAGE: Yvette, this is no time for an inventory, yours or not yours. You promised to talk to the sergeant about Swiss Cheese. There isn't a minute to lose. He's up for court martial one hour from now.

YVETTE: I want to check through these shirts.

MOTHER COURAGE *drags her down the steps by the skirt.*

MOTHER COURAGE: You hyena! Swiss Cheese's life is at stake! And don't say where the money comes from. Pretend he's your sweetheart, or we'll all get it in the neck for helping him.

YVETTE: I arranged to meet One Eye in the bushes. He must be there by now.

CHAPLAIN: And don't give him the whole two hundred. A hundred and fifty should do the trick.

MOTHER COURAGE: You keep your nose out of this! I'm not doing you out of *your* porridge. Now run, and no haggling! Remember his life's at stake! (*She pushes* YVETTE *off.*)

CHAPLAIN: All I meant was: what are we going to live on?

MOTHER COURAGE: I'm counting on that cash-box. At the very least, Swiss Cheese'll get paid out of it.

CHAPLAIN: But d'you think Yvette can manage this?

MOTHER COURAGE: It's in her interest—if I don't pay their two hundred, she won't get the wagon. And she knows the score: she won't have this colonel on the string forever. Kattrin, go clean the knives! And don't you just stand around: wash those glasses: there'll be fifty cavalrymen here tonight . . . I think they'll let us have him. They're not wolves, they're human and after money. God is merciful and men are bribable—that's how His will is done on earth, I don't know about Heaven.

YVETTE (*entering*): They'll do it for two hundred if you make it snappy. He confessed he'd had the cash-box, they put the thumb screws on him, but he threw it in the river when he saw them coming at him. Shall I go get the money from my colonel?

MOTHER COURAGE: The cash-box in the river? How'll I ever get my two hundred back?

YVETTE: You were expecting to get it from the cash-box? I *would* have been sunk. Mother Courage, if you want your Swiss Cheese, you'll have to pay. Or shall I let the whole thing drop—so you can keep your wagon?

MOTHER COURAGE: Now I *can't* pay two hundred. I must hold on to something. Go say I'll pay one hundred twenty or the deal's off. Even at that I lose the wagon.

YVETTE: One Eye's in a hurry. Looks over his shoulder the whole time. Hadn't I better just give them the two hundred?

MOTHER COURAGE: I have her to think of. She's twenty-five and still no husband. I know what I'm doing. One hundred twenty or no deal.

YVETTE: You know best.

YVETTE *runs off. After walking up and down abstractedly,* MOTHER COURAGE *sits down to help* KATTRIN *with the knives.*

MOTHER COURAGE: I *will* pay two hundred if I have to. With eighty guilders we could pack a hamper and begin over. It won't be the end of the world.

CHAPLAIN: The Bible says: the Lord will provide.

MOTHER COURAGE (*to* KATTRIN): You must rub them dry.

YVETTE (*re-enters*): They won't do it. I warned you. He said the drums would roll any second now—and that's the sign they've reached a verdict. I offered one hundred fifty. He didn't even shrug his shoulders.

MOTHER COURAGE: Tell him I'll pay two hundred. Run! (YVETTE *runs,* MOTHER COURAGE *sits,* THE CHAPLAIN *has finished the glasses.*) I believe—I haggled too long.

In the distance: a roll of drums. The CHAPLAIN *stands up and walks away.* MOTHER COURAGE *remains seated. It grows dark; it gets light again.* MOTHER COURAGE *has not moved.*

YVETTE (*re-enters, pale*): You've done it— with your haggling. You can keep your wagon now. He got eleven bullets in him. I don't know why I still bother about you, you don't deserve it, but I just happened to hear they don't think the cash-box is really in the river. They think it's here. And they think you were in with him. I think they're going to bring his body, to see if you give yourself away when you see him. You'd better not know him or we're in for it. And I should tell you straight: they're right behind me. Shall I keep Kattrin out of this? (MOTHER COURAGE *shakes her head.*) Does she know? Maybe she didn't hear the drums or didn't understand.

MOTHER COURAGE: She knows. Bring her.

YVETTE *brings* KATTRIN *who stands by her mother, who takes her hand. Two men come on with a stretcher. There is a sheet over it, and something underneath. Beside them, the* SERGEANT. *They put the stretcher down.*

SERGEANT: There's a man here we don't know the name of, but he has to be registered to keep the records straight. He bought a meal from you. Look at him. See if you know him. (*He draws back the sheet.*) You know him? (MOTHER COURAGE *shakes her head.*) What? You never saw him before he bought that meal? (MOTHER COURAGE *shakes her head.*) Lift him up. Throw him on the garbage dump. He has no one that knows him. *They carry him off.*

IV

MOTHER COURAGE SINGS THE SONG OF THE
GREAT CAPITULATION

Outside an officer's tent. MOTHER COURAGE *waits. A* REGIMENTAL CLERK *looks out of the tent.*

REGIMENTAL CLERK: You want to speak to the captain? I know you. You had a Protestant paymaster with you. He was hiding out. Better make no complaint here.

MOTHER COURAGE: But I'm innocent and if I give up it'll look like I have a bad conscience. They cut my wagon to ribbons with their sabers, and then claimed a fine of five thalers—for nothing, for less than nothing!

REGIMENTAL CLERK (quietly): For your own good: keep your mouth shut. We haven't many canteens, so we let you stay in business, especially if you've a bad conscience and have to pay a fine now and then.

MOTHER COURAGE: I'm going to lodge a complaint.

REGIMENTAL CLERK: As you wish. Wait here till the captain is free.

The CLERK *retires into the tent.* A YOUNG SOLDIER *comes storming in.*

YOUNG SOLDIER: Screw the captain! Where is the son of a bitch? Grabbing my reward, spending it on brandy for his whores! I'll rip his belly open!

OLDER SOLDIER (*following him*): Shut your hole, you'll only wind up in the stocks!

YOUNG SOLDIER: I was the only one in the squad who swam the river and *he* grabs the money. I can't even buy me a beer. Come out, you thief, I'll make lamb chops out of you!

OLDER SOLDIER: Holy Christ, he'll destroy himself.

YOUNG SOLDIER (*pulling himself free of the older man*): Let me go or I'll cut you down too!

OLDER SOLDIER: Saved the colonel's horse and didn't get the reward. He's young. He hasn't been at it long.

MOTHER COURAGE: Let him go. He doesn't have to be chained like a dog. Very reasonable to want a reward. Why else should he go to the trouble?

YOUNG SOLDIER: He's in there pouring it down. I done something special: I want the reward!

MOTHER COURAGE: Young man, don't scream at *me*, I have my own problems.

YOUNG SOLDIER: He's whoring on my money and I'm hungry! I'll murder him!

MOTHER COURAGE: You're hungry. You're angry. I understand.

YOUNG SOLDIER: Talking'll get you nowhere. I won't stand for injustice!

MOTHER COURAGE: How long? How long won't you stand for injustice? One hour? Or two? It's a misery to sit in the stocks: especially if you leave it till then to realize you do stand for injustice.

YOUNG SOLDIER: I don't know why I listen to you. Screw that captain!

MOTHER COURAGE: You listen because you know I'm right. Your rage has calmed down already. It was a short one, and you'd need a long one.

YOUNG SOLDIER: Are you trying to tell me I shouldn't ask for the money?

MOTHER COURAGE: Just the opposite. I only say your rage won't last, you'll get nowhere with it. If your rage was a long one, I'd say: go ahead, slice him up. But what's the use—if you don't slice him up? What's the use if you stand there with your tail between your legs?

OLDER SOLDIER: You're quite right: he's crazy.

YOUNG SOLDIER: All right, we'll see whether I slice him up or not. (*He draws his sword.*) When he comes out, I slice him up.

CLERK (*looking out again*): The captain will be right out. (*A military order:*) Be seated!

The YOUNG SOLDIER *sits.*

MOTHER COURAGE: What did I tell you? Oh, they know us inside out. "Be seated!" And we sit. *I'm* no better. Let me tell you about the great capitulation.

THE GREAT CAPITULATION

Long, long ago, a green beginner
    I thought myself a special case.
(None of your ordinary, run of the mill
girls, with my looks and my talent and
my love of the Higher Things.)
I picked a hair out of my dinner
    And put the waiter in his place.
(All or nothing. Anyway, never the
second best. I am the master of my fate.
I'll take no orders from no one.)
Then a little bird whispers!
        The bird says: "Wait a year or so
        And marching with the band you'll go
        Keeping in step, now fast, now slow,
        And piping out your little spiel.
        Then one day the battalions wheel!
        And you go down upon your knees
        To God Almighty if you please!"

My friend, before that year was over
　I'd learned to drink their cup of tea.
(Two children round your neck and the
　price of bread and what all!)
When they were through with me, more-
　over,
　They had me where they wanted me
(You must get in with people. If you
　scratch my back, I'll scratch yours. Don't
　stick your neck out!)
Then a little bird whispers!
　　　The bird says: "Scarce a year or so
　　　And marching with the band she'd go
　　　Keeping in step, now fast, now slow,
　　　And piping out her little spiel.
　　　Then one day the battalions wheel!
　　　And she goes down upon her knees
　　　To God Almighty if you please!"

Our plans are big, our hopes colossal.
　We hitch our wagon to a star.
(Where there's a will, there's a way. You
　can't hold a good man down.)
"We can lift mountains," says the apostle.

And yet: how heavy one cigar!
(You must cut your coat according to
　your cloth.)
That little bird whispers!
　　　The bird says: "Wait a year or so
　　　And marching with the band we go
　　　Keeping in step, now fast, now slow,
　　　And piping out our little spiel.
　　　Then one day the battalions wheel!
　　　And we go down upon our knees
　　　To God Almighty if you please!"

MOTHER COURAGE: So stay here with your
　sword drawn, if your anger is big enough.
　If it isn't, you'd better go.
YOUNG SOLDIER: Aw, shove it! (*He stumbles
　off, the* OLDER SOLDIER *following him.*)
REGIMENTAL CLERK (*again sticking his head
　out*): The captain is free now. You can
　lodge your complaint.
MOTHER COURAGE: I've thought better of it.
　I'm not complaining. *She leaves. The*
　CLERK *looks after her, shaking his head.*

V

TWO YEARS HAVE PASSED. THE WAR COVERS WIDER AND WIDER TERRITORY.
ALWAYS ON THE MOVE, THE LITTLE WAGON CROSSES POLAND,
MORAVIA, BAVARIA, ITALY, AND AGAIN BAVARIA.
1631. GENERAL TILLY'S VICTORY AT LEIPZIG
COSTS MOTHER COURAGE FOUR SHIRTS.

*The wagon stands in a war-ruined village.
Victory march in the distance.* TWO
SOLDIERS *are being served at a counter by*
KATTRIN *and* MOTHER COURAGE. *One of
them has a woman's fur coat about his
shoulders.*
MOTHER COURAGE: What, you can't pay?
　No money, no schnapps! If they can play
　victory marches, they should pay their
　men.
FIRST SOLDIER: I want my schnapps! I
　arrived too late for plunder. The Chief
　allowed just one hour to plunder the
　town. He's not inhuman, he says—so
　I guess they bought him off.
CHAPLAIN (*staggering in*): There are people
　in the farmhouse. A whole family. Help
　me, someone! I need linen.

The SECOND SOLDIER *goes with him.* KAT-
TRIN, *becoming excited, tries to get her
mother to bring linen out of the wagon.*
MOTHER COURAGE: I have none. I sold all
　my bandages to the regiment. I'm not
　tearing up my officer's shirts for these
　people.
CHAPLAIN (*over his shoulder*): I said: I need
　linen!
　　MOTHER COURAGE *stops* KATTRIN *from
　entering the wagon.*
MOTHER COURAGE: Not on your life! They
　have nothing and they pay nothing.
　The CHAPLAIN *carries in a* WOMAN.
CHAPLAIN: Why did you stay there—in the
　line of fire?
WOMAN (*faintly*): Our farm . . .
MOTHER COURAGE: Think they'd ever let go

of anything? And now *I'm* supposed to pay. Well, I won't!

FIRST SOLDIER: They're Protestants. Why do they have to be Protestants?

MOTHER COURAGE: Protestant, Catholic, what do they care? It's their farm they're thinking of.

SECOND SOLDIER: Anyway, they're not Protestants. They're Catholics.

FIRST SOLDIER: I guess our cannon don't know the difference.

The CHAPLAIN *brings in a* PEASANT.

PEASANT: My arm's shot.

CHAPLAIN: Where's that linen?

MOTHER COURAGE: I can't give you any. With all I have to pay out in taxes, duties, bribes . . . (KATTRIN *picks up a board and threatens her mother with it, making gurgling sounds.*) Are you out of your mind? Put that board down this minute! I'm giving nothing! (*The* CHAPLAIN *lifts her bodily off the wagon steps, then brings the shirts from the wagon, and tears them in strips.*) My shirts! My officer's shirts! *From the house, the cry of a child in pain.*

PEASANT: The child's still in the house.

KATTRIN *runs into the house.*

MOTHER COURAGE: Hey, grab Kattrin, the roof may fall in!

CHAPLAIN: I'm not going back in there.

MOTHER COURAGE: My officer's shirts, half a guilder apiece. I'm ruined! (KATTRIN *comes out with a baby in her arms. To her:*) Never happy till you're dragging babies around! Give it to its mother at once!

KATTRIN *is humming a lullaby to the child.*

CHAPLAIN (*bandaging*): The blood comes through.

MOTHER COURAGE: And, in all this, she's happy as a lark! Stop that music! I don't need music to tell me what victory's like. (*The* FIRST SOLDIER *tries to make off with the bottle he's been drinking from.*) Come back, you! If you want another victory, you'll have to pay for it.

FIRST SOLDIER: But I'm broke.

MOTHER COURAGE *tears the fur coat off his back.*

MOTHER COURAGE: Then leave this. It's stolen goods anyhow.

KATTRIN *rocks the child and raises it high above her head.*

VI

THE CATHOLIC GENERAL TILLY IS KILLED BEFORE THE CITY OF INGOLSTADT
AND IS BURIED IN STATE. MOTHER COURAGE GIVES HER VIEWS
OF HEROES, AND THE CHAPLAIN SINGS A SONG ABOUT
THE DURATION OF THE WAR. KATTRIN GETS THE
RED BOOTS AT LAST. THE YEAR IS 1632.

The interior of a canteen tent. The inside part of the counter is seen at the rear. Funeral march in the distance. The CHAPLAIN *and the* REGIMENTAL CLERK *are playing checkers.* MOTHER COURAGE *and* KATTRIN *are taking inventory.*

CHAPLAIN: The funeral procession is just starting out.

MOTHER COURAGE: Pity about the Chief—twenty-two pairs, socks—getting killed that way. They say it was an accident. There was a fog over the fields that morning, and the fog was to blame. He'd been telling his men to fight to the death, and

was just riding back to safety when he lost his way in the fog, went forward instead of back, found himself in the thick of the battle, and ran right smack into a bullet. (*A whistle from the counter. She goes over to attend to a soldier.*) It's a disgrace—the way you're all skipping your Commander's funeral.

REGIMENTAL CLERK: They shouldn't have handed out the money before the funeral. Now the men are getting drunk instead of going to it.

CHAPLAIN (*to the* REGIMENTAL CLERK): Don't you have to be there?

REGIMENTAL CLERK: I stayed away because of the rain.

MOTHER COURAGE: It's different for you. The rain might spoil your uniform.

ANOTHER SOLDIER *comes to the counter. He sings:*

BATTLE HYMN

One schnapps, mine host, be quick, make haste!
A soldier's got no time to waste:
He must be shooting, shooting, shooting,
His Kaiser's enemies uprooting!

SOLDIER: A brandy.

Two breasts, my girl, be quick, make haste,
A soldier's got no time to waste:
He must be hating, hating, hating,
He cannot keep his Kaiser waiting!

SOLDIER: Make it a double, this is a holiday.

MOTHER COURAGE: Money first. No, you can't come inside, not with those boots on. Only officers are allowed in here, rain or no rain.

CHAPLAIN (*as the funeral music resumes*): Now they're filing past the body.

MOTHER COURAGE: I feel sorry for a commander like that—when maybe he had something big in mind, something they'd talk about in times to come, something they'd raise a statue to him for, the conquest of the whole world, for example— Lord, the worms have got into these biscuits!—he works his hands to the bone and then the common riffraff don't support him because all they care about is a jug of beer or a bit of company. Am I right?

CHAPLAIN: You're right, Mother Courage. Till you come to the riffraff. You underestimate them. Take those fellows outside right now, drinking their brandy in the rain, why, they'd fight for a hundred years, one war after another—if necessary, two at a time.

MOTHER COURAGE: Seventeen leather belts.— Then you don't think the war might end?

CHAPLAIN: Because a commander's dead? Don't be childish. Heroes are cheap. There are plenty of others where he came from.

MOTHER COURAGE: I wasn't asking just for the sake of argument. I was wondering if I should buy up a lot of supplies. They happen to be cheap right now. But if the war's going to end, I might just as well forget it.

CHAPLAIN: There are people who think the war's about to end, but I say: you can't be sure it will *ever* end. Oh, it may have to pause occasionally, for breath, as it were. It can even meet with an accident— nothing on this earth is perfect—one can't think of everything—a little oversight and a war may be in the hole and someone's got to pull it out again. That someone is the King or the Emperor or the Pope. But they're such friends in need, this war hasn't got much to worry about: it can look forward to a prosperous future.

MOTHER COURAGE: If I was sure you're right . . .

CHAPLAIN: Think it out for yourself. How *could* the war end?

REGIMENTAL CLERK: I'm from Bohemia. I'd like to get home once in a while. So I'm hoping for peace.

CHAPLAIN: Peace?

REGIMENTAL CLERK: Yes, peace! How can we live without it?

CHAPLAIN: We don't have to. There's peace even in war. War satisfies all needs—even those of peace. I know a song about that. (*He sings:*)

THE ARMY CHAPLAIN'S SONG

Does war, my friend, stop you from
      drinking?
Does it not give you bread to chew?
To my old-fashioned way of thinking
That much at least a war can do.

And even in the thick of slaughter
      A soldier feels the amorous itch
And many a buxom farmer's daughter
Has lost her virtue in a ditch.

REGIMENTAL CLERK: Maybe. But when shall I get another good night's sleep?

CHAPLAIN: That also has been taken care of.

Somehow we find the bread and brandy

And finding women is a snap.
And when there is a gutter handy
We catch a twenty-minute nap.

As for the sleep that lasts forever
Though it will come in any case
In war more Christian souls than ever
Reach their eternal resting place.

REGIMENTAL CLERK: And when everyone's dead, the war won't stop even then, I suppose?

CHAPLAIN: Let me finish.

What won't a soldier do in wartime
His savage lust to satisfy!
But after all, 'twas said aforetime:
Be fruitful, lads, and multiply!

If you ignore this high injunction,
The war will have to stop, my friend:
Perform your biologic function
And then the war need never end!

REGIMENTAL CLERK: You admit the war *could* stop.

CHAPLAIN: Tsk, tsk, tsk. You don't know where God lives. Listen!

Peacemakers shall the earth inherit:
We bless those men of simple worth.
Warmakers have still greater merit:
They *have* inherited the earth.

I'll tell you, my good sir, what peace is:
The hole when all the cheese is gone.
And what is war? This is my thesis:
It's what the world is founded on.

War is like love: it'll always find a way. Why *should* it end?

MOTHER COURAGE: Then I *will* buy those supplies. I'll take your word for it. (KATTRIN, *who has been staring at the* CHAPLAIN, *suddenly bangs a basket of glasses down on the ground and runs out.* MOTHER COURAGE *laughs*.) She'll go right on waiting for peace. I promised her she'll get a husband when peace comes. (*She follows* KATTRIN.)

REGIMENTAL CLERK (*standing up*): You were singing. I win.

MOTHER COURAGE *brings* KATTRIN *back*.

MOTHER COURAGE: Be sensible, the war'll go on a bit longer, and we'll make a bit more money—then peace'll be all the nicer. Now you go into the town, it's not ten minutes' walk, and bring the things from the Golden Lion. Just the special things for your trousseau: the rest we can pick up later in the wagon. The Clerk will go with you, you'll be quite safe. Do a good job, and don't lose anything, think of your trousseau! (KATTRIN *ties a kerchief round her head and leaves with the* CLERK.) Now you can chop me a bit of firewood. *The* CHAPLAIN *takes his coat off and prepares to chop wood*.

CHAPLAIN: Properly speaking, I am a pastor of souls, not a woodcutter.

MOTHER COURAGE: But I don't have a soul, and I do need wood.

CHAPLAIN: What's that little pipe you've got there?

MOTHER COURAGE: Just a pipe.

CHAPLAIN: I think it's a very particular pipe.

MOTHER COURAGE: Oh?

CHAPLAIN: The cook's pipe in fact. Our Swedish Commander's cook.

MOTHER COURAGE: If you know, why beat about the bush?

CHAPLAIN: I wondered if *you* knew. It was possible you just rummaged among your belongings and just lit on . . . some pipe.

MOTHER COURAGE: How d' you know that's not it?

CHAPLAIN: It isn't! You did know! (*He brings the axe down on the block*.)

MOTHER COURAGE: What if I did?

CHAPLAIN: Mother Courage, it is my duty to warn you. You are unlikely to see the gentleman again, but that's a blessing. Mother Courage, he did not strike me as trustworthy.

MOTHER COURAGE: Really? He was such a nice man.

CHAPLAIN: Well! So that's what you call a nice man! I do not. (*Again the axe falls*.) Far be it from me to wish him ill, but I cannot, cannot describe him as nice. No, he's a Don Juan, a cunning Don Juan. Just look at that pipe if you don't believe me—it tells all!

MOTHER COURAGE: I see nothing special about this pipe. It's been used, of course ...

CHAPLAIN: It's been practically bitten through! Oho, he's a wild man! That is the pipe of a wild man! (*The axe falls more violently than ever.*)

MOTHER COURAGE: Now it's my chopping block that's bitten through!

CHAPLAIN: I told you the care of souls was my field. In physical labor my God-given talents find no adequate expression. You haven't heard me preach. Why, I can put such spirit into a regiment with a single sermon that the enemy's a mere flock of sheep to them and their own lives are no more than a smelly old pair of shoes to be instantly thrown away at the thought of final victory! God has given me the gift of tongues! I can preach you out of your senses!

MOTHER COURAGE: But I need my senses. What would I do without them?

CHAPLAIN: Mother Courage, I have often thought that—under a veil of blunt speech—you conceal a heart. You are human, you need warmth.

MOTHER COURAGE: The best way of warming this tent is to chop plenty of firewood.

CHAPLAIN: Seriously, my dear Courage, I sometimes ask myself how it would be if our relationship should be somewhat more firmly cemented. I mean: now the wild wind of war has whirled us so strangely together.

MOTHER COURAGE: The cement's pretty firm already. I cook your meals. And you lend a hand—at chopping firewood, for instance.

The CHAPLAIN *flourishes the axe as he approaches her.*

CHAPLAIN: Oh, you know what I mean by a closer relationship. Let your heart speak!

MOTHER COURAGE: Don't come at me like that with your axe! That'd be *too* close a relationship!

CHAPLAIN: This is no laughing matter. I have given it careful thought.

MOTHER COURAGE: My dear Chaplain, be sensible, I do like you. All I want is for me and mine to get by in this war. Now chop the firewood and we'll be warm in the evenings. What's that? (MOTHER COURAGE *stands up.* KATTRIN *enters with a nasty wound above her eye. She is letting everything fall, parcels, leather goods, a drum, etc.*) What happened? Were you attacked? On the way back? It's not serious, only a flesh wound. I'll bandage it up, and you'll be better within a week. Didn't the clerk walk you back? That's because you're a good girl, he thought they'd leave you alone. The wound isn't deep. It will never show. There! (*She has finished the bandage.*) Now I have a little present for you. (*She fishes Yvette's red boots out of a bag.*) See? You always wanted them—now you have them. Put them on before I change my mind. It will never show. Look, the boots have kept well, I cleaned them good before I put them away.

But KATTRIN *leaves the boots alone, and creeps into the wagon.*

CHAPLAIN: I hope she won't be disfigured.

MOTHER COURAGE: There'll be quite a scar. She needn't wait for peace now.

CHAPLAIN: She didn't let them get any of the things.

MOTHER COURAGE: I wish I knew what goes on inside her head. She stayed out all night once—once in all the years. I never did get out of her what happened. (*She picks up the things that* KATTRIN *spilled and angrily sorts them out.*) And this is war! A nice source of income, I must say! *Cannon.*

CHAPLAIN: They're lowering the Commander in his grave. A historic moment!

MOTHER COURAGE: It's historic to me all right. She's finished. How would she ever get a husband now? And she's crazy for children. Even her dumbness comes from the war. A soldier stuck something in her mouth when she was little. I'll never see Swiss Cheese again, and where my Eilif is the Good Lord knows. Curse the war!

VII

A highway. The CHAPLAIN *and* KATTRIN *are pulling the wagon. It is dirty and neglected, though new goods are hung around it.*

MOTHER COURAGE (*walking beside the wagon, a flask at her waist*): I won't have my war all spoiled for me! Destroys the weak, does it? Well, what does peace do for 'em? Huh? (*She sings The Song of Mother Courage:*)

So cheer up, boys, the rose is fading!
   When victory comes you may be dead!
A war is just the same as trading:
   But not with cheese—with steel and
      lead!
   Christians, awake! The winter's gone!
   The snows depart, the dead sleep on.
   And though you may not long
      survive
Get out of bed and look alive!

VIII

IN THE SAME YEAR, THE PROTESTANT KING FELL IN THE BATTLE OF LÜTZEN.
THE PEACE THREATENS MOTHER COURAGE WITH RUIN. HER BRAVE
SON PERFORMS ONE HEROIC DEED TOO MANY
AND COMES TO A SHAMEFUL END.

A camp. Summer morning. In front of the wagon, an OLD WOMAN *and her* SON. *The* SON *drags a large bag of bedding.* MOTHER COURAGE *is inside the wagon.*

MOTHER COURAGE: Must you come at the crack of dawn?

YOUNG MAN: We've been walking all night. Twenty miles. We have to get back today.

MOTHER COURAGE: What do I want with bed feathers? Take them to the town!

YOUNG MAN: At least wait till you see them.

OLD WOMAN: Nothing doing here either. Let's go.

YOUNG MAN: And let 'em sign away the roof over our heads for taxes? Maybe she'll pay three guilders if you throw in that bracelet. (*Bells start ringing.*) Hear that, Mother?

VOICE FROM A DISTANCE: It's peace! The King of Sweden got killed!

MOTHER COURAGE *sticks her head out of the wagon. She hasn't done her hair yet.*

MOTHER COURAGE: Bells? Bells in the middle of the week?

The CHAPLAIN *crawls out from under the wagon.*

CHAPLAIN: What's that they're shouting?

YOUNG MAN: It's peace.

CHAPLAIN: Peace?!

MOTHER COURAGE: Don't tell me peace has broken out—I've gone and bought all these supplies!

CHAPLAIN (*shouting*): Is it peace?

VOICE: Yes! The war stopped three weeks ago!

CHAPLAIN (*To* MOTHER COURAGE): Why else would they ring the bells?

VOICE: A big crowd of Lutherans just arrived —they brought the news.

YOUNG MAN: It's peace, Mother. (*The* OLD WOMAN *collapses.*) What's the matter?

MOTHER COURAGE (*back in the wagon*): Kattrin, it's peace! Put on your black dress, we're going to church, we owe it to Swiss Cheese.

YOUNG MAN: The war's over. (*The* OLD WOMAN *gets up, dazed.*) I'll get the harness shop going again now. Everything will be all right. Father will get his bed back. Can you walk? (*To the* CHAPLAIN:) It was the news. She didn't believe there'd ever be peace again. Father always said there would. We'll be going home.

They leave.

MOTHER COURAGE (*from the wagon*): Give them a schnapps!

CHAPLAIN: Too late: they've gone! And who may this be coming over from the camp? If it isn't our Swedish Commander's cook?!

The COOK *comes on, bedraggled, carrying a bundle.*

CHAPLAIN: Mother Courage, a visitor!

MOTHER COURAGE *clambers out of the wagon.*

COOK: I promised to come back, remember? For a short conversation? I didn't forget your brandy, Mrs. Fierling.

MOTHER COURAGE: The Commander's cook! After all these years! Where's Eilif?

COOK: Isn't he here yet? He went on ahead yesterday. He was on his way here.

CHAPLAIN: I'll be putting my pastor's clothes back on. (*He goes behind the wagon.*)

MOTHER COURAGE: Kattrin, Eilif's coming! Bring a glass of brandy for the cook! (*But* KATTRIN *doesn't.*) Oh, pull your hair over your face and forget it, the cook's no stranger! (*To him:*) She won't come out. Peace is nothing to her. It took too long to get here. Here's your schnapps. (*She has got it herself. They sit.*)

COOK: Dear old peace!

MOTHER COURAGE: Dear old peace has broken my neck. On the chaplain's advice I went and bought a lot of supplies. Now everybody's leaving, and I'm holding the baby.

COOK: How could you listen to a windbag like the chaplain? If I'd had the time I'd have warned you against him. But the Catholics were too quick for me. Since when did he become the big wheel around here?

MOTHER COURAGE: He's been doing the dishes and helping me with the wagon.

COOK: And telling you a few of his jokes? He has a most unhealthy attitude to women. He's completely unsound.

MOTHER COURAGE: And you're completely sound?

COOK: And I am completely sound. Your health!

MOTHER COURAGE: Sound! Only one person around here was ever sound, and I never had to slave as I did then. He sold the blankets off the children's beds in autumn. You aren't recommending yourself to me if you claim to be sound.

COOK: Ah well, here we sit, drinking your famous brandy while the bells of peace do ring!

MOTHER COURAGE: I don't see where they're going to find all this pay that's in arrears. Were you people paid?

COOK (*hesitating*): Not exactly. That's why we disbanded. Why stay? I said to myself. Why not look up a couple of friends? So here I am.

MOTHER COURAGE: In other words: you're broke.

COOK (*annoyed by the bells*): I wish they'd stop that racket! I'd like to set myself up in some business.

The CHAPLAIN *enters in his pastor's coat again.*

CHAPLAIN: Pretty good, eh? Just a few moth holes.

COOK: I have a bone to pick with you. You advised a lady to buy superfluous goods on the pretext that the war would never end.

CHAPLAIN: And what business is that of yours?

COOK: It's unprincipled behavior! How dare you interfere with the conduct of other people's businesses?

CHAPLAIN: Who's interfering now, I'd like to know? (*To* MOTHER COURAGE:) I was far from suspecting you had to account to *this* gentleman for everything!

MOTHER COURAGE: Now don't get excited. The cook's giving his personal opinion. You can hardly deny your war was a flop.

CHAPLAIN: You are a hyena of the battlefield! You are taking the name of peace in vain!

MOTHER COURAGE: I'm a what, did you say?

CHAPLAIN: A hyena!

COOK: Who insults my girl friend, insults me!

CHAPLAIN: *Your* intentions are only too transparent! (*To* MOTHER COURAGE:) But when I see *you* take peace between finger and thumb like a snotty old handkerchief, the humanity in me rebels! You want war, do you? Well, don't you forget the proverb: who sups with the devil must use a long spoon!

MOTHER COURAGE: Remember what one fox said to another that was caught in a trap? "If you stay there, you're just asking for trouble." I'm not in love with war, Mr.

Army Chaplain, and when it comes to calling people hyenas, you and I part company!

CHAPLAIN: Then why all this grumbling about the peace? Is it just for the junk in your wagon?

MOTHER COURAGE: My goods are not junk. I live off them.

CHAPLAIN: You live off war. Exactly!

COOK: As a grown man, you should know better than to run around advising people. (*To* MOTHER COURAGE:) In your situation you should get rid of certain goods at once—before prices sink to zero.

MOTHER COURAGE: That's good advice. I think I'll take it. (*She climbs on to her wagon.*)

COOK: One up for me. Anyway, Chaplain, cockfights are unbecoming to your cloth!

CHAPLAIN: If you don't shut your mouth, I'll murder you, cloth or no cloth!

Enter YVETTE, *wearing black, leaning on a stick. She is much older, fatter, and heavily powdered. Behind her, a* VALET.

YVETTE: Hullo everybody! Is this the Mother Courage establishment?

CHAPLAIN: Quite right. And with whom have we the pleasure?

YVETTE: I am Madam Colonel Starhemberg, good people. Where's Mother Courage?

CHAPLAIN (*calling to the wagon*): Madam Colonel Starhemberg to speak with you!

MOTHER COURAGE: Coming!

YVETTE (*calling*): It's me—Yvette!

MOTHER COURAGE: Yvette!

YVETTE: I've come to see how you're getting on! (*The* COOK *turns round in horror.*) Peter!

COOK: Yvette!

YVETTE: Of all things. How did *you* get here?

COOK: On a cart.

CHAPLAIN: Well! You know each other? Intimately?

YVETTE: I'll say! You're fat.

COOK: For that matter, you're no beanpole.

YVETTE: It's good we've met. Now I can tell you what I think of you, tramp.

CHAPLAIN: Do that. Tell him exactly what you think of him. But wait till Mother Courage comes out.

COOK: Now don't make a scene.

MOTHER COURAGE *comes out, laden with goods.*

MOTHER COURAGE: Yvette! (*They embrace.*) But why are you in mourning?

YVETTE: Doesn't it suit me? My husband, the colonel. died several years ago.

MOTHER COURAGE: The old fellow that nearly bought my wagon?

YVETTE: Nah, not him. His older brother.

MOTHER COURAGE: Good to see one person that got somewhere in this war.

CHAPLAIN: You promised to give us your opinion of this gentleman.

COOK: Now, Yvette, don't make a stink!

MOTHER COURAGE: He's a friend of mine, Yvette.

YVETTE: He's Peter Piper, that's what.

COOK: Cut the nicknames!

MOTHER COURAGE: Peter Piper? The one that turned the girls' heads? I'll have to sit down. And I've been keeping your pipe for you.

CHAPLAIN: And smoking it.

YVETTE: Lucky I can warn you against him. He's a bad lot. You won't find a worse on the whole coast of Flanders. He got more girls in trouble than . . .

COOK: That's a long time ago. It's not true any more.

YVETTE: Stand up when you talk to a lady! How I loved that man, and all the time he was having a little bowlegged brunette. He got her in trouble, too, of course.

COOK: I seem to have brought *you* luck.

YVETTE: Speak when you're spoken to, you hoary ruin! And take care, Mother Courage, this type is dangerous even in decay!

MOTHER COURAGE (*to* YVETTE): Come with me. I must get rid of this stuff before the prices fall.

YVETTE (*to* COOK): Miserable cur!

MOTHER COURAGE: Maybe you can help me at army headquarters—with your contacts.

YVETTE: Damnable whore hunter!

MOTHER COURAGE: Kattrin, church is all off, I'm going to market!

YVETTE: Inveterate seducer!

MOTHER COURAGE (*still to* KATTRIN): When Eilif comes, give him something to drink!

YVETTE: I've put an end to your tricks, Peter Piper, and one day, in a better life than this, the Lord God will reward me!

(*She sniffs.*) Come, Mother Courage!
The two leave. Pause.

CHAPLAIN: As our text this morning, let us take the saying: the mills of God grind slowly. And you complain of my jokes!

COOK: I'll be frank with you: I was hoping for a good hot dinner. And now she'll be getting a wrong picture of me. I think I should leave before she comes back.

CHAPLAIN: I think so too.

COOK: Chaplain, peace makes me sick! It's the lot of mankind to perish by fire and sword! Oh, how I wish I was roasting a great fat capon for the Commander—with mustard sauce and those little yellow carrots . . .

CHAPLAIN: Red cabbage. With capon: red cabbage.

COOK: You're right. But he always wanted yellow carrots.

CHAPLAIN: He never understood anything.

COOK: You always put plenty away.

CHAPLAIN: Under protest.

COOK: Anyway, you must admit, those were the days.

CHAPLAIN: Yes, that I might admit.

COOK: And now you've called her a hyena. *You* haven't much future here either . . . What are you staring at?

CHAPLAIN: Why, it's Eilif! (EILIF *enters followed by two soldiers with halberds. His hands are fettered. He is white as chalk.*) What happened?

EILIF: Where's my mother?

CHAPLAIN: Gone to the town.

EILIF: They said she was here. I was allowed a last visit.

COOK (*to the soldiers*): Where are you taking him?

SOLDIER: For a ride.

The OTHER SOLDIER *makes the gesture of throat cutting.*

CHAPLAIN: What has he done?

SOLDIER: He broke in on a peasant. The wife is dead.

CHAPLAIN: Eilif, how could you?

EILIF: It's no different. It's what I did before.

COOK: That was in wartime.

EILIF: Shut your mouth. Can I sit down till she comes?

SOLDIER: No.

CHAPLAIN: It's true. In wartime they honored him for it. He sat at the Commander's right hand. It was bravery. Couldn't we speak with the provost?

SOLDIER: What's the use? Stealing cattle from a peasant, what's brave about that?

COOK: It was just dumb.

EILIF: If I'd been dumb, I'd have starved, smarty.

COOK: So you were bright—and paid for it.

CHAPLAIN: We must bring Kattrin out.

EILIF: Let her alone. Just give me some brandy.

SOLDIER: No.

CHAPLAIN: What shall we tell your mother?

EILIF: Tell her it was no different. Tell her it was the same. Aw, tell her nothing.
The soldiers lead him away.

CHAPLAIN: I'll come with you!

EILIF: I don't need any priest.

CHAPLAIN: You don't know—yet. (*He follows them.*)

COOK: I'll have to tell her, she'll expect to see him.

CHAPLAIN: Tell her he'll be back.
He leaves. The COOK *shakes his head, finally approaches the wagon.*

COOK: Hi! Won't you come out? I'm the cook! Have you got anything to eat in there? (*He looks in.*) She's got a blanket over her head.
Cannon. Re-enter MOTHER COURAGE, *breathless, still carrying her goods.*

MOTHER COURAGE: The peace is over! The war's on again—has been for three days! I didn't get rid of this stuff after all, thank God! The shooting has started in the town already. We must get away. Pack, Kattrin! What's on *your* mind?

COOK: Nothing.

MOTHER COURAGE: But there is. l see it in your face.

COOK: Eilif was here. Only he had to go away again.

MOTHER COURAGE: He was here? Then we'll see him on the march. I'll be with our side this time. How'd he look?

COOK: The same.

MOTHER COURAGE: He'll *never* change. And the war won't get *him*, he's bright. Help me with the packing. (*She starts it.*) Is

Eilif in good with the captain? Did he tell you about his heroic deeds?

COOK: He's done one of them over again.

MOTHER COURAGE: Tell me about it later. (KATTRIN *appears*.) Kattrin, the peace is over. We're on the move again. (*To the* COOK:) What *is* eating you?

COOK: I'll enlist.

MOTHER COURAGE: Where's the Chaplain?

COOK: In the town. With Eilif.

MOTHER COURAGE: Stay with us a while, Cook, I need a bit of help.

COOK: This Yvette matter . . .

MOTHER COURAGE: Hasn't done you any harm in my eyes. Just the opposite. Where there's smoke, there's fire. You'll come?

COOK: I may as well.

MOTHER COURAGE: The twelfth regiment is under way. (THE COOK *gets into harness with* KATTRIN.) Maybe I'll see Eilif before the day is out! Let's go! (*She sings, and the* COOK *joins in the refrain, The Song of Mother Courage:*)

Up hill, down dale, past dome and steeple,
    My wagon always moves ahead.
The war can care for all its people
    So long as there is steel and lead.
Though steel and lead are stout supporters
    A war needs human beings too.
Report today to your headquarters!
    If it's to last, this war needs you!
        Christians, awake! The winter's gone!
        The snow departs, the dead sleep on.
        And though you may not long survive
        Get out of bed and look alive!

IX

THE RELIGIOUS WAR HAS LASTED SIXTEEN YEARS, AND GERMANY HAS LOST HALF ITS INHABITANTS. THOSE WHO ARE SPARED IN BATTLE DIE BY PLAGUE. OVER ONCE-BLOOMING COUNTRYSIDE HUNGER RAGES. TOWNS ARE BURNED DOWN. WOLVES PROWL THE EMPTY STREETS. IN THE AUTUMN OF 1634 WE FIND MOTHER COURAGE IN THE FICHTELGEBIRGE NOT FAR FROM THE ROAD THE SWEDISH ARMY IS TAKING. WINTER HAS COME EARLY AND IS SEVERE. BUSINESS IS BAD. ONLY BEGGING REMAINS. THE COOK RECEIVES A LETTER FROM UTRECHT AND IS SENT PACKING.

In front of a half-ruined parsonage. Early winter. A grey morning. Gusts of wind. MOTHER COURAGE *and the* COOK *at the wagon in rags.*

COOK: There are no lights. No one is up.

MOTHER COURAGE: But it's a parsonage. The parson'll have to leave his feather bed to go ring the bells. Then he'll have himself some hot soup.

COOK: Where'll he find it? The whole village is starving.

MOTHER COURAGE: Why don't we sing him something?

COOK: Anna, I've had enough. A letter came from Utrecht, did I tell you? My mother died of cholera. The inn is mine. Look!

(*He hands her the letter. She glances through it.*)

MOTHER COURAGE: I'm tired of this wandering life. I feel like a butcher's dog, taking meat to the customers and getting none for myself.

COOK: The world's coming to an end.

MOTHER COURAGE: Sometimes I dream of driving through hell with this wagon—and selling brimstone. Or I see myself driving through heaven handing out supplies to wandering souls! If only we could find a place where there's no shooting, me and my children—what's left of 'em—we might rest up a while.

COOK: Why don't we open this inn together?

With you or without you, I'm leaving for Utrecht today. Think it over.

MOTHER COURAGE: I must tell Kattrin. Kattrin! (KATTRIN *comes out of the wagon.*) Listen. We're thinking of going to Utrecht, the cook and me. His mother's left him an inn. We'd be sure of our dinner. And you'd have a bed of your own. What about it?

COOK: Anna, I must speak to you alone.

MOTHER COURAGE: Go back in, Kattrin.

KATTRIN *does so.*

COOK: There's a misunderstanding. I hoped I wouldn't have to come right out with it—but if you're bringing her, it's all off.

KATTRIN *is listening—her head sticking out at the back of the wagon.*

MOTHER COURAGE: You want me to leave Kattrin behind?

COOK: There's no room. The inn isn't a place with three counters. If the two of us stand on our hind legs we can earn a living, but three's too many. Let Kattrin keep your wagon.

MOTHER COURAGE: I was thinking she might find a husband in Utrecht.

COOK: At her age? With that scar?

MOTHER COURAGE: Not so loud!

COOK: The customers wouldn't like it!

MOTHER COURAGE: Not so loud, I said!

COOK: There's a light in the parsonage. We'd better sing. Worthy Master Parson, and all within, we shall now sing the song of Solomon, Holy Saint Martin, and other good men who came to a bad end, so you can see we're good folk too, and have a hard time getting by, especially in winter. (*He sings.* MOTHER COURAGE *joins him in the refrains.*)

THE SONG OF THE WISE AND GOOD

You've heard of wise old Solomon
  You know his history.
He thought so little of this earth
He cursed the hour of his birth
  Declaring: all is vanity.
How very wise was Solomon!
  But ere night came and day did go
This fact was clear to everyone:
  It was his wisdom that had brought
  him low.

(Better for you if you have none.)

For the virtues are dangerous in this world, you're better off without, you have a nice life—some good hot soup included. We're told to be unselfish and share what we have, but what if we have nothing? Unselfishness is a very rare virtue, it simply doesn't pay.

Unselfish Martin could not bear
  His fellow creatures' woes.
  He met a beggar in the snows
And gave him half his cloak to wear:
  So both of them fell down and froze.
What an unselfish paragon!
  But ere night came and day did go
This fact was clear to everyone:
  It was unselfishness that brought him
  low.

(Better for you if you have none.)

That's how it is! We're good, we don't steal, we don't kill, we don't burn the house down, and so, as the song says, we sink lower and lower and there isn't a plate of soup going.

God's Ten Commandments we have kept
  And acted as we should.
  It has not done us any good.
O you who sit beside a fire
  Please help us now: our need is dire!
Strict godliness we've always shown.
  But ere night came and day did go
This fact was clear to everyone:
  It was our godliness that brought us
  low.

(Better for you if you have none.)

VOICE (*from above*): You there! Come up! There's some hot soup for you!

MOTHER COURAGE: I couldn't swallow a thing. Was that your last word?

COOK: The inn isn't big enough. We better go up.

MOTHER COURAGE: I'll get Kattrin.

COOK: If there are three of us the parson won't like it. Stick something in your pocket for her.

The COOK *and* MOTHER COURAGE *enter the parsonage.* KATTRIN *climbs out of the wagon with a bundle. Making sure the others have gone, she lays out on a wagon wheel a skirt of her mother's and a pair of the* COOK'S *pants. She has just finished, and picked her bundle up, when* MOTHER COURAGE *comes down with soup for her.*

MOTHER COURAGE: Kattrin! Where do you think you're going? (*She examines the bundle.*) Ah! So you were listening! I told him: nothing doing—he can have his lousy inn. (*Now she sees the skirt and pants.*) Oh, you stupid girl! Now what if I'd seen that, and you'd been gone! (KATTRIN *tries to leave. Her mother holds her.*) And don't imagine I sent him packing on your account. It was the wagon.

They can't part me from my wagon. Now we'll put the cook's things here where he'll find 'em, that silly man. You and I are leaving. (*She climbs up on the wagon and throws the rest of the* COOK'S *few things down on to the pants.*) There! He's fired! The last man I'll ever take into *this* business! Get into harness, Kattrin. This winter will pass like all the others. *The two women harness themselves to the wagon and start out. A gust of wind. When they have disappeared, the* COOK *re-enters, still chewing. He sees his things.*

X

On the highway. MOTHER COURAGE *and* KATTRIN *are pulling the wagon. They come to a prosperous farmhouse. Someone inside is singing.*

THE SONG OF SHELTER

In March a tree we planted
To make the garden gay.
In June we were enchanted:
A lovely rose was blooming
The balmy air perfuming!
Blest of the gods are they
Who have a garden gay!

In June we were enchanted.

When snow falls helter-skelter
And loudly blows the storm
Our farmhouse gives us shelter.
The winter's in a hurry
But we've no cause to worry.
Cosy are we and warm
Though loudly blows the storm:
Our farmhouse gives us shelter.

MOTHER COURAGE *and* KATTRIN *have stopped to listen. They start out again.*

XI

JANUARY, 1636. CATHOLIC TROOPS THREATEN THE PROTESTANT TOWN OF HALLE. THE STONES BEGIN TO TALK. MOTHER COURAGE LOSES HER DAUGHTER AND JOURNEYS ONWARD ALONE. THE WAR IS NOT YET NEAR ITS END.

The wagon, very far gone now, stands near a farmhouse with a straw roof. It is night. Out of the wood come a LIEUTENANT *and* THREE SOLDIERS *in full armor.*

LIEUTENANT: And there mustn't be a sound. If anyone yells, cut him down.

FIRST SOLDIER: But we'll have to knock—if we want a guide.

LIEUTENANT: Knocking's a natural noise, it's all right, could be a cow hitting the wall of the cowshed.
The soldiers knock at the farmhouse door. An OLD PEASANT WOMAN *opens. A hand*

is clapped over her mouth. Two soldiers enter.

PEASANT'S VOICE: What is it? (*The soldiers bring out an* OLD PEASANT *and his* SON.)

LIEUTENANT (*pointing to the wagon on which* KATTRIN *has appeared*): There's another. (*A* SOLDIER *pulls her out.*) Is this everybody?

OLD PEASANT: That's our son.

PEASANT WOMAN: And that's a girl that can't talk. Her mother's in town buying up stocks because the shopkeepers are running away and selling cheap.

OLD PEASANT: They're canteen people.

LIEUTENANT: I'm warning you. Keep quiet. One sound and you'll have a sword in your ribs. I need someone to show us the path to the town. (*Points to the* YOUNG PEASANT:) You! Come here!

YOUNG PEASANT: I don't know any path!

SECOND SOLDIER (*grinning*): He don't know any path!

YOUNG PEASANT: I don't help Catholics.

LIEUTENANT (*to* SECOND SOLDIER): Show him your sword.

YOUNG PEASANT (*forced to his knees, a sword at his throat*): I'd rather die!

SECOND SOLDIER (*again mimicking*): He'd rather die!

FIRST SOLDIER: We'll soon fix this. (*Walks over to the cowshed.*) Two cows and a bull. Listen, you. If you aren't going to be reasonable, I'll saber your cattle.

YOUNG PEASANT: Not the cattle!

PEASANT WOMAN (*weeping*): Spare the cattle, Captain, or we'll starve!

LIEUTENANT: If he must be stubborn.

FIRST SOLDIER: I think I'll start with the bull.

YOUNG PEASANT (*to his father*): Do I have to? (*The* OLD PEASANT *nods.*) I'll do it.

PEASANT WOMAN: Thank you, thank you, Captain, for sparing us, for ever and ever, Amen.

The OLD PEASANT *stops her going on thanking him.*

FIRST SOLDIER: I knew the bull came first all right!

Led by the YOUNG PEASANT, *the* LIEUTENANT *and the soldiers go on their way.*

OLD PEASANT: What goes on? Nothing good, I guess.

PEASANT WOMAN: Maybe they're just scouts. What are you doing?

OLD PEASANT (*setting a ladder against the roof and climbing up*): I'm seeing if they're alone. (*On the roof:*) Things are moving— all over. I can see armor. And a cannon. There must be more than a regiment. God have mercy on the town and its people!

PEASANT WOMAN: Are there lights in the town?

OLD PEASANT: No, they're all asleep. (*He climbs down.*) It's an attack. They'll all be slaughtered in their beds.

PEASANT WOMAN: The watchman'll give warning.

OLD PEASANT: They must have killed the watchman in the tower on the hill or he'd have sounded his horn before this.

PEASANT WOMAN: If there were more of us . . .

OLD PEASANT: But being that we're alone with that cripple . . .

PEASANT WOMAN: There's nothing we can do, is there?

OLD PEASANT: Nothing.

PEASANT WOMAN: We can't get to the town in the dark.

OLD PEASANT: The whole hillside's swarming with men.

PEASANT WOMAN: We could give a sign?

OLD PEASANT: And be cut down for it?

PEASANT WOMAN: No, there's nothing we can do. (*To* KATTRIN:) Pray, poor thing, pray! There's nothing we can do to stop this bloodshed, so even if you can't talk, at least pray! He hears, if no one else does. I'll help you. (*All kneel,* KATTRIN *behind.*) Our Father, which art in Heaven, hear our prayer, let not the town perish with all that lie therein asleep and fearing nothing. Wake them, that they rise and go to the walls and see the foe that comes with fire and sword in the night down the hill and across the fields. God protect our mother and make the watchman not sleep but wake ere it's too late. And save our son-in-law too, O God, he's there with his four children, let them not perish, they're innocent, they know nothing, one of them's not two years old, the eldest is seven. (KATTRIN *rises, troubled.*) Heavenly Father, hear us, only Thou canst help us or we die, for we are weak and have no sword nor nothing; we cannot trust our own strength but only Thine, O Lord; we are in Thy hands, our cattle, our farm, and the town too, we're all in Thy hands, and the foe is nigh unto the walls with all his power. (KATTRIN, *unperceived, has crept off to the wagon, has taken something out of it, put it under her skirt, and has climbed up the ladder to the roof.*) Be mindful of the children in danger, especially the little ones, be mindful of the old folk who cannot move, and of all Christian souls, O Lord.

OLD PEASANT: And forgive us our trespasses as we forgive them that trespass against us. Amen.

Sitting on the roof, KATTRIN *takes a drum from under her skirt, and starts to beat it.*

PEASANT WOMAN: Heavens, what's she doing?

OLD PEASANT: She's out of her mind!

PEASANT WOMAN: Get her down, quick! (*The* OLD PEASANT *runs to the ladder but* KATTRIN *pulls it up on the roof.*) She'll get us in trouble.

OLD PEASANT: Stop it this minute, you silly cripple!

PEASANT WOMAN: The soldiers'll come!

OLD PEASANT (*looking for stones*): I'll stone you!

PEASANT WOMAN: Have you no pity, don't you have a heart? We have relations there too, four grandchildren. If they find us now, it's the end, they'll stab us to death! (KATTRIN *is staring into the far distance, toward the town. She goes on drumming. To the* PEASANT:) I told you not to let that sort into the farm. What do *they* care if we lose our cattle?

LIEUTENANT (*running back with soldiers and* YOUNG PEASANT): I'll cut you all to bits!

PEASANT WOMAN: We're innocent, sir, we couldn't stop her!

LIEUTENANT: Where's the ladder?

OLD PEASANT: On the roof.

LIEUTENANT (*calling*): Throw down the drum. I order you! (*To peasants:*) You're all in this, but you won't live to tell the tale.

OLD PEASANT: They've been cutting down fir trees around here. If we get a good long trunk we can knock her off the roof . . .

FIRST SOLDIER (*to the* LIEUTENANT): May I make a suggestion? (*He whispers something to the* LIEUTENANT, *who nods. To* KATTRIN:) Listen, you! We'll do you a favor. Everyone in that town is gonna get killed. Come down, go with us to the town, show us your mother and we'll spare her.

KATTRIN *replies with more drumming.*

LIEUTENANT (*pushing him away*): She doesn't trust you, no wonder with your face. (*He calls up to* KATTRIN:) Hey, you! Suppose I give you my word? I'm an officer, my word's my bond! (KATTRIN *again replies with drumming—harder this time.*) Nothing is sacred to her.

FIRST SOLDIER: They'll sure as hell hear it in the town.

LIEUTENANT: We must make another noise. Louder than that drum. What can we make a noise with?

FIRST SOLDIER: We mustn't make a noise!

LIEUTENANT: A harmless noise, fool, a peacetime noise!

OLD PEASANT: I could start chopping wood.

LIEUTENANT: That's it! (*The* PEASANT *brings his axe and chops away.*) Chop! Chop harder! Chop for your life! It's not enough. (*To* FIRST SOLDIER:) You chop too!

OLD PEASANT: I've only one axe.

LIEUTENANT: We must set fire to the farm. Smoke her out.

OLD PEASANT: That's no good, Captain, when they see fire from the town, they'll know everything.

KATTRIN *is laughing now and drumming harder than ever.*

LIEUTENANT: Laughing at us, is she? I'll settle *her* hash if it's the last thing I do. Bring me a musket!

Two soldiers off.

PEASANT WOMAN: I have it, Captain. That's their wagon over there, Captain. If we smash that, she'll stop. It's all they have, Captain.

LIEUTENANT (*to the* YOUNG PEASANT): Smash it! (*Calling:*) If you don't stop that noise, we'll smash up your wagon!

The YOUNG PEASANT *deals the wagon a couple of feeble blows with a board.*

PEASANT WOMAN (*to* KATTRIN): Stop, you little beast!

KATTRIN *stares at the wagon and pauses. Noises of distress come out of her. She goes on drumming.*

LIEUTENANT: Where are those sonsofbitches with that gun?

FIRST SOLDIER: They can't have heard anything in the town or we'd hear their cannon.

LIEUTENANT (*calling*): They don't hear you. And now we're going to shoot. I'll give you one more chance: throw down that drum!

YOUNG PEASANT (*dropping the board, screaming to* KATTRIN): Don't stop now! Go on, go on, go on!

The soldier knocks him down and stabs him. KATTRIN *starts crying but goes on drumming.*

PEASANT WOMAN: You're killing him!

The soldiers arrive with the gun.

LIEUTENANT: Set it up! (*Calling while the gun is set up on forks:*) Once for all: stop that drumming! (*Still crying,* KATTRIN *is drumming as hard as she can.*) Fire!

The soldiers fire. KATTRIN *is hit. She gives the drum another feeble beat or two, then collapses.*

LIEUTENANT: So that ends the noise.

But the last beats of the drum are lost in the din of cannon from the town. Mingled with the thunder of cannon, alarmbells are heard in the distance.

FIRST SOLDIER: She made it.

XII

Toward morning. The drums and pipes of troops on the march, receding. In front of the wagon MOTHER COURAGE *sits by* KATTRIN'S *body. The* THREE PEASANTS *of the last scene are standing near.*

PEASANT WOMAN: The regiments have all left. No, there's still one to go.

OLD PEASANT (*to* MOTHER COURAGE): You must latch on to it. You'll never get by alone. Hurry!

MOTHER COURAGE: Maybe she's asleep. (*She sings:*)

Lullay, lullay, what's that in the hay?
The neighbor's kids cry but mine are gay.
The neighbor's kids are dressed in dirt:
Your silks were cut from an angel's skirt.
They are all starving: you have a cake;
If it's too stale, you need but speak.
Lullay, lullay, what's rustling there?
One lad fell in Poland. The other is—
where?

MOTHER COURAGE: You shouldn't have told her about the children.

OLD PEASANT: If you hadn't gone off to get your cut, maybe it wouldn't have happened.

MOTHER COURAGE: I'm glad she can sleep.

PEASANT WOMAN: She's not asleep, it's time you realized, she's through.

OLD PEASANT: You must get away. There are wolves in these parts. And the bandits are worse.

MOTHER COURAGE (*stands up*): That's right.

OLD PEASANT: Have you no one left?

MOTHER COURAGE: Yes, my son Eilif.

OLD PEASANT: Find him then, leave *her* to us.

PEASANT WOMAN: We'll give her a proper burial, you needn't worry.

MOTHER COURAGE: Here's a little money for the expenses. (*She harnesses herself to the wagon.*) I hope I can pull the wagon by myself. Yes, I'll manage. There's not much in it now. (*The last regiment is heard passing.*) Hey! Take me with you!

The men are heard singing The Song of Mother Courage:

Dangers, surprises, devastations—
    The war takes hold and will not quit.
But though it last three generations
    We shall get nothing out of it.
Starvation, filth, and cold enslave us.
    The army robs us of our pay.
Only a miracle can save us
    And miracles have had their day.
        Christians, awake! The winter's gone!
        The snows depart, the dead sleep on.
        And though you may not long survive
        Get out of bed and look alive!

Perhaps the most buoyant and mercurial talent in the modern theater is that of Eugène Ionesco, the Rumanian-born (in 1912) dramatist who writes in the French language. Ionesco called his first work an "antiplay" to announce his opposition to what seemed to him the tired contrivances of the theater, and he proclaimed his determination to overthrow them by example. At the same time he indicated that his technique would be to make daring use of imagination, subverting the face of reality, exaggerating its forms and distorting its shapes in order to make its banal essence all too recognizable. He would use calculated absurdities in the theater in order to call attention to the less obvious but more dangerous and paralyzing absurdities of real life.

Many of these themes and devices appear in *The Chairs* (1952), perhaps Ionesco's most successful departure from conventional theater. In this play about two old people who make one last attempt to communicate a message to the world before they depart from it, is suggested both the playwright's struggle to break through convention and achieve real, direct communication, and the fear that what he has to communicate may, even if it is heard, be meaningless. Again in this play, man is overwhelmed by the proliferation of objects—the chairs that increasingly fill the stage; and these objects, these rows of emptiness, confront the audience as a vivid and theatrically powerful image. What is their "meaning"? One may speculate on many themes they suggest—the failure of life, the breakdown of communication—but can probably do no better than quote Ionesco himself, who, writing to the director of the first perfomance of *The Chairs*, supplied this comment on the "meaning" he wanted to emerge from the production: "The subject of the play is not the message, nor the failures of life, nor the moral disaster of the two old people, but the chairs themselves; that is to say, the absence of people, the absence of the emperor, the absence of God, the absence of matter, the unreality of the world, metaphysical emptiness. The theme of the play is *nothingness* . . . ; the invisible elements must be more and more clearly present, more and more real (to give unreality to reality one must give reality to the unreal), until the point is reached—inadmissible, unacceptable to the reasoning mind—when the unreal elements speak and move . . . and nothingness can be heard, is made concrete."[1]

Speaking of this sense of nothingness that emerges from Ionesco's plays, and from the plays of other avant-garde dramatists, the critic and producer Harold Clurman wrote: "All these playwrights are antinaturalistic; most of them strike a fundamental note of despair, though their despair wears an ironic grimace. All of them couch their plays in more or less abstract terms in which the depiction of individual characters and the psychology of particular persons are minimized or entirely absent. Thus these plays take on a mythlike character—emblematic of a general human condition in modern society, perhaps even 'universal'.

"The language they employ—though always in prose—is akin to poetry in its attempt to achieve greater concentration and essential meaning (or

---

[1] Quoted in Martin Esslin, *The Theatre of the Absurd* (Garden City, N. Y.: Doubleday & Company, Inc., 1961), p. 100.

meaninglessness!) than ordinary speech. Running through many of these plays—particularly Ionesco's—we find a secondary theme which demonstrates that men today can no longer communicate with one another in any but the most desultory manner. For all values beyond self-preservation have become nebulous or hypocritical to the point of atrophy. What governs our lives are automatic reflexes and the rote of bare utility." In spite of such views, Ionesco turned his back on a theater which depended for its effects on a blackened imitation of life.

He associated realism in the theater with drabness, whereas he believed its more fitting qualities were imagination, amazement, and delight. This sense of wonder is what he has aimed at recapturing in his plays. His early sense of unease, he came to realize, grew not because the theater was too realistic, but because it was not realistic enough—it was too cautious, too inhibited, too slavishly literal. It was not true to man's inventive and imaginative powers, the real source of the pleasure and the insight that give meaning and fulfillment to his existence. Very well, Ionesco said, he would include the circus in the theater—that is, he would restore its lost illusions, he would seek a kind of "beyond-reality"[2] based not on the literal representation of the details of man's existence but on the enlargement and exaggeration of those details in such a way as to reveal hitherto unnoticed absurdities or to provide enlightenment through ridicule. In carrying out these aims, Ionesco within a decade wrote several of the most strikingly original and imaginative plays in the whole range of drama. Seeming at first to defy not only the conventions of the theater but the very logic of human existence, they gradually came to be seen as irresistibly compelling though paradoxical portrayals of man's real dilemmas—the search for identity, the struggle for individuality, the attempt to make something heroic out of his awareness of despair and death. To communicate this vision, Ionesco used all the resources of the theater—stage effects, sounds unrelated to the action, actors stepping in and out of character or forgetting who they were, props like chairs and coffee cups that possessed human characteristics, women who grew additional noses on demand, inanimate objects that talked back, clocks that chimed the hours whenever they felt like it, as well as language that itself often seemed ambiguous and indifferently related to the stage action. It was as if Ionesco had decided that, rather than try to conceal the artifice of the theater under the guise of realism, he would readily admit it was all illusion, and would then show that imagination gave a "truer" account of man's state than did reason. "Fantasy is revealing," he has written; "it is a method of cognition: everything that is imagined is true; nothing is true that is not imagined."[3]

---

[2] The phrase is George E. Wellwarth's, in his book, *The Theater of Protest and Paradox* (New York: New York University Press, 1964), p. 53

[3] Quoted in Martin Esslin *op. cit.*, p. 130

THE CHAIRS

A TRAGIC FARCE

Eugène Ionesco

Translated by
Donald M. Allen

OLD MAN, *aged 95*
OLD WOMAN, *aged 94*
THE ORATOR, *aged 45 to 50*
And many other characters

SCENE: *Circular walls with a recess upstage center. A large, very sparsely furnished room. To the right, going upstage from the pro-* *scenium, three doors. Then a window with a stool in front of it; then another door. In the center of the back wall of the recess, a large double door, and two other doors facing each other and bracketing the main door: these last two doors, or at least one of them, are almost hidden from the audience. To the left, going upstage from the proscenium, there are three doors, a window with a stool in front of it,*

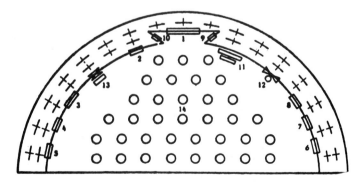

1: Main double door.
2, 3, 4, 5: Side doors on the right.
6, 7, 8: Side doors on the left.
9, 10: Two doors hidden in the recess.

11: Dais and blackboard.
12, 13: Windows, with stools, left and right.
14: Empty chairs.
XXX Corridor, in wings.

opposite the window on the right, then a
blackboard and a dais. See the plan below.
Downstage are two chairs, side by side. A
gas lamp hangs from the ceiling.

[The curtain rises. Half-light. The Old Man
is up on the stool, leaning out the window
on the left. The Old Woman lights the gas
lamp. Green light. She goes over to the
Old Man and takes him by the sleeve.]

OLD WOMAN: Come my darling, close the
window. There's a bad smell from that
stagnant water, and besides the mos-
quitoes are coming in.

OLD MAN: Leave me alone!

OLD WOMAN: Come, come, my darling,
come sit down. You shouldn't lean out,
you might fall into the water. You know
what happened to François I. You must
be careful.

OLD MAN: Still more examples from history!
Sweetheart, I'm tired of French history.
I want to see—the boats on the water
making blots in the sunlight.

OLD WOMAN: You can't see them, there's no
sunlight, it's nighttime, my darling.

OLD MAN: There are still shadows. [He leans
out very far.]

OLD WOMAN [pulling him in with all her
strength]: Oh!... you're frightening me,
my darling... come sit down, you won't
be able to see them come, anyway. There's
no use trying. It's dark...

[The Old Man reluctantly lets himself be
pulled in.]

OLD MAN: I wanted to see—you know how
much I love to see the water.

OLD WOMAN: How can you, my darling?
...It makes me dizzy. Ah! this house,
this island, I can't get used to it. Water
all around us...water under the windows, stretching as far as the horizon.

[The Old Woman drags the Old Man down
and they move towards the two chairs
downstage; the Old Man seats himself quite
naturally on the lap of the Old Woman.]

OLD MAN: It's six o'clock in the evening...
it is dark already. It wasn't like this
before. Surely you remember, there was
still daylight at nine o'clock in the evening,
at ten o'clock, at midnight.

OLD WOMAN: Come to think of it, that's
very true. What a remarkable memory
you have!

OLD MAN: Things have certainly changed.

OLD WOMAN: Why is that, do you think?

OLD MAN: I don't know, Semiramis, sweetheart... Perhaps it's because the further
one goes, the deeper one sinks. It's because the earth keeps turning around,
around, around, around...

OLD WOMAN: Around, around, my little pet.
[Silence.] Ah! yes, you've certainly a fine
intellect. You are very gifted, my darling.
You could have been head president,
head king, or even head doctor, or head
general, if you had wanted to, if only
you'd had a little ambition in life...

OLD MAN: What good would that have done
us? We'd not have lived any better...
and besides, we have a position here.
I am a general, in any case, of the house,
since I am the general factotum.

OLD WOMAN [caressing the Old Man as one
caresses a child]: My darling, my pet.

OLD MAN: I'm very bored.

OLD WOMAN: You were more cheerful when
you were looking at the water... Let's
amuse ourselves by making believe, the
way you did the other evening.

OLD MAN: Make believe yourself, it's your
turn.

OLD WOMAN: It's your turn.

OLD MAN: Your turn.

OLD WOMAN: Your turn.

OLD MAN: Your turn.

OLD WOMAN: Your turn.

OLD MAN: Drink your tea, Semiramis.

[Of course there is no tea.]

OLD WOMAN: Come on now, imitate the
month of February.

OLD MAN: I don't like the months of the
year.

OLD WOMAN: Those are the only ones we
have, up till now. Come on, just to please
me...

OLD MAN: All right, here's the month of
February. [He scratches his head like Stan
Laurel.]

OLD WOMAN [laughing, applauding]: That's
just right. Thank you, thank you, you're
as cute as can be, my darling. [She hugs

him.] Oh, you are so gifted, you could have been at least a head general, if you had wanted to . . .

OLD MAN: I am a general, general factotum. [*Silence.*]

OLD WOMAN: Tell me the story, you know *the* story: "Then at last we arrived . . ."

OLD MAN: Again? . . . I'm sick of it . . . "Then at last we arrived"? That again . . . you always ask for the same thing! . . . "Then at last we arrived . . ." But it's monotonous . . . For all of the seventy-five years that we've been married, every single evening, absolutely every blessed evening, you've made me tell the same story, you've made me imitate the same people, the same months . . . always the same . . . let's talk about something else . . .

OLD WOMAN: My darling, I'm not tired of it . . . it's your life, it fascinates me.

OLD MAN: You know it by heart.

OLD WOMAN: It's as if suddenly I'd forgotten everything . . . it's as though my mind were a clean slate every evening . . . Yes, my darling, I do it on purpose, I take a dose of salts . . . I become new again, for you, my darling, every evening . . . Come on, begin again, please.

OLD MAN: Well, if you want me to.

OLD WOMAN: Come on then, tell your story . . . It's also mine; what is yours is mine! Then at last we arrived . . .

OLD MAN: Then at last we arrived . . . my sweetheart . . .

OLD WOMAN: Then at last we arrived . . . my darling . . .

OLD MAN: Then at last we arrived at a big fence. We were soaked through, frozen to the bone, for hours, for days, for nights, for weeks . . .

OLD WOMAN: For months . . .

OLD MAN: . . . In the rain . . . Our ears, our feet, our knees, our noses, our teeth were chattering . . . that was eighty years ago . . . They wouldn't let us in . . . they might at least have opened the gate of the garden . . . [*Silence.*]

OLD WOMAN: In the garden the grass was wet.

OLD MAN: There was a path which led to a little square and in the center, a village church . . . Where was this village? Do you recall?

OLD WOMAN: No, my darling, I've forgotten.

OLD MAN: How did we reach it? Where is the road? This place was called Paris, I think . . .

OLD WOMAN: Paris never existed, my little one.

OLD MAN: That city must have existed because it collapsed . . . It was the city of light, but it has been extinguished, extinguished, for four hundred thousand years . . . Nothing remains of it today, except a song.

OLD WOMAN: A real song? That's odd. What song?

OLD MAN: A lullaby, an allegory: "Paris will always be Paris."

OLD WOMAN: And the way to it was through the garden? Was it far?

OLD MAN [*dreaming, lost*]: The song? . . . the rain? . . .

OLD WOMAN: You are very gifted. If you had had a little ambition in life you could have been head king, head journalist, head comedian, head general . . . All that's gone down the drain, alas . . . down the old black drain . . . down the old drain, I tell you. [*Silence.*]

OLD MAN: Then at last we arrived . . .

OLD WOMAN: Ah! yes, go on . . . tell me . . .

OLD MAN [*while the Old Woman begins to laugh softly, senilely, then progressively in great bursts, the Old Man laughs, too, as he continues*]: Then at last we arrived, we laughed till we cried, the story was so idiotic . . . the idiot arrived full speed, bare-bellied, the idiot was pot-bellied . . . he arrived with a trunk chock full of rice; the rice spilled out on the ground . . . the idiot on the ground too, belly to ground . . . then at last we laughed, we laughed, we laughed, the idiotic belly, bare with rice on the ground, the trunk, the story of sick from rice belly to ground, bare-bellied, all with rice, at last we laughed, the idiot at last arrived all bare, we laughed . . .

OLD WOMAN [*laughing*]: At last we laughed like idiots, at last arrived all bare, we laughed, the trunk, the trunk full of rice, the rice on the belly, on the ground . . .

OLD MAN AND OLD WOMAN [*laughing toge-ther*]: At last we laughed. Ah! . . . laughed . . . arrived . . . arrived . . . Ah! . . . Ah! . . . rived . . . arrived . . . arrived . . . the idiotic bare belly . . . arrived with the rice . . . arrived with the rice . . . [*This is all we hear.*] At last we . . . bare-bellied . . . arrived . . . the trunk . . . [*Then the Old Man and Old Woman calm down little by little.*] We lau . . . Ah! . . . aughed . . . Ah! . . . arrived . . . Ah! . . . arrived . . . aughed . . . aughed.

OLD WOMAN: So that's the way it was, your wonderful Paris.

OLD MAN: Who could put it better?

OLD WOMAN: Oh! my darling, you are so really fine. Oh! so really, you know, so really, so really, you could have been anything in life, a lot more than general factotum.

OLD MAN: Let's be modest . . . we should be content with the little . . .

OLD WOMAN: Perhaps you've spoiled your career?

OLD MAN [*weeping suddenly*]: I've spoiled it? I've spilled it? Ah! where are you, Mam-ma, Mamma, where are you, Mamma? . . . hi, hi, hi, I'm an orphan. [*He moans.*] . . . an orphan, dworfan.

OLD WOMAN: Here I am, what are you afraid of?

OLD MAN: No, Semiramis, my sweetheart, you're not my mamma . . . orphan, dwor-fan, who will protect me?

OLD WOMAN: But I'm here, my darling!

OLD MAN: It's not the same thing . . . I want my mamma, na, you, you're not my mamma, you . . .

OLD WOMAN [*caressing him*]: You're break-ing my heart, don't cry, my little one.

OLD MAN: Hi, hi, let me go, hi, hi, I'm all spoiled, I'm wet all over, my career is spilled, it's spoiled.

OLD WOMAN: Calm down.

OLD MAN [*sobbing his mouth wide open like a baby*]: I'm an orphan . . . dworfan.

OLD WOMAN [*trying to console him by cajoling him*]: My orphan, my darling, you're breaking my heart, my orphan.

[*She rocks the Old Man who is sitting on her knees again.*]

OLD MAN [*sobbing*]: Hi, hi, hi! My mamma! Where is my mamma? I don't have a mamma anymore.

OLD WOMAN: I am your wife, I'm the one who is your mamma now.

OLD MAN [*giving in a little*]: That's not true, I'm an orphan, hi, hi.

OLD WOMAN [*still rocking him*]: My pet, my orphan, dworfan, worfan, morphan, orphan.

OLD MAN [*still sulky, but giving in more and more*]: No . . . I don't wan't; I don't wa-a-a-ant.

OLD WOMAN [*crooning*]: Orphan-ly, orphan-lay, orphan-lo, orphan-loo.

OLD MAN: No-o-o . . . No-o-o.

OLD WOMAN [*same business*]: Li lon lala, li lon la lay, orphan-ly, orphan-lay, relee-relay, orphan-li-relee-rela . . .

OLD MAN: Hi, hi, hi, hi. [*He sniffles, calming down little by little.*] Where is she? My mamma.

OLD WOMAN: In heavenly paradise . . . she hears you, she sees you, among the flowers; don't cry anymore, you will only make me weep!

OLD MAN: That's not even true-ue . . . she can't see me . . . she can't hear me. I'm an orphan, on earth, you're not my mamma . . .

OLD WOMAN [*he is almost calm*]: Now, come on, calm down, don't get so upset . . . you have great qualities, my little general . . . dry your tears; the guests are sure to come this evening and they mustn't see you this way . . . all is not lost, all is not spoiled, you'll tell them everything, you will explain, you have a message . . . you always say you are going to deliver it . . . you must live, you have to struggle for your message . . .

OLD MAN: I have a message, that's God's truth, I struggle, a mission, I have some-thing to say, a message to communicate to humanity, to mankind . . .

OLD WOMAN: To mankind, my darling, your message! . . .

OLD MAN: That's true, yes, it's true . . .

OLD WOMAN [*she wipes the Old Man's nose,*

dries his tears]: That's it . . . you're a man, a soldier, a general factotum . . .

OLD MAN [*he gets off the Old Woman's lap and walks with short, agitated steps*]: I'm not like other people, I have an ideal in life. I am perhaps gifted, as you say, I have some talent, but things aren't easy for me. I've served well in my capacity as general factotum, I've always been in command of the situation, honorably, that should be enough . . .

OLD WOMAN: Not for you, you're not like other people, you are much greater, and moreover you'd have done much better if you had got along with other people, like other people do. You've quarreled with all your friends, with all the directors, with all the generals, with your own brother.

OLD MAN: It's not my fault, Semiramis, you know very well what he said.

OLD WOMAN: What did he say?

OLD MAN: He said: "My friends, I've got a flea. I'm going to pay you a visit in the hope of leaving my flea with you."

OLD WOMAN: People say things like that, my dear. You shouldn't have paid any attention to it. But with Carel, why were you so angry with him. Was it his fault too?

OLD MAN: You're going to make me angry, you're going to make me angry. Na. Of course it was his fault. He came one evening, he said: "I know just the word that fits you. I'm not going to say it, I'll just think it." And he laughed like a fool.

OLD WOMAN: But he had a warm heart, my darling. In this life, you've got to be less sensitive.

OLD MAN: I don't care for jokes like that.

OLD WOMAN: You could have been head admiral, head cabinet-maker, head orchestra conductor.

[*Long silence. They remain immobile for a time, completely rigid on their chairs.*]

OLD MAN [*as in a dream*]: At the end of the garden there was . . . there was . . . there was . . . there was . . . was what, my dear?

OLD WOMAN: The city of Paris!

OLD MAN: At the end, at the end of the end of the city of Paris, there was, there was, was what?

OLD WOMAN: My darling, was what, my darling, was who?

OLD MAN: The place and the weather were beautiful . . .

OLD WOMAN: The weather was so beautiful, are you sure?

OLD MAN: I don't recall the place . . .

OLD WOMAN: Don't tax your mind then . . .

OLD MAN: It's too far away, I can no longer . . . recall it . . . where was this?

OLD WOMAN: But what?

OLD MAN: What I . . . what I . . . where was this? And who?

OLD WOMAN: No matter where it is—I will follow you anywhere, I'll follow you, my darling.

OLD MAN: Ah! I have so much difficulty expressing myself . . . but I must tell it all.

OLD WOMAN: It's a sacred duty. You've no right to keep your message from the world. You must reveal it to mankind, they're waiting for it . . . the universe waits only for you.

OLD MAN: Yes, yes, I will speak.

OLD WOMAN: Have you really decided? You must.

OLD MAN: Drink your tea.

OLD WOMAN: You could have been head orator, if you'd had more will power in life . . . I'm proud, I'm happy that you have at last decided to speak to every country, to Europe, to every continent!

OLD MAN: Unfortunately, I have so much difficulty expressing myself, it isn't easy for me.

OLD WOMAN: It's easy once you begin, like life and death . . . it's enough to have your mind made up. It's in speaking that ideas come to us, words, and then we, in our own words, we find perhaps everything, the city too, the garden, and then we are orphans no longer.

OLD MAN: It's not I who's going to speak, I've hired a professional orator, he'll speak in my name, you'll see.

OLD WOMAN: Then, it really is for this evening? And have you invited everyone, all the characters, all the property owners, and all the intellectuals?

OLD MAN: Yes, all the owners and all the intellectuals. [*Silence.*]

OLD WOMAN: The janitors? the bishops? the chemists? the tinsmiths? the violinists? the delegates? the presidents? the police? the merchants? the buildings? the pen holders? the chromosomes?

OLD MAN: Yes, yes, and the post-office employees, the innkeepers, and the artists, everybody who is a little intellectual, a little proprietary!

OLD WOMAN: And the bankers?

OLD MAN: Yes, invited.

OLD WOMAN: The proletarians? the functionaries? the militaries? the revolutionaries? the reactionaries? the alienists and their alienated?

OLD MAN: Of course, all of them, all of them, all of them, since actually everyone is either intellectual or proprietary.

OLD WOMAN: Don't get upset, my darling, I don't mean to annoy you, you are so very absent-minded, like all great geniuses. This meeting is important, they must all be here this evening. Can you count on them? Have they promised?

OLD MAN: Drink your tea, Semiramis. [*Silence.*]

OLD WOMAN: The papacy, the papayas, and the papers?

OLD MAN: I've invited them. [*Silence.*] I'm going to communicate the message to them . . . All my life, I've felt that I was suffocating; and now, they will know all, thanks to you and to the Orator, you are the only ones who have understood me.

OLD WOMAN: I'm so proud of you . . .

OLD MAN: The meeting will take place in a few minutes.

OLD WOMAN: It's true then, they're going to come, this evening? You won't feel like crying any more, the intellectuals and the proprietors will take the place of papas and mammas? [*Silence.*] Couldn't you put off this meeting? It won't be too tiring for us?

[*More violent agitation. For several moments the Old Man has been turning around the Old Woman with the short, hesitant steps of an old man or of a child.*]

[*He takes a step or two towards one of the doors, then returns and walks around her again.*]

OLD MAN: You really think this might tire us?

OLD WOMAN: You have a slight cold.

OLD MAN: How can I call it off?

OLD WOMAN: Invite them for another evening. You could telephone.

OLD MAN: No, my God, I can't do that, it's too late. They've probably already embarked!

OLD WOMAN: You should have been more careful.

[*We hear the sound of a boat gliding through the water.*]

OLD MAN: I think someone is coming already . . . [*The gliding sound of a boat is heard more clearly.*] . . . Yes, they're coming! . . .

[*The Old Woman gets up also and walks with a hobble.*]

OLD WOMAN: Perhaps it's the Orator.

OLD MAN: He won't come so soon. This must be somebody else. [*We hear the doorbell ring.*] Ah!

OLD WOMAN: Ah!

[*Nervously, the Old Man and the Old Woman move towards the concealed door in the recess to the right. As they move upstage, they say:*]

OLD MAN: Come on . . .

OLD WOMAN: My hair must look a sight . . . wait a moment . . .

[*She arranges her hair and her dress as she hobbles along, pulling up her thick red stockings.*]

OLD MAN: You should have gotten ready before . . . you had plenty of time.

OLD WOMAN: I'm so badly dressed . . . I'm wearing an old gown and it's all rumpled . . .

OLD MAN: All you had to do was to press it . . . hurry up! You're making our guests wait.

[*The Old Man, followed by the Old Woman still grumbling, reaches the door in the recess; we don't see them for a moment; we hear them open the door, then close it again after having shown someone in.*]

VOICE OF OLD MAN: Good evening, madam, won't you please come in. We're delighted to see you. This is my wife.

VOICE OF OLD WOMAN: Good evening, madam, I am very happy to make your acquaintance. Take care, don't ruin your hat. You might take out the hatpin, that will be more comfortable. Oh! no, no one will sit on it.

VOICE OF OLD MAN: Put your fur down there. Let me help you. No, nothing will happen to it.

VOICE OF OLD WOMAN: Oh! what a pretty suit . . . and such darling colors in your blouse . . . Won't you have some cookies . . . Oh, you're not fat at all . . . no . . . plump . . . Just leave your umbrella there.

VOICE OF OLD MAN: Follow me, please.

OLD MAN [*back view*]: I have only a modest position . . .

[*The Old Man and Old Woman re-enter together, leaving space between them for their guest. She is invisible. The Old Man and Old Woman advance, downstage, facing the audience and speaking to the invisible Lady, who walks between them.*]

OLD MAN [*to the invisible Lady*]: You've had good weather?

OLD WOMAN [*to the Lady*]: You're not too tired? . . . Yes, a little.

OLD MAN [*to the Lady*]: At the edge of the water . . .

OLD WOMAN [*to the Lady*]: It's kind of you to say so.

OLD MAN [*to the Lady*]: Let me get you a chair. [*Old Man goes to the left, he exits by door No. 6.*]

OLD WOMAN [*to the Lady*]: Take this one, for the moment, please. [*She indicates one of the two chairs and seats herself on the other, to the right of the invisible Lady.*] It seems rather warm in here, doesn't it? [*She smiles at the Lady.*] What a charming fan you have! My husband . . . [*The Old Man re-enters through door No. 7, carrying a chair.*] . . . gave me one very like it, that must have been seventy-three years ago . . . and I still have it . . . [*The Old Man places the chair to the left of the invisible Lady.*] . . . it was for my birthday! . . .

[*The Old Man sits on the chair that he has just brought onstage, so that the invisible Lady is between the old couple. The Old Man turns his face towards the Lady, smiles at her, nods his head, softly rubs his hands together, with the air of following what she says. The Old Woman does the same business.*]

OLD MAN: No, madam, life is never cheap.

OLD WOMAN [*to the Lady*]: You are so right . . . [*The Lady speaks.*] As you say, it is about time all that changed . . . [*Changing her tone:*] Perhaps my husband can do something about it . . . he's going to tell you about it.

OLD MAN [*to the Old Woman*]: Hush, hush, Semiramis, the time hasn't come to talk about that yet. [*To the Lady:*] Excuse me, madam, for having aroused your curiosity. [*The Lady reacts.*] Dear madam, don't insist . . .

[*The Old Man and Old Woman smile. They even laugh. They appear to be very amused by the story the invisible Lady tells them. A pause, a moment of silence in the conversation. Their faces lose all expression.*]

OLD MAN [*to the invisible Lady*]: Yes, you're quite right . . .

OLD WOMAN: Yes, yes, yes . . . Oh! surely not.

OLD MAN: Yes, yes, yes. Not at all.

OLD WOMAN: Yes?

OLD MAN: No!?

OLD WOMAN: It's certainly true.

OLD MAN [*laughing*]: It isn't possible.

OLD WOMAN [*laughing*]: Oh! well. [*To the Old Man:*] she's charming.

OLD MAN [*to the Old Woman*]: Madam has made a conquest. [*To the invisible Lady:*] my congratulations! . . .

OLD WOMAN [*to the invisible Lady*]: You're not like the young people today . . .

OLD MAN [*bending over painfully in order to recover an invisible object that the invisible Lady has dropped*]: Let me . . . don't disturb yourself . . . I'll get it . . . Oh! you're quicker than I . . . [*He straightens up again.*]

OLD WOMAN [*to the Old Man*]: She's younger than you!

OLD MAN [*to the invisible Lady*]: Old age is a heavy burden. I can only wish you an eternal youth.

OLD WOMAN [*to the invisible Lady*]: He's sincere, he speaks from the heart. [*To the Old Man:*] My darling!

[*Several moments of silence. The Old Man and Old Woman, heads turned in profile, look at the invisible Lady, smiling politely; they then turn their heads towards the audience, then look again at the invisible Lady, answering her smile with their smiles, and her questions with their replies.*]

OLD WOMAN: It's very kind of you to take such an interest in us.

OLD MAN: We live a retired life.

OLD WOMAN: My husband's not really misanthropic, he just loves solitude.

OLD MAN: We have the radio, I get in some fishing, and then there's fairly regular boat service.

OLD WOMAN: On Sundays there are two boats in the morning, one in the evening, not to mention privately chartered trips.

OLD MAN [*to the invisible Lady*]: When the weather's clear, there is a moon.

OLD WOMAN [*to the invisible Lady*]: He's always concerned with his duties as general factotum . . . they keep him busy . . . On the other hand, at his age, he might very well take it easy.

OLD MAN [*to the invisible Lady*]: I'll have plenty of time to take it easy in my grave.

OLD WOMAN [*to the Old Man*]: Don't say that, my little darling . . . [*To the invisible Lady*]: Our family, what's left of it, my husband's friends, still came to see us, from time to time, ten years ago . . .

OLD MAN [*to the invisible Lady*]: In the winter, a good book, beside the radiator, and the memories of a lifetime.

OLD WOMAN [*to the invisible Lady*]: A modest life but a full one . . . he devotes two hours every day to work on his message.

[*The doorbell rings. After a short pause, we hear the noise of a boat leaving.*]

OLD WOMAN [*to the Old Man*]: Someone has come. Go quickly.

OLD MAN [*to the invisible Lady*]: Please excuse me, madam. Just a moment! [*To the Old Woman:*] Hurry and bring some chairs!

[*Loud ringing of the doorbell.*]

OLD MAN [*hastening, all bent over, towards door No. 2 to the right, while the Old Woman goes towards the concealed door on the left, hurrying with difficulty, hobbling along*]: It must be someone important. [*He hurries, opens door No. 2, and the invisible Colonel enters. Perhaps it would be useful for us to hear discreetly several trumpet notes, several phrases, like "Hail the Chief." When he opens the door and sees the invisible Colonel, the Old Man stiffens into a respectful position of attention.*] Ah! . . . Colonel! [*He lifts his hand vaguely towards his forehead, so as to roughly sketch a salute.*] Good evening, my dear Colonel . . . This is a very great honor for me . . . I . . . I . . . I was not expecting it . . . although . . . indeed . . . in short, I am most proud to welcome you, a hero of your eminence, into my humble dwelling . . . [*He presses the invisible hand that the invisible Colonel gives him, bending forward ceremoniously, then straightening up again.*] Without false modesty, nevertheless, I permit myself to confess to you that I do not feel unworthy of the honor of your visit! Proud, yes . . . unworthy, no! . . .

[*The Old Woman appears with a chair, entering from the right.*]

OLD WOMAN: Oh! What a handsome uniform! What beautiful medals! Who is it, my darling?

OLD MAN [*to the Old Woman*]: Can't you see that it's the Colonel?

OLD WOMAN [*to the Old Man*]: Ah!

OLD MAN [*to the Old Woman*]: Count his stripes! [*To the Colonel:*] This is my wife, Semiramis. [*To the Old Woman:*] Come here so that I can introduce you to the Colonel. [*The Old Woman approaches, dragging the chair by one hand, and makes a curtsey, without letting go of the chair. To the Colonel:*] My wife. [*To the Old Woman:*] The Colonel.

OLD WOMAN: How do you do, Colonel. Welcome. You're an old comrade of my husband's, he's a general . . .

OLD MAN [*annoyed*]: factotum, factotum . . .

[*The invisible Colonel kisses the hand of the Old Woman. This is apparent from the gesture she makes as she raises her hand toward his lips. Overcome with emotion, the Old Woman lets go of the chair.*]

OLD WOMAN: Oh! He's most polite . . . you can see that he's really superior, a superior being! . . . [*She takes hold of the chair again. To the Colonel:*] This chair is for you . . .

OLD MAN [*to the invisible Colonel*]: This way, if you please . . . [*They move downstage, the Old Woman dragging the chair. To the Colonel:*] Yes, one guest has come already. We're expecting a great many more people! . . .

[*The Old Woman places the chair to the right.*]

OLD WOMAN [*to the Colonel*]: Sit here, please. [*The Old Man introduces the two invisible guests to each other.*]

OLD MAN: A young lady we know . . .

OLD WOMAN: A very dear friend . . .

OLD MAN [*same business*]: The Colonel . . . a famous soldier.

OLD WOMAN [*indicating the chair she has just brought in to the Colonel*]: Do take this chair . . .

OLD MAN [*to the Old Woman*]: No, no, can't you see that the Colonel wishes to sit beside the Lady! . . .

[*The Colonel seats himself invisibly on the third chair from the left; the invisible Lady is supposedly sitting on the second chair; seated next to each other they engage in an inaudible conversation; the Old Woman and Old Man continue to stand behind their chairs, on both sides of their invisible guests; the Old Man to the left of the Lady, the Old Woman to the right of the Colonel.*]

OLD WOMAN [*listening to the conversation of the two guests*]: Oh! Oh! That's going too far.

OLD MAN [*same business*]: Perhaps. [*The Old Man and the Old Woman make signs to each other over the heads of their guests, while they follow the inaudible conversation which takes a turn that seems to displease them. Abruptly:*] Yes, Colonel, they are not here yet, but they'll be here. And the Orator will speak in my behalf, he will explain the meaning of my message . . . Take care, Colonel, this Lady's husband may arrive at any moment.

OLD WOMAN [*to the Old Man*]: Who is this gentleman?

OLD MAN [*to the Old Woman*]: I've told you, it's the Colonel.

[*Some embarrassing things take place, invisibly.*]

OLD WOMAN [*to the Old Man*]: I knew it. I knew it.

OLD MAN: Then why are you asking?

OLD WOMAN: For my information. Colonel, no cigarette butts on the floor!

OLD MAN [*to Colonel*]: Colonel, Colonel, it's slipped my mind—in the last war did you win or lose?

OLD WOMAN [*to the invisible Lady*]: But my dear, don't let it happen!

OLD MAN: Look at me, look at me, do I look like a bad soldier? One time, Colonel, under fire . . .

OLD WOMAN: He's going too far! It's embarrassing! [*She seizes the invisible sleeve of the Colonel.*] Listen to him! My darling, why don't you stop him!

OLD MAN [*continuing quickly*]: And all on my own, I killed 209 of them; we called them that because they jumped so high to escape, however there weren't so many of them as there were flies; of course it is less amusing, Colonel, but thanks to my strength of character, I have . . . Oh! no, I must, please.

OLD WOMAN [*to Colonel*]: My husband never lies; it may be true that we are old, nevertheless we're respectable.

OLD MAN [*violently, to the Colonel*]: A hero must be a gentleman too, if he hopes to be a complete hero!

OLD WOMAN [*to the Colonel*]: I've known you for many years, but I'd never have believed you were capable of this. [*To the Lady, while we hear the sound of boats:*] I'd never have believed him capable of this. We have our dignity, our self-respect.

OLD MAN [*in a quavering voice*]: I'm still capable of bearing arms. [*Doorbell rings.*] Excuse me, I must go to the door. [*He stumbles and knocks over the chair of the invisible Lady.*] Oh! pardon.

OLD WOMAN [*rushing forward*]: You didn't hurt yourself? [*The Old Man and Old Woman help the invisible Lady onto her feet.*] You've got all dirty, there's some dust. [*She helps brush the Lady. The doorbell rings again.*]

OLD MAN: Forgive me, forgive me. [*To the Old Woman:*] Go bring a chair.

OLD WOMAN [*to the two invisible guests*]: Excuse me for a moment.

[*While the Old Man goes to open door No. 3, the Old Woman exits through door No. 5 to look for a chair, and she re-enters by door No. 8.*]

OLD MAN [*moving towards the door*]: He was trying to get my goat. I'm almost angry. [*He opens the door.*] Oh! madam, you're here! I can scarcely believe my eyes, and yet, nevertheless . . . I didn't really dare to hope . . . really it's . . . Oh! madam, madam . . . I have thought about you, all my life, all my life, madam, they always called you La Belle . . . it's your husband . . . someone told me, certainly . . . you haven't changed a bit . . . Oh! yes, yes, your nose *has* grown longer, maybe it's a little swollen . . . I didn't notice it when I first saw you, but I see it now . . . a lot longer . . . ah! how unfortunate! You certainly didn't do it on purpose . . . how did it happen? . . . little by little . . . excuse me, sir and dear friend, you'll permit me to call you "dear friend," I knew your wife long before you . . . she was the same, but with a completely different nose . . . I congratulate you, sir, you seem to love each other very much. [*The Old Woman re-enters through door No. 8 with a chair.*] Semiramis, two guests have arrived, we need one more chair . . . [*The Old Woman puts the chair behind the four others, then exits by door No. 8 and re-enters by door No. 5, after a few moments, with another chair that she places beside the one she has just brought in. By this time, the Old Man and the two guests have moved near the Old Woman.*] Come this way, please, more guests have arrived. I'm going to introduce you . . . now then, madam . . . Oh! Belle, Belle, Miss Belle, that's what they used to call you . . . now you're all bent over . . . Oh! sir, she is still Belle to me, even so; under her glasses, she still has pretty eyes; her hair is white, but under the white one can see

brown, and blue, I'm sure of that . . . come nearer, nearer . . . what is this, sir, a gift, for my wife? [*To the Old Woman, who has just come on with the chair:*] Semiramis, this is Belle, you know, Belle . . . [*To the Colonel and the invisible Lady:*] This is Miss, pardon, Mrs. Belle, don't smile . . . and her husband . . . [*To the Old Woman:*] A childhood friend, I've often spoken of her to you . . . and her husband. [*Again to the Colonel and to the invisible Lady:*] And her husband . . .

OLD WOMAN [*making a little curtsey*]: He certainly makes good introductions. He has fine manners. Good evening, madam, good evening, sir. [*She indicates the two first guests to the newly arrived couple:*] Our friends, yes . . .

OLD MAN [*to the Old Woman*]: He's brought you a present.

[*The Old Woman takes the present.*]

OLD WOMAN: Is it a flower, sir? or a cradle? a pear tree? or a crow?

OLD MAN [*to the Old Woman*]: No, no, can't you see that it's a painting?

OLD WOMAN: Oh! how pretty! Thank you, sir . . . [*To the invisible Lady:*] Would you like to see it, dear friend?

OLD MAN [*to the invisible Colonel*]: Would you like to see it?

OLD WOMAN [*to Belle's husband*]: Doctor, Doctor, I feel squeamish, I have hot flashes, I feel sick, I've aches and pains, I haven't any feeling in my feet, I've caught cold in my eyes, I've a cold in my fingers, I'm suffering from liver trouble, Doctor, Doctor! . . .

OLD MAN [*to the Old Woman*]: This gentleman is not a doctor, he's a photo-engraver.

OLD WOMAN [*to the first invisible Lady*]: If you've finished looking at it, you might hang it up. [*To the Old Man:*] That doesn't matter, he's charming even so, he's dazzling. [*To the Photo-engraver:*] Without meaning to flatter you . . .

[*The Old Man and the Old Woman now move behind the chairs, close to each other, almost touching, but back to back; they talk: the Old Man to Belle, the Old Woman to the Photo-engraver; from time to time*] *their replies, as shown by the way they turn their heads, are addressed to one or the other of the two first guests.*]

OLD MAN [*to Belle*]: I am very touched ... You're still the same, in spite of everything ... I've loved you, a hundred years ago ... But there's been such a change ... No, you haven't changed a bit ... I loved you, I love you ...

OLD WOMAN [*to the Photo-engraver*]: Oh! Sir, sir, sir ...

OLD MAN [*to the Colonel*]: I'm in complete agreement with you on that point.

OLD WOMAN [*to the Photo-engraver*]: Oh! certainly, sir, certainly, sir, certainly ... [*To the first Lady:*] Thanks for hanging it up ... Forgive me if I've inconvenienced you.

[*The light grows stronger. It should grow stronger and stronger as the invisible guests continue to arrive.*]

OLD MAN [*almost whimpering to Belle*]: Where are the snows of yester year?

OLD WOMAN [*to the Photo-engraver*]: Oh! Sir, sir, sir ... Oh! sir ...

OLD MAN [*pointing out the first lady to Belle*]: She's a young friend ... she's very sweet ...

OLD WOMAN [*pointing the Colonel out to the Photo-engraver*]: Yes, he's a mounted staff colonel ... a comrade of my husband ... a subaltern, my husband's a general...

OLD MAN [*to Belle*]: Your ears were not always so pointed! ... My Belle, do you remember?

OLD WOMAN [*to the Photo-engraver, simpering grotesquely; she develops this manner more and more in this scene; she shows her thick red stockings, raises her many petticoats, shows an underskirt full of holes, exposes her old breast; then, her hands on her hips, throws her head back, makes little erotic cries, projects her pelvis, her legs spread apart; she laughs like an old prostitute; this business, entirely different from her manner heretofore as well as from that she will have subsequently, and which must reveal the hidden personality of the Old Woman, ceases abruptly*]: So you think I'm too old for that, do you?

OLD MAN [*to Belle, very romantically*]: When we were young, the moon was a living star. Ah! yes, yes, if only we had dared, but we were only children. Wouldn't you like to recapture those bygone days ... is it still possible? Is it still possible? Ah! no, no, it is no longer possible. Those days have flown away as fast as a train. Time has left the marks of his wheels on our skin. Do you believe surgeons can perform miracles? [*To the Colonel:*] I am a soldier, and you too, we soldiers are always young, the generals are like gods ... [*To Belle:*] It ought to be that way ... Alas! Alas! We have lost everything. We could have been so happy, I'm sure of it, we could have been, we could have been; perhaps the flowers are budding again beneath the snow! ...

OLD WOMAN [*to Photo-engraver*]: Flatterer! Rascal! Ah! Ah! I look younger than my years? You're a little savage! You're exciting.

OLD MAN [*to Belle*]: Will you be my Isolde and let me be your Tristan? Beauty is more than skin deep, it's in the heart ... Do you understand? We could have had the pleasure of sharing, joy, beauty, eternity ... an eternity ... Why didn't we dare? We weren't brave enough ... Everything is lost, lost, lost.

OLD WOMAN [*to Photo-engraver*]: Oh no, Oh! no, Oh! la la, you give me the shivers. You too, are you ticklish? To tickle or be tickled? I'm a little embarrassed ... [*She laughs.*] Do you like my petticoat? Or do you like this skirt better?

OLD MAN [*to Belle*]: A general factotum has a poor life!

OLD WOMAN [*turning her head towards the first invisible Lady*]: In order to make crepes de Chine? A leaf of beef, an hour of flour, a little gastric sugar. [*To the Photo-engraver:*] You've got clever fingers, ah ... all the sa-a-a-me! ... Oh-oh-oh-oh.

OLD MAN [*to Belle*]: My worthy helpmeet, Semiramis, has taken the place of my mother. [*He turns towards the Colonel:*] Colonel, as I've often observed to you, one must take the truth as one finds it. [*He turns back towards Belle.*]

OLD WOMAN [*to Photo-engraver*]: Do you

really really believe that one could have children at any age? Any age children?

OLD MAN [*to Belle*]: It's this alone that has saved me: the inner life, peace of mind, austerity, my scientific investigations, philosophy, my message ...

OLD WOMAN [*to Photo-engraver*]: I've never yet betrayed my husband, the general ... not so hard, you're going to make me fall ... I'm only his poor mamma! [*She sobs.*] A great, great [*She pushes him back.*], great ... mamma. My conscience causes these tears to flow. For me the branch of the apple tree is broken. Try to find somebody else. I no longer want to gather rosebuds ...

OLD MAN [*to Belle*]: ... All the preoccupations of a superior order ...

[*The Old Man and Old Woman lead Belle and the Photo-engraver up alongside the two other invisible guests, and seat them.*]

OLD MAN AND OLD WOMAN [*to the Photo-engraver and Belle*]: Sit down, please sit down.

[*The Old Man and Old Woman sit down too, he to the left, she to the right, with four empty chairs between them. A long scene, punctuated at intervals with "no," "yes," "yes." The Old Man and Old Woman listen to the conversation of the invisible guests.*]

OLD WOMAN [*to the Photo-engraver*]: We had one son ... of course, he's still alive ... he's gone away ... it's a common story ... or, rather, unusual ... he abandoned his parents ... he had a heart of gold ... that was a long time ago ... We loved him so much ... he slammed the door ... My husband and I tried to hold him back with all our might ... he was seven years old, the age of reason, I called after him: "My son, my child, my son, my child." ... He didn't even look back ...

OLD MAN: Alas, no ... no, we've never had a child ... I'd hoped for a son ... Semiramis, too ... we did everything ... and my poor Semiramis is so maternal, too. Perhaps it was better that way ... As for me I was an ungrateful son myself ... Ah! ... grief, regret, remorse, that's all we have ... that's all we have left ...

OLD WOMAN: He said to me: "You kill birds! Why do you kill birds?" ... But we don't kill birds ... we've never harmed so much as a fly ... His eyes were full of big tears. He wouldn't let us dry them. He wouldn't let me come near him. He said: "Yes, you kill all the birds, all the birds." ... He showed us his little fists ... "You're lying, you've betrayed me! The streets are full of dead birds, of dying baby birds." It's the song of the birds! ... "No, it's their death rattle. The sky is red with blood." ... No, my child, it's blue. He cried again: "You've betrayed me, I adored you, I believed you to be good ... the streets are full of dead birds, you've torn out their eyes ... Papa, mamma, you're wicked! ... I refuse to stay with you." ... I threw myself at his feet ... His father was weeping. We couldn't hold him back. As he went we could still hear him calling: "It's you who are responsible" ... What does that mean, "responsible"?

OLD MAN: I let my mother die all alone in a ditch. She called after me, moaning feebly: "My little child, my beloved son, don't leave me to die all alone ... Stay with me. I don't have much time left." Don't worry, Mamma, I told her, I'll be back in a moment ... I was in a hurry ... I was going to the ball, to dance. I will be back in a minute. But when I returned, she was already dead, and they had buried her deep ... I broke open the grave, I searched for her ... I couldn't find her ... I know, I know, sons always abandon their mothers, and they more or less kill their fathers ... Life is like that ... but I, I suffer from it ... and the others, they don't ...

OLD WOMAN: He cried: "Papa, Mamma, I'll never set eyes on you again."

OLD MAN: I suffer from it, yes, the others don't ...

OLD WOMAN: Don't speak of him to my husband. He loved his parents so much. He never left them for a single moment. He cared for them, coddled them ... And they died in his arms, saying to him: "You have been a perfect son. God will be good to you."

OLD MAN: I can still see her stretched out

in the ditch, she was holding lily of the valley in her hand, she cried: "Don't forget me, don't forget me" ... her eyes were full of big tears, and she called me by my baby name: "Little Chick," she said, "Little Chick, don't leave me here all alone."

OLD WOMAN [*to the Photo-engraver*]: He has never written to us. From time to time, a friend tells us that he's been seen here or there, that he is well, that he is a good husband ...

OLD MAN [*to Belle*]: When I got back, she had been buried a long time. [*To the first invisible Lady:*] Oh, yes. Oh! yes, madam, we have a movie theatre in the house, a restaurant, bathrooms ...

OLD WOMAN [*to the Colonel*]: Yes, Colonel, it is because he ...

OLD MAN: Basically that's it.

[*Desultory conversation, getting bogged down.*]

OLD WOMAN: If only!

OLD MAN: Thus, I've not ... I, it ... certainly ...

OLD WOMAN [*dislocated dialogue, exhaustion*]: All in all.

OLD MAN: To ours and to theirs.

OLD WOMAN: So that.

OLD MAN: From me to him.

OLD WOMAN: Him, or her?

OLD MAN: Them.

OLD WOMAN: Curl-papers ... After all.

OLD MAN: It's not that.

OLD WOMAN: Why?

OLD MAN: Yes.

OLD WOMAN: I.

OLD MAN: All in all.

OLD WOMAN: All in all.

OLD MAN [*to the first invisible Lady*]: What was that, madam?

[*A long silence, the Old Man and Old Woman remain rigid on their chairs. Then the doorbell rings.*]

OLD MAN [*with increasing nervousness*]: Someone has come. People. Still more people.

OLD WOMAN: I thought I heard some boats.

OLD MAN: I'll go to the door. Go bring some chairs. Excuse me, gentlemen, ladies. [*He goes towards door No. 7.*]

OLD WOMAN [*to the invisible guests who have already arrived*]: Get up for a moment, please. The Orator will be here soon. We must ready the room for the meeting. [*The Old Woman arranges the chairs, turning their backs towards the audience.*] Lend me a hand, please. Thanks.

OLD MAN [*opening door No. 7*]: Good evening, ladies, good evening, gentlemen. Please come in.

[*The three or four invisible persons who have arrived are very tall, and the Old Man has to stand on his toes in order to shake hands with them. The Old Woman, after placing the chairs as indicated above, goes over to the Old Man.*]

OLD MAN [*making introductions*]: My wife ... Mr. ... Mrs. ... my wife ... Mr. ... Mrs. ... my wife ...

OLD WOMAN: Who are all these people, my darling?

OLD MAN [*to Old Woman*]: Go find some chairs, dear.

OLD WOMAN: I can't do everything! ...

[*She exits, grumbling, by door No. 6 and re-enters by door No. 7, while the Old Man, with the newly arrived guests, moves downstage.*]

OLD MAN: Don't drop your movie camera. [*More introductions.*] The Colonel ... the Lady ... Mrs. Belle ... the Photo-engraver ... These are the newspaper men, they have come to hear the Orator too, who should be here any minute now ... Don't be impatient ... You'll not be bored ... all together now ... [*The Old Woman re-enters through door No. 7 with two chairs.*] Come along, bring the chairs more quickly ... we're still short one.

[*The Old Woman goes to find another chair, still grumbling, exiting by door No. 3, and re-entering by door No. 8.*]

OLD WOMAN: All right, and so ... I'm doing as well as I can ... I'm not a machine, you know ... Who are all these people? [*She exits.*]

OLD MAN: Sit down, sit down, the ladies with the ladies, and the gentlemen with the gentlemen, or vice versa, if you prefer ... We don't have any more nice chairs ... we have to make do with what we have ... I'm sorry ... take the one in the middle ... does anyone need a fountain pen? Telephone Maillot, you'll get Monique . . . Claude is an angel. I don't have a radio . . . I take all the newspapers . . . that depends on a number of things; I manage these buildings, but I have no help . . . we have to economize . . . no interviews, please, for the moment . . . later, we'll see . . . you'll soon have a place to sit . . . what can she be doing? [*The Old Woman enters by door No. 8 with a chair.*] Faster, Semiramis . . .

OLD WOMAN: I'm doing my best . . . Who are all these people?

OLD MAN: I'll explain it all to you later.

OLD WOMAN: And that woman? That woman, my darling?

OLD MAN: Don't get upset . . . [*To the Colonel:*] Colonel, journalism is a profession too, like a fighting man's . . . [*To the Old Woman:*] Take care of the ladies, my dear . . . [*The doorbell rings. The Old Man hurries towards door No. 8.*] Wait a moment . . . [*To the Old Woman:*] Bring chairs!

OLD WOMAN: Gentlemen, ladies, excuse me . . .
[*She exits by door No. 3, re-entering by door No. 2; the Old Man goes to open concealed door No. 9, and disappears at the moment the Old Woman re-enters by door No. 2.*]

OLD MAN [*out of sight*]: Come in . . . come in . . . come in . . . come in . . . [*He reappears, leading in a number of invisible people, including one very small child he holds by the hand.*] One doesn't bring little children to a scientific lecture . . . the poor little thing is going to be bored . . . if he begins to cry or to peepee on the ladies' dresses, that'll be a fine state of affairs! [*He conducts them to stage center; the Old Woman comes on with two chairs.*] I wish to introduce you to my wife, Semiramis; and these are their children.

OLD WOMAN: Ladies, gentlemen . . . Oh! aren't they sweet!

OLD MAN: That one is the smallest.

OLD WOMAN: Oh, he's so cute . . . so cute . . . so cute!

OLD MAN: Not enough chairs.

OLD WOMAN: Oh! dear, oh dear, oh dear . . .

[*She exits, looking for another chair, using now door No. 2 as exit and door No. 3 on the right to re-enter.*]

OLD MAN: Hold the little body on your lap . . . The twins can sit together in the same chair. Be careful, they're not very strong . . . they go with the house, they belong to the landlord. Yes, my children, he'd make trouble for us, he's a bad man . . . he wants us to buy them from him, these worthless chairs. [*The Old Woman returns as quickly as she can with a chair.*] You don't all know each other . . . you're seeing each other for the first time . . . you knew each other by name . . . [*To the Old Woman:*] Semiramis, help me make the introductions . . .

OLD WOMAN: Who are all these people? . . . May I introduce you, excuse me . . . May I introduce you . . . but who are they?

OLD MAN: May I introduce you . . . Allow me to introduce you . . . permit me to introduce you . . . Mr., Mrs., Miss . . . Mr. . . . Mrs. . . . Mrs. . . . Mr.

OLD WOMAN [*to Old Man*]: Did you put on your sweater? [*To the invisible guests:*] Mr., Mrs., Mr. . . .
[*Doorbell rings again.*]

OLD MAN: More people!
[*Another ring of doorbell.*]

OLD WOMAN: More people!
[*The doorbell rings again, then several more times, and more times again; the Old Man is beside himself; the chairs, turned towards the dais, with their backs to the audience, form regular rows, each one longer as in a theatre; the Old Man is winded, he mops his brow, goes from one door to another, seats invisible people, while the Old Woman, hobbling along, unable to move any faster, goes as rapidly as she can, from one door to another, hunting for chairs and carrying them in. There are now many invisible people on stage; both the Old Man and Old Woman take care not to bump into people and to thread their way between the rows of chairs. The movement could go like this: the Old Man goes to door No. 4, the Old Woman exits by door No. 3, returns by door No. 2; the Old Man goes to open door No. 7,*]

the Old Woman exits by door No. 8, re-enters by door No. 6 with chairs, etc., in this manner making their way around the stage, using all the doors.]

OLD WOMAN: Beg pardon . . . excuse me . . . what . . . oh, yes . . . beg pardon . . . excuse me . . .

OLD MAN: Gentlemen . . . come in . . . ladies . . . enter . . . it is Mrs. . . . let me . . . yes . . .

OLD WOMAN [*with more chairs*]: Oh dear . . . Oh dear . . . there are too many . . . There really are too, too . . . too many, oh dear, oh dear, oh dear . . .

[*We hear from outside, louder and louder and approaching nearer and nearer, the sounds of boats moving through the water; all the noises come directly from the wings. The Old Woman and the Old Man continue the business outlined above; they open the doors, they carry in chairs. The doorbell continues to ring.*]

OLD MAN: This table is in our way. [*He moves a table, or he sketches the business of moving it, without slowing down his rhythm, aided by the Old Woman.*] There's scarcely a place left here, excuse us . . .

OLD WOMAN [*making a gesture of clearing the table, to the Old Man*]: Are you wearing your sweater?

[*Doorbell rings.*]

OLD MAN: More people! More chairs! More people! More chairs! Come in, come in, ladies and gentlemen . . . Semiramis, faster . . . We'll give you a hand soon . . .

OLD WOMAN: Beg pardon . . . beg pardon . . . good evening, Mrs. . . . Mrs. . . . Mr. . . . Mr. . . . yes, yes, the chairs . . .

[*The doorbell rings louder and louder and we hear the noises of boats striking the quay very close by, and more and more frequently. The Old Man flounders among the chairs; he has scarcely enough time to go from one door to another, so rapidly do the ringings of the doorbell succeed each other.*]

OLD MAN: Yes, right away . . . are you wearing your sweater? Yes, yes . . . immediately, patience, yes, yes . . . patience . . .

OLD WOMAN: Your sweater? My sweater? . . . Beg pardon, beg pardon.

OLD MAN: This way, ladies and gentlemen, I request you . . . I re you . . . pardon . . . quest . . . enter, enter . . . going to show . . . there, the seats . . . dear friend . . . not there . . . take care . . . you, my friend?

[*Then a long moment without words. We hear waves, boats, the continuous ringing of the doorbell. The movement culminates in intensity at this point. The doors are now opening and shutting all together ceaselessly. Only the main door in the center of the recess remains closed. The Old Man and Old Woman come and go, without saying a word, from one door to another; they appear to be gliding on roller skates. The Old Man receives the people, accompanies them, but doesn't take them very far, he only indicates seats to them after having taken one or two steps with them; he hasn't enough time. The Old Woman carries in chairs. The Old Man and the Old Woman meet each other and bump into each other, once or twice, without interrupting their rhythm. Then, the Old Man takes a position upstage center, and turns from left to right, from right to left, etc., towards all the doors and indicates the seats with his arms. His arms move very rapidly. Then, finally the Old Woman stops, with a chair in one hand, which she places, takes up again, replaces, looks as though she, too, wants to go from one door to another, from right to left, from left to right, moving her head and neck very rapidly. This must not interrupt the rhythm; the Old Man and Old Woman must still give the impression of not stopping, even while remaining almost in one place; their hands, their chests, their heads, their eyes are agitated, perhaps moving in little circles. Finally, there is a progressive slowing down of movement, at first slight: the ringings of the doorbell are less loud, less frequent; the doors open less and less rapidly; the gestures of the Old Man and Old Woman slacken continuously. At the moment when the doors stop opening and closing altogether, and the ringings cease to be heard, we have the impression that the stage is packed with people.*]

OLD MAN: I'm going to find a place for you . . . patience . . . Semiramis, for the love of . . .

OLD WOMAN [*with a large gesture, her hands empty*]: There are no more chairs, my darling. [*Then, abruptly, she begins to sell invisible programs in a full hall, with the doors closed.*] Programs, get your programs here, the program of the evening, buy your program!

OLD MAN: Relax, ladies and gentlemen, we'll take care of you . . . Each in his turn, in the order of your arrival . . . You'll have a seat. I'll take care of you.

OLD WOMAN: Buy your programs! Wait a moment, madam, I cannot take care of everyone at the same time, I haven't got thirty-three hands, you know, I'm not a cow . . . Mister, please be kind enough to pass the program to the lady next to you, thank you . . . my change, my change . . .

OLD MAN: I've told you that I'd find a place for you! Don't get excited! Over here, it's over here, there, take care . . . oh, dear friend . . . dear friends . . .

OLD WOMAN: . . . Programs . . . get your grams . . . grams . . .

OLD MAN: Yes, my dear, she's over there, further down, she's selling programs . . . no trade is unworthy . . . that's her . . . do you see her? . . . you have a seat in the second row . . . to the right . . . no, to the left . . . that's it! . . .

OLD WOMAN: . . . gram . . . gram . . . program . . . get your program . . .

OLD MAN: What do you expect me to do? I'm doing my best! [*To invisible seated people:*] Push over a little, if you will please . . . there's still a little room, that will do for you, won't it, Mrs. . . . come here. [*He mounts the dais, forced by the pushing of the crowd.*] Ladies, gentlemen, please excuse us, there are no more seats available . . .

OLD WOMAN [*who is now on the opposite side of the stage, across from the Old Man, between door No. 3 and the window*]: Get your programs . . . who wants a program? Eskimo pies, caramels . . . fruit drops . . . [*Unable to move, the Old Woman, hemmed in by the crowd, scatters her programs and candies anywhere, above the invisible heads.*] Here are some! There they are!

OLD MAN [*standing on the dais, very animated; he is jostled as he descends from the dais, remounts it, steps down again, hits someone in the face, is struck by an elbow, says*]: Pardon . . . please excuse us . . . take care . . . [*Pushed, he staggers, has trouble regaining his equilibrium, clutches at shoulders.*]

OLD WOMAN: Why are there so many people? Programs, get your program here, Eskimo pies.

OLD MAN: Ladies, young ladies, gentlemen, a moment of silence, I beg you . . . silence . . . it's very important . . . those people who've no seats are asked to clear the aisles . . . that's it . . . don't stand between the chairs.

OLD WOMAN [*to the Old Man, almost screaming*]: Who are all these people, my darling? What are they doing here?

OLD MAN: Clear the aisles, ladies and gentlemen. Those who do not have seats must, for the convenience of all, stand against the wall, there, along the right or the left . . . you'll be able to hear everything, you'll see everything, don't worry, you won't miss a thing, all seats are equally good!

[*There is a great hullabaloo. Pushed by the crowd, the Old Man makes almost a complete turn around the stage and ends up at the window on the right, near to the stool. The Old Woman makes the same movement in reverse, and ends up at the window on the left, near the stool there.*]

OLD MAN [*making this movement*]: Don't push, don't push.

OLD WOMAN [*same business*]: Don't push, don't push.

OLD MAN [*same business*]: Don't push, don't push.

OLD WOMAN [*same business*]: Don't push, ladies and gentlemen, don't push.

OLD MAN [*same business*]: Relax . . . take it easy . . . be quiet . . . what's going on here?

OLD WOMAN [*same business*]: There's no need to act like savages, in any case.

[*At last they reach their final positions. Each is near a window. The Old Man to the left, by the window which is beside the dais. The Old Woman on the right. They don't move from these positions until the end.*]

OLD WOMAN [*calling to the Old Man*]: My darling ... I can't see you, anymore ... where are you? Who are they? What do all these people want? Who is that man over there?

OLD MAN: Where are you? Where are you, Semiramis?

OLD WOMAN: My darling, where are you?

OLD MAN: Here, beside the window ... Can you hear me?

COLD WOMAN: Yes, I hear your voice! ... there are so many ... but I can make out yours ...

OLD MAN: And you, where are you?

OLD WOMAN: I'm beside the window too! ... My dear, I'm frightened, there are too many people ... we are very far from each other ... at our age we have to be careful ... we might get lost ... We must stay close together, one never knows, my darling, my darling ...

OLD MAN: Ah! ... I just caught sight of you ... Oh! ... We'll find each other, never fear ... I'm with friends. [*To the friends:*] I'm happy to shake your hands ... But of course, I believe in progress, uninterrupted progress, with some jolts, nevertheless ...

OLD WOMAN: That's fine, thanks ... What foul weather! Yes, it's been nice! [*Aside:*] I'm afraid, even so ... What am I doing here? ... [*She screams:*] My darling, My darling!
[*The Old Man and Old Woman individually speak to guests near them.*]

OLD MAN: In order to prevent the exploitation of man by man, we need money, money, and still more money!

OLD WOMAN: My darling! [*Then, hemmed in by friends:*] Yes, my husband is here, he's organizing everything ... over there ... Oh! you'll never get there ... you'd have to go across, he's with friends ...

OLD MAN: Certainly not ... as I've always said ... pure logic does not exist ... all we've got is an imitation.

OLD WOMAN: But you know, there are people who are happy. In the morning they eat breakfast on the plane, at noon they lunch in the pullman, and in the evening they dine aboard the liner. At night they sleep in the trucks that roll, roll, roll ...

OLD MAN: Talk about the dignity of man! At least let's try to save face. Dignity is only skin deep.

OLD WOMAN: Don't slink away into the shadows ... [*She bursts out laughing in conversation.*]

OLD MAN: Your compatriots ask of me.

OLD WOMAN: Certainly ... tell me everything.

OLD MAN: I've invited you ... in order to explain to you ... that the individual and the person are one and the same.

OLD WOMAN: He has a borrowed look about him. He owes us a lot of money.

OLD MAN: I am not myself. I am another. I am the one in the other.

OLD WOMAN: My children, take care not to trust one another.

OLD MAN: Sometimes I awaken in the midst of absolute silence. It's a perfect circle. There's nothing lacking. But one must be careful, all the same. Its shape might disappear. There are holes through which it can escape.

OLD WOMAN: Ghosts, you know, phantoms, mere nothings ... The duties my husband fulfills are very important, sublime.

OLD MAN: Excuse me ... that's not at all my opinion! At the proper time, I'll communicate my views on this subject to you ... I have nothing to say for the present! ... We're waiting for the Orator, he'll tell you, he'll speak in my behalf, and explain everything that we hold most dear ... he'll explain everything to you ... when? ... when the moment has come ... the moment will come soon ...

OLD WOMAN [*on her side to her friends*]: The sooner, the better ... That's understood ... [*Aside:*] They're never going to leave us alone. Let them go, why don't they go? ... My poor darling, where is he? I can't see him any more ...

OLD MAN [*same business*]: Don't be so impatient. You'll hear my message. In just a moment.

OLD WOMAN [*aside*]: Ah!...I hear his voice!...[*To her friends:*] Do you know, my husband has never been understood. But at last his hour has come.

OLD MAN: Listen to me, I've had a rich experience of life. In all walks of life, at every level of thought...I'm not an egotist: humanity must profit by what I've learned.

OLD WOMAN: Ow! You stepped on my foot...I've got chilblains!

OLD MAN: I've perfected a real system. [*Aside:*] The Orator ought to be here. [*Aloud:*] I've suffered enormously.

OLD WOMAN: We have suffered so much. [*Aside:*] The Orator ought to be here. It's certainly time.

OLD MAN: Suffered much, learned much.

OLD WOMAN [*like an echo*]: Suffered much, learned much.

OLD MAN: You'll see for yourselves, my system is perfect.

OLD WOMAN [*like an echo*]: You'll see for yourselves, his system is perfect.

OLD MAN: If only my instructions are carried out.

OLD WOMAN [*echo*]: If only his instructions are carried out.

OLD MAN: We'll save the world!...

OLD WOMAN [*echo*]: Saving his own soul by saving the world!...

OLD MAN: One truth for all!

OLD WOMAN [*echo*]: One truth for all!

OLD MAN: Follow me!...

OLD WOMAN [*echo*]: Follow him!...

OLD MAN: For I have absolute certainty!...

OLD WOMAN [*echo*]: He has absolute certainty!

OLD MAN: Never...

OLD WOMAN [*echo*]: Ever and ever...

[*Suddenly we hear noises in the wings, fanfares.*]

OLD WOMAN: What's going on?

[*The noises increase, then the main door opens wide, with a great crash; through the open door we see nothing but a very powerful light which floods onto the stage through the main door and the windows, which at the entrance of the emperor are brightly lighted.*]

OLD MAN: I don't know...I can scarcely believe...is it possible...but yes... but yes...incredible...and still it's true ...yes...if...yes...it is the Emperor! His Majesty the Emperor!

[*The light reaches its maximum intensity, through the open door and through the windows; but the light is cold, empty; more noises which cease abruptly.*]

OLD MAN: Stand up!...It's His Majesty the Emperor! The Emperor in my house, in our house...Semiramis...do you realize what this means?

OLD WOMAN [*not understanding*]: The Emperor...the Emperor? My darling! [*Then suddenly she understands.*] Ah, yes, the Emperor! Your Majesty! Your Majesty! [*She wildly makes countless grotesque curtsies.*] In our house! In our house!

OLD MAN [*weeping with emotion*]: Your Majesty!...Oh! Your Majesty!...Your little, Your great Majesty!...Oh! what a sublime honor...it's all a marvelous dream.

OLD WOMAN [*like an echo*]: A marvelous dream...arvelous...

OLD MAN [*to the invisible crowd*]: Ladies, gentlemen, stand up, our beloved sovereign, the Emperor, is among us! Hurrah! Hurrah!

[*He stands up on the stool; he stands on his toes in order to see the Emperor; the Old Woman does the same on her side.*]

OLD WOMAN: Hurrah! Hurrah!

[*Stamping of feet.*]

OLD MAN: Your Majesty!...I'm over here!...Your Majesty! Can you hear me? Can you see me? Please tell his Majesty that I'm here! Your Majesty! Your Majesty!!! I'm here, your most faithful servant!...

OLD WOMAN [*still echoing*]: Your most faithful servant, Your Majesty!

OLD MAN: Your servant, your slave, your dog, arf, arf, your dog, Your Majesty!...

OLD WOMAN [*barking loudly like a dog*]: Arf...arf...arf...

OLD MAN [*wringing his hands*]: Can you see me?...Answer, Sire!...Ah, I can see you, I've just caught sight of Your Majesty's august face...your divine forehead . . . I've seen you, yes, in spite of the screen of courtiers . . .

OLD WOMAN: In spite of the courtiers . . . we're here, Your Majesty!

OLD MAN: Your Majesty! Your Majesty! Ladies, gentlemen, don't keep him—His Majesty standing . . . you see, Your Majesty, I'm truly the only one who cares for you, for your health, I'm the most faithful of all your subjects . . .

OLD WOMAN [echoing]: Your Majesty's most faithful subjects!

OLD MAN: Let me through, now, ladies and gentlemen . . . how can I make my way through such a crowd? . . . I must go to present my most humble respects to His Majesty, the Emperor . . . let me pass . . .

OLD WOMAN [echo]: Let him pass . . . let him pass . . . pass . . . ass . . .

OLD MAN: Let me pass, please, let me pass. [Desperate:] Ah! Will I ever be able to reach him?

OLD WOMAN [echo]: Reach him . . . reach him . . .

OLD MAN: Nevertheless, my heart and my whole being are at his feet, the crowd of courtiers surrounds him, ah! ah! they want to prevent me from approaching him . . . They know very well that . . . oh! I understand, I understand . . . Court intrigues, I know all about it . . . They hope to separate me from Your Majesty!

OLD WOMAN: Calm yourself, my darling . . . His Majesty sees you, he's looking at you . . . His Majesty has given me a wink . . . His Majesty is on our side! . . .

OLD MAN: They must give the Emperor the best seat . . . near the dais . . . so that he can hear everything the Orator is going to say.

OLD WOMAN [hoisting herself up on the stool, on her toes, lifting her chin as high as she can, in order to see better]: At last they're taking care of the Emperor.

OLD MAN: Thank heaven for that! [To the Emperor:] Sire . . . Your Majesty may rely on him. It's my friend, it's my representative who is at Your Majesty's side. [On his toes, standing on the stool:] Gentlemen, ladies, young ladies, little children, I implore you.

OLD WOMAN [echoing]: Plore . . . plore . . .

OLD MAN: . . . I want to see . . . move aside . . . I want . . . the celestial gaze, the noble face, the crown, the radiance of His Majesty . . . Sire, deign to turn your illustrious face in my direction, toward your humble servant . . . so humble . . . Oh! I caught sight of him clearly that time . . . I caught sight . . .

OLD WOMAN [echo]: He caught sight that time . . . he caught sight . . . caught . . . sight . . .

OLD MAN: I'm at the height of joy . . . I've no more words to express my boundless gratitude . . . in my humble dwelling, Oh! Majesty! Oh! radiance! . . . here . . . here . . . in the dwelling where I am, true enough, a general . . . but within the hierarchy of your army, I'm only a simple general factotum . . .

OLD WOMAN [echo]: General factotum . . .

OLD MAN: I'm proud of it . . . proud and humble, at the same time . . . as I should be . . . alas! certainly, I am a general, I might have been at the imperial court, I have only a little court here to take care of . . . Your Majesty . . . I . . . Your Majesty, I have difficulty expressing myself . . . I might have had . . . many things, not a few possessions if I'd known, if I'd wanted, if I . . . if we . . . Your Majesty, forgive my emotion . . .

OLD WOMAN: Speak in the third person!

OLD MAN [sniveling]: May Your Majesty deign to forgive me! You are here at last . . . We had given up hope . . . you might not even have come . . . Oh! Savior, in my life, I have been humiliated . . .

OLD WOMAN [echo, sobbing]: . . . miliated . . . miliated . . .

OLD MAN: I've suffered much in my life . . . I might have been something, if I could have been sure of the support of Your Majesty . . . I have no other support . . . if you hadn't come, everything would have been too late . . . you are, Sire, my last recourse . . .

OLD WOMAN [echo]: Last recourse . . . Sire . . . ast recourse . . . ire . . . recourse . . .

OLD MAN: I've brought bad luck to my friends, to all those who have helped me . . . Lightning struck the hand which was held out toward me . . .

OLD WOMAN [*echo*]: . . . hand that was held out . . . held out . . . out . . .

OLD MAN: They've always had good reasons for hating me, bad reasons for loving me . . .

OLD WOMAN: That's not true, my darling, not true. *I* love you, I'm your little mother . . .

OLD MAN: All my enemies have been rewarded and my friends have betrayed me . . .

OLD WOMAN [*echo*]: Friends . . . betrayed . . . betrayed . . .

OLD MAN: They've treated me badly. They've persecuted me. If I complained, it was always they who were in the right . . . Sometimes I've tried to revenge myself . . . I was never able to, never able to revenge myself . . . I have too much pity . . . I refused to strike the enemy to the ground, I have always been too good.

OLD WOMAN [*echo*]: He was too good, good, good, good, good . . .

OLD MAN: It is my pity that has defeated me.

OLD WOMAN [*echo*]: My pity . . . pity . . . pity . . .

OLD MAN: But they never pitied me. I gave them a pin prick, and they repaid me with club blows, with knife blows, with cannon blows, they've crushed my bones . . .

OLD WOMAN [*echo*]: . . . My bones . . . my bones . . . my bones . . .

OLD MAN: They've supplanted me, they've robbed me, they've assassinated me . . . I've been the collector of injustices, the lightning rod of catastrophes . . .

OLD WOMAN [*echo*]: Lightning rod . . . catastrophe . . . lightning rod . . .

OLD MAN: In order to forget, Your Majesty, I wanted to go in for sports . . . for mountain climbing . . . they pulled my feet and made me slip . . . I wanted to climb stairways, they rotted the steps . . . I fell down . . . I wanted to travel, they refused me a passport . . . I wanted to cross the river, they burnt my bridges . . .

OLD WOMAN [*echo*]: Burnt my bridges.

OLD MAN: I wanted to cross the Pyrenees, and there were no more Pyrenees.

OLD WOMAN [*echo*]: No more Pyrenees . . . He could have been, he too, Your Majesty, like so many others, a head editor, a head actor, a head doctor, Your Majesty, a head king . . .

OLD MAN: Furthermore, no one has ever shown me due consideration . . . no one has ever sent me invitations . . . However, I, hear me, I say this to you, I alone could have saved humanity, who is so sick. Your Majesty realizes this as do I . . . or, at the least, I could have spared it the evils from which it has suffered so much this last quarter of a century, had I had the opportunity to communicate my message; I do not despair of saving it, there is still time, I have a plan . . . alas, I express myself with difficulty . . .

OLD WOMAN [*above the invisible heads*]: The Orator will be here, he'll speak for you. His Majesty is here, thus you'll be heard, you've no reason to despair, you hold all the trumps, everything has changed, everything has changed . . .

OLD MAN: I hope Your Majesty will excuse me . . . I know you have many other worries . . . I've been humiliated . . . Ladies and gentlemen, move aside just a little bit, don't hide His Majesty's nose from me altogether, I want to see the diamonds of the imperial crown glittering . . . But if Your Majesty has deigned to come to our miserable home, it is because you have condescended to take into consideration my wretched self. What an extraordinary reward. Your Majesty, if corporeally I raise myself on my toes, this is not through pride, this is only in order to gaze upon you! . . . morally, I throw myself at your knees.

OLD WOMAN [*sobbing*]: At your knees, Sire, we throw ourselves at your knees, at your feet, at your toes . . .

OLD MAN: I've had scabies. My employer fired me because I did not bow to his baby, to his horse. I've been kicked in the ass, but all this, Sire, no longer has any

importance . . . since . . . since . . . Sir
. . . Your Majesty . . . look . . . I am here
. . . here . . .

OLD WOMAN [*echo*]: Here . . . here . . . here
. . . here . . . here . . . here . . .

OLD MAN: Since Your Majesty is here . . .
since Your Majesty will take my message
into consideration . . . But the Orator
should be here . . . he's making His Majesty
wait . . .

OLD WOMAN: If Your Majesty will forgive
him. He's surely coming. He will be here
in a moment. They've telephoned us.

OLD MAN: His Majesty is so kind. His Majesty
wouldn't depart just like that, without
having listened to everything, heard
everything.

OLD WOMAN [*echo*]: Heard everything . . .
heard . . . listened to everything . . .

OLD MAN: It is he who will speak in my
name . . . I, I cannot . . . I lack the talent
. . . he has all the papers, all the documents
. . .

OLD WOMAN [*echo*]: He has all the documents
. . .

OLD MAN: A little patience, Sire, I beg of
you . . . he should be coming.

OLD WOMAN: He should be coming in a
moment.

OLD MAN [*so that the Emperor will not grow
impatient*]: Your Majesty, hear me, a
long time ago I had the revelation . . . I
was forty years old . . . I say this also to
you, ladies and gentlemen . . . one evening,
after supper, as was our custom, before
going to bed, I seated myself on my
father's knees . . . my mustaches were
longer than his and more pointed . . . I
had more hair on my chest . . . my hair
was graying already, but his was still
brown . . . There were some guests,
grownups, sitting at table, who began to
laugh, laugh.

OLD WOMAN [*echo*]: Laugh . . . laugh . . .

OLD MAN: I'm not joking, I told them, I
love my papa very much. Someone
replied: It is midnight, a child shouldn't
stay up so late. If you don't go beddy-bye,
then you're no longer a kid. But I'd still

not have believed them if they hadn't
addressed me as an adult.

OLD WOMAN [*echo*]: An adult.

OLD MAN: Instead of as a child . . .

OLD WOMAN [*echo*]: A child.

OLD MAN: Nevertheless, I thought to myself,
I'm not married. Hence, I'm still a child.
They married me off right then, expressly
to prove the contrary to me . . . Fortunately,
my wife has been both father and
mother to me . . .

OLD WOMAN: The Orator should be here,
Your Majesty . . .

OLD MAN: The Orator will come.

OLD WOMAN: He will come.

OLD MAN: He will come.

OLD WOMAN: He will come.

OLD MAN: He will come.

OLD WOMAN: He will come.

OLD MAN: He will come, he will come.

OLD WOMAN: He will come, he will come.

OLD MAN: He will come.

OLD WOMAN: He is coming.

OLD MAN: He is coming.

OLD WOMAN: He is coming, he is here.

OLD MAN: He is coming, he is here.

OLD WOMAN: He is coming, he is here.

OLD MAN AND OLD WOMAN: He is here . . .

OLD WOMAN: Here he is!

[*Silence; all movement stops. Petrified, the
two old people stare at door No. 5; this
immobility lasts rather long—about thirty
seconds; very slowly, very slowly the door
opens wide, silently; then the Orator
appears. He is a real person. He's a typical
painter or poet of the nineteenth century;
he wears a large black felt hat with a wide
brim, loosely tied bow tie, artist's blouse,
mustache and goatee, very histrionic in
manner, conceited; just as the invisible
people must be as real as possible, the
Orator must appear unreal. He goes along
the wall to the right, gliding, softly, to
upstage center, in front of the main door,
without turning his head to right or left;
he passes close by the Old Woman without
appearing to notice her, not even when the
Old Woman touches his arm in order to
assure herself that he exists. It is at this*

moment that the Old Woman says: "Here he is!"]

OLD MAN: Here he is!

OLD WOMAN [*following the Orator with her eyes and continuing to stare at him*]: It's really he, he exists. In flesh and blood.

OLD MAN [*following him with his eyes*]: He exists. It's really he. This is not a dream!

OLD WOMAN: This is not a dream, I told you so.

[*The Old Man clasps his hands, lifts his eyes to heaven; he exults silently. The Orator, having reached upstage center, lifts his hat, bends forward in silence, saluting the invisible Emperor with his hat with a Musketeer's flourish and somewhat like an automaton. At this moment:*]

OLD MAN: Your Majesty . . . May I present to you, the Orator . . .

OLD WOMAN: It is he!

[*Then the Orator puts his hat back on his head and mounts the dais from which he looks down on the invisible crowd on the stage and at the chairs; he freezes in a solemn pose.*]

OLD MAN [*to the invisible crowd*]: You may ask him for autographs. [*Automatically, silently, the Orator signs and distributes numberless autographs. The Old Man during this time lifts his eyes again to heaven, clasping his hands, and exultantly says:*] No man, in his lifetime, could hope for more . . .

OLD WOMAN [*echo*]: No man could hope for more.

OLD MAN [*to the invisible crowd*]: And now, with the permission of Your Majesty, I will address myself to all of you, ladies, young ladies, gentlemen, little children, dear colleagues, dear compatriots, Your Honor the President, dear comrades in arms . . .

OLD WOMAN [*echo*]: And little children . . . dreñ . . . dren . . .

OLD MAN: I address myself to all of you, without distinction of age, sex, civil status, social rank, or business, to thank you, with all my heart.

OLD WOMAN [*echo*]: To thank you . . .

OLD MAN: As well as the Orator . . . cordially, for having come in such large numbers . . . silence, gentlemen! . . .

OLD WOMAN [*echo*]: . . . Silence, gentlemen . . .

OLD MAN: I address my thanks also to those who have made possible the meeting this evening, to the organizers . . .

OLD WOMAN: Bravo!

[*Meanwhile, the Orator on the dais remains solemn, immobile, except for his hand, which signs autographs automatically.*]

OLD MAN: To the owners of this building, to the architect, to the masons who were kind enough to erect these walls! . . .

OLD WOMAN [*echo*]: . . . walls . . .

OLD MAN: To all those who've dug the foundations . . . Silence, ladies and gentlemen . . .

OLD WOMAN: . . . 'adies and gentlemen . . .

OLD MAN: Last but not least I address my warmest thanks to the cabinet-makers who have made these chairs on which you have been able to sit, to the master carpenter . . .

OLD WOMAN [*echo*]: . . . penter . . .

OLD MAN: . . . Who made the armchair in which Your Majesty is sinking so softly, which does not prevent you, nevertheless, from maintaining a firm and manly attitude . . . Thanks again to all the technicians, machinists, electrocutioners . . .

OLD WOMAN [*echoing:*] . . . cutioners . . . cutioners . . .

OLD MAN: . . . To the paper manufacturers and the printers, proofreaders, editors to whom we owe the programs, so charmingly decorated, to the universal solidarity of all men, thanks, thanks, to our country, to the State [*He turns toward where the Emperor is sitting:*] whose helm Your Majesty directs with the skill of a true pilot . . . thanks to the usher . . .

OLD WOMAN [*echo:*] . . . usher . . . rusher . . .

OLD MAN [*pointing to the Old Woman*]: Hawker of Eskimo pies and programs . . .

OLD WOMAN [*echo*]: . . . grams . . .

OLD MAN: . . . My wife, my helpmeet . . . Semiramis! . . .

OLD WOMAN [*echo*]: . . . ife . . . meet . . . mis . . . [*Aside:*] The darling, he never forgets to give me credit.

OLD MAN: Thanks to all those who have given me their precious and expert, financial or moral support, thereby contributing to the overwhelming success of this evening's gathering . . . thanks again, thanks above all to our beloved sovereign, His Majesty the Emperor . . .

OLD WOMAN [*echo*]: . . . jesty the Emperor . . .

OLD MAN [*in a total silence*]: . . . A little silence . . . Your Majesty . . .

OLD WOMAN [*echo*]: . . . jesty . . . jesty . . .

OLD MAN: Your Majesty, my wife and myself have nothing more to ask of life. Our existence can come to an end in this apotheosis . . . thanks be to heaven who has granted us such long and peaceful years . . . My life has been filled to overflowing. My mission is accomplished. I will not have lived in vain, since my message will be revealed to the world . . . [*Gesture towards the Orator, who does not perceive it; the Orator waves off requests for autographs, very dignified and firm.*] To the world, or rather to what is left of it! [*Wide gesture toward the invisible crowd.*] To you, ladies and gentlemen, and dear comrades, who are all that is left from humanity, but with such leftovers one can still make a very good soup . . . Orator, friend . . . [*The Orator looks in another direction.*] If I have been long unrecognized, underestimated by my contemporaries, it is because it had to be . . . [*The Old Woman sobs.*] What matters all that now when I am leaving to you, to you, my dear Orator and friend [*The Orator rejects a new request for an autograph, then takes an indifferent pose, looking in all directions.*] . . . the responsibility of radiating upon posterity the light of my mind . . . thus making known to the universe my philosophy. Neglect none of the details of my private life, some laughable, some painful or heartwarming, of my tastes, my amusing gluttony . . . tell everything . . . speak of my helpmeet . . . [*The Old Woman redoubles her sobs.*] . . . of the way she prepared those marvelous little Turkish pies, of her potted rabbit à la Normandabbit . . . speak of Berry, my native province . . . I count on you, great master and Orator . . . as for me and my faithful helpmeet, after our long years of labor in behalf of the progress of humanity during which we fought the good fight, nothing remains for us but to withdraw . . . immediately,

in order to make the supreme sacrifice which no one demands of us but which we will carry out even so . . .

OLD WOMAN [*sobbing*]: Yes, yes, let's die in full glory . . . let's die in order to become a legend . . . At least, they'll name a street after us . . .

OLD MAN [*to Old Woman*]: O my faithful helpmeet! . . . you who have believed in me, unfailingly, during a whole century, who have never left me, never . . . alas, today, at this supreme moment, the crowd pitilessly separates us . . .

> Above all I had hoped
> that together we might lie
> with all our bones together
> within the selfsame skin
> within the same sepulchre
> and that the same worms
> might share our old flesh
> that we might rot together . . .

OLD WOMAN: . . . Rot together . . .

OLD MAN: Alas! . . . alas! . . .

OLD WOMAN: Alas! . . . alas! . . .

OLD MAN: . . . Our corpses will fall far from each other, and we will rot in an aquatic solitude . . . Don't pity us over much.

OLD WOMAN: What will be, will be!

OLD MAN: We shall not be forgotten. The eternal Emperor will remember us, always.

OLD WOMAN [*echo*]: Always.

OLD MAN: We will leave some traces, for we are people and not cities.

OLD MAN AND OLD WOMAN [*together*]: We will have a street named after us.

OLD MAN: Let us be united in time and in eternity, even if we are not together in space, as we were in adversity: let us die at the same moment . . . [*To the Orator, who is impassive, immobile:*] One last time . . . I place my trust in you . . . I count on you. You will tell all . . . bequeath my message . . . [*To the Emperor:*] If Your Majesty will excuse me . . . Farewell to all. Farewell, Semiramis.

OLD WOMAN: Farewell to all! . . . Farewell, my darling!

OLD MAN: Long live the Emperor!

[*He throws confetti and paper streamers on the invisible Emperor; we hear fanfares; bright lights like fireworks.*]

OLD WOMAN: Long live the Emperor!

[*Confetti and streamers thrown in the direction of the Emperor, then on the immobile and impassive Orator, and on the empty chairs.*]

OLD MAN [*same business*]: Long live the Emperor!

OLD WOMAN [*same business*]: Long live the Emperor!

[*The Old Woman and Old Man at the same moment throw themselves out the windows, shouting "Long Live the Emperor." Sudden silence; no more fireworks; we hear an "Ah" from both sides of the stage, the sea-green noises of bodies falling into the water. The light coming through the main door and the windows has disappeared; there remains only a weak light as at the beginning of the play; the darkened windows remain wide open, their curtains floating on the wind.*]

ORATOR [*he has remained immobile and impassive during the scene of the double suicide, and now, after several moments, he decides to speak. He faces the rows of empty chairs; he makes the invisible crowd understand that he is deaf and dumb; he makes the signs of a deafmute; desperate efforts to make himself understood; then he coughs, groans, utters the gutteral sounds of a mute*]: He, mme, mm, mm. Ju, gou, hou, hou. Heu, heu, gu gou, gueue.

[*Helpless, he lets his arms fall down alongside his body; suddenly, his face lights up, he has an idea, he turns toward the blackboard, he takes a piece of chalk out of his pocket, and writes, in large capitals:*]

ANGELFOOD

then:

NNAA NNM NWNWNW V

He turns around again, towards the invisible crowd on the stage, and points with his finger to what he's written on the blackboard.]

ORATOR: Mmm, Mmm, Gueue, Gu, Gu. Mmm, Mmm, Mmm, Mmm.

[*Then, not satisfied, with abrupt gestures he wipes out the chalk letters, and replaces them with others, among which we can make out, still in large capitals:*]

ΛΛADIEU ΛDIEU ΛPΛ

Again, the Orator turns around to face the crowd; he smiles, questions, with an air of hoping that he's been understood, of having said something; he indicates to the empty chairs what he's just written. He remains immobile for a few seconds, rather satisfied and a little solemn; but then, faced with the absence of the hoped for reaction, little by little his smile disappears, his face darkens; he waits another moment; suddenly he bows petulantly, brusquely, descends from the dais; he goes toward the main door upstage center, gliding like a ghost; before exiting through this door, he bows ceremoniously again to the rows of empty chairs, to the invisible Emperor. The stage remains empty with only the chairs, the dais, the floor covered with streamers and confetti. The main door is wide open onto darkness.

We hear for the first time the human noises of the invisible crowd; these are bursts of laughter, murmurs, shh's, ironical coughs; weak at the beginning, these noises grow louder, then, again, progressively they become weaker. All this should last long enough for the audience—the real and visible audience—to leave with this ending firmly impressed on its mind. The curtain falls very slowly.]

April–June, 1951

* In the original production the curtain fell on the mumblings of the mute Orator. The blackboard was not used.